David and Zion

J. J. M. Roberts

David and Zion

Biblical Studies in Honor of
J. J. M. Roberts

edited by
Bernard F. Batto
and
Kathryn L. Roberts

Winona Lake, Indiana
Eisenbrauns
2004

Library of Congress Cataloging-in-Publication Data

David and Zion : biblical studies in honor of J. J. M. Roberts / edited by
Bernard F. Batto and Kathryn L. Roberts
    p.   cm.
Includes bibliographical references and index.
"Bibliography of the writings of J. J. M. Roberts."
ISBN 1-57506-092-2 (hardcover : alk. paper)
    1. Bible. O.T.—Criticism, interpretation, etc. 2. Jerusalem in the
Bible. I. Batto, Bernard Frank. II. Roberts, Kathryn L., 1949–
III. Roberts, J. J. M. (Jimmy Jack McBee), 1939–
BS1192.D285   2004
221.6—dc22
                                2004003313

The paper used in this publication meets the minimum requirements of the American
National Standard for Information Sciences—Permanence of Paper for Printed Library
Materials, ANSI Z39.48-1984. ⊚ ™

Contents

Part 1
David and Zion

Part 2
The Divine King and
the Human King

Part 3
Historical and Lexical Studies

Indexes

Preface

This volume of essays is offered to Professor Jimmy J. Roberts by some of his many former students and closest colleagues on the occasion of his retirement from active teaching. It is a tribute richly deserved.

Professor Roberts needs no introduction to students of the Hebrew Bible and the ancient Near East, because his many books and articles have informed scholars in these areas for nearly forty years. Born in 1939, in tiny Winters, Texas, Jimmy Jack McBee Roberts attended Abilene Christian College, where he received his formal introduction to biblical studies. He continued his study of biblical languages and interpretation at Harvard Divinity School, completing his formal training with a Ph.D. from Harvard University in Assyriology (1969). After short teaching stints at Dartmouth College and the University of Toronto, he has spent the majority of his teaching career at The Johns Hopkins University (1969–1978) and, since 1979, at Princeton Theological Seminary as William Henry Green Professor of Old Testament Literature. Along the way, he has also been Visiting Professor in the Roman Catholic Faculty of Theology of the University of Vienna and at the Yale Divinity School. Despite a long and distinguished career in some of the most distinguished eastern institutions of higher learning, Prof. Roberts has never fully discarded his Texas roots—or charm. Whether in the classroom or at professional conferences, Prof. Roberts invariably can be found standing tall—literally, at six feet—in his Western boots and Stetson, affectionately surrounded by students and colleagues. His white hat, which could be spotted a block away, will be missed on the landscape of Princeton Seminary.

Professor Roberts, in part because of his especially strong expertise in matters Assyriological, has become one of the foremost interpreters of the Hebrew Bible within its ancient Near Eastern setting, especially Mesopotamia. Fortunately, the best of his numerous essays in this area, originally published in many disparate places, have recently been collected and republished in a single volume, *The Bible and the Ancient Near East* (Eisenbrauns, 2002). In addition, the volume also contains a previously unpublished critical edition and translation of the entire corpus of prophetic texts from Mari—a particularly important resource for researchers of ancient Israelite prophecy and prophetic literature.[1]

---

1. J. J. M. Roberts, "The Mari Prophetic Texts in Transliteration and English Translation," in *The Bible and the Ancient Near East: Collected Essays* (Winona Lake, Ind.: Eisenbrauns, 2002) 157–253.

The prophetic literature of the Bible has been of particular interest to Prof. Roberts. One of his earliest publications was a note on Amos 7:14. Beyond numerous articles on a variety of prophetic topics, Roberts has written a commentary on Nahum, Habakkuk, and Zephaniah (1990) and is nearing completion of a major commentary on Isaiah 1–39 for the Hermeneia series. He is also preparing the critical text of Isaiah 1–39 for the Oxford Hebrew Bible.

We pass over in silence the many other projects in which Prof. Roberts has participated or is currently involved. However, we would be remiss in failing to mention his important and ongoing philological contributions to Hebrew lexicography, growing out of his years of work as one of the three co-editors of the Princeton Seminary Classical Hebrew Lexicon Project.

No single theme, thus, can do justice in honoring the broad range of Prof. Roberts's interests, exhibited in his many and variegated publications listed in his bibliography (pp. xv–xxvi). We the editors have selected *David and Zion* as the focus of this volume because the Davidic tradition and the related royal theology of Zion have been at the center of Prof. Robert's research interests throughout his career. The 20 essays by former students and close colleagues are but a token of the respect in which Prof. Roberts is held by his fellow scholars the world over. We are all the richer because of his indefatigable energy and wisdom.

BERNARD F. BATTO
and
KATHRYN L. ROBERTS

Abbreviations

General

A.	siglum for tablets from Mari in the Louvre Museum
adj.	adjective
Akk.	Akkadian
ANE	ancient Near East
Aq.	Aquila
Arab.	Arabic
Aram.	Aramaic
BH	Biblical Hebrew
BM	British Museum
CA	Curse of Agade
DN	divine name
Dtr	Deuteronomistic History
E	Elohistic editor
EA	El-Amarna (tablet)
Eth.	Ethiopic
fem.	feminine
FM	First Millennium
GN	geographical name
Heb.	Hebrew
J	Jahwistic editor
K	*Kethib* (as written)
Lach	siglum for ostraca from Tell Lachish
LN	Nippur Lament
LSUr	Lamentation over the Destruction of Sumer and Ur
LXX	Septuagint
LXX^L	Lucianic Rescension of the Septuagint
masc.	masculine
MB	Middle Babylonian
ms(s)	manuscript(s)
MT	Masoretic Text
NA	Neo-Assyrian
NB	Neo-Babylonian
NEB	New English Bible
NKJV	New King James Version
NRSV	New Revised Standard Version
OL	Old Latin
OT	Old Testament

P	Priestly editor
pl.	plural
Q	*Qere* (as read)
RS	Ras Shamra
RSV	Revised Standard Version
SamP	Samaritan Pentateuch
sing.	singular
Sum.	Sumerian
SV	subject-verb word order
Syr.	Syriac
TEV	Today's English Version (Good News Bible)
Tg.	Targum
Ugar.	Ugaritic
Vg.	Vulgate
VS	verb-subject word order

Reference Works

AB	Anchor Bible
ABD	Freedman, D. N. (editor). *The Anchor Bible Dictionary*. 6 vols. Garden City, N.Y.: Doubleday, 1992
AHw	Soden, W. von. *Akkadisches Handwörterbuch*. 3 vols. Wiesbaden: Harrassowitz, 1965–81
ANEP	Pritchard, J. B. (editor). *The Ancient Near East in Pictures Relating to the Old Testament*. 2nd ed. Princeton: Princeton University Press, 1969
ANET	Pritchard, J. B. (editor). *Ancient Near Eastern Texts Relating to the Old Testament*. 3rd ed. Princeton: Princeton University Press, 1969
AOAT	Alter Orient und Altes Testament
ARE	Breasted, J. H. (editor). *Ancient Records of Egypt*. 5 vols. Chicago, 1905–7. Reprint, New York: Russell & Russell, 1962
ATANT	Abhandlungen zur Theologie des Alten und Neuen Testaments
ATD	Das Alte Testament Deutsch
AUSS	*Andrews University Seminary Studies*
BASOR	*Bulletin of the American Schools of Oriental Research*
BAT	Die Botschaft des Alten Testaments
BDB	Brown, F., S. R. Driver, and C. A. Briggs. *Hebrew and English Lexicon of the Old Testament*. Oxford: Clarendon, 1907
BETL	Bibliotheca ephemeridum theologicarum lovaniensium
BHS	*Biblia Hebraica Stuttgartensia*
Bib	*Biblica*
BibInt	*Biblical Interpretation*
BibOr	Biblica et Orientalia
BiOr	*Bibliotheca Orientalis*
BKAT	Biblischer Kommentar: Altes Testament

BN	*Biblische Notizen*
BR	*Biblical Research*
BWANT	Beiträge zur Wissenschaft vom Alten und Neuen Testament
BZ	*Biblische Zeitschrift*
BZAW	Beihefte zur Zeitschrift für die Alttestamentliche Wissenschaft
CAD	Oppenheim, A. L., et al. (editors). *The Assyrian Dictionary of the Oriental Institute of the University of Chicago.* Chicago: The Oriental Institute of the University of Chicago, 1956–
CANE	Sasson, J. (editor). *Civilizations of the Ancient Near East.* 4 vols. New York: Scribner, 1995
CBC	Cambridge Bible Commentary
CBQ	*Catholic Biblical Quarterly*
CBQMS	Catholic Biblical Quarterly Monograph Series
ConBOT	Coniectanea Biblica, Old Testament
COS	Hallo, W. W. (editor). *The Context of Scripture.* 3 vols. Leiden: Brill, 1997–
CT	Cuneiform Texts from the British Museum
CTA	Herdner, A. (editor). *Corpus des tablettes en cunéiformes alphabétiques.* Paris: Imprimerie Nationale, 1963
CTU	Dietrich, M., O. Loretz, and J. Sanmartín (editors). *The Cuneiform Alphabetic Texts from Ugarit, Ras Ibn Hani, and Other Places.* Münster: Ugarit-Verlag, 1995
DDD	Toorn, K. van der, B. Becking, and P. W. van der Horst (editors). *Dictionary of Deities and Demons in the Bible.* Leiden: Brill, 1995
DNWSI	Hoftijzer, J., and K. Jongeling. *Dictionary of the North-West Semitic Inscriptions.* 2 vols. Leiden: Brill, 1995
EdF	Erträge der Forschung
ErIsr	*Eretz-Israel*
EstBib	*Estudios bíblicos*
ETL	*Ephemerides theologicae lovanienses*
EvT	*Evangelische Theologie*
FAT	Forschungen zum Alten Testament
FOTL	Forms of the Old Testament Literature
FZPhTh	*Freiburger Zeitschrift für Philosophie und Theologie*
GKC	Kautzsch, E. (editor). *Gesenius' Hebrew Grammar.* Translated by A. E. Cowley. 2d ed. Oxford, 1910
HALAT	Koehler, L., and W. Baumgartner, et al. (editors). *Hebräisches und aramäisches Lexikon zum Alten Testament.* 4 vols. Leiden: Brill, 1967–90
HALOT	Koehler, L., W. Baumgartner, and J. J. Stamm. *The Hebrew and Aramaic Lexicon of the Old Testament.* Trans. and ed. under supervision of M. E. J. Richardson. 5 vols. Leiden: Brill, 1994–2000
HAR	*Hebrew Annual Review*
HAT	Handbuch zum Alten Testament
HKAT	Handkommentar zum Alten Testament
HSM	Harvard Semitic Monographs

HSS   Harvard Semitic Studies
HTR   *Harvard Theological Review*
HTS   Harvard Theological Studies
HUCA   *Hebrew Union College Annual*
IBC   Interpretation: A Bible Commentary for Teaching and Preaching
IBT   Interpreting Biblical Texts
ICC   International Critical Commentary
IDB   Buttrick, G. A. (editor). *Interpreter's Dictionary of the Bible.* 4 vols.
          Nashville: Abingdon, 1962
IDBSup   Crim, K. (editor). *IDB Supplementary Volume.* Nashville: Abingdon, 1976
Int   *Interpretation*
JANES   *Journal of the Ancient Near Eastern Society of Columbia University*
JAOS   *Journal of the American Oriental Society*
JBL   *Journal of Biblical Literature*
JBLMS   Journal of Biblical Literature Monograph Series
JCS   *Journal of Cuneiform Studies*
JdI   *Jahrbuch des deutschen archäologischen Instituts*
JNES   *Journal of Near Eastern Studies*
JNSL   *Journal of Northwest Semitic Languages*
Joüon   Paul Joüon. *Grammaire de l'hébreu biblique.* 2d ed. Rome: Pontifical Biblical
          Institute, 1923
JQR   *Jewish Quarterly Review*
JR   *Journal of Religion*
JSOT   *Journal for the Study of the Old Testament*
JSOTSup   Journal for the Study of the Old Testament Supplement Series
JSS   *Journal of Semitic Studies*
JTC   *Journal for Theology and the Church*
JTS   *Journal of Theological Studies*
KAI   Donner, H., and W. Röllig. *Kanaanäische und aramäische Inschriften.*
          Wiesbaden: Harrassowitz, 1962–64
KAR   *Keilinschriften aus Assur religiösen Inhalts.* Edited by E. Ebeling. Leipzig,
          1919–23
KAT   Kommentar zum Alten Testament
KHC   Kurzer Hand-Commentar zum Alten Testament
KTU   Dietrich, M., O. Loretz, and J. Sanmartín. *Die Keilalphabetischen Texte aus
          Ugarit.* Alter Orient und Altes Testament 24. Kevelaer: Butzon &
          Bercker / Neukirchen-Vluyn: Neukirchener Verlag, 1976
LAPO   Littératures anciennes du Proche-Orient
LBS   Library of Biblical Studies
MPAIBL   Mémoires présentés à l'Academie des inscriptions et belles-lettres
NCB(C)   New Century Bible Commentary
NIB   *New Interpreter's Bible*
NICOT   New International Commentary on the Old Testament
NTT   *Norsk Teologisk Tidsskrift*

OBO	Orbis biblicus et orientalis
Or	*Orientalia*
OTG	Old Testament Guides
OTL	Old Testament Library
OTP	Charlesworth, J. H. (editor). *The Old Testament Pseudepigrapha.* Garden City, N.Y.: Doubleday, 1983–85
OTS	Old Testament Studies
OtSt	*Oudtestamentische Studiën*
PRU	Le Palais royal d'Ugarit
RB	*Revue biblique*
ResQ	*Restoration Quarterly*
RHPR	*Revue d'Histoire et de Philosophie Religieuses*
RHR	*Revue de l'histoire des religions*
RLA	Ebeling, E., et al. (editors). *Reallexikon der Assyriologie.* Berlin: de Gruyter, 1932–
SAA	State Archives of Assyria
SANE	Studies on the Ancient Near East
SBLDS	Society of Biblical Literature Dissertation Series
SBLMS	Society of Biblical Literature Monograph Series
SBLSP	Society of Biblical Literature Seminar Papers
SBS	Stuttgarter Bibelstudien
SBT	Studies in Biblical Theology
SEÅ	*Svensk exegetisk årsbok*
SJOT	*Scandanavian Journal of Old Testament*
SJT	*Scandinavian Journal of Theology*
SSS	Semitic Study Series
STDJ	Studies on the Texts of the Desert of Judah
TB	Theologische Bücherei: Neudrucke und Berichte aus dem 20. Jahrhundert
TDNT	Kittel, G., and G. Friedrich (editors). *Theological Dictionary of the New Testament.* 10 vols. Grand Rapids, Mich.: Eerdmans, 1964–76
TDOT	Botterweck, G. J., and H. Ringgren (editors). *Theological Dictionary of the Old Testament.* Grand Rapids, Mich.: Eerdmans
TJ	*Trinity Journal*
TWAT	Botterweck, G. J., and H. Ringgren (editors). *Theologisches Wörterbuch zum Alten Testament.* Stuttgart: Kohlhammer, 1973
TWNT	Kittel, G., and G. Friedrich (editors). *Theologisches Wörterbuch zum Neuen Testament.* Stuttgart: Kohlhammer, 1932–)
TZ	*Theologische Zeitschrift*
UF	*Ugarit-Forschungen*
UT	Gordon, C. H. *Ugaritic Textbook.* Analecta Orientalia 38. Rome: Pontifical Biblical Institute, 1965
VAB	Vorderasiatische Bibliothek
VT	*Vetus Testamentum*

VTSup   Vetus Testamentum Supplements
WBC   Word Biblical Commentary
WMANT   Wissenschaftliche Monographien zum Alten und Neuen Testament
WTJ   *Westminster Theological Journal*
WZKM   *Wiener Zeitschrift für die Kunde des Morgenlandes*
YNER   Yale Near Eastern Researches
ZA   *Zeitschrift für Assyriologie*
ZAH   *Zeitschrift für Althebräistik*
ZAW   *Zeitschrift für die Alttestamentliche Wissenschaft*
ZDMG   *Zeitschrift der deutschen morgenländischen Gesellschaft*
ZDPV   *Zeitschrift des deutschen Palästina-Vereins*
ZRGG   *Zeitschrift für Religions- und Geistesgeschichte*
ZTK   *Zeitschrift für Theologie und Kirche*

Bibliography of the Writings of J. J. M. Roberts

1965

1. "A Note on Amos 7:14 and Its Context." *Restoration Quarterly* 8/3 (1965): 175–78.

1966

2. "The Babylonian Chronicles." *Restoration Quarterly* 9/4 (1966): 275–80.
3. "The Decline of the Wellhausen Reconstruction of Israelite Religion." *Restoration Quarterly* 9/4 (1966): 229–40.
4. Review of the commentaries of Hosea by W. Rudolph (KAT 13/1), H. W. Wolff (BK 14/1), E. Jacob (Commentaire de l'Ancien Testament), and A. Weiser (ATD). *Restoration Quarterly* 9/4 (1966): 304–7.

1967

5. "Antedecents to Biblical Prophecy from the Mari Archives." *Restoration Quarterly* 10/3 (1967): 121–33.
6. "The Geography of Palestine in New Testament Times." Chapter 5 in *The World of the New Testament.* Edited by A. J. Malherbe. Austin, Tex.: Sweet.
7. Review of D. Lys, *The Meaning of the Old Testament. Restoration Quarterly* 10/2 (1967): 110–12.

1968

8. Review of J. Bright, *The Authority of the Old Testament. Restoration Quarterly* 11/4 (1968): 269–71.

1969

9. Review of G. W. Coats, *Rebellion in the Wilderness. Restoration Quarterly* 12/1 (1969): 42–43.
10. Review of G. Fohrer, *Introduction to the Old Testament. Restoration Quarterly* 12/1 (1969): 44–45.
11. Review of P. Ackroyd and B. Lindars (eds.), *Words and Meanings. Restoration Quarterly* 12/2–3 (1969): 128–30.
12. Review of W. W. Hallo (ed.), *Essays in Memory of E. A. Speiser. Journal of Biblical Literature* 88/4 (1969): 504–5.

13. Review of Margaret S. Drower, "Ugarit." Chapter 21 in *History of the Middle East and the Aegean Region c. 1380–1000 B.C.* Volume 2/2 of *Cambridge Ancient History*. Revised ed. *Journal of the American Research Center in Egypt* 8 (1969–70): 96–97.

1970

14. "A New Parallel to 1 Kings 18:28–29." *Journal of Biblical Literature* 89/1 (1970): 76–77.

15. "Recent Trends in the Study of Amos." *Restoration Quarterly* 13/1 (1970): 1–16.

16. Review of James Montgomery, *Arabia and the Bible*; William Robertson Smith, *Lectures on the Religion of the Semites*; and S. R. Driver, A. Neubauer, and E. B. Pusey, *The Fifty-Third Chapter of Isaiah according to the Jewish Interpreters* I–II. *Restoration Quarterly* 13/4 (1970): 265–66.

1971

17. "Erra—Scorched Earth." *Journal of Cuneiform Studies* 24 (1971): 11–16.

18. "The Hand of Yahweh." *Vetus Testamentum* 21/2 (1971): 244–51.

19. Review of Anson F. Rainey, *El Amarna Tablets 359–379*. *Bulletin of the American Schools of Oriental Research* 202 (1971): 30.

20. Review of William H. Römer, *Frauenbriefe über Religion, Politik und Privatleben in Mari*. *Bulletin of the American Schools of Oriental Research* 204 (1971): 41.

21. Review of Margaret S. Drower and J. Bottéro, "Syria before 2200 B.C." Chapter 17 in *Early History of the Middle East*. Volume 1/2 of *Cambridge Ancient History*. *Journal of the American Research Center in Egypt* 9 (1971–72): 141–42.

22. Review of Margaret S. Drower, "Syria, c. 1550–1400 B.C." Chapter 10 in *History of the Middle East and the Aegean Region c. 1800–1380 B.C.* Volume 2/1 of *Cambridge Ancient History*. *Journal of the American Research Center in Egypt* 9 (1971–72): 142.

23. Review of Kathleen M. Kenyon, "Palestine in the Time of the Eighteenth Dynasty." Chapter 11 in *History of the Middle East and the Aegean Region c. 1800–1380 B.C.* Volume 2/1 of *Cambridge Ancient History*. *Journal of the American Research Center in Egypt* 9 (1971–72): 142.

1972

24. *The Earliest Semitic Pantheon: A Study of the Semitic Deities Attested in Mesopotamia before Ur III*. Baltimore: Johns Hopkins University Press, 1972.

25. "Hosea and the Sacrificial Cultus." *Restoration Quarterly* 15/1 (1972): 15–26.

26. Review of Hans-Joachim Kraus, *Die biblische Theologie: Ihre Geschichte und Problematik. Restoration Quarterly* 15/1 (1972): 39–40.

27. Review of Harry T. Frank and W. L. Reed, *Translating and Understanding the Old Testament. Restoration Quarterly* 15/1 (1972): 41–42.

28. Review of James A. Saunders, *Near Eastern Archaeology in the Twentieth Century. Restoration Quarterly* 15/1 (1972): 44–45.

29. Review of Walter Mayer, *Untersuchungen zur Grammatik des Mittel-assyrischen. Bulletin of the American Schools of Oriental Research* 206 (1972): 57.

30. Review of Rykle Borger, *Akkadische Zeichenliste. Bulletin of the American Schools of Oriental Research* 206 (1972): 57.

31. Review of R. K. Harrison, *Old Testament Times*; Leon Wood, *A Survey of Israel's History. Restoration Quarterly* 15/2 (1972): 111–12.

32. Review of Francis I. Andersen, *The Hebrew Verbless Clause in the Pentateuch. Restoration Quarterly* 15/2 (1972): 112–14.

33. Review of Charles C. Torrey, *Ezra Studies*; Christian D. Ginsberg, *Song of Songs and Qoheleth. Restoration Quarterly* 15/2 (1972): 114–16.

34. Review of Thomas O. Lambdin, *Introduction to Biblical Hebrew. Restoration Quarterly* 15/3–4 (1972): 203.

1973

35. "A New Root for an Old Crux: Ps 22:17c." *Vetus Testamentum* (1973): 247–52.

36. "The Young Lions of Psalm 34:11." *Biblica* 54 (1973): 265–67.

37. "The Davidic Origin of the Zion Tradition." *Journal of Biblical Literature* 92 (1973): 329–44.

1974

38. "Job's Summons to Yahweh: The Exploitation of a Legal Metaphor." *Restoration Quarterly* 16 (1974): 159–65.

39. Review of Jans Peter Asmusen, Jorgen Laessøe, and Carsten Colpe, *Handbuch der Religionsgeschichte. Journal of the American Oriental Society* 93 (1974): 282–83.

40. Review of Richard Ellis, *A Bibliography of Mesopotamian Archaeological Sites. Bulletin of the American Schools of Oriental Research* 214 (1974): 43.

1975

41. Hans Goedicke and J. J. M. Roberts (eds.). *Unity and Diversity: Essays in the History, Literature, and Religion of the Ancient Near East.* Baltimore: Johns Hopkins University Press, 1975.

42. "Niškahtî . . . Millēb, Ps. XXXI 13." *Vetus Testamentum* 25 (1975): 797–801.

43. "Divine Freedom and Cultic Manipulation in Israel and Mesopotamia." Pages 181–90 in *Unity and Diversity.*

44. "ṢĀPÔN in Job 26, 7." *Biblica* 56 (1975): 554–57.

45. Review of E. Sollberger, *Pre-Sargonic and Sargonic Economic Texts. Journal of the American Oriental Society* 95/1 (1975): 106–7.

46. Review of Josef Bauer, *Altsumerische Wirtschaftstexte aus Lagasch. Journal of the American Oriental Society* 95/1 (1975): 107.

47. Review of Patrick D. Miller Jr., *The Divine Warrior in Early Israel. Interpretation* 29 (1975): 295–97.

48. Review of Emil Schürer, *The History of the Jewish People in the Age of Jesus Christ (175 B.C.–A.D. 135). American Journal of Philology* 96/3 (1975): 339–40.

49. Review of Siegfried Herrmann, *Geschichte Israels in alttestamentlicher Zeit. Journal of Biblical Literature* 94 (1975): 592–94.

50. Review of G. Johannes Botterweck and H. Ringgren (eds.), Volume 1 of *Theological Dictionary of the Old Testament. Restoration Quarterly* 18 (1975): 236–38.

1976

51. "Myth versus History: Relaying the Comparative Foundations." *Catholic Biblical Quarterly* 38 (1976): 1–13.

52. "The Religio-political Setting of Psalm 47." *Bulletin of the American Schools of Oriental Research* 221 (1976): 129–32.

53. "El." Pages 255–58 in *Interpreter's Dictionary of the Bible, Supplementary Volume.* Nashville: Abingdon, 1976.

54. "Zion Tradition." Pages 985–87 in ibid.

55. "Zaphon, Mount." Page 977 in ibid.

56. Review of *Le temple et le culte* (Compte rendu de la vingtième rencontre assyriologique internationale). *Bulletin of the American Schools of Oriental Research* 223 (1976): 77–78.

1977

57. Patrick D. Miller Jr. and J. J. M. Roberts. *The Hand of the Lord: A Reappraisal of the "Ark Narrative" of 1 Samuel.* Baltimore: Johns Hopkins University Press, 1977.

58. "Nebuchadnezzar I's Elamite Crisis in Theological Perspective." Pages 183–87 in *Essays on the Ancient Near East in Memory of Jacob Joel Finkelstein.* Edited by Maria de Jong Ellis. Connecticut Academy of Arts and

Sciences, Memoir 19. Hamden, Conn.: Published for the Academy by Archon Books, 1977.

59. "Job and the Israelite Religious Tradition." *Zeitschrift für die alttestamentliche Wissenschaft* 89 (1977): 107–14.

60. "Of Signs, Prophets, and Time Limits: A Note on Psalm 74:9." *Catholic Biblical Quarterly* (1977): 474–81.

61. Review of John Van Seters, *Abraham in History and Tradition*. *Journal of Biblical Literature* 96 (1977): 109–13.

62. Review of Volkmar Fritz, *Israel in der Wüste*. *Catholic Biblical Quarterly* 39 (1977): 557–58.

63. Review of Jacob Milgrom, *Cult and Conscience*. *Catholic Biblical Quarterly* 39 (1977): 265–67.

1978

64. Review of Hubert Cancik, *Grundzüge der hethitischen und alttestamentlichen Geschichtsschreibung*. *Catholic Biblical Quarterly* 40 (1978): 233–35.

65. Review of Rivkah Harris, *Ancient Sippar*. *Bulletin of the American Schools of Oriental Research* 230 (1978): 74–76.

66. Review of G. Johannes Botterweck and H. Ringgren, Volume 2 of *Theological Dictionary of the Old Testament*. *Restoration Quarterly* 21 (1978): 237–39.

1979

67. "A Christian Perspective on Prophetic Prediction." *Interpretation* 33 (1979): 240–53.

68. Review of Richard S. Tomback, *A Comparative Semitic Lexicon of the Phoenician and Punic Languages*. *Catholic Biblical Quarterly* 41 (1979): 324–25.

69. Review of G. W. Coats and B. O. Long, *Canon and Authority*. *Journal of the American Oriental Society* 99 (1979): 472–73.

70. Review of William L. Holladay, *Isaiah: Scroll of a Prophetic Heritage*. *Interpretation* 33 (1979): 200.

71. Review of Robert R. Wilson, *Genealogy and History in the Biblical World*. *Journal of Biblical Literature* 98 (1979): 115–17.

72. Review of Werner Mayer, *Untersuchungen zur Formensprache des babylonischen "Gebetsbeschwörungen."* *Bulletin of the American Schools of Oriental Research* 233 (1979): 76–77.

1980

73. "The King of Glory." *Princeton Seminary Bulletin* 3/1 (1980): 5–10.

74. Review of Horst Seebass, *Geschichtliche Zeit und theonome Tradition in der Joseph-Erzählung. Journal of Biblical Literature* 99 (1980): 136–37.
75. Review of Horace D. Hummel, *The Word Becoming Flesh. Theology Today* 37 (1980): 111–13.
76. Review of R. de Vaux, *The Early History of Israel. Princeton Seminary Bulletin* 3 (1980): 76–77.
77. Review of Walter Beyerlin, *Werden und Wesen des 107. Psalms. Catholic Biblical Quarterly* 42 (1980): 531–32.

1981

78. "A Note on Isaiah 28:12." *Harvard Theological Review* (1981): 49–51.
79. Review of E. John Hamlin, *Comfort My People: A Guide to Isaiah 40–66. Theology Today* (April 1981): 131.
80. Review of Othmar Keel (ed.), *Monotheismus im Alten Israel und seiner Umwelt. Catholic Biblical Quarterly* 43 (1981): 622–23.
81. Review of P. Kyle McCarter Jr., *I Samuel* (Anchor Bible 8). *Princeton Seminary Bulletin* 3/2 (1981): 203–4.
82. Review of *The Prophets—Nevi'im: A New Translation of the Holy Scriptures according to the Masoretic Text. Princeton Seminary Bulletin* 3/2 (1981): 204–5.
83. Review of J. A. Thompson, *The Book of Jeremiah. Princeton Seminary Bulletin* 3/2 (1981): 205.
84. Review of Merrill F. Unger, *Israel and the Arameans of Damascus. Princeton Seminary Bulletin* 3/2 (1981): 205–6.

1982

85. "Isaiah in Old Testament Theology." *Interpretation* 36 (1982): 130–43.
86. "Form, Syntax, and Redaction in Isaiah 1:2–20." *Princeton Seminary Bulletin* 3/3 (1982): 293–306.
87. "Zion in the Theology of the Davidic-Solomonic Empire." Pages 93–108 in *Studies in the Period of David and Solomon and Other Essays.* Edited by Tomoo Ishida. Winona Lake, Ind.: Eisenbrauns, 1982.
88. Review of Robert B. Coote, *Amos among the Prophets. Princeton Seminary Bulletin* 3/3 (1982): 312.
89. Review of Claus Westermann, *The Structure of the Book of Job: A Form-Critical Analysis. Princeton Seminary Bulletin* 3/3 (1982): 312–13.
90. Review of Robert Polzin, *Moses and the Deuteronomist: A Literary Study of the Deuteronomic History. Princeton Seminary Bulletin* 3/3 (1982): 313–14.
91. Review of R. E. Clements, *Isaiah 1–39* (The New Century Bible Commentary). *Interpretation* 36 (1982): 84.

92. Review of R. E. Clements, *Isaiah and the Deliverance of Jerusalem. Journal of Biblical Literature* 101 (1982): 442–44.

93. Review of James Barr, *The Scope and Authority of the Bible. Catholic Biblical Quarterly* 44 (1982): 474–75.

1983

94. "The Divine King and the Human Community in Isaiah's Vision of the Future." Pages 127–36 in *The Quest for the Kingdom of God: Studies in Honor of George E. Mendenhall*. Edited by H. B. Huffmon, F. A. Spina, and A. R. W. Green. Winona Lake, Ind.: Eisenbrauns, 1983.

95. "Isaiah 33: An Isaianic Elaboration of the Zion Tradition." Pages 15–25 in *The Word of the Lord Shall Go Forth: Essays in Honor of David Noel Freedman in Celebration of His Sixtieth Birthday*. Edited by Carol L. Meyers and M. O'Connor. Winona Lake, Ind.: Eisenbrauns, 1983.

96. Review of Roland E. Murphy, *The Forms of the Old Testament Literature: Wisdom Literature. Theology Today* 39 (1983): 485.

97. Review of E. Theodore Mullen Jr., *The Assembly of the Gods. Journal of Biblical Literature* 102 (1983): 622–23.

98. Review of G. W. Anderson (ed.), *Tradition and Interpretation. Catholic Biblical Quarterly* 45 (1983): 336–37.

99. Review of James L. Crenshaw, *Old Testament Wisdom. Princeton Seminary Bulletin* 4/1 (1983): 56–57.

100. Review of W. E. Nickelsburg, *Jewish Literature between the Bible and the Mishnah. Princeton Seminary Bulletin* 4 (1983): 57.

101. Review of Marten H. Woudstra, *The Book of Joshua. Princeton Seminary Bulletin* 4 (1983): 124.

102. Review of Richard Adamiak, *Justice and History in the Old Testament. Princeton Seminary Bulletin* 4 (1983): 124–25.

103. Review of Peter C. Craigie, *Psalms 1–50. Princeton Seminary Bulletin* 4/2 (1983): 125–26.

104. Review of Robert P. Carroll, *From Chaos to Covenant. Princeton Seminary Bulletin* 4/2 (1983): 126–27.

105. Review of Dale Patrick, *The Rendering of God in the Old Testament. Princeton Seminary Bulletin* 4/2 (1983): 128–29.

106. Review of Michael E. W. Thompson, *Situation and Theology: Old Testament Interpretations of the Syro-Ephraimite War. Princeton Seminary Bulletin* 4/3 (1983): 201–2.

1984

107. Review of Hermann Spieckermann, *Juda unter Assur in der Sargonidenzeit. Catholic Biblical Quarterly* 46 (1984): 328–30.

108. Review of Moshe Greenberg, *Ezekiel 1–20*, and Peter C. Craigie, *Ezekiel*. *Princeton Seminary Bulletin* 5/2 (1984): 160.
109. Review of Ralph W. Klein, *I Samuel*. *Princeton Seminary Bulletin* 5/3 (1984): 249–50.
110. Review of John Van Seters, *In Search of History*. *Princeton Seminary Bulletin* 5/4 (1984): 250–51.
111. Review of Roland M. Frye, *Is God a Creationist? The Religious Case against Creation-Science*. *Princeton Seminary Bulletin* 5/3 (1984): 261–62.

1985

112. "Amos 6.1–7." Pages 155–66 in *Understanding the Word: Essays in Honor of Bernhard W. Anderson*. Edited by James T. Butler, Edgar W. Conrad, and Ben C. Ollenburger. Journal for the Study of the Old Testament: Supplement Series 37. Sheffield: JSOT Press, 1985.
113. "Isaiah and His Children." Pages 193–203 in *Biblical and Related Studies Presented to Samuel Iwry*. Edited by Ann Kort and Scott Morschauser. Winona Lake, Ind.: Eisenbrauns, 1985.
114. "The Ancient Near Eastern Environment." Pages 75–121 in *The Hebrew Bible and Its Modern Interpreters*. Edited by Douglas A. Knight and Gene M. Tucker. Chico, Calif.: Scholars Press, 1985.
115. The following articles in *Harper's Bible Dictionary* (ed. Paul J. Achtemeier et al.; San Francisco: Harper & Row, 1985):
    "Amoz." 28.
    "Ariel." 63.
    "Dial." 221.
    "Eliakim." 255.
    "Eliphaz." 258.
    "Hittites." 399.
    "Horites." 404–5.
    "Maaseiah." 588.
    "Maher-shalal-hash-baz." 597.
    "Mephibosheth." 626.
    "Mitanni." 642.
    "Pekah." 767.
    "Rezin." 870.
    "Shaving." 934.
    "Shearjashub." 935.
    "Shebna." 935.
    "Talebearing." 1016.

116. "Isaiah 2 and the Prophet's Message to the North." *Jewish Quarterly Review* 75 (1985): 290–308.

117. Review of Claus Westermann, *Genesis 1–11: A Commentary. Princeton Seminary Bulletin* 6/3 (1985): 234–36.

1986

118. Review of Robert McClive Good, *The Sheep of His Pasture: A Study of the Hebrew Noun ʿAm(m) and Its Semitic Cognates. Journal of Biblical Literature* 105 (1986): 325–26.

119. Review of Norman C. Habel, *The Book of Job*, and J. Gerald Janzen, *Job. Princeton Seminary Bulletin* 7/2 (1986): 189–90.

120. Review of Jeffrey H. Tigay, *Empirical Models for Biblical Criticism. Princeton Seminary Bulletin* 7/3 (1986): 293–94.

121. Review of Joel B. Green, *How to Read Prophecy. Theology Today* 43/3 (1986): 464–65.

1987

122. "Yahweh's Foundation in Zion (Isa 28:16)." *Journal of Biblical Literature* 106/1 (1987): 27–45.

123. "In Defense of the Monarchy: The Contribution of Israelite Kingship to Biblical Theology." Pages 377–96 in *Ancient Israelite Religion: Essays in Honor of Frank Moore Cross*. Edited by Patrick D. Miller, Paul D. Hanson, and S. Dean McBride. Philadelphia: Fortress, 1987.

124. Review of Norman K. Gottwald, *The Hebrew Bible: A Socio-Literary Introduction. Theology Today* 43 (1987): 580–81.

125. Review of J. Maxwell Miller and John H. Hayes, *A History of Ancient Israel and Judah. America* 157 (1987): 306–7.

1988

126. "Does God Lie? Divine Deceit as a Theological Problem in Israelite Prophetic Literature." Pages 211–20 in *Congress Volume: Jerusalem, 1986.* Vetus Testamentum Supplements 40. Leiden: Brill, 1988.

127. "The Bible and the Literature of Antiquity: The Ancient Near East." Pages 33–41 in *Harper's Bible Commentary.* San Francisco: Harper & Row, 1988.

1989

128. "Habakkuk." Pages 391–96 in *The Books of the Bible, I.* Edited by Bernhard W. Anderson. New York: Scribner's, 1989.

129. Review of David Damrosch, *The Narrative Covenant: Transformations of Genre in the Growth of Biblical Literature. Princeton Seminary Bulletin* 10 (1989): 64–66.

130. Review of Mordechai Cogan and Hayim Tadmor, *II Kings: A New Translation with Introduction and Commentary* (Anchor Bible). *Princeton Seminary Bulletin* 10/3 (1989): 288–89.

1990

131. *Commentary on Nahum, Habakkuk, and Zephaniah*. Old Testament Library. Louisville: Westminster, 1990.

132. "The Princeton Classical Hebrew Dictionary Project." *Zeitschrift für Althebräistik* 3 (1990): 84–89.

133. "The Meaning of ṣemaḥ in Isaiah 4:2." Pages 110–18 in *Haim M. I. Gevaryahu Memorial Volume*. Edited by Joshua J. Adler. Jerusalem: World Jewish Bible Center, 1990.

134. Review of Jeaneane D. Fowler, *Theophoric Personal Names in Ancient Hebrew: A Comparative Study. Journal of Biblical Literature* 109 (1990): 316–17.

135. Review of Baruch Halpern, *The First Historians: The Hebrew Bible and History*, and Robert Polzin, *Samuel and the Deuteronomist: A Literary Study of the Deuteronomic History—1 Samuel. Princeton Seminary Bulletin* 11/2 (1990): 193–94.

1991

136. "The Translation of Isa 11:10 and the Syntax of the Temporal Expression) והיה ביום ההוא." Pages 363–70 in *Near Eastern Studies Dedicated to H. I. H. Prince Takahito Mikasa on the Occasion of His Seventy-Fifth Birthday*. Edited by Masao Mori. Bulletin of the Middle Eastern Culture Center in Japan 5. Wiesbaden: Harrassowitz, 1991.

1992

137. "Double Entendre in First Isaiah." *Catholic Biblical Quarterly* 54 (1992): 39–48.

138. "The Old Testament's Contribution to Messianic Expectation." Pages 39–51 in *The Messiah: Developments in Earliest Judaism and Christianity*. Edited by James H. Charlesworth. The First Princeton Symposium on Judaism and Christian Origins. Minneapolis: Fortress, 1992.

139. "The Motif of the Weeping God in Jeremiah and Its Background in the Lament Tradition of the Ancient Near East." *Old Testament Essays: Journal of the Old Testament Society of South Africa* 5/3 (1992): 361–74.

1993

140. "An Evaluation of the NRSV: Demystifying Bible Translation." *Insights: A Journal of the Faculty of Austin Seminary* 108 (Spring, 1993): 24–36.
141. "A Future with Hope." *Princeton Seminary Bulletin* 14/2 (1993): 162–64.
142. "Isaiah" [Notes on the Text]. Pages 1011–1109 in *The Harper Collins Study Bible—New Revised Standard Version*. New York: HarperCollins, 1993.
143. Review of A. Murtonen, *Hebrew in Its West Semitic Setting: A Comparative Survey of Non-Masoretic Hebrew Dialects and Traditions. Hebrew Studies* 34 (1993): 168–69.
144. Review of B. Metzger, R. Dentan, and W. Harrelson, *The Making of the New Revised Standard Version of the Bible. Princeton Seminary Bulletin* 14/2 (1993): 184–85.
145. Review of Ehud ben Zvi, *A Historical-Critical Study of the Book of Zephaniah. Journal of Biblical Literature* 112 (1993): 524–25.
146. Review of Steven L. McKenzie, *The Trouble with Kings: The Composition of the Book of Kings in the Deuteronomistic History. Restoration Quarterly* 35 (1993): 53–54.

1994

147. Review of Daniel E. Fleming, *The Installation of Baal's High Priestess at Emar: A Window on Ancient Syrian Religion. Critical Review of Books in Religion* 1993 (1994): 109–10.
148. Review of Jon D. Levenson, *The Hebrew Bible, the Old Testament, and Historical Criticism: Jews and Christians in Biblical Studies. Princeton Seminary Bulletin* 15/3 (1994): 294–95.

1995

149. "Historical-Critical Method, Theology, and Contemporary Exegesis." Pages 131–41 in *Biblical Theology: Problems and Perspectives in Honor of J. Christiaan Beker*. Edited by Steven J. Kraftchick, Charles D. Myers Jr., and Ben C. Ollenburger. Nashville: Abingdon, 1995.
150. Review of Bernard F. Batto, *Slaying the Dragon: Mythmaking in the Biblical Tradition. Journal of Religion* 75 (1995): 102.
151. Review of Leander Keck et al. (eds.), Volume 1 of *The New Interpreter's Bible. Princeton Seminary Bulletin* 16/3 (1995): 363–64.

1997

152. "Whose Child Is This? Reflections on the Speaking Voice in Isaiah 9:5." *Harvard Theological Review* 90 (1997): 115–29.

153. "Blindfolding the Prophet: Political Resistance to First Isaiah's Oracles in the Light of Ancient Near Eastern Attitudes toward Oracles." Pages 135–46 in *Oracles et Prophéties dans l'Antiquité: Actes du Colloque de Strasbourg, 15–17 juin 1995*. Edited by Jean-Georges Heintz. Université des Sciences Humaines de Strasbourg, Travaux du Centre de Recherche sur le Proche-Orient et la Grèce antiques 15. Strasbourg: De Boccard, 1997.

1999

154. "The Legal Basis for Saul's Slaughter of the Priests of Nob (1 Samuel 21–22)." *Journal of Northwest Semitic Languages* 25 (1999): 21–29.
155. "Contemporary Worship in the Light of Isaiah's Ancient Critique." Pages 265–75 in *Worship and the Hebrew Bible: Essays in Honor of John T. Willis*. Edited by M. P. Graham, R. R. Marrs, and S. L. McKenzie. Journal for the Study of the Old Testament Supplement Series 284. Sheffield: JSOT Press, 1999.
156. Review of Doris Prechel, *Die Göttin Išḫara: Ein Beitrag zur altorientalischen Religionsgeschichte*, and Tilde Binger, *Asherah: Goddesses in Ugarit, Israel and the Old Testament*. *Journal of the American Oriental Society* 119 (1999): 693–94.

2000

157. Review of William R. Gallagher, *Sennacherib's Campaign to Judah: New Studies*. *Review of Biblical Literature* (10/31/2000).

2001

158. "God's Imperial Reign according to the Psalter." *Horizons in Biblical Theology* 23/2 (2001): 211–21.

2002

159. *The Bible and the Ancient Near East: Collected Essays*. Winona Lake, Ind.: Eisenbrauns, 2002.
160. "The Enthronement of Yhwh and David: The Abiding Theological Significance of the Kingship Language of the Psalms." *Catholic Biblical Quarterly* 64 (2002): 675–86.
161. "Melchizedek (11Q13 = 11QMelch)." Pages 264–73 in vol. 6B of *Hebrew, Aramaic, and Greek Texts with English Translations: Pesharim, Other Commentaries, and Related Documents*. Edited by James H. Charlesworth. The Princeton Theological Seminary Dead Sea Scrolls Project. Tübingen: Mohr Siebeck, 2002 / Louisville: Westminster John Knox Press, 2002.
162. Review of Gerald L. Keown, Pamela J. Scalise, and Thomas G. Smothers, *Jeremiah 26–52* (Word Biblical Commentary 27). *Restoration Quarterly* 44/1 (2002): 63–64.

Part 1

David and Zion

The "History of David's Rise to Power" and the Neo-Babylonian Succession Apologies

MICHAEL B. DICK

Siena College

Since the publication of L. Rost's book *Die Überlieferung von der Thronnach-folge Davids* in 1926[1] many scholars have accepted the thesis that 1 Sam 16:14–2 Sam 5:10 represents an independent source detailing the History of David's Rise to power (HDR). This document was then redacted into the Deuter-onomistic History. Subsequent exegetes have either refined or contested this thesis. Mettinger and Grønbæk would expand the beginning of the HDR to include the rejection of Saul and David's anointing (1 Sam 15:1–16:13, minus vv. 15, 10–26, and 35b, which were inserted by DtrP).[2] The classical position of Rost and Weiser[3] would end the HDR with 2 Sam 5:19, although a few scholars would include some form of Nathan's oracle in 2 Samuel 7.[4] Cer-tainly 2 Samuel 8 was added by the Deuteronomistic Historian. Mettinger ar-gues that the HDR contained at least an early version of the Nathan oracle, and so the HDR would begin with David's election and anointing and end with the transferal of this preferential status to the Davidic Dynasty.

The purpose of the HDR is to portray David as the legitimate successor of the Northern king Saul and to justify the usurpation of Saulide rule by the

---

Author's note: With great pleasure I dedicate this article to a friend, teacher, and *Doktorvater*, Jimmy Jack Roberts, whom I met in my first year of graduate studies at The Johns Hopkins University. For six years he taught me Hebrew, Phoenician, Akkadian, and Ugaritic. Earlier I had studied Ugaritic and Northwest Semitic inscriptions in Rome under Mitchell Dahood. I suspect that Jim had been assigned by the Hopkins faculty of Near Eastern Studies to nudge me away from my putative early "Pan-Ugaritic" upbringing. Clearly, Jim's interests in seeing the Hebrew Bible against its broader ancient Near Eastern milieu—in particular his interests in Assyriology and King David—make this contribution particularly germane.

1. L. Rost, *Die Überlieferung von der Thronnachfolge Davids* (BWANT 3/6; Stuttgart: Kohl-hammer, 1926).

2. T. N. D. Mettinger, *King and Messiah: The Civil and Sacral Legitimation of the Israelite Kings* (ConBOT 8; Lund: CWK Gleerup, 1976) 33.

3. See A. Weiser, "Die Legitimation des Königs David: Zur Eigenart und Enstehung der sogen. Geschichte von Davids Aufstieg," *VT* 16 (1966) 324–54.

4. Mettinger, *King and Messiah*, 48–62, esp. 62.

Judahite David. Since David's family is portrayed as having legitimate claim to both Israel and Judah, the work might well have been a polemic dating back to the beginnings of the divided monarchy. The German novelist Stefan Heym (1913–2001) wrote a historical novel in 1972 (*Der König David Bericht*) about a fictional ninth-century Ethan ben Hoshaya who was commissioned by Solomon to explain the rise to power of the Davidides over the Saulides. In Heym's insightful novel, the propaganda document sponsored by Solomon was to be called *The One and Only True and Authoritative, Historically Correct and Officially Approved Report on the Amazing Rise, God-Fearing Life, Heroic Deeds, and Wonderful Achievements of David, Son of Jesse, King of Judah for Seven Years and of Both Judah and Israel for Thirty-Three, Chosen of God, and Father of King Solomon.*[5]

For the thesis of this essay, it is not really germane whether the HDR is a discrete literary unit, where it begins or ends, or even when it may have been written. I am solely interested in the content of the apology in HDR defending the Davidic claim to legitimate succession of Saul's kingship. Saul was an anointed king, chosen by Yahweh (1 Sam 10:1). Although he and three of his sons died in the battle at Gilboa, he had a surviving offspring, Ishbaal, who actually carried on the dynasty in Transjordan (2 Sam 2:10).[6] David's challenge is clear: What right does he have to usurp the throne? The HDR represents that political apology. The rhetoric of the HDR has a twofold goal: (1) to discredit Saul; (2) to raise David in his stead while exonerating him from complicity in regicide (2 Sam 1:1–16).[7] It approaches each of these two points from both religious and more-secular[8] perspectives. The elements shown in the table on the top of p. 5 are the most important in that defense.

In his 1967 Brandeis Ph.D. dissertation, Herbert Wolf rightly drew our attention to the similarity of these and other points in the HDR with the political *Thronbesteigungsbericht* of the Hittite King Hattušili III (1290–1265 B.C.E.). Wolf even suggested a possible relationship between the two. Harry Hoffner

---

5. For a study of Heym's novel, see Walter Dietrich, "Von einem, der zuviel wußte: Versuch über Stefan Heyms 'König David Bericht,'" *Von David zu den Deuteronomisten: Studien zu den Geschichtsüberlieferungen des alten Testaments* (BWANT 8/16; Stuttgart: Kohlhammer, 2002) 100–112.

6. There were also other surviving Saulides who could have continued the dynasty: his sons Ahinoam, Armoni, and Mephibaal; an infant grandson born to Jonathan; and five grandsons born of Merab, Saul's eldest daughter.

7. However, the Shimei incident in 2 Samuel 15 indicates that David was not successful in exonerating himself from the death of the Saulides.

8. Of course the categories "religious" and "secular" are etic and not emic.

	Discredit Saul	Credit David
Religious	1. Saul loses Yahweh's approval (1 Sam 13:13–14; 15:1–34) 2. Saul kills priests of Nob (1 Sam 22:6–19) 3. No communication from Yahweh (1 Sam 28:6); lack of ידע 4. Disrespect for the dead (1 Samuel 28)	1. Yahweh approves David and anoints him (1 Sam 16:12–13) 2. David protects last surviving priest (Abiathar) (1 Sam 22:20–23) 3. David receives communication from Yahweh (1 Sam 30:7–8); use of the ephod 4. David's respect for dead (2 Sam 1:11–16) 5. Religious concern for cult objects and sacrifices (2 Sam 6:1–18)
Secular	1. Jealousy of Saul (1 Sam 18:8) 2. Evil spirit on Saul (1 Sam 19:9; 16:14) 3. Lost military battle of Gilboa (1 Samuel 31) 4. Saul loses the מעיל (1 Sam 24:4) to David	1. David marries Michal (1 Sam 18:20–21, 22–27) 2. David and Jonathan (1 Sam 20:31; 23:17) 3. David loyal to Saul (1 Sam 16:16–23) 4. David defeats Amalekites (1 Sam 30) 5. David receives the מעיל from Jonathan (1 Sam 18:4)[a]

a. See R. Alter, *The David Story: A Translation with Commentary of 1 and 2 Samuel* (New York: Norton, 1999) 112.

Jr., who also added the Telepinu Proclamation for consideration, further developed Wolf's work.[9]

In my ongoing research on the Neo-Babylonian kings I was struck by how many of these sixth-century kings had usurped power from the previous dynast: Neriglissar (560–556) replaced Nebuchadnezzar II's son Amēl-Marduk (562–560); Nabonidus usurped rule from Neriglissar's son Lā-abâši-Marduk (May 3, 556–June 20, 556); and one could even continue with Cyrus, who took over power from Nabonidus and his son Belshazzar.

---

9. H. Hoffner, Jr., "Propaganda and Political Justification in Hittite Historiography," in *Unity and Diversity: Essays in the History, Literature, and Religion of the Ancient Near East* (ed. H. Goedicke and J. J. M. Roberts; Baltimore: Johns Hopkins University Press, 1975) 49–62.

Similar Apologetic Structures

David	Nabonidus	Cyrus
Power was in the hands of a king no longer wanted by the deity	Power was in the hands of a king no longer wanted by the deity	Power was in the hands of a king no longer wanted by the deity
Yhwh searches for a worthy and pious substitute	Marduk searches for a worthy and pious substitute	Marduk searches for a worthy and pious substitute
He finds him in David	He finds him in Nabonidus	He finds him in Cyrus
David obtains power by the will and consent of Yhwh	Nabonidus obtains power by the will and consent of Marduk	Nabonidus obtains power by the will and consent of Marduk
Acclamation by the people	Acclamation by the people	Acclamation by the people
Political, religious, and moral reestablishment of *status quo ante*	Political, religious, and moral reestablishment of *status quo ante*	Political, religious, and moral reestablishment of *status quo ante*

In the surviving apologies for these usurpations, I discovered interesting and specific parallelisms between the Neo-Babylonian political apologies that have survived[10] and the HDR. I propose that these similarities do not argue for any literary dependence whatsoever (it is amusing to imagine the Neo-Babylonian scribes carefully perusing the HDR to justify their monarch's legitimacy!). Rather the nature of sacral kingship itself dictates such correspondences. To legitimize usurpation the new king had to establish that the previous monarch had lost divine approval (and why) and that the new monarch had received (especially unwillingly) this divine approval in his stead. The "usurper" also had to establish why he had been so chosen rather than others. In the cases both of Israel and of the Neo-Babylonian Empire usurpation was undoubtedly facilitated by the fact that in the former case the dynastic principle had not been deeply established and in the latter instance it had been lost through cen-

10. This would also include the Cyrus Cylinder (Schaudig K2.1) which seems to have been from the same Neo-Babylonian school of scribes as drafted Nabonidus's Babylonian stele (Schaudig 3.3). Hanspeter Schaudig, *Die Inschriften Nabonids von Babylon und Kyros' des Grossen samt den in ihren Umfeld entstandenen Tendenzschriften: Textausgabe und Grammatik* (AOAT 256; Münster: Ugarit-Verlag, 2001). See further Franco D'Agostino, *Nabonedo, Adda Guppi, il deserto e il Dio luna: Storia, ideologia e propaganda nella Babilonia del VI sec. a.C.* (ed. G. Del Monte; Quaderni di Orientalistica 2; Pisa: Giardini, 1994) 39.

turies of outside domination.[11] (Here a politically connected marriage is help-ful to provide a degree of continuity!) In a casual examination of such Tudor apologists as Polydore Vergil (ca. 1470–ca. 1555) in his *Anglica Historia* (books 23–25) and Thomas More in his 1557 *History of King Richard III*,[12] I have even found similar arguments in defense of Henry Tudor's seizing of the kingship from Richard III. But these latter examples lie beyond the scope of this paper.

Since so little information exists about Neriglissar's coup-d'état,[13] I shall focus on Nabonidus, for whom we have political apologies similar to the biblical HDR.

Lā-abâši-Marduk, Son of Neriglissar

Nabonidus was clearly a usurper. In the Dynastic Prophecy, which probably dates from Hellenistic times, Nabonidus is called a *rubû ḫammā'u* "rebel prince" (line 11) of the Haran dynasty[14] (line 12). We are not told much there about his unlucky predecessor, Lā-abâši-Marduk, the son of King Neriglissar, only that "he . . . [verb erased]."[15] Babylonian legal documents are dated by the reign of the king. The earliest document attesting to Lā-abâši-Marduk's rule is dated May 3, 556 B.C.E.; the last document dates to June 20 of that same year. There seems to be an overlap of about one month between the reigns of Lā-abâši-Marduk and Nabonidus.[16] (This of course is quite a bit less than the six and one-half year overlap of the Saulide Ish-baal and David.)

The most revealing comments about the so-called legitimate Lā-abâši-Marduk are found in the Babylon Stele (Schaudig 3.3), which Beaulieu[17] dates

---

11. D'Agostino, ibid., 29.

12. Richard S. Sylvester (ed.), *The Complete Works of St. Thomas More*, vol. 2: *The History of King Richard III* (New Haven: Yale University Press, 1963).

13. There are some intriguing snippets that suggest parallelisms between Neriglissar and David, but they are minimal. In a fragment of a Historical Epic (BM 34113 = sp 213) published by A. K. Grayson (*Babylonian Historical-Literary Texts* [Toronto Semitic Texts and Studies 3; Toronto: University of Press, 1975] 87), Amēl-Marduk is faulted for religious lapses (as was Saul). According to the Ionian historian Megasthenes (cited in both Eusebius and Berossus), Neriglissar had married Amēl-Marduk's sister. Like David, Neriglissar might also have been a successful military commander before assuming kingship (Jer 39:3, 13). All of these features would have been exploitable to justify his coup, but in fact we lack such explicit propaganda for Neriglissar.

14. Perhaps *palû* is better translated here as "rule" and not necessarily "dynasty."

15. *lu i-*(erasure) [   ] (line 10).

16. According to the Uruk King List (*ANET* 566), Lā-abâši-Marduk ruled three months. The nine months of the *Babyloniaca* seems in error.

17. P.-A. Beaulieu, *The Reign of Nabonidus, King of Babylon* (YNER 10; New Haven: Yale University Press, 1989) 22.

to the middle of the first year of Nabonidus's reign but Schaudig to the thir-
teenth year, when the temple Ehulhul was rebuilt in Haran.

IV 37′ ᵐ*la-a-ba-ši-*ᵈAMAR.[UTU] 38′ DUMU-*šu ṣa-aḫ-ri* 39′ *la a-ḫi-iz*
ri-id-di 40′ GIN₇ *la* ŠÀ DINGIR-*ma* 41′ *ina* ᴳᴵˢGU.ZA LUGAL-*ti* 42′ *ú-ši-im-ma*

Lā-abâši-Marduk, his [Neriglissar's] young son, who was wont to accept
no guidance, assumed the royal throne against the divine will.

The use of the Akkadian participial *āḫiz* instead of the usual preterite verb
tense here would seem to suggest an ongoing generalized, persistent character
flaw: he was wont to accept no *riddu/ridu*.[18] The *CAD* (R 324) translates this
"untutored in mores, ascended the throne against the divine will." However,
this should not be understood in the sense of Oppenheim's "youthful inexpe-
rience," "a minor who had not yet learned how to behave."[19] Schaudig is
probably correct that this flaw is a willful failure to acquiesce to the conduct
expected by both gods and humans.[20] Thus we have here the equivalent of
Berossus's judgment of Lā-abâši-Marduk in the *Babyloniaca* of κακοήθεια,
which is always conscious, intentional malice. "Because his wickedness became apparent in many ways he was plotted against and brutally killed by his
friends."[21] Furthermore, his becoming king was against the divine will, so he
failed from both secular and sacral perspectives.

Although the text is quite damaged, to some scholars the Haran Stele
(V 25–34) suggests that both Amēl-Marduk and Lā-abâši-Marduk were militarily incompetent.[22] Furthermore, in the famous basalt stele from Haran
(Schaudig 3.2) Nabonidus's mother, Adad-Guppi, also implies that both
Amēl-Marduk and Lā-abâši-Marduk neglected their responsibilities toward
their dead royal ancestors—a very serious charge in Babylonia. Certainly, it
should be noted, a usurper normally breaks the dynastic nexus between father
and son. The accusation of Adad-Guppi, Nabonidus's mother, would suggest
that her solicitude for the dead kings Nebuchadnezzar II and Neriglissar makes

---

18. Perhaps the use of this somewhat uncommon word is meant to invoke a pun on the
word *ridûtu* which means "royal succession."

19. *ANET* 309. In fact, if the reference to a son of Neriglissar in Nrg 39 (dated to the
second day of the month of *elūlu* of his fourth year) refers to Lā-abâši-Marduk, then that
son would probably not have been a minor. See D'Agostino, *Nabonedo, Adda Guppi, il diserto e il Dio luna*, 32 n. 64.

20. Schaudig, *Die Inschriften Nabonids*, 524 n. 813.

21. Berossus the Chaldean, *The Babyloniaca of Berossus* (trans. Stanley Mayer Burstein;
SANE 1; Malibu, Calif.: Undena, 1978) 170.

22. Neither D'Agostino nor Schaudig sees a military reference in this line (*Die Inschriften
Nabonids*, 518 n. 778); they eliminate Beaulieu's and Oppenheim's [*um-ma-na-a*]*t-šú*.

Adad-Guppi more these monarchs' offspring than were their natural sons. Clearly this would entitle her to be the mother of a king.

II 47 ⌜*ur-ri u mu-ši* EN.NUN-*tì-šú-nu iṣ-ṣur-ma*⌝

II 48 *šá e-li-šú-nu ṭa-a-bi i-te-⟨né⟩-ep-pu-šú ka-a-a-na*

II 49 ⌜MU-*a bab-ba-nu-ú*⌝ *ina pa-ni-šú-nu iš-ku-un ki-*[*ma*]

II 50 [DUMU.MUNUS *ṣi-it šà-b*]*i-*⌜*šú-nu ul-lu-ú re-ši*⌝-[*ia*]

BREAK

III 11 *ár-ka-niš šim-ti ú-bil-šú-nu-t*[*i*]

III 12 *ma-na-ma ina* DUMU^MEŠ-*šú-nu u mam-ma ni-š*[*ì-šú-nu*]

III 13 *u* ^LÚGAL^MEŠ-*šú-nu šá* ⌜*i*⌝-*nu-ma re-ši-*[*šú-nu*]

III 14 *ul-lu-ú ina bu-šu-ú ù* NÍG.GA

III 15 *ú-at-*TIR-*šú-nu-tú la iš-tak-*⌜*kan*⌝-*šú-nu-*[*tú*]

III 16 *qut-rin-nu ia-a-tú* ⌜ITI⌝-*sam-ma la na-par-k*[*a-a*]

III 17 *ina lu-bu-ši-ia dam-qu-ú-tú* GU₄^MEŠ

III 18 UDU.NÍTA^MEŠ *ma-ru-tú* NINDA^ḪI.A KAŠ.SAG GEŠ[TIN]

III 19 Ì.GIŠ LÀL *u* GURUN ^GIŠKIRI₆ ⌜*ka*⌝-*la-ma ki-is-p*[*i*]

Day and night he (Nabonidus) watched over them (Nebuchadnezzar and Neriglissar) and constantly performed their wills. He established my [Adad-Guppi] good name before them and they raised me up as if I were their own real daughter . . . [*break*] . . . Later, fate carried them away, but no one among their sons, none of their courtiers nor nobles, whom they had raised up with goods and possessions, made incense offerings to them. I, however, monthly without ceasing in my good raiment brought them offerings of cattle, sheep, bread, beer, wine, oil, honey, fruit of all sorts as an offering for the dead . . . (*kispu*).

Nabonidus

Like David, Nabonidus descended from modest familial antecedents. In 1 Sam 20:27 Saul's use of the term "son of Jesse" for David is clearly a derogatory reference to David's humble ancestry.[23] Nabonidus refers to himself as "I am Nabonidus, the only son,[24] who has nobody. In my mind there was no

23. Hans Joachim Stoebe, *Das erste Buch Samuelis* (KAT 8/1; Gütersloh: Mohn, 1973) 378. See 1 Sam 30:31; 2 Sam 20:1. Of course, the phrase "son of Jesse" will later undergo an elevation to Messianic status.

24. This DUMU *e-du* is not however just a sign of modesty; it is also a topos for the solitary child raised by the gods to kingship; see Schaudig, *Die Inschriften Nabonids*, 488 n. 695. Schaudig, however, takes the epithets *rubû emqu* and *rubû gitmalu* as referring to Nabonidus and not to his father. The lack of inflection in Neo-Babylonian texts makes the referent ambiguous.

thought of kingship" (3.1.7–9).[25] His father was Nabû-balātsu-iqbi, who is described as a *rubû emqu* "wise prince" and *rubû gitmalu* "perfect prince"; however, we have no information about his father from any cuneiform records (unlike the situation for Neriglissar's father).[26] Nabonidus, however, in the Eigikalamma Cylinder (Schaudig 2.5) compensates for his nonregal human ancestry by citing a long list of deities who have called him to the throne: Marduk, Anu, Enlil, Ea, Bēlet-ilī, Nabû, Nannar, Shamash, Erragal, Zababa, and Nusku. Only then does Nabonidus interject his father, "the wise prince."[27]

Nabonidus's mother, the famed Adad-Guppi (Aramaic Hadad-Happe), also fails to provide any ancestry in her famed autobiographical Haran inscription. Although clearly Nabonidus wished to establish linkage (e.g., in his dress) with the Assyrian Sargonids, it is gratuitous (pace Walter Mayer) to suggest that he was related to King Ashurbanipal. If David suffered from Moabite origins (book of Ruth and perhaps 1 Sam 22:3), Nabonidus grew from Aramean roots (Haran in north Syria). His mother's name is Aramaic. For example, he did not actually worship the Mesopotamian god Sîn, but rather his Aramaic *Erscheinungsform* El Šahr/Ilteri, "a deity which nobody had ever seen in this country," as the hostile Verse Account of Nabonidus derisively recounts.[28]

The Persian King Cyrus highlights the modest, nonroyal origins of Nabonidus. The Cyrus Cylinder (Schaudig's K2.1) has a political goal similar to those dynastic *apologiae* of Nabonidus. The Cyrus Cylinder has to justify Cyrus's right to the throne of Babylon. Cyrus contrasts his origins from a long line of kings (22 NUMUN *da-ru-ú ša* LUGAL-*ú-tu*) with those of Nabonidus. Cyrus refers to Nabonidus as *maṭû* "insignificant."[29]

---

25. The text references are to Schaudig.

26. That name, however, can be found in records from Haran, though they do not name Nabonidus's father.

27. By contrast Cyrus in the Cyrus Cylinder can boast that each of his ancestors was a "great king," that he came from an eternal royal seed (lines 20–23).

28. Schaudig P1 V 11′ ᵈ*il-te-ri*. Similarly David will promote a new form of the patriarchal deity as King Enthroned on Zion, the City of David; see B. C. Ollenburger, *Zion the City of the Great King: A Theological Symbol of the Jerusalem Cult* (ed. David J. A. Clines and Philip Davies; JSOTSup 41; Sheffield: JSOT Press, 1987) 63–64.

29. Years ago in 1884, G. Rawlinson suggested that Nabonidus's wife was an (unnamed) daughter of Nebuchadnezzar II; this would fit in with Dan 5:2 that Belshezzar was Nebuchadnezzar's (grand)son. If this were true, then the usurpers Neriglissar and Nabonidus would both have come to the throne through marriage to daughters of Nebuchadnezzar. This would of course recall David's helpful marriage to Saul's daughter Michal (and maybe was promised the elder daughter, Merab). D'Agostino (*Nabonedo, Adda Guppi, il diserto e il Dio luna*, 23 n. 19) seems to refute this suggestion rather effectively, however.

The Adad-Guppi pseudoautobiography,[30] two exemplars of which survive from Haran (Schaudig's 3.2), offers some interesting details about Nabonidus's life. Nabonidus was probably born between 620 and 615 in Haran, while it was still Assyrian. (David too was born outside of Saul's kingdom.) He probably accompanied his mother to Babylon when Nabopolassar sacked the city in 609.

In Babylon, much like David in the court of King Saul, Nabonidus served the kings as a lower functionary. His mother states that she introduced her son to Nebuchadnezzar and to Neriglissar: "Day and night he performed duties before them and regularly did whatever pleased them" (3.2 II 47–48). As we have already seen, Nabonidus's mother accused their sons of neglecting the expected *kispu* rites, which provides an important political statement and is certainly part of Nabonidus's political propaganda. First of all, it suggests that both Amēl-Marduk and Lā-abâši-Marduk were negligent in providing for their royal parents. This negligence would justify their replacement.

Remember, of course, David's grief for Saul and his sons in 2 Sam 1:17–2:7; 21:14. There, David's lament for Saul and his sons is recorded in the Book of Jashar and to be taught to the Judahites. Then David praises the men of Jabesh-gilead for rescuing the bodies of Saul and his sons and providing them a proper burial.

> David sent messengers to the people of Jabesh-gilead, and said to them, "May you be blessed by the Lord, because you showed this loyalty to Saul your lord, and buried him! Now may the Lord show steadfast love and faithfulness to you! And I too will reward you because you have done this thing. Therefore let your hands be strong, and be valiant; for Saul your lord is dead, and the house of Judah has anointed me king over them." (2 Sam 2:5–7, NRSV)

David reminds them that he is now an anointed king, even if for the moment just over Judah. They showed חֶסֶד to Saul and should now, David suggests, transfer that חֶסֶד to him. Later, when the two sons of Rimmon assassinate Ishbaal, Saul's son and successor, David executes Ishbaal's killers and buries Ishbaal's severed head (2 Sam 4:12). This act of piety not only disassociates David from the murder but also shows his respect to Saul's dead son. Later, in 2 Samuel 21, David brings back the ashes of Saul and Jonathan from Jabesh-gilead and reburies them with the seven Saulide sons of Rizpah and Merob in their family tomb. After this act of piety, fertility is restored to the land (2 Sam 21:14).[31]

---

30. See Tremper Longman III, *Fictional Akkadian Autobiography: A Generic and Comparative Study* (Winona Lake, Ind.: Eisenbrauns, 1991) 97–103.

31. It must be admitted, however, that nowhere does it say he reburied Ishbaal, whose head was in Hebron (with Abner) and whose body remained buried in Transjordan.

Second, Adad-Guppi indirectly reveals the relative court status of her son, who was clearly not included in the above list of *nišū* or *rabûti* "(their) people or their high officials." Thus he was a third-level bureaucrat. That he could read and write, a very unusual skill, is clear from his claim in the Eigikalamma Cylinder (2.5): "Nabû, who oversees all, gifted him with the scribal skill (*šukāma*)" (I 10). It is also clear from his frequent learned debates with oracular scholars that he was well trained in these esoteric arts.[32] (Perhaps this is analogous to David's role in ritual song, which by the time of Qumran is going to make him a "prophet.")[33]

After becoming king, Nabonidus, like David, spent a good deal of his time in the desert with his army, even though he must have been around 60 years old when he assumed the throne of Babylon. Herodotus suggests that Nabonidus had played important roles even during the time of Nebuchadnezzar II.

> They were still warring with equal success, when it chanced, at an encounter, which happened in the sixth year, that during the battle the day was suddenly turned to night. Thales of Miletus had foretold this loss of daylight to the Ionians, fixing it within the year in which the change did indeed happen. So when the Lydians and the Medes saw the day turned to night they ceased from fighting, and both were the more zealous to make peace. Those who reconciled them were Syennesis of Cilicia and Labynetus the Babylonian. (*Historiae* 1.74)

Astronomy would date this eclipse to May 28, 585 B.C.E. It is clear from Herodotus 1.77 that "Labynetus" is Nabonidus. However, military prowess does not seem to occupy as important a role in Nabonidus's *apologia* as it does in David's.[34]

The Rhetoric of "Legitimate" Usurpation

The strongest arguments for the royal legitimacy of both David and Nabonidus is that (1) their predecessor had lost divine approval; (2) they had not sought out or connived for rule; (3) they both had divine approbation, that is, they were called by the gods; and (4) they were dressed as kings: clothes make the king!

---

32. The hostile Verse Account of Nabonidus (Schaudig's P 1) specifically denies Nabonidus's proficiencies in writing (V 10).

33. 2 Sam 11:14 might suggest that David too was literate. See P. Kyle McCarter, Jr., *II Samuel* (AB 9; Garden City, N.Y.: Doubleday, 1984) ad loc. W. Dietrich (*Von David zu den Deuteronomisten*, 11, 18) emphasizes the importance of music as a royal skill and cites the example of Shulgi.

34. W. Dietrich (*Von David zu den Deuteronomisten*, 13) stresses the importance of military success in the ascendancy of the Near Eastern monarch.

1. Their Predecessor Had Lost Divine Approbation

Lā-abâši-Marduk, Nabonidus's predecessor, had "assumed the royal throne against the divine will" (3.3 IV 40–41). Similarly, David's predecessor, Saul, had lost his original divine calling (1 Sam 16:1). Because of Saul's "sin," doubly reported in 1 Samuel 13 and 1 Samuel 15, Yahweh rejects Saul's kingship.

> The Lord said to Samuel, "How long will you grieve over Saul? I have rejected him from being king over Israel. Fill your horn with oil and set out; I will send you to Jesse the Bethlehemite, for I have provided for myself a king among his sons." (1 Sam 16:1, NRSV)

2. They Had Not Sought Out Kingship

Even though Nabonidus had entertained "no thought of kingship" (3.1 I 8), he was both sought out by his troops[35] and called by the gods—he himself was totally passive (even grammatically). In his early apology (according to Beaulieu's dating) 3.3 V 1–9,

> 1. *a-na qé-ʳreb* É.GAL⌐ 2. *ub-lu-ʾi-in-ni-ma* 3. *kul-lat-sú-nu a-na* GÌRI-*iá*
> 4. [*i*]*š-šap-ku-nim-ma* 5. *ú-na*⌐(*šá*)-*áš-ši-qu še-pa-a-a* 6. *ik-ta-na-ar-ra-bu*
> 7. LUGAL-*ú-ti*

They brought me into the palace and all threw themselves at my feet and kissed my feet and thereby blessed my kingship.

This Babylonian stele continues by claiming that Nabonidus was raised (*našû*)[36] to lordship (*bēlūti*) of the land at the word of Marduk "my Lord."[37] Both a dream and an astrological sign (the conjunction of the "Great Star" and the moon) immediately reinforced this statement.

The HDR also presents David as passive, as being brought to kingship without having sought it. At first David too was sent for (by Samuel) and brought in to be anointed.

> Samuel said to Jesse, "Are all your sons here?" And he said, "There remains yet the youngest, but he is keeping the sheep." And Samuel said to Jesse, "Send and bring him; for we will not sit down until he comes here." He sent and brought him in. Now he was ruddy, and had beautiful eyes, and was handsome. The Lord said, "Rise and anoint him; for this is the one." Then Samuel took the horn of oil, and anointed him in the presence of his brothers; and the spirit of

---

35. In the text, the referent of the 3rd pl. verb is not specified: courtiers, palace guard, etc.

36. The use of the N of *našû* reinforces the passivity of Nabonidus.

37. The fact that Nabonidus gives priority here to Marduk rather than to Sîn is one reason why Beaulieu would date it so early in Nabonidus's reign.

the Lord came mightily upon David from that day forward. Samuel then set out and went to Ramah. (1 Sam 16:11–13, NRSV)

In 2 Samuel 5 the tribes of Israel approach David in Hebron to ask him to assume kingship to replace the Saulide Dynasty.

Then all the tribes of Israel came to David at Hebron, and said, "Look, we are your bone and flesh. For some time, while Saul was king over us, it was you who led out Israel and brought it in. The Lord said to you: It is you who shall be shepherd of my people Israel, you who shall be ruler over Israel." So all the elders of Israel came to the king at Hebron; and King David made a covenant with them at Hebron before the Lord, and they anointed David king over Israel. (2 Sam 5:1–3, NRSV)

3. Divine Approbation

Apparently, Nebuchadnezzar appears to Nabonidus in a dream and reassures him of the auspicious interpretation of the celestial signs. This dream clearly reinforces his function as the legitimate successor of Nebuchadnezzar. In fact, earlier Nabonidus had called himself the *našparu dannu* of both Nebuchadnezzar and Neriglissar (3.3 V 17–18). The *CAD* N/2 renders this unusual phrase as "legitimate envoy"; Nabonidus is the legitimate heir/representative of these undisputed Neo-Babylonian kings, even if he is not the actual fruit of their loins. Here Nebuchadnezzar legitimates Nabonidus. This is the equivalent of 1 Sam 24:20, where Saul acknowledges David as king because he has honorably spared his life: "Now I know that you shall surely be king, and that the kingdom of Israel shall be established in your hand."

Nabonidus fulfills the duties of Babylonian kingship by tending to the shrines of the gods. Nabonidus's pious cultic works began in Mesopotamia upon his assumption of the throne and culminated for him in the restoration of his native Haran and the Ehulhul temple of Sîn. Of course David restores the Ark from oblivion in Kiriath-jearim/Baalah to its new resting place in Jerusalem (2 Sam 6:2; Psalm 132); David also wished to build a house for Yahweh (2 Samuel 7), which had to await his son.

This divine approval manifests itself in the success and prosperity of the country ruled.[38] Cyrus the Great replaced Nabonidus by the call of Marduk (Schaudig K2.1, line 12) and immediately released the Babylonians from their hardships, including corvée labor (lines 17–19). Nabonidus's numerous building inscriptions document his claim stated in the Imgur-Ellil Cylinder (Schaudig 2.1, lines 13–14):

---

38. W. Dietrich, *Von David zu den Deuteronomisten*, 14.

uru ká.dingir.ra^{ki} *a-na dam-qa-a-ti aš-te-né-ʾe-e*

I constantly sought the welfare of Babylon

Similarly a summary of David's reign claims:

> So David reigned over all Israel; and David administered justice and equity to all his people. (2 Sam 8:15)

4. Clothes Make the King!

Curiously both the Davidic and Nabonidus political *apologiae* make use of clothing to establish their respective royal claims. Throughout the HDR the מעיל-cloak symbolizes the transfer of power. Samuel began ministering before the Lord wearing the מעיל from his mother (1 Sam 2:19).[39] In 1 Samuel 15 that symbolism is explicit: Saul has just been rejected as king by Samuel, whose cloak (מעיל) is torn by the panicky Saul.

> As Samuel turned to go away, Saul caught hold of the hem of his robe, and it tore. And Samuel said to him, "The Lord has torn the kingdom of Israel from you this very day, and has given it to a neighbor of yours, who is better than you. (1 Sam 15:27–28, NRSV)

In a short time, we discover who this "neighbor of yours" is who will assume kingship. Jonathan, the crown prince, cedes kingship by giving David his מעיל (1 Sam 18:4). Later, in the cave at En-Gedi the stealthy David cuts away a piece of Saul's מעיל, "and so David is in symbolic effect 'cutting away' Saul's kingship."[40] When David confronts Saul with his deed in 1 Sam 24:12, it is clear that "taking away the מעיל" involves no sin or פשע—perhaps used here in its sense of rebellion.

Nabonidus also lays subtle claim to kingship by the clothes he wears. This time the vehicle is not text but iconography. Nabonidus takes great pains to link himself with the earlier Assyrian kingship. There is no evidence whatsoever that Nabonidus was related to the Sargonid Dynasty; nevertheless, he wishes to portray his roots in their soil. Not only was he born in the last capital city of Assyria (Haran) while it was still Assyrian, his mother's pseudoautobiographical text takes great pains to link Nabonidus with the time of Ashurbanipal. Nabonidus portrays himself in his iconography as both Babylonian and an Assyrian king. He revises the dual monarchy of the Assyrian Sargonids. As symbols of Babylonian royalty, Nabonidus wears the royal cap, the staff, and no

---

39. Although this passage is outside of the boundaries of the HDR, it already adumbrates the motif of this robe in the Samuel-David story. In 1 Sam 28:14 the spectral Samuel at En-Dor will be immediately recognizable by this cloak.

40. Robert Alter, *The David Story*, 148.

Fig. 1. Nabonidus wears the kuzippu before the "Assyrian" deities (BM 90837). Used by permission of the Trustees of the British Museum.

Fig. 2. Ashurbanipal wearing the kuzippu as temple builder (BM 90865). Used by permission of the Trustees of the British Museum.

earrings; as an heir to the Assyrian monarchy, he wears the Assyrian wrapped cloak ("Schalgewand Nr. 2"), with which he—like the young Samuel in his מְעִיל before the Lord—worships the Assyrian symbols of divinity including the winged, caudate sun disk. Notice the similarity in royal dress between Nabonidus in fig. 1 and the portrayal of the Assyrian kings in figs. 2 and 3 (on the central medallion). In Neo-Assyrian times this garb, already an archaism, was an important symbol of royal power that depicted the Assyrian king as *sangû*-priest.[41] This wrap is probably the *kuzippu* (Sumerian t ú g m a₆) referred to in NA texts, made out of red or white wool (see figs. 2 and 3). For Nabonidus his unusual portrayal wearing

---

41. Ursula Magen, *Assyrische Königsdarstellungen, Aspekte der Herrschaft: Eine Typologie* (Baghdader Forschungen 9; Mainz am Rhein: von Zabern, 1986) 92. We can judge the importance of clothing for symbolizing power in both of the myths "The Descent of Ishtar" and "Inanna and Enki."

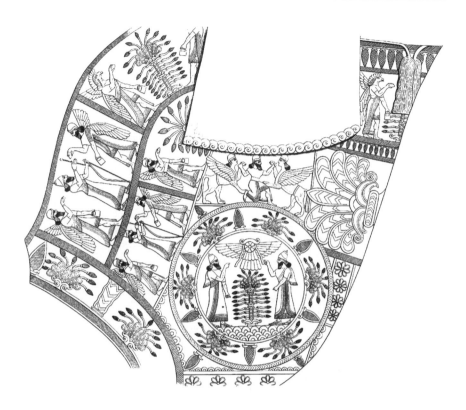

Fig. 3. Ashurnasirpal II Medalion from a Garment on an orthostat in NW Palace at Nimrud Room G Nr. 3. This figure was provided as a digitally enhanced copy by Gorgias Press from their forthcoming reproduction of A. H. Layard's Monuments of Nineveh.

the *kuzippu* (fig. 1) graphically bolsters his reuse of Ashurbanipal's titulary as "great king, powerful king, king of the universe, king of Babylon, king of the four corners (of the earth), provider for the Esagila and Ezida, whom Sîn and Ningal called to kingship in his mother's womb" (Ehulhul Cylinder 2.12 1–5).[42] The iconography of Nabonidus clearly differentiates him from that of more typical Babylonian monarchs such as Marduk-apla-iddina II (biblical Merodach-Baladan, 715 B.C.E.; see fig. 4, a *kudurru* of Marduk-apla-iddina). This represents the more-traditional royal attire of a Babylonian king.

---

42. See M. Streck, *Assurbanipal und die letzten assyrischen Könige bis zum Untergange Nineveh's* (VAB 7/1–3; Leipzig: Hinrichs, 1916) 2.2–3, text I, col. I 3–5; R. Borger, *Beiträge zum Inschriftenwerk Assurbanipals* (Weisbaden: Harrassowitz, 1996) 14–15.

Fig. 4. Kudurru of Marduk-apla-iddina II (biblical Merodach-Baladan 715 B.C.E.). Used by permission of the Photoarchiv des Vorderasiatischen Museums der Staatlichen Museen zu Berlin.

It is well known and can be amply documented that Nabonidus saw himself in the tradition of the Assyrian king. This is archaeologically quite clear on his stele. This form of royal stele is an unambiguous display of Assyrian royal ideology. It is politically significant that the Late Babylonian kings did not take up this Assyrian stele-type that had indeed been used earlier in Babylon. But add to this the fact that Nabonidus has himself portrayed precisely in the old traditional royal robe, which had been used for centuries in Assyrian stele and statues. Up to this point the Babylonian royal attire had been a skirt without a robe over it. In this case Nabonidus clearly abandons the Babylonian tradition.[43]

Summary

If kingship comes from the gods, then this theologoumenon places definite restraints on any usurper. The royal apologies of a David, Nabonidus, or even

43. E. A. Braun-Holzinger and E. Frahm, "Liebling des Marduk: König der Blasphemie Große Babylonische Herrscher in der Sicht der Babylonier und in der Sicht anderer Völker," in *Babylon: Focus mesopotamischer Geschichte, wiege früher Gelehrsamkeit, Mythos in der Moderne* (Colloquien der Deutschen Orient-Gesellschaft 2; Saarbrücken: Saarbrücker, 1999) 131–56, esp. 141. Translation by the author.

a Cyrus or Darius for "usurping" royal power from a legitimate dynast must of necessity be similar. Such similarities, which I have investigated above, stem not from monogenesis (my mimetic borrowing) but from the very nature of ancient kingship. The natural heir must lose divine approbation, often through some type of cultic sacrilege; the usurper gains it, even—or should I say, always—unwillingly. He remains passive to the active choice of the gods. Often such devices as iconography compensate for the absence of a legitimate dynastic claim to the throne and attempt to gap the absence of dynastic succession. Since most of the subjects of the new king would be illiterate, the iconographic claim might easily remain the paramount *apologia*.

R(az/ais)ing Zion in Lamentations 2

F. W. Dobbs-Allsopp
Princeton Theological Seminary

That the Zion tradition was one of the informing influences on the Lamentations poet[1] has been generally recognized.[2] Telltale signs of its key themes and concepts may be found throughout the various poems that the biblical book comprises. But it is above all in Lamentations 2 where the governing tenets of this tradition—especially Yahweh's presence in Zion and the inviolability of Jerusalem—are encountered most forthrightly. The Zion tradition and its central dogmas could not be maintained in the face of the catastrophic events surrounding the Babylonian destruction of Jerusalem. The poem's opening movement (vv. 1–8) depicts Yahweh's assault on Jerusalem. The city, its temple, and supporting mythologies are razed. What survives this verbal carnage is the uneasy figuration of Yahweh as enemy and the literary image of personified Zion. It is in the latter, through sheer vocativity (vv. 13–19) and defiant vocality (vv. 20–22), that the poem seeks to counterfeit the Zion tradition. In raising Zion, preserving her person(a), and provoking her voice, even as her material vestments of municipality and her once-enlivening mythologies are razed, the poem incarnates within its readership a potentially

---

1. As a convenience I refer to the poet as "he" throughout. The odds seem good that the poet in all likelihood was male. However, S. D. Goitein ("Women as Creators of Biblical Genres," *Prooftexts* 8 [1988] 23–27) raises the interesting possibility that the Lamentations poet may have been a woman or at least that much of the poetry was "spoken in a style" customary among female mourners. Goitein bases this principally on the fact that in antiquity women were counted among the professional mourners and on the strong "female colorization" given to much of the imagery in Lamentations, especially in the first, second, and fourth poems. Short of possessing signed autographs or reliable historical observations, I remain skeptical of our abilities to discern gender from linguistic and literary cues alone. Still, the thesis has heuristic value, for the gender of an author may well have an impact on the way that readers interpret specific phrases and passages. And it is for this reason that Goitein's thesis is worth keeping in our minds as we read through these poems. Besides, our earliest-known named author is in fact a woman, Enheduanna, daughter of Sargon of Akkad (ca. 2300 B.C.E.) and priestess of the moon god at Ur.

2. B. Albrektson, *Studies in the Text and Theology of the Book of Lamentations* (Lund: CWK Gleerup, 1963) 219–30.

life-bequeathing memory of hope and liberation. Zion *razed* and *raised* are the twin themes I tease out in the reading of Lamentations 2 that follows.[3]

Razing Zion

The opening section of Lamentations 2, unified by a parade of clauses exhibiting a remarkably uniform syntactic profile[4] and a high density of com-

3. The present essay draws (explicitly in places) on the reading of Lamentations 2 offered in my *Lamentations* (IBC; Louisville: Westminster John Knox, 2002) 78–104. It is at once narrower and more comprehensive than that reading, however. It is narrower thematically, because it focuses most pointedly on the poem's engagement with and reformulation of the Zion tradition, and more comprehensive in its coverage of philological details—this shows up mostly in the notes. On the whole, the essay aims to exemplify the kind of historicist literary reading that I have called for elsewhere ("Rethinking Historical Criticism," *BibInt* 7 [1999] 235–71). That is, the reading enacted here is at once thoroughly literary in orientation and informed throughout by philological and historical concerns. The notes, then, are all important insofar as it is there that I try to ground my reading historically—mostly in terms of philology and linguistics, but some attention is also given to iconography and archaeology. Much of the initial research for the present paper was carried out while I was on leave in Jerusalem during the 1997–98 academic year and was supported in part by a National Endowment for the Humanities Fellowship awarded under the auspices of the Albright Institute and in part by a Special Junior Faculty Leave from Yale University. Most of the actual writing has taken place during a leave (2002–3) supported by Princeton Theological Seminary. My thanks to all of these institutions for making it possible to carry out the research and writing reflected in the present paper. Finally, it is a great privilege for me to be able to offer this essay in celebration of the life and work of J. J. M. Roberts, someone I am proud to call teacher, colleague, and, most of all, friend. Jim was the one who first opened my eyes to the world of the Hebrew Bible. In particular, it was his habitual accent on history and his relentless need to read comparatively that brought the biblical texts to life for me. These are aspects that remain central to my own scholarly ambitions. The essay at almost every step has been enacted with Jim in mind—in its thematic treatment of the Zion tradition (a subject central to much of Jim's own writing), its grounding in history, philology, and comparative studies, and its broader engagement with the religious thought of Israel and Judah. Even my diction, here and there, gestures to Jim or his work. Only my own habitual preoccupations with lyric and strange fascination with Levinas fall outside of Jim's orbit of interests. For these I beg his indulgence.

4. Most consist of Yahweh as subject, a masculine singular verb of violence or devastation, and Zion (or one of the city's parts) as object. The second enjambed line of the poem's opening couplet (*ʾădōnāy ʾet-bat-ṣiyyôn* "the Lord, the Daughter of Zion") frames the main characters featured in the poem, Yahweh and personified Zion, and underscores the primary roles they play, actor and patient. This entails a subtle but significant switch from the roles the two played in Lam 1:1–11, where Zion was the grammatical subject of most of the verbs and Yahweh was hardly mentioned. The *nota accusativi* (*ʾet*), which otherwise appears infrequently in poetry, jumps out at the reader to brand Zion as the passive object—

mon vocabulary,[5] enacts one of the boldest theological innovations of the exile, the figuration of Yahweh as enemy. The catastrophic destruction of Jerusalem and its temple called into question the set of beliefs and myths that had grown up around Zion.[6] The Zion tradition, as this mythic complex is known to scholars, crystallized during the Davidic-Solomonic era[7] and exerted a special influence on certain biblical writings, such as the Psalms and Isaiah. The tradition's conceptual linchpin was the belief that Yahweh, conceived as the great warrior-king who was enthroned and thus made present in the temple (Isa 6:1; Ps 46:5; 47:3; 48:3; cf. Exod 15:18; Num 23:21; Deut 33:5), chose Jerusalem as his dwelling place (Ps 78:68; 132:13; cf. Ps 46:5, 6; 48:2–3, 4, 8–9; 76:3; 87:2).[8]

Two important implications were derived from this central dogma. On the one hand, Yahweh's choice of Jerusalem was thought to implicate a beatific life for Jerusalem's inhabitants, characterized above all by security, joy, and peace. Indeed, Mount Zion and its structures, in all of their architectural materiality, became the visible token of Yahweh's beneficence, a visual testimony to the great king's invincibility, sovereignty, and reliability (Ps 48:6, 9, 13–14).[9] On the other hand, Jerusalem, its temple, and the hill on which it stood were endowed with cosmic characteristics and potencies befitting the permanent

---

even victim! Here, then, the poet makes his grammar mirror the imagery, in which Yahweh is portrayed as inflicting, attacking, hurting Zion.

5. For example, words for anger (ʾap [2:1a, c, 3a, 6c], ʿebrâ [2:2b], ḥēmâ [2:4c]), Yahweh featured as enemy (2:4a, b, 5a), blʿ "to destroy" (2:2a, 5a, b, 8b), frequent use of the title type bat GN (2:1a, 2b, 4c, 5c, 8a), and prominent focus on the Temple Mount ("Daughter of Zion" [2:1a, 4c, 8a], "Glory of Israel" [2:1b], "footstool" [2:1c], "tent of the Daughter of Zion" [2:4a], "his covert" [2:6a], "his assembly" [2:6a], "festival and sabbath" [2:6b], "king and priest" [2:6c], "his altar" [2:7a], "his sanctuary" [2:7a], "house of Yahweh" [2:7c], and "day of assembly" [2:7c]).

6. For the characterization of the Zion tradition that follows, see especially J. H. Hayes ("The Traditions of Zion's Inviolability," *JBL* 82 [1963] 419–26); J. J. M. Roberts ("The Davidic Origin of the Zion Tradition," *JBL* 92 [1973] 329–44; and "Zion in the Theology of the Davidic-Solomonic Empire," in *Studies in the Period of David and Solomon and Other Essays* [ed. T. Ishida; Winona Lake, Ind.: Eisenbrauns, 1982] 93–108; both reprinted in Roberts, *The Bible and the Ancient Near East: Collected Essays* [Winona Lake, Ind.: Eisenbrauns, 2002] 313–30 and 331–47, respectively); and J. D. Levenson ("Zion Traditions," *ABD* 6.1098–1102). One can find ample references to the older literature especially in Roberts's work.

7. See especially, Roberts, "Davidic Origin of the Zion Tradition," 324–30; "Zion in Theology," 343–47.

8. Roberts, "Zion in Theology," esp. p. 332.

9. J. D. Levenson, *Sinai and Zion: An Entry into the Jewish Bible* (Minneapolis: Winston, 1985) 148–51.

residence of the High God (Ps 132:8, 13–14). Zion was thought to lie at the center of the world (Ezek 5:5; 38:12) and on top of Yahweh's holy mountain, whose base was rooted in the depths of the underworld and whose highest reaches—"the heights of Zaphon" (Isa 14:13)—stretched into the farthest heavens. And thus, like other cosmic mountains the world over,[10] Jerusalem became for Judeans the axis mundi, the point of junction between heaven and earth, the preeminent locus of communication between the heavenly and terrestrial realms. As such Isaiah, for example, could stand in the temple and gain access to Yahweh's heavenly divine council (Isa 6:1–8, esp. v. 5).[11]

As B. Albrektson reasons, the probability that the Lamentations poet knew the Zion tradition seems good: the poet in all likelihood hails from Jerusalem or its immediate environs, he laments the fall of the temple, and the fate of the city is the central interest of these poems.[12] Still more specific evidence of the Zion tradition (i.e., standard themes, allusions) is apparent throughout Lamentations. One of the fundamental conceptions of the Zion tradition is Yahweh as the great king. For example, the chief subject of Psalm 48—a *locus classicus* for Zion theology[13]—is Yahweh. The psalm opens in praise of Yahweh (48:2) and closes by professing "our God's" perpetuity (48:15). Indeed, Yahweh is even called "the great King" (*melek rāb*, 48:3). Though the image of Yahweh as warrior dominates in Lamentations, and especially here in 2:1–8, the image of the great king literally "sitting enthroned" (*tēšēb*) appears in 5:19 ("But you, O Lord, reign forever, / your throne endures to all generations")[14] and is im-

---

10. See R. J. Clifford, *The Cosmic Mountain in Canaan and the Old Testament* (HSM 4; Cambridge: Harvard University Press, 1972); M. Eliade, *The Myth of the Eternal Return, or, Cosmos and History* (trans. W. R. Trask; Princeton: Princeton University Press, 1971).

11. Nabu-apla-iddina's relief in the Shamash temple at Sippar provides an exquisite iconographic expression of this notion (*ANEP*, no. 529). In the upper half of the relief Shamash sits on his throne above the heavenly ocean, while the lower panel depicts a procession in the temple of the deity.

12. Albrektson, *Studies*, 223.

13. Roberts, "Davidic Origin of the Zion Tradition," 323–24; Levenson, "Zion Traditions," 1099.

14. The contrastive sense here ("But") is implicit in the juxtaposition with the rehearsal of earthly misery in vv. 2–18 (similarly at 3:42; see my *Lamentations*, 123). This is registered by the addition of a disjunctive *waw* in the LXX (*su de*) and the Syr. (*w'nt*) (and in several late Hebrew MSS as well). The force of this contrast has been well noted by C. Westermann. He observes that the line is not uttered in "straightforward jubilation" but contains definite notes of "bitterness" (and even rebuke), as Yahweh's heavenly and exalted enthronement leaves the deity "at an unfathomable distance from the earthly scene," apparently unable to view the human misery just figured (Westermann, *Lamentations: Issues and Interpretation* [Minneapolis: Fortress, 1994] 216; see also my *Lamentations*, 148). For similar deconstructions of key elements of the Zion tradition, see below.

plied in the reference to Yahweh's "footstool" (*hădōm raglāyw*) in 2:1c.[15] Deities, like kings, in ancient Syria–Palestine were commonly portrayed sitting on lion-footed or cherubim-sided thrones.[16] The so-called "El Stela" from Ugarit is an especially good iconographic representation of the enthroned divine king.[17] It shows the bearded high god El sitting on a lion-footed throne with his feet propped on a footstool. Some such image ultimately lies behind the depiction of the mourning El in the Ugaritic tablets as well:

> Then the Beneficent One, Kindly El
> Descends from his throne, sits on his footstool,
> [And] from the footstool, sits on the ground. (CTU 1.5.VI.11–14)

In Israelite thought, Yahweh is imagined in similar fashion, sitting (albeit invisibly) on an immense cherubim throne located in the temple (1 Kgs 6:23–28; Isa 6:1–8), with his feet propped on the ark of the covenant, which serves as his "footstool" (Ps 99:5; 132:7; 1 Chr 28:2).

The conflated titles in 2:15c, "the perfection of beauty" (*kĕlîlat yōpî*)[18] and "the joy of all the earth" (*māśôś lĕkol-hāʾāreṣ*) clearly reflect the beatific description of the Temple Mount in the Zion tradition.[19] The language of "perfection" and "exemplariness" underscores Zion's ideal nature, her paradisiacal

---

15. T. D. N. Mettinger sees similar implications in the iconography of the cherubim throne ("The Name and the Glory: The Zion-Sabaoth Theology and Its Exilic Successors," *JNSL* 24 [1998] 3).

16. T. N. D. Mettinger, "YHWH SABAOTH: The Heavenly King on the Cherubim Throne," in Ishida, *Studies in the Period of David and Solomon and Other Essays* (ed. T. Ishida; Winona Lake, Ind.: Eisenbrauns, 1982) 109–38.

17. Ibid., fig. 6.

18. M. Wagner (*Die lexikalischen und grammatikalischen Aramaismen im altestamentlichen Hebräisch* [BZAW 96; Berlin: Alfred Töpelmann, 1966] 64–65), considering *kĕlîlat* an Aramaism based on the common Aramaic term *klyl* "crown," suggests that *kĕlîlat yōpî* here is to be understood as "crown of beauty" instead of "perfection of beauty," as has usually been suggested. The LXX in fact translates *kĕlîlâ* as "crown" (*stephanos*). There is much to commend such a construal (see my "Linguistic Evidence for the Date of Lamentations," *JANES* 26 [1998] 26–28). Nevertheless, Albrektson's observation that, if the LXX's construal is original, then the failure of the Aramaic-speaking translators of the Peshitta and the Targum to recognize the Aramaism is troubling (*Studies*, 113). For the purposes of the present discussion, I assume the traditional understanding of the phrase, while recognizing the possibility of the alternative construal.

19. Following D. R. Hillers (*Lamentations* [AB 7A; New York: Doubleday, 1992] 100–101). It is very likely that the MT (and the versions) is a conflation of variant versions of the line, though there is no real basis for preferring one variant over the other. In fact, the MT appears to preserve a number of variant readings—the four-couplet stanzas in 1:7 and 2:19, 2:3c, 9a (so ibid., 99–100), 5:5.

status (like the Garden of Eden).[20] Ezekiel, drawing on the Zion tradition,[21] applies Zion's epithet *kĕlîlat yōpî* to personified Tyre (27:3) and describes the king of Tyre as "flawless in beauty" (*kĕlîlat yōpî*, 27:12). Elsewhere Ezekiel notes the spread of Zion's fame "on account of her beauty, which was perfect" (*bĕyopyēk kî kālîl hû*, 16:14). A related epithet is used of Zion in Ps 50:2 (*miklal yōpî* " the perfection of beauty").[22] In Ps 48:3 Zion is described just as in Lam 2:15c as "the joy of all the earth" (*mĕśôś kol-hā*ʾāreṣ*). As J. Levenson notes,

> it is not surprising that joy . . . should be a prominent feature of the Zion tradition. . . . [I]n the ANE it was not unusual for a king upon his accession or the anniversary of it to give his subjects a very tangible cause for joy by issuing a decree that would cancel debts, release prisoners, repatriate prisoners of war, and the like.[23]

Similarly, the rule of Yahweh, the "great King," and his human viceroy, David, would result in "righteousness and justice," security, and abundant life.[24] The title "the splendor of Israel" (*tipʾeret yiśrāʾēl*) in 2:1b may also refract something of this more-general characterization (i.e., perfection, beauty, joy) of Zion in the Zion tradition, albeit this is not as obvious as with the two titles in 2:15c. Note, though, the closely comparable epithet *tipʾeret gĕʾôn kaśdîm* "Proud beauty of the Chaldeans" (Isa 13:19) and the designation of Yahweh's sanctuary as *tipʾeret* (Isa 60:7; 63:15; 64:10).

Even the close ties (historically and figuratively) between the Davidic monarch and the divine king exhibited within the Zion tradition (esp. Ps 2:6–7) may be reflected in 4:20. "Yahweh's anointed" (*mĕšîaḥ yhwh*; cf. 1 Sam 24:7, 11; 26:9, 11; 2 Sam 1:14, 16; 19:22), "the breath of our nostrils" (*rûaḥ ʾappênû*; cf. EA 141, 143, 144, 147), and "under his shadow" (*bĕṣillô*; cf. Ps 17:8; 91:1) are all traditional royal epithets. The explicit messianism in the first title clearly points to roots in the Zion tradition,[25] but even the other two titles, as Albrektson observes, "belong to the whole complex of traditions with its roots in Canaanite cult, in which the Zion traditions are also included."[26] And thus one may conclude with Albrektson that the passages just reviewed (as well as others to be taken up below) are sufficient to show that it is probable not only

20. Levenson, *Sinai and Zion*, 128.
21. Ibid., 128–29.
22. Ibid., 91.
23. Ibid., 1099.
24. Roberts, "Zion in Theology," 342–43; Levenson, "Zion Traditions," 1099.
25. See Roberts, "Zion in Theology," 337, 342–43; Levenson, "Zion Traditions," 1100.
26. Albrektson, *Studies*, 229–30.

on general grounds that the Lamentations poet was from Jerusalem and knew well its temple traditions but

> in the text itself there are several indications, both in ideas and in characteristic expressions, to support the thesis that it is the cultic traditions of Jerusalem, particularly those conceptions connected with Zion, which constitute the background to the reaction of the author in the face of the catastrophe of 587.[27]

But with Jerusalem and its temple lying in ruins, the conceptual foundation of the Zion tradition, the visible token of Yahweh's beneficence and potency, was wrecked and with it the validity of the tradition's entire theological enterprise. As a consequence, the exile generated alternatives to or reinterpretations of the Zion tradition, such as the "name" theology of the Deuteronomistic history and the *Kabod* ("glory") theology of Ezekiel.[28] However, none was as radical as that found in Lam 2:1–8. Drawing principally on the mythic complex associated with the Day of Yahweh, the poet figures Yahweh as enemy and depicts the destruction of Zion, especially the Temple Mount, mythopoetically in terms of the deity's divine assault, and in the process, the Zion tradition is all but completely razed.

The concept of the Day of Yahweh was well known in ancient Judah.[29] It entailed the belief that at some point (in the future) Yahweh would intervene in history and defeat his enemies in battle. It is clear from Amos that this Israelite prophet's audience had positive expectations concerning the Day of Yahweh (Amos 5:18–20), suggesting that Yahweh's enemies were assumed to be the same as Israel's. Amos, however, turns this popular belief on its head, making it clear that Israel, too, can be numbered among Yahweh's enemies. No doubt that, despite Amos' prophecy, the positive associations with the Day of Yahweh remained popular in later Judah (e.g., Isa 13:1–22). The poet in Lamentations, like Amos, uses the concept to figure spectacularly Yahweh's battle against his own people and beloved city,[30] though in Lamentations Yahweh's day of wrath is viewed as already having happened (esp. 1:12c).

---

27. Ibid., 230. While affirming Albrektson's general line of argument, I. Provan (*Lamentations* [NCBC; Grand Rapids: Eerdmans, 1991] 60) 20–25) and R. B. Salters (*Jonah and Lamentations* [OTG; Sheffield: JSOT Press, 1994] 109–20) rightly stress that the Zion tradition was only one of the theological streams assumed by our poet.

28. Mettinger, "Name and Glory," 1–24.

29. The seminal study is by G. von Rad ("The Origin of the Concept of the Day of Yahweh," *JSS* 4 [1959] 97–108); but also see M. Weiss, "The Origin of the 'Day of the Lord'—Reconsidered," *HUCA* 37 (1966) 29–60.

30. F. W. Dobbs-Allsopp, *Weep, O Daughter of Zion: A Study of the City-Lament Genre in the Hebrew Bible* (BiOr 44; Rome: Pontifical Biblical Institute, 1993) 63.

The Day of Yahweh is characterized in Hebrew literature by a variety of identifiable and recurrent features:

- an initial call to wail (Isa 13:6; Ezek 30:2 [MT]; Joel 1:5, 13; Zeph 1:11) or cry of terror (*hāh*, Ezek 30:2; *'āhāh*, Joel 1:15; *hôy*, Amos 5:18)
- a day of battle and war (Isa 13:2, 4–5; 34:3; Ezek 7:14; 13:5; 30:4, 16–17; Joel 2:1–2, 4–5, 7–9; Zeph 1:14, 16; Obad 15; Ps 78:9)
- Yahweh, envisioned as the Divine Warrior, both stands at the head of the invading army, as their divine general, and himself actively takes part in the onslaught (e.g., Isa 13:3–5; 34:5–6; Joel 2:11)
- divine anger (Isa 13:1, 5, 9, 13; Ezek 7:3, 8, 12, 14; Zeph 1:15, 18)
- fire (Ezek 30:8, 14, 16; Joel 2:3, 5; Zeph 1:18)
- darkness and gloom (Isa 13:10; Ezek 30:3, 18; Joel 2:2, 10; 3:4; 4:15; Amos 5:18; Zeph 1:15)
- attribution of sin (Isa 13:11; Ezek 7:3, 4, 8, 9; Amos 5:21–24; Zeph 1:17)
- haunt of the wild animals (Isa 13:19–22; 34:11, 13–16)
- reaction to the devastation (Isa 13:7–8; Ezek 7:17, 27; Joel 2:6)

Many of these features show up in the initial stanzas of Lamentations 2. The poem as a whole is framed by an inclusio (*běyôm 'appô* "on the day of his anger" [2:1c] / *běyôm 'ap-yhwh* "on the day of the anger of Yahweh" [2:22b; cf. *běyôm 'appekā*, 2:21c]) that names the day portrayed with a not-so-veiled reference to the "Day of Yahweh" (*yôm yhwh*, e.g., Amos 5:18).[31] The introductory ejaculation, *'êkâ* "How!" (2:1a), is principally a token of glossolalia or pure sound that voices in a pre- or postreferential kind of language the complex set of emotions death and loss trigger in human beings—emotions that in a very real sense can never be fully articulated. It is commonly found in funeral dirges (Isa 1:21; Jer 48:17; *'êk*: 2 Sam 1:19; Isa 14:4; Jer 9:18; Ezek 26:17; 1 Mac 9:21) and here, as elsewhere in Lamentations (1:1a; 4:1a), imparts to these poems a sad and somber tonal coloring. However, with the predominance of battle imagery in what immediately follows, and not funeral imagery as in Lam 1:1–2, *'êkâ* doubles as a cry of terror (Ezek 30:2; Joel 1:15; Amos 5:18). Imagery of battle abounds: dwellings are destroyed (2:2a[32]), palaces and

---

31. See esp. Weiss, "Day of the Lord," 60, where the related expressions for the Day of Yahweh are charted (also K. J. Cathcart, "Day of Yahweh," *ABD* 2.84), including *yôm 'ap-yhwh* (Lam 2:22b; cf. *yôm 'appô*, 2:1c).

32. *Nāwâ/nāweh* in the singular can refer either to "pastureland" (2 Sam 7:8; 15:25; Jer 33:3; 49:20; Ps 23:1–2; Job 18:15; cf. Akk. *nawûm* "pastureland," esp. in MB and NB; *CAD* N/1 249–51) or to a "habitation" of some kind (Exod 15:13; Isa 27:10; 33:20; Jer 10:25;

strongholds broken down and laid in ruins (2:2b,[33] 5b[34]), walls toppled (2:7b,[35] 8a,[36] 8c[37]), city gates demolished (2:9a[38]), and the temple profaned

---

49:19; Job 5:24; Prov 3:33). And while I. Provan (*Lamentations*, 60) would appear to be correct in his contention that the plural *nĕ'ōt*, as attested (Jer 9:9; 23:10; 25:37; Joel 1:19, 20; 2:22; Amos 1:2; Ps 23:2; 65:13; 74:20; 83:13), does seem always to refer to "pasture-lands," it does not follow that it could not potentially refer also to habitations, and thus the possibility that *nĕ'ōt* here may refer to habitations must be left open (so Hillers, *Lamentations*, 97). Compare, especially Isa 33:20: "Look upon Zion, the city of our assembly! / . . . / a secure habitation (*nāweh ša'ănān*)." The use of *'ēt* further underscores the syntactic pattern followed throughout this opening section of the poem (verb of destruction + Yahweh as subject + Zion, or, as here, some aspect of the city or temple, as object) and mimes the syntactic framing of the initial couplet of the poem.

33. The root *hrs* denotes the physical destruction of overturning of walls (Jer 50:15; Ezek 26:12), towers (Ezek 26:4), foundations (Ezek 30:4; Ps 11:3), and, as here, "strongholds" (Mic 5:10). By extension whole cities may be thought of as being torn down or overthrown (2 Sam 11:25; 2 Kgs 3:25; 1 Chr 20:1; Isa 14:17; Ezek 13:14). Sometimes the root takes an animate object (Ps 28:5; Jer 1:10; 31:28; Job 12:14). In particular, note Exod 15:7, where Yahweh treats the enemies as he is here treating Judah's strongholds. Given the personification of Judah here, the poet obviously means effectively to combine both architectural and personal imagery. The closest parallel is Ezek 16:39, in which Jerusalem is sexually abused in the prophetic motif of the punishment of the harlot (see Lam 1:8–9). The imagery in Ezekiel is especially horrific. Our poet keeps the architectural imagery to the fore (compare the Tg. [= Urb. 1], which totally sublimates the architectural language in some versions; see E. Levine, *The Aramaic Version of Lamentations* [New York: Hermon, 1976] 109), but the more personal aspects of his language haunt the line from the background. For the turning over of this imagery in more hopeful contexts, see Isa 49:17 and Ezek 36:35. The term *mibṣĕrê* ("fortifications") is typically used to designate a fortified city (esp. Num 32:17, 36; Josh 10:20; 19:29, 35; 1 Sam 6:18; 2 Kgs 3:19; 10:2; 17:9; 18:8; Jer 4:5; 5:17; 8:14; 34:7; Ps 108:11; 2 Chr 17:19; Dan 11:15). Of course, not all cities and towns in ancient Judah were fortified. A city's fortifications included city walls, gate complex, towers, and glacis (see P. J. King and L. E. Stager, *Life in Biblical Israel* [Louisville: Westminster/John Knox, 2001] 231–39). Some of the more prominent of Judah's fortified cities included Jerusalem, Tel Beit Mirsim, Lachish, and Azekah. These would have provided Judah with its first line of defenses and thus the cities that would hold any enemy's primary attention (N.B.: "And let him know that for the fire-signal of Lachish we are keeping watch according to all the signals which my lord gave, because we cannot see Azekah," *Lach* 4.rev.2–4). The choice of "Judah" as the specific geographical name here of course inscribes the whole country into the poet's discourse. Here is one of those places where the personified city's identity enlarges to take in the whole country. City laments as well, while focusing most intently on one city, have the larger country ultimately in view (Dobbs-Allsopp, *Weep, O Daughter of Zion*, 101, 106, 136–37). Of course, the poet likely has the fortifications of Jerusalem and perhaps the acropolis temple-complex more specifically in mind as well.

34. Following the lead of some of the versions (LXX[L,A], Tg.), many commentators alter the suffixes so that they agree (e.g., A. Ehrlich, *Randglassen zur hebräischen Bibel* [Leipzig:

(2:7c[39]) and ruined (2:6a,[40] 7a,[41] 8). Yahweh, enraged (2:1a, 1c, 2b, 3a,[42] 4c, 6c)[43] and armed with fire (2:3c,[44] 4c)[45] and a bow (2:4a),[46] does not so much

---

Hinrichs, 1907–14] 7.36; W. Rudolph, "Der Text der Klagelieder," *ZAW* 56 [1938] 106; A. Weiser, *Klagelieder* [ATD 16/2; Göttingen: Vandenhoeck & Ruprecht, 1958] 59). However, such a change is not necessary. Nor should one distinguish literally between what is considered Zion's and what belongs to Israel (e.g., H.-J. Kraus, *Klagelieder* [BKAT 20; 3rd ed.; Neukirchen-Vluyn: Neukirchener Verlag, 1968]; Albrektson, *Studies*, 93; Provan, *Lamentations*, 64; Hillers, *Lamentations*, 98). The 3rd masc. sing. suffix refers to Yahweh— there are no unambiguous references in this part of the poem to Israel/Jacob via 3rd masc. sing. suffixes (see 2:3b). The use of the distinct suffixes effectively shows how what is Yahweh's is also personified Zion's (she is explicitly mentioned in 2:4c and 5c), and vice versa. For *rmnwt*, see S. M. Paul ("Cuneiform Light on Jer 9, 20," *Bib* 49 [1968] 374; *Amos* [Hermeneia; Minneapolis: Fortress, 1991] 50). The root *šḥt* "to ruin" is used three times in this poem (2:5b, 6a, 8a). Elsewhere it is typically used, as here, to denote the physical destruction of buildings, walls, cities, and the like (e.g., Gen 13:10; 18:28; 19:13, 29; 2 Sam 20:15; 24:16; Jer 5:10; 48:18; Ezek 26:4; 43:3).

35. The MT's *ḥômōt ʾarmĕnôteyhā* ("her fortresses") should be retained. The LXX's singular "wall" (*teichos*) aligns the MT with the singular *ḥômat* in 2:8a, while the Syr. in 2:8a (*šwryh*) smoothes the MT there in the other direction. The 3rd fem. sing. suffix refers to Zion, as Hillers notes (*Lamentations*, 99), and there is no good rationale (and certainly no textual support) for emending the text to read a 3rd masc. sing. suffix, as so many contend (e.g., Rudolph, "Text," 107; Weiser, *Klagelieder*, 59; Kraus, *Klagelieder*, 58).

36. The LXX's *kai epetrepse* likely reflects the scribe's anticipation of *ḥēšîb* in the second couplet. The constraints of the acrostic require a *ḥet*, and thus MT (*ḥāšēb*) should be preferred.

37. LXX (*kai teichos omothumadon ēsthenēsen*) and Syr. (*wšwryh ʾkḥd, ṣdw*) divide MT (*wayyaʾăbel-ḥēl wĕḥômâ / yaḥdāw ʾumlālû* "he caused wall and rampart to mourn / together they languished") differently, even though the parallelism shows the lineation clearly. The couplet is parallel and formed chiastically: VS/SV. The *wayyiqtol* form closes the stanza and the section as a whole. Good parallels to Jerusalem's groaning walls are found in the Mesopotamian laments (LSUr 380; LN 141; CA 227). The city gate and surrounding walls were evidently characteristic sites for lamentation (Dobbs-Allsopp, *Weep, O Daughter of Zion*, 89). The image evoked is as if one were sitting far off in the dark of night and could only hear the lamentations emanating from the city's walls, as if the walls themselves were mourning. And of course the walls do have reason to mourn because they have been breached and destroyed—they are literally in a weakened state. The *ḥēl* was specifically the outer, surrounding wall (see King and Stager, *Life in Biblical Israel*, 231). The closest parallel is Jer 14:2, where Jerusalem's gates are said to be languishing (*ʾumlĕlû*) and dark (*qādĕrû*) to the ground (see W. L. Holladay, *Jeremiah 1* [Hermeneia; Philadelphia: Fortress, 1986] 429–30). Otherwise *ʾml* is always used predicated of organic—animal or vegetation—subjects. Here Jerusalem's multi-leveled identity comes to the fore again. The poet is thus able to play on both Jerusalem's physical and personal identities at the same time. The image of a languishing woman (1 Sam 2:5; Jer 15:9) stands behind this imagery (so also in Jer 14:2 according to Holladay [*Jeremiah 1*, 429]; cf. Jer 15:9; 1 Sam 2:5). The topic change with the second line of the couplet—wall and rampart become the subject of the plural verb—

lead the enemy invasion as do battle himself, all but single-handedly, against Jerusalem—the actual human enemies are relegated to performing a mop-up

breaks the tight syntactic pattern that otherwise holds sway in this opening section. This anticipates the shift in focus that begins in v. 9, while simultaneously signaling the close of the poem's initial movement. Lam 2:8c–9a form a hinge that joins the two sections and initiates the transition:

> *wayya²ăbel-ḥēl wĕḥômâ*
> *yaḥdāw ²umlālû*
> *ṭābĕ⁶û bā²āreṣ šĕ⁶āreyhā*
> *²ibbad wĕšibbar bĕrîḥeyhā*

> He caused rampart and wall to lament;
> they languish together.
> Her gates have sunk into the ground;
> he has ruined and broken her bars.

The imagery throughout these couplets retains the architectural focus of 2:1–8, while the two outer lines (joined by matching nominal and verbal compounds) mimic the opening section's tight clause structure. In the two inner lines, this clause structure is exploded, and the first three lines feature gestures of personification that anticipate the shift to a more human-centered focus in the rest of the poem.

38. The image in 2:9a (*ṭābĕ⁶û bā²āreṣ šĕ⁶āreyhā* "her gates are sunk in the earth") is of the destroyed gate structure, either of the battered gate doors themselves lying in the dirt (as in CA 168) or perhaps of the ruined gate towers, whose decapitation would make them appear as if they had sunk down in the earth (Jer 14:2; see the image of fallen gates in Y. Yadin, *The Art of Warfare in Biblical Lands* [London: Weidenfeld and Nicolson, 1963] 96). In either case, it does not appear, especially in light of the second line (where the "bars" have been shattered or destroyed), that the poet had the image of a burned-out city gate in mind (cf. Nah 3:13), the other common means for gaining access through the city gate (see Yadin, *Art of Warfare*, 392–93, 421–22). Here it seems that the gates have been broken through by a battering ram (King and Stager, *Life in Biblical Israel*, fig. 120).

39. When this couplet (*qôl nātĕnû bĕbêt-yhwh / kĕyôm mô⁶ēd* "an uproar was heard in the house of Yahweh / as on a feast day") is commented on, most observe that it is the enemy who is making a ruckus while plundering the temple. Provan is typical: "the enemy, having gained access to the temple, engaged in a boisterous celebration of the kind normally associated in Israel with the day of an appointed feast" (*Lamentations*, 67; Hillers, *Lamentations*, 105). While this is surely the reality that stands behind the poetry, it is not so obvious that it is the image most prominently on display in the poetry itself. In the first place, the enemy is nowhere topicalized. Second, only here in the first 24 couplets is the main verb something other than a 3rd masc. sing. form, and only here and 2:4b does a couplet begin with a part of speech other than a verb. In each of the other 23 couplets Yahweh is the subject. Finally, of the 23 occurrences of the phrase *ntn qôl* in the Bible (according to Even-Shoshan's tabulation), 8 refer to the thunderous roar of Yahweh (2 Sam 22:14; Joel 2:11; 4:6; Amos 1:2; Ps 18:14; 46:7; 68:34; 77:18). Together all of these suggest that the noise referred to here is caused as much by Yahweh as by the enemy. Here, then, the 3rd masc. pl. verb

operation after the real fighting is already over (2:3b, 7b[47]).[48] Indeed, the poet
seems intent on accenting the ferocity of Yahweh's onslaught. The initial cou-

---

nātĕnû is interpretable as an impersonal passive, as in 2 Chr 24:9 (see the translations by
W. Rudolph, *Klagelieder* [KAT 17/3; Gütersloh: Mohn, 1962] 216; Kraus, *Klagelieder*, 31).
Again the poem's irony is apparent. Yahweh's voice is usually a positive sign for Israel. Here
the "uproar" caused is of course negative. The second line of the couplet, *kĕyôm mô'ēd*,
turns the irony tragic. The "house of Yahweh" should be filled with shouts of jubilation (Ps
26:7); instead it is filled with the din of battle (Exod 32:17; Jer 50:22, 46; 51:55).

40. The verb *ḥms* is always used in the Hebrew Bible to denote violent and ethically
wrongful actions (Jer 22:3; Ezek 22:26; Zeph 3:4; Job 15:33; 21:27; Prov 8:36), epito-
mized by the rape of a woman (Jer 13:22). The more common nominal form of the root,
ḥāmās, supports this basic sense. Only here in the Hebrew Bible is *ḥms* predicated of Yahweh. This of course underscores the severity of the catastrophe. But it also casts Yahweh's
actions rather ambivalently. Here the image of Jerusalem as widow (1:1b) and rape victim
(1:8–10; cf. F. W. Dobbs-Allsopp and T. Linafelt, "The Rape of Zion in Lam 1:10," *ZAW*
113/1 [2001] 77–81; Dobbs-Allsopp, *Lamentations*, 63–67) hovers especially close in the
background. Widows are not to be treated thusly (Jer 22:3), and the heinous nature of rape
has already been mentioned. The first line in the MT (*wayyaḥmōs kaggan śukkô*) is difficult
and presumed corrupt by many commentators (e.g., Rudolph, "Text," 106; McDaniel,
"Philological Studies, I," 36–38; Hillers, *Lamentations*, 99). However, the versions do not
attest to a materially different text (LXX's *ōs ampelon to skēnōma autoi* likely reflects a harmonization and then corruption of *ampelōni* in the Greek of the more transparent Isa 1:8). Albrektson (*Studies*, 95–97; cf. 82) defends the grammar of the MT by assuming that the
preposition *kĕ-* "like" has absorbed the preposition *bĕ-* "in" (**kĕbaggan*, lit., "as in a garden"). The linguistic phenomenon involved is not unique (B. K. Waltke and M. O'Connor, *Introduction to Biblical Hebrew Syntax* [Winona Lake, Ind.: Eisenbrauns, 1990] §11.2.9c)
and the resulting imagery—comparison of a destroyed temple to the dilapidated temporary
harvest shelters after they have been abandoned following the harvest—has good parallels
in the Mesopotamian city laments (Dobbs-Allsopp, *Weep, O Daughter of Zion*, 69–70; cf.
Isa 1:8). Thus, Yahweh is here imagined as violently destroying the temple as if it were a
temporary garden hut, with *śukkô* refracting both the normal meaning of Hebrew *suk/sukkâ*
as a "temporary shelter" (Job 27:18; Jonah 4:5) and its more specialized usage as a designation for the temple itself (Ps 27:5).

41. *Zānaḥ* "he spurned" likely has the notion of Yahweh's abandonment in its purview—compare *lāmâ 'ĕlōhîm zānaḥtā lāneṣaḥ* "why, O God, have you spurned so long?" (Ps
74:1) with *lāmâ lāneṣaḥ tiškāḥēnû* "why have you forgotten so long?" (Lam 5:20). See also
the comparable use of *znḥ* in Ps 44:24; 88:15; 89:39; and Lam 3:31.

42. The MT (followed by the Tg.) reads *boḥŏrî-'ap* "in burning anger," while the versions
(LXX, Syr., Vg.) add a suffix. The MT is clearly the *lectio difficilior*. The proclivity for the versions in Lamentations, and especially the Peshitta, to add pronominal suffixes has been noted
(esp. Albrektson, *Studies*, 210). The prominence of *'appô* elsewhere in Lamentations (1:12c;
2:1a, 1c, 6c; 4:11a) may have contributed to the additions here (Albrektson, *Studies*, 89).

43. For the strong accent on divine anger in this opening section of the poem and the
resulting depiction of Yahweh, in the words of K. O'Connor ("Lamentations" in *NIB*
6.1038), as an "out of control" and "mad deity," see Dobbs-Allsopp, *Lamentations*, 80–81.

plet of 2:2 stresses that Yahweh destroys "without mercy" (*lo' ḥāmal*;[49] literally counterpointing Zion's desire for "compassion" expressed throughout the

---

44. MT *kĕ'ēš lehābâ*; LXX *kai katephage panta ta kyklō*; Syr. *wšbq nwr' by'qwb wšlmbyt' 'klt 'ydwhy*. LXX's *kai* and *panta* are expansive, the latter likely through dittography with *kl* at the end of *'kl*—note that the LXX has understood the final *he* on *'klh* as the definite article of the final word *sbyb* (*ta kyklō*; cf. Albrektson, *Studies*, 90–91). Otherwise, both the LXX and the Syr. are attempting to make sense out of the MT. The Syr. turns MT's enjambment into parallelism. The second line in MT (*k'š lhbh 'klh sbyb*) seems suspiciously long. Given MT's occasional tendency toward conflation elsewhere in Lamentations (esp. 1:7b, 21b), Hillers (*Lamentations*, 98) is probably correct to understand the MT here as resulting from a conflation of two variant readings: *kĕ'ēš lehābâ* (cf. Hos 7:6; Isa 4:5; Ps 105:32) and *kĕ'ēš 'akĕlâ sābîb* (cf. Exod 24:17; Isa 30:27). The latter has been preferred on the basis of its uniqueness, but either could be original. Furthermore, after the expansion, MT remains intelligible. The addition of *lehābâ* simply increases the intensity of the image.

45. The word *'ēš* "fire" is a common manifestation of divine theophanies (Gen 15:17; Exod 19:18; Deut 4:11; 2 Sam 22:9, 13; Ezek 1:4; Amos 5:6), is used as an instrument of war to destroy buildings and cities (Num 21:28; Deut 13:17; Josh 6:24; 8:8; Judg 9:49; 12:1; 1 Sam 30:1; 1 Kgs 16:18; Isa 1:7; 64:10; Jer 49:27; 50:32; 51:38; Ezek 16:41; Amos 1:4, 7), and frequently occurs as a symbol of divine anger (Isa 66:15; Ezek 21:36; 22:31; 36:5; 38:19; Nah 1:6; Ps 79:5; 89:47), all of which resonate here. See D. R. Hillers, "Amos 7,4 and Ancient Parallels," *CBQ* 26 (1964) 221–24; P. D. Miller, "Fire in the Mythology of Canaan and Israel," in *Israelite Religion and Biblical Theology: Collected Essays* (JSOTSup 267; Sheffield: Sheffield Academic Press, 2000) 18–23; O. Keel, *The Symbolism of the Biblical World: Ancient Near Eastern Iconography and the Book of Psalms* (New York: Seabury, 1978; repr. Winona Lake, Ind.: Eisenbrauns, 1997) fig. 294.

46. The divine warrior is portrayed with bow and arrow (2 Sam 22:15; Hab 3:9; Ps 7:14). In Ps 7:13 and Lam 3:12 Yahweh is imagined bending (*drk*) his bow as here (cf. Zech 9:13). Cf. Keel, *Symbolism*, figs. 296, 303–4; pl. XX.

47. The idiom *hsgyr byd* "to deliver into the hand of" is common in BH (Josh 20:5; 1 Sam 23:11, 12, 20; 30:15; Ps 31:8; and in the *Piel*, 1 Sam 17:46; 24:19; 26:8), as is the related idiom *ntn bĕyad-* (Lam 1:14c); cf. A. Even-Shoshan, *A New Concordance of the Old Testament* (Jerusalem: Kiryat Sefer, 1985) 789; note that Syr. translates both idioms (1:14c; 2:7b) *'šlm*. Here the image is that of Yahweh giving Jerusalem into the power of its enemies. This motif has an especially long history in city laments. The Sumerian equivalent of this phrase, s u m (= ES z é - è m; Akk. *nadānu*), occurs frequently in the Mesopotamian city laments (LSUr 63, 181, 239; balags 2:37; 8:34–35 [FM]; 10:a+71–72; 16:a+16–17 [FM]; 50:b+ 179–80), as does the related Sum. phrase š u(-a) . . . gi₄ "to hand over" (LSUr 172-, 175–77; LN 96; Dobbs-Allsopp, *Weep, O Daughter of Zion*, 65). The gesture is one way by which a vanquished people can interpret a defeat so that their god's autonomy remains intact (B. Albrektson, *History and the Gods* [Lund: CWK Gleerup, 1967] 38–39). Here, then, the poet shows Yahweh very much in control of history. Jerusalem's fall was no accident. He orchestrated the whole affair.

48. For the "synergism" (i.e., human combatants were considered a part of Yahweh's hosts) that typifies the mythopoetic presentation of the Divine Warrior in biblical tradition, see P. D. Miller, *The Divine Warrior in Early Israel* (Cambridge: Harvard University Press,

first poem),[50] a sentiment that is not only repeated two more times in the poem (2:17b, 21c[51]) but is strongly realized in this initial section through syntax. Yahweh is the overt subject of 29 out of the first 31 verbs. He has "beclouded" (see below), "thrown down," "not remembered," "destroyed," "broken down," "brought down," "cut down," "withdrawn (his protective hand)," "burned," "bent his bow," "killed," "poured out his fury," "become like an enemy," "destroyed," "multiplied . . . mourning," "broken down," "destroyed," "abolished," "spurned," "scorned," "disowned," "delivered into the hand of the enemy," "determined to lay into ruins," "stretched the line," "not withheld his hand from destroying," and "caused . . . to lament." The intensity and mercilessness of Yahweh's assault is chillingly communicated (and represented). In-depth commentary is not required by even the most casual reader to sense and feel the savagery of Yahweh's attack. The use of perfective verb forms in the Hebrew throughout this section does not so much emphasize the "past-ness" of Yahweh's actions (as suggested, for example, by the NRSV's translation) as view them as a totality, thus implicating a sense of certainty and completeness—that is, there is no question that Yahweh's actions have achieved their terrible goal! The poet even goes to the extreme not only of portraying Yahweh as the enemy (as in 1:13–15)[52] but also of calling him an "enemy," not once, but three times in the space of only four couplets (2:4a, b; 5a). In 2:4a the Tg. makes the image most explicit (*ʾtʿtd ʾl ymynyh dnbwkdnṣr wsyyʿyh* "He [= Yahweh] stood ready at the right of Nebuchadnezzar and aided him"), while at the same time softening its implications (*kʾylw hwh mʿyq lʿmmyh byt yśrʾl* "as if he himself were oppressing his people, the house of Israel").[53] The simile is fronted and thus emphasized in 2:4b (*kĕṣār wayyahărōg*

1973); cf. Keel, *Symbolism*, pls. XXI–XXII. Note the explicitness of the Tg. at 2:4a: "He (= Yahweh) stood ready at the right of Nebuchadnezzar and aided him" (*ʾtʿtd ʾl ymynyh dnbwkd-nṣr wsyyʿyh*).

49. Whether one should read with the K (as cited; followed by LXX) or the Q (= *wĕlōʾ ḥāmal*; followed by Syr., Tg., Vg.) is impossible to tell. The syntagma "verb plus *lōʾ ḥml*" occurs both asyndetically (2:21c; 3:43) and syndetically (2:17b) in Lamentations. The meaning is the same regardless. Both are to be interpreted adverbially as "without mercy" (R. Gordis, "A Commentary on the Text of Lamentations" in *The Seventy-Fifth Anniversary Volume of the Jewish Quarterly Review* [ed. A. A. Neuman and S. Zetlin; Philadelphia, 1967] 279). I have followed the K here based chiefly on the customary literalness of the LXX.

50. See my "Tragedy, Tradition, and Theology in the Book of Lamentations," *JSOT* 74 (1997) 56–58; *Lamentations*, 25, 56.

51. Read with the MT and the LXX. The Syr., Tg., and Vg. read the syndetic version of the phrase (*wĕlōʾ ḥāmāltā*), as they do in 2:2a.

52. See my *Lamentations*, 67–70.

53. Levine, *Aramaic Version of Lamentations*, 111.

"foe-like, he kills").[54] But 2:5a is the most pointed of the three references, be-cause the "like" (*kĕ-*) in the MT (followed by the LXX) is probably a later theological addition, not preserved in the Syr. (*hw᾿ mry᾿ b᾿ldbb᾿* = Heb. *hyh ᾿dny l᾿wyb*), designed to stress that Yahweh is only acting "as if" he were an enemy but has not in reality "become" an enemy![55] Only in Job (16:9; cf. Isa 63:10) is Yahweh comparably designated. That a Judean poet could call Yah-weh "enemy" is a telling sign of the deep distress and unparalleled suffering brought on by the catastrophe.

A reference to the darkness and gloom that so typifies the Day of Yahweh likely inheres in the Hebrew verb *yā᾿îb* in 2:1a. The verb itself only occurs here in the Hebrew Bible, and therefore its meaning is disputed. However, the

---

54. Most have judged the lineation suggested in *BHS* to be faulty. The versions (LXX, Syr., Tg.) generally lineate so that *kĕṣār* comes at the end of the second line of the first cou-plet in the stanza (e.g., NRSV: "He has bent his bow like an enemy, / with his right hand set like a foe"). That such lineation was not original is suggested by the impossibility of con-struing what remains in 2:4b as a couplet (i.e., it would violate the minimum constraint ["no unit can stand alone as a line"] on line composition in Hebrew verse; see M. O'Con-nor, *Hebrew Verse Structure* [Winona Lake, Ind.: Eisenbrauns, 1980] 67) and the resulting parallelism, which is not the dominant trope in Lamentations (see my "Enjambing Line in Lamentations: A Taxonomy [Part I]," *ZAW* 113/2 [2001] 219–39; "The Effects of Enjamb-ment in Lamentations [Part 2]," *ZAW* 113/5 [2001] 370–85). However, there is no reason that one cannot construe MT (as lineated in *BHS*) as a focusing construction—similar in many respects to the *casus pendens* construction. Here Yahweh's enemy status is being fore-grounded. As I noted, the Tg. effects similar heightening functions, though usually through prosaic elaborations (e.g., 2:4a; 5a). Such a solution makes good sense, and it is eminently preferable to the range of alternate lineations, transpositions, and emendations otherwise prominent in the literature.

55. The Syr. preserves the unique reading. Elsewhere, whenever the MT has the con-struction *hyh k-* it is represented in the Syr. with *᾿yk* (1:1b, 6b; 4:8b; cf. Albrektson, *Studies*, 93). By contrast, the syntagma *hyh l-* is sometimes rendered without the preposition *l-* (1:8a, 17c). All the other versions, including the MT, appear to have made the text conform to the larger context, in which *kĕ-* is used four times (2:3c, 4a, b, c)—twice with words for enemy (2:4a, b)! There is also the added theological motivation, which (as noted above) would want to stress that Yahweh is only acting *like* an enemy. He has not in reality *become* an enemy. This line of interpretation is made most explicit in the Tg., where, as in 2:4a, the Hebrew is translated in such a way (i.e., it uses *dmy l-* to translate the simple Hebrew prepo-sition *kĕ-*) as to reinforce the notion "that God is *as* an enemy, rather than an enemy" (Le-vine, *Aramaic Version of Lamentations*, 111). The Syr. is certainly more provocative and thus the *lectio difficilior* and should be preferred. Here, then, Yahweh's change of status mirrors Jerusalem's change of status in 1:1—both in content and in form. R. Gordis's suggestion ("Commentary," 279) that the MT's *k-* is asseverative in this line amounts to the same sense as suggested here, though his understanding of the syntax seems unlikely, especially in col-location with *hyh*.

larger poetic context of these first eight stanzas, in which Yahweh as the Divine Warrior who battles against Jerusalem on "the day of his anger" factors so centrally, suggests understanding *yāʿīb* as a denominative verb meaning "to becloud, overcloud, engulf in clouds" derived from the common noun *ʿāb* "darkness, cloud," an interpretation in fact found in the versions (LXX [*egnophōsen*] and Syr. [*ʾyb*]; cf. RSV) and supported by many commentators.[56] The darkness associated with the Day of Yahweh both portends calamity and catastrophe and figures the cosmic upheavals that typically accompany Yahweh's theophany (Exod 19:16–19; Deut 4:11; 5:23–24).[57] That is, as a typical ancient Near Eastern storm god,[58] the literary depiction of Yahweh's theophany customarily involves the dark clouds associated with thunderstorms (Exod 3:22; 13:21–22; 14:14; 19:9; 40:38; Lev 9:15, 16; 14:14; Deut 1:33; 4:11; 5:4, 5, 22; 1 Kgs 8:10, 11; Isa 4:5; Ps 78:14; 105:39). And as a warrior deity, Yahweh is frequently imagined as wrapped in clouds (2 Sam 22:12, 13; Ps 97:2; Lam 3:44) or riding upon them through the skies (2 Sam 22:11; Isa 19:1; Ps 68:5, 33; 104:3) or as otherwise associated with them (Judg 5:4). Indeed, the stunning vision that opens the book of Ezekiel portrays Yahweh's war chariot (which is en route to do battle against Jerusalem) as enshrouded with "a great storm cloud" (*ʿānān gādôl*, 1:4). Fittingly, then, Joel (2:2) and Zephaniah (1:15) refer to the Day of Yahweh as "a day of densest cloud" (*yôm ʿānān wāʿărāpel*, NJPS; cf. Ezek 30:2), and Ezekiel (30:18) envisions it as a time when "the city shall be covered by a cloud." Thus, the image of Yahweh "beclouding" Jerusalem is especially well suited to the context. Not only are the clouds a harbinger of impending doom, but also they are the visible manifestation of the Divine Warrior's menacing presence.[59]

---

56. Ewald, *Randglossen*, 331; K. Budde, "Die Klagelieder" in *Die fünf Megillot* (KHC; Tübingen: Mohr, 1898) 85; M. Haller, *Die Klagelieder: Die fünf Megilloth* (HAT; Tübingen: Mohr [Paul Siebeck], 1940) 98; Albrektson, *Studies*, 85–86; Weiser, *Klagelieder*, 58, 62; Kraus, *Klagelieder*, 32; Provan, *Lamentations*, 58–59; Dobbs-Allsopp, *Weep, O Daughter of Zion*, 64; Westermann, *Lamentations*, 140, 144.

57. Mettinger ("Name and Glory," 18–22) notes the centrality of theophany to the Zion tradition and its exilic successors.

58. For the seminal treatment of this theme with special reference to the relationship between Yahweh and Baal, see F. M. Cross, *Canaanite Myth and Hebrew Epic* (Cambridge: Harvard University Press, 1973) 147–95; for an updated discussion and ample bibliographic references, see M. S. Smith, *The Early History of God* (San Francisco: Harper & Row, 1987) esp. 49–55.

59. Hillers's complaint that this explanation "is suspiciously ad hoc, and the meaning is not especially suited to this context, nor is 'beclouding' otherwise an image for punishment" (*Lamentations*, 96) seems to me to be misspoken. To the contrary, the image of storm clouds seems especially well suited to the context of Lam 2:1–8, as noted above. Moreover, destruction narratives in the Bible are frequently set at night (e.g., Genesis 19, Joshua 2,

Of the remaining features associated with the Day of Yahweh motif, only the attribution of sin is conspicuously missing.[60] The reaction to the bad news

Judges 19–21) so as to evoke the malevolent, foreboding, and ominous feelings associated with darkness (W. W. Fields, "The Motif 'Night as Danger' Associated with Three Biblical Destruction Narratives," in *"Sha'arei Talmon": Studies in the Bible, Qumran, and the Ancient Near East Presented to Shemaryahu Talmon* (ed. Michael Fishbane and Emanuel Tov; Winona Lake, Ind.: Eisenbrauns, 1992) 17–32. Furthermore, poets down through the ages can be shown to be rather fond of creating neologisms. In this case, the verb *yā'îb* offers an economy of language that would be unachievable with the nominal *'āb*. And it also results in a striking image: that of Yahweh intentionally beclouding. It lends a dynamism to the otherwise natural process—one that economically captures the image of a fast-moving thunderhead moving across the valley in a mountainous region. In fact, the image is lent a further degree of depth, as Provan notes (*Lamentations*, 59), when one remembers that elsewhere, when Yahweh makes contact with Israel through the medium of a cloud (Exod 19:9; 34:5–6; 1 Kgs 8:10–13), it is usually something positive (cf. Weiser, *Klagelieder*, 62; Albrektson, *Studies*, 86). Hence, the conventional theophany of Yahweh is compellingly turned on its head. Finally, one can observe a similar development of a denominative verb from the noun *'ānān* "cloud" in Gen 9:14: "When I bring clouds (*bĕ'annî 'ānān*) over the earth, and the bow is in the clouds, I will remember my covenant . . . and the waters will never again become a flood to destroy all flesh." Indeed, one wonders whether or not the allusion is intentional, pointing up the broken covenant and Yahweh's revoking of his promise.

Two other explanations of *yā'îb* are less commendable. The comparison with Arab. *'āba* "to dishonor, disgrace" (Ehrlich, *Randglassen*, 35; Rudolph, "Text," 105; T. J. Meek, "The Book of Lamentations," *IB* [Nashville: Abingdon, 1956] 6.16; H. H. Gottlieb, *A Study of the Text of Lamentations* [Acta Jutlandica 48, Theology Series 12; Arhus: Det laerde Selskab, 1978] 23; O. Kaiser, *Klagelieder* [ATD 16/2; Göttingen: Vandenhoeck & Ruprecht, 1992] 124) results in the rather banal line, "he disgraced Zion in anger," and has no good parallels. McDaniel's ("Philological Studies, I," 34–35) and Hillers's (*Lamentations*, 96) contention that *y'yb* is best derived from **w'b* "to show contempt" (presumably the root that stands behind Heb. *tô'ēbâ* "abomination") is potentially more interesting. However, the parallel they cite, "The anger of Yahweh was kindled against his people, / and he abhorred (*waytā'ēb*) his inheritance" (Ps 106:40), while tantalizing close to our passage, also bears a glaring weakness: why form a new denominative, when a perfectly good denominative verb already exists, *t'b*, which appears 22 times in the Hebrew Bible?

60. The absence of attributions of sin or guilt to Zion is not insignificant. It robs, at least momentarily, Yahweh's terrible assault of any obvious justification. Indeed, as K. O'Connor notes ("Lamentations" in *NIB* 6 [Nashville: Abingdon, 2001], the reader gains the impression of a mad deity, who is out of control. Yahweh's ferocious anger is lacking any explicit justification (citations). To be sure, themes of sin and guilt will be raised at least once later in the poem (2:14b) and appear elsewhere in the sequence—they are especially prominent in Lamentations 1 (see my *Lamentations*). So it is not the case that the poet fails to attend to Jerusalem's sin or that the reader who comes to Lamentations 2 through Lamentations 1 will assume that Yahweh's actions are totally unmotivated; but neither can we simply read concepts of sin (Deuteronomic or otherwise) into this section of the poem, as is usually done. The suppression of the sin theme (especially in light of the otherwise wholesale use of the Day of Yahweh traditions) and the resulting lyric rendition of Yahweh's onslaught

of the coming Day of Yahweh appears in a modified and adapted form in 2:9–
12,[61] and the haunt of the wild animals theme turns up emblematically else-

---

must be encountered, at least initially, on their own terms. And on this reading Yahweh's
turning against Jerusalem takes on a decidedly sinister feel, which is only mollified somewhat retrospectively as readers wonder about sin and justification—whether because of its
obvious lack or because of the theme's greater prominence in Lamentations 1.

61. Lam 2:9–12 is loosely shaped by the reaction-to-bad-news motif that is found in
some Day of Yahweh passages (e.g., Isa 13:6–8). The heart of the poet's refiguration of the
bad-news motif begins with 2:9b–c, where the poem shifts to focus more intently on the
city's population and their reaction to the catastrophe. The description of dismay at the approach of bad news is a commonplace in Ugaritic and biblical literature. See D. R. Hillers,
"A Convention in Hebrew Literature: The Reaction to Bad News," *ZAW* 77 (1965) 86–
90. The convention is comprised of a variety of elements, including most prototypically:
(1) approach of the bad news; (2) hands falling helpless; (3) pains in the loins; and (4) melt-
ing or overturning of the heart. Jer 6:24 (cf. Isa 21:3–4; Jer 49:23; 50:43; Ezek 21:11–12)
contains most of these:

> We have heard news of them,
>   our hands fall helpless;
> anguish has taken hold of us,
>   pain as of a woman in labor.

Most interestingly for our purposes, the convention is used to figure both the general dismay at the approaching Day of Yahweh (Isa 13:7–8; Ezek 7:17–18, 25–27; Joel 2:6) and
the response of the attacking enemy kings to the sight of cosmic Zion (Ps 48:5–8). Ezekiel
7 is especially enlightening because it adds two additional elements to the four mentioned
above: people in mourning (vv. 18, 27) and the paralysis of the ruling elite (v. 26):

> All hands shall grow feeble,
>   all knees turn to water.
> They shall put on sackcloth,
>   horror shall cover them.
> Shame shall be on all faces,
>   baldness on all heads.
>   . . . .
> Disaster comes upon disaster,
>   rumor follows rumor;
> they shall keep seeking a vision from the prophet,
>   instruction shall perish from the priest,
>   and counsel from the elders.
> The king shall mourn,
>   the prince shall be wrapped in despair,
>   and the hands of the people of the land shall tremble. (Ezek 7:17–18, 26–27)

Five out of the six groups of people mentioned in both Lam 2:9–10 and Ezek 7:26–27 are
the same: priests, prophets, king, princes (*śār* vs. *nāśî'*), and elders. Both passages agree on the
failure of the prophets to obtain visions and the perishing of the Torah (NRSV "guidance"/

where (esp. 5:18; cf. 4:3). Thus, the centrality of the motif to this section of the poem is beyond doubt. But what is most significant is how the poet uses the Day of Yahweh motif, in modified form (e.g., Jerusalem is the target instead of some enemy nation, and Yahweh is a menacing enemy instead of an avenging savior), to effect an overturning or undoing of the Zion tradition and not simply a reinterpretation thereof.

First, the poem's opening stanza effects a kind of stripping away of the cosmic potency that became associated with Zion. The language in 2:1b, casting down "from heaven to earth," is usually understood figuratively as symbolizing

---

"instruction"). The differences in these passages come, in the first place, in who is depicted as mourning. In Lam 2:10 the "elders" (i.e., the old men) and "young girls," as a merism meant to represent the entire surviving population, are depicted as performing conventional mourning gestures, whereas in Ezek 7:27 the king and princes are so depicted. The other major difference—itself very telling—is the temporal perspective from which these passages are presented. Ezekiel 7, following the reaction-to-bad-news motif more closely, shows these as a response to the news of an event still in the future—note, for example, the future tense of the NRSV's translation of the Hebrew imperfective verb forms. Psalm 48, as well, shows the enemy responding to the mere sight of God's cosmic mountain, Zion, prior to any attempted assault:

> Then the kings assembled,
>   they came on together.
> As soon as they saw it, they were astounded;
>   they were in panic, they took to flight;
> trembling took a hold of them there,
>   pains as of a woman in labor,
> as when the east wind shatters
>   the ships of Tarshish.
> As we have heard, so we have seen
>   in the city of the Lord of hosts,
> in the city of our God,
>   which God establishes forever. (Ps 48:5–8)

In Lam 2:9–10, however, the reaction has been transposed to a time after the destruction of Jerusalem. Thus, the people do not "keep seeking a vision from the prophet" in hopes of countering Ezekiel's prophesy. Rather, the prophets themselves cannot "find" a vision from (or even "because of") Yahweh. And the Torah will not only "perish from the priests," but it simply is no more, nonexistent. The king and princes suffer the same fate as does personified Zion in 1:3b—they are (exiled) "among the nations," and the elders and young girls mourn for real, not just in anticipation of some foretold, future calamity. Finally, it is the sad sight of ruined Jerusalem, not the awe-inspiring sight of the impregnable fortress of the "Lord of hosts," that triggers these reactions—again the perspective is *post eventum*. Thus, our poet skillfully transforms the bad-news motif from a frightening portent of future calamity into a sad memorial to a past catastrophe.

Zion's humiliation (especially in readings, such as that of the NRSV, in which yā'ib in 2:1a is construed to mean "humiliated"). However, the language, though figured and certainly implying humiliation (cf. Ps 102:11), is to be taken quite literally as well. The verb "to throw down, cast aside" signifies rejection, spurning; literally, a casting out of one's presence (2 Kgs 13:23; 17:20; 24:20; Ps 51:13; 71:9; Jer 52:3; cf. Jer 22:28; Ezek 16:3). In particular, the verb is used with reference to Yahweh's rejection and destruction of the Shiloh sanctuary (Jer 7:15) and of personified Tyre (Ezek 28:17). The latter is especially remarkable in that Tyre is depicted very similarly to that of Zion in the Zion tradition: Tyre is called "signet of perfection" and "perfect in beauty" (Ezek 28:12), imagined as sitting enthroned (Ezek 28:2) atop God's "holy" and cosmic mountain (Ezek 28:14, 16) and in his dwelling place ("Eden, the garden of God," Ezek 28:13), and ultimately "cast" off God's heavenly mountain to the "earth" in a fashion very reminiscent of the ejection and banishment from heaven of the rebellious "Day Star" in Isaiah 14 (esp. v. 12).

Thus, Yahweh's treatment of the personified "splendor of Israel" (cf. Isa 13:19; 22:2; 23:7; 28:1, 4; Jer 48:2; 49:25; Ezek 26:17; 27:3; Nah 2:8a; Zeph 2:15; Lam 2:15c) in 2:1b enacts emblematically what is elaborated in Ezekiel 28 (and Isaiah 14), namely: a rejection of Zion, a stripping of the cosmic status with which she was imbued in the Zion tradition, and thus a denigration of an important part of that tradition. Yahweh does not so much abandon Zion—a theme prevalent elsewhere in Lamentations (1:1a; 5:20) and the Mesopotamian city laments—as remove her, spatially, physically, from his presence. The net result, however, is the same as divine abandonment. Zion is denied access to Yahweh's protective presence.

The reference to "his footstool" in the following couplet points in the same direction. As already noted, the ark of the covenant could be understood as forming Yahweh's footstool (Ps 99:5; 132:7; 1 Chr 28:2), but by metonymic extension (synecdoche) it also comes to represent the Jerusalem temple as a whole (Isa 60:13). The thought behind such imagery is that Yahweh's throne is in heaven—that is, his dwelling is remote, transcendent—but humans may gain access to the divine presence through the earthly temple, envisioned as a footstool (cf. Isa 6:1–13; 66:1). By not remembering his footstool, Yahweh effectively cuts off access to his divine presence—the temple no longer functions as the vehicle permitting access to Yahweh (as, for example, in Isaiah 6).[62]

---

62. The ark's function is similarly rethought in the Deuteronomistic history. According to Mettinger ("Name and Glory," 6), it "loses its old numinous role as the footstool of God, reappearing as a storage chest for the tablets of the Law."

One of the central implications of the Zion mythos was security for Jerusalem and the city's inhabitants. As the deity's dwelling place, Jerusalem was believed to be protected by Yahweh himself. Such a belief is dramatically displayed in texts such as Isa 29:1–8, where Yahweh appears at the last moment to defend and save Jerusalem:

> And in an instant, suddenly,
> you will be visited by the Lord of hosts
> with thunder and earthquake and great noise,
> with whirlwind and tempest, and the flame of a devouring fire.
> And the multitude of all the nations that fight against Ariel,
> . . . .
> shall be like a dream, a vision of the night.

And the presumption of Jerusalem's inviolability clearly lies behind the dismay and astonishment voiced in Lam 4:12:[63]

> The kings of the earth did not believe,
> nor did any of the inhabitants of the world,
> that foe or enemy could enter
> the gates of Jerusalem.

However, in Lam 2:1–8 the withdrawal of Yahweh's divine protection is dramatically enacted. Throughout the ancient Near East the expression "hand of DN" designated the "disastrous manifestation of supernatural power."[64] The "disastrous manifestations" of Yahweh's "right hand" are usually reserved for Israel and Judah's enemies in Hebrew literature, and thus the hand of Yahweh is primarily a symbol of divine protection, power, and might (Exod 13:21–22; 15:6, 12, 16; Isa 41:10; Ps 20:7; 44:4; 48:11; 60:7; 89:14; 98:1; 118:11). However, in Lamentations 2 Yahweh's hand has apparently undergone a "change" (cf. Ps 77:11). In 2:3b Yahweh's "right hand" is withdrawn from before the invading enemy, leaving the city defenseless and open to attack.[65] The lineation

---

63. Albrektson, *Studies*, 225–26.

64. J. J. M. Roberts, "The Hand of Yahweh" in *Bible and the Ancient Near East*, 96 (= *VT* 21 [1971] 246).

65. The *Hiphil* (or *Hophal*) of *šwb* and *swg* with *'āḥôr* is used elsewhere with the meaning "to turn away, repudiate, reject, disavow" (Isa 44:25; 59:14; Ps 44:11; Lam 1:13b). For the specific sense to "refrain from" with the preposition *min*, see Isa 58:13; Ezek 18:8, 17; and 20:22. For the specific imagery of hands being "withdrawn" using the *Hiphil* of *šwb*, see Gen 38:29; Josh 8:26; 1 Kgs 13:4; and Ps 74:11. What is at issue here is the intended referent of the 3rd masc. sing. suffix on *yĕmînô*: does it refer back to Israel (Ehrlich, *Randglassen*, 35; N. K. Gottwald, *Studies in the Book of Lamentations* [London: SCM, 1954] 10 n. 10; Hillers, *Lamentations*, 98) or Yahweh (Tg. ["He drew back his right hand and did not

in 2:3b, enforced by the enjambment (*hēšîb ʾāḥôr yĕmînô / mipnê ʾôyēb*), even reflects this thematic content.[66] The pause between *yĕmînô* and *mipnê* effectively mirrors what Yahweh's withdrawal of support brings about: the enemy is unencumbered and thus free to attack the city. Yahweh's hand is literally separated from the enemy by the pause at line-end.

In the second line of 2:4a we have another reference to Yahweh's "right hand." The line is slightly garbled so the ultimate significance of the reference is not transparent, and thus open to varying interpretations.[67] Many emendations have been proposed. Among the most compelling are those suggested by W. Rudolph, who reconstructs *ḥiṣṣāw bîmînô* "with his arrows in his right

---

help his people from before the enemy"]; Weiser, *Klagelieder*, 63; Rudolph, *Klagelieder*, 218; Kraus, *Klagelieder*, 42; Gottlieb, *Studies*, 25–26; Provan, *Lamentations*, 62; Dobbs-Allsopp, *Weep, O Daughter of Zion*, 64; Westermann, *Lamentations*, 123)? Decontextualized, the reference could be to either. As some have noted, *yāmîn* and *qeren* both symbolize strength, and thus the image here is analogous to that of 2:3a; Yahweh is humbling Israel. In support of this interpretation, note Jer 48:25 ("the horn [*qeren*] of Moab is cut off, and his arm [*zĕrōʿô*] is broken, says Yahweh") and Ps 44:11 (*tĕšîbēnû ʾāḥôr minnî-ṣār* "you turned us back from the enemy"), which is especially close to the sense implied if the suffix refers to Israel. And yet, without dismissing the potential resonance of this interpretation, it nevertheless seems apparent in the present context that the implied referent is most prominently Yahweh. As noted, the first eight stanzas of this poem focus on Yahweh as the divine warrior, and it is by Yahweh's right hand that his saving power is routinely manifested on behalf of Israel (Isa 41:10; Ps 20:7; 44:4; 48:11; 60:7; 77:11; 89:14; 98:1; 118:15, 16; Job 40:14), especially in the Song of the Sea and elsewhere in Exodus (13:21–22; 15:6, 12, 16). Indeed, the *Hiphil* of *šwb* is used with hand to signify Yahweh's judgment (Isa 1:25; 14:27; Amos 1:8; Zech 13:7; Ps 81:15). Moreover, the 3rd masc. sing. suffix occurs 14 other times in these opening eight stanzas (2:1a, b [twice]. 2b, 4a [twice], 4c, 5b, 6a [twice], 6c, 7a [twice], 8b), and without a single exception they all refer back to Yahweh (including *yĕmînô* in 2:4a). Thus, it is hard to dispute the strong contextual presumption of a highly prominent reference to Yahweh here. Ps 74:11 provides an especially close parallel to the sense presumed here: "Why dost thou hold back (*tāšîb*) thy hand (*yādĕkā*), / why dost thou keep thy right hand (*wîmînekā*) in thy bosom?" (RSV). And, as if to bring the point home, note how the protective "right hand" that Yahweh withholds from before the attacking enemy here is not withheld (*lōʾ-hēšîb / yādô*) from consuming Zion in 2:8b. As Provan notes (*Lamentations*, 62), all the traditional symbols of Yahweh's past presence with Israel—cloud, fire, and now his right hand—in these first several verses of the second poem are perverted and turned against Israel. The hand that saved Israel in the past is the same hand that now destroys her.

66. See my "Effects of Enjambment," 385.

67. MT *niṣṣāb*; LXX *estereōse dexian autou*; Syr. *ʾqym ymynh*; Vg. *firmavit dexteram suam*. The mismatch of gender in the MT (*niṣṣāb*—masc.; *yĕmînô*—fem.) suggests that as it stands the MT is not original.

hand" (cf. Ezek 39:3),[68] and D. R. Hillers, who reads *niṣṣāb bîmînô* "the sword hilt was in his right hand" (cf. Judg 3:22).[69] Both are eminently possible, but neither inspires complete confidence. Rudolph's emendation is based on the assumption that the LXX, Syr., and Vg. are reading the causative form *hiṣṣîb*. He emends because the idiom **hṣyb ymyn* is not otherwise attested in BH. While he may be correct that the idiom itself is not otherwise attested, neither is it nonsensical.[70] The *Hiphil* of *nṣb* is used in 3:12 in the sense of setting up or preparing a target and in Jer 5:26 to set a trap. And the synonymous verb *kwn* is used with the same basic semantic range in both the *Hiphil* (to ready a net in Ps 57:7 and more generally to prepare weapons for battle in Ps 7:14 and 2 Chr 26:14) and the *Polel* (to aim a bow, as in Ps 21:13, or otherwise get it ready, as in Ps 7:13; and, more specifically, to set an arrow on the string in Ps 11:2).[71] And thus, a solution involving the root *nṣb* is imaginable. One possibility is to read *yaṣṣēb yĕmînô* "he poises his right hand."[72] If this proposal is on the right track, the image in 2:4a is that of Yahweh's readying his "right hand"—his weapon par excellence!—for battle. Thus, not only does Yahweh deny Judah his divine protection, but also the chief symbol of that protection, "his right hand," may be poised to do battle against Judah.

And finally, in 2:8b, as if to bring the point home, Yahweh's protective "right hand," having been withdrawn from its defensive posture and then (possibly) readied for battle, is finally engaged and not withheld "from destroying," from displaying the full extent of Yahweh's brutal and disastrous power. However the garbled line in 2:4a is finally resolved, in 2:8b there is a reversal in the hand imagery introduced in 2:3b. In the latter Yahweh withdrew his protective hand from before the enemy. Now in 2:8b he refuses to withdraw his hand from destroying Zion. So that the use of the negative here formally suggests the opposite of the earlier positive phrase (*hēšîb . . . yĕmînô //*
lōʾ-hēšîb yādô), by changing the objects (enemy in 2:3b and Zion [implied] in 2:8b), the sense of the two phrases turns out to be equivalent, dare I say even

---

68. Rudolph, "Text," 106; cf. Wesier, *Klagelieder*, 59.

69. Hillers, *Lamentations*, 98.

70. Cf. Kraus, *Klagelieder*, 32.

71. Albrektson's interpretation ("the right hand holds the arrow and stretches the string") is especially close to the general sense of these latter passages, though his analysis of the syntax is extremely forced (*Studies*, 91–92).

72. In supposing the prefix form of the verb (instead of the suffix), which both the LXX and the Syr. (see Lam 3:12; Gen 21:28; 33:20) are capable of supporting, I assume that the MT has resulted from a confusion between *nun* and *yod*. Otherwise there is no obvious way to explain how the MT was corrupted from a putative *hṣb*. For other prefix forms in this poem, see *yāʿîb* (2:1a) and perhaps *yēšĕbû* (2:10a).

parallel! Note that *yad* and *yāmîn* are classic A and B terms in Hebrew poetry (e.g., Judg 5:26; Ps 21:9), the reversal of their normal order perhaps signifying the overturning of expectations as contained in the phrases themselves.[73] In each case, the hand that saved Judah in the past is the same hand that now destroys her, leaving the myth of Zion's inviolability wrecked in its wake.

Other aspects of the Zion tradition are similarly and intentionally debunked in this section of the poem. The reign of peace that was to be inaugurated by Yahweh's victory (e.g., Ezek 39:10–11; Ps 46:10–11; 76:4–9) is in little evidence in Lam 2:1–8. Joy (Ps 48:2) is replaced by "mourning and moaning" (*ta'ăniyyâ wa'ăniyyâ*,[74] 2:5c), and weapons are brandished (2:4a) instead of broken (Isa 2:2–4; Mic 4:1–4). The enemies (Ps 46:7; 48:5–7; 76:6–8), who were to have been turned back by Yahweh's thunderous voice (Ps 46:7; 76:7, 9) and made to grovel before him, acknowledging his sovereignty (Ps 76:11–13; Zech 14:16–19), instead, rejoice and their "might" is exalted (Lam 2:17c). In fact, Yahweh has become one of them (2:4a, b; 5a), he himself cutting down the "might of Israel" (2:3a; cf. Ps 132:17), with echoes of his thunderous voice resounding in the ruined temple (2:7c). Hebrew *qeren* "might"[75] in both 2:3a and 17c literally refers to a "horn" (of a bull or wild ox) and is always used as a metaphor for power and authority and "is usually associated with divine deliverance from one's enemies."[76] That Yahweh cuts

---

73. As in 2:3b, the enjambment in 2:8b is also representational (see my "Effects of Enjambment," 385). As lineated in *BHS* (*lō'-hēšîb / yādô mibbalēaʿ*), the hand, which here is not withdrawn, straddles the pause and thus effectively mimes Yahweh's ongoing consumption. If one lineates more conservatively (*nātâ qāw / lō'-hēšîb yādô mibbalēaʿ*), then the enjambment remains representational, though of a different kind. The lack of a pause within the second clause mirrors the continuity of action, Yahweh's refusal to withdraw his consuming hand.

74. This is a wonderful example of the poet's conscientiousness of sound play (cf. Isa 29:2). The Syr.'s more prosaic rendering (*twny' w'wlyt'*; see also NRSV's "mourning and lamentation") points this up effectively.

75. Curiously, though most commentators recognize the figurative use of *qeren* here as a symbol for power or might (e.g., Weiser, *Klagelieder*, 63; Rudolph, *Klagelieder*, 222–23; Kraus, *Klagelieder*, 37; Provan, *Lamentations*, 61; Hillers, *Lamentations*, 97–98), many still insist on translating it literally as "horn" (e.g., Weiser, *Klagelieder*, 58; Rudolph, *Klagelieder*, 216; Provan, *Lamentations*, 61; Hillers, *Lamentations* 93; notable exceptions include Kraus, *Klagelieder*, 31; Kaiser, *Klagelieder*, 325; Westermann, *Lamentations*, 141; cf. NRSV, NJPSV). The presence of *kōl* (only here), of course, makes a literal rendering nonsensical. What sense could "every horn of Israel" possibly have? Rather, the only interpretation is the figurative one. For close parallels to the reduction of "power" envisioned here, see Jer 48:25 and Ps 75:11. The humiliation will be compounded in 2:17c because the enemy's "might" will be lifted up instead of Judah's (as in 1 Sam 2:10; Ezek 29:21; Zech 2:4; Ps 89:18, 25; 132:17; 148:14).

76. C. L. Seow, *Myth, Drama, and the Politics of David's Dance* (HSM 46; Atlanta: Scholars Press, 1989) 197.

down Judah's "might" and magnifies the "might" of the enemy encapsulates, emblematically, the overturning of the Zion tradition that is accomplished in this opening section. Finally, in 2:8, the very architecture that served as the visible token of everything for which the Zion tradition stood and about which the psalmist implores his audience to "walk" and "go all around," to "count its towers," "consider well its ramparts," and "go through its citadels" (Ps 48:13–14) is razed.[77] The language of intentionality (2:8a)[78] and of stretching a measuring line (2:8b),[79]

---

77. Levenson ("Zion Traditions," 1099) stresses that Mount Zion itself and its structures provide "visual testimony" to and "geographical and architectural" affirmation of the Zion tradition.

78. The LXX (kai epetrepse) likely reflects the scribe's anticipation of hēšîb in the second couplet. The constraints of the acrostic require a ḥet, and thus the MT (ḥāšab yhwh lĕhašḥît) should be preferred. The Syr.'s plural (šwryh) collapses the difference in number evidenced in the MT here and in 2:7b (the LXX does the same in the other direction in 2:7b, i.e., teichos). The MT is to be retained as lectio difficilior. The verb ḥāšab, in the first place, stresses the fact that Yahweh's destruction is planned and intentional (Jer 18:11; 29:11; 26:3; 36:3; 49:20; 50:45; Mic 2:3). Compare especially 2 Chr 25:16: "God has determined (yāʿaṣ) to destroy (lĕhašḥîtekā) you." The motif of Yahweh's "divine plan" occurs elsewhere in the poem (2:17a, especially zāmam) and is generally associated with the divine-word motif throughout the Hebrew Bible and, even, in the Mesopotamian laments (Albrektson, History and the Gods, 68–97; Kraus, Klagelieder, 47–48; Dobbs-Allsopp, Weep, O Daughter of Zion, 61). In this way the poet wants to stress that the destruction of Jerusalem was not accidental, thus preserving Yahweh's integrity and omnipotence. In light of the idiom nāṭâ qāw in the succeeding couplet, ḥšb may well take on retrospectively the more specific nuance of Yahweh's active planning of the demolition of the city and temple—metonymically represented here by the "wall" of personified Zion. Though never used with this precise nuance, note that the root ḥšb is used of the work of crafts people and artisans, especially concerning the construction of the tabernacle in P (Exod 26:1, 31; 28:6, 15; 31:4; 35:32, 35; 36:8, 35; 38:23; 39:8; Amos 6:5; 2 Chr 2:13; 26:15). The root is used in the Niphal in 4:2b. As earlier in the poem (2:5b, 6a), the root šḥt (here used in the Hiphil) is used to designate the destruction of an architectural unit, a wall (cf. Gen 13:10; 19:14, 29; 2 Sam 24:1; Jer 48:1; Ezek 43:3—all with Yahweh as subject; Gen 19:13; 1 Sam 23:10; 2 Kgs 18:25; Jer 6:5; Ezek 26:4; Dan 9:26). In Ezek 26:4 the walls of Tyre are destroyed.

79. The possibility of an alternative lineation (breaking the initial line after nāṭâ qāw) to the lineation represented in BHS should be considered. Aside from hendiadys constructions (2:2a, 9a, 15b, 16c, 17b, 19a, 21c,) or other reduced complement structures (2:8a, b) or contiguously conjoined verb phrases, the bulk of multiverb couplets in Lamentations 1–4 split the verbs among both lines (note the examples in Lamentations 2: vv. 5a, b, 6a, 7a, 8c, 9a, 10b, 11a, 13c, 14b, 16b, c, 17a, b, c, 18b, 21c; vv. 13a, b, and 20a are the notable exceptions). The qaw is a line used for measuring (mdd, Ezek 47:3; sbb, 1 Kgs 7:23) things: the circumference of a bowl of some sort (ḥayyām mûṣāq, 1 Kgs 7:23), the course of the river in Ezekiel's temple vision (Ezek 47:3), land (Isa 34:17), wood for an idol (Isa 44:17), the foundations of the earth (Job 38:5), and materials and such for building a city or the like (Jer 31:39;

though prototypically the vocabulary of building,[80] is on occasion (2 Kgs 24:13; Isa 34:11) used to figure destruction and demolition, because "demolition itself requires careful planning."[81] Thus, there can be no denying the exactness and forethought that goes into Yahweh's actions. Jerusalem's destruction is no accident, nor the result of some divine lapse of mind.

And beyond the obvious literal resonances that the image of razing and demolition is meant to conjure—a ruined Jerusalem completely devoid of any physical reminders of its glorious past—there is an allusion to, or even a parody of, the very kind of sanctuary-razing ceremonies for which the Mesopotamian city laments and *balags* were originally composed. Before old temples could be renovated or completely rebuilt, any walls remaining visible would have to be demolished. During this demolition, offerings were made and lamentations (i.e., the city laments or *balags*) sung in front of a brick from the old temple until the foundations of the new temple were laid. The purpose of this ritual was to placate the god's anger. Our poet, in the spirit of Second Isaiah's more famous parody of idol-making (Isa 44:9–20), though much more somberly, parodies this kind of sanctuary-razing ceremony.[82] Here it is Yahweh, instead of the master builder, who does the necessary measuring in preparation for the demolition, and the first part of the poem is intent on showing

---

Zech 1:16). The syntagma *nāṭâ qāw* simply indicates the process of stretching the measuring line—that is, the act of measuring itself (2 Kgs 21:13; Isa 34:11; 44:13; Zech 1:16; Job 38:5). Hillers, noting that stretching a line is prototypically the action of a builder, wonders how "a phrase from the vocabulary of building becomes a synonym for destruction" (*Lamentations*, 99), as it does here and in 2 Kgs 24:13 and Isa 34:11. At one level, irony may be intended. That is, the measuring and other things that normally accompany building are turned on their head and used antithetically to indicate demolition and destruction. Our poet's ironic tendencies have already been abundantly noted. Moreover, Isa 34:17 generally supports this line of interpretation. There Edom is to be turned into a ruin inhabited only by jackals, hyenas, and so forth, which, of course, is the antithetic image of an otherwise flourishing city or nation. But Provan (*Lamentations*, 68; following Kaiser, *Lamentations*, 336) is equally correct to think that "demolition itself requires careful planning," and measurements are needed when buildings are to be demolished. However, I cannot follow Provan when he concludes that "God first checks the wall and condemns it. Only then does he proceed to destroy it" (*Lamentations*, 68). The stretching of the line has nothing to do with determining guilt or innocence (Provan's checking and condemning)—which was determined already in the past (cf. Paul, *Amos*, 235 n. 78)—but rather is prefatory to the execution of judgment.

80. Hillers, *Lamentations*, 99.

81. Provan, *Lamentations*, 68; cf. Kaiser, *Klagelieder*, 336.

82. Demolition and razing are also the exact opposite of the duty to build Yahweh's city that is one of the chief implications associated with the Zion tradition; see Roberts, "Theology in the Davidic-Solomonic Empire," 342–43.

that Yahweh's anger is anything but placated. The parody brings into relief the distinction between Lamentations and the classic city laments from Mesopotamian. The latter eventually look forward to renewal and rebirth. A similar trajectory is reflected in the latter part of Psalm 78 (esp. vv. 56–72), where, in good city-lament fashion, Yahweh abandons "his dwelling at Shiloh" and delivers "his glory" (*tip*ʾ*artô*; cf. 2:1b) into captivity. Shiloh was destroyed (as the archeological evidence well attests)[83] and its inhabitants killed. And though Shiloh was not rebuilt, Yahweh chose a new dwelling place, Zion, and there he built a new sanctuary "like the high heavens, / like the earth" (Ps 78:69).[84] In Lamentations, by contrast, the city and its temple, once destroyed, remain in ruins (esp. 5:18), and there is no evidence for any kind of rebuilding.

After the *blitzkrieg* of these opening stanzas, the one aspect of the Zion tradition that remains intact is the image of Yahweh as the enthroned warrior-king, though, significantly, he has now changed sides and become an enemy of Judah, and his heavenly dwelling place (5:19) no longer has an earthly anchor. As C. Westermann recognizes, the latter verse in Lamentations 5 is not spoken with its customary jubilation but stands almost as a rebuke of the divine, since Yahweh's perpetual enthronement in heaven renders the deity practically inaccessible (with the earthly temple demolished), and thus locates Yahweh far away from the human misery that is the subject of the poem.[85] Here, then, the mythic charter authorizing Jerusalem's special status is shattered. Unlike either the earlier Isaiah of Jerusalem or the later anonymous author of Zechariah 9–14, both of whom envision Yahweh's battle against Jerusalem as a purgation necessary for the city's ultimate salvation, our poet cannot (yet) foresee a future for the city or its temple and thus has them and their attendant ideological superstructure completely razed.

---

83. For details, see I. Finkelstein, "Excavations at Shiloh 1981–1984," *Tel Aviv* 12 (1985) 123–80, esp. 170, 173–74.

84. For details and the plausibility of finding city-lament imagery and motifs in Psalm 78, see E. L. Greenstein, "Qinah ʿal hurban ʿir umiqdaš besifrut hayisraʾelit ha-qedumah," in *Homage to Shmuel: Studies in the World of the Bible* (ed. Z. Talshir et al.; Jerusalem: Ben Gurion University Press, 2001) 88–97. [in Hebrew]

85. C. Westermann, *Lamentations: Issues and Interpretation* (Minneapolis: Fortress, 1994) 216; see my *Lamentations*, 148. Indeed, all of the elements of the Zion tradition refracted in Lamentations are rhetorically framed so as to show their current bankruptcy: Yahweh's footstool is no longer remembered (2:1c), the proclamations of Zion's idyllic perfection and joy are turned into derisive taunts in the mouths of the passersby (2:15c), the kings of the land are astonished by Jerusalem's violation (4:12), and even Yahweh's *měšíaḥ*, his earthly regent, is ignominiously captured in a pit (5:20).

This initial part of the poem is thick with meaning. The blending of the two mythic complexes, the Day of Yahweh and the Zion tradition, makes for a fabulous figuration of Yahweh's assault on and destruction of Jerusalem and its temple. It also maintains a connection with Judah's broken past that both validates and memorializes that past and lends meaning and significance to the community's present experience.[86] The traditions themselves as they are modified (and, in the case of the Zion tradition, all but obliterated) and fitted to current circumstances are shown to be vital and life-enhancing. The twin anomalies (from the standpoint of the Zion tradition) of Jerusalem's destruction and of Yahweh's failure to rescue it are directly confronted, and a new pattern of reality is created in order to reduce the perceived dissonance between Judah's present historical reality and its mythic traditions of the past. This new emerging pattern of reality, or as N. K. Gottwald describes it, this "new ethical and spiritual foundation for community,"[87] remains fragmented and very much in flux.

Perhaps its most startling aspect is the metaphorical depiction of Yahweh as enemy. Imagining Yahweh as enemy has both pragmatic and metaphorical effects. Perhaps the most pragmatic effect of such a move is to align Yahweh with the winning side and thereby enact a wonderful strategy for safeguarding Yahweh's potency. By simply switching Yahweh's allegiance from Judah to Judah's enemies, the poet is able to show Yahweh in all his power and might as a still-vital force, able to maintain absolute authority and control of historical events. Indeed, he is no otiose or even a semi-otiose deity who must be aroused into action as if from sleep. And concerning this god, there is no gap between historical reality and the myths of old. The destruction suffered by Jerusalem was not an aberration; it did not come about because of some mysterious lapse in divine life or because the divine life itself had been extinguished. Rather, it was the methodical and measured action of a still-vigorous and menacing deity, who remains capable of realizing the kind of pyrotechnic grandeur recounted in Judah's ancient lore.[88]

But the consequences of this highly pragmatic move ultimately become measured in the metaphor's rich surplus of meaning. Metaphor is a figurative expression "in which a word or phrase ordinarily and primarily used of one

---

86. This is done in a way not dissimilar to the dignity-lending function of the multiple allusions to the Egyptian captivity in Lamentations 1; see my *Lamentations*, 75–77.

87. N. K. Gottwald, "The Book of Lamentations Reconsidered," *The Hebrew Bible in Its Social World and in Ours* (Atlanta: Scholars Press, 1993) 165.

88. My language here reflects that of J. Levenson in *Creation and the Persistence of Evil* (Princeton: Princeton University Press, 1989).

thing is applied to another,"[89] the net effect of which is to ascribe the attributes of the former to the latter. In this case, the enemy metaphor attaches
the attributes of the enemy to Yahweh. Beyond portraying Yahweh as poised
to do battle (2:4a, b), the metaphor is never explicitly developed. Rather, it is
left for the reader to fill in any significance that might be attached to the poet's
so naming of Yahweh. For ancient and modern readers alike there is little positive that is to be associated with referring to somebody as an enemy. An
enemy is someone who hates, despises, and curses and thus who is hated, despised, and cursed; someone who intends harm or injury and therefore is to be
harmed or injured; who is not to be trusted but feared.

P. Ricoeur defines metaphor as a "redescription of reality."[90] The poet in
Lamentations 2, by metaphorizing Yahweh as "enemy," significantly shifts the
way the human-divine relationship is perceived. It now gains a pronounced
adversarial coloring to it. Yahweh may remain potent, but his is a potency that
is to be actively feared, guarded against, not trusted. Here we do not meet the
kindly and compassionate God so often preached in church and synagogue.
Nor do we even have to do with the fearsome but righteous God of justice,
whose punishments, though severe, are always just and appropriate. Rather,
here the only presence of the deity offered by this poet is that which is manifested in the raw and malevolent power of an enemy, a power that aims only
to maim, murder, and break. Here there is no consideration of just cause (recall the thematic prominence of Yahweh's anger and the corresponding absence of any mention of human sin!). Only Job's imagery of the Divine
Enemy as a mad beast (16:9) is more terrifying. Through the enemy metaphor
the poet finds a language that expresses a terror and hurt that is ultimately beyond expressing, that gives some bite to the heart and senses, that jolts and ultimately induces in the reader a "sense of complicity with the extremity"[91] of
the cruelty and suffering that the destruction of Jerusalem unleashed on the
city's human population.

The image of the familiar God of beneficence and compassion must be
(momentarily) exploded if the audience is to comprehend bodily and cogni-
tively the extremity of the atrocity herein figured. This is definitely not a
metaphor for God that the biblical traditions luxuriate in. And yet its service-
ability to this poet's larger project cannot be denied. The wager that the poet

---

89. *Webster's New World Dictionary.*

90. P. Ricoeur, *The Rule of Metaphor* (Toronto: University of Toronto Press, 1977) 229–
39; cf. C. Newsom, "Job," *NIB* 4.416–17.

91. L. Langer, *The Holocaust and the Literary Imagination* (New Haven: Yale University
Press, 1975) 175.

makes here is that Yahweh must be confronted as a dangerous enemy if he is to remain foundational for the post-destruction community. That is, by the end of the sequence Yahweh remains the central pillar of communal life but in so doing has become the God of both good and evil (Lam 3:36) and thus a force to be wary of and no longer beyond human reproach.

Raising Zion

The other notable aspect of interest in the poem's opening section is the metaphorical survival of the ruined city's persona even after the material city's ruin. If not as arresting as Yahweh's being imagined as enemy, it is every bit as significant, theologically and otherwise. The action at the surface of the poem through these first eight stanzas, as we have seen, concentrates most fixedly on the *razing* of municipal Zion—buildings destroyed, walls torn down, the temple measured and demolished. But amidst the resulting verbal carnage, the *raising* of personified Zion is also at work. This happens, initially in these stanzas, under the poem's surface, or, perhaps more accurately, at its margins and will be appreciated most fully by readers retrospectively, once cues of Zion's survival are brought explicitly to the surface of the poem (e.g., when she is invoked in v. 13 or directly addressed in vv. 18–19; or when she finally speaks in vv. 20–22). But for those attentive readers—readers who, perhaps, come to this poem through the first poem, where Zion's survival is made explicit from the outset, or who anticipate her centrality from familiarity with the city-lament genre (e.g., scribes!)—the work of *raising* Zion, of gathering her scattered (linguistic) traces, first, into vocativity and, then, into vocality, begins almost immediately.

The personified-city metaphor conveys significance at several different levels in Lamentations.[92] In particular, there is the female persona, who is brought to life in the opening stanza of Lamentations 1,[93] and the physical, material city itself. In the first poem both levels of meaning are consciously evoked, though it is the persona that is clearly foregrounded, especially since she is the speaker for the entire second half of that poem. But regardless of which is more prominent in particular contexts, both dimensions of the metaphor are always being juggled. The strategy in 2:1–8 is radically different. The two levels of meaning are progressively and intentionally differentiated as we move through the section. The focus is chiefly on the destruction of the physical city itself. Just note the high density of terms such as dwellings, strongholds, palaces, and

---

92. For discussion, see my *Weep, O Daughter of Zion*, 87–88; *Lamentations*, 50–53.
93. See my *Lamentations*, 53–56.

walls. This shift in focus to the material city is already initiated in 2:1. Recall that Lamentations 1 ends with personified Zion groaning but still alive, exhausted by both what she has suffered and the articulation of her suffering. It is this sad figure, "Daughter Zion" (*bat-ṣiyyôn*), whom Yahweh so ruthlessly casts out of heaven at the outset of 2:1. The eviction dramatically symbolizes Zion's dethronement, if you will, the stripping away of her cosmic privileges and status.

But it also symbolizes the poet's removal of the city's persona from the foreground of this part of the poem, a feat that is achieved verbally in this first stanza by the progressive materialization of the names by which the city–temple complex is referred. "Daughter Zion" in 2:1a can only be predicated of a personified, animate figure.[94] In 2:1b, the reference to the "splendor of Israel" is more (creatively) ambiguous. It is both another epithet of the personified city–temple complex (cf. Isa 13:19; 22:2; 23:7; 28:1; Jer 48:2; 49:25; Ezek 26:17; 27:3; Nah 2:8a; Zeph 2:15; Lam 2:15c) and a more depersonalized reference to Yahweh's heavenly and earthly abode (Isa 60:7; 63:15; 64:10)—thus both the persona and the material city are intentionally evoked. And in 2:1c reference to Yahweh's "footstool" can only signify the actual temple, thus effectively pushing the city's persona out of view, offstage as it were, at least for the time being. At this point the poem, moving in its highly uniform clause structure, eerily suggesting (at least to those of us living on the other side of the twentieth century) the lock-step march and methodical precision of a well-trained infantry division, proceeds in its mostly bloodless (cf. 2:2c, 4b, 5c) demolition of the city's physical architecture, with special attention given to the temple itself, culminating in 2:8 with explicit reference to the temple's ritualized razing.

And yet, if personified Zion has been pushed out of the foreground of the poem's action, she is nonetheless never really allowed to vanish altogether, as her trace is preserved linguistically. Though beclouded, cast down, and forgotten in 2:1, she herself, in her metaphorical person, survives. And she is kept alive throughout the poem's opening movement through incantation, through the repeated voicing of Zion's various epithets (2:1a, b, 2b, 4c, 5c, 8a). The "strongholds of *Maiden Judah*"[95] are broken down (2:2b), fury like

---

94. See my "Syntagma of *bat* Followed by a Geographical Name in the Hebrew Bible: A Reconsideration of Its Meaning and Grammar," *CBQ* 57 (1995) 451–70.

95. Reading *mibṣĕrê bĕtûlat-yĕhûdâ* following the Vg. (*virginis Juda*). The MT reads *bat-yĕhûdâ* (followed by LXX, Syr., Tg.). The Vg.'s reading is unique, which, in light of the almost (*bat-ʿammî* in 2:11b) exclusive preference for *bat* GN as the long epithet of choice in this poem (2:1a, 4c, 5c, 8a, 10a, 13a, 15b, 18a), the appearance of *bĕtûlat* in Lamentations as only a part of the extended epithet *Bĕtûlat bat GN* (1:15c; 2:13b), and the rarity of the

fire is poured into "the tent of *Daughter Zion*" (2:4c), lamentation is "multiplied in *Daughter Judah*" (2:5c), and the "wall of *Daughter Zion*" is demolished
(2:8a), but the personified figure herself, as is made abundantly clear in the
grammar of the Hebrew, remains, nonetheless; traces of the city's otherwise
battered walls and demolished infrastructure are here preserved in language
and laid as a foundation for linguistic making—*poiesis*.

Still, any notion of Zion's raising is only embryonic in 2:1–8. Though personified Zion and material Zion are successfully differentiated and the trace of
the former inscribed linguistically, it will take the remainder of the poem to
raise Zion, to enchant Zion's persona, in all of her vocality, to the poem's surface. In the poem's next section (2:9–12),[96] the figure of Zion's persona continues to hover ghost-like in the background. Verse 9 is punctuated by four
3rd-person fem. sing. pronominal suffixes (*sĕ'āreyhā, bĕrîheyhā, wĕśāreyhā, nĕbî-
'eyhā*), and Zion's titles appear two more times in the succeeding stanzas (*bat-
ṣiyyôn*, 2:10a; *bat-'ammî*, 2:11b). In addition, the poem's rhetoric now begins
(intentionally) to mime language used elsewhere (mostly in Lamentations 1)
of Zion. The king and princes find themselves "among the nations" (*baggôyīm*)
just like personified Zion (1:3b). The elders' and young girls' performance of
ritual acts of mourning reminds us of Zion's own acts of mourning (1:2, 8c, 9b,
16a, 17a). The phrase "the young girls of Jerusalem" (*bĕtûlōt yĕrûśālāim*) puns
the kind of epithet used for naming the personified city elsewhere in the poem
(e.g., *bĕtûlat yĕhûdâ* [2:2b Vg]; *bĕtûlat bat-ṣiyyôn* [2:13b]). The elders "sit on the
ground (*lā'āreṣ*)" (2:10a) and the young girls bow "their heads to the ground
(*lā'āreṣ*)" (2:10c; and even the "bile" of the speaker in v. 11 "is poured out on
the ground [*lā'āreṣ*]" [2:11b]) in sympathetic identification with the fate of the
personified city, who was "thrown down from heaven to earth (*'ereṣ*)" (2:1b)

---

title *bĕtûlat* GN in the Hebrew Bible more generally (Jer 18:13; 31:4, 21; Amos 5:2), is
surely the *lectio difficilior*. The term *btlt 'nt* is, of course, one of Anat's most common epithets
in the Ugaritic texts (Dobbs-Allsopp, *Weep, O Daughter of Zion*, 83; "Syntagma," 464–65).
That the biblical tradition knew of the Anat traditions is suggested, not only by the other
appearances of this title type, but also by Joel 1:8: "Lament like a maiden dressed in sack-
cloth for the husband of her youth" (see D. R. Hillers, "'The Roads of Zion Mourn' [Lam
1:4]," *Perspective* 12 [1971] 127–30). The title *bĕtûlat* is especially appropriate here because
it foregrounds the image of a nubile young woman who is no longer a little girl but not yet
a wife (see N. H. Walls, *The Goddess Anat in Ugaritic Myth* [SBLDS 135; Atlanta: Scholars
Press, 1992]). The specific epithet thus projects an image of personified Judah as a woman
who falls between the cracks of the Judean social system in her liminal state; she literally has
no obvious means of security—an image, then, that is graphically mimicked as her protective "fortifications" are torn down by Yahweh.

96. See my *Lamentations*, 91–95.

and whose gates—symbolizing the city's architectural edifice as a whole—were "sunk into the ground (*bā'āreṣ*)" (2:9a). And the speaker's visceral response to the death of the children in 2:11a–b,

> My eyes are spent with weeping;
>   my stomach churns;
> my bile is poured out on the ground
>   because of the destruction of the Daughter of My People,

eerily mirrors Zion's own reaction voiced earlier in 1:20a–b,

> See, O Yahweh, how distressed I am;
>   my stomach churns,
> my heart is wrung within me,
>   how bitter I am![97]

Here, then, the poem's incantatory magic begins to take effect. Zion's presence, personified and conjured through repeated naming, stirs about in the afterwash of the poem's lyric play, though *she* is still not made (directly) a part of the poem's conversation. All of this changes in the third section (2:13–19).[98] Incantation gives way, first, to invocation (2:13), and, eventually, to direct address (2:18–19). Zion, whose (personal) presence to this point has lurked mostly at the edges of the poem's discourse, or hovered just under its surface, is now invited into the center of that discourse. In 2:13a–b the speaker refers to Zion using the vocative:

> How may I bear witness to you,[99] to what compare you,
>   O Daughter Jerusalem (*habbat yĕrûšālaim*[100])?

---

97. Reading *kî mārô mārôtî*, following Vg. for MT's *kî mā'rô mārîtî* "for I have been very rebellious" (see C. L. Seow, "A Textual Note on Lamentations 1:20," *CBQ* 47 [1985] 416–19).

98. See my *Lamentations*, 95–98.

99. The Vg.'s reading (*cui comparabote* = Heb. *'e'ĕrōk*) is possible in light of the frequent confusion between *dalet* and *reš* in the Hebrew script of most historical periods, and in other respects, too, is very attractive, especially in light of the good parallels (Isa 40:18; Ps 40:6; 89:7; Job 28:17, 19; note that Ehrlich's [*Randglossen*, 37; followed by Albrektson, *Studies*, 107 n. 1; Gottlieb, *Study*, 32 n. 81] objection to this construal of the Vg. is rendered vacuous in light of all of the examples beside Isa 40:18; so Provan, *Lamentations*, 72 [ultimately]; Hillers, *Lamentations*, 100; Dobbs-Allsopp, *Weep, O Daughter of Zion*, 35 n. 20). Equally plausible is Gordis's suggestion ("Commentary," 282; cf. Rudolph, "Text," 108; Gottlieb, *Study*, 32) that the *Hiphil* of *'wd* means "to revive, restore, fortify" as it does in the *Polel* (Ps 146:9; 147:6) and the *Hithpolel* (Ps 20:9). In support of this thesis, Gordis notes that the four verbs in the first two couplets are chiastically structured, "the first and fourth (*'ā'îdēk* and *'ănahămēk*) are parallel to each other, as are the second and the fourth [*sic*! third] (*'ădammeh* and *'ašweh*)"

To what can I liken you, that I may comfort you,
   O Maiden Daughter Zion (*bĕtûlat bat-ṣiyyôn*)? (2:13a–b)

Not surprisingly Zion is here (and in vv. 15b [*bat-yĕrûšālāim*], 15c [*kĕlîlat yōpî/ māśôś lĕkol-hā'āreṣ*], 18a [*bat-ṣiyyôn*]) invoked with the very title-types that here-tofore have been used to keep her alive, to mark her trace in the poetry's discourse. A liberal sprinkling of 2nd-person fem. pronominal suffixes through-out these stanzas (2:13a [twice], 13b [twice], 13c [twice], 14a [twice], 14b [twice], 14c, 15a, 16a [twice], 17c [twice], 18c [twice], 19b, 19c [twice]) makes clear Zion's emergence as a "You" instead of a "She"—or, indeed, as is more often the case in the first portion of the poem, instead of a "Her" (i.e., grammatical object, victim).[101] The culmination comes in 2:18–19, with personified Zion being addressed directly for the first time. Fittingly, 2:18a gathers together in one place most of the stylistic devices so far used to sustain Zion's poetic presence, her trace (e.g., imperative, title, vocative): "Cry out wholeheartedly to the Lord, / O wall of Daughter Zion!"[102] And then in 2:19a personified Zion is beckoned

---

("Commentary," 282)—this squares with the other chiasms within the stanza—and that the *Hiphil* of *'wd* is attested with just this sense in Sir 4:11: "Wisdom exalts her sons and strengthens (*wt'yd*) those who seek her." One might further note that the chiastic verb pairs also rhyme. Either reading makes sense within the context, and neither is stylistically ob-jectionable. Nevertheless, the MT (followed by the LXX, Syr., Tg.) may be preferred on the basis that stylistically it provides a better fit with the rest of the stanza. Moreover, one also has the suspicion that the Vg. may ultimately represent an attempt to make sense of a verb that the scribe did not know or thought did not fit the context, which would mean that the MT is the *lectio difficilior*. In the final analysis, the Hebrew may be playing on two meanings: "to be parallel to, like" (NRSV; Albrektson, *Studies*, 108) and "to witness" (LXX; Syr.; Tg.; Dobbs-Allsopp, *Lamentations*, 96–97; cf. *Arad* 24.rev.7–9). Of the two, "to wit-ness" is perhaps the more prominent.

100. LXX *hē ti omoiōsō soi, thygater Ierousalēm*; Syr. *wmn 'dm' lky brt 'wršlm*; Tg. *wmh 'hy dmy lmk knšt' dyrwšlm*. The out-of-place *he* in the LXX (which the Syr. and Tg. have con-strued as the conjunction *w-*) calls attention to the abnormal definite article in the MT, which the LXX obviously did not understand. The definite article in BH can be used as a marker of the vocative (Waltke and O'Connor, *Biblical Hebrew Syntax*, §13.5.2c), as it likely does here (cf. *hā'ēl bêt-'ēl* in Gen 31:13 and *hammelek 'aššûr* in Isa 36:16; see my *Weep, O Daughter of Zion*, 34 n. 21).

101. For the use of pronouns and pronominal suffixes as a structuring device, see my *Lamentations*, 49.

102. The couplet has been thought corrupt by most commentators (e.g., Hillers, *Lam-entations*, 101). However, aside from emending the MT's *ṣā'aq* (*Qal* perfect 3rd masc. sing.) to *ṣa'ăqî* (*Qal* imperative fem. sing.), which in light of the five imperatives (*hôrîdî, 'al-tittĕnî, qûmî rōnnî, śipkî, śĕ'î*) in the five immediately following couplets is almost universally ac-cepted, the MT is eminently construable. The final affix on *libbām*, -*ām*, understood by MT

literally to "rise up,"[103] as if out of the very ruins of her materiality, and "cry out" in the full vocality of personhood.

Here, then, we have, in a Levinasian idiom, a language of "sheer vocativ-ity."[104] A language, that is, made up of vocatives, imperatives, and 2nd-person references. For Levinas the fact of invocation itself—no matter the content—is all important:

> The other is maintained and confirmed in his heterogeneity *as soon as one calls upon him,* be it only to say to him that one cannot speak to him to classify him as sick, to announce to him his death sentence. At the same time as grasped, wounded, outraged, he is "respected." The invoked is not what I comprehend. He is not under a category. He is the one to whom I speak.[105]

Of course, Levinas's overriding ambition is to think the other in a way that pre-serves the other's heterogeneity, in a way that does not reduce the relation with the other to comprehension. The language of invocation is the ethical means (par excellence) to such a thinking otherwise. And what is ultimately at stake

---

and the versions as a 3rd masc. pl. suffix and thus often found problematic, is most likely an adverbial morpheme. Adverbial *-m* was clearly productive in Ugaritic and Amarna Akka-dian (see D. Sivan, *A Grammar of the Ugaritic Language* [Leiden: Brill, 1997] 179), and its ves-tigial use has been plausibly identified in several passages in the Hebrew Bible, including *rêqām* "empty-handed" (Gen 31:42; cf. *ri-qa-mi* [EA 245.6]), *yômām* "daily" (as a separate entry in BDB, 401), and *gam* in Num 11:4; Isa 13:3; Jer 48:2; Ps 71:22, 24; 137:1; and Prov 1:26 (see McDaniel, "Philological Studies, I," 31–32). Adverbial *-m* is present elsewhere in Lamentations, occurring in the very next couplet (*yômām* "daily," 2:18b) and in 1:8c (*gam* "aloud"; so ibid.; Hillers, *Lamentations*, 70–71). The word *libbām*, then, literally would mean "heartily, from the heart, wholeheartedly," that is, "from the gut," because the heart was considered to be one of the centers of the emotions (cf. 1:20b; 2:19b; T. F. McDaniel, "Philological Studies in Lamentations, II" *Bib* 49 [1968] 203–4; Hillers, *Lamentations*, 101). *Ḥômat bat-ṣiyyôn*, the other phrase believed troublesome, is surely a synecdoche for Zion as a whole, as Provan (*Lamentations*, 76) has argued. The synecdoche works at many levels. As already noted, the city walls in antiquity were a prominent site for the uttering of lamenta-tions, and it was the literal "wall of Daughter Zion" that Yahweh laid in ruins earlier in the poem (2:8a). Moreover, the phrasing, here turned into a vocative, plays on the language employed throughout 2:1–8 to keep Zion's persona alive and distinct from her physical and municipal raiment.

103. In all likelihood *qûmî* here is used as an aspectualizer marking ingressive aspect; see my "Ingressive *qwm* in Biblical Hebrew," *ZAH* 8 [1995] 51). However, this does not pro-hibit the language from signifying more literally, etymologically. Indeed, poets the world over and throughout history have been fond of playing on etymologies.

104. See J. Robins, *Altered Reading: Levinas and Literature* (Chicago: University of Chi-cago Press, 1999) esp. 10–11.

105. E. Levinas, *Totality and Infinity: An Essay on Exteriority* (trans. A. Lingis; Pittsburgh: Duquesne University Press, 1985) 69.

for Levinas (why ethics as first philosophy) is, S. Critchley notes, "that unless our social interactions are underpinned by ethical relations to other persons, then the worst might happen, that is, the failure to acknowledge the humanity of the other."[106] "Such, for Levinas," continues Critchley, "is what took place in the Shoah," where the other person became "a faceless face" and "whose life or death . . . a matter of indifference."[107] The poem's language of vocativity, then, is a Levinasian gesture of absolute giving; in speaking the world *to* Zion, life—survival—is effectuated and, just as significantly, respect and *other*ness is imputed to her. She is faced as a face. Here we gain a glimpse at what this poem ultimately has to offer in the place of the Zion tradition's mythic guarantee of inviolability: "speaking to," as a model for approaching the other in all of his/her heterogeneity, is the only true guarantee of (bodily) inviolability. It is in the face of the other, after all, that for Levinas the primordial prohibition "Thou shalt not kill" rises to speech. And thus it is in the very fact of discourse (conversation, speaking to) that Zion in this poem, mirroring how "the other comes from behind his appearance" in Levinasian conversation,[108] emerges from her scattered poetic traces into vocality.

   In 2:20–22 the poem comes full circle, then. Razing turns into raising. The irony-laden, though finally tragic, "sounds" (*qôl*, lit., "voice") that filled the "house of Yahweh" (on Mount Zion) as it was despoiled and demolished (2:7c) here morph into the up-raised voice of personified (and now houseless) Zion as she (angrily) confronts Yahweh with the consequences of his "day of anger." Vocality becomes the final trace left of Zion for the future. Suffering's aversive corrosion of language is here countered by uplifted voice—voice, a central aspect of all lyric poetry, here evokes the presence of an other in the face of God (and the readerly community). If the poem memorializes the tragic destruction of city and temple (as surely it does), in the end its ultimate witness is to survival, to an upraised voice that refuses to be silenced, that exposes and decries the atrocity it cannot undo in its vocal preservation of the trace of an other.

   Zion speaks! She does so not as a contrite and defeated prisoner of war, or even as a convicted felon pleading on the mercy of the court. There is none of the hair-tearing, skin-gouging, or loud hysteria that the conventional liter-

---

106. S. Critchley, "Introduction," in *The Cambridge Companion to Levinas* (ed. S. Critchley and R. Bernasconi; Cambridge: Cambridge University Press, 2002) 13.
   107. Ibid.
   108. Robins, *Altered Reading*, 65; cf. D. Glowacka, "Disappearing Traces: Emmanuel Levinas, Ida Fink's Literary Testimony, and Holocaust," in *Between Ethics and Aesthetics: Crossing the Boundaries* (ed. D. Glowacka and S. Boos; Albany: State University of New York Press, 2002) 103, 107.

ary portrayal of mourning women (and goddesses) in antiquity comprises.[109] Nor do we even meet the broken and spent persona who concluded the previous poem. Instead, the words that we hear are cold and pointed, steeled, it would seem, by the flames of Zion's own anger at the humiliation and hurt of suffering. She begins by "speaking to" Yahweh: "Look, O Yahweh, and consider" (cf. 1:9c, 11c, 20a), confident that to see suffering "face to face" (embodied in real people) is, de facto, to say "No!" to that suffering, to respond compassionately to end it. And the "speaking to" itself—despite the hardness of what is spoken—insists on coming before Yahweh ethically, approaching the deity as an other, as a "You," and thus passing on to Yahweh the gesture of absolute giving that the poem has just bequeathed to her.

The second line of the couplet ("whom you have violated so!") provides the object of the initial address—identifies those at whom the deity is to look—and again echoes language from Lamentations 1. Here the poet chooses the same verb of violence, *ʿll*,[110] that was used so strategically in the first poem (1:12b, 22b). Indeed, the charges leveled are identical—the only difference being that in 1:12b and 22b the reference was to Zion's own pains, while here it is in reference to the pains of its inhabitants. The similarity of language equates the two in a way implied by Zion's identity as the personification of her people: Zion's pains *are* her people's pains and vice versa. And again (cf. 1:22a–b) the poet matches the violence (*ʿôlaltā* "you have acted violently," 2:20a) and the victims of the violence, the children (*ʿôlālayik*, 2:19c; *ʿōlălê*, 2:20b), by means of a horrific pun.

In the rest of this stanza Zion asks rhetorical questions (matching those of the speaking voice in 2:13). The answers are only too obvious. Verse 20b raises the specter of cannibalism (so LXX, Tg.; cf. *Lam. Rab.* 2:23) and with it

---

109. See B. Alster, "The Mythology of Mourning," *Acta Sumerologica* 5 (Hiroshima, 1983) 1–16.

110. The verb *ʿll*, when not used in the sense of "to glean" (e.g., Lev 19:10), has a strongly violent coloring to it. It is used in the Exodus story to refer to Yahweh's infliction of the plagues on the Egyptians (Exod 10:2; 1 Sam 6:6) and in the Balaam story to depict the way the ass deals with Balaam (Num 22:29). More menacing is a type of "sporting" envisioned in 1 Sam 31:4; Jer 38:19; and Judg 19:25. The first two envision torture and the latter rape. The use of *ʿll* in Lamentations likely cleaves more closely to the violent end of the semantic range. The irony, of course, is that Yahweh's "sporting," which was to be retold throughout the generations so that Israelites would know the power of their God (Exod 10:2), is rendered unnecessary by the events of 586. The inhabitants of Jerusalem and Judah experienced firsthand the violence of Yahweh's "sporting." Here again the poet is intent on replacing the exodus story as Judah's paradigm charter myth. Note that as in 1:12b, 22b, the NRSV anesthetizes the violence in its translation "done."

the heinous thought that one person's life can be purchased at the expense of another's. The added horror here is that those who die are babes—the community's literal and physical future—and they are killed by their own mothers! The language here is quite evocative. The term for "offspring" in Hebrew (*pĕrî*) is literally "fruit," and while it is true that this term is frequently used figuratively for offspring (cf. Gen 30:2; Deut 7:32; Ps 21:11), as indeed it is here, nevertheless the poet means through his choice of diction to color the mother's act of cannibalism with the lush enjoyment and everyday occurrence of eating fruit: "Should women have to eat their fruit?"[111] The resulting contrast of images, especially once the second line of the couplet is encountered (*ʿōlălê ṭippūḥîm* "the babes they have reared"), is jarring and very effective. This tainting of the inhumane, the bestial with sensuous (even erotic) delight continues even through the end of the couplet, as the hapax legomenon translated here as "reared" puns on the erotically charged (esp. Song 2:3, 5; 7:9) Hebrew word typically (though uncertainly) glossed as "apple" (*ṭippūḥîm* // *tappûaḥ*, pl. *tappûḥîm*). The answer to the question is, of course, no! Women should not have to eat their own children, ever. The whole image is grotesque and revolting. That it could be thought, let alone voiced, again speaks volumes about the depth of Zion's misery and anger.

In the next question, Zion asks should "priest and prophet" be murdered (*hrg*)[112] in the very place where presumably they were to serve Yahweh and expected his divine protection, "in the sanctuary of the LORD." Again the negative answer is only too obvious, and the chief culprit is implicit (in both questions) in the address to Yahweh.[113] In the first two couplets of 2:21 Zion continues to identify human casualties, though she has now dropped the false face of the earlier rhetorical questions. Young and old "lie" (dead) on the ground/earth (*lāʾāreṣ*)—again alluding to Zion's own treatment at the beginning of the poem. Young men and women (i.e., those in the prime of their lives) fall by the sword. This abbreviated catalog, which moves from rhetorical questions (2:20b–c) to plain, declarative statements (2:21a–b), ends in direct accusation: "You murdered on the day of your anger! / You slaughtered without mercy!" (2:21c). Elsewhere in the Hebrew Bible, Yahweh's sacrificial victims are usually envisioned as Israel's and Judah's enemies (Isa 30:25; 34:6;

---

111. The LXX (*karpon koilias autōn*) and the Tg. (*pyry bṭnyhwn*) make this interpretation explicit and in the process show (quite effectively!) the playful ambiguity inherent in the Hebrew original.

112. The LXX's *apokteneis* is either an inner Greek corruption (Albrektson, *Studies*, 121) or a harmonization to the larger context (e.g., direct address in 2:20a, *hāragtā* in 2:21c).

113. This, of course, is made explicit in the LXX's *apokteneis* (if the latter is not an inner Greek corruption).

Jer 12:3; 46:10; Ezek 39:17), though in Zeph 1:7–8, as here, Judah and Jerusalem, too, become sacrificed. Zion's speech in this stanza, as it gathers traces of Jerusalem's human inhabitants, epitomizes (to borrow from D. Głowacka's work on the Shoah) the power of (literary) speech to effectuate the passage of the dead and the victimized into remembrance.[114]

The final stanza is one long complex sentence, which sets it apart from the poem's tendency to keep sentences confined mostly to individual lines and couplets. This change of pattern helps signal the poem's impending conclusion, but it also underscores the feeling of climax. Parataxis joins the separate clauses, piling one thought onto another, until they overwhelm Zion and simply need to be gotten out. It begins ("You invited . . . as if for a day of festival") by continuing to play on the image of sacrifice. The announcement of a festival (cf. 2:7c) is normally a joyous event,[115] involving festivities of all sorts, including a festal meal. This day of festivities, however, takes a phantasmagorical turn in the second line. Instead of calling all (surviving) Judeans to a celebratory feast, Yahweh calls all of Zion's "enemies from all around" (cf. 1:17b) to make a feast of the city's inhabitants. That this "day of festival" is in reality the Day of Yahweh is made clear by the explicit references to the latter in 2:21c and 22b and the lexical play on the earlier phrase, "the day you have announced" (1:21c). The dark cloudiness that angrily threatened the poem's opening (2:1) reveals its terrible significance: "on the day of Yahweh's anger there were / no survivors, no one escaped" (cf. 2:22b). "Enemies" (so NRSV) is a gloss for an obscure Hebrew word (*měgûray*). Suggestions for its meaning include "those who lie in wait" (cf. Ps 59:4), "attackers" (cf. Job 18:19), or "dread, terrors," with particular reference to the "terror is on every side" found frequently in Jeremiah (6:25; 20:3, 10; 46:5; 49:29).[116] Whichever of these is correct, the Hebrew bears connotations of a surrounding enemy and the feelings of terror that this would arouse.

In 2:22b by delaying the substantivized adjectives till the second line of the couplet (*pālîṭ wěśārîd*), the poet enhances the syntactic pull felt in the couplet and effectively renders, through juxtaposition, the final couplet ("those whom . . .") as an appositive (this sense is further enforced through implication associated with the use of the standard Hebrew relative particle *ʾăšer*, which here functions almost like a substantive). The first line of the last couplet contains

---

114. D. Głowacka, "Disappearing Traces," 98–99.

115. Note the long and positive "midrashic injection" (Levine, *Aramaic Version of Lamentations*, 121).

116. For these and other proposals, see Albrektson, *Studies*, 124–25; McDaniel, "Philological Studies, I," 42–44; Hillers, *Lamentations*, 102.

the same rare verb for "child rearing" (*ṭpḥ*) found in 2:20b, thus effectively alluding back to the portrayal of cannibalism there. The verb also plays on (through a change in the middle labial) the verb for "slaughter" (*ṭbḥ*) in 2:21c.[117] Thus, as with the wordplay in 2:20, victimizing activity and victim are equated here, further heightening the incongruity and horror of the situation.

The word order of the final couplet is also important. First, by demoting the verb to final position, the poet effects the most violent form of enjambment found in Lamentations[118] and thus increases yet again the palpability of the syntax's tug as it drags the reader ever more insistently through to the stanza's end. It is as if this is where the poem had been heading all along—that is, a certain naturalness attends the poem's denouement, even though, as we will see, in one sense the end is anything but natural. Second, this use of verbal enjambment further enhances the sense of closure in the poem by effecting a chiasm with the poem's opening couple: V/SO::OS/V:[119]

> *ʾêkâ yāʿîb bĕʾappô* / *ʾădōnay ʾet-bat-ṣiyyôn* (2:1a)
> V / S + O
> *ʾăšer ṭippaḥĕtî wĕribbîtî* / *ʾōyĕbî killām* (2:22c)
> O / S + V

This long-range chiasm also establishes a set of correspondences that further complicates the poem's meaning. Both verbs are destructive in nature, and the poet's pattern of identifying Zion's experience as victim with that of her inhabitants is exemplified once again (Zion is victimized by Yahweh's beclouding in the same way that those whom Zion bore and reared are destroyed). This leaves the final correspondence to relate "my Lord" (*ʾădōnāy*) in 2:1a with "my enemy" (*ʾōyĕbî*) in 2:22c. The equation is quite striking at first glance, but after some consideration, quite brilliant as well. Throughout Lamentations the identity of the enemy is constantly and intentionally blurred (e.g., 1:2). In this poem, alone, in addition to references to Zion's historical enemies (2:3b, 7b, 16a, 17c), Yahweh is called an enemy (2:4a, b, 5a) and shown both acting like an enemy (esp. 2:1–8) and collaborating with the actual (human) enemy (2:3b, 7b, 17c). Through such strategic lexical manipulation, the poet gives this final reference to the "enemy" the capacity to refer to both Zion's actual human enemies and Yahweh. And of the two it is the latter, Yahweh, who is most prominently in view here, as suggested by the chiasm with 2:1a, the more immediate context of 2:20–22 in which only Yahweh is

---

117. Positive evidence for this kind of wordplay may appear in the LXX's mistaken reading in 2:20b: Gk. *mageiros* (= Heb. *ṭbḥ*) for MT *ṭippūḥîm*.

118. Dobbs-Allsopp, "Enjambing Line," 227–28.

119. See my "Effects of Enjambment," 374–75.

addressed, and the specific reference to "enemy" in the singular (contrast the plural of Syr. and Tg., and, for example, 1:21b). Here Zion dramatically affirms the designation given to Yahweh in 2:1–8.

The poem's final word, *killām*, provides one last twist. The verb itself literally means "to bring to an end, complete, finish"—and thus is most fitting as the poem's concluding word!—and the typical translation as "destroy" (so NRSV) rightly emphasizes that the kind of completion in mind here involves the destruction of human life. But this misses the sad irony of the poem's diction. The feat of child-rearing that Zion had begun (giving life and then giving the cultural and physical means to live that life) Yahweh literally and ghastly completes, not by producing healthy and productive adults but by murdering and killing.

There is much that can be said about this final portion of the poem.[120] But for our purposes the vocality that erupts here at poem's end is the culmination of the "raising" trope that I have been teasing out of the poem over the course of the last several pages. The significance of Zion's coming to voice, which may be appreciated variously,[121] lies above all in the resounding "No!" said to suffering and in its implications of survival. It is through Zion's speech, and specifically in the latter's (constative) content, that the poem constructs a memory of resistance and transcendence to counter the literal reality of destruction and suffering. The hint of defiance in Zion's words—which hides behind the thin veneer of the rhetorical questions of 2:20b–c and explodes ever so briefly in the acrid accusation of 2:21c—creates the necessary space for an emergent sense of resistance that gestures ever so faintly toward the nonfinality of suffering and the evil that caused it. Suffering and destruction constitute the tragic dimension of human existence that can never be completely overcome or abolished. But they can be resisted and therefore transcended. The maintenance of human dignity embodied in Zion's final words, as she contests the hurtful actions of Enemy Yahweh, not only creates a basis for resistance, but is already a part of such resistance,[122] a cry of defiance and protest against the unforgivable reality of human suffering—as Levinas says, the suffering in an other.

Voice is also the poem's quintessential trope of life—in this case, its chief sign of survival. The poem itself, and especially here at the end, literally recuperates Zion's voice from the silence of oblivion, and in so doing subdues the horrors of atrocity and facilitates physical survival: true justice is "a right to

---

120. See my *Lamentations*, 98–104.
121. Ibid., esp. pp. 35–36.
122. Cf. W. Farley, *Tragic Vision and Divine Compassion: A Contemporary Theodicy* (Louisville: Westminster/John Knox, 1990) 57.

speak."[123] The linguistic traces of Zion's survival, as I have tried to show
above, are apparent throughout the poem (e.g., in the frequent naming of
personified Zion, in the miming of her words, and in the vocativity of the
poem's language) and are appreciated especially retrospectively. But it is in the
"speaking voice"[124] of 2:20–22 that Zion's aliveness becomes unmistakable.
Vocality is the governing trope of lyric poetry, as R. Pinsky, a former Poet
Laureate of the United States, reminds us. He writes that "poetry is a vocal,
which is to say a bodily, art. The medium of poetry is a human body: the column of air inside the chest, shaped into signifying sounds in the larynx and the
mouth."[125] Such physical vocality is itself being troped when Zion speaks. In
her imagined articulation of speech she too must bring "the column of air"
into her chest and in the process of shaping the sounds of verse in larynx and
mouth she must breathe and therefore live. Her vocality is her survival. And
what is more, continues Pinsky, "when I say to myself a poem . . . , the artist's
medium is my breath. The reader's breath and hearing embody the poet's
words."[126] And thus, the gift of life bequeathed through voice to Zion is given
again and again as the poem's auditors—ancient and modern alike—breathe
in Zion's words and revocalize them for themselves.

Such vocality is ultimately enabled tropologically through personification
and prosopopoeia. That is, personified Zion can come to voice only because
the geographical entity that Zion literally names—the Temple Mount and, by
extension, all of Jerusalem—has been imbued anthropomorphically with various human attributes, voice chief among them. The Lamentations poet surely
did not invent personified Zion de novo but likely inherited the trope.[127] Yet
to say this is not to take anything away from the genius of the poet's utilization
and manipulation of the trope, however traditional is the latter. It is Zion as
persona that becomes the crux of what the poem has to offer in place of the
now-bankrupt Zion tradition. The Zion mythos was centrally concerned with
geography: the geography of Yahweh's chosen place of dwelling. To be sure,
the notions attached to this interest in geography were not unsophisticated.[128]
Still, the tangible, physical geography of Mount Zion—the temple with all of

---

123. The quotation is from Levinas, *Totality and Infinity*, 298. The general sentiments
expressed here I have taken from Glowacka, "Disappearing Traces," esp. 107.

124. See the seminal observations of W. F. Lanahan, "The Speaking Voice in the Book
of Lamentations," *JBL* 93 (1974) 41–49.

125. R. Pinsky, *The Sounds of Poetry: A Brief Guide* (New York: Farrar, Straus, and Giroux, 1998) 8.

126. Ibid.

127. See my *Weep, O Daughter of Zion*, esp. pp. 75–90.

128. For details, see Levenson, *Sinai and Zion*, esp. 111–84; cf. Mettinger, "Name and
Glory," 1–2.

its supporting architectural accoutrements—was not insignificant either. Geography and architecture provided visible confirmation of Zion's cosmic status
(Ps 48:9) and visual concreteness to the notion of divine presence so central to
the Zion tradition (namely, that Yahweh was enthroned invisibly as king in the
innermost sanctum of the temple). And, indeed, there were those who believed quite literally that physically standing in the temple was sufficient to
guarantee their bodily safety (Jer 7:10; cf. Lam 2:20c). With Zion in ruins
after 586, however, this emphasis on geography and its implied notions of divine presence would have to be reimagined, as the ruination visibly belied the
central thrust of the mythology. Many of the exilic writers struggled with the
resulting dissonance. The response of the Deuteronomistic historian(s), according to T. N. D. Mettinger,[129] was to stress the fact that Yahweh actually
dwells in heaven, with only his "name" (*šēm*) available on earth,[130] and to
deny the numinous roles of old played by the ark and cherubim throne.

The Priestly writer, as another example, refashions the temple as a "tabernacle" (*miškān*), a specifically movable entity, so as not to be tied down to one
particular geographical location.[131] Ezekiel, on the other hand, shows the
"glory" of Yahweh abandoning the temple and Jerusalem (Ezekiel 8–11) and
has Yahweh declare that he himself has become either a "little sanctuary"
(*miqdāš mĕʿaṭ*) or a "sanctuary for a little while" (so NRSV) for his people in exile (11:16)[132]—in either case the availability of Yahweh's presence is no longer
dependent on the existence of the Jerusalem temple, on a specific geographical
locale. And Jeremiah reminds his listeners that Yahweh had once before rav-
aged his own shrine, in Shiloh, and thus could do it again (Jer 7:12–15; cf. Ps
78:56–72).[133] Indeed, one of the principal ideological premises motivating the
composition of the classic Mesopotamian city laments was to celebrate Ibbi-
Sin's restoration of the major cult centers that had been destroyed at the end
of the Ur III period, a kind of reactivation or revitalization of their sacred
functions—a perspective which these compositions share with the Priestly
writer and Ezekiel, both of whom also look forward to the Jerusalem temple's
eventual restoration and reactivation.[134]

---

129. Ibid., 6–11.

130. Recall that Lamentations (esp. 5:19), too, enacts a similar (if much less positive)
shift in emphasis toward divine transcendence.

131. C. L. Seow, "The Designation of the Ark in Priestly Theology," *HAR* 8 (1984)
185–98.

132. For discussion of this passage, see W. Zimmerli, *Ezekiel 1* (Hermeneia; Philadelphia: Fortress, 1979) 262; M. Greenberg, *Ezekiel 1–20* (AB 22; New York: Doubleday,
1983) 190.

133. Cf. Levenson, *Sinai and Zion*, 165–69.

134. For an understanding of the last portion of Psalm 78 in relation to the city-lament
genre, see Greenstein, "Qinah ʿal hurban ʿir," 88–97.

Lamentations 2 also reimagines the significance of geography, though the tack taken contrasts significantly with these other biblical and extrabiblical compositions. In separating persona from material city[135] and then systematically wrecking the latter, the poem accomplishes two feats. First, the importance that was attached to geography, to place, was displaced and decentered—literally demolished! In doing so the poem strikes an utterly realistic tone. It does not deny the testimony of the eye. Just as the temple architecture itself once provided a visible token of Zion's mythic vibrancy, so now the visible ruination of that same architecture is not to be refused: Zion is no longer the earthly site of divinity.[136] The temple, like the city, is totally demolished and Yahweh is no longer to be found there—since he himself was the one who did the demolishing! There is a finality about this wrecking that does not share the anticipation of rebuilding common to an Ezekiel or the Mesopotamian city laments.[137] In this respect, Lamentations very closely resembles the "Curse of Agade," a city-lament kind of composition that memorializes the destruction of Agade instead of celebrating its eventual restoration.

Second, in place of geographical Zion, the poem gives a figure of the imagination, personified Zion. The material act of rebuilding temple and city, physically gathering up the scattered and battered rubble (the architectural traces of broken Zion) and reforming them into a new physical structure, which after all is the narrative rationale for all city laments in the first place, is eschewed and a different kind of building is engaged: a gathering up of linguistic and textual traces of an imagined Zion—a nonphysical though not immaterial making of the imagination, poesy.[138] Here the imagination gives

---

135. A similar separation strategy is evident in the Deuteronomistic history as well. Only there the divorce focuses on the conception of Yahweh's dwelling: the fusion of earthly and heavenly abodes in the temple (expressed wonderfully, for example, in Nabu-apla-iddina's Sippar relief) is consciously severed, with Yahweh's actual habitation being confined to heaven (Mettinger, "Name and Glory," 7–9).

136. This need not entail, necessarily, the debunking of Zion's cosmic dimensions as well. As Levenson, for one, well notes (*Sinai and Zion*, 125), Zion always was more than an earthly place and at any rate Yahweh's dwelling in Zion was never "gross and tangible." And thus Zion's cosmic dimension could be emphasized in compensation for the literal lack of an earthly temple. For example, in the exile the Israelites only needed to direct their prayers to the place where the temple once stood in order to activate cosmic communication (1 Kgs 8:28–29; cf. Dan 6:11; Mettinger, "Name and Glory," 7–9). However, the emphasis in Lamentations is otherwise.

137. Recall that in Ezekiel the "glory" of Yahweh eventually returns (Ezekiel 40–48); in Psalm 78 Shiloh is replaced by Jerusalem; and in the Mesopotamian city laments the temple is rebuilt.

138. Here we should emphasize the very materiality of poetry as a making with words,

what cannot as yet be realized on the ground. If the Judeans remaining in Palestine after 586 cannot rebuild the real temple, cannot literally *reconstruct* the geographical Zion of old, they can reconstitute it imaginatively. The power of this linguistic and textual gesture should not be undervalued. As E. Scarry observes, the imagination is a person's "last resource for the generation of objects" that the world fails to provide, and as such it potentially wields tremendous power. For example, if there is no actual food available for a hungry person, imagining berries and grain, at least temporarily, can transform the aversive sensations of hunger into potentially positive feelings and in so doing perhaps motivate action that will eventually alleviate the hunger itself.[139] Here personified Zion is still very much the site of divine presence and communication, a functional equivalent to Eliade's geographical axis mundi. She is the intermediary who beseeches Yahweh on behalf of the larger community; she is the common voice of suffering and pain and expresses the people's desire for relief and new life. And thus, personified Zion serves the temple-less community as an imaginative surrogate—a *place*holder, if you will—until such a time as a more material temple of mud and brick can be rebuilt; a Zion of the mind and text is substituted (quite literally before the eyes of the poem's readers) for the Zion of myth and cult that now lies in ruin.

As important as the fact of the imagination's intrusion in reality here (what S. Heaney calls the "redress of poetry"[140]) is the way that it intrudes—and the way it intrudes is as a person. Imagined Zion is also *personified* Zion. The trope of *personi*fication carries with it (however covertly) the power of the *personal*, and it is the promotion of the personal as the premier site of divine accessibility and redemption that one senses ever so subtly in the figure of personified Zion as she is concretized in Lamentations 2 and especially as she is juxtaposed with her former, material embodiment.[141] If Yahweh is to still be

---

with language. In the case of Lamentations, the words themselves emerge on the page out of the very letters of the alphabet that encase the poem through the acrostic.

139. E. Scarry, *Body in Pain* (New York: Oxford University Press, 1985) 166–67.

140. S. Heaney, *The Redress of Poetry* (New York: Farrar, Straus, and Giroux, 1995) 1–16.

141. Both Gottwald, in his perception that Lamentations is struggling toward a "new ethical and spiritual foundation for community" ("Reconsidered," 169) and Provan, in his feeling (never elaborated upon) that the poet is somehow seeking "to lead Israel back to faith in a person rather than a place" (*Lamentations*, 21), appear, at least intuitively, to sense the importance of the *personal* in Lamentations more generally. And indeed, from this point on in the sequence, the poetry's focus narrows rather fixedly to the human consequences of the destruction—here in the figure of the personified city (2:20–22), then in the suffering "man" of Lamentations 3, and finally in the larger post-destruction community in Lamentations 4 and 5. The material city, with the exception of an occasional allusion here and there (e.g., 3:7, 9; 5:18), no longer represents a prominent concern of these poems. And a

engaged—and that he must be is implicit in the very composition of the poem itself—it will not be via the mechanism of sacrifice at the Temple Mount but through human voice and prayer. Vocal Zion has only "prayer" and "upraised hands" to offer Yahweh (Ps 141:2; cf. Lam 2:18a, 19a, 19c), trusting that it is enough to "call upon" Yahweh in order to become present before the deity (Ps 145:18; cf. Deut 4:7). The personal, as a matter of pragmatics (i.e., the temple no longer exists), becomes the foremost site for encountering divinity. Expressed in a Levinasian idiom, it is the "face" of (personified) Zion, whose epiphany comes in the poetry through "voice" ("Look and see!"),[142] that bears both the surviving trace of the former (geographical) Zion and "the trace . . . [that] is the proximity of God."[143] The epiphany of God, according

---

similar heightening of the human may be detected in other exilic writings. For example, Jeremiah writes about a "new covenant" that Yahweh will write on the people's hearts (31:31–34) and Ezekiel speaks of Yahweh's giving the people a "new heart" and a "new spirit" (36:26–27). In Second Isaiah the figure of a "suffering servant" features prominently (esp. Isa 52:13–53:12) and the people themselves are explicitly identified with the temple complex (Isa 51:16). And then there is the incarnation of the divine within humanity itself in the person of Jesus of Nazareth as figured in the New Testament. But perhaps the most telling parallels for our appreciation of the personified figure of Zion in this poem are the Hellenistic *tychē poleōs* and the rabbinic Shekinah. While both of these latter figures partake of the divine in ways not realized by personified Zion in Lamentations—the *tychē* becomes fully divinized, while the Shekinah remains a hypostasization of Yahweh—their parallels to the figure of Zion in etymology and function are striking. Like Zion, both are abstractions of geographical phenomena (e.g., the name "Shekinah" is derived from the Semitic root *škn* "to dwell," which suggests that she was originally that aspect of the deity that was ap-prehensible and accessible to humans, thus functioning very much in a way analogous to the older *miškān* "sanctuary"), both are female persona, and both have compassionate na-tures and advocate on behalf of their human subjects vis-à-vis God (in the case of the She-kinah) or other gods.

142. Levinas himself is often dismissive of literature and art, forever wary of their innate capacities to disfigure the other. And yet, as J. Robins compellingly shows, there are many ways "in which Levinas needs the resources of literature to say his philosophy" (*Altered Read-ing*, xxiii; and see especially Levinas's *Proper Names* [Stanford: Stanford University Press, 1996] where Levinas is often more appreciative of particular literary artists). In reality, of course, there is no real possibility of ethical language without rhetoric and figures (Glo-wacka, "Disappearing Traces," 102–3; Robins, *Altered Reading*, 19), and thus there is always a certain "duplicity" and risk in speaking, however indebted to the literary the latter may be. Still, it is worth noting that this poem's evocation of the "face" of the other, of Zion, is es-pecially Levinasian, and thus especially ethical, insofar as it is accomplished through voice, thus minimizing the risk to disfiguring characterizations—speaking to ("voice"), we recall, is after all the Levinasian paradigm for ethical relations: "the face speaks" (Levinas, *Totality and Infinity*, 66).

143. E. Levinas, "A Man-God," *Entre Nous* (New York: Columbia University Press, 1998) 57.

to Levinas, is embodied (primordially) in the face of the other who calls forth (my) responsibility. The upraised voice of Zion in these last several stanzas, then, is the calling forth of the other that gives witness to the "invisible God," the Infinite which is itself revealed "through what it is capable of doing in the witness";[144] Zion's angry protestations against human hurt and suffering constitute her own "never, never, again,"[145] and as such are "the very coming of God to the idea."[146] That is, both the representation of Zion (as victim and witness) in which the plastic "face" of an other is effected and the feat of witnessing that is not "a recording from an objectifying vantage point but an incessant traversing of the distance toward the event"[147] constitute movements of approach toward the other that for Levinas are the essence of responsible (ethical) relations, and thus "the fall of God into meaning."[148]

* * *

In the end, however, and by whatever idiom, the two basic trajectories that I have been tracing throughout this paper—the razing and raising of Zion—complement and mirror one another: the *razing* of Zion's foundations, represented at the poem's (semantic) surface, is matched perfomatively by the mostly tropological *raising* of Zion's voice (her vocativity and vocality). But ultimately, it is the latter that the poem literally (literarily) offers in compensation for the former: *raising* finally trumps and tropes *razing*. The Zion at the outset of Lamentations 2 (material Zion, the Zion of temple and cult, the place of divine habitation memorialized in the songs of Zion) is razed and demolished and at poem's end replaced by a different kind of Zion—a Zion of the mind and text who nevertheless through impersonation maintains a site for divinity, whose speaking voice tokens survival and preserves and sustains the ever-fragile trace of her former architectural self until such a time in the future as geography and architecture can once again channel divinity.[149]

---

144. E. Levinas, *Ethics and Infinity* (Pittsburgh: Duquesne University Press, 1985) 109.

145. Cf. T. Des Pres, *The Survivor* (New York: Oxford University Press, 1976) 47.

146. E. Levinas, *Time and the Other* (Pittsburgh: Duquesne University Press, 1987) 115.

147. Glowacka, "Disappearing Traces," 106.

148. Levinas, *Time and the Other*, 115. I am very much indebted here for my Levinasian musings on the significance of Zion's personification to Robins's *Altered Reading*, Glowacka's "Disappearing Traces," and M. L. Baird's "Emmanuel Levinas and the Problem of Meaningless Suffering: The Holocaust as a Test Case," *Horizons* 26 (1999) 73–84.

149. Interestingly, after the exile, some of the resurrected versions of the Zion tradition (e.g., Isaiah 60–62) feature the personified figure raised to (and through) poetic expression here (and elsewhere in the sequence; see Levenson, "Zion Traditions," 1102). Personified Zion also features significantly in the prophecies of Second Isaiah, whose work more generally exhibits an indebtedness to Lamentations; see P. T. Willey, *Remember the Former*

This reappreciation of Zion in Lamentations 2 did not take place in a vacuum. As I have tried to indicate, many of those writing in the wake of 586 (P, DtrH, Jeremiah, Ezekiel) were similarly forced to confront the disjunctions of myth and history. Nowhere were these disjunctions more pronounced than in the claims of the once proud and dominant Zion tradition. For our poet, the tradition could no longer be taken at face value. Its governing ideologies are shown (lyrically) to be wanting, suddenly nonconsonant with the hard realities of the day. Only the tradition's twin peaks, Yahweh and Zion, survive the poem's linguistic onslaught, and they are necessarily refigured, reimagined. Yahweh remains central to the poet's thought, yet, without an earthly venue for habitation, he is strangely distant and his metaphorization as enemy makes approaching this deity problematic.

Of the two, though, it is with Zion that the poet makes his most positive and long-lasting contribution. She, too, in this poet's hands is not what she once was. The geographical site of Yahweh's chosen dwelling, whose architecture alone used to inspire laud and descriptions of mythic splendor, is here depicted as having been ruthlessly razed by the deity himself. And in place of this (former) holy place the poet raises through word and trope a personified and vocal Zion; an imagined alter ego for the temple–city complex, capable of surviving without stone and mortar; an image whose pragmatic appeal and imaginative power, though composed originally for the temple-less community of post-destruction Jerusalem and surrounding environs, continues to reverberate and inspire these many centuries later, as my own Levinasian interruptions and allusions have been intended to show. The raising of Zion in this poem is one of those feats of literary imagination, and thus world creation (poesy), whose intervention in history both then and now more than holds its own, effecting a compelling counterweight capable (to use Heaney's words and Simone Weil's image) of "tilting the scales of reality towards some transcendent equilibrium."[150] Zion raised in the imagination is this poem's answer to the reality of razed Zion.

Things: The Recollection of Previous Texts in Second Isaiah (SBLDS 161; Atlanta: Scholars Press, 1997); B. D. Sommer, *A Prophet Reads Scripture: Allusion in Isaiah 40–66* (Stanford: Stanford University Press, 1998). Ultimately, of course, we cannot know just how indebted these later writings are to Lamentations.

150. Heaney, *Redress of Poetry*, 3–4.

Sinai and Zion in Psalm 93

John S. Kselman
Weston Jesuit School of Theology

As many commentators have shown, Psalm 93 replicates a mythic pattern derived from Canaanite prototypes, specifically the myth of the cosmic battle of the creator god with the chaotic forces of the sea. After his triumph, the divine victor is hailed as king by the other gods, who construct for him a heavenly palace. The emergent from this theomachy is the habitable created world, by the creator's imposition of order upon chaos. In Canaanite myth, the creator and king of the gods is Baal.

In Psalm 93, all of these elements are present: Yahweh is the divine warrior doing battle with chaotic powers, variously described as *nĕhārôt* "rivers/streams" three times in v. 2 and as *mayim rabbîm* "many/mighty waters" and *yām* "sea" in v. 4. An instance of the artistry of Psalm 93 is shown in the way the poet balances these five epithets for the forces of chaos with the five occurrences of the divine name Yahweh in vv. 1 (twice), 3, 4, and 5. In v. 1c the poet takes up the theme of the creation of a stable world. Yahweh's acclamation as king and his enthronement are described in v. 2: *Yhwh mālāk . . . nākôn kis'ăkā* "[It is] Yahweh [who] is king [and no other god] . . . your throne is established."[1]

The final element in this Canaanite-Israelite mythic pattern is the provision of a palace for the divine victor in v. 5 ("your house"). Traditionally v. 5b is translated "holiness is fitting (*na'ăwâ*) to your house."[2] If this translation is correct, Psalm 93 would conclude with a somewhat banal and flat statement, out of harmony with the artistry and drama of the rest of the poem.

Some commentators have proposed alternative understandings. Buttenwieser takes the verb *nā'â/nāwâ* to mean "be beautiful," whose *Pilel* form means "beautify/adorn" and translates "holiness adorns your house."[3] J. D.

---

1. The change of person from 3rd (*mālāk* "he is king") to 2nd ("your throne") is not uncommon in Hebrew poetry; see Ps 5:6–7.

2. Analyzed as a *Pilel* form of the verb *nā'â/nāwâ* ("be fitting, becoming, suitable"); so, e.g., Delitzsch, Briggs, Kraus, and many others.

3. M. Buttenwieser, *The Psalms Chronologically Treated with a New Translation* (LBS; New York: Ktav, 1969 [1938]) 341. He compares the form to *'anwēhû* ("I will acclaim him") in Exod 15:2.

Shenkel and M. Dahood take a different tack in determining the meaning of Ps 93:5. Like Buttenwieser, they analyze the MT form *na'āwâ* as a finite form of *nā'â/nāwâ*, whose object "you" is supplied by the double-duty suffix of *lĕbêtĕkā*. The preposition *l-* is taken to mean "in"; *qōdeš* "holiness" is a collective reference to the pantheon or heavenly council ("holy ones"). Finally, Shenkel and Dahood find in *'ēdōteykā* the Ugaritic noun *'d/'dt* "throne":

> Your throne has been firmly established;
> in your temple the holy ones shall glorify you,
> O Yahweh, for length of days.[4]

This interpretation is not impossible. The praise of the king of the gods by the heavenly court is a motif found elsewhere in archaic Hebrew poetry. In Psalm 29, the "sons of God" (divine beings) praise Yahweh (vv. 1–2), acclaiming him as king in his palace (vv. 9c–10) after his victory over the sea (vv. 3–9b, 10). In Psalm 89, the praise of Yahweh by the other gods is followed by his victory over the chaotic sea (vv. 10–11) and the creation of the world (vv. 12–13). He is enthroned in v. 15, and his acclamation as king (v. 19) closes this first section of Psalm 89. However, Shenkel's analysis depends on the discovery of a Ugaritic noun in *'ēdōteykā*, a term that, as we will see, can be understood without recourse to Ugaritic; and on a rare, if not unparalleled, meaning ("in") of the preposition *l-*.

The key to a simpler and more elegant solution is provided by a Qumran variant (4QPs^b) that has *nwh* in place of *n'wh*.[5] This variant produces in v. 5 the reading *nĕwēh qōdeš* "holy habitation/dwelling place," a phrase that also occurs in Exod 15:13: "You led them by your might (*'ozzĕkā*)[6] to your holy habitation." Two scholars have noted the consonance of Ps 93:5 and Exod 15:13. Commenting on Exod 15:13, W. H. C. Propp notes that *nāweh* (and the Akk. cognate *nāwûm*) means primarily "shepherd's abode, pasture." From this meaning it developed the meaning of "abode" in general, a dwelling place, a place of habitation: "A *nāwe(h)* is generally the goal of a journey or a place of rest . . . and bears the additional connotations of 'camp' (Isa 32:8) and 'tent' (Isa 33:20; Job 5:24; 18:15). . . . But a permanent habitation such as Jerusalem can be a metaphorical *nāwe(h)* and Yahweh's holy *nāwe(h)* may even

---

4. J. D. Shenkel, "An Interpretation of Ps 93:5," *Bib* 46 (1965) 401–16; M. Dahood, *Psalms II* (AB 17; Garden City, N.Y.: Doubleday, 1968) 342–44.

5. P. Flint, *The Dead Sea Scrolls and the Book of Psalms* (STDJ 17; Leiden: Brill, 1997) 95. As M. L. Barré has pointed out to me, the *'alep* of *n'wh* in the MT may be a mater lectionis for the original long *a* vowel; see F. I. Andersen and A. D. Forbes, *Spelling in the Hebrew Bible* (BibOr 41; Rome: Pontifical Biblical Institute, 1986) 49, 81–91.

6. Note that in Ps 93:1 Yahweh is clothed and girded with might (*'ōz*).

be the whole land of Canaan."[7] Although Propp points out the relationship of *něwēh qodšekā* "your holy habitation" in Exod 15:13 and *něwēh qōdeš* "holy habitation" in Ps 93:5, he does not supply a full translation of the psalm verse. D. M. Howard, another scholar who recognizes the relationship of the psalm verse to Exod 15:13, does provide a translation:

> Your decrees are affirmed, O Mighty One,
> in your house, (your) holy habitation,
> O Yahweh, for length of days.[8]

While Howard's analysis is a step forward in identifying the construct phrase *nwh qdš* in Ps 93:5, the result produced sounds more like prose than poetry.

I would like to make an alternative proposal: the proclitic *l-* of *lěbêtěkā* is not a preposition (to which Howard, like Shenkel, attaches the unusual meaning "in"), as other commentators assume; it is, rather, an emphatic particle, the so-called *lamed* emphatic. This emphatic particle was first identified over a century ago by P. Haupt and was recently and exhaustively treated by J. Huehnergard: "In the majority of the most probable instances [in Biblical Hebrew], proclitic *l-* is prefixed to nouns. Usually it is an emphasizing element: e.g. in nonverbal clauses."[9] This is exactly the syntactic situation is Ps 93:5, which I would render: "Surely your house is a holy habitation," where the noun *bêt* "house" with the emphatic *lamed* is the subject of a nonverbal clause. Psalm 89, which has linguistic and thematic connections with Psalm 93 (see above), also uses the emphatic *lamed* in the concluding bicolon of the first section of the poem (vv. 2–19): "Surely Yahweh (*laYhwh*) is our shield; surely the Holy One (*liqdôš*) of Israel is our king" (Ps 89:19).[10]

The final controverted word in v. 5 is *ʿēdōteykā*. Taking up a suggestion of Johannes Pedersen, Albright and Cross understand the word to be cognate

---

7. W. H. C. Propp, *Exodus 1–18* (AB 2; New York: Doubleday, 1998) 532–33. Among the other possible meanings of *nāweh*, Propp lists the pasturage of Sinai and its environs, the desert tent (Exodus 25–31; 35–40), and David's sacred tent (2 Sam 6:17; 15:25), the predecessor of Solomon's temple.

8. D. M. Howard, *The Structure of Psalms 93–100* (Biblical and Judaic Studies from the University of California, San Diego 5; Winona Lake, Ind.: Eisenbrauns, 1997) 35, 41.

9. J. Huehnergard, "Asseverative *la and Hypothetical *lu/law in Semitic," *JAOS* 103 (1983) 591. Even T. Muraoka, who questions the very existence of emphatic *lamed*, admits that it remains a possibility in several places (e.g., Ps 89:19) where it is prefixed to the subject or predicate of a nominal clause (*Emphatic Words and Structures in Biblical Hebrew* [Jerusalem: Magnes / Leiden: Brill, 1985] 123).

10. Huehnergard proposes that the vocalization of emphatic *lamed* is *la-*. Is it merely a coincidence that this emphatic particle occurs in Psalm 89 at the end of the first section of the poem and in Psalm 93 at the end of the poem?

with Arabic *ʿahd*, the primary term for covenant among early Arabs. The development of the form can be schematized as follows:

ʿahd > *ʿādōt* (fem. pl., with elision of *he*)
ʿādōt > *ʿôdōt* (Canaanite shift of *ā* to *ō*)
ʿôdōt > *ʿēdōt* (dissimilation)[11]

Cross understands *ʿēdūt* to be a secondary form, representing an original *ʿēdōt*, a *plurale tantum* meaning "covenant." Note Exod 31:18 and 32:15, where the two tablets of the covenant are termed *šĕnê luḥōt hāʿēdūt*; in Deut 9:11 and 15, the tablets are *šĕnê luḥōt habbĕrît*. Similarly, the ark of the covenant is *ʾărôn hāʿēdūt* in Exod 25:21; 26:33, etc., and *ʾărôn habbĕrît* in Deut 10:18; 31:9, 25, etc.

Besides Arabic *ʿahd*, there are two other important cognates of Hebrew *ʿēdōt/ʿēdūt*: the Assyrian technical term *adû/adê* (*plurale tantum*) for a vassal treaty,[12] and Aramaic *ʿdy* (*ʿadayyā*) with the same meaning.[13] The plural usage of the related Hebrew, Akkadian, and Aramaic technical treaty or covenant terms may have originally referred to "stipulations," an essential part of a treaty; they come to mean "covenant" by synechdoche, or pars pro toto. Note the series *hāʿēdūt* [*hāʿēdōt*] *wĕḥuqqîm wĕhammišpātîm* "stipulations, statutes, and ordinances" in Deut 4:45 and 6:20, where the synonymous terms suggest the meaning "stipulations" for *hāʿēdūt/hāʿēdōt*.[14]

11. W. F. Albright, *Yahweh and the Gods of Canaan* (Jordan Lectures 1965; Garden City, N.Y.: Doubleday, 1968) 106–7; F. M. Cross, *Canaanite Myth and Hebrew Epic* (Cambridge: Harvard University Press, 1973) 266–67; idem, *From Epic to Canon* (Baltimore: Johns Hopkins University Press, 1998) 16. See also B. Volkwein, "Masoretisches *ʿēdūt, ʿēdwōt, ʿēdōt*: 'Zeugnis' oder 'Bundesbestimmung'?" *BZ* 13 (1969) 18–40; T. Veijola, "Zu Ableitung und Bedeutung von *hēʿîd* im Hebräischen: Ein Beitrag zur Bundesterminologie," *UF* 8 (1976) 343–51; J. A. Thompson, "Expansions of the עד Root," *JSS* 10 (1965) 222–40. Thompson notes that the third form of the Arabic verb *ʿhd* means "swear to someone, enter into a treaty, agree with someone" (p. 234).

12. R. Frankena, "The Vassal-Treaties of Esarhaddon and the Dating of Deuteronomy," *OtSt* 14 (1965) 134–36.

13. J. A. Fitzmyer, *The Aramaic Inscriptions of Sefîre* (BibOr 19; Rome: Pontifical Biblical Institute, 1967) 23–24.

14. See also Deut 6:17: *šāmôr tišmĕrûn ʾet miṣwōt yhwh ʾĕlōhêkem wĕʿēdōtāyw wĕḥuqqāyw ʾăšer ṣiwwāk* "you shall keep the commandments of Yahweh your God and his stipulations and his statutes which he commanded you"; Ps 81:5–6: *ḥōq . . . mišpāṭ . . . ʿēdūt* "statute . . . ordinance . . . stipulations"; Ps 99:7: *šāmĕrû ʿēdōtāyw wĕḥōq nātan lāmô* "they kept his stipulations and the statutes he gave them"; Ps 25:10: *lĕnōṣĕrê bĕrîtô wĕʿēdōtāyw* "to those who keep his covenant and his stipulations." And note also 2 Kgs 17:13, 15: *wĕšimrû miṣwōtay ḥuqqōtay kĕkol hattôrâ ʾăšer ṣiwwîtî ʾet ʾăbōtêkem . . . wayyimʾăsû ʾet ḥuqqāyw wĕʾet bĕrîtô ʾăšer kārat ʾet ʾăbōtām wĕʾet ʿēdōtāyw ʾăšer hēʿîd bām* "keep my commandments [and] my statutes

Having noted the occurrence in both Exod 15:13 and Ps 93:5 of *nĕwēh qōdeš* "holy habitation/dwelling place," we can now turn our attention to the issue of the *function* of the new reading of Ps 93:5 proposed here. In the ancient hymn of Exodus 15, the deity's holy habitation is located in the area of Sinai. When the poet of Psalm 93 uses the same phrase for Yahweh's dwelling place in the temple on Mount Zion, the psalmist is engaging in a process found elsewhere, the transfer of the role and status of Sinai to Yahweh's new dwelling place, Zion.[15] Other examples of the transfer of motifs from Sinai to Zion can be found, for instance, by comparing Exod 40:34–35 with 1 Kgs 8:10–11:

> *waykas heʿānān ʾet ʾōhel môʿēd*
> *ûkĕbôd yhwh mālēʾ ʾet hammiškān*
> *wĕlōʾ yākōl mōšeh lābôʾ ʾel ʾōhel môʿēd*
> *kî šākan ʿālāyw heʿānān*
> *ûkĕbôd yhwh mālēʾ ʾet hammiškān*

> The cloud covered the Tent of Meeting,
> and the glory of Yahweh filled the tent.
> Moses was unable to approach the Tent of Meeting,
> because the cloud settled on it,
> and the glory of Yahweh filled the tent.

Compare this description of the cloud and the glory of Yahweh upon the Sinai tent in Exodus 40 to that of Solomon's dedication of the temple on Mount Zion:

> *wayhî bĕṣēʾt hakkōhănîm min haqqōdeš*
> *wĕheʿānān mālēʾ ʾet bêt yhwh*
> *wĕlōʾ yākĕlû hakkōhănîm*
> *laʿămōd lĕšārēt mippĕnê heʿānān*
> *kî mālēʾ kĕbôd yhwh ʾet bêt yhwh*

> When the priests came out of the holy place,
> the cloud filled the house of Yahweh.
> The priests were not able
> to stand or minister because of the cloud,
> because the glory of Yahweh filled the house of Yahweh.

according to all the torah which I commanded your fathers . . . but they rejected his statutes and his covenant which he made with their fathers and his covenant (stipulations) which he imposed on them." This series is reinforced by *miṣwōt* "commandments" in v. 16 and by *miṣwōt* and *ḥuqqōt* ("statutes") in v. 19.

15. R. J. Clifford, *The Cosmic Mountain in Canaan and the Old Testament* (HSM 4; Cambridge: Harvard University Press, 1972) 154–58; J. D. Levenson, *Sinai and Zion: An Entry into the Jewish Bible* (Minneapolis: Winston, 1985) 187–217.

Both passages describe theophanies involving the cloud of Yahweh and his glory, the divine luminescence that envelops and emanates from the deity and that makes Moses in Exodus 40 and the priests in 1 Kings 8 unable to enter this place of intense and life-threatening holiness. The reuse of the Exodus language in 1 Kings 8 is a clear and unassailable instance of the transfer of motifs from Sinai to Zion.

Another important witness to this process is Isa 2:2–4. In the poem, the "mountain of Yahweh's house" is elevated to become the highest mountain, to which all peoples will stream, "to the mountain of Yahweh, to the house of the God of Jacob." The climax of the poem is reached when Zion replaces Sinai as the source of divine instruction:

> *kî miṣṣiyyōn tēṣēʾ tôrâ*
> *ûdĕbar yhwh mîrûšālāim*
>
> For from Zion will go forth torah,
> and the word of Yahweh from Jerusalem.[16]

Finally, we turn our attention to *ʿēdōteykā* in Ps 93:5. As discussed above, *ʿēdōt/ʿēdūt* has been identified as a term for "covenant" by Albright and Cross. In the Pentateuch, referring to the Sinai covenant, it appears in such constructions as *ʾōhel hāʿēdūt* "the tent of the covenant" (Num 9:15; 17:22, etc.), *ʾărôn hāʿēdūt* "the ark of the covenant" (Exod 25:22; 26:33, etc.), *luḥōt hāʿēdūt* "the tablets of the covenant" (Exod 31:18; 32:15; 34:29), and *miškan hāʿēdūt* "the tent of the covenant" (Exod 38:21; Num 1:50, etc.). In the context of Ps 93:5, *ʿēdōteykā* "your covenant" refers to the royal covenant that Yahweh entered into with David and his descendants. This is indicated by two texts, Ps 89:29 (in a psalm with several other points of contact with Psalm 93) and Ps 132:12; in both texts Yahweh is the speaker, addressing David (and the dynasty):

> *lĕʿôlām ʾešmôr lô ḥasdî*
> *ûbĕrîtî neʾĕmenet lô*
>
> Forever I will keep my covenant loyalty to him,
> and my covenant will stand firm for him.
>
> *ʾim yišmĕrû bāneykā bĕrîtî*
> *wĕʿēdōtî zô ʾălammĕdēm*
> *gam bĕnêhem ʿădê ʿad*
> *yēšĕbû lĕkissēʾ lāk*

---

16. For the parallelism of *ʿēdūt* and *tôrâ*, see Pss 19:8 and 78:5; in Ps 78:10 *bĕrît* and *tôrâ* are parallel terms.

> If your sons keep my covenant,
> and my stipulations which I will teach them,
> then their sons forever
> shall sit on your throne.[17]

The eternal covenant offered by Yahweh to David and his successors in Pss 89:29 and 132:12 is also the covenant spoken of in Ps 93:5. In all three cases the covenant (*ʿēdōteykā* in Ps 93:5, *bĕrîtî* in Ps 89:29; *ʿēdōtî*[18] in Ps 132:12) is described as reliable, enduring (*neʾemnû/neʾĕmenet*),[19] something the Davidic king and his descendants can count on "forever."

So the Zion tradition relocates Yahweh's holy dwelling place from Sinai to Zion; Mount Zion succeeds Mount Sinai to become the source of Torah, the preeminent role of Sinai; and the Sinai covenant is succeeded by the royal covenant, reliable and enduring. The new reading of Ps 93:5 aligns this hymn with the emerging Zion tradition and probably with Solomon's temple-building in the tenth century B.C.E. We can probably even see the tradition at its beginning in 2 Samuel 6, with David's transfer of the ark, symbol of Yahweh's presence with and guidance of the premonarchic tribal confederacy, to the Davidic tent in Jerusalem, and ultimately to Solomon's temple.

Based on the analysis of *lĕbêtĕkā* "Truly your house" and *ʿēdōteykā* "your covenant" argued for above, the translation proposed for Ps 93:5 is:

---

17. The similar language used for the inauguration of the royal covenant in 2 Sam 7:16 confirms this interpretation of Ps 93:5: *wĕneʾman bêtĕkā ûmamlaktĕkā ʿad ʿôlām lĕpāneykā kisʾăkā yihyeh nākôn ʿad ʿôlām* "Your house and your kingdom will endure forever before me; your throne will be established forever." *Lĕpāneykā* ("before you") is emended to *lĕpānay* ("before me").

18. On *ʿēdōtî*, Johnson suggests that the vocalization shows some uncertainty on the part of the Masoretes about whether to point it as a singular (*ʿēdūtî*) or a plural (*ʿēdōtay*); see A. R. Johnson, *Sacral Kingship in Ancient Israel* (2nd ed.; Cardiff: Wales University Press, 1967) 23 n. 2.

19. Besides Ps 93:5, there is one other instance of *ʿēdūt/ʿēdōt* as a subject of a *Niphal* of *ʾmn*, in Ps 19:8: *ʿēdût yhwh neʾĕmanâ* "The decrees of Yahweh are sure." The noun *ʿēdūt/ʿēdōt* is in parallelism with preceding *tôrat* and with following *piqqûdê* "precepts," *miṣwat* "commandment," and *mišpĕṭê* "ordinances." This context for *ʿēdût* in Psalm 19 may indicate that its specific nuance here is "stipulations," that is, covenant obligations. The apparent fem. sing. verb *neʾĕmānâ* with fem. pl. subject *ʿēdût* can be explained in several ways (so Volkwein, "Masoretisches," 38): The verb may be a sing. construction with a pl. subject, emphasizing the unitary character of the subject. Or one may emend the final mater lectionis *he* to *waw*, producing the plural *neʾemnû*; the *he* may have come into the text when *ʿēdût* was mistakenly derived from *ʿwd* "witness/testify" and was understood as an abstract fem. sing. noun meaning "testimony." Finally, *neʾĕmānâ* may be an archaism, a fem. pl. verb with *ā* ending, as in Aramaic (GKC 44m; Joüon 42f).

Your covenant is entirely reliable;
truly your house is a holy habitation,
O Yhwh, for length of days.[20]

---

20. M. L. Barré (private communication) has suggested to me an alternative understanding of v. 5b: "Truly your house, the Holy Habitation, O Yhwh, will be [i.e., will endure] forever." "Holy Habitation" is taken to be an epithet of the temple, in apposition to the subject of the nonverbal sentence, "your house"; "for length of days/forever" is the predicate. In this rendering v. 5b is parallel to "your throne is established forever" in v. 2a, and together they form an inclusion around the body of the poem. This inclusion is strengthened by the distant parallelism of *tikkôn* "is established" in v. 1c and *nākôn* "established" in v. 2a with *ne'emnû* ("reliable, trustworthy") in v. 5a. For *'āmēn* "reliable" // *kûn* "establish," see 2 Sam 7:16; Pss 78:8, 37; 89:38; see also M. L. Barré, "The Seven Epithets of Zion in Ps 48,2–3," *Bib* 69 (1988) 557–63.

"Back to the Future": Zion in the Book of Micah

Rick R. Marrs

Pepperdine University

Luke 7:36–50 relates the memorable encounter of the sinful woman and Jesus at the party of Simon the Pharisee. At a crucial moment, Jesus delivers the parable of the two debtors. The parable is well known: two debtors, neither able to repay his loan, experience "deliverance" and a new beginning through the cancellation of a debt. Perhaps more significant is the *social context* in which Jesus delivers this parable and the diverse audience receiving this word. By means of this parable, Jesus deftly pronounces judgment upon Simon, a powerful figure needing to realize his own indebtedness and failure, while simultaneously announcing forgiveness and deliverance to the powerless woman. The contrast is striking: a stinging rebuke for Simon, a comforting word of hope for the sinful woman. Jesus in a single move ably offers a multivalent message to two listeners based upon their variant social and theological *Sitzen im Leben.*

I offer this compelling Lukan scene as a window through which we might view Micah's proclamation in the eighth century B.C.E. Micah finds himself preaching to widely divergent audiences with dramatically different social settings. On the one hand, he must address the urban power-brokers of Jerusalem. On the other hand, he hails from the rural environs of the Judean countryside and likely knows firsthand the sense of powerlessness and hopelessness felt there. As a faithful prophet of God, he has at his disposal rich, but dramatically diverse, theological resources. On the one hand, he knows well the theological riches of the Exodus and Sinai traditions. On the other hand, he breathes the air of the Zion and Davidic traditions. The book of Micah reflects the agile movement of Micah between these varied audiences and theological traditions.

Author's note: It is a pleasure and honor to dedicate this article to Professor Roberts. His consistent and careful attentiveness to the text and its theological significance has served admirably as a model for me as a former student. More importantly, his willingness to give of his time and himself continues unabated. I fondly remember and appreciate everything he did for me while a student at The Johns Hopkins University. He is truly a mentor worthy of emulation.

77

I propose to review and analyze the function and theological importance of Zion in the book of Micah. As a backdrop to this task, several ancillary matters need addressing. First, some attention to the current status of Micah studies (specifically redaction criticism and literary criticism) will be given. Second, the theological dynamics of Zion theology, especially as articulated in the scholarly work of Professor J. J. M. Roberts, will be noted. Against this backdrop, the place and theological importance of Zion in the book of Micah will follow.

Background Matters

The book of Micah has received significant scholarly attention in recent years, resulting in radically disparate interpretations.[1] Numerous recent analyses of the book of Micah take a diachronic approach.[2] The redaction history of the book appears complex and merits serious detailed study.[3] Not surprisingly, determining the dates both for individual pericopes and for the final form of the book often rests upon crucial decisions regarding vocabulary, style, theological themes and motifs, and presumed social conditions. Although each interpretation diverges widely in specific details, a typical redactional analysis of Micah envisions the book as a (most likely late) postexilic

---

1. For excellent summaries of the key issues in contemporary Micah studies, see J. Willis, "Fundamental Issues in Contemporary Micah Studies," *ResQ* 13 (1970) 77–90; K. Jeppesen, "New Aspects of Micah Research," *JSOT* 8 (1978) 3–32; F. Andersen and D. Freedman, *Micah* (AB 24E; New York: Doubleday, 2000).

2. For a sampling of diachronic analyses of the book of Micah, see J. Mays, *Micah* (OTL; Philadelphia: Westminster, 1976) 21–33; H. Wolff, *Micah: A Commentary* (Minneapolis: Augsburg/Fortress, 1990) 26–28; T. Lescow, "Redaktionsgeschichtliche Analyse von Micha 1–5," *ZAW* 84 (1972) 46–85; idem, "Redaktionsgeschichtliche Analyse von Micha 6–7," *ZAW* 84 (1972) 182–212; idem, "Zur Komposition des Buches Micha," *SJOT* 9 (1995) 200–222; B. Renaud, *La formation du livre de Michée* (Paris: Gabalda, 1977); idem, *Michée-Sophonie-Nahum* (Paris: Gabalda, 1987) 74–119; I. Willi-Plein, *Vorformen der Schriftexegese innerhalb des Alten Testaments* (BZAW 123; Berlin: de Gruyter, 1971) 70–114; J. Jeremias, "Die Bedeutung der Gerichtsworte Michas in der Exilszeit," *ZAW* 83 (1971) 330–53; W. McKane, *The Book of Micah* (Edinburgh: T. & T. Clark, 1998) 1–8.

3. Most recently scholarly attention has turned toward the redaction history of the twelve. For a sampling of the place of Micah in this discussion, see *Reading and Hearing the Book of the Twelve* (ed. J. Nogalski and M. Sweeney; Atlanta: Society of Biblical Literature, 2000). Especially pertinent articles from this volume include: M. Biddle, "'Israel' and 'Jacob' in the Book of Micah: Micah in the Context of the Twelve," 146–65; B. Curtis, "The Zion-Daughter Oracles: Evidence on the Identity and Ideology of the Late Redactors of the Book of the Twelve," 166–84; K. Cuffey, "Remnant, Redactor, and Biblical Theologian: A Comparative Study of Coherence in Micah and the Twelve," 185–208.

product containing updatings, additions, accretions, and modifications to a modest original body of Mican oracles from the eighth century.[4]

Conversely, several recent analyses take a more synchronic approach to the book of Micah.[5] In these studies, issues of the form and function of the various oracles, as well as their relationship to the larger whole, are paramount. Again, not surprisingly, rather diverse arrangements and divisions of the book are suggested.[6]

Although both approaches remain valid and valuable, this study will proceed primarily against a synchronic backdrop. Since my primary focus involves determining and delineating a theological understanding of the place

---

4. When one analyzes the specifics of much of the argumentation, the conclusion of B. Childs (*Introduction to the Old Testament as Scripture* [Philadelphia: Fortress, 1979] 430) is apt: "Although these scholars all agree on a complex history of redaction which passed through many stages, the analyses are so strikingly different that no common conclusions have emerged." Numerous redactional studies begin with the assumption that authentic material from Micah appears only in chaps. 1–3. (How much of these initial chapters derives from Micah is disputed.) Disagreement occurs in determining the origin and redactional history of the remaining chapters. Although most scholars regard these chapters (i.e., chaps. 4–7) as decidedly later than the eighth century, a minority of scholars continue to regard significant portions of this material as also stemming from the prophet Micah (see, e.g., E. Sellin, *Das Zwölfprophetenbuch* [KAT 12/1; Leipzig: Deichertsche, 1929]; L. Allen, *Joel, Obadiah, Jonah, and Micah* [NICOT; Grand Rapids: Eerdmans, 1976]; J. Willis, *The Structure, Setting and Interrelationship of the Pericopes in the Book of Micah* [Ph.D. diss., Vanderbilt University, 1966]; D. Hillers, *Micah* [Hermeneia; Philadelphia: Fortress, 1984]). A comprehensive treatment of this discussion is beyond the scope of the present article; for further discussion, one may consult the standard commentaries and dictionaries.

5. For a sampling of synchronic analyses of the book, see L. Allen, *Joel – Micah*; J. Willis, "The Structure of the book of Micah," *SEÅ* 34 (1969) 5–42; idem, "Fundamental Issues," 77–90; idem, "Thoughts on a Redactional Analysis of the Book of Micah," *SBL 1978: Seminar Papers* (SBLSP 1; Chico, Calif.: Scholars Press, 1978) 87–109; L. Luker, "Beyond Form Criticism: The Relation of Doom and Hope Oracles in Micah 2–6," *HAR* 11 (1987) 285–301.

6. Several scholars propose a tripartite arrangement of judgment (Micah 1–3), hope (Micah 4–5), and further admonitions and comfort (judgment and hope [Micah 6–7]). Others (e.g., Willis ["Structure," 5–42]; Allen [*Joel – Micah*]) propose a tripartite arrangement wherein each section begins with "hear ye" (1:2; 3:1; 6:1), and judgment gives way to hope (chaps. 1–2; 3–5; 6–7). Alternately, Mays (*Micah*, 2–12) suggests a bipartite division: chaps. 1–5 address a universal audience of all peoples; chaps. 6–7 address Israel. For a fuller discussion of the "coherence" of the book of Micah literarily, see Cuffey, "Remnant, Redactor . . . ," 185–97. For an alternate reading, see K. Jeppesen, "'Because of You!': An Essay about the Centre of the Book of the Twelve," in *In Search of True Wisdom: Essays in Old Testament Interpretation in Honour of Ronald E. Clements* (ed. E. Ball; JSOTSup 300; Sheffield: Sheffield Academic Press, 1999) 196–210.

and role of Zion in the book of Micah, articulating this understanding against the larger backdrop of the whole book is most desirable.[7]

Before proceeding to an analysis of the particular passages in Micah that are germane to understanding the place of Zion in the book, I will mention two recent relevant sociological analyses of the prophet Micah and his career. Two significant interpretations of the prophet have emerged in the writings of Hans Wolff and Delbert Hillers.

Simply put, Hans Wolff argues that Micah originated as a prophet from the Judean countryside and traveled to metropolitan Jerusalem to speak on behalf of his rural compatriots. Utilizing insights from the larger dynamics present in the waning days of the eighth century B.C.E. in Judah (and Israel), Wolff theorizes that the villages surrounding Jerusalem (specifically those in the Shephelah) were dramatically (and disastrously) impacted by social policies implemented by the central Jerusalem authorities. These policies were not value free; they crippled the economy and socially destabilized several of these towns. Tragically, these villagers lost any "voice" in cosmopolitan Jerusalem. Micah became their voice. As Yahweh's spokesman on behalf of the beleaguered and despairing poor of the countryside, Micah caustically denounced the political, social, and cultic abuses of the capital city. Wolff's thesis has significant implications for reading the book of Micah.[8] Precise identification of

---

7. From this point on, the use of "Micah" will refer to the canonical book, unless otherwise noted.

8. Wolff's argumentation is intriguing. He contends that Micah clearly is working "away from home" since he is designated "the Moreshite." (Other prophetic cases where hometowns are mentioned include Amos [from Tekoa] and Jeremiah [from Anathoth], both prophets best known for their oracles delivered away from their villages.) Jeremiah 26 is central to Wolff's thesis. Jeremiah avoids a death sentence when the "elders of the land" arise and cite Micah as precedent for proclaiming doom against Jerusalem without receiving a judgment of death. Wolff conjectures that Micah may have belonged to the "elders of the land" (cf. the "elders of Judah," 1 Sam 30:36), who possibly lost all authority with the influx of Jerusalem authorities into the Shephelah. For Wolff, this hypothesis explains many characteristics of Micah's language and appearance. Micah addresses the Jerusalem leaders as "the heads of the house of Jacob and rulers of the land of Israel" (3:1, 9). He reserves the designation "my people" for his rural compatriots (1:9; 2:9; 3:3, 5). Micah forcefully decries the abuse of the Jerusalem officials who have entered towns such as Moresheth and confiscated the finest properties and houses for their private use. Against such outrage, Micah stridently proclaims God's "justice" (מִשְׁפָּט). For a complete detailing of Wolff's thesis, see *Micah*, 1–9; "Micah the Moreshite: The Prophet and His Background," in *Israelite Wisdom: Theological and Literary Essays in Honor of Samuel Terrien* (ed. J. Gammie et al.; Missoula, Mont.: Scholars Press, 1978) 77–84; *Micah the Prophet* (Philadelphia: Fortress, 1981) 3–25.

the various audiences and speakers in the book becomes crucial.[9] Specifically identifying Micah's adversaries, as well as his followers, is paramount. Secondarily, passages treating Micah's credibility and authority as a divine emissary take on added meaning.

Moving in a somewhat different direction, while traveling a similar sociological highway, Delbert Hillers intriguingly reads Micah's prophetic work against the backdrop of contemporary understandings of millenarian groups. As prophet of a "new age," Micah was instrumental in initiating and implementing a "revitalization movement." Hillers theorizes that Micah belonged to the group that had been disenfranchised and rendered powerless by the Jerusalem hierarchy. He became God's prophetic voice for this abandoned and excluded segment of Judean society.[10] This thesis also has important implications for reading the book of Micah. Given the apparent inability of most diachronic readings of Micah to win adherents, Hillers adopts a more synchronic approach.[11] He compellingly argues that several oracles, typically judged post-Mican by most redaction-critical analyses, may in reality derive from Micah. As God's spokesperson of a new age, Micah would have certainly voiced God's multivalent message to the various audiences in attendance. To the Jerusalem power-brokers, doom clouded the horizon; to the disaffected and

---

9. For variant views to that of Wolff, see A. Schart, *Die Entstehung des Zwölfprophetenbuchs: Neubearbeitungen von Amos im Rahmen schriftenübergreifender Redaktionsprozesse* (BZAW 217; New York: de Gruyter, 1998); M. Biddle, "'Israel' and 'Jacob,'" 146–65; R. Kessler, "Zwischen Tempel und Tora: Das Michabuch im Diskurs der Perserzeit," *BZ* 44 (2000) 21–36.

10. Hillers (*Micah*, 4–8) defines "revitalization" as a "deliberate, organized, conscious effort by members of a society to construct a more satisfying culture." He notes that in other societies leaders of such movements need not belong to the lower class. (In medieval Europe millennial movements often derived from lower clergy or nobility.) A major factor in the rise of millennarian groups is deprivation, deprivation resulting from the refusal of the traditional authorities to maintain and regulate the social conditions necessary for meaningful and productive life. Hillers lists five elements in the book of Micah with parallels in revitalization movements: (1) the removal of foreign elements (in preparation for a coming righteous kingdom); (2) a pre-"messianic" age of distress; (3) a reversal of social classes (with the expectation of the dominance of the pariah class); (4) the idea of a righteous, peaceable ruler; (5) a new age characterized by triumph over enemies.

11. Hillers (*Micah*, 4) argues that a synchronic reading does not necessarily presume that all the material derives from the career of Micah. Rather, it may presume a recurrent social situation to which the materials, viewed as a product of the community of faith, continue to speak (see also J. Mays, "The Theological Purpose of the Book of Micah," in *Beitrage zur alttestamentlichen Theologie: Festschrift für W. Zimmerli zum 70. Geburtstag* [ed. H. Donner, R. Hanhart, and R. Smend; Göttingen: Vandenhoeck & Ruprecht, 1977] 276–87).

deprived of the community, hope would surely follow and overwhelm the immediate debacle.

Zion in the Book of Micah

Like the compositional history of the book of Micah, so the dating and traditiohistorical development of the Zion traditions within the Hebrew Bible has been much debated. The work of Roberts has figured prominently in this discussion. In contrast to those who date the Zion traditions late (exilic or postexilic), he has consistently and cogently argued for an early dating of both the Zion and the David traditions.[12] Typically four (or five) key components are cited in connection with this tradition: (1) Zion as the divine mountain; (2) Zion and the river of paradise; (3) Zion and the conquest of chaos; (4) Zion and the defeat of the nations; (5) Zion and the pilgrimage of the nations.[13]

Against this backdrop, my thesis is relatively simple. Although the prophet Micah is often devalued as a theologian and rhetorician in comparison to his eighth-century compatriots (Amos, Hosea, Isaiah), the book bearing his name reflects considerable theological sensitivity and rhetorical interplay. Zion is the object of considerable theological reflection and attention. Theologically, Zion appears in two settings. On the one hand, Micah talks of Zion as a current reality. This Zion has witnessed rampant social injustice and either has recently experienced or will soon experience harsh treatment. Because of the injustices committed within its walls by the power-brokers of Micah's day, Yahweh launches a counteroffensive on behalf of beleaguered Zion. This results in a second view of Zion in the book. Zion appears not solely as it currently exists but as an object of divine intent. As an object in the hands of Yahweh, Zion undergoes a transformation. This transformation, although envisioned as a future event, in actuality captures Yahweh's *original* intent for Zion and its inhabitants. Ultimately, Zion has a future, but it is a future embodied in her past.

---

12. For a brief sampling, see J. J. M. Roberts, "The Davidic Origin of the Zion Tradition," *JBL* 92 (1973) 32–44; "Zion tradition," *IDBSup* (Nashville: Abingdon, 1976) 985–87; "Zion in the Theology of the Davidic-Solomonic Empire," in *Studies in the Period of David and Solomon and Other Essays* (ed. T. Ishida; Tokyo: Yamakawa-Shuppansha/Winona Lake, Ind.: Eisenbrauns, 1982) 93–108; "Isaiah 33: An Isaianic Elaboration of the Zion Tradition," in *The Word of the Lord Shall Go Forth: Essays in Honor of David Noel Freedman in Celebration of His Sixtieth Birthday* (ed. C. Meyers and M. O'Connor; Winona Lake, Ind.: Eisenbrauns, 1983) 15–25.

13. In the book of Micah, the first, fourth, and fifth of these motifs figure most prominently. See also J. Levenson ("Zion Traditions," *ABD* 6.1099–1101), who articulates the theology of Zion under three headings: (1) Enthronement of Yahweh after Victory; (2) The Election of Zion and David; (3) Visions of Peace.

Significantly, these two dramatically divergent pictures of Zion are portrayed in starkest contrast in immediately adjacent oracles in 3:9–12 and 4:1–4.

Zion: Present Reality

The most notable passage in the book of Micah reflecting the current status of Zion is 3:9–12.[14]

> Hear this, you rulers of the house of Jacob and chiefs of the house of Israel,
> Who abhor justice and pervert all equity,
> Who build Zion with blood and Jerusalem with wrong!
> Its rulers give judgment for a bribe,
> Its priests teach for a price, its prophets give oracles for money;
> Yet they lean upon the Lord and say,
> "Surely the Lord is with us! No harm shall come upon us."
> Therefore because of you Zion shall be plowed as a field;
> Jerusalem shall become a heap of ruins,
> and the mountain of the house a wooded height.

This third oracle in the triad of oracles in Micah 3[15] poignantly captures the plight of Jerusalem evidenced in Micah 1–3. Zion suffers the consequences of rampant injustice among the entire power structure, civil ("rulers," "chiefs") and religious ("prophets," "priests"). The reversal motif in the oracle is striking. Because the leaders arrogantly and wrongfully trust in Zion's (or their own?—"surely the Lord is with us! No harm will come upon us") inviolability (cf. Jeremiah 7), Yahweh will destroy the base of that false trust (Zion). Since these oppressive leaders "build Zion with blood" (בנה ציון בדמים),[16]

---

14. For many scholars, this is not simply the *present* reality, but the *only* reality for Zion attributed to the prophet Micah (so, e.g., H. Preuss, *Old Testament Theology* [Louisville: Westminster John Knox, 1996] 2.44–45; E. Jenni and C. Westermann, "צִיּוֹן," *TLOT* 2.1075). Alternately, J. Jeremias ("Tradition und Redaktion in Micha 3," in *Verbindungslinien: Festschrift für Werner H. Schmidt zum 65. Geburtstag* [ed. A. Groupner, H. Delkurt, and A. Ernst; Neukirchen-Vluyn: Neukirchener Verlag, 2000] 137–51) dates Micah 3 to the period of Jeremiah.

15. Mic 3:1–4 treats the judicial abuses present in the courts; 3:5–8 decries the absence of justice in the ministry of the false prophets; 3:9–12 addresses the breakdown of justice throughout the governmental system.

16. Surely this reference intends more than simply building spacious dwellings. The "blood" most certainly intends oppressive bloodshed, similar to Isa 5:7. Hillers (*Micah*, 48) captures the sense nicely. Since building a holy city (with fortifications, palaces, and temple) is a divine prerogative (cf. Pss 51:20[18]; 102:17[16]), the human agents involved must act with justice and righteousness every step of the way. Reading "blood" and "wrong" as

Yahweh counters by returning Zion to a plowed field and heap of ruins (צִיּוֹן שָׂדֶה תֵחָרֵשׁ . . . עִיִּין תִּהְיֶה).[17] This oracle captures the essence of Micah 1–3 both structurally and theologically. In Micah 1–3 announcement oracles with accompanying reasons predominate. Structurally, Micah moves from the general accusation (v. 9) to the specific charges (v. 11). Notably, the oracle even documents an awareness of criticism on the part of the adversaries (v. 11b). Theologically, the pattern is consistent. Micah's judgment oracles often open with an unjust act on the part of the powerful that Yahweh forcefully counters. In Mic 1:2–7, Yahweh departs his heavenly holy temple to counter the havoc wrought in the capital cities (Samaria, Jerusalem) by the respective oppressive leaders. The imagery is graphic. In response to the abuse inflicted upon these cities by their leaders, Yahweh wreaks withering devastation. The surrounding mountains melt and the valleys split open (1:4). These symbols of power lay exposed and bare before foreign invaders (1:7).[18] Perhaps most striking is the reversal depicted in 1:7. The religious trappings (idols and images) acquired for security Micah labels "whore's fees" (אֶתְנַן זוֹנָה). For Micah, these religious securities dotting the landscape of Samaria were none other than symbols of prostitution gained through illicit activities.[19] In 3:9–12, Micah envisions for the Southern capital what the Northern capital experienced.[20]

Clearly, 3:9–12 paints Zion in tragic colors, yet colors that change before our eyes. The red tones of the bloodshed of oppression resulting from the corrupt and self-serving activities of the civil and religious leaders give way to the

hendiadys for oppression of the weak by the mighty, he argues that Micah regards this activity a sacrilege of the worst kind.

17. The motif of returning a city to a ruin heap and wooded height for wild animals to reinhabit is well attested in the prophetic literature and in ancient Near East (see Isa 13:19–22; 34:11–17; Zeph 2:13–15; Jer 50:39; Sefire I.A.32–33).

18. For a fuller discussion of this text, see my "Micah and a Theological Critique of Worship," in *Worship and the Hebrew Bible* (ed. M. Graham, R. Marrs, and S. McKenzie; JSOTSup 284; Sheffield: Sheffield Academic Press; 1999) 184–203.

19. For a fuller discussion of this verse, see P. Miller, *Sin and Judgment in the Prophets* (SBLMS 27; Chico, Calif.: Scholars Press, 1982) 28.

20. Although Zion goes unmentioned, Mic 2:1–5 reflects a similar pattern of human injustice countered forcefully by a reciprocal divine justice. The scene depicts a blatant miscarriage of justice. The rich lie awake at night "devising" ways in which they can engage in land extortion from the defenseless poor (חֹשְׁבֵי־אָוֶן וּפֹעֲלֵי רָע); however, Yahweh "devises" his own plan (חֹשֵׁב . . . רָעָה). These powerful land-extorters will themselves experience loss of land at the hands of a more powerful invader! In similar fashion to 3:11b, voice is given to Micah's opponents. In 2:4, these former oppressors cry foul when they experience a similar injustice from the other side!

earth tones of plowed fields and wooded heights. The uncivilized behavior of those in power results in a dramatic return of Zion from a center of civilization to an uncivilized habitat fit only for wild animals and demanding agrarian endeavors.

Zion: Divine Intent

Although clearly in dire straits at the close of chap. 3, Zion's most glorious moments lie ahead. As chap. 4 opens, the painting changes dramatically once again. Here we encounter Micah's compelling and creative use of the Zion traditions. Micah 4 opens with the well-known vision of a transformed Mt. Zion. The motif of the pilgrimage of the nations comes to the fore. In contrast to the imminent destruction foreseen for Jerusalem (3:9–12), Mic 4:1–4 portrays a secure and stable Jerusalem.[21] The imagery is dramatic. Mt. Zion, topographically overshadowed by the Mount of Olives, is elevated in stature and grandeur.[22] In striking contrast to the military devastation envisioned in Mic 1:2–7 and 3:9–12, Jerusalem is characterized as a haven of peace and security. War implements lose functional reality; the people dwell unafraid among their vineyards and orchards.[23]

Most noteworthy is the activity of the nations in this vision. The nations flow to Jerusalem and the temple, not for battle, but for instruction (תורה) and the word of the Lord (דבר־יהוה).[24] However, completely absent are the traditional brokers of those commodities; no mention is made of either priests or prophets (or their "props").[25] Instead, Yahweh himself functions as sole judge

---

21. The contrasts between 4:1–4 and 3:9–12 have been oft noted. Jerusalem, soon to become a "heap of ruins" swarming with animals (3:12), will ultimately become a "house of instruction" teeming with foreign nations (4:1–2). Zion, formerly destructively "plowed" as a field, will now be farmed with transformed war implements (4:3). Zion, formerly noted for her abhorrence of justice and perversion of equity (3:9), will become the center of equity and justice.

22. Echoes with 1:2–7 may also be implicit. Whereas Samaria experienced the meltdown of her mountains, the rupture of her valleys, and the exposure of her foundations, Mt. Zion rises in elevation, with the temple gloriously perched atop her summit.

23. This language may reflect a "peasant ideal" (cf. 1 Kgs 4:25; Zech 3:10; for a fuller discussion, see Wolff, *Micah*, 122–23; Hillers, *Micah*, 51). Such activity could only occur with the absence of war and an extensive period of agrarian productivity.

24. Just as the nations secondarily experience God's judgment and punishment (1:2; 4:11–12; 5:4b–5, 8[5b–6, 9]), so now they are recipients of God's salvation and blessings. These militaristic nations experience lasting peace as they acknowledge the invincibility of Yahweh and experience the exaltation of the Temple Mount. (For a fuller discussion, see H. Wildberger, "Die Völkerwallfahrt zum Zion: Jes 11,1–5," *VT* 7 [1957] 62–81.)

25. See Mic 1:2–7; 5:9–14.

and arbiter. Not surprisingly, this vision is far from imminent reality. Strikingly, the promise concludes with a confessional affirmation (v. 5):

> For all the peoples walk, each in the name of its god, but we will walk in the name of the LORD our God forever and ever.[26]

To a community battered and beset by corruption and abuse among its leadership, Mic 4:1–4 presents a transformed Jerusalem, a city indwelt by the divine judge. To such a promise of hope, the beleaguered community responds with faithful hope (4:5).

Theologically, part of the power of this passage lies in its complete disconnection with the present reality.[27] However, this transformation will be neither immediate nor without anguish. Micah's vision of this transitional period involves two different perspectives. One set of texts treat this transitional period from the perspective of the people of God. In these texts Micah envisions a moment of departure from the city and period of seeming vulnerability in the countryside (4:9–10; 2:12–13; cf. 4:6–8). The theological motif that dominates these texts is the royal sovereignty of Yahweh. The other set of texts treat this transitional period from the perspective of the invading foreign nations. In these texts, daughter Zion withstands the onslaught of the predator nations, turning the tables upon her opponents (4:11–13; 5:2–6; cf. 5:7–9). The theological Zion motif that dominates these texts is the defeat of the nations.

The transition from Zion as current reality and Zion as God intends involves struggle and anguish. Mic 4:9–10 graphically captures the intensity of

---

26. Although not without problems, Mic 4:1–5 may plausibly be read within the context of a worshiping community. To the liturgical promise (vv. 1–4), the congregation affirmingly responds (v. 5). Perhaps implicit is the notion that the success of the nations' learning the ways of Yahweh lies indissolubly intertwined with Israel's faithfulness to the ways of Yahweh. J. Limburg ("Swords to Plowshares: Text and Contexts," in *Writing and Reading the Scroll of Isaiah* [VTSup 70/1; ed. C. Broyles and C. Evans; Leiden: Brill; 1997] 286) notes the fitting link between the appeal to walk (הלך) in v. 2 and the resolve of the faithful to do so in v. 5.

27. Hillers (*Micah*, 52) notes that protest movements often are accompanied with visions of an ideal future, visions often appearing most unrealistic. Again, geographic and social location may impact profoundly one's theological message (so B. Birch, T. Fretheim, and W. Brueggemann, *Theological Introduction to the Old Testament* [Nashville: Abingdon, 1999] 310–11). In "The Rhetoric of Hurt and Hope: Ethics Odd and Crucial," in *Old Testament Theology: Essays on Structure, Theme, and Text* (Minneapolis: Fortress, 1992) 54–55, Brueggemann argues that this promissory oracle may have functioned to counteract the prevailing despair created by harsh doom oracles. For an early dating of this material, based on its associations with the psalms of Zion, see J. Willis, "Isaiah 2:2–5 and the Psalms of Zion," in *Writing and Reading the Scroll of Isaiah* (VTSup 70/1; ed. C. Broyles and C. Evans; Leiden: Brill, 1997) 295–316.

this transition. The scene opens addressing Zion as a young woman in the final throes of childbirth. In agony she cries out.[28] With a final push her "child(ren)" go(es) forth; however, the exit from the womb of Zion brings not joy, but the sorrow of exile.[29] Leaving the "plowed field" and "wooded height" that Jerusalem is to become, she finds herself encamped in the open countryside. However, when the horizon appears darkest, the remnant of Zion experiences divine redemption. The reality of potential exile gives way to the conviction of divine deliverance.

This scene echoes an earlier declaration in Mic 2:12–13. In the midst of doom oracles and seeming hopelessness, Micah declares that the survivors do not go forth leaderless. Although seemingly a helpless and powerless flock of sheep, Micah declares that none other than Yahweh will lead his battered flock.

I will surely gather all of you, O Jacob, I will gather the survivors of Israel;
I will set them together like sheep in a fold, like a flock in its pasture;
 It will resound with people.
The one who breaks out will go up before them;
 they will break through and pass the gate, going out by it.
Their king will pass on before them, the Lord at their head. (2:12–13)[30]

---

28. The question "Is there no king in you?" may be intentionally ambiguous. On the one hand, it may exude sarcasm, chiding the Jerusalemites for placing their hopes in a now-impotent earthly leader. On the other hand, it may refer to Yahweh as king (see v. 7), a king who has power to transform even the bleakest moments.

29. The reference to Babylon remains problematic. Although most regard the citation either as evidence of the late date of the oracle or a later scribal insertion (possibly from the period of Jeremiah), a few scholars consider Babylon simply a reference to the *location* of the departure, not the *conqueror* (so P. C. Craigie, *Twelve Prophets* [Philadelphia: Westminster, 1985], who cites 2 Kgs 17:24, where the Assyrians colonize North Israel with Babylonian captives. He considers this a possible reversing of that movement).

30. Without question this short hope oracle jarringly interrupts the cacophony of doom oracles in Micah 1–3. Though most scholars simply label the oracle a later postexilic insertion and move on, the placement and function of this oracle may serve rhetorically in a pastoral capacity. If Micah truly is addressing two decidedly different sociological groups, this oracle may affirm Yahweh's care for his faithful, yet seemingly powerless, band of followers. In the midst of disaster and devastation of the wicked, Yahweh exhibits a concern for the poor and oppressed. More specifically, in 2:12–13 Micah may utilize an oracle originally depicting refugee flight from Northern Israel and reapply it meaningfully to his Judean audience. Later passages specifically envision Yahweh functioning as shepherd for his beleaguered people when their human leaders fail them (see Ezek 34:1–16; Isa 40:1–11). (This interpretation seems preferable to that of A. van der Woude ["Micah in Dispute with the Pseudo-Prophets," *VT* 19 (1969) 256], who places these words in the mouth of the false prophets.) For an entirely different reading, based on emendation of the text, see J. Wagenaar, "'From Edom He Went Up . . .': Some Remarks on the Text and Interpretation of Micah II 12–13," *VT* 50 (2000) 531–39.

It is noteworthy that Micah uses common Near Eastern shepherd imagery to depict Yahweh's royal protection of his people. Zion's ultimate destiny cannot be divorced from the vision of Yahweh as royal protector and triumphant leader.[31]

The imagery of Yahweh gathering his battered survivors and leading them triumphantly reappears in 4:6–8. Whereas 2:12–13 envisions a departure at its inception, with no successful resolution, 4:6–8 depicts a return. In 2:12–13 the identity of the departees is left unspecified; they are simply labeled "the flock." In 4:6–8 their identity is made clear; they are the lame, the afflicted, and the cast off. The picture is memorable. Through Yahweh's transformative royal power, this rag-tag remnant, beaten and crippled, becomes a "strong nation" (גוי עצום). Those once cast off return to dwell in the shadow of Yahweh's reigning presence. Perhaps even more striking is the image of daughter Zion and the direction to which this image points. Daughter Zion, formerly an exposed and vulnerable flock away from the security of Zion, now dwells securely in the shadow of the tower and reaps the benefits of Zion's *former dominion, the sovereignty of daughter Jerusalem* (v. 8). Surely the reference looks back to the glorious days of the Davidic Empire, although David goes unmentioned.[32] The transformation of Zion is complete, a transformation rooted securely in the theology of Yahweh as victorious king enthroned in Jerusalem.

Another set of texts in the book of Micah emphasizes the failure of the nations to exploit ultimately the vulnerability of Zion. In Mic 4:11–13, the nations have gathered to defile Zion. In a marvelous twist of fate, Micah declares that events are not as they seem. Here the nations, not the remnant, are gathered; however, this assembling carries polar purposes. The nations assemble intending to harm Zion and exploit its apparent precarious situation. However, in actuality Yahweh has assembled the nations so that Zion might exploit them!

Now many nations are assembled against you, saying, "Let her be profaned,
    And let our eyes gaze upon Zion."
But they do not know the thoughts of the Lord;
    They do not understand his plan,
    That he gathers them as sheaves to the threshing floor.
Arise and thresh, O Daughter Zion, for I will make your horn iron
    And your hoofs bronze;
You shall beat in pieces many peoples,
    And shall devote their gain to the Lord,
    Their wealth to the Lord of the whole earth.

---

31. Here the triumphant victory march is still on the distant horizon. At this stage it is simply enough to affirm that the survivors do not wander abandoned and unprotected.

32. The absence of David from Micah's Zion oracles is striking.

The imagery is stark; the nations, having come to plunder, suddenly find themselves harvest victims. They have been gathered to the threshing floor so that daughter Zion may thresh them. The oracle concludes with a shift from agrarian imagery to the gathering of spoils after a decisive military victory. The nations are not only defeated; they are decisively despoiled and their wealth given to Yahweh, "Lord of the whole earth."[33] The deciding factor in the outcome involves the nations' failure to recognize and acknowledge Yahweh's plan. Just as earlier Yahweh devised a plan to counter the evil machinations of the oppressive land barons within his own community (2:1–5), now he executes his plan against the nations.[34]

Mic 5:1–5[35] reflects a theology akin to 4:11–13, while reintroducing the royal shepherd imagery of 2:12–13 (and 4:6–8) and the childbirth metaphor of 4:9–10. Mic 5:1–5 envisions both ends of the victorious return of the remnant. Similar to 4:9–10, the beginning of the painful transition of Zion from present reality to future divine intent involves the agony of birthing labor (5:2). Like 4:6–8, the victorious return involves Zion dwelling securely in the land with borders secure (5:4b–5).[36] However, Mic 5:1–5 introduces a striking new element to the restoration of Zion. For the first (and only time) in the book of Micah, a human agent arises to implement and exercise Yahweh's victorious sovereignty over the land. Although the figure is certainly intended to conjure images of King David, David nowhere receives explicit mention. Rather, his geographical and rural origins are highlighted! Even with the introduction of a specific ruler, Micah's creative use of the Zion tradition remains consistent. Just as Yahweh shepherded his people as a royal monarch during their darkest days, so now Yahweh brings forth a ruler away from the

---

33. Earlier Yahweh, in punishment, "returned" (שוב) the wages of prostitution (1:7).

34. Theologically, Mic 4:11–13 sounds like Psalm 2 in prophetic dress. Although the imagery varies, the scene is similar. There the nations assemble to exploit a royal transition in leadership; however, Yahweh the enthroned one laughs at their ill-fated intentions.

35. The versification between the Hebrew text of Micah 5 and the English versions varies by one verse. The verses cited follow the Hebrew versification.

36. The reference to the potential entrance of the Assyrians into the land remains enigmatic. What seems clear is the conviction that any Assyrian threat will be easily repulsed; new leaders (seven shepherds, eight leaders) will be sufficient, not only to thwart any invasion, but also to launch a counteroffensive against Assyria! See D. Hillers ("Imperial Dream: Text and Sense of Micah 5:4–5," in *The Quest for the Kingdom of God: Studies in Honor of George E. Mendenhall* [ed. H. Huffmon, F. A. Spina, and A. R. W. Green; Winona Lake, Ind.: Eisenbrauns, 1983] 137–39) for a fuller discussion of possible interpretations of this passage. While "David" is explicitly absent from Micah's theological articulation, Davidic theology is implicitly present in the securing of the borders of the land.

corrupt capital city, Jerusalem. Jerusalem may be bankrupt as a source for
faithful leadership, but the small village of Bethlehem once again will produce! Two aspects of this Davidic oracle merit attention. First, it is noteworthy
that even though David goes unmentioned, his humble origins do not. Surely
such a reminder must have brought hope to Micah's compatriots in the small
and seemingly insignificant rural villages. Just as Yahweh formerly brought his
people to greatness through the rule of a most unexpected leader, so again
Yahweh would manifest his majestic power through the raising of a shepherd
king from a most unexpected location.[37] Just as Mic 4:8 harkened back to
Zion's *former dominion* to envision its future rule, so Mic 5:2 emphasizes the
ancient origin (מקדם מימי עולם) of the one coming to rule.[38] For Micah, a secure future lies in capturing the glorious past.

Just as Mic 4:6–8 presents a radical reversal of the fortunes of the remnant
of Daughter Zion, so Mic 5:6–8 depicts a radical role reversal for the activity
of that remnant.

> Then the remnant of Jacob, surrounded by many peoples,
> Shall be like the dew from the Lord, like showers on the grass,
> > Which do not depend upon people or wait for any mortal.
> And among the nations the remnant of Jacob, surrounded by many peoples,
> Shall be like a lion among the flocks of sheep, which, when it goes through,
> > Treads down and tears in pieces, with no one to deliver.
> Your hand shall be lifted up over your adversaries,
> And all your enemies shall be cut off.

The remnant, having survived the pain of the birthing process and the tenuous
sojourn away from the secure environs of Zion, now experience the ultimate
reversal of fortunes regarding the nations. They are no longer victims; they are
now like dew and a lion (among the flock of sheep!). Numerous scholars
maintain that the two images (dew, lion) do not cohere. They consider the
former a beneficent image while the latter suggests harm and destruction.[39]
However, D. Hillers cogently argues that dew functions elsewhere in the Hebrew Bible as a metaphor for irresistibility (see 2 Sam 17:12) rather than beneficence. He argues that in this aspect both images cohere—the dew and the

---

37. The addition of Ephrathah to Bethlehem may suggest a contrast between the "fertility" of this little village and its environs and the barrenness and devastation of formerly
powerful Jerusalem (3:12).

38. In Amos 9:11 the Davidic period is spoken of as the "ancient days" (ימי עולם).

39. Cf. M. Anbar, "Rosée et ondées ou lion et lionceau (Michée 5,6–7)?" *BN* 73
(1994) 5–8. Biddle ("Israel and Jacob," 162) unconvincingly argues that dew suggests "indifference" (i.e., the indifference of the remnant to its exilic surroundings).

lion are irresistible and beyond human control.[40] Such an interpretation fits nicely with the other remnant passages in Micah.[41] The vulnerable and seemingly powerless remnant flock emerges invincible and unstoppable among the nations.

Micah, Zion, and Old Testament Theology

A cursory review of works on Old Testament theology reflects little attention given to Micah. If cited at all, Micah usually receives credit for his memorable articulation of obedience to the will of Yahweh (6:6–8).[42] Until recently, with rare exception, Micah took a back seat to his eighth-century compatriots (Amos, Hosea, Isaiah).[43] The place of Micah in the work of G. von Rad epitomizes the second-class status of Micah. Micah is cited primarily as a stepchild to von Rad's hero Isaiah.[44] We may speculate that part of the reason for this neglect involves the difficult text of Micah and its most complicated redaction history. Although the sociological setting of the prophet Micah and the redaction history of the book have received extensive attention more recently, a comprehensive theology of the book remains lacking.[45]

---

40. Alternately, Craigie (*Micah*) suggests a theological contrast. He links this passage to the Abrahamic promise of Gen 12:3. Depending on the reaction of the nations to Yahweh's plan, the nations will either experience the beneficence of Yahweh's activity (through his people) as dew or the punishment of Yahweh's activity as a lion.

41. These passages also stand in striking contrast to the earlier depiction (1:10–16) of the havoc wreaked upon the Shephelah by the nations.

42. Five of the seven Mican citations in B. Childs (*Old Testament Theology in a Canonical Context* [Philadelphia: Fortress, 1985]) reference Mic 6:6–8. The bulk of these appear in Childs's sections "Knowing and Doing the Will of God" and "The Shape of the Obedient Life."

43. Micah appears largely in the footnotes of W. Eichrodt's (*Theology of the Old Testament* [2 vols.; Philadelphia: Westminster, 1961, 1967]) work. He does not appear at all in J. Barr's (*The Concept of Biblical Theology* [Minneapolis: Fortress, 1999]) recent work.

44. G. von Rad, *Old Testament Theology* (New York: Harper & Row, 1965) 2.171. Interestingly, von Rad considered the fate of Zion the major difference between Isaiah and Micah. Whereas Isaiah envisioned a restoration of Zion, Micah simply saw a complete obliteration of Jerusalem from the pages of history (so also Preuss, *Old Testament Theology*, 44–45, et passim).

45. My understanding of the theology of the book of Micah is similar to that presented in the recent work of D. Gowan (*Theology of the Prophetic Books: The Death and Resurrection of Israel* [Louisville: Westminster John Knox, 1998] 50–59). In response to the majority tendency to attribute only the threatening doom oracles to Micah, Gowan bluntly argues that Micah would then become an extremely minor and unworthy prophet for memory. He contends that the most creative section of Micah appears in chaps. 4–7. For Gowan, the

I would suggest we encounter in Micah's use of the Zion traditions a theological scenario strikingly similar to the one found in Isa 1:21–26. There, Isaiah paints a picture of Jerusalem present, past, and future.[46] Current Jerusalem is riddled with rampant sin and infidelity. The level of injustice is so high that one cannot distinguish Jerusalem, *Yahweh's city*, from the cities of the surrounding pagan nations. Isaiah laments the tragic slippage of Jerusalem from her former (Davidic) greatness. The once faithful and righteous city now traffics in social oppression. However, Jerusalem is a city with more than a past and a present. It has a future. Realizing that future will be excruciating and fraught with struggle.[47] The end of that pain and struggle will result in a return to Jerusalem's *glorious past*. Jerusalem, Yahweh's city, will once again be that faithful and righteous city. I would suggest that canonically the book of Micah provides a theological exposition of Isaiah's vision in 1:21–26.

The bulk of Micah 1–3 depicts present Jerusalem. Jerusalem currently manifests the activities and behavioral attitudes of its Northern counterpart, Samaria. Micah graphically proclaims the tragic outcome awaiting Jerusalem. It will experience a similar devastation. Micah effectively uses the fall of Samaria to address current ills within his own community. Just as Jerusalem found itself in tenuous circumstances following the fall of the North,[48] now the rural countryside is reeling from the devastating social injustices of the Jerusalem elite. Micah unleashes a series of judgment oracles against Jerusalem that rival earlier oracles delivered against the Northern Kingdom.[49] The capital city Jerusalem will experience "meltdown" (1:2–7); the powerful and

---

book in its present form reflects the situational ambiguity and need for theological reflection present at the close of the eighth century. He argues that chaps. 4–7 were formulated originally to deal with the reality that, although severely punished by the Assyrians, Jerusalem survived and the Davidic dynasty continued. Like J. J. M. Roberts, Gowan argues that the closest parallels to the Zion traditions in Micah 4–5 are not to be found in Second Isaiah, Jeremiah, or Ezekiel, but in the (earlier) psalms of Zion (e.g., Psalms 46, 48, 84, 87, 122) and (less so) in the royal psalms. Like Gowan, I consider the book of Micah not a mere repository of disparate and disconnected oracle fragments but largely the studied responses of a Judean prophet to the crises of Samaria and Jerusalem.

46. Although not without difficulties, in some ways the book of Micah is organized largely around oracles treating the present (chaps. 1–3), the future (chaps. 4–5), and the past (chaps. 6–7).

47. Isaiah exploits the imagery of smelting ore (to remove the impure slag from the precious metal) to depict the transition from present reality to future divine intent.

48. Jerusalem absorbed a significant refugee population from the North and found itself only a few miles from Assyrian military presence.

49. The similarity between the opening chapters of Micah and Amos has been frequently noted. Both begin with theophanies in which Yahweh's arrival generates cataclysmic topographical consequences.

abusive elite will experience disastrous retribution (2:1–5). No offender will escape punishment (3:1–7). Micah concludes his depiction of present Jerusalem with a poignant portrayal of the capital city made uninhabitable (3:9–12). The city most recently built through bloody oppression will become a furrowed field and the Temple Mount a lair for wild animals.[50]

However, this is not the theological end of the saga.[51] Like Isa 1:21–26, Yahweh intends a future for his city and his faithful remnant. Micah 4–5 articulates that future. Like Isaiah, Micah envisions a glorious return of Zion to its former status and stature (5:1–5). Like Isaiah, Micah affirms that this "return to the future" will be neither easy nor painless. In chaps. 4–5, Micah begins with a powerful portrayal of Zion as God intends (4:1–4). The scene belies current reality. In a city and countryside riddled with the markings of war and violence, Micah unveils a vision of Zion as a harbinger and harbor of peace. The peace is so extensive that nations come to learn from it and to experience it; even war implements become unnecessary and are transformed into implements useful for cultivation and productivity. Strikingly, Yahweh sits exalted in the royal city, but it is his *Torah*, not the royal scepter, that casts the dominant shadow over the landscape.

The bulk of the remainder of Micah 4–5 recounts the chief components in the transition from present Jerusalem to Zion as Yahweh intends. Like Isaiah, Micah knows the transformation will be a time of agony and testing. Where Isaiah uses smelting imagery, Micah uses the imagery of childbirth. New life only comes through the excruciating pain of childbirth. Through a powerful interplay of metaphors, Micah comforts his despairing audience with ringing assurances that, though the period seems quite precarious, Yahweh is ever-present with his faithful remnant. Though childbirth places one in a most vulnerable and life-threatening situation, Micah affirms God's protective presence through the use of royal shepherd imagery (4:6–7). Ultimately this seemingly powerless and unprotected assemblage of discards will enjoy the royal rule of Yahweh in Zion. Even more radically, Micah depicts a turning of the tables on the nations. The nations come to exploit and inflict harm upon defenseless Zion; in shocking contrast, this powerless remnant will exercise agrarian harm upon the attacking nations (4:11–13).[52]

---

50. The imagery is strikingly similar to Psalm 129, although the tone is notably different.

51. Throughout the book of Micah, Zion is the object of human and divine action. Regarding the actions of the wicked oppressors and foreign nations, Yahweh's activity is largely reactive (1:2–7, 8–9; 2:1–5; 3:5–8, 9–12); in contrast, his activity toward the remnant he will return to Zion is largely proactive (2:12–13; 4:1–5, 6–7; 5:1–5, 6–8).

52. Micah appropriately uses common agrarian imagery for punishment (threshing) to depict the reversal of Zion's fortunes, since earlier Zion suffered agrarian harm for its sins (3:12).

Against this backdrop, Micah's use of the Davidic tradition emerges. Given the current corruption of the Jerusalem leadership, Micah mutes this element of the royal Zion tradition.[53] The theology is significant. For Micah, it is the *origin* of the future Davidic ruler that is most important. For a scattering of small countryside villages feeling powerless to effect their own escape from destruction, Micah reminds his audiences that theological hope for the future lies in the past. The former glory of Jerusalem finds its origins not in a powerful and prestigious capital city, but in the seemingly insignificant environs of Bethlehem. Just as David previously secured borders vulnerable to external threats and invasion, so another royal figure will arise and shepherd Yahweh's flock. The image captures the grandeur of the transformation:

> And he shall stand and feed his flock in the strength of the Lord,
> In the majesty of the name of the Lord his God.
> And they shall live secure, for now he shall be great to the ends of the earth;
> And he shall be the one of peace. (4:3–4a)

Yahweh the royal shepherd (2:12–13; 4:6–7) now rules through his faithful earthly agent.

The first oracle of Micah 5 relates the place and function of the Davidic ruler in the transformation of Zion from present predicament to future glory. The midsection of Micah 5 relates the utter reversal of fortunes for the remnant of Yahweh in this transformation (5:6–8). No longer the vulnerable and defenseless flock, the remnant becomes an irresistible force.

The preceding theological reading of Micah 1–5 has intentionally limited its scope and focus to the place and function of Zion in the present book of Micah. Several implications follow from this analysis. Micah matches nicely with his Jerusalem counterpart, Isaiah. Both envision a future for Zion rooted in the past. Contrary to von Rad, who finds their difference in the fate of Zion, I find that their difference lies more in the quantitative and qualitative attention given to the Davidic agent in the execution of Zion's future. Not unexpectedly, rural Micah gives less attention to the Jerusalem associations of the Davidic ruler and instead emphasizes his humble, rural origins.

Second, given the contrast between present Jerusalem and future Zion, the book of Micah merits further attention regarding the possible theological interplay of Sinai theology and Zion theology.[54] Given current interest in the

---

53. Brueggemann (*Theology of the Old Testament*, 594) notes that the nations come to Zion not as the seat of David, but as the locus of Yahweh's *Torah*.

54. The classic study of the Sinai tradition in Micah is that of W. Beyerlin (*Die Kulttraditionen Israels in der Verkundigung des Propheten Micah* [Göttingen: Vandenhoeck & Ruprecht, 1959]). Beyerlin argues that the primary influence upon Micah was the cultic tradition of

theological streams and trajectories in the prophetic literature, the book of Micah may prove a most valuable resource in charting the interaction of those two traditions at the close of the eighth century in Judah.[55]

Finally, the consistent and long-standing endeavor of Roberts to demonstrate that the Zion tradition surfaced earlier rather than later in Israelite and Judean theology may receive additional support from the book of Micah. Micah effectively interweaves powerful elements of the Zion tradition. In

---

Sinai. He finds Sinai echoes in 6:1–8 and 1:2–7 (with which he compares Psalm 81) and argues that Micah uses the name "Israel" exclusively as a designation for the twelve-tribe configuration (like the Pentateuch). J. Levenson (*Sinai and Zion* [Minneapolis: Winston, 1985]) significantly tempers Beyerlin's views. He rejects the late dating of the Zion tradition and the tendency among critics to pit the Northern Sinai tradition against the Southern Zion tradition. Levenson argues that Micah allowed the two traditions to coexist, suggesting that the Mican Messianic oracle may have offered hope to Israel after the covenant curses had been actualized, and concludes that the two traditions may reflect a sociological rather than a geographical distinction. More recently, S. Cook ("The Tradition of Mosaic Judges: Past Approaches and New Directions," in *On the Way to Nineveh: Studies in Honor of George M. Landes* [ed. S. Cook and S. Winter; ASOR Books 4; Atlanta: Scholars Press, 1999] 286–315) has attempted to draw close connections between Exodus 18 and Micah 3–5.

55. Numerous avenues for discussion lay before us. R. Dentan (*Knowledge of God in Ancient Israel* [New York: Seabury, 1968] 72–73) surmises that the Exodus/Sinai traditions may have fared better in the countryside while the David/Zion traditions flourished among the urban elites. I would suggest an alternate view. Micah appears to utilize the Sinai tradition to judge the present social injustice rampant among the urban elite; in contrast, he effectively utilizes the Zion tradition to offer comfort and hope to the dispossessed and disadvantaged dwellers in the countryside. H. Gese (*Essays on Biblical Theology* [Minneapolis: Augsburg, 1981] 81) contrasts the old Sinai revelation with the new, eschatological revelation of Zion addressed to all peoples (who acknowledge the kingship of God). The Sinai revelation is transformed into the state of *shalom* offered in the new Zion revelation. For Gese, the *Torah*s of Sinai and of Zion are qualitatively different. Psalm 50 articulates the Zion *torah*. The essence of Zion *torah* is *todah* (50:23). Again, I would argue that the book of Micah reflects an attempt to keep the Sinai and Zion traditions in dialogue, rather than having one tradition eclipse the other. In actuality, the book of Micah may serve as effective supplementary testimony to the work of J. Levenson (*Sinai and Zion*). Levenson argues that theologically the Sinai and Zion traditions must be kept in dialogical tension and balance. Within a larger discussion of covenant renewal and the cosmic mountain (pp. 206–8), he places Psalms 81 and 50 in dialogue with Jer 7:1–15, arguing that the covenant breach described in Psalm 81 is transferred to Zion in Psalm 50. Similarly, in Psalm 50 the Zion and Sinai traditions reverse Jer 7:1–15. Where Jeremiah uses Sinai to critique a misinterpreted Zion tradition, Psalm 50 uses Zion (the temple tradition) to critique a misinterpreted Sinai tradition. It may not be insignificant that it is an earlier oracle from the prophet Micah that delivers the later prophet Jeremiah from disaster (Jer 26:18). Each demonstrates the life-threatening nature of attempting to keep both traditions in faithful dialogue.

Micah's oracles we find the exaltation of Yahweh, the defeat of the nations, and the pilgrimage of the nations. Interestingly, Micah seems focused almost exclusively on the historical dynamics of the Zion tradition rather than its cosmic dynamics.[56] Such a limiting of focus to the historical dynamics may reflect Micah's current sociological setting. Engulfed in conflict with the powerful urban elite of his day, and needing to speak a word of hope to his seemingly powerless rural compatriots, Micah utilizes those elements of the tradition most germane to his immediate historical and social circumstances. Like his later prophetic successor (Jesus with Simon and the sinful woman) Micah delivers scathing rebuke to one audience and comforting hope of deliverance to another audience. In the present, Yahweh stands against the powerful elite and is judging present Jerusalem as he judged its Northern counterpart, Samaria. However, once that punishing judgment is complete, Yahweh will turn to redeem and restore his remnant, taking it back to the future. Against this backdrop, the conclusion of Roberts (from another context) is most fitting:

> The fundamental point necessary for the formation of the Zion tradition was the belief that Yahweh had chosen Jerusalem for his permanent abode. . . . Certainly the political ascendancy of Jerusalem in the imperial period had a great deal to do with both the imperial conception of Yahweh's suzerainty and the glorification of his capital. The Zion tradition was basically fixed by the end of this period. It was reinforced by Jerusalem's deliverance from Sennacherib, though the interpretation of that event was largely colored by the preexisting Zion tradition; however, about this time the first major innovations in the tradition were introduced by Isaiah and Micah. Working from within the tradition, they introduced the notion of Yahweh's fighting against Zion, in order through judgment to realize the ideals embodied in the tradition.[57]

---

56. The closest one gets to a cosmic hint is the theophany in 1:2–7.
57. Roberts, "Zion in the Theology of the Davidic-Solomonic Empire," 108.

"Who Knows? Yahweh May Be Gracious": Why We Pray

KATHRYN L. ROBERTS
Austin Presbyterian Theological Seminary

David is remembered in the biblical tradition as a man of piety and prayer. Over against Saul who leads the troops into battle before Samuel can arrive to offer sacrifices and pray for the troops, David seeks an oracle from Yahweh before embarking on his military campaigns. David gives sanctuary to Abiathar when he flees Nob after the slaughter of the priests there by Saul's partisans. In the face of death David is the first among mourners, offering up laments for King Saul and his son Jonathan, later for Abner, and most poignantly, for Absalom, David's eldest son. In addition to the narrative accounts of his piety, almost half of the 150 psalms in the Psalter are attributed to David, as is the Psalter itself.

David's prayer for his and Bathsheba's dying child in 2 Samuel 12 is different from the other prayers attributed to him. He does not go through the traditional motions of prayer. Instead, his are the actions of mourning and lament: fasting and lying prostrate on the ground in extreme distress. Unlike the lament for Saul and Jonathan or the cries of anguish over the death of Absalom, our text provides no words as David pleads for his infant son. But, it is not what David might say in prayer that is the focus of this paper; rather, it is what he says about prayer and the motivation for prayer and what this affirmation says about God.

2 Samuel 11–12: Literary Issues

Before we address these issues, however, it is necessary to discuss the historicity of the events that lie behind this narrative. Many scholars have argued that the report of the death of the unnamed infant is an apologetic fiction, intended to save Solomon from charges of illegitimacy and strengthen his claim to the Davidic throne.[1] If they are correct, there was no dying child, hence no

---

Author's note: For Jimmy. Partner, friend, teacher, and man of prayer.

1. There is a long history behind this question. For a fuller discussion of these earlier views, see Tomoo Ishida, *History and Historical Writing in Ancient Israel: Studies in Biblical Historiography* (Studies in the History and Culture of the Ancient Near East 16; Leiden: Brill, 1999).

prayer of David on his behalf, and therefore, no model here of prayer that per-
severes in the face of loss. There are genres in which nonhistorical stories and
parables function as efficacious guides for religious behavior, but the genre
here purports to be narrating real events. It is questionable whether in such a
genre a pure fiction, made up to serve other purposes, can provide a paradigm
for prayer.

The person and reputation of the biblical David has fallen on hard times
lately. Gone is the Sunday School David who followed after the sheep; the ro-
manticized little boy whose music calmed the savage Saul; the brave kid who,
with a slingshot and unwavering faith in Yahweh, confronted the giant Goli-
ath; and the pious "man after God's own heart," the cleaned-up version of the
usurper who refrained from harming God's anointed in the struggle for the
kingdom. Recent "biographies" of David have employed a hermeneutic of
suspicion in looking beneath the narrative surface in the books of Samuel.[2] In
fleshing out the person and times of David they have artfully made the results
of critical historical and literary tools accessible to biblical scholars of varying
levels of expertise. The biographies have, at the least, rounded David out as a
person and, at their best, offered more nuanced interpretations of an admittedly complex man, along with an appreciation for the court historian's literary and theological art. The biographies have torn the apologetic veil from his
face, revealing an often self-serving, self-absorbed man.

Nowhere is the grasping, self-centered king more visible than in 2 Samuel
11 and 12. Here the narrative of David's blatant abuse of power in adultery
and murder in chap. 11 and the death of the child of that union a chapter later
is a sad story with long-term implications for the king and his household. The
theologian in Samuel starkly narrates a cautionary tale, warning that the wages
of royal sin can indeed be death, though not necessarily the death the reader
might expect. In their present position, the shocking events in these two
chapters glorify neither the king nor his attractive neighbor. David's flagrant
abuse of royal power is portrayed for all to see. What David had convinced
himself was done in secret plays itself out in his family and before all Judah in
all its sordid detail. David's actions and their results provide an example and a

---

2. Most notably, Baruch Halpern, *David's Secret Demons: Messiah, Murderer, Traitor, King*
(Grand Rapids: Eerdmans, 2001); Stuart Lasine, *Knowing Kings: Knowledge, Power, and Nar-
cissism in the Hebrew Bible* (SSS 40; Atlanta: Society of Biblical Literature, 2001); and Steven
L. McKenzie, *King David: A Biography* (New York: Oxford University Press, 2000). Although not a biography, Robert Alter's *David Story: A Translation with Commentary of 1 and
2 Samuel* (New York: Norton, 1999) also interprets Israel's most notorious king and his
times.

warning of the surety that the stain of murder is not easily washed away; that it is pervasive, tainting those closest to him far into the future. Interestingly, it is at chaps. 11–12, where David's sins are most blatant and least ambiguous, that the king's modern biographers are the most skeptical and suspicious regarding their historicity. To their way of thinking the narrator "doth protest too much." Samuel chronicles so many murders separated from David by a few degrees or a convenient piety, that one directly attributed to him raises suspicions. Citing its apologetic nature Halpern calls all of 2 Samuel David's "Broadway Alibi," but where the apologetic is least obvious, Halpern is the most skeptical.[3] "Oddly enough, the one case in which the text proclaims David's guilt is implausible. But the presentation is nonetheless revealing."[4]

McKenzie is skeptical for the same reasons. "The negative portrait of David in the Bathsheba narrative differs radically from the apologetic material that surrounds it."[5] But McKenzie ultimately concludes that the literary event probably has its origins in the historical David's activities. "The story accords well with the image of David" that emerges from a critical reading of the earlier narratives, such "as the Nabal-Abigail episode, only without the cover-up." Therefore, the Bathsheba story "may be based on a historical event. It is also a masterfully told tale that prods its audience to 'read between the lines' to discern the motives of the characters."[6]

In their present location these two chapters play an integral role in the events that follow: the murder of Amnon, Absalom's revolt and subsequent death, the murder of Adonijah, and Solomon's succession (2 Samuel 13– 1 Kings 2). "The sword" mentioned in Nathan's oracle of judgment links David's murder of Uriah the Hittite by the "sword of the Ammonites" with the ensuing bloodshed and treachery among his own children, resulting ultimately in Solomon's successful accession to the throne (11:25, 12:10–12). The theory of this Succession Narrative as an extended account chronicling the struggle for dynastic succession within David's house, encompassing 2 Samuel 9–20 plus 1 Kings 1–2, was first articulated by Leonhard Rost.[7] David's biographers

---

3. Halpern, *David's Secret Demons*, 97.
4. Ibid., 93.
5. McKenzie, *King David*, 156.
6. Ibid.
7. Rost actually thought that the events justifying the confinement of Michal, with its assurances that "the daughter of Saul had no child to the day of her death" (2 Sam 6:23), formed the beginning of the story of succession, and were, by a later editor, worked into the fuller narrative sequence in chaps. 6–7. See Leonhard Rost, *The Succession to the Throne of David* (trans. Michael D. Rutter and David M. Gunn; Sheffield: Almond, 1982; trans. of *Die Über-lieferung von der Thronnachfolge Davids* [BWA(N)T 3/6; Stuttgart: Kohlhammer, 1926]) 98.

agree with Rost's view of the apologetic nature of this narrative block but come to widely divergent conclusions regarding its provenance and its particular agenda. They agree that these chapters put David in an unattractive light, but for very different reasons.

In McKenzie's view the Deuteronomist created a Succession Narrative that validated Solomon over his older brothers as heir to the Davidic dynasty by adding 1 Kings 1–2 to an earlier Court History source.[8] This Court History, much of 2 Samuel, had sought to portray David as a "too gentle and loving" parent, unable to discipline his out-of-control, unruly sons, thereby explaining Absalom's murder of Amnon and his later revolt.[9] The apologetic focus of the narrative thus shifted from an attempt to soften David's indulgent parenting in the Court History to the legitimation of Solomon and his claim to the throne in the Succession Narrative. The events narrated in chaps. 11 and 12 are probably rooted in an actual event but are a postdeuteronomistic addition to this Succession Narrative. McKenzie makes a point of saying that the Bathsheba affair as narrated in chaps. 11–12 "is not apologetic," thus maintaining its status as an insertion and thereby distinguishing it from the narrative block into which it was inserted. This distinction is confusing, because regardless of its label, it seems to function apologetically for McKenzie, though on Solomon's behalf, and not David's. McCarter, in his commentary on 2 Samuel agrees that 11:2–12:25 "is a later composition with a prophetic point of view comparable to that of similar materials in 1 Samuel" but dates the composition to the eighth century.[10]

When it comes to dating these chapters, McKenzie follows Van Seters, who finds the Deuteronomist's idealization of David and the Chronicler's omission of these troubling events suspicious. Rather than an argument for Solomon's accession, Van Seters says, "the Court History is a post-Dtr addition to the history of David from the postexilic period" and "must be seen, therefore, as the product of an antimessianic tendency in certain Jewish circles" in the postexilic period.[11] Van Seters's view is representative of a host of recent minimalist interpretations of the united monarchy that have called into question the

---

8. McKenzie, *King David*, 34.

9. Ibid., 162.

10. P. Kyle McCarter, Jr., *2 Samuel: A New Translation with Introduction, Notes and Commentary* (AB 9; Garden City: Doubleday, 1984) 275; and *1 Samuel: A New Translation with Introduction, Notes and Commentary* (AB 8; Garden City: Doubleday, 1980) 12–14, 288–91, 302.

11. John Van Seters, *In Search of History: Historiography in the Ancient World and the Origins of Biblical History* (New Haven: Yale University Press, 1983; repr. Winona Lake, Ind.: Eisenbrauns, 1997) 290.

biblical claims of a golden Davidic age.[12] According to proponents of this view the scarcity of tenth-century inscriptional and epigraphical evidence, coupled with a skeptical eye to archaeological remains, casts doubt on the actions of David, his dynastic claims, and consequently the narratives themselves.

> The Court History was not a piece of history writing. There is no reason to believe that any other sources, traditional or archival, were at the author's disposal when he composed the various scenes and episodes of his work. They may all be contrived. The notion of an eye witness account of events has to be abandoned and with it the reconstruction of the rise of history writing in Israel. There is no such historiography in Samuel–Kings prior to the work of the Dtr Historian.[13]

For Van Seters the so-called Succession Narrative is polemical, the reaction of a postmonarchical time against the deuteronomistically inspired dynastic promises to David found in 2 Samuel 7.[14] McKenzie agrees with Van Seters regarding the late date for the narrative's incorporation into the received text but parts company with him over the issue of genre. When it comes to narrative function, McKenzie agrees with Halpern that the Succession Narrative is a propaganda piece for Solomon's accession.[15] For Halpern its function as apologetic requires that its origins be early and rooted, however tenuously, in actual events. Halpern answers Van Seters and the minimalists:

> The point is, 2 Samuel is early, and very much in earnest—for after the loss of the north, and after the passage of the years, much of its detail would surely have been omitted, as it was later in Chronicles. It concerns itself with accusations that David murdered his way to the throne, accusations not suddenly invented in a later period. Its portrait of Israel's struggle to unseat David is actuated by an intention to rally elites hostile to David to Solomon's side.[16]

Halpern takes apologetic so seriously that, like McKenzie, he is suspicious when the narrative of chaps. 11 and 12 indicts David in a straightforward manner. The forthrightness of the events as they are related must then cut against their having a basis in fact. Employing a circuitous logic, Halpern holds David responsible for events from which the text removes him and exonerates him for the more blatant of his sins. "Second Samuel alibis David for his murders, and frames him for Uriah's death, which is the spark that ignites the fires of

---

12. Christopher Shea, "Debunking Ancient Israel: Erasing History or Facing the Truth?" *The Chronicle of Higher Education* 44/13 (1997) A12–14.

13. Van Seters, *In Search of History*, 290–91.

14. Ibid.

15. McKenzie, *King David*, 171–72.

16. Halpern, *David's Secret Demons*, 99–100.

Absalom's revolt. We know that Samuel is accurate because it is nothing but lies."[17] After all of the excuses proffered by the Court History for earlier offenses, a straightforward recitation of the king's sins raises this biographer's suspicions. In light of the honesty of the narrative, David cannot have taken Uriah's wife and his life.

Despite their frequent appeals to the apologetic nature of 2 Samuel, Halpern and McKenzie apply it rather arbitrarily. They find its effects persuasive when it comes to the marriage of the public David to the beautiful widow Abigail after her husband Nabal's sudden and financially-convenient death. But, when it comes to adultery and the murder of Uriah the Hittite, events that would seemingly require a great deal of careful, skillful spin, these biographers discount the role of apologetic, finding instead even more sinister events at work. For each, the questions of whose interests are being served in the telling and the sources of such private, household information are key. Each makes different assumptions based on his interpretation of which acts remained relatively private and which were more widely known and required a public apology.

Though their historical reconstructions end up widely divergent, Halpern and McKenzie find new life in the person and actions of the narratively inactive Bathsheba. In their scenarios, it is Bathsheba who orchestrates events to her advantage, creating an atmosphere conducive to the elevation and ultimate accession of her son, Solomon. Both are suspicious of her apparent passivity in this narrative and in events surrounding the succession.

In Halpern's view, the adultery and murder as narrated in chaps. 11–12 are "Bathsheba's revenge" for her grandfather Ahithophel's, along with probably her father's, abortive support of Absalom in his palace coup. Halpern's own reconstruction places Absalom's revolt chronologically before an adultery and murder that never really happened anyway.[18] In his view, this apologetic was written to legitimize Solomon's dynastic claims, since he was, in actuality, not the issue of Bathsheba and David, but of Bathsheba and Uriah. The name *Solomon*, meaning "his replacement," refers to his dead father, who died previously

---

17. Ibid., 100.

18. In 11:3 Bathsheba is identified as the daughter of Eliam. Ahithophel, the Gilonite, who played a prominent role as one of David's partisans and later as Absalom's advisor, is mentioned as having a son named Eliam at 23:34. Uriah, the Hittite, appears further down in the same list (23:39). Whether Eliam, father of Bathsheba, is Eliam, son of Ahithophel, is a matter of much speculation and the beginning point for many creative reconstructions of events. For a cursory review of some of the more prominent views, see Randall C. Bailey, *David in Love and War: The Pursuit of Power in 2 Samuel 10–12* (JSOTSup 75; Sheffield: JSOT Press, 1990) 172 n. 27.

under ordinary circumstances, instead of to an unnamed infant brother who died soon after birth.[19]

In a final chapter entitled "Poetic Justice," McKenzie forwards the notion that the last laugh is truly Bathsheba's. The silent, passive pawn of the earlier narratives is unmasked as the keeper of the tradition, the one who reminds the reader that the great King David's final days were spent bundled up for physical warmth with a young woman who remained a virgin until after his death (1 Kgs 1:1–4). Bathsheba's strength is in her shrewdness and her staying power. It is she who orchestrates events and uses the prophet Nathan to further her ends: placing her son, Solomon, on the throne in Jerusalem.

> Historically, Bathsheba may have been involved in the conspiracy to seat her son Solomon on the throne after David in place of the rightful heir, Adonijah. David's one-time "victim" took advantage of him at the end of his life for her political purposes. The possibility that David's supposed victim used him and his reign more than he used her provides a highly ironic ending to the life of David.[20]

While offering no novel historical reconstructions, Alter brings a close reading of the text to bear and he, too, speculates that Bathsheba's role as victim may be purely narrative art. He finds a clue at 11:4 where it says, "So David sent messengers to get her, and she came to him, and he lay with her." Her active coming to him causes this biographer to wonder whether the writer of 2 Samuel is

> boldly toying with this double meaning, intimating an element of active participation by Bathsheba in David's sexual summons. The text is otherwise entirely silent on her feelings, giving the impression that she is passive as others act on her. But her later behavior in the matter of her son's succession to the throne (1–2 Kings) suggests a woman who has her eye on the main chance, and it is possible that opportunism, not merely passive submission, explains her behavior here as well. In all of this, David's sending messengers first to ask about Bathsheba and then to call her to his bed means that the adultery can scarcely be a secret within the court.[21]

While crediting Bathsheba with political acumen, Halpern and McKenzie both underestimate the significance of household and harem gossip as important sources of insider information. Halpern is especially skeptical that anyone

---

19. Halpern's (*David's Secret Demons*, 391–406) conclusion that Solomon's royal ancestry comes under considerable doubt has far-reaching implications: "Ironically, in Matthew, as distinct from Luke, Jesus' lineage descends through Solomon, the beneficiary of Yahweh's dynastic promise to David in 2 Sam 7. A cloud on Solomon's paternity affects Jesus's genealogical claim to be the Davidic messiah" (p. 404).

20. McKenzie, *King David,* 183.

21. Alter, *The David Story,* 251 n. 4.

outside of David and Bathsheba could have known about private moments between them. "So long as David and Joab kept silent, divine revelation was the only possible means of exposure. For real certainty, in this case, could not follow from a coincidence of an affair between David and Bathsheba and the subsequent death of Uriah."[22] Maybe not "real certainty," but innuendo and gossip feed on less coincidence than is present here. The fact that service personnel in a large household (servants, messengers, including wives with lesser status) are, in effect, invisible does not mean they are oblivious to what is happening around them. As Alter points out at several junctures in his commentary, the things the king had hoped were remaining private matters were indeed public knowledge.

> The verb "to send"—the right verb for "messengers"—occurs eleven times in this chapter, framing the beginning and the end. This episode is not a moral parable but a story anchored in the realities of political history. It is concerned with the institutionalization of the monarchy. David, now a sedentary king removed from the field of action and endowed with a dangerous amount of leisure, is seen constantly operating through the agency of others, sending messengers within Jerusalem and out to Ammonite territory. Working through intermediaries, as the story will abundantly show, creates a whole new order of complications and unanticipated consequences.[23]

Among Lasine's contributions is an examination of biblical narratives concerning rulers, human and divine, in terms of the power of public and private information. Using an interdisciplinary, comparative approach, he makes distinctions between what can be said about the public persona of a given leader, based on state-controlled propaganda versus private information gleaned from gossip. "The control of gossip and the maintenance of a firm boundary between the private and public realms play a much larger role in the success of kings than one might expect."[24] Gossip about private lives can play an important role in shaping public opinion. Until 2 Sam 11:2 the David on display is largely the public man, the beloved king who repeatedly wins the approval and blessing of his subjects and of the deity (1 Sam 18:5–7). He is the "man after God's own heart" (1 Sam 13:14). Narrative perspective shifts dramatically after 11:1, highlighting the motives of the king's heart and the actions that take place in his bedroom and his palace. The private life of the king in chaps. 11 and 12 not only explains the very public turmoil in the subsequent chapters, it also calls into question the earlier unarticulated motives of the more public David.

---

22. Halpern, *David's Secret Demons*, 94.
23. Alter, *The David Story*, 249–50 n. 1.
24. Lasine, *Knowing Kings*, 103.

Applying McKenzie's own criteria for the identification of apologetic literature, particularly what he calls "overstress," the repetition of a particular idea, I think it is clear that for the public David the History of David's Rise is indeed David's "Broadway alibi."[25] It is the newly crowned king whose political-religious interests are being served. As McCarter puts it, "everything the young man did that might be interpreted as wrong was described in terms carefully chosen to gainsay such an interpretation. Most of his private motivation was set forth in detail in order to contradict the impression his public deeds might give."[26]

At 2 Sam 11:2 the story moves into the realm of the private King David. In chap. 11, where the reader might expect an elaboration of his private motivations and feelings, there are none. The king's obviously selfish actions are all that matter. He is decisive and his motives are left unexplained. In chap. 12 Yahweh intervenes through the prophet Nathan, holding David publicly accountable for his private deeds. With the prophetic indictment at 12:7–12 the narrative takes the long view, making this narrative block Solomon's "Broadway alibi." Among its functions is an attempt to explain and exonerate the means of Solomon's accession to the throne and even his very person from charges of ruthless fratricide and persistent whispers of illegitimacy. From the ominous "it happened, late one afternoon" (11:2), to the "therefore the sword shall never depart from your house" (12:10), the events in between ultimately work to "establish the kingdom in the hand of Solomon" (1 Kgs 2:46).

2 Samuel 12:1–15: Crime and Punishment

"But the thing that David had done displeased Yahweh, and Yahweh sent Nathan to David" (12:1). The prophet Nathan's parable of the rich man's appropriation of the poor man's little ewe lamb tricks the king into pronouncing his own guilt and punishment. "Then David's anger was greatly kindled against the man. He said to Nathan, 'As Yahweh lives, the man who has done this deserves to die; he shall restore the lamb fourfold, because he did this thing, and because he had no pity'" (12:5, 6). In his zeal David calls for fourfold restitution and unwittingly declares his own actions capital crimes. Nathan's response, "You are the man!" turns David's reflexive, hasty judgment back on himself, confirming for David that Yahweh has taken his treachery personally. Yahweh's response is one of indignation, "I anointed you . . . I rescued you . . . I gave you your master's house, and your master's wives into

---

25. McKenzie, *King David*, 33–36.
26. McCarter, *II Samuel*, 289.

your bosom" (12:7, 8). Like the rich man who had much and wanted more, David took and killed to satisfy his appetite.

The called-for restitution and punishment, as represented by "the sword," will rise up against him from within his own palace and from among the king's own children, in full public view. The treachery and murder that David perpetrated in secret will be reenacted before all Israel, even before the sun. "Yahweh's punishment of David underscores the element of secrecy in David's sins, partly by highlighting the fact that the punishment will be public and shameful, visible not only to God but to the people from whom he had hidden his sinful acts."[27] The prophet's words connect David's adultery and murder with Absalom's revolt (chaps. 13–18). According to Nathan's oracle, as the Succession Narrative develops David's household feels the strain, as four of his sons die on their way to the throne.[28]

When confronted with his sin, David repents. "'I have sinned against Yahweh.' Nathan said to David, 'Now Yahweh has put away your sin; you shall not die. Nevertheless, because by this deed you have utterly scorned Yahweh, the child that is born to you shall die" (12:13).[29] In response to David's repentance, Yahweh "puts away, passes over" (הֶעֱבִיר) his sin and strikes the unnamed infant, who becomes fatally ill. This death of the innocent child "helps expiate David's sin and thus continue his kingship."[30] Levenson goes on to say that the unnamed infant is, in effect, his father's sin-offering. The child's death "inadvertently—indeed, against his will—did just that, paying for the murder and adultery with the first fruit of his beloved Bathsheba's womb."[31]

As noted above, the account of the substitutionary death of the infant first born to David and Bathsheba has drawn skepticism from the king's biogra-

---

27. Ibid., 106.

28. David's sons are not the only ones to pay dearly for the sins of their father. Due to David's complicity beforehand and his leniency afterward, Tamar, the king's daughter and Absalom's sister, is raped with impunity by Amnon, her half-brother. This event is the pretext for Absalom's later murder of Amnon (2 Samuel 13). Interestingly, the Talmud (Yoma 22b) makes the association between the fourfold restitution required at the killer's hand and the violent fate of four of David's children, listing Tamar among the deaths of her half-brothers: the unnamed infant son, Amnon, and her brother Absalom. Adonijah is not counted among them. See Alter, The David Story, 258 n. 5.

29. See my exegesis of Psalm 51, a penitential psalm of David "when the prophet Nathan came to him, after he had gone in to Bathsheba," "My Tongue Will Sing Aloud of Your Deliverance: 'A Living Sacrifice' in the Psalms" in Psalms and Practice: Worship, Virtue, and Authority (ed. Stephen B. Reid; Collegeville, Minn.: Liturgical Press, 2001) 99–110.

30. Jon D. Levenson, The Death and the Resurrection of the Beloved Son: The Transformation of Child Sacrifice in Judaism and Christianity (New Haven: Yale University Press, 1993) 29–30.

31. Ibid.

phers and other commentators. In Halpern's extreme view, the narrative concerning David's repentance, the substitutionary death of the infant, and the subsequent birth of Solomon have long been misunderstood, if one holds to the dominant view that this sequence of events assures Solomon's Davidic paternity. "The death of the first son of David and Bathsheba has long drawn a wink and a nod from scholars. It would appear that they have been right, and that Solomon was Bathsheba's first son after Uriah's death," as long as the reader understands that the story of the death of the nonexistent firstborn is intended to mask the truth that Uriah was really Solomon's father.[32]

McKenzie does not agree. He argues against the frequent scholarly assertion that "Solomon was the real offspring of the adulterous union between David and Bathsheba," the charge that the Succession Narrative was supposed to have addressed in its apology.[33] As far as one is able to reconstruct events, he is sure that Solomon was certainly David's son, his birth following soon after the death of the first infant. The account of the child's death makes the connection between David's "double crime involving both adultery and murder. His punishment is also a double one. It includes not only his loss of the throne [temporarily in Absalom's coup] but also the death of the newborn child, the product of the adultery. A death was necessary because David was guilty of shedding innocent blood; this could only be atoned for by the life of another. Since Yahweh had intended not to kill David, his guilt was transferred to his newborn son. The baby's life substituted for his father's."[34]

The outright rejection of the historicity of 2 Samuel 11–12 by some modern biographers needs to be abandoned. While recognizing the apologetic nature of this narrative block, I conclude that the bounds of such skepticism are out of proportion. Even as apologetic, these narratives concerning David can be dismissed as purely fanciful only with difficulty. The very definition of apologetic requires that public knowledge of private events in a public household needs to be addressed. Private events that are able to be denied will be, but what has become public often cannot be denied and therefore must be spun to the best possible advantage. As apologetic for Solomon these stories are able to go only so far; they are not able to create a dead baby that was never born.

2 Samuel 12:16–23: David's Prayer for the Dying Child

In among the king's self-condemnation and the death of the child and the birth of Solomon is David's prayer for the dying child. David's prayer for his

---

32. Halpern, *David's Secret Demons*, 401.
33. McKenzie, *King David*, 161.
34. Ibid.

and Bathsheba's unnamed child is different from other prayers attributed to him. Rather than evidencing a posture of prayer, his seven days of fasting and lying prostrate on the floor speak of lament, mourning, and death. Unlike other laments attributed to him, such as the lament for Saul and Jonathan (2 Sam 1:17–27), the public expression of mourning over Abner (3:31–35), or cries of anguish when Absalom dies (19:1–5), there are no eloquent or wrenching words from David's mouth, to be taken up later in worship or in song. There are no words at all, only the distress of fasting and prostrate prayer.

This atypical prayer of David has received relatively little attention in the literature. Within the agenda of the Succession Narrative the prayer makes the shock of the oracle of judgment more acute and heightens the suspense of the deathwatch. David's attitude of prayer also testifies to his piety. It does not offer a new formula or ritual, an innovative stance toward prayer. As Calvin says in his sermon on this passage, to mourn the dead is a necessary ritual. "It is natural to weep over those who are close to us, as we have seen earlier in the mourning of David over Saul and Jonathan" and as he will weep again over Absalom; "in that situation, he acted like a man who had totally lost control of himself. Yet he says here: 'Since the child is dead, I must no longer be grieved.' Now here is a contradiction which is extremely peculiar. It seems that David has completely stripped off any human affection when he says: 'The child is dead, he will no longer return to me.'"[35] Calvin raises the same question as David's servants: "What is this thing that you have done? You fasted and wept for the child while it was alive; but when the child died, you rose and ate food" (12:21). David's behavior is incomprehensible to those around him. "David and his servants have differing views of the death of the child, because David alone knows that it has been foreordained by Yahweh as atonement for David's sin."[36] The elders in his house are confused by his actions and probably also embarrassed. They can't understand why David mourns while the child is alive and ceases when he dies. They see David's mourning as premature and his acceptance of the child's death as easy or calloused. From David's way of looking at things, however, he is not mourning. By his self-humiliation and distress he begs God for the life of the infant. What the servants don't know, but what the reader knows, along with David, is that the

35. John Calvin, "On Facing Affliction and Bereavement," *Sermons on 2 Samuel, Chapters 1–13* (trans. Douglas Kelly; Edinburgh: Banner of Truth Trust, 1992) 590.

36. McCarter (*2 Samuel*, 301), citing G. Gerleman, "Schuld und Sühne: Erwägungen zu 2 Sam 12," in *Beiträge zur alttestamentlichen Theologie: Festschrift für Walther Zimmerli zum 70. Geburtstag* (ed. Herbert Donner, Robert Hanhart, and Rudolf Smend; Göttingen: Vandenhoeck & Ruprecht, 1977) 132–39.

situation is hopeless. David's punishment has been transferred to the child, and he will die. The prophet Nathan has told him this, and events are hurtling in that direction.

It is amazing that, despite this knowledge of the certainty of his child's death, David nonetheless spends seven days and nights on the floor, hungry and dirty, pleading with God to change a judgment that he knows he "deserves," that he has brought upon himself, that seems irrevocable. In answer to his servants' questions, David responds, "While the child was still alive, I fasted and wept; for I said, 'Who knows? Yahweh may be gracious to me, and the child may live'" (12:22). David's prayer arises not only from the knowledge of his own helplessness but also from a strong faith in the God who has stood with him in the past (12:7–9). His prayer's hope is built upon confidence that God can be affected by his prayers, that God can be moved. "Who knows?" David says, "perhaps. . . ." David has experienced the grace and mercy of God in the past, and those experiences give him hope that God will once again be gracious and merciful. David's prayer depends upon what he personally knows of the prior faithful activity of God. His very kingdom is not built upon remote generalities but on his awareness of the presence of God, and he calls out, knowing that God is the One who is affected by human need.

"Who knows? Perhaps. . . ." This is the foundation of the life of faith: believing in a God whose mind is able to be changed on our behalf. The child dies and David rises from the ground, washes and anoints himself, and worships God. His actions leave the reader and the king's household breathless. David continues to believe in God, and worship is his response. He does not lose faith or shake his fist. Who God is has not changed for him. He has experienced God's presence as judging and as gracious, and he sees them both as saving, that is, as restorative of relationship with God.

"Who knows? Perhaps God will be gracious" is the same flicker that drives Jesus to the garden to pray in the face of a hopeless situation. Its utterance arises from a passionate, profound faith in the goodness of God. "Who knows? Perhaps . . ." believes God hears and cares and can be moved. David holds out to others who pray a God whose mind is not closed to human tears and weeping.

Rabbi Harold Kushner's response to the problem of pain and suffering in the book of Job is representative of a school of thought that says that prayer doesn't change God; it changes, instead, the one who prays. God is too removed, too unchanging, unable to be moved by human need or want. Instead, prayer changes the one who prays and that one's attitudes and responses. Prayer creates community and solidarity. Faced with a premature, tragic death despite the earnest prayers of many people of all faiths and creeds, a devout woman asked Kushner the critical question, "How can anyone be expected to take prayer

seriously?" Pastorally, the rabbi pointed to the many graces that had come into
the new widow's life during her husband's illness and since his death.

> And what about *your* prayers?, I asked her. Were they left unanswered? You
> faced a situation that could easily have broken your spirit, a situation that could
> have left you a bitter, withdrawn woman, jealous of the intact families around
> you, incapable of responding to the promise of being alive. Somehow that did
> not happen. Somehow you found the strength not to let yourself be broken.
> You found the resiliency to go on living and caring about things. Like Jacob in
> the Bible, like every one of us at one time or another, you faced a scary situa-
> tion, prayed for help, and found out that you were a lot stronger, and a lot better
> able to handle it, than you ever would have thought you were. In your despera-
> tion, you opened your heart in prayer, and what happened? You didn't get a
> miracle to avert a tragedy. But you discovered people around you, and God
> beside you, and strength within you to help you survive the tragedy. I offer that
> as an example of a prayer being answered.[37]

In 1 Samuel the onlookers, the elders and the servants in the king's house,
would appear to share Kushner's viewpoint: the child has died and David
seems rejuvenated. But, it is not clear that David would agree. Without the
"perhaps" David would hardly have spent seven days and nights on the floor,
and had Kushner's new widow shared Kushner's theology, she probably
would not have prayed the prayers he said were answered. David's act of
prayer says that David took seriously the possibility that God's judgment
might be averted by human prayer.

"The biblical God, unlike the static, eternally unchanging god of Greek
philosophy, can change his mind. He repents of proposed plans of action, reacts to the changing attitudes of God's human subjects, and this may result in
a divinely inspired prediction failing to materialize."[38] The king of Nineveh's
conviction that Jonah's God was intent on the city's destruction evokes a repentance unparalleled in scripture. The Assyrian king's "Who knows?" sounds
very much like his earlier royal counterpart in great distress. "God may relent
and change his mind; God may turn from his fierce anger, so that we do not
perish." David's "Who knows? Yahweh may be gracious to me" releases us all
to pray and challenge God. The ability to pray this prayer is founded on a faith
that keeps us coming back and storming heaven with our prayers.

---

37. Harold S. Kushner, *When Bad Things Happen to Good People* (New York: Schocken,
1981) 130–31.

38. J. J. M. Roberts, "A Christian Perspective on Prophetic Prediction," *Int* 33 (1979)
240–53, esp. 245.

"And Lot Went with Him":
Abraham's Disobedience in Genesis 12:1–4a

Andrew G. Vaughn
Gustavus Adolphus College

It has long been noted that Abraham's life of obedience to God gives David and subsequent Davidic kings a paradigm for following God. Some years ago, Ronald E. Clements developed this connection by exploring the connections between the Yahwist's account of the Abrahamic Covenant in Genesis and 2 Samuel 7.[1] This essay seeks to expand the connection between David and Abraham by offering a corrective in a common interpretation of Abraham's call in Gen 12:1–4a. I suggest that, like David, Abraham from the beginning is not completely obedient to God. Rather, there is a movement from promise to fulfillment of a different type than commonly noted. Abraham comes on the scene in Genesis 11 and 12 as a promising man who is capable of responding to God like no other human to date. Yet, a reexamination of the Abraham cycle reveals that the theme of Abraham as a paradigm of unreserved obedience is not completely actualized or fulfilled until Genesis 22.[2]

Problems with Viewing Abraham in
Genesis 12:1–4a as a Paradigm for David

While it is clear that there are parallels between David and Abraham, a problem occurs with an attempt to make the connection too strong because

---

Author's note: This essay originated in coursework with Patrick D. Miller and later in a collaboration with Michael T. Davis. I also benefited from comments from J. J. M. Roberts, Bernard Batto, Terence Fretheim, David Janzen, Susan Schumacher, and members of the Lenox Colloquium. I am especially pleased to be able to include this essay in a volume in honor of J. J. M. Roberts because my ideas about Genesis and Abraham originated in Roberts's course on Genesis more than 15 years ago. Roberts's course on Genesis instilled a love for Genesis in me that continues today.

1. Ronald E. Clements, *Abraham and David: Genesis 15 and Its Meaning for the Israelite Tradition* (SBT 5; London: SCM, 1967).

2. This essay is part of a larger work that explores the connection between David and Abraham. While the parallels between David and Abraham will be apparent in the treatment below, the focus of this essay is on the portrayal of Abraham.

Abraham is often held to be completely faithful and trustworthy from the very beginning, whereas David's lapses in moral fortitude or complete trust in God are more apparent. This perceived difference between Abraham and David is perhaps most apparent in Gen 12:1–4a (the call of Abraham) where Abraham typically has been viewed as a model of complete trust or obedience in God. The present essay seeks to correct this traditional interpretation. The correction presented in this essay reveals that the parallels between Abraham and David are actually stronger than previously noted.

The response of Abraham[3] in Gen 12:1–4a is taken by both Christian and Jewish traditions as paradigmatic of obedience to God. Next to the binding of Isaac in Genesis 22, Gen 12:1–4a is held by many exegetes as a narrative of Abraham's absolute obedience. Indeed, the Apostle Paul highlights Abraham's obedience and willingness to follow God as paradigmatic in Romans 4 and Gal 3:6–18. Gerhard von Rad follows this Pauline interpretation in his commentary on Genesis and gives a common assessment of the merit of Abraham's action in leaving his people and homeland:

> Abraham obeys blindly and without objection . . . The one word *wayyēlek* ('and he set out') is more effective than any psychological description could be, and in its majestic simplicity does greater justice to the importance of the event.[4]

Although von Rad has no reservations in his praise of Abraham's response in Gen 12:1–4a, just a few pages later in his comments on the material in the latter part of chap. 12, he must struggle to contain his perplexity over Abraham's behavior in this narrative. He states: "The composition of the Abraham stories begins with a narrative that is offensive and difficult to interpret."[5] Indeed, von Rad is correct; in Gen 12:10ff., Abraham leaves the land that he has been promised (Canaan) because, the reader is to suppose, there is a great famine. The reader must assume that Abraham does not rely completely on God to provide in the face of the famine. The patriarch travels to Egypt in order to find food, and while there he allows Pharaoh to take Israel's ancestress as a wife in order to save his own skin. It is at this point that von Rad characterizes Abraham's behavior sharply but accurately:

---

3. In order to avoid confusion, I use the names "Abraham" and "Sarah" throughout this essay (except in direct quotation from scripture) even when the text uses "Abram" or "Sarai." This choice does not of course mean that the name change is unimportant but rather that the main point of this essay concerns the actions of Abraham and Sarah both before and after their names were changed.

4. Gerhard von Rad, *Genesis: A Commentary* (rev. ed.; trans. J. H. Marks; Philadelphia: Westminster, 1972) 161.

5. Ibid., 167.

Was the departure from Canaan already an act of unbelief in the sense of the narrative? Perhaps so. But what concerns us most is the betrayal of the ancestress, and one must not exactly restrain one's thoughts if they recognize in the bearer of the promise himself the greatest enemy of the promise.[6]

It is disconcerting that within a few verses Abraham is transformed from a model follower in Gen 12:1–4a to "the greatest enemy of the promise" at the end of chap. 12.

A similar observation that highlights both the paradigmatic import of Gen 12:1–4a and the contrast found in Gen 12:10ff. is made by Hans W. Wolff in his essay "The Kerygma of the Yahwist." Wolff notes that Gen 12:1–4a sets forth much of the Yahwist's theological purpose or *kerygma*—Abraham succeeds in blessing all the nations of the earth and establishing the nation of Israel when he is obedient to God.[7] In a manner similar to von Rad, Wolff also notes that Abraham's actions in Gen 12:10ff. do not exhibit a reliance on God, and because of this other nations (here Egypt) are cursed instead of blessed. Wolff implies that if the purpose of the Yahwistic narratives is to be carried out, Abraham must be obedient as he had been in Gen 12:1–4a.[8]

Alternative Assessments of Abraham's Obedience in Genesis 12:1–4a

It should be noted that, even though most commentators hold up Gen 12:1–4a as an example of Abraham's complete and absolute obedience, there are notable exceptions. In his comprehensive commentary, Claus Westermann urges restraint in evaluating Abraham's level of obedience at this point in the narrative. He observes:

> The commentaries here [Gen 12:4a] laud Abraham's obedience, at times in too fulsome a way (F. Delitzsch, H. Gunkel, O. Procksch, A. Dillmann, B. Jacob, G. von Rad, and others); but this is the outlook of a secularized world where obedience or faith has become abnormal. This cannot be the intention of 12:4a. It is the normal and natural thing that Abraham should go as God commanded him; he would be putting himself at risk were he not to go.[9]

---

6. Ibid., 169.

7. Hans Walter Wolff, "The Kerygma of the Yahwist," in *The Vitality of Old Testament Traditions* (ed. Walter Brueggemann and Hans W. Wolff; Atlanta: John Knox, 1975) 41–82.

8. Ibid., 56.

9. Claus Westermann, *Genesis 12–36: A Commentary* (trans. John J. Scullion; Minneapolis: Augsburg, 1985) 152.

Building on Westermann's words of caution, one sees that a more modest evaluation of Abraham's level of obedience is in order at this point in the narrative flow of Genesis 12–22—and it is this more modest evaluation of Abraham that supports attempts to describe parallels between David and Abraham. The instances where Abraham and Sarah play the role of "enemy of the promise" are not limited to the stories of the endangering of the ancestress in Gen 12:10–12 (and the story's doublet in Gen 20:1–8). Throughout the Abraham Cycle, both the patriarch and his wife, Sarah, at various times play the role of "enemy of the promise." On multiple occasions Abraham and Sarah either hesitate before they obey God or question the plans of God or attempt to "assist" God in bringing about the promise of progeny rather than trusting solely on God. All of these instances of less-than-model faith cause one to question how Abraham's character could change so dramatically if Abraham were really so completely and blindly faithful in Gen 12:1–4a as von Rad and the majority of commentators argue. How could Abraham move from this paradigm of complete trust and reliance on God in Gen 12:1–4a to a person who questions and has a difficult time trusting completely in God just six verses later?

Westermann is not the only commentator to present a more modest view of the level of Abraham's obedience in Gen 12:1–4a. Rabbinic tradition refers to Abraham's faith development in terms of the ten trials of Abraham. Abraham is seen to have faith all along, but the degree of his faith and commitment to God grows through each of these trials, culminating with the binding of Isaac in chap. 22. There is no consensus among the rabbis about which events actually comprise the ten trials, but they do agree that these trials begin with Abraham's call in Gen 12:1–4a and culminate with Abraham's near sacrifice of Isaac in Genesis 22. James Kugel explains:

> Surveying the whole of Abraham's life as it is narrated in Genesis, ancient readers could not help thinking that the incident with Isaac was not the first time that Abraham had been tested. In fact, his whole life seemed to be one long series of divinely instituted challenges. From the very start, when God had first told Abraham to leave his homeland, it was to go "to the land that I will show you" (Gen. 12:a). Why did not God say "to the land of Canaan? This order sounded as if it was deliberately worded to test Abraham's faith, as if God were saying, "Follow! I will not even tell you where we are going."[10]

Something intrinsic about the nature of the narratives in Genesis 12–22 caused the rabbis to see Abraham's development itself as a model or paradigm of faith,

---

10. James L. Kugel, *Traditions of the Bible: A Guide to the Bible as It Was at the Start of the Common Era* (Cambridge: Harvard University Press, 1998) 296.

development that evolved through a series of "tests." Building on this obser-vation, one may anticipate that within the narrative of Genesis 12–22, even though Abraham possesses the potential for absolute obedience already at the story of his call (Gen 12:1–4a), he will not actually achieve that complete re-liance on God until his ultimate testing (Genesis 22).

Literary Evidence for Abraham's Development toward Complete Trust

A brief summary of some of the major events in Genesis 12–22 highlights this development in the character of Abraham. Throughout chaps. 12–22, the final redactor of Genesis uses a technique of repeating the promise in ever-stronger terms following instances of Abraham's display of deepening trust in God. At the same time, the redactor includes indications that Abraham does not trust completely or blindly, in that he questions God and at times attempts to move the divine promise forward through various devices of his own making.

Upon examining those instances where Abraham trusts God, one is not surprised that the rabbis would refer to these events as the ten trials of Abra-ham. In Gen 12:1–4a Abraham does trust God, even if not completely, whereupon he receives a promise of land, progeny, and fame. In Gen 13:7, after Abraham shows faith in God's promise by giving his nephew Lot the better land, the promise is reiterated to Abraham in no uncertain terms. In chap. 14, after fighting foreign kings on behalf of Lot, Abraham refuses to take booty from the battle lest anyone other than God receive credit for his estab-lishment. Immediately following, in Gen 15:1 the promise is presented again in even stronger language.

Yet alongside such positive depictions of Abraham's actions, one discovers that the final redactor of Genesis has included indications that Abraham's faith is far from complete. An example may be observed in Genesis 15, through an alternation of promise and foreboding punishment. Immediately following a restatement of the promise (15:1), Abraham questions the promise by asking if his adopted son will be the means by which the promise is carried out (vv. 2–3). The dissonance created by the juxtaposition of promise and ques-tioning of that promise is surely no coincidence. The redactor appears to em-phasize that at this point in time Abraham is not completely sure of the promise and needs reassurance. Reassurance comes in vv. 4–5 and 17–21, but there is also a pronouncement of punishment for generations after Abraham (vv. 13–16). One observes that this must be a literary technique to show that Abraham's lack of blind faith results in complications for the completion of the promise further down the line. This literary technique is found at least six times throughout the Abrahamic Cycle:

1. Abraham endangers the ancestress/mother of the promise (Gen 12:10–20). As Wolff points out, Abraham's lack of complete obedience results in a complication of the blessing of the other nations because Egypt is cursed.[11]
2. Abraham's second endangering of the ancestress/mother of the promise (Genesis 20). Once again, instead of another nation being blessed through Abraham, Gerar is cursed.
3. The incident in Genesis 15 described above illustrates how Abraham's lack of complete trust results in a complication of the promise.
4. The attempt by Sarah and Abraham to have a surrogate child through Hagar produces a complication to the promise in the person of Ishmael and his descendents. Here Abraham and Sarah apparently try to take matters into their own hands by "helping" God to establish the promise, but a complication is the result.
5. The laughter of Abraham in Gen 17:17 at the prospect of God's providing an heir through Sarah is followed in Gen 17:18–20 with an emphasis on Ishmael and how he will also be made into a great nation. In the future Ishmael and his descendents will prove to be a complication for the promise that was given to Abraham and his descendents through Isaac.
6. Anticipating my conclusion below, I include here the taking of Lot in Gen 12:4a as another example of Abraham's lack of complete obedience. Abraham was commanded to leave the entire household of his father, but the taking of Lot creates a complication in chap. 13 that necessitates Abraham's being allotted the less desirable land.

This same pattern continues until chaps. 21–22, when Abraham finally begins to show complete and unqualified trust and obedience.

Something changes by chap. 21. Following another episode of a sojourn where the ancestress is put in danger in chap. 20, Isaac is finally born in chap. 21. Abraham then does as God commands him and, as if to emphasize the rewards of such obedience, he is successful in his negotiations with the wells. The narrative then reaches a crescendo with the final "trial" noted by the rabbis—the binding of Isaac in chap. 22. It is at this point that Abraham finally shows complete reliance on God.[12] Given the benefit of hindsight, one can

---

11. See Wolff, "Kerygma of the Yahwist," 56.

12. I thank one of the editors of this volume, Bernard Batto, for pointing out that even in Genesis 22 Abraham's moral character is ambiguous until the very end. In private communication, Batto observes, "First, he does not inform Sarah of the command from God nor of his intention to sacrifice Isaac. Second, he lies to his servants, telling them that he and 'the boy' will go 'worship' and then 'we will come back to you,' knowing full well that if he carries out God's command, he alone—not 'we'—will return. Third, Abraham equivocates in his reply to Isaac's question, Where is the oblation? 'God will provide' could just

see that the reader was being prepared already at the beginning of the narrative in 12:1–4a to see in Abraham the potential for such paradigmatic faith but not to expect its realization until much later in the patriarch's career. Such a development in character from incomplete reliance upon God to a person who in the end actually exhibits complete reliance makes Abraham much more closely parallel to David. Both Abraham and David have their lapses but eventually rise to the stature of model believers.

The several examples of Abraham's not exhibiting complete reliance on God lead one to question von Rad's interpretation of Abraham as completely obedient from the beginning and to side instead with Westermann in his assessment of Gen 12:4a. The existence of different sources does not allow one to sidestep this problem because the theme of incomplete faith stretches across the different sources of Genesis, being found in J, E, and P passages. This phenomenon leads to further questioning of the thesis that Abraham was intended to be a model of obedience from the very start. Upon closer examination it is apparent that in the J text of Gen 12:1–4a Abraham *only partially obeys* God's command. Moreover, it appears that this theme of a lack of total faith present in the J narratives becomes even more pronounced when the final redactor of Genesis reworks the P and E texts and juxtaposes them with the J texts. However, before such a conclusion can be established, it is necessary to revisit Abraham's response to the divine command as presented in the J text of Gen 12:1–4a.

Reevaluating Abraham's Response in Genesis 12:1–4a

Initially it seems difficult to identify just where Abraham is at fault. His response to the requirements in Gen 12:1 (to leave his country, his kindred and the house of his father) seems to be faultless, emphasized by the phrase in Gen 12:4a: *wayyēlek ʾabrām kaʾăšer dibber ʾēlāyw yhwh* "and he went just as Yhwh told him." However, immediately after this assertion we find what might seem to be an afterthought: *wayyēlek ʾittô lôṭ* "and Lot went with him."

But is Lot's role merely an afterthought? When one glances back at the divine command to leave land (*ʾereṣ*), kindred (*môledet*), and the house of the father (*bêt ʾāb*), one is moved to wonder why this individual, Abraham's nephew

---

as easily refer to the boy Isaac whom God has indeed provided to Abraham. Moreover, is Abraham equivocating even within his own mind over whether he will or will not carry out God's command? The narrative itself suggests that this is the case, since God's messenger only stays Abraham's hand when Abraham actually begins to plunge the knife downward to kill Isaac."

and a member of the household (*bêt ʾāb*) of Abraham's father, Terah, accompanies Abraham on the journey to Canaan. Gen 11:26–32 (a combination of J and P texts) anticipates Gen 12:4a by emphasizing Lot's inclusion within the household (*bêt ʾāb*) that Abraham must leave. I will evaluate Gen 11:26–32 in some detail below, but for the moment it is sufficient to note that this P genealogy (Gen 11:26–27, 31–32) together with the J narrative in Gen 11:28–30[13] describe the household of Terah in such a way as to include both Abraham *and* Lot.

Context of Genesis 12:4a:
Evidence for Lot's Inclusion in Terah's Household

The genealogy in Gen 11:26–32 contains both J and P elements. The idea of Lot's inclusion in the household of Terah is found already in the base text (Gen 11:28–30) from the J tradition; the later insertion of the P genealogy continues and emphasizes this point. Turning first to the references in the J narrative, one notes the description in Gen 11:28a: "And Haran died before (*ʿal pěnê*) Terah, his father." Although the mention of Lot has dropped out in the extant J passages, the report of Haran's dying before his father makes it clear that Haran died while a member of Terah's house.[14] This description prevents conjecture that Haran left the household of Terah before his death to establish a new household.[15] Moreover, the end of Gen 11:28 specifies that Haran died "in the land of his birth, in Ur of the Chaldees." This specification prevents speculation that Haran might have set out on his own to form a new household only to die in the presence of his father at some later time. Even in the extant J passages in Gen 11:28–30, the impression is given that any son of Haran (Lot) would still be a member of the household of Terah.

That J understands Lot as a member of Terah's household and as separate from Abraham's own household is reinforced by Gen 13:1,

wayyaʿal ʾabrām mimmiṣrayim hûʾ wěʾištô wěkol ʾăšer lô wělôṭ ʿimmô hannegbâ

---

13. For a convincing argument for the common attribution of Gen 11:28–30 to J, see J. A. Emerton, "The Source of Genesis XI 27–32," *VT* 42/1 (1992) 37–46.

14. One should note that the Hebrew idiom for "before" has the same connotations as the English word "before." Hebrew *ʿal pěnê* can mean either "before" with the sense of "in the presence of" or "before" in a temporal sense. In either meaning, Haran died while still a part of Terah's house.

15. For a discussion of the makeup of the *bêt ʾāb* "household," see N. K. Gottwald, *The Tribes of Yahweh: A Sociology of the Religion of Liberated Israel, 1250–1050 b.c.e.* (Maryknoll, N.Y.: Orbis, 1979) 316–17; and L. E. Stager, "The Archaeology of the Family in Ancient Israel," *BASOR* 260 (1985) 22–23.

And Abram went up from Egypt, he and his wife, and all that he had, and Lot with him, into the Negev.

Here we have a clear distinction between Lot and Abraham's goods. Lot is listed separately in clear anticipation of the separation of Abraham and Lot later in the chapter. Moreover, Abraham's wife and possessions are marked with a singular suffix. One concludes from these indications that J intended to say that Lot originated, as did Abraham, from the household of Terah and now comprises his own household, separate from Abraham.

The inclusion of Lot in the household of Terah is similarly emphasized in the P texts that are later juxtaposed with the J texts in Genesis 11–12.[16] The first reference to Lot in the P narrative occurs in Gen 11:27. The text reads, "These are the generations of Terah: Terah begat Abram, Nahor, and Haran; Haran begat Lot." Lot is described as being Terah's grandson, a part of the household of Terah. When juxtaposed with Gen 11:28a (the J text that details the death of Lot's father before Terah [Lot's grandfather]), there is little doubt that the combined narratives of J and P describe Lot as belonging to the household of Terah.

Immediately following the J narrative (Gen 11:28–30) is a P notation that Terah took "Abram his son (*ʾet ʾabrām běnô*), Lot, the son of Haran, his grandson (*wě ʾet lôṭ ben hārān ben běnô*), and Sarai his daughter-in-law, the wife of his son Abram (*wě ʾet śāray kallātô ʾēšet ʾabrām běnô*)" (Gen 11:31). The relationship of Terah's kin is given in detail. Both Abraham and Lot are clearly natural members of the household of Terah, whereas Sarah belongs to this household because of her relationship to Abraham. Abraham is a part of Terah's household because he is Terah's son. Lot is a part of the household because he is Terah's grandson. Sarah, by contrast, is included only because of her relationship to Abraham and not because an intrinsic relationship to Terah.

A subsequent P text (Gen 12:4b) states that Abraham was 75 years old when he set out from Haran. Given the datum that Terah was 70 when he begat Abraham (Gen 11:26), and the notice that Terah did not die until he was 205 (Gen 11:31), one must conclude that Abraham and Lot left Terah in Haran some 60 years before Terah's death.[17] Again, the fact that Terah is still alive

---

16. For a discussion of how the juxtaposition of P texts with J and E texts changes the overall flow and themes of Genesis, see Richard E. Friedman, *Who Wrote the Bible?* (Englewood Cliffs, N.J.: Prentice Hall, 1987) 234–35.

17. The fact that Terah remains in Haran is puzzling in the narrative. This awkward detail is a large part of the reason that the MT and Greek chronologies with a lifespan of 205 years for Terah is to be preferred over the Samaritan Pentateuch, which harmonizes the passages by lowering Terah's lifespan to 145 years. For support of this text-critical analysis, see the

when Abraham leaves Haran emphasizes the fact that the association with Lot
at least partially breaks the command to leave behind completely the household of Terah.

Gen 12:5 states that "Abram took Sarai, his wife, and Lot, the son of his
brother," as he traveled to the land God would show him. This verse squarely
places the responsibility upon Abraham for Lot's inclusion in the move. Moreover, the wording parallels exactly Terah's "taking" of his household. Um-
berto Cassuto notes that the language of Gen 11:31 and Gen 12:5 is a
common formula used in the Hebrew Scriptures and other Canaanite literature to describe the departure of the head of a household along with all his
family in order to settle elsewhere.[18] Consequently, the description in Gen
12:5 would seem to remove any doubt that Lot's presence in Abraham's company in Gen 12:4a is due to a decision of Abraham.

Nevertheless, the description in Gen 12:5 raises a question that must be
dealt with—has Lot become a legitimate member of Abraham's household
because adoption by Abraham was either expected or required? If so, this
would indicate that, although Abraham takes Lot with him of his own accord,
he may have been obliged to do so by social law. This does not seem to be the
case, however. As Roland de Vaux comments in his book *Ancient Israel*, "The
Old Testament laws contain no directive about adoption. The historical books
record no example of adoption in the strict sense, *i.e.*, the legal acknowledg-
ment of one born outside the family as having the rights of a child born into
the family."[19] De Vaux points to several instances that might be considered
types of adoptions. Yet, even in these cases the issue of "adoption" is really
more an issue of recognition of a child that might be considered "foreign"

---

convincing arguments by Ronald S. Hendel, *The Text of Genesis 1–11: Textual Studies and
Critical Edition* (New York: Oxford University Press, 1998) 73–74. However, see also J. A.
Emerton ("When Did Terah Die [Genesis 11:32]?" in *Language, Theology, and the Bible: Essays in Honour of James Barr* [ed. by S. E. Balentine and J. Barton; Oxford: Clarendon, 1994]
170–81) who argues that the text-critical question is ambiguous and cannot be resolved.

    18. Umberto Cassuto (*A Commentary on the Book of Genesis* [2 vols.; trans. Israel Abra-
hams; Jerusalem: Magnes, 1984] 2.278) cites the following formula: (a) the name of the
head of the family, (b) a verb for the movement, (c) a list of the family members, and (d) a
list of possessions. Verse 31 fits this formula in that it (a) describes Terah as the head of the
family (*bêt 'āb*), (b) uses the verb "to go" (*hālak*) and thus emphasizes that Terah as the head
of the family was responsible for the move, and (c) indicates that Abraham and Lot are both
members of Terah's household. For other examples of this formula in the Hebrew Bible, see
Gen 36:6; 46:6; Exod 38:2–4. See also the Ugaritic text in Tablet I AB v 6–13 and Tablet
BH i 17–2

    19. Roland de Vaux, *Ancient Israel: Its Life and Institutions* (trans. J. McHugh; New York:
McGraw-Hill, 1961) 51.

(e.g., the "adoption" of Bilhah's two children by Rachel [Gen 30:3–8]). All such instances describe the recognition by a grandparent or family head of children born to a clan member who has married outside of Israel or obtained a child by a surrogate mother.[20] These cases clearly do not apply to Lot despite the fact that he has lost his father, a brother to Abraham. Moreover, the need for adoption by Abraham is even less likely in this case because Lot's grandfather, Terah, was still living when he and Abraham left Haran. So it would appear as indicated by Gen 11:26–32 that Lot is primarily a member of Abraham's father's household and that his presence in Abraham's company implies that, while Abraham has left his land and clan relations, he has not completely broken ties with Terah's household.

That Lot should not be considered part of Abraham's household is also evident from the descriptions of the possessions in Gen 12:5. In observing the list of what at first glance appears to be solely the possessions of Abraham (*wĕʾet kol rĕkûšām ʾăšer rākāšû* "and all their possessions which they possessed"), one is puzzled by the occurrence of a plural suffix and verb. The plural suffix and verb can only refer to *both* Abraham and Lot. This verse thus emphasizes that there are *two* households, traveling in tandem. Given the fact that later texts describe Lot as having his own flocks, herdsman, and fighting men, one is left to suppose that the practical reason for Lot's inclusion in Abraham's journey to Canaan is to ensure their mutual survival by pooling their resources. If this is the case, it is a clear violation of God's design to have no one other than God responsible for the establishment of Abraham and Sarah, and Lot's inclusion is a clear sign of Abraham's lack of complete reliance on God at the initial stage and a harbinger of ill consequences to follow. This feature calls for closer analysis.

Abraham's Lack of Complete Reliance on God
in Genesis 12:1–4a and Its Consequences

From the evidence presented above it is clear that Lot is understood to be a member of Terah's household, *not* Abraham's. Further, the terms of the command in Gen 12:1 explicitly state that there is to be a complete separation from both the geographical location of the patriarch's people and all ties with his kinspeople, both the most distant and those of Terah's *bêt ʾāb* (household). Consequently, mere geographical relocation is not sufficient to fulfill the command; the command requires that Abraham leave everyone—the entire household (*bêt ʾāb*) of Terah. As the above discussion shows, this includes Lot.

---

20. Ibid., 51–52.

Abraham's "disobedience" (or lack of complete trust and obedience) can also be recognized in the J narratives from the consequences that result from taking a proscribed kinsperson with him. Lot and his shepherds almost immediately fall into strife with Abraham's shepherds. This leads to an inevitable split, and we find Lot subsequently associated with the cities of the plain. Abraham has to come to Lot's rescue in chap. 14, as does God, in chap. 19. Lot's presence poses a complication to the promise presented to Abraham in Gen 12:1–4a, following a pattern described above. Not only are Abraham and his descendants left the less fertile land following the split between Abraham and Lot in Gen 13:10ff., but also Lot's two sons conceived through his daughters turn out to be the ancestors of Moab and Ammon—two of the national enemies of later Israel. Although the text does not specifically draw the connection between Abraham's lack of complete faith and the creation of these nations that later are enemies of Abraham's descendants, it is a logical consequence.[21] Moreover, this consequence is similar to the enmity that results following the creation of Ishmael and his descendants. As noted above, such consequences, which constitute punishments or at least impediments to the fulfillment of the promise, are found at least six times in the Abrahamic Cycle and occur each time Sarah and Abraham lack complete trust in God or carry out an act of self-assertion.

One must ask why is it so important for Abraham to separate himself completely from his household, a separation emphasized by the juxtaposition of the P texts with the J texts. The answer is straightforward: so Abraham's deity alone can receive credit for carrying out the promises given to Abraham in Gen 12:1–4a. The whole idea of separating out Abraham's household from others distinguishes Israel's God from other clan gods. In the case of Abraham, the biblical writer apparently thinks it important to emphasize Abraham's separation from the household of Terah, since tradition, as is shown in Josh 24:2, holds that Terah and his household worshiped other deities. The exilic redactor who juxtaposed the P texts with the J texts is well aware of such a tradition. Since, in Genesis, Israel's deity is identified as the God of Abraham, Isaac, and Jacob, it is imperative to leave no doubt that the deity responsible for the establishment of the new household of Abraham is *his* deity alone. The only way this can be done is for there to be a complete separation between Abraham and his past. Only then may Israel's deity act on behalf of Abraham

---

21. While the connection is beyond the scope of this paper, one notes that these descendents are the very enemies that David must contend with generations later. Again, Abraham is a true paradigm for David because his lack of complete obedience results in complications that David must deal with as well.

and his descendants, establishing them as a great nation and blessing the world through them.

Given the above, I propose the following translation of Gen 12:1–4a:

> Yhwh said to Abram, "Go out from your land, your kindred, and from the house of your father, to the land which I will show you so that I might make you a great nation, bless you, and make your name great, in order that you will be a blessing. Then I will bless those who bless you, but anyone who holds you in contempt, I will curse; in order that through you all the families of the earth might be blessed." Abram went as Yhwh told him, *and* Lot went with him.

In the end, Abraham *does* completely separate himself and *does* show complete trust in Yhwh. However, in the redacted narratives of Genesis, this manifestation of "complete faith" does not occur until Genesis 22. In this chapter the patriarch demonstrates his complete trust in the deity through the willingness to sacrifice the very means by which the promise will be carried out—his son Isaac. Up until this point, however, neither Abraham nor Sarah completely trusts Yhwh.

Conclusion

Abraham's actions in answering the commands found in Gen 12:1–4a constitute only a partial display of reliance on God. To be sure, Abraham does exhibit reliance on God, but his reliance on God is incomplete. The lack of complete reliance may not be as pronounced as it is in Gen 12:10–20 when Abraham leaves Canaan and denies that Sarah is his wife, yet the fact remains that his reliance on God is not complete. This reading of the ancestral narratives solves an apparent contradiction of how an apparently obedient Abraham in Gen 12:1–4a could subsequently exhibit an incomplete obedience that must be continually tested right up to and including the ultimate test of the binding of Isaac in Genesis 22. Moreover, this reading shows how the combined narratives of J, E, and P work together to present a theme of movement from developing obedience and faith to complete obedience and faith. Read in this light, one sees that God's observation in Gen 22:12 ("For *now* I know that you are a God-fearer") is the first point in the final form of the ancestral narratives that God recognizes Abraham's absolute reliance on God. The reader sees that with the juxtaposition of the E and P texts into J's narrative flow, the theme of "incomplete reliance" beginning in Gen 12:1–4a becomes even clearer in the final, "integrated" form of Genesis.

David and Zion in the Theology of the Deuteronomistic History: Theological Ideas in 2 Samuel 5–7

JOHN T. WILLIS
Abilene Christian University

Sections of narrative throughout the Bible, including the Deuteronomistic History (Dtr), vary strikingly in their theological density or compactness. The author(s) of 2 Samuel 5–7 bring together several theological themes or concepts that are central to his (their) predilections and purposes throughout the Dtr. Hence, these chapters are quite dense or compact theologically.

In the present study I accept three working hypotheses. First, Deuteronomy–2 Kings is a unified work written in its present final form in the exilic period. Although its author or authors used earlier sources (both oral and written), and although it may very well be that this work is the result of a major editing by an advocate (or advocates) of Josiah's reform around 620 B.C.E. and a minor editing by exilic redactors ca. 550 B.C.E., it is valid to seek to understand this work in its completed form.[1] T. E. Fretheim writes:

> It is important to note that, even if the dual redaction hypothesis proves to be the most convincing, it is necessary to understand how the entire history may have functioned in the exilic context. . . . Because it is the exilic redactor through whose hands the material was finally passed, we have to reckon with how the material would have functioned in that situation.[2]

Second, the authors or redactors who produced this literary piece had strong theological concerns that they sought to present through the narrative they constructed. Third, the author or authors of this work targeted a specific Jewish

---

Author's note: It is a great pleasure to present this essay to my friend of many years, J. J. M. Roberts. Like many others, I am indebted to him for numerous insights that have shaped my thinking on several issues. And the way he has conducted himself, especially under adverse conditions, has made a significant impact on my life.

1. See W. Brueggemann, "Samuel, Book of 1–2 (Narrative and Theology)," *ABD* 5.966b.

2. T. E. Fretheim, *Deuteronomic History* (IBT; Nashville: Abingdon, 1983) 17.

audience as its receptive community and intended to shape the ideals and actions of that community by what they narrated.

2 Samuel 5–7 appears to be programmatic in this literary work. The three chapters express theological ideas that are crucial in the overall compass of the work. They narrate seven distinct incidents or sets of incidents:

- The ten North Israelites tribes make a covenant with David to become their king, in addition to being king over Judah—(5:1–5).
- David and his men capture Jerusalem from the Jebusites and then occupy and expand the city—(5:6–12).
- David's wives and concubines bear David eleven children in Jerusalem—(5:13–16).
- David defeats the Philistines in two battles in the valley of Rephaim—(5:17–25).
- David brings the ark of the covenant to Jerusalem and houses it in a tent—(chap. 6).
- Yahweh promises to establish David's dynasty forever—(7:1–17).
- David thanks Yahweh for all his blessings and petitions Yahweh to keep his promise to establish David's dynasty—(7:18–29).

Four entities stand out in these chapters: Yahweh, David, Jerusalem or Zion, and the ark of the covenant. I will attempt to bring out the significance of each of these within the narrative structure of 2 Samuel 5–7.

Yahweh

Commenting on 1 and 2 Samuel, W. Brueggemann writes:

> This literature is intensely theonomous. It understands that ultimately the historical process is not shaped by political-economic factors, nor by inventive personalities, but by the purposes and governance of Yahweh, which may operate visibly or unnoticed. The literature is committed to this perception of reality and neither apologizes for it nor explains it. The modern reader is not free to regard this central motive as an intrusion or an embarrassment. Yahweh is a central character in the narrative, a quite expected presence in the drama, and a proper agent of historical events.[3]

Indeed, Yahweh plays an important role in 2 Samuel 5–7, as evidenced in five ways.

---

3. Brueggemann, "Samuel, Book of 1–2," 967a–b.

1. Yahweh as the Source of David's Authority

According to the North Israelites—the old Saul party—who came to Hebron to make David their king, Yahweh had said to David while Saul was still king, "It is you who shall be shepherd of my people Israel, you who shall be prince over Israel" (2 Sam 5:2). This promise does not appear earlier in the narrative. Some scholars think the reference is to Samuel's anointing of David at Bethlehem in 1 Sam 16:1–13.[4] But it is more likely that this is an instance of Deuteronomistic theology.[5] Both the statement that Yahweh designated David as ruler of Israel and the use of the expression "my [Yahweh's] people Israel" (see further 5:12; 6:21; 7:7, 8, 10, 11, 23 [2×], 24 [2×], 27) point to the Deuteronomic view that Yahweh had already established a covenantal relationship with Israel long before he made a covenant with David and his dynasty. "Israel is not David's kingdom, the subjects of his sovereignty, but Yahweh's people, the objects of his care and concern; . . . therefore all Yahweh does for David is done with a view to Israel's benefit."[6] Like all the people, the king is subject to Yahweh and must obey his will. The pericope stating Yahweh's requirements for Israel's king in Deut 17:14–20 includes such instructions:

> When he [the king] has taken the throne of his kingdom, he shall have a copy of this law written for him in the presence of the levitical priests. It shall remain with him and he shall read in it all the days of his life, so that he may learn to fear Yahweh his God, diligently observing all the words of this law and these statutes, neither exalting himself above other members of the community nor turning aside from the commandment, either to the right hand or to the left, so that he and his descendants may reign long over his kingdom in Israel (17:18–20).[7]

Accordingly, the Davidic covenant is subject to and complementary to the Mosaic covenant. As M. D. Guinan writes:

> The Mosaic covenant is the basic covenant that gives Israel its distinct identity. No text in the OT suggests that this covenant is ever replaced by the Davidic. The two covenants cannot be contrasted on the basis of covenant obligations;

---

4. So W. Brueggemann, *First and Second Samuel* (Interpretation; Louisville: John Knox, 1990) 237.

5. So P. K. McCarter, Jr., *II Samuel* (AB 9; Garden City, N.Y.: Doubleday, 1984) 132.

6. D. F. Murray, *Divine Prerogative and Royal Pretension: Pragmatics, Poetics and Polemics in a Narrative Sequence about David (2 Samuel 5.17–7.29)* (JSOTSup 264; Sheffield: JSOT Press, 1998) 179.

7. On this point, see A. D. H. Mayes, *Deuteronomy* (NCB; Grand Rapids: Eerdmans, 1979) 270; and G. N. Knoppers, "The Deuteronomist and the Deuteronomic Law of the King: A Reexamination of a Relationship," *ZAW* 108 (1996) 329–46, esp. 330, 332.

the king, too, is expected to be a faithful Yahwist and to obey the covenant commandments, especially in their concern for justice. . . . Both covenants were accepted in Israel and appear in the canon of Scripture; responsible exegesis must do justice to this fact. It is better to view the two not as contradictory but as complementary. . . . Deuteronomy, with its overriding Mosaic concerns, admits kingship but stresses that the king is simply one of the people, "one of your kinsmen" (Deut 17:14–20).[8]

A. H. J. Gunneweg argues that the Sinai tradition is one of the oldest sacral traditions of Israel, with roots in the Autumn or Tabernacle Festival celebrated at Shechem. It was the basis of a premonarchical tribal league or amphictyony called "Israel," grounded in the conviction that Israel was in covenant relationship with Yahweh, who promised to be Israel's God by certain historical acts and by virtue of which Israel had become Yahweh's people. The Davidic tradition, Gunneweg continues, is an addition to the Sinai tradition; it reflects an attempt to incorporate the development of central leadership within Israel into the older traditions of the amphictyony and by interpreting the sacral kingship as a part of the Yahwistic religion. The cult legend in 2 Samuel 6 of the transfer of the ark sanctuary of the amphictyony to Jerusalem, the city of David, celebrates the Davidide on the throne as being the guardian of the ark.[9] Even though the amphictyonic hypothesis is untenable, as scholars have shown convincingly,[10] the Dtr does present a story line about a loosely organized tribal confederation called "Israel" that preceded the establishment of the monarchy in Israel and that attained stable and solid existence under David.

2 Sam 5:3 states that the North Israelites made a covenant with David *lipnê yhwh* "before Yahweh." This expression occurs often in the Dtr. It appears 10 or 11 times in 2 Sam 5–7: 5:3; 6:5, 14, 16, 17, 21 [2×]; 7:16 [?], 18, 26, 29. The context of all the passages in chap. 6 and in 7:18 suggests that in these passages it means "before the ark," assuming that invisible Yahweh is seated enthroned "on" (above? between?) the cherubim, which served as the "handle" for the "mercy seat," the lid on the ark (note especially 6:4–5). This can hardly

---

8. M. D. Guinan, "Davidic Covenant," *ABD* 2.71. Similarly L. Eslinger, *House of God or House of David: The Rhetoric of 2 Samuel 7* (JSOTSup 164; Sheffield: JSOT Press, 1994) 32–33.

9. A. H. J. Gunneweg, "Sinaibund und Davidsbund," *VT* 10 (1960) 335–41. For additional discussion on this issue, see D. R. Hillers, *Covenant: The History of a Biblical Idea* (Baltimore: Johns Hopkins University Press, 1969) 154–56; and D. J. McCarthy, *Old Testament Covenant: A Survey of Current Opinions* (Richmond: John Knox, 1972) 49–52, 58, 80–85.

10. See, among others, R. de Vaux, "La thèse de l'amphictyonie israélite," *HTR* 64 (1971) 415–36; and M. C. Astour, "Amphictyony," *IDBSup* 23–25.

be the meaning in 5:3; 7:16, 26, 29, however. For example, the setting in 5:3 is Hebron (see also v. 1), and the context here suggests that at that time the ark was at Baale-judah (6:2)—that is, Kiriath-jearim (1 Sam 7:1–2).

Ian Wilson has made an extensive study of the expression *lipnê yhwh* "before Yahweh" in Deuteronomy, where it occurs 25 times. He concludes that it signifies "the localized Presence of the Deity at the 'chosen place.'"[11] In other words, in Deuteronomy the meaning lies somewhere between the idea that "before Yahweh" refers to Yahweh's transcendence, on the one hand, and the idea that it refers to the sanctuary or the ark itself, on the other. The intention is to portray Yahweh as present "in person" but not to portray him as transcendent. Such an understanding seems to be sufficient for some occurrences in 2 Samuel 5–7, but it is not suitable for 2 Sam 7:16, 26, 29, which affirm that David's "house" (dynasty) will continue "forever" "before Yahweh." Here, surely, "before Yahweh" signifies something much broader than Yahweh's presence at a certain locality. D. F. Murray offers a more acceptable explanation for the meaning of the expression "before Yahweh" in these passages:

> [it] is used very frequently of ritual and liturgical acts, very often but not exclusively performed at a recognized shrine, to express (1) the orientation of the actions as performed in the interests of Yahweh; (2) the associated sense of an actual audience with Yahweh thereby created; (3) the relative status of Yahweh and of the worshipper as the powerful and the dependent respectively.[12]

First and foremost, the Deuteronomic writer(s) is (are) emphasizing that David and his dynasty are subject to and totally dependent on Yahweh.

2. Yahweh Was <u>with</u> David

After the brief account of David capturing Jerusalem from the Jebusites, occupying the stronghold, and building the city all around, the narrator comments: "And David became greater and greater, for Yahweh, the God of Israel, was with him" (2 Sam 5:10). Then, after noting that Hiram king of Tyre built David a palace, the narrator comments further: "David then perceived that Yahweh had established him king over Israel, and that he had exalted his kingdom for the sake of his people Israel" (2 Sam 5:12). Citing 1 Sam 16:18;

---

11. Ian Wilson, *Out of the Midst of the Fire: Divine Presence in Deuteronomy* (SBLDS 151; Atlanta: Scholars Press, 1995) 204, similarly 159, 197, and the entire section on "before Yahweh," 131–97.

12. Murray, *Divine Prerogative*, 124 n. 39; see also 142–44, 157–58, 226. For further discussion of the expression "before Yahweh," see R. Sollamo, "Den bibliska formeln 'Inför Herren/Inför Gud,'" *SEÅ* 50 (1985) 21–32; and M. D. Fowler, "The Meaning of *lipnê Yhwh* in the Old Testament," *ZAW* 99 (1987) 384–90.

18:12, 14, 28, McCarter affirms that the expression "Yahweh was with him [i.e., David]"

> is the theological leitmotif of the apology of David [i.e., 1 Sam 16:14–2 Sam 5:10], and the decisive influence of Yahweh's special favor for David runs throughout the narrative, the end of which is marked by a final repetition of the expression in connection with a glance ahead: "And David continued to grow greater and greater, for Yahweh Sabaoth was with him" [2 Sam 5:10].[13]

3. Yahweh as the One Who Makes David Victorious

Both times before David fights the Philistines in the valley of Rephaim, he "inquires of Yahweh" (2 Sam 5:19, 23), Yahweh tells David what to do, David does it, and Yahweh gives him the victory (2 Sam 5:19–20, 24). After the first victory, David exclaims, "Yahweh has burst forth against my enemies" (v. 20), and the name of the place is called "Baal-perazim," that is, "The Lord of Burstings Forth." This shows that Baal (= Lord) is a proper term for Yahweh in the OT. In fact, Baal (= Yahweh) is the real victor over the Philistines in the valley of Rephaim. However, it is significant that this victory is also a victory over the gods of the Philistines. 2 Sam 5:21 states that "the Philistines abandoned their idols there, and David and his men carried them away."[14] In preparation for the second battle, Yahweh says to David, "When you hear the sound of marching in the tops of the balsam trees, then be on the alert; for then Yahweh has gone out before you to strike down the army of the Philistines" (v. 24). Again, it is Yahweh who gives David victory over the Philistines.[15]

4. The Ark as Symbol of Yahweh's Kingship

According to 2 Samuel 6, David resolves to bring the ark of the covenant from Baale-judah, that is, Kiriath-jearim (cf. 1 Sam 7:1–2), to Jerusalem. This incident is closely connected to the previous paragraph, which describes Da-

---

13. P. K. McCarter, Jr., "The Apology of David," *JBL* 99 (1980) 489–504, esp. 503–4.

14. See Murray, *Divine Prerogative*, 97.

15. N. L. Tidwell ("The Philistine Incursions into the Valley of Rephaim [2 Sam. v 17ff.]," *Studies in the Historical Books of the Old Testament* [VTSup 30; Leiden: Brill, 1979] 190–212) approaches this text from a form-critical and traditiohistorical perspective and seeks to recover the "original historical reference." He concludes that 2 Sam 5:17–25 consists of "short battle-reports" (pp. 193–94): 2 Sam 5:17–21, still largely in its original form, relates a minor successful routing of a Philistine raiding party to confiscate grain during David's days at Hebron similar to that related in 2 Sam 23:13–17 (pp. 209–11), whereas 2 Sam 5:22–25 relates a "major confrontation between Israel and the Philistines which either paved the way for or resulted from the capture of Jerusalem" (p. 212). Tidwell recognizes that "the message of the present text is that by these two encounters Yahweh through David finally opened the way to the total fulfillment of the ancient promise of the Land" (p. 191).

vid's victory over the Philistines (2 Sam 5:17–25), because the transporting of the ark from Kiriath-jearim to Jerusalem is a triumphal march celebrating Yahweh's victory over the Philistines. In the days of Eli and Samuel the Philistines had defeated the Israelites in two battles, killed the two sons of Eli, Hophni and Phinehas, and captured the ark, bringing it to the temple of their god Dagon in Ashdod (1 Sam 4:1–5:5). After tumors devastated the Philistines in their city-states, they returned the ark to the Israelites, who finally housed it in the house of Abinadab the priest in Kiriath-jearim, which apparently was a sanctuary (1 Sam 5:6–7:2). But now, the Israelites under David had defeated the Philistines in two victories. David and the Israelites are convinced that this was due to Yahweh's intervention and help, and thus they celebrate Yahweh's critical role in those victories by transporting the ark in a victory march to Jerusalem.[16] The ark is "called by the name of Yahweh of hosts who is enthroned on the cherubim" (2 Sam 6:2; cf. 1 Sam 4:4), that is, the ark symbolizes the presence of Yahweh as king among his people, and the king leads his "hosts," in this case apparently the Israelites, in battle against their enemies.[17] This understanding is compatible with McCarter's suggestion that David's bringing the ark to Jerusalem agrees with "other ancient Near Eastern accounts of the introduction of a national god to a new royal city."[18] But contrary to McCarter, who apparently understands 2 Samuel 6 as essentially disconnected from 2 Sam 5:17–25 literarily, historically, and theologically, there is a close connection between the two passages.

As the ark proceeds, David and all the house of Israel dance "before Yahweh" (2 Sam 6:5). When David leaves the ark in the house of Obed-edom, Yahweh blesses the house of Obed-edom. Interpreting this blessing as a sign of approval, David transports the ark a second time, to Jerusalem, again dancing "before Yahweh" with all his might (2 Sam 6:14, 16, 21). When David finally deposits the ark in the tent he had prepared for it, he offers burnt offerings and

---

16. Murray, *Divine Prerogative*, 118–22.

17. H. Gese ("Der Davidsbund und die Zionserwählung," *ZTK* 61 [1964] 11–14) reasons that, when David captured Jerusalem, he did not want it to appear that this city was a foreign element in the Israelite tribal league, so he brought the ark to Jerusalem, which had been the center of that tribal league when it was at Shiloh. But when the Philistines captured the ark and burned down the amphictyonic central sanctuary at Shiloh, respect for the ark greatly diminished. By defeating the Philistines, David restored respect for the ark as the cultic center of Israel. While some of the points Gese makes go beyond the textual evidence, it does seem clear that by bringing the ark to Jerusalem David was trying to maintain a continuity between Israel's submission to Yahweh prior to the establishment of the Israelite monarchy and his own submission to Yahweh.

18. McCarter, *II Samuel*, 181.

offerings of well-being "before Yahweh," and he blesses the people in the name of Yahweh of hosts. When David defends his actions in response to Michal's criticisms, he reminds her that Yahweh had chosen him in place of her father, Saul (2 Sam 6:21). "David knows that he has been appointed ruler by the Lord. . . . Therefore the Lord is to be praised, and David purposely serves the Lord, who is the only great one, precisely by making himself contemptible."[19]

5. Yahweh Asserts His Will over David

2 Samuel 7 recounts Yahweh's promise to make David a house, that is, a dynasty, forever and David's response to Yahweh with a prayer of thanksgiving for this promise. In his prayer, David acknowledges the connection between Yahweh's deliverance of Israel from Egyptian slavery and gift of the promised land (2 Sam 7:23–24) and Yahweh's choice of David and his dynasty to rule over Israel forever (2 Sam 7:25–29).

All of these particulars suggest a close amicable relationship between Yahweh and David. But this is not the whole story. 2 Samuel 5–7 describes two sharp conflicts between Yahweh and David. 2 Sam 6:6–10 states that, as David and the Israelites were bringing the ark of the covenant to Jerusalem on a cart, the oxen pulling the cart shook it; the priest Uzzah reached out his hand to steady the ark; Yahweh became angry with Uzzah and struck him, and Uzzah died. David was angry with Yahweh for striking Uzzah, and David was afraid to continue the journey with the ark, and so left it in the house of Obed-edom. Murray thinks the point of these verses is that David thought he was in control of the ark when he set out from Kiriath-jearim to bring it to Jerusalem, but Yahweh quickly showed him that Yahweh was in control of both David and the ark. By blessing the house of Obed-edom, Yahweh was indicating he wanted the ark to remain there. But a second time, David takes matters into his own hands, and transports the ark from the house of Obed-edom to Jerusalem.[20] Whether this explanation is correct or not, the author(s) of 2 Sam 6:6–10 is (are) seeking to demonstrate that Yahweh's will prevails over David's will even if Yahweh's actions are displeasing to David.

2 Sam 7:1–17 declares that David told the prophet Nathan that he wanted to build Yahweh a house, that is, a temple for the ark (note especially v. 2). It was customary in the ancient Near East for a king to support his tutelary deity. Yet, more than this lies underneath the surface here. David is trying to control the always potentially dangerous ark and its deity by housing them in a build-

---

19. H. W. Hertzberg, *I & II Samuel* (trans. J. S. Bowden; OTL; Philadelphia: Westminster, 1964) 281.

20. Murray, *Divine Prerogative*, 126–29, 157.

ing. But Yahweh told David through Nathan the prophet that Yahweh would not allow David to build him a house, that is, a temple; his son (Solomon) would do that. Instead, Yahweh would build David a house, that is, a dynasty.[21] "Whatever David's motives, his action [building a temple] would have the twofold consequence of installing Yahweh's symbol in a house of David's making and thus obliging the deity to David—a single move both obliges and potentially puts the deity at the king's disposal. Yahweh will have none of it."[22]

Since Yahweh prevails and David must comply in both of these cases, apparently the author(s) of this narrative is a Yahwist (are Yahwists) who advocate(s) that Yahweh was responsible for David's success and that Yahweh chose and maintained David and his dynasty, but that Yahweh did not approve of all of David's ideas and actions and restricted or punished David when it was necessary to carry out Yahweh's purposes.

David

The second major player in the narrative in 2 Samuel 5–7 is David. This narrative presents David in three ways.

1. David Stands in Bold Contrast to Saul

According to 2 Sam 5:2, when the tribes of North Israel come to David at Hebron, they say to him: "For some time, while Saul was king over us, it was you who led out Israel and brought it in," that is, even during Saul's reign, David was the real leader of Israel's troops (see 1 Sam 18:5, 13).

While the Philistines essentially ruled Israel during the reign of Saul (see 1 Sam 13:1–14:46; chaps. 17–18; 23; 27–29), and finally defeated the Israelites, and killed Saul and three of his sons on Mount Gilboa (1 Samuel 31), David decisively defeats the Philistines in two battles in the valley of Rephaim (2 Sam 5:17–25).

The biblical narrative often reports that David "inquired of Yahweh" before making a decision or acting (1 Sam 22:6–19; 23:1–14; 30:7–8; 2 Sam 2:1–7; 5:17–25; 21:1–14). But Saul's experiences of "inquiring of Yahweh" are all flawed in one way or another. When he realizes there is confusion in the Philistine camp, he summons the priest Ahijah with the ephod apparently to "inquire of Yahweh," but while Ahijah is in the process of "inquiring," Saul charges him, "Withdraw your hand" (1 Sam 14:19), apparently from the ark

---

21. The issues raised by 2 Sam 7:5–7 are very difficult to explain in light of the rest of chap. 7 as well as other OT texts such as 1 Kgs 5:17–19[Eng. 3–5] and 8:17–19. On this matter, see McCarter, *II Samuel*, 219–20, 225–29.

22. Eslinger, *House of God or House of David*, 24.

or the ephod, from which he was about to extract the Urim and the Thummim or the lots. Here Saul decides what to do without consulting Yahweh.[23] Later, Saul commands his men to pursue the Philistines by night while they are fleeing from Israel, but the priest admonishes him to "inquire of Yahweh" first. Saul does this, but there is no answer from Yahweh (1 Sam 14:36–37). Saul then suspects that the reason Yahweh is not answering is that someone in Israel has sinned; so again he "inquires of Yahweh" to find out who it is. The lot falls on Jonathan (who had eaten honey in violation of his father's oath, which he had not heard), and Saul commands his men to kill Jonathan. But the soldiers intervene on Jonathan's behalf and save his life (1 Sam 14:38–45). Later, the Philistines advanced on Saul and the Israelites and, feeling their pressure, Saul "inquired of Yahweh" again. But "Yahweh did not answer him, not by dreams, or by Urim, or by prophets" (1 Sam 28:5–6). In desperation, Saul consulted the medium of Endor, who brought up Samuel from the dead. Samuel told Saul the Philistines would defeat the Israelites and that he and his sons would die in the battle (1 Sam 28:7–19). Tidwell remarks: "From the traditio-historical point of view the consultation of the oracle in both battle-reports, drawing attention as it does to David's reliance on Yahweh and setting him thus in contrast with Saul . . . may be the most important element in the stories in their present context."[24]

When David brings the ark into Jerusalem, Michal the daughter of Saul strongly reproves him for exposing himself before the eyes of his servants' maids, and David responds: "It was before Yahweh, who chose me in place of your father and all his household, to appoint me as prince over Israel" (2 Sam 6:20–21). The final redactors (editors, compilers, authors) are making the point here that Yahweh has rejected the house of Saul in favor of the house of David.[25]

Yahweh's speech to David through Nathan, promising David that Yahweh would establish his dynasty over Israel forever, contains the announcement that, when David's son Solomon sins, Yahweh will "punish him with a rod such as mortals use, with blows inflicted by human beings. But I will not take my steadfast love from him, as I took it from Saul, whom I put away from before you" (2 Sam 7:14–15; cf. 1 Sam 13:7–14; 15:17–29).

---

23. On this passage, see P. K. McCarter, Jr., *I Samuel* (AB 8; Garden City, N.Y.: Doubleday, 1980) 240.

24. Tidwell, "The Philistine Incursions into the Valley of Rephaim," 208.

25. See Hertzberg, *I & II Samuel*, 281.

2. David Bears Certain Significant Programmatic Epithets

David "leads out and brings in Israel" (2 Sam 5:2). This is a technical phrase meaning that David exercises military leadership over Israel (cf. 1 Sam 18:13, 16).

David is "shepherd" of God's people Israel (2 Sam 5:2). "The term 'shepherd' is a conventional metaphor in the ancient world for king, indicating the responsibility of the king to guard, feed, nurture, and protect the flock: that is, the community over which he presides."[26] (See 2 Sam 7:7; Pss 78:70–72; 80:2[1].)

David is "prince" (*nāgîd*) over Israel (2 Sam 5:2; 6:21). Scholars have debated the meaning of *nāgîd* extensively. W. F. Albright argued that it means a "military commander," thus one less than a king, a charismatic figure.[27] W. Richter thought it meant a "savior-judge," a carryover of the idea of "judge" of the period of the judges into the monarchic period. A. Alt, B. Halpern, P. K. McCarter, and others think it means "the designated heir" to the throne, "king-designate."[28] It is likely that the meaning of *nāgîd* changed over the years and that its initial significance related to Saul, David, and Solomon withered. However, Brueggemann is undoubtedly correct in his comments on 2 Sam 5:3:

> The precise meaning of the term 'prince' (*nagid*) is much disputed. At the least, it is a word used to avoid the title 'king' (*melek*). To be sure, the narrative commentary of verse 3 uses the term 'king,' but the actual wording of the elders seems to want to avoid that high title. Two reasons for such avoidance are likely. First, to call David 'prince' leaves room for the kingship of Yahweh. This *nagid* is one way out of the vexed notion that human kingship is a rejection of the kingship of Yahweh. Second, the elders apparently do not wish to overlegitimate or excessively exalt David in office.[29]

This agrees with the much earlier assessment of A. Alt: "As the chosen of Yahweh he was merely called *nāgîd*, and it was the nation that conferred upon him

---

26. Brueggemann, *First and Second Samuel*, 237.

27. W. F. Albright, *Samuel and the Beginnings of the Prophetic Movement* (Cincinnati: Hebrew Union College Press, 1961) 15: "We may be quite certain that the appearance of *nagid* instead of *melekh* in the formula of installation was intentional. In other words, Saul and David were not meant by Samuel or the tribal heads of Israel to be enthroned as kings but only to be anointed as military leaders of the tribal confederation."

28. A. Alt, "The Formation of the Israelite State in Palestine," in *Essays in Old Testament History and Religion* (trans. J. A. Wilson; Oxford: Blackwell, 1966 [first published in German in 1930]) 195, 214; B. Halpern, *The Constitution of the Monarchy in Israel* (HSM 25; Chico, Calif.: Scholars Press, 1981) 9–11; McCarter, *II Samuel*, 132.

29. Brueggemann, *First and Second Samuel*, 238–39.

the title of *melek*, 'king.' A clear distinction is made between his divine ordination and his human rank. They are both essential constituents of the monarchy in Israel."[30] D. F. Murray also deals with the contrast between *nāgîd* and *melek* extensively, and reaches basically the same conclusions as Alt and Brueggemann.[31]

David is Yahweh's "anointed one" (Heb. *māšîaḥ*, 2 Sam 5:4). It is true that "the elders of (North) Israel" anoint David at Hebron to be king over them. However, the reader of the Samuel narrative (or of the Dtr) is aware of two previous "anointings" of David. First, at Yahweh's instruction, Samuel anointed David privately in Bethlehem (1 Sam 16:3, 12–13), connoting that David was "Yahweh's anointed one" (compare the anointing of Saul, 1 Sam 9:15–16; 10:1). Second, the people of Judah anointed David king over the house of Judah after the Philistines killed Saul and three of his sons on Mount Gilboa (1 Samuel 31), and David and his companions left Ziklag and settled in the towns of Hebron (2 Sam 2:3–4). That David is "Yahweh's anointed one" (messiah) has important symbolic meaning.

> By strength of anointment, the king became a theocratic vassal of the Lord, as texts like I Sam 9:16; 16:3 indicate. . . . The theocratic character of the anointment is also exemplified by the fact that the king was the Lord's anointed (I Sam. 24:6, 10—H 24:7, 11; 26:16), and a vassal of God who reigned in God's stead over his people (I Sam. 10:1 LXX; II Sam. 6:21).[32]

In David's prayer in 2 Sam 7:18–29, he refers to himself as "your [Yahweh's] servant" ten times. In the preceding paragraph, Yahweh refers to David as "my servant David" twice in the message he gives Nathan to deliver to David (2 Sam 7:5, 8). Alluding to the same set of incidents, Ps 89:20 uses similar language. The context of 2 Samuel 7, in which this expression is couched, suggests that the narrator is emphasizing that, in the same setting in which Yahweh is ensuring the continuation of David and his dynasty, Yahweh is reminding David that Yahweh is actually king and that David is his "servant," his vassal.

3. David Deals Wisely with Those Who Oppose Him

(a) David defeats the Jebusites and captures Jerusalem for his capital (2 Sam 5:6–9). The Canaanites had controlled this city in the midst of Israelite incursions into the land (cf. Judg 19:10–12), probably because it did not lie on the main north–south trade route and because it was built on and amidst hilly

---

30. Alt, "The Formation of the Israelite State," 195.
31. Murray, *Divine Prerogative*, 142–44, 155–59, 178–83, 238–49, 280–316.
32. S. Szikszai, "Anoint," *IDB* 1.139.

slopes and was well fortified.[33] It seems likely, in light of David's purchase of the threshing floor from Araunah the Jebusite (2 Sam 24:15–25), that David spared the Jebusites who survived the conquest of the city and provided places for them to live in or near the city.

(b) David negotiates with King Hiram of Tyre (in Phoenicia) to build David a palace (2 Sam 5:11).

(c) David defeats the Philistines in two significant battles in the valley of Rephaim, south of Jerusalem (2 Sam 5:17–25). Prior to these victories, the Philistines had controlled much territory in the land of Israel (see 1 Sam 13–14, 17–18, 23, 29, 31). David's capture and carrying off of the Philistine idols (2 Sam 5:21) probably stands as the literary counterpoint to the Philistines' capturing the ark of the covenant and carrying it off into their land and depositing it in the temple of Dagon in Ashdod (1 Sam 4:10–5:2).[34] These two victories over the Philistines also function as the fulfillment of Yahweh's promise related by Abner to the North Israelites according to 2 Sam 3:18.

(d) On both occasions that David disagrees with Yahweh—that is, when Yahweh kills Uzzah for trying to steady the ark (2 Sam 6:6–15) and when Yahweh refuses to let David carry out his dream of building a temple for the ark (2 Sam 7:1–17), David nonetheless yields to Yahweh's will.

(e) When Saul's daughter Michal chastises David for acting shamefully before his servants' maids by dancing with all his might before the ark, David declares that he had danced before Yahweh, that he would not hesitate to do it again, and that the maids she had in mind would hold him in honor for his actions (2 Sam 6:16, 20–23).

(f) David remains very cordial to Nathan the prophet when Nathan delivers Yahweh's message to him, denying him the privilege of building the temple but announcing that Yahweh would establish David's dynasty (2 Sam 7:1–17). G. W. Ahlström argues at length that Araunah was the king of Jerusalem, Zadok was the Jebusite priest of the deity there, and Nathan was a Jebusite prophet; and that David took over and Israelitized or Yahwicized the Jebusite cult, thus achieving an amicable relationship with the Jebusites.[35]

Zion or Jerusalem

2 Samuel 5–7 are crucial for understanding the role of Zion or Jerusalem in OT theology. They emphasize two things about Zion. First, when David

---

33. See Hertzberg, *I & II Samuel*, 268.
34. See McCarter, *II Samuel*, 154, 159.
35. G. W. Ahlström, "Der Prophet Nathan und der Tempelbau," *VT* 11 (1961) 113–27, esp. 117–22.

captures Jerusalem from the Jebusites, he uses only "his [own] men," his "body of personal retainers," his "professional soldiers," "the professional military force which belonged to him personally from his earliest days" (see 1 Sam 22:1–2; 23:3, 5, 13; 24:4–5, 7–8, 23[3–4, 6–7, 22]; 25:5, 8–13; etc.).[36] And when he occupies the stronghold, he names it "the city of David" (2 Sam 5:9), indicating it is his personal possession. Therefore, politically neither North Israel nor Judah has any claim to it.[37]

Second, Zion or Jerusalem is located geographically between Israel and Judah, but belongs to neither. David is dealing with a very delicate and complex political situation at this point. The ten tribes of North Israel and the tribe of Judah have been hostile to each other for a long time, and Jerusalem has been in foreign hands. David seeks to unite these three entities by ruling each of them personally simultaneously.[38] Hertzberg describes the condition well:

> As 'the city of David', the captured city was not given to one of the tribes, but remained the property of the throne. . . . David was now master of an easily defensible capital which in addition—an exceptionally important point for him—lay right on the border between 'Judah' and 'Israel' and was extra-territorial to the land belonging to the tribes, so that neither of the two partners in the kingdom could feel themselves at a disadvantage.[39]

The issue about whether Israel or Judah should be the first to bring David back to Jerusalem after the overthrow of Absalom's rebellion and Absalom's death (2 Sam 19:41–43) shows that North Israel and Judah were still not a united nation after David had ruled as king in Jerusalem for several years. In fact, David's betrayal to Saul by the people of Keilah (1 Sam 23:12) and the Ziphites on two different occasions (1 Sam 23:19–28; 26:1–5), David's conflict with Nabal (1 Sam 25:1–38), and Absalom's rebellion (2 Sam 15:7–12) indicate that only certain groups in Judah supported David.

The Ark of the Covenant

David's transfer of the ark of the covenant from Kiriath-jearim to Jerusalem has very important theological implications. First, prior to the housing of the ark in Jerusalem, it resided in the temple in Shiloh (1 Sam 3:3; 4:3–4). By

---

36. Alt, "The Formation of the Israelite State in Palestine," 208–9. See also K. Gutbrod, *Das Buch vom Reich: Das zweite Buch Samuel* (BAT 11/2; Stuttgart: Calwer, 1958) 68–69.

37. See esp. Gese, "Der Davidsbund," 11.

38. Alt ("The Formation of the Israelite State," 208–17) describes this situation in detail. See also J. R. Porter, "The Interpretation of 2 Samuel VI and Psalm CXXXII," *JTS* 5 (1954) 161–73, esp. 163.

39. Hertzberg, *I & II Samuel*, 270. See further McCarter, *II Samuel*, 141.

bringing the ark to Jerusalem to play a central role in the cult he would establish there, David is attempting to strengthen both his position with and his support from the ten North Israelite tribes.[40]

Second, the ark symbolizes the presence of Yahweh among his people as "king," since He "sits enthroned" above the ark on the cherubim (1 Sam 4:4; 2 Sam 6:2).[41] Hence, David's transporting the ark to Jerusalem is a symbolic way of saying both that he as human king is willfully submitting himself to Yahweh as divine king and also that Yahweh is choosing Jerusalem for his dwelling place. Indeed, Ps 132:13–14 (most scholars call attention to the close relationship between 2 Samuel 6 and Psalm 132) affirms:

> For Yahweh has chosen Zion;
> he has desired it for his habitation:
> "This is my resting place forever;
> here I will reside, for I have desired it."[42]

B. C. Ollenburger goes to great lengths to try to show that the Zion tradition connected with the ark is totally separate from and prior to the Davidic tradition, which is concerned with legitimacy, succession, and hegemony. The Psalms of Zion (Psalms 46, 48, 76) connect Zion with Yahweh's kingship, not with any earthly kingship. The author of Psalm 132 uses the earlier Zion tradition to enforce David's legitimacy and Davidic succession.[43] In its present form, however, the narrative in 2 Samuel 5–7 reflects a close connection between the Zion tradition and the Davidic tradition.

Third, the ark is strongly connected to the divine epithet "Yahweh Sabaoth," "Yahweh of hosts" (1 Sam 4:4; 2 Sam 6:2), that is, Yahweh of the armies of Israel (cf. 1 Sam 17:45). Thus, when Israel goes into battle against its enemies, its divine king Yahweh is leading into battle, riding on his chariot, the ark. Thus he fights Israel's battles against its enemies (cf. Josh 10:14; 1 Sam 18:17).[44]

---

40. See Alt, "The Formation of the Israelite State," 218.

41. See Porter, "The Interpretation of 2 Samuel VI and Psalm CXXXII," 171–73; T. N. D. Mettinger, "YHWH SABAOTH: The Heavenly King on the Cherubim Throne," in *Studies in the Period of David and Solomon and Other Essays* (ed. T. Ishida; Winona Lake, Ind.: Eisenbrauns, 1982) 117.

42. On this see Gese, "Der Davidsbund," 16–19; and especially J. J. M. Roberts, "Zion in the Theology of the Davidic-Solomonic Empire," in *Studies in the Period of David and Solomon and Other Essays* (ed. T. Ishida; Winona Lake, Ind.: Eisenbrauns, 1982) 99.

43. B. C. Ollenburger, *Zion the City of the Great King: A Theological Symbol of the Jerusalem Cult* (JSOTSup 41; Sheffield: JSOT Press, 1987) 59–66.

44. See Mettinger, "YHWH SABAOTH," 109–38.

Conclusion

In 2 Samuel 5–7 the narrator pulls together several theological themes that he has introduced and partially developed in prior chapters. But here he brings them into sharper focus. Yahweh is undisputed king of his people Israel. Through his earthly vassal, "prince" or "shepherd" or "servant" David, he "chooses" Zion-Jerusalem as his dwelling place. He has David and his followers defeat the Jebusites, occupy the city, and bring the ark of the covenant there to reside temporarily within a tent but ultimately within a temple. David, relying always on Yahweh's guidance of power, defeats or makes friendly alliances with Israel's traditional or potential enemies, specifically, the Jebusites, the Philistines, and the Phoenicians. Yahweh makes it quite clear that it is David's dynasty, and not Saul's, that he has chosen and that thus will prevail. The closing verses of Psalm 78 summarize these themes in a remarkable way:

> [Yahweh] abandoned his dwelling at Shiloh,
> the tent where he dwelt among mortals,
> and delivered his power to captivity,
> his glory to the hand of the foe. . . .
> He rejected the tent of Joseph,
> he did not choose the tribe of Ephraim;
> but he chose the tribe of Judah,
> Mount Zion, which he loves.
> He built his sanctuary like the high heavens,
> like the earth, which he has founded forever.
> He chose his servant David,
> and took him from the sheepfolds;
> from tending the nursing ewes he brought him
> to be the shepherd of his people Jacob,
> of Israel, his inheritance.
> With upright heart he tended them,
> and guided them with skillful hand. (vv. 60–61, 67–72)

Part 2

The Divine King and the Human King

The Divine Sovereign:
The Image of God in the Priestly Creation Account

BERNARD F. BATTO
DePauw University

It is commonplace among critical biblical scholars to contrast the two creation accounts in the opening chapters of Genesis by asserting that the first account, the Priestly account, is much less anthropomorphic in its depiction of
the deity than is the following, Yahwistic account. Indeed, outside of "actions" such as "making," "saying," "naming," and the like, the only other supposedly anthropomorphic characterization of אלהים "God" in Gen 1:1–2:3 is
that on the seventh day he "rested" (שבת, 2:2); and even this term can be
translated more neutrally as "he ceased (from working)."[1] So without any explicit description of the deity, can one "flesh out"—to continue the metaphor
of anthropomorphism—the Priestly Writer's conception of the deity?

Moreover, to shift the focus slightly, in Gen 1:26 the Priestly Writer says
that God proposes נעשה אדם בצלמנו כדמותנו "let us make humankind in our
image according to our likeness" and in Gen 1:27, acting on that proposal,
ויברא אלהים את־האדם בצלמו "God created humankind in his image." Clearly,
here P suggests that the deity is imaged at least partially through human form
or human attributes, as many commentators from ancient to modern times
have recognized. There is little agreement among these commentators, however, about how humans actually image the deity.

Author's note: This paper is dedicated to J. J. M. Roberts, whose friendship extends back to
my graduate school days at The Johns Hopkins University, where he first introduced me to
Amarna Akkadian and later directed my 1972 dissertation, *Studies on Women at Mari: Politics
and Religion*—his first directed dissertation but certainly not his last. His judicious use of Assyriology to shed light on the Hebrew Bible inspired me to attempt a similar path in my
own career.

1. Use of the vocable ברא 'to create' is generally not considered an anthropomorphism
because this vocable "is never used in the Hebrew Old Testament with other than God as
its subject"; so Bruce Vawter (*On Genesis: A New Reading* [Garden City, N.Y.: Doubleday,
1977] 39), echoing the nearly unanimous voice of modern commentators. Gerhard von
Rad (*Genesis: A Commentary* [OTL; 2nd ed.; London: SCM, 1963] 47) goes so far as to
claim, mistakenly, that ברא implies *creatio ex nihilo*.

In this paper I will argue that one can put a humanlike form to P's conception of God, namely, that of the divine sovereign. P may have been conscious of the theological limitations inherent in this anthropomorphism. Nevertheless, within P's world view, divine sovereignty was the most transcendent characterization of God available, and P readily employed it to further his theological agenda.[2] Corollary to P's characterization of God as the divine sovereign is P's further point that God created humans to serve as his regents in administering this world. If God is the divine sovereign, then humankind is his viceroy on earth. (The ambiguity in the phrase "the image of God"—referring to the Priestly portrayal of the deity per se as well as to humankind being created in the deity's image and likeness—is therefore intentional in the title of this paper.)

Given P's parsimonious language regarding the deity, one is forced to use an oblique method in teasing out P's conception of God. Thus, in developing my thesis I will proceed along three auxiliary lines of argument: (1) an examination of ancient Near Eastern literature and iconography wherein creator and creation are presented as constituent elements or subsidiary metaphors of a more fundamental metaphor of divine sovereignty, (2) comparative evidence from cognate biblical texts concerning God's kingship in relation to creation, and (3) an analysis of the Priestly creation account itself for indications of an implied image of God.

Divine Sovereignty in the Ancient Near East

In the ancient Near East, the concept of divine sovereignty had reference to the absolute and universal rule of the chief deity over heaven and earth. Since early in the second millennium B.C.E. at least, the concept of one deity's being supreme over the other gods and controlling the cosmos was well established across the ancient Near East, even if the identity of this divine sovereign varied from region to region and from period to period, for example, in Egypt: Atum, Horus, or Amun-Re; in Mesopotamia: Anu, Enlil, Ea-Enki,

---

2. It is a pleasure to acknowledge J. J. M. Roberts's important contributions to the question of God's kingship, including his most recent article "The Enthronement of Yahweh and David: The Abiding Theological Significance of the Kingship Language of the Psalms," *CBQ* 64 (2002) 675–86. His earlier essays are now conveniently collected in his volume *The Bible and the Ancient Near East: Collected Essays* (Winona Lake, Ind.: Eisenbrauns, 2002); from these on the kingship of Yahweh note in particular his essay "Zion in the Theology of the Davidic-Solomonic Empire," 331–47, esp. 332–37 (originally published in *Studies in the Period of David and Solomon and Other Essays* [ed. T. Ishida; Winona Lake, Ind.: Eisenbrauns, 1982] 93–108).

Marduk, or Ashur; in Canaan: El or his associate Baal. In Israel and Judah, of course, the role of divine sovereign was ascribed to Yahweh, also known as אלהים "God."

Creator as a Subsidiary Metaphor of the Divine Sovereign

The metaphor of the divine sovereign involved a number of associated subsidiary metaphors. Principal among these was that of *creator*. The association between the divine sovereign and the creator has a long history in ancient Near Eastern tradition.

In Mesopotamia, since at least the third millennium B.C.E., myths involving divine sovereignty have been used to undergird the political hegemony of particular city-states over neighboring states, without necessarily involving a subsidiary metaphor of creation per se. The Sumerian myth Enmerkar and the Lord of Aratta, in which Inanna is said to favor Kulab in Uruk over a rival sanctuary, served to justify Uruk's preeminence within the Sumerian confederation. The Akkadian myth of Anzu served a similar function for the city-state of Girsu; by defeating the chaos monster Anzu, Ninurta, the god of Girsu, was able to rescue the "tablets of destiny" and restore order in the world.

To judge from its wide distribution and long life, the Old Babylonian myth Atrahasis may be regarded as the standard Mesopotamian cosmology from the Old Babylonian period through the Neo-Assyrian period (from ca. 1700 to ca. 600 B.C.E.). The story of Atrahasis opens with a rebellion of the worker gods against Enlil, recognized as the divine sovereign in this text, as frequently in ancient Mesopotamia.[3] To satisfy the lesser gods' grievances, Enlil directed Ea, the god of wisdom noted for his craftsmanship, to devise a substitute for the worker gods; the result was the creation of primeval humankind from clay mixed with the blood of the principal rebel god. The primeval humans, however, like the rebel god from whose blood they were partially made, seem not to have acknowledged the authority of the divine sovereign. The latter, in turn, attempted in various ways to wipe them out, ultimately by means of a flood. Enlil relented only when a solution was found by recasting humankind as a naturally mortal species. Though Ea was the craftsman, the plan ultimately had to have Enlil's stamp of approval. Here the divine sovereign motif is closely linked to that of the creation of humankind. The creation of the physical universe is not addressed in this myth, however, since it assumes the preexistence of a world populated only with divine beings, divided into two classes: a small cadre of ruler deities and a large group of lesser, worker gods.

---

3. See my "Sleeping God: An Ancient Near Eastern Motif of Divine Sovereignty," *Bib* 58 (1987) 153–77.

The development of the motif of the divine sovereign in Mesopotamia underwent a dramatic shift with the rise of the nation-states of Babylon and Assyria during the second millennium B.C.E. and continuing into the first millennium B.C.E. In each case the national deity, namely, Marduk in Babylon and Ashur in Assyria, were touted by their respective devotees as the supreme deity, with the obvious purpose of justifying their country's political ascendancy as the ruler of the "world." In the Old Babylonian period, when Babylon first rose to prominence under the aggressive West-Semitic Hammurabi (ca. 1792–1750 B.C.E.), Babylonian propagandists were not so bold as to claim that Marduk had displaced Anu or Enlil, the traditional two contenders for the role of head of the Mesopotamian pantheon. Nevertheless, according to the prologue to the Law Code of Hammurabi (i 1–26), both Anu and Enlil did cooperate in elevating Marduk to preeminence among the Igigu gods, giving Marduk "supreme power over all the peoples" and establishing for him at Babylon an "eternal kingship whose foundations are as fixed as heaven and earth."[4] Succeeding generations of Babylonians were not so restrained, however. In a kind of incipient monotheism, literature was rewritten and hymns composed that ascribed to Babylon's patron deity most of the important functions and the major attributes of the other gods. This process is perhaps most explicit in a Babylonian text that equates Marduk with all of the other gods and their functions:

Ninurta (is)	Marduk of the pickaxe
Nergal (is)	Marduk of battle . . .
Enlil (is)	Marduk of lordship and consultations
Nabu (is)	Marduk of accounting
Sin (is)	Marduk who lights up the night
Shamash (is)	Marduk of justice
Adad (is)	Marduk of rain

                                    (CT 24, 50; BM 47406, obverse)[5]

And so on.

The campaign to promote Babylon's patron deity to the rank of divine sovereign is most blatant in the Babylonian theogonic myth Enuma Elish.[6]

---

4. Trans. Martha Roth, "The Laws of Hammurabi," *COS*, 2.131, p. 336.

5. Translation by W. G. Lambert, "Historical Development of the Mesopotamian Pantheon: A Study in Sophisticated Polytheism," in *Unity and Diversity: Essays in the History, Literature, and Religion of the Ancient Near East* (ed. Hans Goedicke and J. J. M. Roberts; Baltimore: Johns Hopkins University Press, 1975) 191–200, esp. 197–98.

6. See my "Creation Theology in Genesis," in *Creation in the Biblical Traditions* (ed. Richard J. Clifford and John J. Collins; CBQMS 24; Washington, D.C.: Catholic Biblical Association, 1992) 16–38, esp. 25–26.

Borrowing heavily from the traditions of Anzu[7] and Atrahasis, the author of Enuma Elish gave expression to a new religiopolitical paradigm. This myth tells how Marduk became the divine sovereign when the older, established gods of Mesopotamia failed to meet new threats to world order.[8] The former authority of those gods is acknowledged by allowing that one of their number, namely Ea (Sumerian Enki), had been successful previously in establishing a kind of primeval order. Ea had defeated Apsu, the first husband of Tiamat (Primeval Ocean), and built a palace within Apsu as a symbol of his power to control chaos. But when Tiamat reemerged in an even more threatening form—symbolized by her new marriage to the even more ferocious Qingu—Ea and the older gods proved unequal to the task. Thereupon Marduk—here, for obvious propagandistic reasons, said to be Ea's own fulgent son—offered to subdue Tiamat and Qingu in return for the right to be the divine sovereign. Marduk not only vanquished Tiamat and her cohorts, he went one better over the old regime. Out of the carcasses of the slain gods, Marduk created the world and peopled it with humans who are to act as servants to the gods, thereby allowing the gods the rest or leisure befitting their divine status.[9] In short, Enuma Elish claims to supplant all previous cosmologies by reaching back before them to the very beginning of existence to tell the true story of how the whole of creation came to be: the physical universe, humankind, even the origin of the gods. And in this new story Marduk demonstrates his superiority over all the gods; he alone was able to overcome the threat of annihilation by turning chaos into the completed cosmos, which includes the establishment of the human realm. The other gods gratefully acknowledged Marduk as their divine sovereign by proclaiming his fifty titles of kingship.

When Enuma Elish reached Assyria, Neo-Assyrian theologians appropriated this myth of divine sovereignty for their own national god simply by substituting everywhere the name of Ashur in place of Marduk. Much like Babylonian theologians did for Marduk, Assyrian theologians elevated Ashur to the rank of divine sovereign, at first somewhat tentatively by modeling Ashur on the pattern of Enlil during the second millennium and then more

---

7. "The direct borrowing in *Enūma elish* from the *Myth of Anzu* in effect makes Marduk not only the new Anu, Enlil, and Ea, but the new Ninurta as well." So Richard J. Clifford, *Creation Accounts in the Ancient Near East and in the Bible* (CBQMS 26; Washington, D.C.: Catholic Biblical Association, 1994) 85.

8. For this interpretation of Enuma Elish, see T. Jacobsen, *Treasures of Darkness: A History of Mesopotamian Religion* (New Haven: Yale University Press, 1976) 163–91.

9. On the motif of divine rest as a symbol of divine authority, see my article "The Sleeping God," 153–77.

aggressively under Sennacherib by replacing the cult of Marduk with a cult of Ashur as head of the pantheon.[10]

The Ugaritic myth of Baal and Anat is also a myth of divine sovereignty, though of a different kind. In the Ugarit versions of the Combat Myth, Baal does not so much replace the elder El as the king of the gods as he becomes El's associate in ruling the world. In one version Baal overcomes Death (Mot); in another version Baal subdues Sea (Yam), alternately called River. Either way, Baal wins the right to build his palace from which he rules with thunderous voice, the symbol of his divine authority.

The ancient Near Eastern motif of the divine sovereign could be fleshed out with considerably more detail and through additional examples.[11] But enough has been said to allow a sketch of some of the principal features of the motif. The divine sovereign was the deity who as king of the gods ruled both heaven and earth. How he became the divine sovereign varies according to myth type. In cases such as Anu and Enlil in Sumer, Atum in Egypt, or El in Canaan, the deity seems to have been acknowledged as head of the pantheon through long-standing tradition. In the Combat Myth type, however, a deity earned the rank of divine sovereign by defeating in battle the chaos-dragon, usually symbolized as primeval Sea, though others were also possible, for ex-

---

10. See J. J. M. Roberts, "The Davidic Origin of the Zion Tradition," 326–27; W. G. Lambert, "The God Aššur," *Iraq* 45 (1983) 82–86, esp. p. 86.

11. Egypt is ignored here for several reasons: (1) There are no extant Egyptian cosmologies; our knowledge of Egyptian myth is limited to allusions in various texts. Moreover, it is likely that knowledge of such myths was the secret domain of specialized priests who used them in healings, rituals, and funerary preparations. (2) Each major religious center had its own mythic tradition revolving around its own deity, even if at core they shared certain common features. Also, traditions even at the same center often evolved considerably over Egypt's long history. Such diversity makes generalizations difficult. (3) While one may attribute the role of divine sovereign to Amun, Amun-Re, or Aten-Re, or to Horus as a manifestation of Re, there is no unanimity in Egyptian tradition about either the creator or the process of creation. (4) Although Egyptian influence is patent in other biblical texts, for example, Psalm 104, there is no clear evidence that Egyptian ideas directly influenced the Priestly creation account. (5) The creation of humankind is a minor theme in extant Egyptian literature. See Clifford, *Creation Accounts in the Ancient Near East and in the Bible,* 99–116; B. Batto, "The Ancient Near Eastern Background for Hebrew Conceptions of Creation," in *The Epic of Creation,* ed. Karl E. Peters et al. (forthcoming). Regarding (4), Jon D. Levenson (*Creation and the Persistence of Evil: The Jewish Drama of Divine Omnipotence* [San Francisco: Harper & Row, 1988] 59–65) argues for a trajectory from the Egyptian "Hymn to Aten" to Psalm 104 to Genesis 1; assuming Levenson is correct, any Egyptian influence upon P has been mediated through Psalm 104.

ample, Death, Desert, and Night or Darkness.[12] One consequence of this victory is that the divine sovereign was thought to be responsible for making an inhabitable world possible. In Babylon Marduk was made out to be the principal architect of creation, the controller of all destinies. Should this divine sovereign ever relax his authority, the forces of anticreation could win out and the world would fall into the realm of chaos.[13] In Assyria this same function was assigned to Ashur. At Ugarit Baal kept the powers of noncreation at bay in a precariously balanced world. Meanwhile, in Egypt similar powers were ascribed to Horus/Re. But whatever the country, in the ancient Near East creation—the displacement of absolute chaos with cosmic order—was usually understood to be a primary function of the divine sovereign. "Creator," accordingly, may be considered a submotif (subsidiary metaphor) of the divine sovereign motif (metaphor).

The King as Viceroy of the Divine Sovereign

Throughout the ancient Near East human kingship was viewed as complementary to divine sovereignty. The human king ruled on earth in the name of the gods, and more specifically, in the name of the divine sovereign. This was nowhere more evident than in Egypt, where the pharaoh was put forth in life as the embodiment or incarnation of Horus—later, Amun-Re—and in death as the embodiment of Osiris. Accordingly, the decrees of the king had the force of the divine will. Though less explicit elsewhere, similar conceptions prevailed throughout the ancient Near East. Here I shall confine consideration just to Mesopotamia and within Mesopotamia principally to Assyria during the Neo-Assyrian period, which provides perhaps the closest extant parallels to ancient Israel.

The Assyrian King as Viceroy of the Divine Sovereign
Discussion of the Assyrian king as viceroy of the divine sovereign may begin with consideration of the winged anthropomorphic figure that hovers within a

---

12. *Death*: for example, Mot in the Ugaritic myth of Baal and Anat. *Desert*: for example, in the second part of the Sumerian myth of Enki and Ninhursag, water (Enki) penetrates and makes fertile the arid land (Ninhursag). For the latest edition of this myth, see P. Attinger, "Enki et Ninhursaga," *ZA* 74 (1984) 1–52. For another translation, see T. Jacobsen, *The Harps That Once . . . : Sumerian Poetry in Translation* (New Haven: Yale University Press, 1987) 181–204. *Night or Darkness*: for example, in the Egyptian text known as "The Repulsing of the Dragon"; see S. Morenz, *Egyptian Religion* (Ithaca, N.Y.: Cornell University Press, 1973) 167–69.

13. See Batto, "The Sleeping God," esp. 163 and 169–72.

Fig. 1. Watercolor painting by W. Andrae of fragmentary glazed polychrome tile from Ashur.

fiery nimbus since, as will be demonstrated, that figure represents the divine power working through the king. Perhaps the best-known instance of the winged anthropomorphic figure is a fragmentary polychrome glazed tile from Ashur found in the Anu-Adad Temple (fig. 1), dating to the time of Tukulti-Ninurta II (890–884 B.C.E.).[14] This fragmentary polychrome tile was found in a garbage dump, probably discarded in ancient times because of its broken condition. It depicts a winged anthropomorphic figure within a nimbus, surrounded by heavy storm clouds[15] and holding a drawn bow. The figure hovers above the Assyrian army, only the heads of which are preserved in the fragmentary lower portion of the tile. The figure within the nimbus is depicted in human form from the waist upward. Faint markings indicate that it wears the horned cap symbolic of divinity. From the waist downward the figure termi-

---

14. BM 115706. See Walter Andrae, *Farbige Keramik aus Assur und ihre Vorstufen in altassyrischen Wandmalereien* (Berlin: Scarabaeus, 1923) 13, pl. 8; reproduced in *ANEP*, no. 536.

15. The clouds that surround the deity are more than "rain clouds," as suggested by the excavator; more likely the artist's intention was to portray storm clouds containing huge hailstones, a conventional component of a storm god's arsenal (Josh 10:11; Ps 18:13–14 [Heb.]; 78:47–48; 148:8; Isa 30:30; Job 38:22; cf. Isa 28:2; Hag 2:17).

nates in a broad feathery tail.
Likewise upon his back are large
feathered wings that extend well
beyond the circular nimbus. Together with fiery flames erupting outward from the nimbus,
the multicolored feathers of amber, blue, and white project an
atmosphere of awesome brilliance—the graphic equivalent
of *melammu*, that "awe-inspiring
radiance" surrounding deities
and kings, the sight of which can
cause enemies to capitulate and
throw down their weapons in
surrender.[16] The form of the
projectiles that the anthropomorphic figure shoots cannot be

*Fig. 2. Broken obelisk (drawing of central panel).
Drawing by the author.*

made out. Given the storm clouds, however, O. Keel is perhaps correct in pos-
iting that the projectiles that the figure shoots are lightning bolts, as in a relief
from the palace of Ashurnasirpal II (883–859 B.C.E.).[17]

In the past this winged anthropomorphic figure within the nimbus has often been mistakenly identified as Ashur, the national god of Assyria. I will return to the question of the identity of this figure below, after consideration of
additional examples.

The earliest instance of an anthropomorphized sun disk is the "broken obelisk" from tenth-century Nineveh (see fig. 2).[18] Herein four enemies hunker

---

16. On this concept, see A. Leo Oppenheim, "Akkadian pul(u)ḫ(t)u and melammū,"
JAOS 63 (1943) 31–34; Elena Cassin, *La splendeur divine: Introduction à l'étude de la mentalité
mésopotamienne* (Civilisations et sociétés 8; Paris: Mouton, 1968).

17. Othmar Keel, *The Symbolism of the Biblical World: Ancient Near Eastern Iconography and
the Book of Psalms* (New York: Seabury, 1978; repr. Winona Lake, Ind.: Eisenbrauns, 1997)
215, with drawing on p. 217, fig. 296, reproduced from B. Meissner, *Babylonien und Assy-
rien* (Heidelberg: Carl Winter, 1925) 2.40, fig. 10. Keel is followed by Martin Klingbeil,
*Yahweh Fighting from Heaven: God as Warrior and as God of Heaven in the Hebrew Psalter and
Ancient Near Eastern Iconography* (OBO 169; Fribourg, Switzerland: Éditions Universitaires /
Göttingen: Vandenhoeck & Ruprecht, 1999) 260–62.

18. BM 118898; from Kuyunjik. Photo in E. A. W. Budge and L. W. King, *Annals of
the Kings of Assyria* (London: British Museum Dept. of Egyptian and Assyrian Antiquities,
1902) 1.xi; *ANEP*, no. 440.

Fig. 3. Ashurnasirpal at War (scene no. 1). BM 124555 (Room B, slab 3a). Used by permission of the British Museum.

Fig. 4. Detail of the scene in fig. 3, showing anthropomorphic figure and king; drawing by the author.

submissively before an unidentified Assyrian king. In the left hand, the king displays his ring and mace (scepter), traditional symbols of divinely conferred sovereign authority. The king extends his open right hand as a symbol of magnanimous pardon and graciousness. At the top of the panel appear the symbols of the principal high gods, indicating divine approbation. In the midst of these heavenly symbols is an anthropomorphized sun disk. There is no human figure per se, but two hands project downward from the sun disk. The left hand holds a relaxed (i.e., undrawn) bow, the right hand is extended open, as if in blessing. The relaxed bow symbolizes a cessation of hostilities, as I will demonstrate below. The intention, therefore, seems to be to suggest that (cosmic) peace and weal has been achieved through the king's use of divinely conferred authority.

Fig. 5. Ashurnasirpal at war (scene no. 2). BM 124540 (NW Palace, [Throne] Room B, slab 11a). Used by permission of the British Museum.

A fully anthropomorphized sun disk does not appear in Assyria until the ninth century. Apart from seal impressions, the anthropomorphic winged figure occurs only on the wall reliefs and paintings in the palaces of three Neo-Assyrian kings, Tukulti-Ninurta II, Ashurnasirpal II, and Shalmaneser III.

The most instructive reliefs come from the northwest palace of Ashurnasirpal II at Nimrud (Kalhu). In two different reliefs depicting similar scenes (figs. 3, 4, 5), Ashurnasirpal attacks the fortified city of an enemy.[19] Appropriate to royal propaganda, the Assyrian king dominates the scene. Riding in his war chariot, he leads the charge with drawn bow. In both reliefs just over the head of Ashurnasirpal or slightly in front of him hovers the winged anthropomorphic figure in his nimbus, in form and posture almost identical to that of the figure on the polychrome tile discussed above. The horned cap of a divinity is clearly visible. A fiery radiance issuing forth from the nimbus is not drawn, however, though it most likely is implied. But this time one can see a detail that was lost in the broken portion of glazed tile. The Assyrian king's actions are replicated almost exactly in the actions of the winged anthropomorphic figure. It holds a drawn bow and shoots a three-pronged (lightning) bolt at the enemy, just as does the human monarch. One is reminded of the boasts by Assyrian kings such as Ashurnasirpal ("I thundered against them like

---

19. Figure 4 is my drawing, providing details of similarities between the anthropomorphic winged figure and the Assyrian king. For another interpretation of these scenes, see George Mendenhall, *The Tenth Generation* (Baltimore: Johns Hopkins University Press, 1973) 46–47.

Fig. 6. Ashurnasirpal returning from battle. BM 124551 (Room B, slab 5a). Used by permission of the British Museum.

Fig. 7. Anthropomorphic winged figure (detail from fig. 6). Used by permission of the British Museum.

the god Adad of the Devastation (and) rained down flames upon them. With might and main my combat troops flew against them like the Storm Bird")[20] or Shalmaneser III ("By the ferocious weapons which Ashur, my lord, has presented to me, I inflicted a defeat upon them . . . descending upon them like Adad when he makes a rainstorm pour down")[21] or Tiglath-pileser III

---

20. A.0.101, translation by A. Kirk Grayson, *Assyrian Rulers of the Early First Millenniun B.C.* (Royal Inscriptions of Mesopotamia, Assyrian Periods 2/1; Toronto: University of Toronto Press, 1991) 1.210. Similarly, in the "standard inscription" of Ashurnasirpal: "With the help of the gods Shamash and Adad, the gods my supporters, I thundered like the god Adad, the devastator, against the troops of the land of . . ." (ibid., 1.275; followed by John Malcolm Russell, *The Writing on the Wall: Studies in the Architectural Context of Late Assyrian Palace Inscriptions* [Mesopotamian Civilizations 9; Winona Lake, Ind.: Eisenbrauns, 1999] 25).

21. Trans. A. Leo Oppenheim, in *ANET* 277.

Fig. 8. Ashurnasirpal receiving official. BM 124549 (Room B, slab 7b). Used by permission of the British Museum.

Fig. 9. Detail from fig. 8. Used by permission of the British Museum.

("I pursued them, and in the very course of the march I swept over them like a downpour of the god Adad").[22]

Another relief (figs. 6, 7) depicts Ashurnasirpal returning victorious from battle, carrying a "relaxed" or undrawn bow at his side in a nonthreatening position. Here, too, the winged anthropomorphic figure in his horned cap is depicted accompanying the king, hovering over and a bit to the fore, as if leading the king home in triumph. Partially replicating the action of Ashurnasirpal, the winged anthropomorphic figure carries at his side in the left hand a relaxed bow, exactly as does the king. His open right hand is extended in blessing, however, whereas the king displays two arrows in his extended right hand, apparently symbolic of "purified" weapons that have received divine approval.[23]

22. Hayim Tadmor, *The Inscriptions of Tiglath-Pileser III King of Assyria* (Jerusalem: Israel Academy of Sciences and Humanities, 1994) 73.

23. On the symbolism of "purified" weapons, see Ursula Magen, *Assyrische Königsdarstellungen: Aspekte der Herrschaft* (Baghdader Forschungen 9; Mainz am Rhein: von Zabern, 1986) 81–91.

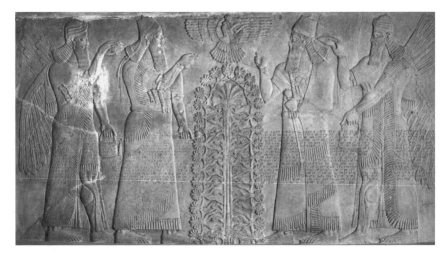

Fig. 10. Ashurnasirpal purifying sacred tree. BM 124531 (Room B, slab 23). Used by permission of the British Museum.

Fig. 11. Detail of fig. 10. Used by permission of the British Museum.

As in the battle reliefs, there is near identification between the king and the winged anthropomorphic figure, even though patently the former is still "human" while the latter is "divine."

Yet another relief (figs. 8, 9) depicts Ashurnasirpal receiving an official, perhaps a subdued enemy king, after the battle.[24] The king holds "purified" arrows in his right hand; in his left hand he holds his relaxed bow at his side. The winged anthropomorphic figure hovers above and slightly forward of the king. Although the hands of the figure are in the same position as those of the king, in this case neither hand of the winged anthropomorphic figure fully replicates the king's action. Rather, here the winged anthropomorphic figure indicates complete divine approbation of the king, since, facing in the same direction as the king (i.e.,

24. See also Samuel M. Paley, *King of the World: Ashur-nasir-pal II of Assyria 883–859 B.C.* (New York: Brooklyn Museum, 1976) 102, pl. 18a.

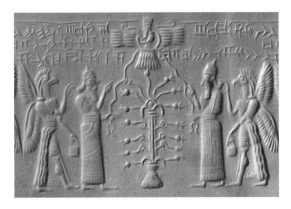

Fig. 12. Seal of Mushezib-Ninurta (BM 89135). Used by permission of the British Museum.

having a similar "outlook") it extends the open right hand in blessing and holds in the left hand the ring symbolizing divinely bestowed royal authority.

But the most important relief of all is one that served as the backdrop to the throne, thus dominating the throne room and setting its theme. As in the preceding cases, there is both identity and distance between the king and the winged anthropomorphic figure. It portrays Ashurnasirpal before a "sacred tree" (figs. 10, 11).[25] The king, flanked by a winged genius (*apkallu*) that sprinkles him with a purifying cone, is depicted on both sides of a sacred tree (i.e., he ritually circles it) in a gesture of reverence. The king's pointer finger of his right hand is extended in the traditional position of humble supplication (*ubānu tarāṣu*).[26] Above the tree hovers the winged anthropomorphic figure within its characteristic nimbus—this time with erupting flames clearly drawn—and wearing its horned cap to emphasize its divinity. It again holds in the left hand the ring while extending the right hand outward in a gesture of blessing, indicating divine approbation of the king's actions. This scene is replicated in a Neo-Assyrian cylinder seal (fig. 12), except that in this case water flows forth in a double stream from the winged nimbus to either side of the

---

25. Commenting on this relief, J. M. Russell (*The Writing on the Wall*, 12–13) observes that "the images of the king and a winged deity are shown twice, symmetrically flanking a stylized palm tree (called the 'sacred tree' in modern literature). Variations of this motif, which must represent the role of the king in assuring the prosperity of Assyria, are repeated in the palace decoration of later kings. In the corners of the throne room and beside doorways are more images of sacred trees and winged deities." A nearly identical scene, preserved in fragmentary condition, is found on slab 13, also in Room B. Moreover, in some rooms in the Northwest Palace the "sacred tree," often attended by *apkallus*, is itself the dominant theme of the wall reliefs, contributing to the ornamentation of what has been called a "rhetoric of abundance" in Assyrian royal propaganda; see Irene J. Winter, "Ornament and the 'Rhetoric of Abundance' in Assyria," *ErIsr* 27 (Hayim and Miriam Tadmor Volume; 2003) 252*–64*.

26. See Magen, *Assyrische Königsdarstellungen*, 45–55.

sacred tree.[27] This flowing stream is a frequent motif in Neo-Assyrian cylinder seals. The meaning is the same in both cases: the abundance and well-being that the king has effected throughout the kingdom, which in Assyrian royal rhetoric includes the whole world. Taken as a whole, Ashurnasirpal's "acts," especially his removal of every threat to the realm has resulted in (re)establishing peace and cosmic order in an otherwise chaotic world. The resultant blessings flow not only to the Assyrian homeland but also to the whole world.[28]

This motif had a long life and appeared in many forms. Naturally one is reminded of the Yahwistic primeval myth in which a stream arising in Eden issues forth into a fourfold river that encircles all the lands (Gen 2:10–14). But nearly a thousand years prior to Ashurnasirpal II, in the Old Babylonian kingdom of Mari, Zimri-Lim's artists decorated his palace walls with a (partially preserved) depiction of idyllic harmony and abundance, at the center of which is a two-paneled fresco (fig. 13).[29] In the upper panel the goddess Ishtar invests the king with his symbols of authority. In the lower panel to either side stands a goddess with a vase from which flows a fourfold stream. It is doubtful that two goddesses and two streams are intended. Rather, through the symmetry of a flowing vase on either side with their respective streams conjoined at the center of the panel, the intent is to suggest a mythical four-branched stream encircling the whole of the inhabitable land to water it, exactly as in Genesis 2. This interpretation seems to be confirmed by the single statue of a woman (goddess) found in the adjoining courtyard; the woman holds a vase from which water apparently flowed, to judge from the bored hole that runs from the base of the statue through the center of the statue and opens into the vase (fig. 14).[30] Etched on the torso of this statue are a series of wavey lines suggesting flowing water, through which fish swim upward toward the source vase, similar to the depiction in the lower panel of the fresco. The point is that

---

27. See Dominique Collon, *First Impressions: Cylinder Seals in the Ancient Near East* (London: British Museum Publications, 1987) 76–77, pl. 341.

28. For additional discussion of the winged nimbus in conjunction with the sacred tree, see Klingbeil, *Yahweh Fighting from Heaven*, 211–16.

29. Mari, third campaign, 1935–1936; see A. Parrot, *Syria* 18 (1937) 335–46, pl. 39, fig. 8 (drawing of central panels, after a copy by J. Lauffray), from which fig. 13 here is reproduced with permission of the Institut Français d'archéologie du Proche-Orient; see also Marie-Thérèse Barrelet, "Une peinture de la cour 106 du palais de Mari," in *Studia Mariana* (ed. A. Parrot; Leiden: Brill, 1950) 16, fig. 4; *ANEP*, no. 610.

30. Drawing from Barrelet, "Une peinture de la cour 106 du palais de Mari," 32, fig. 12c, after *Syria* 18, pl. 12. For photos, see E. Strommenger, *Fünf Jahrtausende Mesopotamien* (Munich: Hirmer, 1962) pls. 162–63; André Parrot, *Nineveh and Babylon* (trans. S. Gilbert and J. Emmons; London: Thames & Hudson, 1961) 74–75, pls. 82, 83.]; or *ANEP*, no. 516 (partial view only).

Fig. 13. Central panels from the Throne Room of the palace at Mari.

kingship itself implies peace, security, and fruitfulness in the earth, and this weal stems ultimately from the sovereignty of the deity, effected through the earthly king as viceroy.

The identity of the anthropomorphic figure within the nimbus has been the subject of considerable discussion. Among the proposals are (1) a specific deity—namely, Ashur, the national deity of Assyria, the sun god Shamash or his

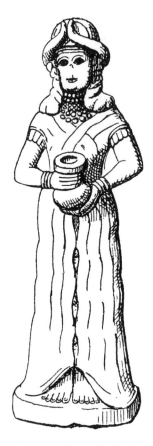

Fig. 14. Goddess with flowing vase. Aleppo National Museum no. 1659. Mari palace. Drawing by M. Barrelet; used with permission.

vizier Bunene, Ṣalmu, or Ninurta; (2) a representation of the awe-inspiring brilliance of Ashur; and (3) an iconographic depiction of the sunlike *alter ego* of the Assyrian king.[31] Ruth Mayer-Opificius has demonstrated that this winged anthropomorphic figure is interchangeable with the more ancient and more common winged sun disk and that the roots of this artistic convention go back to older Egyptian depictions of the solar deity. Although the sun disk originally was the symbol of the sun god, with time the sun disk acquired additional meanings. Because of an increasing "cosmic competence" attributed to the solar deity, the sun disk came to symbolize universal divine power and as such could be used to signify the beneficent presence of the highest deity. In the process the winged sun disk came to be used in three ways: (1) as a simple representation of the heavens, (2) as a symbolic representation of the relationship between the solar god in the heavens and the fruitfulness of the earth, and (3) to suggest a constellation of *sun god–king–sacred tree* involving religious implications for the office of kingship.[32]

Thomas Podella has taken this insight even further to demonstrate that the winged anthropomorphic figure within the nimbus is a specific adaptation of this solar imagery by Assyrian kings of the ninth century B.C.E. Podella has made a careful study of this figure in the northwest palace of Ashurnasirpal II at Nimrud, where the wall reliefs are relatively well preserved, thereby allowing the Assyrian adaptation of this motif to be studied in context. The anthropomorphic winged figure occurs in scenes depicting major

31. For a discussion of the identity, see Thomas Podella, *Das Lichtkleid JHWHs: Untersuchungen zur Gestalthaftigkeit Gottes im Alten Testament und seiner altorientalishchen Umwelt* (FAT 15; Tübingen: Mohr [Siebeck], 1996) 26–31, 132–54. See further Ruth Mayer-Opificius, "Die geflügelte Sonne: Himmels- und Regendarstellungen im alten Vorderasien," *UF* 16 [1984] 189–236; P. Calmeyer, "Fortuna-Tyche-Khvarnah," *JdI* 94 (1979) 358 with n. 26; S. Dalley, "The God Ṣalmu and the Winged Disk," *Iraq* 48 (1986) 85–101.

32. T. Podella, *Das Lichtkleid JHWHs*, 147.

phases in the life of the king. The anthropomorphic winged figure replicates exactly the actions of the Assyrian king in the attack of a city (figs. 3–5) and at the conclusion of a successful military campaign and return from battle (figs. 6–9). The figure also appears in a cultic context hovering over the sacred tree (figs. 10–11). The figure does not appear in less significant scenes such as in the hunting of wild animals or at the crossing of a river. From such discriminate employment by the Assyrian artists, Podella concludes that the anthropomorphic winged figure in the nimbus represents a symbiotic and thoroughgoing equivalence between the king and the highest deity. This anthropomorphic winged disk is thus an expression of the power of the king as the nexus between heaven and earth wherein peace, security, and the weal of the kingdom are accomplished.[33]

The anthropomorphic winged figure in the nimbus thus represents the power of the Assyrian king to mediate heavenly realities to his earthly realm, that is, to make the divine order present on earth. Analogous to the physical sun's rays bringing beneficence daily to the whole earth, the king as a kind of double of the solarized (or highest) deity was believed to be responsible for ensuring the weal of the kingdom. The king was said to be the "image" of the divine sovereign.[34] One may recall also the epithet of the king, *šamšu ša nišēšu /*

---

33. Ibid., 134–40. Podella follows the reconstructed order of the panels in the throne room in Janusz Meuszyński, *Die Rekonstruktion der Reliefdarstellungen und ihrer Anordnung im Nordwestpalast von Kalḫu (Nimrūd)* (Baghdader Forschungen 2; Mainz am Rhein: von Zabern, 1981). Caution should be exercised, however, not to assume that this new symbolism of the winged anthropomorphic figure was adopted in a univocal manner by all artists, even within Assyria. A Neo-Assyrian seal from the time of Sargon II (Seal ANE 130865 in the British Museum) seemingly employs the winged anthropomorphic figure as a novel equivalent of the (older and more universal) winged sun disk. In this instance the winged anthropomorphic figure is supported by a humanoid genius flanked by two bull-men in a manner equivalent to the way the winged sun disk (symbolizing the solar deity) is supported outside of Assyria by bull-men and a humanlike genius or by a single genius; see the discussion below (esp. n. 73, with figs. 15–17). It is significant that, although the provenance of Seal ANE 130865 is Nimrud, its maker was apparently a transplanted Babylonian seal cutter; so Dominique Callon, "Seals of Merodach-Baladan," in *ErIsr* 27 (Hayim and Miriam Tadmor Volume; 2003) 10*–17*, esp. 16*, fig. 7.

34. In the Tukulti-Ninurta Epic it is said of Tukulti-Ninurta I that this heroic king was formed in the divine womb (I A 17′); he was "the eternal image of Enlil (*ṣalam* ᵈE), attentive to the voice of the people, to the counsel of the land" (I A 18′); translation by P. Machinist, *The Epic of Tukulti-Ninurta I: A Study in Middle Assyrian Literature* (Ph.D. diss., Yale University, 1978) 67–69; followed by Benjamin R. Foster, *Before the Muses: An Anthology of Akkadian Literature* (2 vols.; Bethesda, Md.: CDL, 1993) 1.213. The epic goes on to say (I A 19′–20′) that Enlil had exalted Tukulti-Ninurta as if he were Enlil's own son, second only to Enlil's firstborn son (i.e., the god Ninurta; so Machinist, pp. 206–7). See also Podella, *Das*

šamšu kiššat nišē "sun of his people / sun of all the people."[35] It is no wonder that the "standard inscription" engraved repeatedly on the walls of Ashurnasirpal's palace and on the base of his throne proclaims him to be the "viceregent of Ashur" and "king of the universe."[36]

During the Neo-Assyrian period, when Assyrian hegemony extended across the whole of the eastern Mediterranean, use of the anthropomorphic winged figure spread to the Levant, where it manifestly also influenced both popular religion and the royal cults of the kingdoms of Judah and Israel. Perhaps through this channel P also was influenced by the motif, albeit in an indirect fashion.

Summary

Conceptions of divine sovereignty varied in the ancient Near East from society to society and from period to period, and to a great extent mirrored developments in the political realm. In earlier periods, divine power was thought to be distributed between several gods. But with the advent of Babylonian hegemony over Mesopotamia and even over the whole of the ancient Near East at times during the second and first millenniums B.C.E., new theological conceptions evolved, according to which one deity, namely the patron god of Babylon, came to be regarded as the sole, absolute ruler of heaven and earth. Meanwhile, Assyrian propagandists similarly promoted the god Ashur as the divine sovereign, particularly in the first millennium B.C.E. during the period of Neo-Assyrian hegemony. To judge from the Babylonian myth Enuma Elish, one of the principal functions of the divine sovereign was to bring order into the midst of chaos, to establish conditions under which meaningful existence was not only possible but even guaranteed both for gods and for humans—or in equivalent Priestly terminology, to "create the heavens and the earth." Creation was a function of divine sovereignty. To be the divine sovereign is also to be the creator. The divine sovereign does not rule the world directly, however. Instead, he normally governs the human realm through

Lichtkleid JHWHs, 255. The idea that the king was the son of the (chief) deity was not limited to Mesopotamia; such a conception figured even more prominently in Egyptian royal propaganda; see W. H. Schmidt (*Die Schöpfungsgeschichte der Priesterschrift* [WMANT 17; Neukirchen-Vluyn: Neukirchener Verlag, 1964] 127–48) and H. Wildberger ("Das Abbild Gottes, Gen 1:26–30," *TZ* [1965] 245–59, 481–501), cited by Claus Westermann, *Genesis 1–11: A Commentary* (trans. John J. Scullion; Minneapolis: Augsburg, 1984), 152–53.

35. *CAD* Š/1 337, s.v. *šamšu* 1.e.b′.

36. Russell, *The Writing on the Wall*, 24. Russell (pp. 41–47) notes that despite much writing throughout Ashurnasirpal's palace there was only one basic inscription, repeated over and over with small variations. Note, too, that one of the gates in Ashurbanipal's palace was named "Long live the viceroy of Ashur" (p. 160).

divinely established kingship. The human king was the "image" of the divine sovereign, his viceroy on earth, charged with perfecting the divine sovereign's work of creation by promoting right order, justice, and the human weal.

Yahweh's Kingship in the Hebrew Bible

The Vocabulary of Yahweh's Kingship

In the Hebrew Bible the concept of divine sovereignty is usually referenced under the rubric the "kingship" of God/Yahweh, from the frequent appellation of Yahweh using the vocable *melek* "king" and from the related phrase in the Psalter *yhwh mālak*, variously rendered with a durative meaning, that is, "Yahweh is king," or with an ingressive meaning, that is, "Yahweh has become king." Reference to the absolute and universal rule of Yahweh is sometimes also made without use of the root מלך, for example, in expressions such as "God of heaven" and "enthroned on the cherubim," or even in conceits such as the divine council and the judge of the other gods.[37] The term "king" need not imply universal rule, however. Ancient Near Eastern peoples, including biblical authors, often conceived of a national deity's authority as confined to the territorial boundaries of that nation (e.g., Deut 8:32; Judg 11:24; 1 Sam 26:19; 2 Kgs 5:17; 18:33; Mic 4:5). Accordingly, when Yahweh/God is given the appellation "king of Israel" (Isa 44:6; Zeph 3:15), "king of Jacob" (Isa 41:21), or "your king" (1 Sam 12:12; Isa 43:15), there is not necessarily any implication of Yahweh's being the divine sovereign. When Yahweh overcomes and judges the gods of other nations, the assumption is that these gods are powerful rulers in their own national territories who may even be willing to concede to Yahweh the right to govern his own people but not sovereignty over the other gods (e.g., Exod 12:12; Num 33:4; Jer 49:1–3; Isa 24:21).[38] Because of these possible limitations on the terms "king" and "kingship," the terms "divine sovereign" and "divine sovereignty" are to be preferred to express P's conception of Yahweh's absolute rule over heaven and earth.

The kingship of God/Yahweh in the Hebrew Bible has been the subject of numerous studies.[39] Particularly controversial has been Mowinckel's hypothesis concerning the cultic actualization of Yahweh's kingship during an annual Israelite enthronement festival, analogous to the ritual enactment of the kingship

---

37. Simon B. Parker, "The Beginning of the Reign of God: Psalm 82 as Myth and Liturgy," *RB* 102 (1995) 532–59.

38. Ibid., 548–52.

39. See the recent surveys by Keith W. Whitelam, "King and Kingship," *ABD* 4.40–48; Henri Cazelles, "Sacred Kingship," *ABD* 5.863–66.

of Marduk during the Babylonian New Year *akitu* ritual.[40] Some have tried to illuminate Israel's conception of Yahweh's kingship by comparing how the kingship of various national gods was conceived of in other ancient Near Eastern societies.[41] Still others have tried to illuminate what "God is king" meant by examining this metaphor in terms of human kingship within ancient Israel. T. N. D. Mettinger has posited that the root metaphor for God in the official cult of Judah was *basileomorphic,* combining characteristics of Canaanite El and Baal.[42] M. Z. Brettler finds the metaphor "God is king" to be the predominant relational metaphor for God in the Hebrew Bible, with which were associated a number of subsidiary metaphors such as "shepherd," "master," and "judge" that helped to flesh out what this basic metaphor meant according to the ancient Israelite way of thinking.[43] For the purpose of this essay such issues need not be decided, because my concern is less with Israel's precise conception of Yahweh's kingship than with the principle of Yahweh's universal kingship within P's theology.

There are many expressions of Yahweh's divine sovereignty in the Hebrew Bible. Constructs using מלך as the nomen rectum include מלך הגוים "king of the nations" (Jer 10:7), מלך עולם "everlasting king" (Jer 10:10; Ps 10:16), מלך כל־הארץ "king of the whole earth" (Ps 47:8; cf. Zech 14:9), and מלך שמיא "king of heaven" (Dan 4:34).[44] Ps 95:3 asserts that אל גדול יהוה ומלך גדול "Yahweh is a great god, a great king[45] over all the gods."[46] על־כל־אלהים

---

40. Sigmund Mowinckel, *Psalmstudien II: Das Thronbesteigungsfest Jahwës und der Ursprung der Eschatologie* (Amsterdam: Schippers, 1961); *The Psalms in Israel's Worship* (trans. D. R. Ap-Thomas; 2 vols.; Nashville: Abingdon, 1961–79).

41. Werner Schmidt, *Königtum Gottes in Ugarit and Israel* (BZAW 80; Berlin: Alfred Töpelmann, 1961); Gary V. Smith, "The Concept of God/the Gods as King in the Ancient Near East and the Bible," *TJ* 3 (1983) 18–38.

42. In contrast to the Northern Kingdom of Israel, where covenant served as the root metaphor; see T. N. D. Mettinger, "The Study of the Gottesbild: Problems and Suggestions," *SEÅ* 54 (1989) 133–45; Martin Klingbeil, *Yahweh Fighting from Heaven,* 26.

43. Marc Zvi Brettler, *God Is King: Understanding an Israelite Metaphor* (JSOTSup 76; Sheffield: Sheffield Academic Press, 1989) 160. By contrast, M. Klingbeil (*Yahweh Fighting from Heaven*) argues that the root metaphor for God in ancient Israel was not king but warrior.

44. The phrase "King of heaven" continued in popularity into the Apocrypha (1 Esd 4:46, 58; Tob 13:7, 11); note also the occurrence of the phrase "the kingdom of heaven" in the Gospel of Matthew rather than "the kingdom of God" found in the other New Testament gospels.

45. Kings of powerful ancient Near Eastern countries, especially those who subjugated lesser nations and made vassals of their kings, were referred to as "great kings" (using either the adjective גדול [Jer 25:14; 27:7; Ps 136:17; Eccl 9:14] or the adjective רב [Jer 50:41; Dan 2:10; cf. Hos 5:13; 10:6]). Because in Hebrew רב is normally used quantitatively (in

Surprisingly, the term "king of kings," while used of human overlords (Ezek 26:7; Ezra 7:12; Dan 2:37), is never applied to God in the Hebrew Bible.[47]

Yahweh's divine sovereignty is at times also expressed through the epithet אלהי השמים 'the God of heaven' (Gen 24:3, 7; Jonah 1:19; Ezra 1:2; Neh 1:4, 5; 2:4, 20; 2 Chr 36:23).[48] "God of heaven" is a shorthand for the ruler of all that is, both in heaven and on earth, as witnessed by the interchangeability of "God of heaven" with "God of heaven and (God of) earth" (cf. Gen 24:3 and 24:7; Ezra 5:11 and 5:12) and by the frequent declarations that the God of heaven directs the affairs of all the nations throughout the earth (e.g., Josh 2:11; 2 Chr 36:23; Ezra 1:2). The implication is that there is only one such deity (Deut 4:39) and that this incomparable majestic deity controls everything, both in heaven and on earth.[49]

Yahweh as the Divine Sovereign in the Hebrew Bible

Biblical authors were right at home in the mythic world of the divine sovereign. They also readily linked their belief in Yahweh's universal rule to the

---

the sense of "many") rather than qualitatively (i.e., "great), it is likely that the phrase *melek rab* is a calque of the Akkadian *šarru rabû* "great king," mediated through a Northwest Semitic language (see M. Brettler, *God is King*, 30–31). In 2 Kgs 18:19, 28 = Isa 36:4, 13, Rabshakeh, in the name of his master, "the great king (מלך גדול)", the king of Assyria," boasts of the invincibility of the Assyrian army. It was almost inevitable that Israel's theologians should ascribe the epithet "great king" to Yahweh, whether using the adjective גדול (Mal 1:14) or the adjective רב (Ps 48:3).

46. The phrase "King of the gods" is also found in Add Esth 14:72.

47. But see in the New Testament: "the Lamb will conquer them, for he is the Lord of lords and the King of kings" (Rev 17:16).

48. Variants include Heb. אל השמים Ps 136:26; Aram. אלה שמיא Ezra 5:11, 12; 6:9, 10; 7:12, 21, 23 or, alternatively, האלהים בשמים 'the God in heaven' (Deut 4:39; Ps 115:3; Eccl 5:1; 2 Chr 20:6; cf. Josh 2:11; 1 Kgs 8:23; Ps 115:3; 2 Chr 6:14).

49. Rahab, the Canaanite prostitute, reflecting on how Yahweh had already defeated Egypt and the two Transjordanian kingdoms of Sihon and Og, spoke not only for herself but all "the nations" in acknowledging how useless it was to resist the Israelites because "Yahweh your God is indeed God in heaven above and on earth below" (Josh 2:11). By putting this statement of faith in the mouth of an outsider, the Deuteronomist emphasizes the universality of Yahweh's rule. Other biblical theologians employ this same literary conceit of having outsiders acknowledge Yahweh as the God who controls both heaven and earth and as the one who empowers them: Cyrus (2 Chr 36:23; Ezra 1:2), Artaxerxes (Ezra 7:21 + 23); Nebuchadnezzar (Dan 2:18 + 47; cf. 4:1–3, 34–37 [note "King of heaven" as Yahweh's title in v. 37]). Patently, the God of heaven is the divine sovereign. The phrase "God of heaven" retained its currency throughout the intertestamental period and into the New Testament; e.g., Tob 10:11; Jdt 5:8; 6:19; 11:17; 3 Macc 6:28; 7:6; Rev 11:13; 16:11. See also C. J. Labuschagne, *The Incomparability of Yahweh in the Old Testament* (Leiden: Brill, 1966).

myth of the divine sovereign's having slain the chaos dragon in primeval time and to the defeat of national enemies in their own day. Psalm 74, for example, links Yahweh's kingship to his having slain the many-headed chaos dragon in primeval time. This psalm was clearly composed in the shadow of the destruction of the temple by the Babylonians. This exilic psalmist's anguished cry, "How long, O God is the foe to scoff?" is an appeal to Yahweh to defend his honor as divine sovereign by vanquishing the present Babylonian foe as he defeated its counterpart Leviathan in primeval days. The psalmist then abruptly turns to recounting God's acts of creation:

> Yours is the day, yours also the night;
> you established the luminaries and the sun.
> You have fixed all the bounds of the earth;
> you made summer and winter. (Ps 74:16–17, NRSV)

The linking of Yahweh's kingship here with creation motifs (vv. 15–17) is particularly noteworthy since creation per se does little to advance the psalmist's case; their presence seems to derive solely from the fact that creation is part and parcel of the divine sovereign metaphor. The defeat of chaos and the establishment of order is an acknowledged function of the divine sovereign.

A similar condition prevails in other Psalms. In Psalm 93 the theme of Yahweh's kingship (v. 1) is linked with the establishment of an orderly world (v. 1) and the subjugation of the chaotic Sea (vv. 3–4). In Psalm 89 Yahweh's kingship is not explicitly mentioned, but it is implied in the statement that Yahweh is incomparable within the divine council (vv. 6–9), "great and awesome above all that surround him" (v. 8). First to be mentioned among his mighty deeds are the conjoined themes of the defeat of chaotic Sea (vv. 10–11) and the "founding" of "the world and all that is in it" (vv. 12–13). Indeed, in the 16 psalms in which reference to Yahweh's kingship is either explicit or implicit,[50] creation themes are found in 8, or exactly one-half. Such a high degree of consistency, when compared with other themes, argues well for my thesis that the creator metaphor is but a subsidiary aspect of the divine sovereign metaphor.

A similar situation prevails also in Second Isaiah. This anonymous exilic prophet appealed to the cosmogonic myth of the divine sovereign to give hope to the discouraged Jewish exiles. Yahweh is "the Creator of Israel, your

---

50. Explicit: 5:3; 10:16; 44:5; 47:3, 7, 8, 9; 74:12; 84:4; 93:1; 96:10; 97:1; 98:6; 99:1; 146:1; 149:2; as listed by Klingbeil, *Yahweh Fighting from Heaven*, 31, and correcting the typographical error from 145:1 to 146:1. Implicit: "great," "our Lord (above) all gods," 135:5; "God of gods" and "Lord of lords," 136:2, 3; "alone . . . exalted," "above earth and heaven," 148:13.

King" (Isa 43:15; cf. 43:1). Israel can have confidence in Yahweh because as divine sovereign he defeated chaotic Sea in primeval time (Isa 44:27; 50:2 51:9–10) and is "the Creator of the ends of the earth" (Isa 40:28) and "of the heavens" (42:5; cf. 45:18). It is he who placed humankind upon the earth (45:12). He is the creator of absolutely everything, even light and darkness, weal and woe (45:7). Only Yahweh has such power; he has no rival among the gods, who in the final analysis are nothing more than worthless idols (Isa 41:21–24; 44:6–20). Yahweh confers human kingship upon whom he wills, even the mighty Persian Cyrus, in order to further Yahweh's purpose (Isa 41:25–26; 44:28). Thus, Yahweh is not just Israel's king (41:21; 43:15; 44:6; cf. 51:22), but also the very divine sovereign (52:7). Even now the divine sovereign is preparing a new creation and a new exodus (e.g., Isa 41:17–20; 43:16–21; 52:11–12; et passim) in which he will reestablish control over the forces of chaos and recreate Israel as his special people. It is Yahweh's power to create at will, then, which proves that he is the divine sovereign, the absolute ruler of all.[51]

Jeremiah 10 similarly links Yahweh's sovereignty with his role as creator. In a scathing attack on the gods of the nations as powerless idols, Jeremiah proclaims Yahweh's incomparability among the gods as "the king of the nations" (10:7) and as "the living God and the everlasting King" (10:10) precisely in his role as the creator. In contrast to the gods "who did not make the heavens and the earth," Yahweh is "he who made the earth by his power, who established the world by his wisdom" (10:12). "None of these is like Yahweh . . . the one who formed all things" (10:16). For Jeremiah, too, Yahweh's sovereignty is self-evident from the fact that he is creator of heaven and earth.

Additional evidence could be adduced.[52] But even from the limited data presented here it is clear that in the Hebrew Bible, as in ancient Near East generally, creation and divine sovereignty are frequently linked, with the metaphor of the creator being an aspect of the divine sovereign metaphor.

The Image of the Deity in the Priestly Creation Story

As already observed, within the primeval story the Priestly Writer provides no description whatever of God (אלהים) or his characteristics. Nevertheless,

---

51. I explored these themes at length in "The Motif of Exodus in Deutero-Isaiah," (paper presented at the Fifty-Seventh General Meeting of The Catholic Biblical Association of America, University of San Diego, San Diego, Calif., August 13–16, 1994, in the Task Force "Theology of the Hebrew Bible/Old Testament").

52. See, among other texts, Gen 14:19; Deut 10:14; 2 Kgs 19:15; Jonah 1:9; 1 Chr 29:11; 2 Chr 2:11.

the Priestly Writer's conception of God may be gleaned indirectly from various clues in the passages traditionally attributed to P. In one way or another they all support the portrait of God as the divine sovereign.

God as the Divine Sovereign

One of the contributions of a comparative literary approach to the Bible is the recognition that, contrary to traditional renderings, Gen 1:1 is a temporal clause grammatically connected with v. 2, rather than being an independent sentence that summarizes the work of creation to be presented in greater detail in following verses.[53] Together, these first two verses lay out the state of things when the creator began to create.

> In the beginning when God created the heavens and the earth, the earth was a formless void and darkness covered the face of the deep, while a wind from God swept over the face of the waters. (Gen 1:1–2, NRSV)

The Priestly Writer thus follows a typical pattern of ancient Near Eastern cosmologies such as Atrahasis and Enuma Elish, both of which begin with a temporal clause describing conditions prior to the events that led the divine sovereign (Enlil in Atrahasis and Marduk in Enuma Elish) to inaugurate the whole chain of activities that established the cosmos as it is now constituted. Ever since Gunkel proposed the theory that a common "Combat Myth" (*Chaoskampf*) underlies both Enuma Elish and Genesis 1,[54] scholars have debated whether or not the Priestly creation story is dependent upon the Mesopotamian myth. Heidel's further outline of structural similarities in Enuma Elish and Gen 1:1–2:4a was particularly influential in convincing a whole generation of biblical scholars that the biblical account was in part dependent upon the Babylonian myth.[55] More recently the pendulum has swung in the opposite direction, however, with claims that P is devoid of such mythic conceptions, or at minimum that P deliberately rejected them.[56] The reality seems to lie somewhere in between these two poles: like other biblical theo-

---

53. For a concise discussion of the controversy surrounding the interpretation of this verse, see Gordon J. Wenham, *Genesis 1–15* (WBC 1; Waco, Tex.: Word, 1987) 11–14.

54. Hermann Gunkel, *Schöpfung und Chaos in Urzeit und Endzeit: Eine religionsgeschichtliche Untersuchung über Gen 1 und Ap Joh 12* (Göttingen: Vandenhoeck & Ruprecht, 1895).

55. Alexander Heidel, *The Babylonian Genesis* (2nd ed.; Chicago: University of Chicago Press, 1951) 82–140, with diagram on p. 129, followed by, among others, E. A. Speiser, *Genesis* (AB 1; New York: Doubleday, 1969) 10.

56. E.g., W. Lambert, "A New Look at the Babylonian Background of Genesis," *JTS* 16 (1965) 287–300; Wenham, *Genesis 1–15*, 8–9. Westermann (*Genesis 1–11*, 132 et passim) takes a middle approach, suggesting that P manifests both "originality" and "its place in the stream of tradition" within the ancient Near East.

logians and poets, P's world view was grounded in the cultural idiom of a common Semitic Combat Myth,[57] even as he manifestly struggled to find his own distinctively "Yahwistic" voice—part of which involved muting as much as possible competing theological ideas from both within and without Israel, especially any suggestion that Yahweh's absolute control over heaven and earth was compromised by the existence of other deities wielding even limited power over specialized domains.

It is important to recognize that the Priestly creation account does not stand alone as an isolated pericope but is part and parcel of the larger Priestly primeval narrative (Genesis 1–9) that concludes with God establishing a covenant with all flesh, following the cosmic Flood. Failure to recognize the integrity of this narrative unit is one of the principal reasons why a number of scholars have been mislead into denying too facilely the presence of Combat Myth motifs in the Priestly creation account. Combat Myth motifs are readily evident in, among others, the breaking out of the Great Deep from its divinely imposed bounds (1:6–10; cf. Job 38:8–10; Ps 104:6–9) during the cosmic flood (7:11), and the deity's subsequent (re)mastery over the chaotic waters by means of his storm wind (8:2; cf. 1:2), and the deity's retirement of his war bow (9:13–17). Whether there is any direct dependency running from Enuma Elish to P is unclear, but there seems to be at least indirect influence because the structure and motifs in the Priestly primeval story are closer to Enuma Elish than to any other extant form of the Combat Myth.

True, P lacks an actual battle against a chaos dragon. Nevertheless, similarities between Genesis 1 and Psalm 8, where the vestigial battle motif is even more obvious,[58] as well as P's conscious efforts to mute Combat Myth themes

---

57. Jon D. Levenson (*Creation and the Persistence of Evil*) does a masterful job of showing the pervasiveness of the Combat Myth throughout the whole of the Hebrew Bible, although in my opinion he attempts to demythologize too much P's use of Combat Myth themes. The idea of a Combat Myth as an explanation of the cosmos—itself seen as delicately balanced between existence and nonexistence, between creation and noncreation, between order and chaos—was widely diffused in the Ancient Near East, forming part of a common cultural world view. To postulate that P—or any biblical writer, for that matter—could have been ignorant of such conceptions flies in the face of everything we know about the ancient Near East. The Combat Myth was as pervasive of ancient Near Eastern world views as are "Darwinian" theories of evolution at the beginning of the twenty-first century, even if individuals reject these as an authentic explanations of "the origin of the human species." See my aforementioned forthcoming essay, "The Ancient Near Eastern Background for Hebrew Conceptions of Creation."

58. Note especially, "You built a fortress for your habitation, having silenced your adversaries, the foe and the avenger" (Ps 8:2); see M. Dahood, *Psalms I* (AB 16; Garden City, N.Y.: Doubleday, 1965) 45–51.

by depicting a divided (i.e., ordered) תהום "Great Deep" and the tamed התנינים הגדלים "great sea dragons" (compare the taming of Leviathan in Job 41 and of Egypt in Ezek 29:3–4), confirm that the Combat Myth was never far from the mind of the Priestly Writer as he rewrote his primeval story; neither was the metaphor of God as the divine sovereign, one of the foundational themes of the Combat Myth.

This explains the presence of the bow motif in Gen 9:10–17. In Enuma Elish, when Marduk "hangs up" his bow after defeating the last of his enemies, the symbolism is clear. Since every foe, including Tiamat, has been vanquished, Marduk no longer has need of weapons, so he is able to place his powerful bow in the heavens as the "bow star"—perhaps to be identified as the constellation Sirius—where it will forever shine as a symbol of Marduk's everlasting sovereignty. In the Priestly account the Great Deep has not yet been fully subdued by the end of chap. 1, even though God "rests," in keeping with the traditional divine sovereignty motif. In the Priestly telling, the flood is a resurgence of the Great Deep. Like the seven-headed chaos monster that it symbolizes, the Great Deep breaks out of its prison to challenge once more the divine sovereign's creative will (compare Gen 1:2, 6, 9 with 7:11 and 8:2). At the conclusion of the flood the Great Deep has been fully mastered, however, and the divine sovereign can permanently retire his bow by setting it in the sky where it can be seen as the nonthreatening rainbow—a symbol of cosmic blessings that come with this "covenant of peace" newly established with "all flesh."[59] With this act God demonstrates that he is firmly in control as the divine sovereign, similar to the actions of Marduk in Enuma Elish.

One may now also suggest additional symbolism for the Assyrian scenes mentioned previously. There the king, the earthly counterpart of the heavenly high god, has put aside his war bow used to subdue the enemy (figs. 3–5) and carries it in a "relaxed" condition as a symbol of triumph following the battle (figs. 6, 7). But in the cultic scene before the sacred tree suggestive of the universal weal that pervades in the kingdom after the enemy has been vanquished (figs. 10, 11), there is no need of such a bellicose symbol as the war bow. In "the covenant of peace" tradition that I have written about elsewhere, the divine sovereign, after an initial period of enmity with unruly humankind, ultimately lays aside his war equipment and establishes cosmic peace in the earth and with humankind. Examples of this "covenant of peace" tradition can be adduced from Mesopotamian, Canaanite, and Egyptian mythic texts.[60] It is just

---

59. Bernard F. Batto, "The Covenant of Peace: A Neglected Ancient Near Eastern Motif," *CBQ* 49 (1987) 187–211.
60. Ibid.

to such a tradition of cosmic peace that Assyrian royal propagandists apparently were appealing in portraying the Assyrian king and his divine alter ego before the sacred tree. As the agent of the divine sovereign, the Assyrian king establishes universal weal within the realm, such that there is no longer any need of war equipment.

In Genesis the goal of cosmic weal is the same. In Gen 9:14 the deity says, "Whenever I bring a cloud over the earth, the bow will appear in the cloud." At first blush the deity's remark might seem to flow from the metaphor of God as creator, in this case as creator of atmospheric conditions. But when viewed from within the tradition of the divine sovereign who rides upon clouds, with its subsidiary metaphor of God as warrior, who uses storm clouds as a vehicle or, alternatively, as a weapon, God's statement in 9:14 takes on a different meaning.

At Ugarit, one of the principal epithets for Baal is "cloud-rider." Within biblical tradition Yahweh, similarly, is a cloud-rider. In Ezekiel's vision (Ezekiel 1) Yahweh appears in a storm cloud. In Psalm 18 (= 2 Sam 22):10–22 the deity is depicted as "soaring on the wings of the wind," with "thick (clouds) under his feet" and shrouded in darkness (= black clouds). Other passages also describe God's epiphany in equally ominous meteorological terms (e.g., Exod 15:7–10; Judg 5:4–5; Ps 68:7–8; Hab 3:3–5). Gen 9:14, too, should be understood within this storm epiphany tradition. In the immediately preceding flood scene God has just used his wind (8:2; cf. רוח אלהים, 1:2) to subdue the chaotic Great Deep (8:3). The reference to the "wind of God" hovering over the Deep in Gen 1:2 likely should also be understood as the deity using his storm winds as a weapon with which to bring the chaotic water into submission.[61] If elsewhere P's God is accustomed to using meteorological phenomena as personal equipment, then also in Gen 9:14. God's "bringing" of a "cloud over the earth" very likely stems from this same tradition of the divine warrior who from the midst of his storm cloud overwhelms the foe. In Gen 9:13–17, however, the appeal is not to that part of the tradition in which the deity overcomes his foe. That has already been accomplished twice over, in the subduing of the chaotic waters in Genesis 1 and again in the flood story in Genesis 8. Rather, in Genesis 9 the appeal is to the establishment of cosmic peace that results from the divine sovereign's victory. God enters into a covenant of peace with "all

---

61. Compare the description of Yahweh's employing a hail storm to defeat the enemy in Josh 10:11, "Yahweh hurled huge stones from heaven . . . so that more died from the hail stones than the Israelites killed with the sword." Not unrelated is the scene depicted in the aforementioned Assyrian polychrome tile (fig. 1), where the winged anthropomorphic figure, as the earthly counterpart of the heavenly highest god(s), fights from the midst of storm clouds, reminiscent of Adad's "thundering" against the enemy.

flesh." Since there is no longer any foe to overcome, God converts his bow from an implement of war into a symbol of the covenant of peace. From now on, whenever the divine sovereign makes an appearance on earth from within his majestic cloud, the bow—visible now as a rainbow—will serve as a reminder of this covenant of peace. Just as the bow has been transformed from a threatening implement of war into a symbol of hope and comfort, so also an epiphany of the "Cloud-rider" henceforth will be an event of cosmic joy rather than of dread. When the divine sovereign appears, it will not be as a warrior but as one whose presence causes peace to flourish in the earth.

Corollary to this passage is Gen 2:1–3, with its notation that upon completion of a perfect creation in six days, God "rested." It is now well accepted that this scene has implications of temple-building.[62] Like Baal after his combat with Yam, Ea-Enki after his victory over Apsu, and Marduk after vanquishing Tiamat (and Qingu), so God after dividing *tĕhōm* appears to rule his newly ordered cosmos from a cosmic temple, his palace—one more bit of evidence that P thinks of God as the divine sovereign.

Elsewhere I have shown this "rest" to be an aspect of the "sleeping god" motif, which is yet another subsidiary metaphor of the divine sovereign metaphor. Just as retiring the war bow is an aspect of the metaphor of divine sovereignty, so also is the sleeping or resting deity.

The motif of the divine sleep is double edged, however. On the one side are texts that describe sleep as the prerogative of the divine sovereign. In Enuma Elish, Marduk rested after slaying the chaos monster Tiamat. He next built his palace Esagila on Temenanki ("the foundation of heaven and earth"), not only as the abode of his own enthronement but also as a place of rest for all the gods. In Atrahasis the lesser gods disturb Enlil's sleep by their outcries, which is tantamount to challenging his authority. In Egyptian Memphite theology, after creating humankind, Ptah rested. In Zion royal theology Yahweh desired Zion as "his place of rest" (Ps 132:13–14). But on the other side are texts that claim that the divine sovereign does not, or ought not, sleep. Thus, the psalmist calls upon Yahweh to "wake up" because the enemy is at the door (Ps 44:24; note that Yahweh is called king in v. 4). The divine sovereign may not "rest" because the foe is still at large. Deutero-Isaiah makes much the same plea in the so-called Ode to Yahweh's Arm (Isa 51:9–11).

---

62. See Jon D. Levenson, *Creation and the Persistence of Evil,* 78–99, and the bibliography cited there. See also Victor (Avigdor) Hurowitz, *I Have Built You an Exalted House: Temple Building in the Bible in Light of Mesopotamian and Northwest Semitic Writings* (JSOTSup 115; JSOT/ASOR Monograph 5; Sheffield: Sheffield Academic Press, 1992) 242.

If God rests in Gen 2:1–3, therefore, it is because, as divine sovereign who has just completed a perfect world, there are no threats to his authority.[63] No palace or throne is mentioned here, but a "resting place" or a throne seems to be implied nonetheless.

It may be suggested, further, that P envisions God as "enthroned upon the cherubim" (Ps 80:2; 99:1), similar to Ezekiel's vision of Yahweh seated on a cherub throne (Ezek 1:26; 10:1) Because P seems to allow absolutely no other deity into this creation story, one wonders to whom God is talking when he says, "Let us create humankind in our image, according to our likeness" (Gen 1:26). As with Deutero-Isaiah (41:28), P's God has no counselor and needs none. All of his works are perfect. Nevertheless, in biblical tradition the divine monarch is never alone. In Isaiah 6 he is attended by seraphs with whom he deliberates: "Whom shall I send, and who will go for us?" (Isa 6:8). In 1 Kgs 22:19–23 Yahweh, seated on his throne in the presence of כל־צבא השמים "the whole heavenly host," deliberates with various "spirits" about how best to get rid of Ahab in Israel. Jeremiah, too, knows of such deliberations within the divine council (Jer 23:18, 22). A heavenly court is also much in evidence in the prologue of Job (1:6–27; cf. 38:7). Westermann claims that P "was not familiar with the idea of a heavenly court," because "angels or any sort of intermediary beings are found nowhere in P."[64] But P's emphasis upon Yahweh's uniqueness does not necessarily exclude divine attendants, as evident from Ezekiel where God, despite being characterized by a similar transcendence, is

---

63. For details of this metaphor, see my "Sleeping God," 153–57. It is important to keep in mind that in the Hebrew Bible the term היכל "temple/palace" is used equally of both the deity's "house" and the royal residence, as was Akkadian *ekallu* (Sum. é.gal) in Mesopotamia.

64. Claus Westermann, *Genesis 1–11*, 144–45. Westermann's own preferred explanation of the plural constructions here and elsewhere as a "plural of deliberation" is unconvincing, because the examples proffered as evidence may be better explained otherwise. The alternation between singular and plural in Isa 6:8 ("Whom shall *I* send, and who will go for *us*?") may be construed as the deity deliberating not with himself but with the seraph attendants mentioned in the immediately preceding verses. Similarly, the shift from plural to singular in David's choice of a punishment in 2 Sam 24:14 ("Let *us* fall into the hand of the Lord . . . but let *me* not fall into human hands") may be motivated by the scope of the referent: in the first case "three days of pestilence" would afflict the entire nation, while in the second case "three months of pursuit before your foes" would affect primarily David himself. A third alleged attestation of a plural of deliberation, from Gen 11:7, is even less persuasive; the deity's remark ("Come, let *us* go down. . . .") is from the Yahwistic tradent, which contains additional allusions to the deity's speaking with or interacting with other divine beings (e.g., "like gods" ‖ "like one of us" [Gen 3:5, 22]; "the cherubim" [2:24]; "the sons of the gods/God" [6:2, 4]).

never alone but always borne about by his cherubim attendants. In Ezekiel's vision the cherubim, like Yahweh himself, have humanlike forms. If Ezekiel is dependent upon P for his imagery, as I argue in the following section, then one may take a cue from Ezekiel and assume that for P also the divine sovereign both possesses a humanlike form and speaks to anthropomorphic cherub attendants when he proposes, "Let *us* make humankind in *our* image, according to *our* likeness" (Gen 1:26).[65]

Ezekiel's Vision of God's Majesty and
Its Significance for Understanding P

Because Ezekiel and P appear to share some common traditions and in particular overlapping traditions regarding creation, Ezekiel has the potential to confirm or to negate at least partially the Priestly portrait of God that I have been sketching. Ezekiel 28 and Genesis 2–3 share mythical elements of a common primeval story, for example, the Garden of God/Eden, precious stones, a primeval humanlike figure, who though innocent on the day of creation became presumptuous in a desire to be Godlike, and guardian cherub(s) who drive out the protagonist, "fallen" because of hubris. A strong case can be made, as well, for identifying the wise serpent of Genesis 3—a kind of seraph[66]—with the condemned proud cherub of Ezekiel 28. Because Ezekiel 28 seems to presuppose elements not only of the Yahwistic primeval story but also the idea of perfection imposed upon this story through the secondary Priestly frame of Genesis 1, it seems necessary to conclude that Ezekiel 28 is subsequent to and dependent upon the completed P+J version of Genesis 1–3, rather than being a completely independent tradition.[67]

A close relationship between Ezekiel and the Priestly primeval story can also be discerned from Ezekiel's vision of God—more exactly, of Ezekiel's vision of "the glory of Yahweh" (v. 28)—in Ezekiel 1. First, apart from late passages (Ps 19:2; 150:1; Dan 12:3) that seem to be derivative from Genesis 1 or Ezekiel 1, the word רקיע 'firmament/dome' occurs in the Bible only in the P creation story of Genesis 1 and in Ezekiel's vision of God's glory or majesty in Ezekiel 1 and the related vision in 10:1. Second, the Ezekielian phrase to describe the deity, דמות כמראה אדם "a likeness like the appearance of a human" (1:26), patently bears some relationship to the Priestly statement in Gen 1:26 that God created אדם "humankind" בצלמנו כדמותנו "in our image, according

---

65. Similarly Jon D. Levenson, *Creation and the Persistence of Evil*, 5.

66. On the serpent as a seraph, see my *Slaying the Dragon: Mythmaking in the Biblical Tradition* (Louisville: Westminster John Knox, 1992) 59–60 with n. 46, and pp. 95–96.

67. For this interpretation of Ezekiel 28 and its relation to Genesis 1–3, see ibid., 94–97, with the documentation there.

to our own likeness." The Ezekielian metaphor of God's having a human likeness is the reverse of the Priestly statement that God created humankind in the likeness of God. Third, Ezekiel's likening of the brilliance of Yahweh's majesty to "the appearance (מראה) of the bow (הקשת) in a cloud (בענן) on a rainy day" (Ezek 1:28) is reminiscent of the Priestly conclusion to the primeval story, that after the flood God placed his bow in the cloud(s) as a perpetual sign of the covenant between himself and the earth/all flesh (Gen 9:13–17). This cloud is to be seen not only by the deity but also by those on earth. "When I bring cloud(s) over the earth, the bow in the cloud will be visible" (נראתה הקשת בענן, 9:14). This bow motif does not appear elsewhere in the Hebrew Bible.[68] Moreover, in 9:14 the difficult phrase בענני ענן על־הארץ, usually translated "when I bring clouds over the earth," may be more literally translated "when I cloud a cloud over the earth" and probably means approximately "when I bring my storm cloud over the earth." If correct, then this is another reference to God as the cloud-rider who appears in his storm cloud as he maneuvers across the sky, just as in Ezekiel 1 "the heavens opened" and in his "visions of God" (1:1) the prophet saw רוח סערה באה מן־הצפון ענן גדול "a storm wind approaching from the north, an awesome cloud" (1:4).

Clearly, there is intertextuality functioning between Ezekiel and Genesis.[69] Their shared viewpoints make it legitimate, therefore, to use Ezekiel 1 as a key to unlocking P's understanding of the deity in the Genesis narrative.

Ezekiel's own conception of the deity needs elucidation first, however, because the prophet makes it very clear that he is not giving a literal description of Yahweh or even of the throne of Yahweh and the four "living creatures" that bear up the throne—identified finally as cherubs in 10:1. Repeatedly Ezekiel tells the reader that his descriptions are only approximate, "something like X," where X is itself only a point of comparison. The visual and auditory imagery that the prophet employs may be difficult for moderns to comprehend but is not outside the range of symbolism attested in the ancient Near East. Moshe Greenberg[70] correctly notes that much of Ezekiel's vision derives

---

68. The bow as an aspect of the motif of God's throne does reappear again in the New Testament in Rev 4:3 and 10:1; cf. Sir 43:11; 50:7.

69. Determining in which direction the dependency flows is more difficult, though I argue that Ezekiel is dependent upon the completed P+J primeval story rather than the other way round. If so, then Ezekiel would be one of the first commentators on the Priestly primeval story, and nearly contemporary in time. I addressed this issue in an unpublished paper, "Intertextuality and the Dating of the Primeval Creation Accounts" (presented at the Fifty-Ninth General Meeting of the Catholic Biblical Association of America, University of St. Thomas, St. Paul, Minn., August 10–13, 1996).

70. Moshe Greenberg, *Ezekiel, 1–20: A New Translation with Introduction and Commentary* (AB 22; Garden City, N.Y.: Doubleday, 1983) 52–58.

from stock ancient Near Eastern descriptions. The closest literary analogue is Ps 18 (= 2 Sam 22):8–14, where in response to the psalmist's cry for help,

> The earth quaked and trembled . . .
> [God] tilted the sky and came down
> Thick clouds were under his feet
> He rode on a cherub and flew
> He appeared [var. soared] on wings of wind
> He put darkness about him as his pavilion . . .
> In the radiance before him fiery coals burned
> YHWH thundered from heaven
> The Most High gave forth his voice.[71]

Fig. 15. Bull-men and humanoid genius support winged disk, from eighth-century Karatepe. Drawing by the author.

The motif of a deity riding upon cherubs or composite animals is commonplace both in the Bible and in the ancient Near East. Ezekiel is very insistent that the cherubim in his vision had humanlike bodies (v. 5), despite having three additional faces of various animal forms and four wings (v. 6). They have human hands (v. 8) and straight—that is, human—legs (v. 7), not like some "cherubs" of this ancient world having bulllike or lionlike bodies with the characteristic "hooked" rear legs of bulls or lions.[72] Ezekiel's cherubim thus bear greater resemblance to the tradition of the semidivine creatures that bear up the winged sun disk (figs. 15 [middle figure], 16, 17).[73] By insisting upon the humanoid features of the

---

71. Translation by M. Greenberg, ibid., 53.

72. For representative examples, see *ANEP*, nos. 500, 501, 522, and 534.

73. Figure 15: drawing by the author of three genii—a humanoid flanked by two bull-men—supporting a winged disk (*ANEP*, no. 855). For a similar Neo-Assyrian example, except that the winged disk has been "modernized" into a winged anthropomorphic figure within the nimbus, see Seal ANE 130865 (British Museum) from Nimrud, published by Max Mallowan (*Nimrud and Its Remains* [3 vols.; New York: Dodd, Mead, 1966] 1.48, #12); repr. Dominique Callon (*First Impressions*, 78, #352) and most recently restudied by idem, "Seals of Merodach-Baladan," in *ErIsr* 27 (Hayim and Miriam Tadmor Volume;

Fig. 16. Humanoid genius with uplifted hands. Drawing by the author.

Fig. 17. Eagle-headed humanoid supporting winged disk. Drawing by the
author.

cherubs, Ezekiel perhaps intended to suggest a degree of likeness between these bearers of כבוד יהוה "the majesty of Yahweh" and Yahweh himself, who is described in 1:26 as having a partially humanlike form: דמות כמראה אדם "a likeness of appearance of a human."

The continuing depiction of the deity in v. 27 is further veiled in very guarded language. The syntax of this verse is convoluted and difficult to ascertain; the author seemingly deliberately avoids straightforward descriptions here in order to protect the transcendence of the deity. Nevertheless, one aspect of

---

2003) 10*–17*, esp. 16*, fig. 7. For another example (from tenth-century Ain Dura in Aleppo National Museum) of a homonoid genius similarly flanked by two bull-men supporting a now missing sun disk, see André Chouraqui, L'univers de la Bible, 3.537; for a scene of just two bull-men supporting the winged disk, minus the humanoid in the center, see M. von Oppenheim, Tell Halaf (ed. Anton Moortgat; 4 vols.; Berlin: de Gruyter, 1955) vol. 3, pl. 98 (A 3,171). Fig. 16: drawing by the author of winged humanoid genius with uplifted arms, presumably supporting a now missing deity, from Tell Halaf, ninth century; see photo in M. von Oppenheim, Der Tell Halaf: Eine neue Kultur im ältesten Mesopotamien (Leipzig: Brockhaus, 1931) 152, pl. 32a. Fig. 17: drawing by the author of a winged disk supported by a four-winged humanoid genius with an eagle's head, from Tell Halaf, ninth century (= ANEP, no. 653).

the vision is clear, namely, the radiance of the divine being. As Greenberg notes, the basic structure of v. 27 is chiastic:

> I saw X / from his loins up
> From his loins down / I saw Y,

where X is "the like of *ḥašmal*" (amber?) and Y is "the semblance of fire." In other words, the whole of the humanlike figure upon the throne is completely shrouded in brilliance.[74]

Ezekiel's portrait of Yahweh is intentionally opaque—an unfocusable but searing glimpse of the majestic deity enthroned above the (heavenly) dome (v. 26), engulfed in awesome brilliance and surrounded by a radiant rainbow. But even this limited vision of כבוד יהוה "the majesty of Yahweh" is so overwhelming that the prophet's only defense is to fall upon his face in reverence (v. 28).

On one key point, however, Greenberg has missed the mark. He compares Ezekiel's vision of Yahweh's majesty to the winged anthropomorphic figure in the previously mentioned fragmentary polychrome glazed tile from Ashur found in the Anu-Adad Temple from the time of Tukulti-Ninurta II (fig. 1). Greenberg, following the lead of a number of other scholars, incorrectly identified the figure within the nimbus as the god Ashur and assumed, therefore, that as a representation of the Assyrian god the winged anthropomorphic figure may be used to elucidate the Ezekielian conception of God's majesty.[75] As noted above, however, the winged anthropomorphic figure is not so much the divine sovereign himself, as it is the manifestation of the divine sovereign's power exercised through his human viceroy, the Assyrian king.

Nevertheless, the winged anthropomorphic figure may illustrate Ezekiel's image of the deity indirectly. If the Assyrian winged anthropomorphic figure is symbolic of the Assyrian king as the representative or image of the divine sovereign on earth then the corollary is that the divine sovereign himself bears some resemblance to the earthly king and especially to the anthropomorphic figure in the nimbus. Ezekiel seems to depict the "majesty of Yahweh" as a similarly anthropomorphic portrayal of a totally transcendent deity. Insofar as the deity can be apprehended by human senses at all, it is possible to do so only indirectly through recognizing the divine image as manifested in human form. Something similar seems to have been the view of the Priestly Writer;

---

74. Greenberg, *Ezekiel, 1–20*, 50–51. See also the similar conclusion on the basis of ancient Near Eastern iconography of Othmar Keel and Christoph Uehlinger, *Gods, Goddesses, and Images of God in Ancient Israel* (trans. Thomas H. Trapp; Minneapolis: Fortress, 1998) 296–97.

75. Greenberg, *Ezekiel, 1–20*, 54.

the deity's statement "Let us create humankind *in our image*" would seem to imply that the human form images something of the deity and the beings that surround the deity.[76]

The Democratization of Kingship in the Priestly Creation Account

If it is correct that for P the deity is first and foremost the divine sovereign, then the fact that humankind bears the divine image must mean that P understood humans to be the earthly embodiment of the divine sovereign. In other words, on earth humankind serves as viceroy of the divine sovereign, similar to the way that in Assyria the king was understood to be the divine sovereign's viceroy. According to P, האדם "humankind" was given authority over all the earth to *subdue* (כבש) it and to *exercise dominion* (רדה) over the animals (Gen 1:26, 28). This is of course royal language and royal ideology.[77]

In the ancient Near East ultimately the goal of cosmogonic myth was the creation of humankind. Moreover, in Mesopotamian myth at least, kingship was a necessary part of—even the apex of—the creation of humankind.[78] In royal propaganda everywhere, kingship was divinely instituted, the divine instrument for maintaining justice and right order in the earth—as Lipit-Ishtar and Hammurabi stated so eloquently in the prologues to their respective law codes,[79] and as expressed in various Neo-Assyrian benedictions over the king.[80]

---

76. For a survey of the many interpretations of the phrase "image of God," see Westermann, *Genesis 1–11*, 147–58; and more recently, Wenham, *Genesis 1–15*, 29–32.

77. On this widely recognized aspect, see the discussion, with references to previous scholarship, in Westermann, *Genesis 1–11*, 151–54, 159; and Victor P. Hamilton, *The Book of Genesis: Chapters 1–17* (NICOT; Grand Rapids: Eerdmans, 1990) 137–38. S. G. F. Brandon (*Creation Legends of the Ancient Near East* [London: Hodder and Stoughton, 1963] 1150, followed by Westermann [*Genesis 1–11*, 159], suggests that the point of the Genesis account here is that humans are being liberated, so to speak, from the servile burden imposed upon them by the Mesopotamian mythic creation tradition "to bear the yoke of the gods." This may be true, but it misses the full import of humankind's royal function being developed here by P.

78. W. R. Mayer, "Ein Mythos von der Erschaffung des Menschen und des Königs," *Or* 56 (1987) 55–66. For English translations of this text, see Clifford, *Creation Accounts in the Ancient Near East and in the Bible*, 69–70; and Alasdair Livingstone, "A Late Piece of Constructed Mythology Relevant to the Neo-Assyrian and Middle Assyrian Coronation Hymn and Prayer," in *COS* 1.146, pp. 476–77.

79. Lipit-Ishtar of Isin (2017–1985 B.C.E.) claimed that the high gods An and Enlil appointed him king of Sumer and Akkad "in order to establish justice in the land, to eliminate cries for justice, to eradicate enmity and armed violence, to bring well-being to the lands of Sumer and Akkad" (The Laws of Lipit-Ishtar 1.1–37 [trans. Martha Roth, in *COS* 2.154, p. 411]; similarly in the epilogue, 21.5–17). For his part, Hammurabi of Babylon

Not unrelated is the well-attested literary and iconographic conceit that the king is "master of the animals." Assyrian kings are often depicted killing ferocious lions and wild bulls. To take just the example of Ashurnasirpal II, one notes that in the throne room of the Northwest Palace at Nimrud, two contiguous slabs (B-19 and B-20) in their upper panels depict the king killing lions in the one case and wild bulls in the other. In the panels immediately below, the king is shown standing over a slain lion and a slain wild bull, respectively, holding his hunting bow in his left hand and a libation a bowl in his raised right hand, indicative of a successful hunt (fig. 18).[81] Also, four of the sixteen bronze bands on Ashurnasirpal's gate in the Temple of Mamu at Balawat (ancient Imgur Enlil) were dedicated to showing the king hunting lions and wild oxen; the accompanying text reads "wild oxen by the Euphrates, I killed" and "Lions by the Balih River, I killed."[82] Moreover, the inscription chiseled on the base of Ashurnasirpal's throne in his (Northwest) Palace at Kalhu diverges from the "standard text" on the walls by adding accounts of

---

(1792–1750 B.C.E.) claimed that Anu and Enlil promoted Marduk and his city Babylon "and made it supreme within the regions of the world" and that "Anu and Enlil, for the enhancement of the well-being of the people, named me by my name: Hammurabi . . . to make justice prevail in the land, to abolish the wicked and the evil, to prevent the strong from oppressing the weak, to rise like the sun-god Shamash over all humankind, to illuminate the land" (The Laws of Hammurabi 1.27–49 [trans. Martha Roth; *COS* 2.131, p. 336]; see also the epilogue, 47.9-780). Ur-Namma (2112–2095 B.C.E.), founder of the Third Dynasty of Ur, earlier had claimed that the gods had similarly commissioned him to establish justice in the land (The Laws of Ur-Namma 104–13 [idem, *COS* 2.153, p. 409]).

80. Representative examples from coronation prayers include prayers for Tukulti-Ninurta I ("May Assur give you authority, obedience, concord, justice and peace!" [trans. Alasdair Livingstone; *COS* 1.140, p. 472]) and for Ashurbanipal ("May eloquence, understanding, truth and justice be granted him [Ashurbanipal] as a gift! . . . May concord and peace be established in Assyria!" [idem, *COS* 1.142, p. 473]). Likewise, in a hymn to Shamash, Ashurbanipal prays for himself: "May he constantly shepherd over your peoples, whom you gave him, in justice" (idem, *COS* 1.143, p. 474).

81. Figure 18: drawing by Halina Lewakowa, in J. Meuszyński, *Die Rekonstruktion der Reliefdarstellungen*, fig. 1.3. The reliefs themselves are, for the upper panels, BM 124534 (B-19a, killing lions), and BM 124532 (B-20a, killing wild bulls); for photos, see *Assyrian Palace Reliefs*, fig. 26 [= ANEP, no. 184] and fig. 27, respectively. The lower panels are BM 124535 (B-19b, the slain lion), and BM 124533 (B-20b, the slain wild bull; photo in Paley, *King of the World*, 102, pl. 18b). Photos of B-19a, B-19b, and B-20a are also available in Strommenger, *Fünf Jahrtausende Mesopotamien*, pl. 202. The theme of the king hunting wild animals is even more extensively depicted in the reliefs of Ashurbanipal; see Paley, figs. 55–104. For a systematic listing and discussion of the theme of the king as hunter, see Magen, *Assyrische Königsdarstellungen*, 29–36.

82. Russell, *The Writing on the Wall*, 55–57.

B-20   B-19

Fig. 18. Ashurnasirpal killing lions (B-19) and wild bulls (B-20). Drawing of bas reliefs on walls of the throne room of the Northwest Palace at Nimrud. Used by permission of R. P. Sobelewski, Polish Mission to Nimroud/Iraq/Polish Center of Archaeology.

the king hunting wild beasts and breeding herds of them.[83] Undoubtedly there was an element of the thrill of hunting wild animals involved, and the Assyrian artists are careful to show the skill and the daring of the monarch.[84] But there is more involved, because these scenes also convey the image of the king as the lord and master of the animals, the one who protects the land from every threat, including the threat of wild animals that might ravage the land and take away its security.[85] A threat of attack by wild beasts can be as debilitating as the threat of an armed enemy.

83. Ibid., 42–44. In addition, other scenes depict animals brought as tribute from far-flung parts of the empire or captured on hunting expeditions; regarding these Russell comments: "Viewing these animals, [Ashurnasirpal's] subjects would be reminded in a very direct way of the king's role as shepherd, and may well have seen in these heterogeneous animals from diverse regions, brought together in the capital and cared for by the king of the realm, a metaphor of the various peoples of the empire, united and protected by that same authority" (p. 44).

84. In the case of Ashurbanipal, where text and image are coordinated on the same relief, the element of sport in the lion hunt is acknowledged; see ibid., 201–2. The coordination of text and image in the same panel is a novel practice begun with Ashurbanipal (ibid., 216); for earlier kings, motives must be inferred.

85. Commenting on two similar Neo-Assyrian seals that depict a deity/hero with his foot resting upon a domestic animal and defending it from an attacking lion, Othmar Keel (*The*

Lev 26:5–6 speaks of the security that God bestows in precisely these terms: "I will grant peace in the land and you shall lie down, and no one shall make you afraid; I will remove dangerous animals from the land, and no sword shall go through your land" (NRSV). Ezekiel (34:25–31) in speaking of the eschatological covenant of peace that God will establish on earth echoes similar sentiments: "I will make with them a covenant of peace and banish wild animals from the land, so that they may live in the wild and sleep in the woods securely. . . . They shall no longer be plunder for the nations, nor shall the animals of the land devour them; they shall live in safety, and no one shall make them afraid. . . . You are my sheep, the sheep of my pasture and I am your God, says the Lord God" (Ezek 34:25–31; cf. Hos 2:20[2:18]).[86] When kings killed wild beasts, symbolically they were acting in place of the divine sovereign, divinely appointed shepherds ridding the earth of threats to the divinely willed peace.[87]

In creating humankind, P says, God gives humankind mastery over all the animals, both domesticated and wild (Gen 1:26, 28); in Gen 9:2, the writer elaborates on this motif, saying that animals will be in "fear and dread" of humankind, apparently because humans bear the "image" of God (9:6). Others have noted that the "fear and dread" that humankind wreaks upon the animal kingdom is analogous to the *puluḫtu* that Mesopotamian kings generated in their foes.[88] But in P's revisioning of creation, kingship has been democratized. Not just kings but all humans bear this royal badge of divinity.

Symbolism of the Biblical World, 58) says: "The foot placed upon the weaker animal expresses 'dominion' (cf. Ps 8:6). As in the case of the king, however, this dominion consists not only in holding subject, but also in defense of the weaker animal against the attacking lion."

86. For the linkage between the themes of removal of wild beasts and the establishment of security in the land, see Katherine M. Hayes, "Lord of the Animals: God and ʾādam" (paper presented at the Sixty-Third General Meeting of the Catholic Biblical Association of America, Loyola Marymount University, Los Angeles, Calif., August 5–8, 2000) 1–40; see also my "Covenant of Peace," 187–211.

87. That the killing of wild animals was intimately linked with the establishment of cosmic weal is graphically represented on an ivory bed-head from Nimrud whereon the king is depicted slaying a wild bull, amid other panels decorated with various motifs indicating universal harmony and abundance; see Max Mallowan, *Nimrud and Its Remains,* 2.491–92, ##385–87.

88. Despite a reputation for "calculated frightfulness," Ashurnasirpal II, like other Neo-Assyrian kings, used a careful balancing of carrot and stick to assure the submission of vassal kingdoms; see Barbara N. Porter, "Intimidation and Friendly Persuasion: Re-evaluating the Propaganda of Ashurnasirpal II," in *ErIsr* 27 (Hayim and Miriam Tadmor Volume; 2003) 180*–91*.

Perhaps the best commentary on P's vision of all humankind's being imbued with royal divine status is Psalm 8, which, as noted above, bears obvious similarities to Genesis 1. This psalm opens with hymned praise of God as the divine sovereign (אדון): "How majestic is your name in all the earth!" It then moves quickly to the divine sovereign's role as creator but dwells on humankind as the culmination of the deity's creative design:

> You have made [humankind] barely lower than God,[89]
> crowning them with glory and honor.
> You have given them dominion[90] over the works of your hands.
> You have placed all things under their feet:
> all sheep and oxen,
> and also the wild beasts,
> the birds of the sky and the fish of the sea—
> whatever courses through the sea.

The psalmist then reiterates his opening line praising the divine sovereign for his marvelous works "in all the world." As in P, the divine sovereign has made אדם "humankind" his viceroy and given it responsibility for this world and everything in it.

One cannot help but contrast Psalm 8 with royal psalms such as Psalms 2, 89, and 110. In Psalm 89 the psalmist extols the divine sovereign for choosing David and his descendants to bear the mantel of royal divinity. The king is imbued with the status of divine sonship and entrusted with the deity's own work of maintaining order in a threatening and chaotic world:

> I will set his hand on Sea,
> and his right hand on Rivers.
> He shall cry to me, "You are my Father,
> my God, and the Rock of my salvation!"
> I will make him the firstborn,
> the highest of the kings of the earth. (Ps 89:26–28)

According to this royal psalm, the Davidic king alone wears the mantel of the divine sovereign and exercises divine rule on earth. In a burst of poetic exuberance, the psalmist claims that God has even commissioned the king to have dominion over the powers of chaos (ים "Sea" ‖ נהרות "Rivers"), a role traditionally reserved for the divine sovereign alone, as in Ps 24:1–2, where Yahweh is celebrated as the king of glory, who subdues these waters of chaos:

---

89. Or: "gods" (אלהים).

90. A different root (משל) is used here than in Gen 1:26 + 28 (רדה, כבש), but the meaning is identical.

> To Yahweh belong the earth and its fullness,
> The world and those who dwell therein;
> For he has founded it upon Sea,
> And established it upon Rivers.

Prior to the psalmist, the Canaanite author of the Baal epic celebrated Baal as king of the gods by virtue of his victory over Prince Sea ‖ Judge River.[91]

Psalm 2 is no less expansive in asserting that the divine sovereign has exalted the Davidic king alone. Scholars have long considered v. 7 ("You are son; today I have begotten you") a statement of adoptive divine sonship for the Davidic king, presumably pronounced at his coronation. Recently, however, Jeffrey Tigay has recognized in v. 6 a formula of divine creation of the king through a special נסך "casting" by the deity. Although unique in biblical literature, similar claims that the king was specially created in a divine "casting" are found in Mesopotamian, specifically Assyrian royal propaganda.[92] Accordingly, Psalm 2 appears to go beyond a mere claim of adoptive or fictive sonship for the king to assert instead that the Davidic king is literally God's own specially created son:

> "But I myself created my king on Zion, my holy mountain."
> Let me tell of Yahweh's decree;
> He said to me: "You are my son;
> Today I have begotten you." (vv. 6–7)

Given such credentials, it is no wonder that the psalmist warns the nations against conspiring "against Yahweh and his annointed," since the two form but a single ruling unit. Ps 110:1 similarly claims that the divine sovereign has seated the king at his right hand and placed his enemies under his feet as a footstool.

Psalm 8, then, with its democratization of kingship is a radical departure from the royal psalms. In Psalm 8 the whole of humankind has been "crowned with glory and honor" and given "dominion" over creation because the divine sovereign has "put all things under their feet." Similar to P, however,

---

91. On the connection between Psalm 24 and the Baal epic, see the perceptive commentary by J. J. M. Roberts, "The King of Glory," *PSB* n.s. 3/1 (1980) 50; reprinted in idem, *The Bible and the Ancient Near East,* 104–9. I have diverged from Roberts's translation of Ps 24:2 by reading ימים "Sea" (ים + enclitic *mem*) and נהרות "River" instead of "the seas" and "the rivers," respectively; the lack of the definite article in each case convinces me that more rather than less of the older mythological tradition has been retained in this poetic formulation. Compare Ps 89:26.

92. Jeffrey H. Tigay, "Divine Creation of the King in Psalms 2:6," *ErIsr* 27 (Hayim and Miriam Tadmor Volume; 2003) 246*–50*.

Psalm 8 has toned down the mythical imagery of creation. Gone, for example, are references to subduing the chaos dragon Sea-Rivers, replaced instead by more secular references to ruling "whatever courses through the sea." Psalm 8 echoes conceptually and theologically P's view that all humans were created in the image of the divine sovereign.

P evidently writes out of the shadow of the Babylonian exile, by which time the shortcomings of not only the Israelite monarchy but also the Davidic monarchy in Zion-Jerusalem have been made patently evident. Hence in Genesis 1, P seeks to ground the divine image elsewhere than in the king, as the royal Zion theology would have it. Humankind itself may be flawed, as P will make clear in subsequent chapters. Indeed, the divine image is already greatly tarnished by Genesis 5, because P puts some distance between Adam's descendants and God's image by noting that Adam's sons were begotten in Adam's image rather than in the image of God, as Adam himself had been (5:1–3). Nevertheless, tarnished as the divine image in humankind may be, it is still the divinely willed avenue by which to apprehend the transcendent deity. The divine sovereign has delegated his authority to humankind. This is both privilege and duty, it would appear. Every human is anointed to continue the agenda of the divine sovereign by working to eliminate from this world every form of oppression and injustice (chaos) so that peace and universal weal (cosmos) may prevail throughout this universe that God created "perfect" (טוב מאד).[93]

Conclusion

When cultural clues within the Priestly primeval story are pursued, it becomes obvious that P's God exhibits many of the characteristics of the high gods observable in other ancient Near Eastern societies. God is clearly the creator of heaven and earth. But Near Eastern cosmologies, especially those of the latter part of the second millennium and the first millennium, attribute the work of creation primarily to the king of the gods, that is, to the divine sovereign. Moreover, creation frequently involved a clash of wills, the divine sovereign against an archfoe—which conflict is of cosmic proportions, that is, what Gunkel dubbed a *Chaoskampf.* Such Combat Myth motifs are downplayed in P but not wholly absent. P's deity is the divine sovereign who rules from his temple above the heavens. At especially critical junctures when his creation is threatened God emerges from his transcendent abode amid awesome clouds to (re)impose order over chaos and to (re)establish a kingdom befitting this

---

93. The Priestly tradition recognized that humankind frequently fell short of its royal vocation, however. For this reason the Priestly tradition posited the necessity of priesthood for bridging the gap between the sinful manner in which humans act and their royal vocation.

majestic divine sovereign. Because of his totally transcendent nature, however, it is difficult to observe the divine sovereign directly. The divine sovereign is always "on duty," so to speak, but after an initial ordering of chaos, he has turned over the duty of maintaining peace and harmony in the world to humans, who as the deity's representatives have been charged with promoting the welfare of creation.

The Priestly Writer used the primeval narrative to introduce God as universal ruler. The ancient Near Eastern metaphor of the divine sovereign provided the Priestly Writer with an excellent foundation upon which to build a theology in which both the transcendence and the universality of the deity clearly emerge. But at the same time this exalted deity is very close to his world. His providence extends to all things and all beings, whether in heaven or on earth. Nevertheless, the divine sovereign chooses to exercise his dominion on earth largely through humankind. There is no attempt to link any of this either to the king or to Zion, however, because in P's new universalizing theology each person is endowed with the divine image and each person is charged with actualizing and maintaining this world in the perfection that the divine sovereign intended.

The Ruler in Zion and the Hope of the Poor: Psalms 9–10 in the Context of the Psalter

PATRICK D. MILLER
Princeton Theological Seminary

In the recent investigation of the Psalter as a book, a strong case has been made for seeing its center and climax in its declaration of the rule of the Lord, explicitly articulated in a number of places in the expression "the Lord is king" (*yhwh melek,* e.g., Ps 29:10) and variants (e.g., Pss 24:10, 95:3, 98:6, 99:4, 149:2) or "the Lord reigns" (*yhwh/ʾĕlōhîm mālak,* e.g., Pss 47:9, 93:1, 96:10, 97:1, 99:1) but evident in many other ways throughout the Psalter, including the personal reference "my king" (e.g., Pss 5:3, 44:5, 68:25, 74:12, 84:4).[1] In three significant ways, this centering on God's rule of the world, including Israel, the nations, and the whole of creation, is strongly connected to David and his successors as the human rulers charged with representing the rule of God in the human community.

One is the presence of a number of psalms that seem to focus on the human ruler, that is, the so-called *Royal Psalms,* some of which are strategically placed within the Psalter to help make the connection between the divine rule and human rule.[2] That the Psalter has this conjoining of divine and human rule at its center is reinforced by the presence of the first Royal Psalm as part of the

---

1. Gerald Wilson has presented a cogent and persuasive argument that the climax of the Psalter is in the Enthronement Psalms in Book IV, announcing the enduring rule of the Lord of Israel in the face of the failure of the monarchy (*The Editing of the Hebrew Psalter* [SBLDS 76; Chico, Calif.: Scholars Press, 1985]). James L. Mays has suggested that "The Lord Reigns" is the center of the Psalms, its root metaphor (*The Lord Reigns: A Theological Handbook to the Psalms* [Louisville: Westminster John Knox, 1994]).

2. Wilson, *The Editing of the Hebrew Psalter,* 207–8. See also the summary discussion and further reflections of J. Clinton McCann, Jr., "Books I–III and the Editorial Purpose of the Hebrew Psalter," in *The Shape and Shaping of the Psalter* (ed. J. C. McCann, Jr.; JSOTSup 159; Sheffield: JSOT Press, 1993) 93–107. There may be other Royal Psalms than those traditionally so designated (2, 18, 20, 21, 45, 72, 89, 101, 110, 132, 144:1–11) in that there are clearly other psalms that refer to the human king, and there seem to be some others that express the voice of the king, a point to be argued here with reference to Psalms 9 and 10. For a strong effort to identify a more expanded role for the king in the Psalter, see John H. Eaton, *Kingship and the Psalms* (SBT second series 32; London: SCM, 1976).

introduction to the Psalter, that is, Psalm 2, appropriately included in the introduction because it, more than any other psalm, explicitly lays out the connection between God's rule and the rule of the king.[3] A second way the connection is emphasized is in the attribution of a large number of the psalms to David, Israel's king par excellence, in the superscriptions that precede many of the psalms. Third is the shared association of the rule of the Lord and of the king with Zion, a point that is made at the beginning of the Psalter (Ps 2:6) and constantly reaffirmed.

The introduction to the Psalter, however, is not simply a pointer to the rule of the Lord over the nations and kings as exercised through David and his line. Psalm 1, which makes up the first part of the two-part introduction to the Psalter, says nothing about the king or about human and divine rule. It is rather about the Lord's way as the way of the righteous and the contrast of that way with the way of the wicked, a way that will end in judgment and destruction.

Two notes are sounded, therefore, in the introduction, notes that reverberate throughout the rest of the Psalter. The contrast between the righteous and the wicked and the conflict between them occupies much attention in the psalms that follow. This is especially evident in the many Psalms of Lament, in which those who are righteous or innocent cry out for God's help against their enemies, against the wicked, against evil doers.[4] So also, God's rule and its exercise by and through the anointed of the Lord pervade the psalms that follow. By and large, these two themes are articulated in different genres and different psalms (prayers for help or Laments versus Royal Psalms, and Enthronement Psalms), though this is not always the case, especially inasmuch as the Royal Psalms are not really a distinctive genre but a thematic category comprising various genres. Where they come together first in the Psalter is in Psalms 9 and 10, a psalm combination that is probably quite late in its composition and apparently artfully constructed and intentionally set within its context. It may be argued that no other psalm so fully joins the basic themes of the Psalter—the rule of God, the representative rule of the king, the plea for help in time of trouble, the ways of the wicked and the righteous, and the justice of God

---

3. For the place of Psalm 2 as formally a part of the introduction to the Psalter, see, e.g., my "Beginning of the Psalter," in McCann (ed.), *The Shape and Shaping of the Psalter*, 83–92; reprinted in *Israelite Religion and Biblical Theology* (JSOTSup 267; Sheffield: Sheffield Academic Press, 2000) 269–78.

4. Some of the laments or cries for help do acknowledge some sin and consequent guilt and see what has happened to the one(s) praying as reflective of divine anger, punishment, or judgment (e.g., the so-called Penitential Psalms). But such psalms are in a minority and balanced by those that assert an innocence before God (e.g., Psalms 7, 17, 139). Even among the Penitential Psalms, while a sense of sin and guilt may dominate a psalm like Psalm 51, it is more muted in other psalms, for example, Psalm 6.

on behalf of the weak and the poor. It is likely that the psalm was created precisely to bring all these notes into a single and powerful chord.[5]

That Psalms 9 and 10 represent a single psalm originally that has been split into two psalms in the Hebrew tradition is widely acknowledged. Some of the indicators of the unity of these two psalms are obvious.[6] They are developed around an acrostic pattern that sets up the first word of each verse according to the sequence of the Hebrew alphabet and continues through both psalms; there is no superscription at the beginning of Psalm 10, a feature uncommon to Book I of the Psalter except with regard to Psalms 1 and 2 and Psalms 32 and 33, where also one is to read these pairs as a conjoined set and not as discrete and individual psalms;[7] and the Greek translation treats the two psalms as a single psalm.

There are still other indicators of the fact that the two psalms are to be read together. Thematically, the Lord's rule holds the psalms together. It is the starting point and assumption of Psalm 9 (vv. 5, 8),[8] and it is the conclusion and hope of Psalm 10 (v. 16). The call to the Lord, "Rise up!" which occurs ten times in the Psalter, is the dominant petition in both psalms (9:20 and 10:12). The expression "in times of trouble" (*lĕ'ittôt baṣṣārâ*), a somewhat peculiar Hebrew expression, occurs only here, and it appears in both Psalms (9:10; 10:1). Its occurrence in Psalm 9 in the midst of the declaration that "the Lord is a stronghold for the oppressed[9] // a stronghold in times of trouble" is

---

5. Hossfeld has suggested that these two psalms provide a kind of "small theology of the rule of Yʜᴡʜ" (Frank-Lothar Hossfeld and Erich Zenger, *Die Psalmen I: Psalm 1–50* [Die Neue Echter Bibel; Würzburg: Echter, 1993] 82). For other treatments of these two psalms, see in addition to the commentaries: Walter Brueggemann, "Psalms 9–10: A Counter to Conventional Social Reality," in *The Bible and the Politics of Exegesis: Essays in Honor of Norman Gottwald* (ed. David Jobling et al.; New York: Pilgrim, 1991), reprinted in Brueggemann, *The Psalms and the Life of Faith* (ed. P. D. Miller; Minneapolis: Fortress, 1995) 217–34; Notker Füglister, "'Die Hoffnung der Armen ist nicht für immer verloren': Psalm 9/10 und die sozio-religiöse Situation der nachexilischen Gemeinde," in *Biblische Theologie und gesellschaftlicher Wandel: Festschrift für Norbert Lohfink S.J. zum 65 Geburtstag* (ed. Georg Braulik, Walter Gross, and Sean McEvenue; Freiburg: Herder, 1993) 101–23; Robert Gordis, "Psalm 9–10: A Textual and Exegetic Study," *JQR* 48 (1957) 104–22; Klaus Koenen, "Völkervernichtung und Völkermission: Die theologische Bedeutung der Textgeschichte erläutert am Beispiel von Ps 9, 21," *BN* 54 (1900) 22–27.

6. See the brief but helpful discussion of Wilson, *The Editing of the Hebrew Psalter*, 173–74.

7. Compare Psalms 42 and 43, which are also to be read as a single psalm.

8. The versification used here for Psalm 9 is according to the Hebrew Bible.

9. As is often the case in the Psalms, it is difficult to be sure what aspect of time is implied in the verbs. The presence of *wayĕhî* at the beginning of this sentence has led Hans-Joachim Kraus to read this as a past action sentence: "Then Yahweh *became* a fortress for the oppressed" (*The Psalms* [Minneapolis: Augsburg, 1988] 1.189).

the grounds for the complaint/question at the beginning of the lament in
Psalm 10: "Why, O Lord, do you stand afar off? // Hide yourself in times of
trouble?" Further, one notes that while Psalm 9 seems to focus upon "the
nations" (gôyîm) as the enemy and Psalm 10 on "the wicked" as the ones doing in the petitioner, both psalms identify the wicked and the nations with one
another (9:6, 16–17, 18; 10:15–16). And those who are being done in by
whatever group are regularly called the "afflicted" ('ānî/'ānāw) in both psalms
and more specifically identified as "oppressed" (dak) and "poor" ('ebyôn) in
Psalm 9 and as "oppressed" (dak), "innocent" (nāqî), "hapless"/"helpless"
(ḥēlĕkâ/ḥēlkā'îm),[10] and "orphan" (yātôm) in Psalm 10.

The unity of the two psalms is an important factor in their interpretation
and to be firmly maintained in light of all these signals, precisely because the
two psalms are not easy to read together and do not flow smoothly into one
another or create a single entity that looks like any other psalm or even represents, as a whole, any typical genre. Psalm 9 begins in song of thanksgiving and
moves then to a prayer for help, a move that is heightened in Psalm 10, a reverse of the cultic movement from lament to thanksgiving.[11] If indeed the
two psalms have been constructed carefully as a unit, and possibly in the latest
stages of the formation of the Psalter, then one must make a serious effort to
read them as a whole.[12] While there are many issues on the way to working
out a full and complex interpretation of these psalms, the focus here is on the
speaker of the psalms and the implications for thinking about the psalm's
meaning in the light of who it is that speaks and how the psalm fits into the
Psalter as a whole.

The identity of the one who sings and prays in this psalm would seem to
be the human ruler, the king.[13] There are two obvious pointers to this con-

---

10. On this unusual word, see Füglister, "'Die Hoffnung der Armen ist nicht für immer
verloren,'" 122 n. 59.

11. See Walter Beyerlin, "Die tôdā der Heilsvergegenwärtigung in den Klageliedern des
Einzelnen," ZAW 79 (1967) 208–24; and Patrick D. Miller, They Cried to the Lord: The
Form and Theology of Biblical Prayer (Minneapolis: Fortress, 1994), chap. 5. There is a similar
reversal of the customary and logical order in Psalm 40.

12. The date of Psalms 9–10 is no more to be determined precisely than is the case for
most psalms. The usual assumption, in light of terminology, e.g., the frequent reference to
the 'ānî, the use of the acrostic form, and the like, is that the psalm belongs to the postexilic
period and may even be Hellenistic. See, for example, Klaus Seybold, Die Psalmen (HAT
1/15; Tübingen: Mohr, 1996) 55; and Hossfeld in Hossfeld and Zenger, Die Psalmen I, 82.

13. See the comment of Peter Craigie, "The substance of the psalms lends itself to a
royal interpretation, at least in the initial stage of their history" (Psalms 1–50 [WBC; Waco,
Tex.: Word, 1983] 117). John Eaton argues also for a royal interpretation of the speaker in
Psalm 9–10 (Kingship and the Psalms, 32–33).

clusion. One is the superscription that ascribes these psalms, along with the other psalms in Book I of the Psalter, to David. The second basis for assuming that we hear in these psalms the voice of the king is the prominent place that the nations and peoples have in the two psalms, especially in Psalm 9 but also in Psalm 10, as noted above.[14] The psalm is couched in 1st-person sing. style with the nations identified as both the enemies of the one who prays and also the wicked before God. In the context of the Psalter and more immediately Book I, this opposition is especially to be heard as reflective of conflict between the Lord's appointed ruler and the nations of the earth.[15]

There has been resistance to seeing the king as the speaker because the nations-as-enemy seems to be a theme confined to Psalm 9, and Psalm 10 seems to be more of a cry for help from one of the oppressed or poor.[16] It is this shift in subject matter as well as the reverse order of the genres of thanksgiving and lament that have led interpreters to treat the psalms separately and to hear in their words different voices. But if the psalm is a constructed and intentional unity, then one would expect to encounter a single, common voice throughout unless there were explicit indicators to the contrary. Such indicators, however, are not present.[17] A single "I" speaks throughout the psalm, one whose personality and specifics are carefully hidden but whose place and stature are indicated directly by the criteria mentioned above. There is nothing in Psalm 10 to counter this assumption. Certainly it is not the case

---

14. In an excursus in his dissertation, Gert Kwakkel takes up the question of the possible royal reading of psalms not traditionally assigned to the genre of Royal Psalms, particularly the ones with which he is dealing in his study of the theme of upright behavior as grounds for deliverance (e.g., Psalms 7, 17, and 26). He does not think that a strong case can be made for regarding these and other psalms as royal, as some have suggested. In his discussion, however, he says: "The arguments taken from the nature of the enemies are most convincing in those cases in which foreign peoples are responsible for the hostilities (as in Ps. 9 and Ps. 118)" (Gert Kwakkel, *"According to My Righteousness": Upright Behaviour as Grounds for Deliverance in Psalms 7, 17, 18, 26, and 44* [Groningen: Rijksuniversiteit Groningen, 2001] 290).

15. This is especially the case in the light of Psalm 2, where the *gôyîm* and the *lĕ'ummîm* stand in opposition to the Lord's anointed, as is the case in Psalms 9–10.

16. See, e.g., Seybold, *Die Psalmen*, 56.

17. In his investigation of the possibility of Royal Psalms outside the generally accepted number, Kwakkel argues that a royal interpretation is appropriate for parts of a psalm in which there seem to be no elements indicating the involvement of a king if there are other places in the psalm in which the king is involved. That is, the editors assume that all of the psalm could be read and used as parts of a Royal Psalm even if the king is absent from large parts of the psalm. The particular example Kwakkel uses to illustrate this is Psalm 18, which has large sections that do not explicitly or by implication assume the involvement of the king, but is regularly regarded as a Royal Psalm because of its conclusion, which clearly points to the king as the speaking voice (Kwakkel, *"According to My Righteousness,"* 287).

that the increased focus on the poor or the afflicted, which begins already in Psalm 9 and continues throughout the whole, suggests that the psalm has to be by an individual member of the community who has suffered assaults of some sort at the hands of wicked brothers and sisters. A deep concern for the poor and the oppressed, for the needy and the orphan, was a cardinal responsibility of the ruler of ancient Israel. Throughout the Royal Psalm 72, the king's responsibility for the maintenance of the cause of the poor and needy and oppressed is central. And Jeremiah essentially defines kingship in terms of whether or not the king attends to the needs of the poor. Psalms 9 and 10 are a cardinal example of the incorporation of the poor into the king's prayer and his identification with their need.

If the royal character of these psalms is most evident in the first one and the cry for help on the part of or on behalf of the oppressed and the needy is most evident in the second one, neither element is missing from the other psalm. The accomplishment of this psalm in its artful composition is precisely the joining of these themes, indeed of the major themes of the Psalter in one whole. Psalm(s) 9–10 is the psalm that most fully joins the two primary features of the Psalter in one: the lament dimension—the fate of the righteous and the wicked at the center of a cry for help by one in trouble—and the theme of the Lord's rule (and the king) and the fate of the nations. These are generally treated as separate psalmic themes, though they come together more often than recognized. Here their joining in one is in a large way. The psalm(s) are almost a cardinal example of an Enthronement Psalm with the declaration of the Lord's kingship and the call for the Lord to rise up in judgment against the nations and peoples of the earth to manifest a righteous rule in the whole of the universe, as evidenced especially in the protection of the poor and needy from their oppressors, whoever they may be. At the same time, there is hardly any psalm that better embodies the typical lament prayer for help, with its complaint against God (e.g., 10:1ff.), its complaint against the wicked who threaten to do in the righteous, the poor/needy/helpless/afflicted (e.g., 10:2–11), and its petitions to the Lord to rise up against the wicked/enemies/nations (9:20–21; 10:12, 15). Only in Psalm 14 do we hear anything equivalent to the challenge to the Lord's power and presence in the midst of a wicked and oppressive world as is heard in the various quotations of the wicked in Psalm 9–10:

"God will not seek" (10:4)
"There is no God" (10:4)
"I will not be moved from generation to generation" (10:6)
"God has forgotten. He has hidden his face. He will not see forever" (10:11)
"You [God] will not seek it out" (10:13)

The quotations of the wicked are an implicit complaint on the part of the faithful ruler, who prays and who has asked the questions himself first (10:1). The continued capability of the wicked to oppress and do in the afflicted and helpless is seen as a reflection of a godless spirit, but the evidence is visible to the psalmist/king who prays. So the hidden thoughts of the wicked expressed by the psalmist become the psalmist's own fears, his own complaint against God.

As in all the prayers for help (except Psalm 88), there are words of trust that express the confidence of the ruler in the midst of the cry for help (e.g., 9:16–19; 10:14, 16–18). Indeed the psalm begins with a song of thanksgiving that sets all that follows in the context of the experience of divine deliverance already known and experienced (9:1–7).

The complex joining of powerful complaint and cry for help with assertions of the Lord's rule means that these different kinds of voices, these different kinds of claims, are not to be heard apart from one another. One may talk about distinctive themes in this regard and recognize that one theme dominates a particular psalm while the other theme is prominent in other psalms. But the affirmation of the Lord's kingship is articulated in the context of and in the face of precisely all the human questions and fears that come to expression in the psalms of complaint and lament. Here lament and complaint are encompassed in praise and thanksgiving at the beginning (9:1–13) and the declaration of the eternal reign of God over the nations of the earth (10:16) and on behalf of the weak (10:17–18) at the end. As Psalm 72 asserts that the claim of the king to rule over the nations and the kings of the earth is found in his deliverance of the needy and the afflicted (Ps 72:1–4, 8–14), so Psalm(s) 9–10 answers the cry of the poor for help with the conviction that the Lord is ruler and as ruler will hear and answer. Theodicy and sovereignty are not at odds with each other but are two sides of the same coin.

Divine sovereignty, therefore, is the weighty word of the psalm, on which depend the hopes and fears of the afflicted, the poor, the weak, and the king as one of these or as representative in their behalf. Three powerful images or metaphors convey its force. The most prominent one is the picture of God as *king*. The rule of the Lord is directly affirmed in language that speaks of the rule as eternal (10:16a), over the nations and peoples (9:12, 10:16b), effected from the divine throne in Zion (9:12; cf. v. 15). What is most critical and at the heart of the joining of the two themes is the fact that the Lord's rule is particularly manifest in power to deliver the weak and the afflicted from their oppressors, from the wicked and the evil one (9:12–13; 10:16–18). Divine rule is always an exercise in power, but that is not a neutral power. It always has a moral content to it. According to this psalm, divine rule and power are most evident in God's attention to those who cry out in pain, shame, hurt, and affliction.

The moral character of the divine rule is further indicated with the metaphor of the Lord as *judge*. This is not distinct from the royal image. On the contrary, twice the judging activity of the Lord is specifically identified as a royal activity:

> You have sat on the throne giving righteous judgment (9:5)
> He has established his throne for judgment (9:8)

But it is specifically as judge that the Lord recognizes and adjudicates the right of the weak and the afflicted. The image dominates the psalm as much as the picture of God as ruler (9:5, 8–9, 17, 20; 10:5). Because the Lord is a righteous judge, the just cause of the one who is oppressed by the wicked/nations will be upheld (9:5). The one who "judges the world with righteousness" and "judges the peoples with equity" (9:9) is the hope of the lowly and the afflicted (9:8–11), an assumption one can take up in confidence and against all the assumptions of the wicked (whether nation or evil person) that they can get away with their evil deeds because the psalmist king has experienced God's deliverance and just judgment as redemptive in the past.

The power of this divine ruler to effect justice for the afflicted is indicated with the imagery of the *warrior* God. This is evident especially in 9:6–7:

> You have rebuked (*gāʿar*)[18] the nations, you have destroyed the wicked;
>   you have blotted out their name forever and ever.
> The enemies have vanished in everlasting ruins;
>   their cities you have rooted out;
>   the very memory of them has perished.

So the king can call on the Lord to rise up and strike fear into the nations (9:20–21). The one who decides in behalf of justice also exercises a just power to carry out the judgment and thus to undo the wicked and destroy them and their power over the weak and the lowly.[19]

---

18. The verb *gāʿar* "to rebuke, blast" has strong mythopoeic overtones of the divine battle against the chaotic enemies. For discussion of texts from Ugarit as well as the Old Testament, see the discussion of André Caquot in his essay on the root in *TDOT* 3.49–53. Note his summary comments: "The derivatives of *gaʿar* frequently appear in poetic references to the victory that God won over the waters" (p. 51) and: "When the etymology and secular use of *gāʿar* ('to utter a cry') are taken into account, it seems that the central point in the religious use of *gaʿar* and *geʿarah* lies in the fearful and threatening voice of Yahweh, which he utters in the thunder, and which functions as a battle cry when he puts various enemies to flight" (p. 53).

19. For further elaboration of the way in which these three metaphors are central to the Old Testament depiction of Israel's God, see my *Religion of Ancient Israel* (The Library of

The mediator of the Lord's deliverance is in some way the king, whose rule over the nations is affirmed here. Zion is the throne of the king and judge of the nations of the earth and the throne of the one through whose actions this rule is carried out. The king is recipient of this powerful deliverance as much as the dispenser of it. No explicit word is said about the king's role in the psalm. For that, one must read Psalm 2 and 72 and other psalms. It is important, however, that the rule of the Lord is not apart from its manifestation through the human ruler. The point set forth in Psalm 2 is underscored here where we find the first reference to Zion and specifically to God's rule from Zion after the introductory reference to Zion as the throne of God's human ruler in Psalm 2. Whereas Psalm 2 focused more on the human ruler, Psalms 9–10 focus on the divine ruler enthroned in Zion.

The ultimate aim of Psalm(s) 9–10, therefore, is to declare the rule of the Lord as enduring, powerful over all, and the hope of the afflicted, whose deliverance from the wicked is evidence of the Lord's rule. All the references to the divine throne, the abode of the Lord in Zion, and the depiction of the Lord as king, judge, and warrior indicate that this psalm is an early anticipation of the psalms that make up the center of Book IV and the climax of the Psalter. When it is heard much later in the Psalter, the claim that "the Lord is king" or "the Lord reigns" and the character of this claim as grounding all the hope of the afflicted, and specifically of the human ruler as afflicted and protector of the afflicted, is not a new thing in the Psalter. It has been prepared for at the beginning.

While no single psalm or set of psalms in Book I of the Psalter can be said to mark an unequivocal center or controlling point, this powerful combination of cry for help and affirmation of divine power and rule flows directly out of the introductory psalms and stands very much at the center of the first collection of psalms in Book I, that is, Psalms 3–14. The ways of righteousness and wickedness and the ultimate vindication of the former and perishing of the latter are what Psalm 1 sets forth as the subject matter of the Psalter. It is in this combination psalm that these motifs, already anticipated in Psalm 7, come to strong prominence with both the words about God's vindication of the just cause of the righteous and the several references to the wicked/enemies' perishing (*'ābad*, 9:4, 6, 7; 10:16; cf. 9:19).

So also the protection and support of the poor and needy, of the orphan and the oppressed that is so much at the heart of the Torah in which the righteous one delights (Ps 1:1–3) arises first here as a strong theme that will continue

---

Ancient Israel; Louisville: Westminster John Knox, 2000) 6–12; and idem, "The Sovereignty of God," in *Israelite Religion and Biblical Theology*, 406–21.

throughout the Psalter. Indeed Psalm(s) 9–10 contains one of the largest cluster of terms for the poor and needy of any psalm in the Psalter, including the following words: *dak* ("oppressed"—9:10, 10:18), *ʿānî/ʿānāw* ("afflicted/affliction"—9:13, 14, 19; 10:2, 9 [2×], 12, 17), *ḥēlĕkâ* ("helpless"—10:8, 10, 14), *nāqî* ("innocent"—10:8), *yātôm* ("orphan"—10:14, 18), and *ʾebyôn* ("poor"— 9:19).[20] Furthermore, *all* of these terms make their *first* appearance in the Psalter in Psalm(s) 9–10. That is, it is with this psalm that the *Armentheologie* of the Psalter begins.[21] The prayer for the poor, the weak, the needy, and the oppressed first arises in Psalm(s) 9–10, and it happens with such vigor that it places *the protection and support of the poor and the needy* as the fundamental content of the *sovereignty of God*.

That justice and the help of the poor and afflicted is also fundamental to the rule of the human king is evident in the way in which some of these same terms, specifically *ʿānî* (72:1, 4, 12) and *ʾebyôn* (72:4, 12, 13 [2×]), cluster in Psalm 72 as that psalm sets the king's protection and justice for the poor and the weak as the basis of his claim to rule the nations, a protection manifest by the king's just judgment, a reflection of the judging activity of the Lord. The first occurrence of the divine epithet "helper" (*ʿōzēr*) is Ps 10:14, where the Lord is the helper of the orphan.[22] The same epithet is then applied to the

---

20. On these terms for the poor as they are present in Psalms 9–10, see the summary comment of F. Hossfeld:

> Der Psalm fällt auf durch ein reiches und verstreutes Vokabular zum Thema "Armut": Leitwort ist *ʿani* "der Arme" (9[13.19] 10[2.9.12.17]), einmal in 9[19] begleitet vom Synonymbegriff *ʾaebyon* "der Elende"; daneben tauchen fast singuläre Austauschbegriffe auf wie *dak* "der Bedrückte" (9[10] 10[18]) und *ḥēlʿkāh* "der Schwache" (10[8.10.14]). Dadurch weist sich der Psalm aus als einer der typischen Armenpsalmen (9/10 25 34 37 69 72 109), die im ersten Davidpsalter zugleich identisch sind mit der Reihe der akrostischischen Psalmen (9/10 25 34 37). Der Psalm wechselt mühlos zwischen dem Blick auf den einzelnen Armen (9[10.14.19] 10[2.8.9.14.18]) und dem Blick auf das Kollectiv der Armen (9[13.19] 10[10.12.17]). Die Armut hat viele Facetten: soziale Not und Ausbeutung (9[10.13]), Verfolgung (10[2]) Rechtsnot (10[7.8]) und Ausgeliefertsein an die hinterhältige feindliche Übermacht (10[9f]). Der Beter bedenkt die Armut in all ihren Dimensionen und schildert die eigene wie die der Gruppe der Armen. Er überschaut Vergangenheit, Gegenwart und Zukunft und sieht die Armut sowohl unter sozialem als auch religiösem Aspekt. (*Die Psalmen I*, 81–82)

21. On the theology of the poor in the Psalter, see Hossfeld and Zenger, *Die Psalmen I*, passim, and the earlier classic work of Albert Gelin (1953) translated into English as *The Poor of Yahweh* (Collegeville, Minn.: Liturgical Press, 1964).

22. On this word and its possible association with a second *ʿzr* root, from an original *ǵzr*, preserved in Ugaritic and meaning "hero," "warrior," "protector," or the like, see Jerome Creach, *Yahweh as Refuge and the Editing of the Hebrew Psalter* (JSOTSup 217; Sheffield: Sheffield Academic Press, 1996) 35, and the references in n. 34.

king in Psalm 72 with reference to the king's support of the "afflicted" (*ʿānî*), "who has no helper."

The rule of the Lord's anointed over the nations of the earth is set as a theme of the Psalter in Psalm 2, which, like Psalm(s) 9–10, understands the rule of the human king from Zion as a manifestation of the eternal rule of the one enthroned in Zion and heaven.[23] If the focus of Psalm 2 is on the human ruler, the derivative character of this rule is clear. If Psalm(s) 9–10 focus on the Lord as king, the working out of this rule is implicit in the voice of the king as the one who prays and whose rule is defined in the same way as the rule of the Lord—the help and deliverance of the poor, the afflicted, and the oppressed.

The central subject matter of the Psalter is thus fully underway in this lately but carefully crafted Psalm. At the beginning of the Psalter, its climax is already anticipated. In the first group of psalms, the juxtaposition of human cries for help and shouts of praise because the Lord reigns lets the reader know that these cannot be separated. The one receives its answer in the other. But the questions of the one are always a test of the other. The sovereignty of God is seen to be nothing other than a protection of the just cause of the afflicted, for whom God's judgment is a safe haven and refuge (9:10). The human ruler will be—in this book as in human experience—both the one who voices the cry for help and the one who brings the power of God on behalf of the weak.

---

23. See my "Beginning of the Psalter," 276–77.

Buber, Kingship, and the Book of Judges: A Study of Judges 6–9 and 17–21

DENNIS T. OLSON
Princeton Theological Seminary

It is a great pleasure and honor to dedicate this essay to my good friend over many years of our teaching together at Princeton Seminary, Jim Roberts. This native Texan's work among us as a scholar, teacher, and colleague has enriched our lives, stretched our minds, and deepened our souls.

Buber, Kingship, and Judges

In his 1967 book *Kingship of God*, the well-known Jewish scholar Martin Buber included an essay entitled "Books of Judges and Book of Judges."[1] Buber argued that the biblical book of Judges contained within itself two separate "books" or subplots. These two "books" within Judges held together different viewpoints on the institution of the monarchy in an intentional dialectical tension.

> The work is composed of two books. . . . Each of the two books is edited from a biased viewpoint, the first from an anti-monarchical, the second from a monarchical. We have in 'Judges' the result of a compositional balancing of two opposing editorial biases, each of which had been represented in a complete book form.[2]

One book encompassed Judges 1–16. This antikingship "book" began in chap. 1 with the account of the defeated Canaanite King Adoni-bezek. With the king's thumbs and big toes mutilated by his Israelite captors, the king confessed, "Seventy kings with their thumbs and big toes cut off used to pick up scraps under my table; as I have done, so God has paid me back" (Judg 1:7). Buber observes that this story of the humbling of royal hubris was "the typical legend of derision, and the motif word is 'king.'"[3] Subsequent stories portrayed the humbling of other enemy kings who oppressed Israel. The obese

---

1. Martin Buber, *Kingship of God* (London: Humanities, 1967) 66–84.
2. Ibid., 68.
3. Ibid., 69.

Moabite King Eglon is humiliated in a grotesque assassination by the judge Ehud (Judg 3:17, 21–22). Buber interprets the Canaanite General Sisera in Judges 4–5 as a stand-in for the Canaanite King Jabin. His ignominious death at the hands of Jael who hammers her tent peg through his skull becomes a metaphor for King Jabin's eventual fate (Judg 4:21–24).

For Buber, however, the high point of this antimonarchical "book" within Judges is the figure of Gideon in Judges 6–8. "The anti-monarchical book centers plainly in him," and "he is the genuine hero of the primitive-theocratic legend."[4] Called by God as a judge-deliverer, Gideon defeats the enemy, but then he renounces the people's offer to make him a king with words that Buber understands as genuine humility and piety: "I will not rule (Heb. *māšal*) over you, and my son will not rule over you; Yhwh will rule over you" (Judg 8:23). In Buber's judgment, Gideon's refusal to take up kingship exemplifies the preferred vision advocated by the first "book" within Judges: the exclusive kingship of God with no human royal rival. This theme is reinforced in the next story of Gideon's misbegotten son Abimelech, who establishes himself as a rogue Israelite king by killing 70 of his own brothers (Judges 9). One brother, Jotham, escapes the massacre and proclaims a fable that indicts Abimelech as nothing but a worthless bramble bush in a forest of majestic trees. "The Jotham fable," writes Buber, is "the strongest anti-monarchical poem of world literature."[5] The illicit King Abimelech met an appropriately disgraceful demise when a woman standing on a besieged city wall threw a millstone upon his head and crushed his skull (Judg 9:53–54). The antikingship "book" ends with the stories of Jephthah and Samson, who return to the mold of genuine deliverers or judges who like Gideon make no claim to be king (Judges 10–16).

"In chapters 17–21," writes Buber, "a monarchical book appears at the side of the anti-monarchical Book of Judges, or rather, in opposition to it."[6] The two major episodes within these chapters recount corrupt priests leading people in idolatry and the brutal rape and murder of an Israelite woman and its resulting civil war within Israel. These stories signal Israel's descent into religious and social chaos and anarchy. The prime cause of this Israelite disintegration is expressed, according to Buber, in the refrain that both begins and ends this second, prokingship "book" within Judges. The refrain reads, "In those days there was no king in Israel; all the people did what was right in their own eyes" (Judg 17:6; 21:25). Part of the refrain, "In those days there was no

---

4. Ibid., 70.
5. Ibid., 75.
6. Ibid., 77.

king in Israel," also appears in 18:1 and 19:1. Buber restates the meaning of the refrain in these words: "That which you pass off as theocracy [God alone is king] has become anarchy. . . . Only since this people . . . took unto itself a human being for a king, has it known order and civilization."[7] Buber contends, however, that it is not any kingship in view here but specifically and only the kingship of David as opposed to Saul. Several details within Judges 17–21 echo places and events in Saul's life and thus implicitly associate Saul with all the negative events that occurred in Israel's social and religious meltdown at the end of Judges. Gibeah, Mizpah, Jabesh-Gilead, the tribe of Benjamin, and the act of cutting an ox into twelve pieces and sending them out as a call to war are all associated with King Saul in 1 Samuel 10–31, and these same details have echoes in the disastrous events of Judges 17–21, especially in chaps. 19–21 (e.g., compare Judg 19:29–30 and 1 Sam 11:7).

But how and why does the one book of Judges hold together these two opposing "books," one antikingship and the other prokingship, specifically a pro-Davidic kingship? Buber's answer was that the holding together of these two perspectives prepared the reader for a similar tensive dialectic that would occur in the next cycle of stories about the rise of Israel's monarchy in 1–2 Samuel. On one hand, the prophet Samuel was angered by the Israelites' demand that he appoint for them "a king to govern us, like other nations" (1 Sam 8:5). God instructed Samuel to give in to their demands "for they have not rejected you, but they have rejected me from being king over them" (1 Sam 8:7). The people's desire for a human king like the nations is here clearly condemned. On the other hand, this antimonarchical theme is counterbalanced by God's love and commitment to King David as "a man after his own heart" (1 Sam 13:14), to whom God promised an eternal dynasty through the prophet Nathan: "I will establish the throne of his kingdom forever" (2 Sam 7:13). Human kingship here is enthusiastically embraced. Buber suggests that Israel learned from these two unresolved voices to balance (1) a worthwhile and partially attainable vision of human freedom and individual decision embodied in primitive theocracy, which historically always threatened to devolve into anarchy, and (2) the realistic and ongoing need for earthly government and continuity of leadership and structure embodied in kingship.

Buber believed that the present form of Judges with its two opposing "books" originated already in the early monarchical period, the time of Samuel the prophet. In this, Buber strongly disagreed with the earlier formulations of Julius Wellhausen, who accounted for the pro- and antimonarchial traditions in both Judges and 1 Samuel 7–12 as reflective of different literary sources

---

7. Ibid., 78.

202 Dennis T. Olson

from widely different historical periods. For Wellhausen, the promonarchical sections originated during the Israelite monarchy, and the antikingship traditions of Judges and 1–2 Samuel emerged only later, in the postexilic period of Israel's history. With the Babylonian exile and return to the land under Persian auspices in the sixth and fifth centuries B.C.E., Israel's human kingship ended. Wellhausen contended that the image of "king" was then transposed to God in a postexilic theocracy, a theocracy that was retrojected back centuries earlier into the period of the judges by a later redactor.[8] In contrast to Wellhausen, Buber understood these disparate traditions to coexist in the same book already in the early monarchy. Yet Buber also recognized that the biblical stories continued to resonate with new audiences and readers in later contexts. "In this view of history which caused the compositional balancing to succeed," Buber concluded, "post-exilic Judaism read the Book of Judges."[9]

Although we will disagree below with much of Buber's construction concerning the book of Judges, there are some aspects of his proposal worth preserving and to which we will return at the conclusion of this essay.

The Structure of Judges, the Character of Gideon, and the Concluding Refrain: Responses to Buber's Proposal

Our analysis of Buber's treatment of Judges provides much of the raw data and lines of argument that set the stage for analyzing more recent proposals about the ideology of Judges in regard to kingship. Our survey of these proposals will not be exhaustive. Several previous studies have summarized the variety of positions in regard to the book of Judges and its ideological assessment of the institution of kingship.[10] We will isolate three key elements that respond to Buber's proposal and relate to the view of kingship in the book of Judges: (a) an alternative proposal for the overall editorial structure of the book of Judges, (b) an alternative reading of Gideon's refusal to accept kingship for himself and his statement that "Yhwh will rule over you" (Judg 8:23), and

---

8. Ibid., 82. See Julius Wellhausen, *Die Composition des Hexateuchs und der historischen Bücher des Alten Testaments* (3rd ed.; Berlin: Georg Reimer, 1899) 229.

9. Ibid., 84.

10. Marvin Sweeney, "Davidic Polemics in the Book of Judges," *VT* 46 (1997) 517–29; Andrew D. H. Mayes, "Deuteronomistic Royal Ideology in Judges 17–21," *BibInt* 9 (2001) 241–58; David Howard, "The Case for Kingship in Deuteronomy and the Former Prophets," *WTJ* 52 (1990) 101–15; and Frank Crüseman, *Der Widerstand gegen das Königtum: Die antiköniglichen Texte des Alten Testaments und der Kampf um den frühen israelitischen Staat* (Neukirchen-Vluyn: Neukirchener Verlag, 1978) 19–53, 155–66.

(c) a reconsideration of the refrain that brackets the final chapters of Judges, "In those days there was no king in Israel; all the people did what was right in their own eyes" (Judg 17:6; 21:25). We will consider each element in turn.

The Editorial Structure of Judges

Buber argued that Judges could be divided into two halves or "books," chaps. 1–16 and 17–21. For him, the singular theme of kingship—whether pro or con—was the single determining factor in his proposal for the structure of Judges. He was forced to acknowledge that several parts and details of the book did not deal with kingship at all and had to be ignored in determining the book's structure.[11] More recent redaction-critical and literary studies of Judges have laid the groundwork for an alternative proposal for the overall structure and movement of the book of Judges.[12] This alternative proposal accommodates many more of the details and sections of Judges than Buber's thesis was able to incorporate. The book of Judges likely began as a loose collection of local hero tales carried by individual clans or tribes. These and other parts of Judges were shaped and gathered in two or more stages of editing in which the local stories were generalized to include "all Israel." Moreover, later redactors shaped the entire book into a fairly coherent and generalized pattern of a series of Israelite generations who experienced a downward political and religious spiral in their leadership, in their religious adherence, and in their social unity. This pattern of gradual and progressive deterioration is evident (a) in the shape of the book's introduction (1:1–3:6), (b) the progression of the six major judge stories, (c) the sequence of the six so-called minor judges, and (d) the overall geographical movement from Southern to Northern Israel evident throughout the book.

The introduction in 1:1–3:6 provides the defining pattern for understanding the movement and structure of the entire book of Judges as it moves from initial military success and religious faithfulness to increasing failure and apostasy. This pattern is presented twice in these introductory chapters. The first

---

11. Buber, *Kingship of God*, 69. Concerning the antikingship "book" of Judges 1–16, Buber writes: "If one eliminates . . . the sketchy sections, the general reflections and the speeches of the 'messenger' (2:1–5) and of the 'interpreter' (6:7–10), as well as the statements concerning the 'minor' judges of whom nothing is really related, then one obtains a succession of seven stories, . . . every one of which expresses the anti-monarchical bias."

12. See my "Judges: Introduction, Commentary and Reflections," *NIB* 2.721–888, esp. 762–65, 791–819; Lawson Stone, *From Tribal Confederation to Monarchic State: The Editorial Perspective in the Book of Judges* (Ph.D. diss., Yale University, 1987) 260–391; and Barry Webb, *The Book of the Judges: An Integrated Reading* (Sheffield: JSOT Press, 1987) 123–79.

section in 1:1–2:5 focuses on Israel's increasing *military* failure to conquer Canaan. It portrays the last stages of Israel's conquest of Canaan after the death of Joshua as a downward spiral that moves from moderate successes by the Southern tribe of Judah (1:1–21) to increasingly negative failures by the Northern tribes of "the house of Joseph" (1:22–36). This movement from fairly positive associations with the Southern tribe of Judah and more negative associations as one moves geographically into the Northern tribes of Israel is also reflected in the sequence of major judges and their tribes of origin in Judges 3–16, as we will note below.

Judg 2:6–3:6 provides a second instance of the introductory pattern that focuses on Israel's growing *religious* failure to obey the covenant with God. The cyclical pattern in 2:11–19 of Israel's apostasy, God's handing them over to an oppressor, their cry to God, God's deliverance through a judge, and Israel's return to apostasy is reshaped into a pattern of decline. This reshaping is accomplished by the redactional additions of 2:17 (increasing failure of judges as religious leaders) and 2:20–3:6 (in light of Israel's escalating lack of faith, God abandons the conquest strategy and instead allows Canaanites to remain in the land, 2:20–21).[13]

The six major judge narratives in chaps. 3–16 have been edited and shaped in their present form to conform to this same introductory paradigm of military, political, and religious decline. The tales of the individual judges begin with the model judge Othniel (3:7–11), who stands apart from the rest and provides the standard of proper judgeship by which all the other judges may be evaluated. Six elements in the Othniel account become the criteria by which subsequent judges are evaluated: (1) the nature of the evil done by Israel, (2) description of the enemy's oppression, (3) divine reaction to the Israelites' cry, (4) the judge's success in uniting and delivering Israel, (5) a focus on God's victory versus a focus on the judge's personal life and desire for vengeance, and (6) the proportion of years of peace versus years of oppression. As we move from the earlier to the later judges in chaps. 3–16, the reader notes the progressive deterioration in actualizing these six criteria of the model judges.

(1) The nature of Israel's evil moves from an unspecified evil in the early judge stories (3:12; 4:1a) to a more and more explicit charge of idolatry and worshiping foreign gods in the later judge stories (6:10; 8:24–27, 33–35; 10:6).

---

13. For more details and arguments for this redactional shaping of the introduction to Judges, see E. Theodore Mullen, "Judges 1:1–3:6: The Deuteronomistic Reintroduction of the Book of Judges," *HTR* 77 (1984) 33–54; Stone, "From Tribal Confederation," 190–259; and Olson, "Judges," 731–61.

(2) The descriptions of the enemy's oppression in the early judge narratives are relatively short and generic (3:13; 4:2), but the descriptions of the oppression in the latter judge narratives become longer and more severe (6:1–6; 10:6–16).

(3) God's reaction to the Israelite cry of distress is immediate and positive in the early judge tales (3:15; 4:3–7). In contrast, Israel's cry in the later stories evokes a prophetically mediated divine rebuke (6:7–10) and then a direct and unmediated divine rejection (10:10–14), a sign of Israel's increasing sinfulness and the judges' increasing failure to lead. This decline culminates in the Samson narrative, which has no cry from Israel at all; Israel has lost its social and religious capacity even to cry in distress as a community to God (13:1).

(4) The judges' success in uniting and saving Israel begins on a high note. The early judges are victorious (3:29–30; 4:23–24). They united Israel, including the Northern Ephraimites, to their cause (3:27; 5:14). The degree to which the Israelite tribe of Ephraim (likely a metonym for the Northern Kingdom of Israel) is included or excluded becomes an indicator of Israel's health throughout these narratives. The later judges have some success against external enemies (8:28). However, Gideon is the first judge to become entangled in a brief internal conflict with his fellow Israelite tribe of Ephraim (8:1–3). Gideon's conflict with Ephraim is quickly resolved without bloodshed, but this intra-Israel conflict escalates with the later judges who begin killing fellow Israelites. Abimelech murders 70 of his own brothers (9:5). Jephthah kills his own daughter and then kills 42,000 members of the tribe of Ephraim (12:1–6). The last judge, Samson, is a one-man army who does not unite or lead any tribes of Israel in battle. His success is limited, because he will only "begin to deliver Israel from the hand of the Philistines" (13:5).

(5) The focus of the early judge narratives is on the praise and activity of God (3:15, 28; 4:23; 5:1–11, 31). We know very little about the origins, divine call, or personal lives of the early judges—Othniel, Ehud, and Deborah. In contrast, the later judge stories gradually lessen the attention on God's role in achieving victory and increase the amount of biographical detail dedicated to the individual judges, beginning with Gideon. By the time we reach Jephthah and Samson, their personal stories and desire for personal revenge simply crowd out the actual account of any military victory or God's role in it.

(6) The decreasing proportion of the number of years Israel had rest or peace under each judge to the number of years of enemy oppression is another marker of the decline of the judges period. The ideal standard is set in the Othniel account with a long 40 years of peace in contrast to only 8 years of oppression (3:8, 11). The early judges all meet or exceed this standard while the later judges fall short. Thus, the proportions of years of peace to years of

oppression run as follows: Othniel—40/8, Ehud (3:14, 30)—30/18, Deborah (4:3; 5:31)—40/20, Gideon (6:1; 8:28)—40/7, Jephthah (10:8; 12:7)—6/16, and Samson (13:1; 16:31)—20/40. Gideon's role as a transition figure is marked by his meeting the standard set by Othniel of at least 40 years of peace (8:28), but this notice is marred by an accompanying indictment that "all Israel prostituted themselves" to an idolatrous ephod made by Gideon (8:27). Note how the initial standard of 40 years of peace under Othniel's ideal judgeship has turned into 40 years of oppression by the time we have reached Samson, the last of the judges.

Thus, we may outline the major judge cycle as composed of three stages that move from moderate success to gradual decline. The first stage includes the model judge Othniel and the positive judgeships of Ehud and Deborah (Judg 3:7–5:31). Stage two is a transitional phase in which Gideon is both positively and negatively portrayed, culminating in his son Abimelech, who is uniformly condemned (6:1–10:5). The third and final phase of the major judges includes Jephthah and Samson, both of whom increasingly fail to unite Israel or to win lengthy periods of peace (10:6–16:31).

The same sense of gradual decline appears in the sequence of the six so-called minor judges. The brief notices about these judges intrude at three junctures among the major judge narratives: Shamgar in 3:31, Tola and Jair in 10:1–5, and Ibzan, Elon, and Abdon in 12:8–15. Scholars have often puzzled about the significance of these minor judges, including Buber, who excluded them as in any way significant to his own vision of the structure or movement of Judges. However, the three junctures in which the minor judges occur correspond to the three stages in the decline of the major judges. The first minor judge, Shamgar, successfully kills 600 Philistines and is said to have "delivered Israel" (3:31). His success corresponds with the positive portraits of the early major judges, who were successful and faithful. The next two judges, Tola and Jair in 10:1–5, appear at the end of the second transitional stage with Gideon and Abimelech. Gideon is a transitional figure, militarily successful but religiously unfaithful in the end. Gideon's son, Abimelech, is a dismal failure on all counts. The two minor judges listed in this section are similarly a mixed bag. The narrator reports that Tola "rose to deliver Israel," but the narrator provides no indication that Jair accomplished anything for the well-being of Israel. All that is reported is that Jair had 30 sons who rode 30 donkeys and possessed 30 towns. Jair exemplifies the gradual shift from the judges as focused on God and Israel to leaders focused on themselves and their possessions.

The third interpolation of minor judges (Ibzan, Elon, and Abdon) in 12:8–15 appears between the stories of Jephthah and Samson. In line with the decline and failure of these last judges, no mention of delivering Israel or any other beneficial effect is reported for these three minor judges. Moreover, the length of their successive judgeships is relatively short: 7, 10, and 8 years. The relative shortness of their tenure corresponds to the relative brevity of the judgeships of Jephthah and Samson. Moreover, the focus of the reports of these minor judges is exclusively on their personal lives and individual concerns (finding spouses for their children, the number of their children riding on donkeys and the like). The early judges' focus on Israel's deliverance and praise of God is gradually diluted into personal agendas, individual and family concerns, and trivial pursuits in the later judges, both the minor judges (Ibzan, Elon, and Abdon) and the major judges (Jephthah and Samson).

One other major indicator of the structure of overall decline in the book of Judges is the geographical sequence of the judges as the reader moves from the early to later judges. We already noted above in our discussion of the introductory section of Judges (1:1–3:6) that a progression from Southern tribes to Northern tribes is detectable and corresponds to a gradual decline as one moves from south to north. A similar geographical movement from Southern Judah through middle and Northern Israelite tribes and clans is evident in the sequence of individual judge stories in 3:6–16:31. The sequence begins with the positive model of Othniel, who is related to Caleb from the tribe of Judah (1:10–15; 3:9). Then we move in sequence through the tribes of Benjamin (Ehud, 3:15), Ephraim (Deborah, 4:4), Issachar (Tola, 10:1), Zebulun (Elon, 12:12), and the far Northern tribe of Dan (Samson, 13:2).[14] These geographical progressions from Southern Judah to the far Northern Dan are accompanied by a deteriorating progression in the effectiveness and faithfulness of the judges and the Israelites. This progression suggests a shaping of the book at some stage that is ideologically tilted toward Southern Judah.

At the same time, however, the book is not simply anti-North. The judges' varying relationship with the dominant Northern tribe of Ephraim is an important motif throughout the book of Judges. The treatment of Ephraim by the individual judges functions as a barometer of Israel's cohesion and social unity as a people. In the earliest and most positive phase of the judges era, the individual judges called on the tribe of Ephraim to join in the conflict against

---

14. Some of the other judges, especially in the later stages are not listed by their affiliation with one of the major twelve tribes of Israel. Rather, they are listed by their minor clan or village designations: Gideon is an Abiezrite, the weakest clan in Manasseh (6:11, 15), Jephthah is from Gilead (11:1), Ibzan is from Bethlehem (12:8), and Abdon is from Pirathon (12:13). These increasingly minor clan designations clustered among the later judges further contribute to the sense of growing disunity and social fragmentation as one moves through the book.

the enemy, and they immediately responded (3:27; 4:5; 5:14). In the second transitional phase under the judge Gideon, the tribe of Ephraim is called into the conflict against Midian at a late stage. The Ephraimites complain bitterly to Gideon about not being invited earlier to join in the battle. Gideon soothes their hurt feelings and peacefully resolves the internal dispute with Ephraim (7:24–25; 8:1–3). In the third and most negative phase of the judges era, beginning with Jephthah, the Ephraimites are again bitterly disappointed that they were not invited to join Jephthah's fight against the Ammonites. Jephthah's response is to kill 42,000 members of the tribe of Ephraim. This violence against Ephraim, an act that clearly underlines the inadequacy of Jephthah as a judge, prefigures the full-scale civil war within Israel that will erupt at the end of the book in Judges 19–21. The overall ideology of the book, although "tilted" toward being pro-South and pro-Judah, seems at the same time to promote the inclusion of Ephraim, the leader among the Northern tribes, as an important and respected member of the community of Israel.

We have noted, then, the ways in which the double introduction in Judg 1:1–3:6 and the narratives of the major and minor judges in 3:7–16:31 suggest a coherent structure which moves from success and faithfulness to increasing failure, both militarily and religiously. The overall effect is the gradual unraveling of Israel's cohesion as a community by the end of the judges era. The final judge, Samson, neither leads nor unifies any Israelites. His judgeship is strictly a one-man show motivated by personal desires and personal vengeance. In fact, the tribe of Judah betrays Samson by binding him (albeit with Samson's permission!) and delivering him over to the Philistines (15:9–17). This unraveling of Israel's social fabric climaxes in the concluding section of Judges. These final chapters form a two-part conclusion to Judges. Chapters 17–18 recount the rise of idolatry and religious disintegration. Chapters 19–21 recount the chaos of social violence and civil war as a sign of Israel's social and military disintegration. This two-part conclusion mirrors the two-part introduction to Judges, which likewise deals with Israel's increasing military (1:1–2:5) and religious (2:6–3:6) failure. Thus, contrary to Buber's proposal, the book of Judges is not structured as two opposing "books." Rather, Judges is one book with a fairly coherent structure narrating a gradual but progressive religious, social, and military decline during the time of the judges.

Gideon and Kingship

"I will not rule over you, and my son will not rule over you; Yhwh will rule over you" (Judg 8:23). Buber interpreted these words of Gideon as pious and humble advocacy for a pure theocracy devoid of human kingship. However, more recent redactional and literary analyses of Judges suggest a rather

different portrait of Gideon's character and intentions as he speaks these allegedly antiroyal words. A fuller analysis of the shift that takes place in Gideon's
character over the three chapters, 6–8, as well as the role of the Gideon cycle
in the structure of Judges conspire to raise a reader's suspicions about Gideon's
motives as he utters the words of Judg 8:23.

As the reader moves through the Gideon story and comes to 8:23, the character of Gideon changes considerably. He begins as a timid, humble servant of
God who tears down idols. But Gideon gradually changes into an arrogant and
vengeful leader who adopts the benefits of leadership but does not carry out
its responsibilities in a faithful manner. In the first phase of the Gideon story,
Gideon was fearful and hid from the Midianite enemy (Judg 6:11). Gideon felt
unworthy and incapable of accepting God's commission to deliver the Israelites (Judg 6:15). He broke down his father's bull idol and altar "but because
he was too afraid of his family and the townspeople to do it by day, he did it
by night" (Judg 6:27). God reduced Gideon's large army of 32,000 to 300 in
order to demonstrate that the victory over the Midianites would depend primarily on God's power, not human strength (Judg 7:1–8). God is concerned
that "Israel would only take the credit away from me, saying, 'My own hand
has delivered me'" (7:2).

Yet just before entering into battle with the Midianites, Gideon begins to
take some of the credit and inserts his own name into the shout of praise and
glory associated with the victory to come: "For Yhwh *and for Gideon*" (Judg
7:18–20). The typical model of the judges cycle in the other narratives of
Judges would conclude the story of Gideon with a brief note about the victory
won and the number of years of rest that followed (e.g., Judg 3:30). But the
Gideon narrative does not end in this usual way. Rather, Judg 8:4 begins a
new scene as Gideon crosses the Jordan River out of Canaan in hot pursuit of
two Midianite kings. Gideon's 300 soldiers are "exhausted and famished"
from all their fighting. Yhwh plays no role in the action of these last episodes.
The reader gets a sense that Gideon has begun to overstretch his proper
boundaries literally (the Jordan River) and figuratively. It is Gideon alone, not
his soldiers and not Yhwh, who is pushing the action and calling the shots. He
takes disproportionate and violent revenge on two towns that refuse to give
him food. After the two enemy kings confess that Gideon looks like a king
(8:18), Gideon kills the two monarchs and takes for himself their royal cres-
cents (8:21). Gideon has begun to cross over the line from temporary judge to
dynastic king.

This now is the narrative context for the Israelites' request to Gideon,
"Rule (Heb. *māšal*) over us, you and your son and your grandson also; for *you*
[not God!] *have delivered us* out of the hand of Midian" (8:22). Although the

word "king" (Heb. *melek)* is not used, the people invite Gideon into what
sounds very much like royal dynastic rule. Moreover, the Israelites seem to be
taking credit away from God and giving it exclusively to Gideon. In effect,
they and Gideon say what God had earlier warned against, "My own hand has
delivered me" (7:2; see also the prophet's warning in 6:7–10). Gideon *appears*
to turn down the request to become their ruler in words that sound on the
surface quite pious: "I will not rule . . . Yhwh will rule over you" (8:23). But
Buber and others fail to see that the narrator has placed Gideon's claim—that
God alone rules Israel with no room for human leadership—in a literary context that casts considerable doubt on the sincerity of the statement. First of all,
Gideon has been acting more and more like an independent and improper
king. He took the law into his own hands in a personal and violent vendetta
(8:13–17). He accumulated gold (8:24–26), a sign of a bad king according to
the law in Deut 17:17. Gideon crafts an ephod or idol to which "all Israel prostituted themselves" (8:27). This, too, is a sign of a bad king, according to the
law in Deut 17:20.[15]

The ephod that Gideon fashioned is a device for receiving divine oracles
and guidance from the deity. Is Gideon thus hiding his own de facto royal
power behind the cloak of a divination device that he controls, all the while
claiming that it is not he but "Yhwh" who "will rule over you"? Or has
Gideon simply abandoned all responsibility to lead in partnership with God,
leaving a power vacuum inadequately filled by a mechanical and idolatrous
oracular device? Either reading of Gideon's actions—that he is a covert king
or that he has abandoned all responsibility for leadership—indicates that something has begun to go terribly wrong with the system of the judges.

Indeed, the figure of Gideon is a pivot point in the entire sequence of
judges in the book of Judges. The early judge stories begin with military success and the praise of God (e.g., the Song of Deborah and Barak in Judges 5).
The Gideon story marks a transitional phase in which the early Gideon relies
on God but gradually moves to replace God with himself and his own constructed idol. In the beginning of his career, Gideon had broken down pagan
altars and idols in his hometown of Ophrah (6:24–27). At the end of his life,
Gideon constructs an idol, which leads Israel astray in the same hometown,
Ophrah (8:27). This shifting and dual character of Gideon (faithful, unfaithful;
timid, arrogant) is marked by his dual names that appear throughout the story,
Gideon and Jerubbaal (e.g., 8:29–30). Moreover, Gideon has "many wives"

15. David Jobling, "Deuteronomic Political Theory in Judges and 1 Samuel 1–12," in
The Sense of Biblical Narrative: Structural Analyses in the Hebrew Bible (JSOTSup 39; Sheffield:
JSOT Press, 1986) 1.66–67.

and 70 sons (8:30), further signs of a kingship like the nations (Deut 17:17; 1 Kgs 11:3; 2 Kgs 10:1). Gideon names one son "Abimelech," which means "My Father Is King" (8:31)! Gideon is an ambiguous figure, refusing to accept the office of ruler or king and yet acting very much like a covert king. He was successful militarily but religiously misled the people. He died "at a good old age" and brought 40 years of peace, but his people did not "exhibit loyalty" to his family "in return for all the good that he had done in Israel" (8:35). In particular, Gideon's son, Abimelech, will overtly and violently seize the kingship that his father only covertly assumed in Judges 9 by killing 70 of Gideon's sons.

What our analysis of the Gideon narrative suggests is that the words of Gideon, "I will not rule over you. . . . Yhwh will rule over you," cannot be taken at face value as a straightforward antimonarchical statement spoken by an utterly reliable and pious Gideon. The statement in 8:23 and the context of the whole Gideon story turn out to be, in fact, somewhat critical of monarchy. More accurately, the Gideon tale is critical of a particularly abusive form of royal leadership that Gideon covertly, and his son Abimelech overtly, practiced. The narrator clearly condemns Abimelech, not for being king per se, but for "the crime he committed against his father in killing his seventy brothers" (9:56). This assessment spills over into a not-so-subtle condemnation of Gideon for the excessive violence he perpetrated against the two towns (possibly Israelite towns?) that refused him food (8:13–17) and the two kings he pursued beyond the borders of Canaan (8:18–21). This exorbitant violence is a harbinger of the vengeful violence that will mark the judgeships of Jephthah and Samson and the civil war in the closing chapters of Judges (Judges 19–21). Moreover, Gideon's erection of the idolatrous ephod (8:24–28) is a literary echo to a later time of increasing anarchy and chaos in the story of Micah and his idolatrous "ephod," which marks the culminating endpoint of Israel's downward spiral into religious disintegration (Judges 17–18).

What then are we to make of Gideon's statement that refuses kingship and affirms that Yhwh will rule over the people (8:23) in assessing the view of kingship in Judges? Scholars have offered at least three different options for understanding Gideon's statement.[16] Many argue, in agreement with Buber, that Gideon's statement is an outright and proper rejection of the offer of kingship or any type of leadership. Some have argued that the statement is not a refusal but a politely worded acceptance of kingship.[17] Others argue that Gideon refused the title of king but accepted a position of leadership that gave

16. See the review of scholarship in Gerald Gerbrandt, *Kingship according to the Deuteronomistic History* (SBLDS 87; Atlanta: Scholars Press, 1986) 124.

17. G. Henton Davies, "Judges VIII 22–23," *VT* 13 (1963) 151–57.

him virtually the same power and benefits as that of a king, only without the title. Our reading of the full Gideon episode suggests that, however one reads Gideon's words in 8:23, they should be construed as in some way negative. At least two plausible possibilities exist. Gideon's statement may well be an outright rejection of kingship, but the rejection actually represents in the narrator's view an abrogation of responsibility and needed leadership in an unsettled time. By refusing kingship, Gideon is contributing along with his other actions to the religious and social disintegration of his time. On the other hand, Gideon's statement may just as plausibly be interpreted as false piety and humility behind which Gideon in fact claims the powers and benefits of a de facto kingship for himself, although he does not formally claim the royal title. These two options seem to be almost equally possible as readings of Gideon's character.

The Concluding Refrain to the Book of Judges and Kingship

Buber argued that the refrain that begins and ends the final section of the book of Judges (17:6; 21:25; see also 18:1; 19:1) puts a promonarchical stamp on the book's final chapters (chaps. 17–21): "In those days there was no king in Israel; all the people did what was right in their own eyes." The refrain seems to suggest that the social and religious chaos in Israel in these final chapters would have been avoided had there been a king in place. Moreover, Buber saw the refrain as specifically pro–Davidic and anti-Saul in light of the negative associations with Gibeah and Benjamin in the latter chapters in Judges, especially 19–21 (Saul was from Gibeah of the tribe of Benjamin— 1 Sam 10:26).

Most scholars have followed Buber in seeing the later chapters of Judges framed by the refrains of 17:6 and 21:25 as in some way promonarchical.[18] Many have agreed that the material is specifically pro-Judah, pro-David, and anti-Saul in light of the immediate literary context of 1 Samuel.[19] Gale Yee has argued that the later chapters of Judges with the refrain were composed not to address the time of David and Saul but the time of King Josiah. She

18. See the survey in Gerbrandt, *Kingship*, 134–38.
19. Recent examples include Yairah Amit, "Literature in Service of Politics: Studies in Judges 19–21," in *Politics and Theopolitics in the Bible and Postbiblical Literature* (JSOTSup 171; ed. H. G. Reventlow et al.; Sheffield: JSOT Press, 1994) 28–40; idem, *Hidden Polemics in Biblical Narrative* (Biblical Interpretation 25; Leiden: Brill, 2000); Marc Zvi Brettler, "The Book of Judges: Literature as Politics," *JBL* 108 (1989) 395–418; idem, *The Book of Judges* (New York: Routledge, 2002) 97–102, 111–16; Sweeney, "Davidic Polemics," 517–29; Robert H. O'Connell, *The Rhetoric of the Book of Judges* (VTSup 63; Leiden: Brill, 1996) 266–68.

maintains that Judges 17–21 functioned as ideological propaganda supporting the political, economic, and religious reforms of Josiah, which subverted tribal kinship ties and economic structures by centralizing authority in the king.[20] Yee's proposal situates the context later in the monarchy rather than earlier. But even in her interpretation, Judges remains pro-Judah (Southern Kingdom) and pro–Davidic Dynasty (Josiah was in David's line).

A small minority of scholars have disagreed with Buber and others. They have interpreted the refrains at the end of Judges as not consistently prokingship but in some way as critical of monarchy, whether Davidic or otherwise. For example, R. G. Boling interprets the two refrains in 17:6 and 21:25 as having two different aims or meanings.[21] He argues that the first refrain in 17:6 applies only to chaps. 17–18, where religious chaos prevails: idols are erected, priests work for the highest bidder, and a wandering tribe violently takes over a city that does not belong to it. The message of the refrain in 17:6, originating in the monarchical period in Israel's history, is that a king would have prevented such chaos. Boling would concede that 17:6 is prokingship. In contrast, however, Boling sees the second refrain in 21:25 as linked only to chaps. 19–21, which, according to Boling, demonstrate the ability of the tribal confederation to come together and resolve what begins as a chaotic social situation of inhospitality, murder, and the near-extinction of one of the Israelite tribes. At the end of chap. 21 where the refrain occurs, Boling maintains, Israel is unified and restored. This concluding refrain about there being no king and everyone doing what is right in their own eyes is understood as a positive affirmation of the kingless community and its ability to govern itself. Boling understood the refrain in 21:25 to be the product of an exilic redactor who urged the exiles to accept the demise of kingship and return to the kingless structure of the judges era when they relied on God alone to ensure their survival.

W. J. Dumbrell built in part on Boling's work but read both refrains in 17:6 and 21:25 as critical of Israel's dependence on monarchy or any other system of human institutional government, including the tribal confederacy. "What [alone] had preserved Israel had been the constant interventions of Israel's

---

20. Gale Yee, "Ideological Criticism: Judges 17–21 and the Dismembered Body," in *Judges and Method: New Approaches in Biblical Studies* (ed. Gale Yee; Minneapolis: Fortress, 1995) 146–70. See the helpful comparison and analysis of Yee's ideological reading and O'Connell's literary-rhetorical interpretation (see n. 19 above) by Mayes, "Deuteronomistic Royal Ideology in Judges 17–21."

21. R. G. Boling, *Judges* (AB 6A; Garden City, N.Y.: Doubleday, 1975) 29–38, 293; idem, "In Those Days There Was No King in Israel," in *A Light Unto My Path: Old Testament Studies in Honor of Jacob M. Myers* (ed. H. N. Bream et al.; Philadelphia: Temple University Press, 1974) 33–48.

deity."[22] At the same time in agreement with Boling, Dumbrell believes the
refrain reflects positively on the judges era as a preferred system of governance
without the corruptions of a king and a time when all are involved in deciding
what is right in their own eyes. The exilic author

> is suggesting that the pattern of direct divine intervention, with theocratic lead-
> ership, upon which Israel's well-being had always hung, had been never so really
> demonstrated as it had been in the age of the judges. It is the revival of this man-
> ner of leadership which alone would hold the key to Israel's future.[23]

Dumbrell here seems to waver between two different positions. On one hand,
he understands Judges 17–21 as critical of all human systems of government.
On the other hand, he argues that Judges 17–21 promoted one particular
form of human governance, a loosely structured theocracy exemplified at the
end of Judges that involved direct divine intervention and everyone doing
what was right in his/her own eyes.

My own study of Judges 17–21 and the role it plays in the overall structure
and movement of the book of Judges suggests that it cannot be read as in any
way an affirmation of the actions or governance of Israel at the end of Judges.
The book of Judges is a story of gradual decline, which comes to a dismal and
destructive climax in the religious and social chaos of chaps. 17–21. That one
of Israel's tribes, Benjamin, is snatched just in the nick of time from extinction
at the end of the book is no great mark of success but simply the bare thread
that allows the story of Israel's twelve tribes to move to its next phase intact.
When it occurs elsewhere in the Bible, the phrase "all the people did what was
right in their own eyes" is consistently either neutral or negative when applied
to humans. For example, Proverbs teaches that "the way of fools is right in
their own eyes, but the wise listen to advice" (Prov 12:15; 21:2). This negative interpretation is further supported by the use of the same phrase for Samson's errant and misguided yearning for a Philistine wife: "she is right in my
eyes" (14:3, 7). The flip side of the refrain about the absence of a king and all
the people doing what was right in their own eyes is the frequently repeated
phrase throughout Judges: "the Israelites did what was evil in the eyes of
Yhwh" (2:11; 3:7, 12; 4:1; 6:1; 10:6; 13:1). In the present form of Judges, the
Israelites' doing "evil in the eyes of Yhwh" is functionally equivalent to doing
"what was right in their own eyes." Thus, I would agree with Buber and
others who see this section of Judges as largely prokingship in the general

---

22. W. J. Dumbrell, "In Those Days There Was No King in Israel; Every Man Did
What Was Right in His Own Eyes: The Purpose of the Book of Judges Reconsidered,"
JSOT 25 (1983) 31.

23. Ibid.

sense of promoting the need for human communities to have some institutional mechanisms of order, authority, and restraint in order to live together and minimize anarchy and violence.

But I would disagree with Buber and others who suggest that these later chapters of Judges are specifically, thoroughly, and uncritically pro-David, pro-Judah, or pro–Southern Kingdom, at least in the book's final form. Some of these intra-Israelite rivalries of tribes, kings, and kingdoms may have played some role in earlier stages in the writing and shaping of these stories. But in their present form, these narratives intentionally include all tribes and groups as taking part in and being responsible for the social and religious collapse of Israel at the end of the judges period. One idolatrous Levite or priest is from the South and the tribe of Judah (17:7), and the other callous and self-absorbed Levite is from the North and the tribe of Ephraim (19:1). "All Israel" is involved in the misguided civil war and the killing and kidnapping of women that follow (20:1, 8). All the tribes of Israel experience a defeat in the battle, a sign of God's judgment against them (20:17–25). Benjamin (the tribe of King Saul) experiences defeat (20:33–36), but so does the tribe of Judah when it takes the lead (the tribe of King David—20:18–25). This blanket condemnation of "all Israel" echoes the angel's words of judgment against "all the Israelites" at the beginning of the book in Judg 2:4, a general condemnation that includes Judah, who is at the same time elevated as the leading tribe in Judg 1:2. Just as Judah went up first in fighting against the Canaanites in 1:2, so too Judah goes first in the calamitous fighting against Judah's own brother tribe, Benjamin (20:18). We have noted that a consistent sign of the deterioration of the judges era was the increasing intra-Israelite violence and attacks against fellow Israelites, especially the Northern tribe of Ephraim. Judah participates in a prominent way in the violent civil war against Benjamin at the end of Judges, a sign that Judah is viewed critically along with the other tribes.

Conclusion:
The Double-Voiced Assessment of Kingship in the Book of Judges

Buber argued that the book of Judges contained two "books," one antimonarchical in chaps. 1–16 and the other promonarchical in chaps. 17–21. I have argued against several elements of Buber's analysis of Judges. Judges does not contain two "books" with diametrically opposed viewpoints on kingship as Buber maintained. The carefully crafted and edited structure of Judges suggests a fairly coherent perspective moving through the whole book. Nor are Buber's promonarchical chapters of Judges 19–21 uncritically pro-Davidic or pro-Judah in their present form as he suggested. I noted that his reading of

Gideon's character and refusal of kingship attributed too much piety and humility to Gideon, whose character changes by the end of his story and thus
renders suspicious his words of refusal. I noted that at least two different readings of the narrator's point of view were possible: either Gideon wrongly refused to take up the responsibilities and chores of leadership when his people
needed him, or he covertly took on the benefits and power of being king even
while his words seemed to suggest otherwise. In any case, Gideon's character
at the end of the story is portrayed at least as mixed: he did succeed militarily
in delivering Israel for a time, but he failed religiously by leading Israel astray
in the worship of the idolatrous ephod.

But Buber remains helpful in suggesting that our description of the view
of kingship in Judges must be double-voiced, both yes and no. Most scholars
before and after Buber have tended to say that Judges is either entirely promonarchical or antimonarchical. Buber may help us to see that in some way it
must be both. But how do we then describe the view of human kingship in
Judges, and how do we account for its double-voiced attitude toward the
monarchy?

The entire book of Judges had a long history of composition and editing.
Early stories of individual judges were collected and edited over many generations, probably extending from a time early in the Israelite monarchy to the
exilic or postexilic period. At an earlier stage, the book of Judges likely functioned as an apologetic piece to support kingship in Israel, particularly the
Southern Judean dynasty of King David and his successors. The geographical
progression of both the introduction in Judg 1:1–2:5 and the individual judge
stories in 3:7–16:31 suggests a preference for the Southern tribe of Judah as
success and faithfulness among the Southern tribes gradually decline into failure and disobedience as one moves farther North among the tribes of Israel.
The introduction concludes with the expulsion of what will be the northern-
most tribe of Dan from its land (1:34–36), and the individual judge stories
conclude with the tragic death of the judge Samson, who is also from the
Northern tribe of Dan (13:2; 16:23–31). This pro-Judean and prokingship
perspective may well have been the product of the editors who worked on the
books of the Deuteronomistic history (Deuteronomy–2 Kings) during the
reigns of King Hezekiah (2 Kings 18–20), King Josiah (2 Kings 22–23), or at
other times during the monarchy.

However, the narratives of the exile of the Northern Kingdom (2 Kings 17)
and especially the exile of the Southern Kingdom of Judah (2 Kings 24–25)
suggest that the final form of Judges came to be read within the broader perspective of the whole Deuteronomistic history that extended from Deuteronomy to 2 Kings. That history encompassed Israel's narrated experience

through a number of different political contexts: the unique office of Moses as covenant mediator, Joshua's leadership of the conquest and the temporary judges who followed him, Israel's kings in both Northern Israel and Southern Judah, and the time of the exile and the end of kingship. Looking back from the perspective of the exile, Israel came to know that each of these human political contexts and institutions were initially moderately successful but in the end ultimately flawed. Each period of leadership (Moses, Joshua–Judges, Kings) followed a similar pattern of initial success followed by deterioration and the ultimate dissolution of the old system. Moses successfully led Israel out of Egypt, but Israel in its trek through the wilderness grew increasingly rebellious against God (Deut 31:27–29). The old wilderness generation of Israelites, including Moses himself, was condemned to die in the desert without entering the promised land. An entirely new generation would be the ones to inherit the land of Canaan (Deut 1:22–45; see Numbers 13–14). During the period of Joshua and the judges, Israel experienced initial success in its conquest in the book of Joshua. However, the book of Judges traced the gradual decline of the judges era from moderate success into gradual decline culminating in social and religious chaos and disintegration (Judges 17–21). During the period of the kings in Israel, the initial success of King David and King Solomon in the united monarchy gradually deteriorated into the divided kingdoms of North and South (1 Kings 11–12), the exile of the Northern Kingdom (2 Kings 17), and finally the exile of the Southern Kingdom of Judah and the apparent end of the Davidic kingship in its traditional form (2 Kings 24–25).

Thus, Judges within the final form of the Deuteronomistic history functions as a sober and realistic example of what eventually happens to any form of human governance or polity among the people of God. Every form of human leadership or power, whether a Mosaic covenant mediator or a judge or a king, may be moderately appropriate and helpful for a given time and context. But no human institution or structure is immune from the larger and deeper problem that infects humanity itself, namely, human sinfulness, rebellion against God, and self-absorbed quests for power, vengeance, and resources through strategies of violence, delusion, and theft. The book of Judges is not simply an apology for kingship as if the presence of kings would be the one ideal guarantee of Israel's long-term adherence to the covenant with God. Rather, the institution of Israelite judges was a paradigm of the way in which God must work in an imperfect world through necessary but inevitably flawed human structures, ideologies, and institutions. Such human structures and arrangements of power and resources may work for a time in given contexts and periods, but they will eventually deteriorate. God allows such institutions and structures to run their course and die in order that new arrangements and structures may be born. God allowed the structure of leadership through temporary judges to "hit bottom" in the social and religious chaos of Judges 17–21. Israel would struggle to find a new way of governance through the new institution of kingship in Israel (1–2 Samuel, 1–2 Kings). Like the judges, the institution of kingship would function effectively for a time but eventually disintegrate in the exile. Israel would then need again to struggle to find an appropriate polity and structure to reconstitute itself as the people of God, whether it remained in Diaspora or returned to the land. Aspects of kingship remained alive in Judaism in the form of a hope for the messiah, but leadership in the community took other forms in the meantime. Thus, the book of Judges is a sober and mature portrait of the necessity of human structures of leadership and power, the inevitability of their corruption and eventual decline, and the gracious willingness of God to work in and through such flawed human structures and communities in order to accomplish God's purposes in the world.

The Rule of God in the Book of Daniel

C. L. SEOW

Princeton Theological Seminary

It has been observed that the theme of the rule of God dominates the book of Daniel as it does nowhere else in the Old Testament.[1] The standard Hebrew and Aramaic terms for kingship (מַלְכוּ/מַלְכוּת) occur about 70 times—by far the heaviest concentration anywhere in the Bible—along with Aram. שָׁלְטָן / Heb. שִׁלְטוֹן (cf. Arab. *sulṭān*) and other derivatives of the root שׁלט, as well as other terms for royal power and majesty. Divine sovereignty is staked out at every turn, whether explicitly or implicitly, and the deity is repeatedly called "the God of gods" (2:47; 11:36), "the lord of kings" (2:47), and "the Most High God" (3:26, 32; 4:14, 21, 22, 29, 31; 5:18, 21; 7:18, 22, 25 [2×], 27), all of which are appropriately reminiscent of the role of the deity, whose name is part of Daniel's name—El, the high god of the Canaanite pantheon, the quintessential divine ruler of heaven and earth.[2] Yet, despite the obvious importance of the theme, there is considerable ambivalence regarding the book's perspective on the manifestation of divine rule on earth, particularly in the predicted emergence of a stone hewn not by hand (chap. 2) and in the vision of one who comes with the clouds "as a human one" (chap. 7). This ambivalence is evident in the history of interpretation, where the former has been interpreted as an individual (typically the Jewish Messiah or Christ in his first or second advent) or a corporate entity (the Jewish nation or the church),[3]

---

1. So, for instance, J. Boehmer, *Reich Gottes und Menschensohn im Buch Daniel* (Leipzig: Hinrichs, 1899) 16–17; J. E. Goldingay, *Daniel* (WBC 30; Dallas: Word, 1989) 330.

2. In the Ugaritic texts, El is frequently called *mlk* (*CTU* 1.2.III.5; 1.3.V.8, 36; 1.4.I.5, IV.24, 38, 48; 1.6.I.36; 1.17.VI.49; 1.117.2–3) and portrayed as an enthroned figure presiding over the divine council. See F. M. Cross, Jr., "אֵל ʾēl," *TDOT* 1.242–61 (= *TWAT* 1.259–79); idem, *Canaanite Myth and Hebrew Epic: Essays in the History of the Religion of Israel* (Cambridge: Harvard University Press, 1973) 1–75. In light of Cross's study, too, it is not amiss to note that the God of Daniel (etymologically meaning "My Judge Is El"), like El in Canaanite literature, is depicted as an ageless deity enthroned in the divine council (7:9–10), a deity whose will is communicated to humans through dreams and visions and the agency of various intermediaries.

3. See the surveys in G. Pfandl, "Interpretations of the Kingdom of God in Daniel 2:44," *AUSS* 34 (1996) 249–68; J. A. Montgomery, *Daniel* (ICC; New York: Scribner's, 1927)

while the latter has also been interpreted as an individual (the Messiah, Christ in his incarnation or his return to earth, an angel, a political or religious leader) or a symbol for a group (the Jewish people or Christian believers).[4]

This essay is an attempt to gain some clarity on these passages within the book's broader perspective on the rule of God. More specifically, I wish to argue here that there is substantial coherence in the characterization of the rule of God in the book. This may seem, at first blush, to be all too trivial a point to make. Yet, to my knowledge, there has been no attempt to link the various characterizations of the reign of God in the book, no doubt because of the widespread view about the composite origin of the book and its complicated editorial history. In particular, the two most prominent images for the reign of God—the image of the stone hewn not by human hands in chap. 2 and the one who comes with the clouds in chap. 7—are seen as figures that are totally unrelated one to the other. With regard to the latter, J. J. Collins has already shown that there is coherence between the image and the second half of the book.[5] Yet Collins unnecessarily dissociates the chapter from the stories of Daniel 1–6. By contrast, I will first demonstrate that there are significant links in the portrayal of the reign of God between Daniel 1–6 and Daniel 7. Then I will show how this reading of the text is consonant with the reading already set forth by Collins.

A Threefold Divine Giving

We may begin with the introductory chapter, even though there is no explicit mention of the rule of God there, for this chapter, by virtue of its present position, sets the tone for the book, whatever its compositional and redactional history may have been.[6] Arguably the most significant theological claim of this chapter is found in the recurrence of the verb נתן used in connection with divine initiative. It is the deity who *gave* (וַיִּתֵּן) King Jehoiachin of Judah into the power of Nebuchadnezzar (1:2), who also *gave* (וַיִּתֵּן) Daniel, an exile, "to grace

185–92; E. F. Siegman, "The Stone Hewn from the Mountain (Daniel 2)," *CBQ* 18 (1956) 364–79.

4. See A. J. Ferch, *The Son of Man in Daniel Seven* (Andrews University Doctoral Dissertation Series 6; Berrien Springs: Andrews University Press, 1979) 4–39; J. Eggler, *Influences and Traditions Underlying the Vision of Daniel 7:2–14* (OBO 177; Fribourg, Switzerland: Universitätsverlag / Göttingen:Vandenhoeck & Ruprecht, 2000) 88–95.

5. J. J. Collins, "The Son of Man and the Saints of the Most High in the Book of Daniel," *JBL* 93 (1974) 54–66; idem, *Daniel* (Hermeneia; Minneapolis: Fortress, 1993) 294.

6. Daniel 1 was probably composed as an introduction to the Aramaic tales of chaps. 2–6, if not to the entire book. See Collins, *Daniel*, 24–38.

and mercies" (וּלְרַחֲמִים לְחֶסֶד, 1:9) before the prison warden,[7] and *gave* (נָתַן) the exiles "knowledge and insight" (וְהַשְׂכֵּל מַדָּע) to survive and even thrive in their context (1:17). Divine sovereignty, as expressed in this threefold giving, is the theological thread that holds the literary unit together, suggesting that the God of judgment who permits the exile is, paradoxically, also the God of "grace and mercies" who enables the survival of faith and even grants the possibility of success for the faithful. The introductory story is, therefore, not so much about the courage of the youngsters (although that is surely included) as it is about the sovereignty of God and how that sovereignty is made manifest through God-given knowledge and insight. Importantly, too, this threefold giving also anticipates other references to divine giving, most notably the giving of divine rule and majesty (2:28; 4:14, 22, 29; 5:18–19; 7:6, 14, 27), even to "the lowliest of humanity" (4:14; cf. 2:21, 27).[8] Here in the introduction, then, is a clue for the interpretation of the rule of God in the rest of the book.

A Stone Hewn Not by Hands

The first explicit reference in the book to the rule of God appears in the vision of the four regimes in Daniel 2, where it is predicted that God will establish after their demise "a regime that shall never be impaired" (דִּי מַלְכוּ תִתְחַבַּל לָא עָלְמִין, 2:44). The event will apparently take place sometime in the indefinite future (2:28, 29, 45).[9] Exegetes through the centuries have, for the most part, assumed that four successive empires in history are at issue, although there is considerable debate over the precise identities of the four.[10] To

---

7. The reference to "grace and mercies" points not so much to the favor granted *by* the warden (so NJPSV, NRSV, NIV, and many commentators) but to the "grace and mercies" of God evident *before* the warden (cf. RSV, NASV). Indeed, one may compare this account with the story of Joseph in Egypt, a story that has many parallels with the accounts of Daniel's experience. Joseph was also in captivity in a foreign land, but Yhwh was with him, extending to him חֶסֶד and showing him favor *in the eyes of* (בְּעֵינֵי) the prison warden (Gen 39:21). So, too, the story in Daniel 1 implies that God was with Daniel, granting him "grace and mercies *before* (לִפְנֵי) the chief warden." Cf. 1 Kgs 8:50; Neh 1:11; Ps 106:46; *T. Jos.* 2:3 (εἰς οἰκτιρμούς); Jdt 10:8 (εἰς χάριν).

8. References to Daniel are to the Hebrew system of versification.

9. See G. W. Buchanan, "Eschatology and the End of Days," *JNES* 20 (1961) 188–93; J. T. Willis, "The Expression *be'acharith hayyamin* [*sic*] in the Old Testament," *ResQ* 22 (1979) 54–71. For a survey of the literature on the pertinent idioms, see G. Pfandl, *The Time of the End in the Book of Daniel* (Adventist Theological Society Dissertation Series 1; Berrien Springs: Adventist Theological Society Publications, 1996).

10. See the classic review in H. H. Rowley, *Darius the Mede and the Four World Empires in the Book of Daniel: A Historical Study of Contemporary Theories* (Cardiff: University of Wales Press, 1959) 61–182.

support this view, modern critics have adduced possible analogues, including Hesiod's *Works and Days* (1.109–201), which speaks of periods in human history in terms of four different metals, and the *Bahman Yasht*, a ninth-century C.E. Iranian prophetic text describing a vision of a tree with branches of various metals representing various periods in history.[11] It is hardly assured, however, that the text has to do with successive empires.

The first regime in this dream is incontrovertible, for Nebuchadnezzar is named. One may take the cue from the opening verse in the chapter, which refers to the second year of Nebuchadnezzar's מַלְכוּת (2:1), that the מַלְכוּתָא that God has given to him (2:37) is simply that—Nebuchadnezzar's own reign—and not the Babylonian Empire, and the text confirms this: "You are the head of gold" (2:38). The idea that the dream concerns successive empires spanning centuries is, in fact, belied by the prediction that the fourth regime is to destroy "all these," implying that all the other regimes will still be in existence when it comes to be. The text may, therefore, be referring not to four empires extending over several centuries but to four *reigns*.[12] Indeed, the same word used here is found elsewhere in the book for the reign of Nebuchadnezzar (4:23, 28, 33), the reign of Belshazzar (5:18, 26, 28; 8:1), the reign of Darius (6:27, 29), the reign of Cyrus (6:29), as well as the eternal reign of God (3:33; 4:31; 7:27). Thus, the passing of Nebuchadnezzar's מַלְכוּת mentioned in 4:28 is not the end of the Babylonian Empire per se, since Nebuchadnezzar's empire, according to the book's historiography, is continued through the reign of his "son" Belshazzar. Accordingly, the second regime is that of Belshazzar, who is portrayed as inferior to Nebuchadnezzar (5:22–29; cf. 2:39). Moreover, although the second regime is said to be inferior to Nebuchadnezzar's, no such thing is suggested of the others. On the contrary, the third power will be universal in scope: "it shall have dominion over all the earth" (תִּשְׁלַט בְּכָל־אַרְעָא, 2:39). And this assessment is corroborated later in the book by the edict of Darius the Mede to "all peoples, nations, and languages inhabiting the earth," invoking his own dominion over them (בְּכָל־שָׁלְטָן מַלְכוּתִי; see 6:26–27). This Darius, the third ruler after Nebuchadnezzar and the inferior Belshazzar, has dominion over all the earth, just as it is predicted in Daniel 2.

As for the fourth reign, it must be the fourth and last king mentioned in the first half of the book, namely, Cyrus (6:29), who is portrayed in the introduc-

---

11. For a challenge to the view that the "four-kingdom" schema is a result of such external influences, see G. F. Hasel, "The Four World Empires of Daniel 2 against Its Near Eastern Environment," *JSOT* 12 (1979) 17–30.

12. See the observation of B. D. Eerdmans, "Origin and Meaning of the Aramaic Part of Daniel," *Actes du XVIIIᵉ congrès international des orientalistes* (1932) 198–202. This position has been defended most recently by Goldingay, *Daniel*, 49–52.

tory chapter as the last king in whose reign Daniel served (1:21). Historians might point out, too, that it was during the reign of Cyrus that the regimes of Belshazzar, the de facto ruler of Babylon when it fell at the hands of the Persian army, and the last Median kings were destroyed once and for all.[13] Thus, historically, Cyrus, the fourth reign named in the book, did destroy "all these" (2:40). Herodotus, who notes the different ethnic backgrounds of the Persians and the Medes (1.130), also says that Cyrus himself was the product of a mixed marriage (1.107). The narrator of Daniel 2 may well be alluding to this background, for in Cyrus and his political coalition, there was a "mixing of human seed" (2:43), something that would have been an anathema to the Jews.[14] It is he who will bring about the unification of the mighty Persians and the disintegrating Median kingdom—thus, an alliance of two unequal powers, a mixing of the strong (תַּקִּיפָה) with the brittle (תְּבִירָה), as it were (2:42).

Accordingly, it is "in the days of those kings"—presumably the three after Nebuchadnezzar, since he is being addressed—that God will establish yet another rule, one that will never be impaired and not be left to another people (2:44). That rule is symbolized in the vision by a stone "from the mountain" (מְטוּרָא, 2:45), hewn from it "not by hands" (2:34, 45), meaning probably that it will be by divine will and power (cf. Job 34:20). Oddly, even though the four regimes are represented in the dream by metals, the stone hewn not by hand is supposed to crush (דקק) them all (2:34, 35, 44, 40, 44, 45); indeed, to the extent that what is left of them will become "like chaff from the threshing floor of summer," carried away by a wind until not a trace of them is left (2:35). The statue of metal is supposed to become that finely pulverized!

The oddity of the imagery is perhaps evidence that metaphors have been imported from other "frames," in the language of metaphor theorist Max Black, and are now being set in a new "frame."[15] The narrator in Daniel 2 is here adapting two figures from Deutero-Isaiah, a text with which it shares

---

13. There is, as far as we know from historical records, no Median king by the name of Darius. Since "Darius" is the name of several Achaemenid rulers, however, it has been suggested that the name in Old Persian, *Dārayarahu* ("He who holds firm the good"), may have been a throne name for someone—possibly Gobryas. See K. Koch, "Dareios, der Meder," in *The Word of the Lord Shall Go Forth: Essays in Honor of David Noel Freedman in Celebration of His Sixtieth Birthday* (ed. C. L. Meyers and M. O'Connor; Winona Lake, Ind.: Eisenbrauns, 1983) 287–99.

14. See M. Mallowan, "Cyrus the Great (558–529 B.C.)," in *The Cambridge History of Iran* (ed. I. Gershevitch; Cambridge: Cambridge University Press, 1985) 2.404. On the mixing of human seed, see Ezra 9:2; Ps 106:35.

15. M. Black, *Models and Metaphors: Studies in Language and Philosophy* (Ithaca: Cornell University Press, 1962) 27–34.

many affinities.[16] The first is the quarry metaphor in Isa 51:1b: "Look to the rock (צוּר) whence you were hewn, to the excavation of the pit whence you were dug."[17] Interestingly, the metaphor in Deutero-Isaiah is itself borrowed from yet another frame, Deut 32:18, where the צוּר is a reference to the deity, as the parallelism clarifies: "You have neglected the צוּר who begot you; you have forgotten the God who brought you forth."[18] Indeed, in at least 33 other instances, including one from Deutero-Isaiah (Isa 44:8), צוּר is used as a metaphor for the deity as a reliable source of strength and vital sustenance. It is remarkable, therefore, that the exilic poet should then apply the metaphor to Israel's ancestors, boldly attributing to them the role typically played by the deity. Accordingly, whereas the divine צוּר is elsewhere portrayed as a progenitor (Deut 32:18a; Ps 89:27) and as one who endures labor pains to bring forth the people (see מְחֹלְלֶךָ in Deut 32:18b), it is now Abraham who is the progenitor and Sarah who is the one who births them (תְּחוֹלֶלְכֶם, Isa 51:2). The divine צוּר is, in this view, represented on earth by Israel's earliest ancestors, the recipients of God's promise of election.

In similar fashion, then, the stone hewn from *the* rock/mountain (note the determinate מְטּוּרָא in Dan 2:35!) points to Abraham's descendants, who, like their progenitor to whom they are to look (Isa 51:2), will somehow mediate divine sovereignty on earth. As Deutero-Isaiah envisions it, the lowly exiles will, through the mysterious workings of God, bring about the demise of the powerful foreign nations, threshing the mountains and crushing (דקק) them, turning them into chaff that will be carried away and scattered by the winds (Isa 41:15–16). Even the despised and lowly suffering servant may be so empowered to humble the lofty and powerful. To the exilic poet, this is possible because Israel is none other than Yhwh's elect, the seed of Abraham, before

---

16. See P. von der Osten-Sacken, *Die Apokalyptik in ihrem Verhältnis zu Prophetie und Weisheit* (Theologische Existenz heute 157; Munich: Chr. Kaiser, 1969) 18–27; H. L. Ginsberg, "The Oldest Interpretation of the Suffering Servant," *VT* 3 (1953) 400–404; J. G. Gammie, "On the Intention and Sources of Daniel I–VI," *VT* 31 (1981) 287–91; G. W. E. Nickelsburg, *Resurrection, Immortality and Eternal Life in Intertestamental Judaism* (HTS 26; Camridge: Harvard University Press, 1972) 19–26, 61–66; I. Fröhlich, "Daniel 2 and Deutero-Isaiah," in *The Book of Daniel in the Light of New Findings* (ed. A. S. van der Woude; BETL 106; Leuven: Leuven University Press, 1993) 266–70.

17. Everywhere else in Biblical and Postbiblical Hebrew מַקֶּבֶת refers to a tool ("hammer"), but here it apparently refers to the act or result of excavation. So also Syr., *maqqabtā* "pit, excavation" (see *HALOT* 2.625). Hence, the Peshitta, apparently perceiving a redundance, omits בּוֹר.

18. See M. P. Knowles, " 'The Rock, His Work Is Perfect': Unusual Imagery for God in Deuteronomy XXXII," *VT* 39 (1989) 307–22.

whom foreign potentates will become as nothing and perish (Isa 41:11; cf. 40:23–24).

So, too, Daniel alludes to a stone hewn without hands from *the* rock/ mountain (מְטוּרָא), a stone that will crush (דקק) the foreign powers, even if they be symbolized by durable metals. The stone hewn without hands from the mountain represents the rule of God that will never be impaired (2:44). On the contrary, it will itself grow to be a great mountain filling the whole earth (2:37), an imagery that on the one hand recalls the Isaianic vision of what will be sometime in the future (בְּאַחֲרִית הַיָּמִים; cf. בְּאַחֲרִית יוֹמַיָּא; in Dan 2:28),[19] when the nations of the world will come together to glorious Mount Zion, the abode of Yhwh's sovereignty (Isa 2:1–4; cf. Mic 4:1; Ps 22:28–29), and on the other hand is reminiscent of Isaiah's vision of the glory of God or the knowledge of God filling all the earth (Isa 6:3; 11:9; cf. 60:14). This stone hewn from the mountain will grow to become, again, the great mountain!

The story of Nebuchadnezzar's dream then ends with the peculiar scene of his obeisance before Daniel, a scene that has long embarrassed interpreters because the king's gestures suggest worship: he falls upon his face, bows to Daniel, and orders cereal offering (מִנְחָה) and oblations (נִיחֹחִין) to be offered him (2:46). The foreign ruler, who is called "the king of kings" (2:26) is now fallen, his face upon the ground, prostrate before the lowly captive. The prediction of the collapse of the mighty statue (representing human kingship) by a mere stone is foreshadowed, even set in motion in this event, for the "head of gold," as it were, is now on the ground before Daniel. The gestures of worship poignantly convey the message that the rule of God is manifested in Daniel the Judean exile, who, as the rhetorical links with the Joseph story imply, is the seed of Abraham. Thus, just as Deutero-Isaiah predicted the prostration of foreign rulers before the lowly exiles (Isa 45:14; 49:7, 23; 60:14), Nebuchadnezzar is now prostrate before the Judean exile. Indeed, as the doxology earlier in the chapter anticipates, the *wisdom and power* of God are evident in the *wisdom and power* of the lowly (2:20, 23). The reign of God is, in this way, already effected. The promise that human power will be excelled by the enduring rule of God is already coming to pass in this implausible way—through a human being, and a lowly one at that. The sacerdotal language of Nebuchadnezzar's obeisance before Daniel shocks the reader into the realization that the powerless may yet represent the eternal and indestructible rule of God.

Furthermore, the predicted growth of the stone is also foreshadowed and its fulfillment initiated in this event. Daniel had predicted that the stone will

---

19. Note, too, Deutero-Isaiah's use of אַחֲרִית in reference to the telling of events before they happen, "things not yet accomplished" (Isa 41:22; 46:10; 47:7).

grow to be "a great mountain" (טוּר רַב, 2:35). So Nebuchadnezzar "made Daniel great" (לְדָנִיֵּאל רַבִּי), gave him a "great gift" (מַתְּנָן רַבְרְבָן), and made him chief (רַב) of the governors (2:48). Three times in the span of just one verse the narrator implies that the lowly exile is becoming "great" (רַב), just as the stone is supposed to become great (רַב). To be sure, that greatness is not yet to the extent predicted; the "stone" is not yet a mountain that fills all the earth. The greatness of this servant of God is, for now, only over "all the province of Babylon" and "all the sages of Babylon." Still, the prediction has been set in motion in this preliminary way. Not only does Daniel become great, at his behest, three other Judean exiles—known by their humiliating, nonsensical captive names (2:49)—are promoted with him, again fulfilling in a nascent manner the promised growth of the stone. This stone may, indeed, be an individual or a community of faith.

The Reign of God That Cannot Be Impaired

It has been suggested that the literary units of Aramaic Daniel (chaps. 2–7), whatever their individual histories and chronological priorities may have been, now appear as components of an intentionally structured anthology manifesting what Lenglet calls a "concentric symmetry":[20] the two passages concerning the four regimes match one another on the outside (chap. 2 // chap. 7), the stories of miraculous deliverance from death—from the fiery furnace and from the den—are parallel (chap. 3 // chap. 6), and the two accounts of admonition to the kings—one penitent, the other recalcitrant—mirror one another on the inside (chap. 4 // chap. 5). Whether or not one accepts such an architectonic structure, it seems clear that chaps. 3 and 6 are, indeed, parallel accounts: the former relates how Daniel's friends (with Daniel noticeably absent) survive an ordeal; the latter concerns the survival of Daniel alone in an analogous ordeal. Both accounts, in fact, continue the story of the enduring rule of God as manifested in the survival and growth of the lowly exiles, either individually (like Daniel) or as a community (like Daniel's three friends). As Gammie observes in linking Daniel with Deutero-Isaiah's portrayal of the suffering servant, Daniel is called "servant of the living God" (6:21), and his friends are called "the servants of the Most High God" (3:26).[21] As in Deutero-Isaiah, too, the suffering servant is at once one and many, at once individual and collective.

20. A. Lenglet, "La structure littéraire de Daniel 2–7," *Bib* 53 (1971) 169–90. Cf. R. Albertz, *Der Gott des Daniel: Untersuchungen zu Dan 4–6 in der Septuagintafassung sowie zu Komposition und Theologie des aramäischen Danielbuches* (SBS 131; Stuttgart: Katholisches Bibelwerk, 1988) 170–93.

21. Gammie, "Intention and Sources," 289.

Despite having been thrown into a furnace superlatively fired up (3:19), Daniel's friends walk about in the furnace "free and without impairment," their company presently including a mysterious someone who "resembles a divine being" (דָּמֵה לְבַר־אֱלָהִין, 3:25). Especially noteworthy here is the assertion that they suffer no impairment (חֲבָל, 3:25), the term being related to the characterization of the rule of God that cannot be impaired (לָא תִתְחַבַּל, 2:44). Indeed, even the most intense fire had no power (לָא שְׁלֵט) over these exiles (3:27). They who had trusted God unconditionally (see 3:16–17, 28) had been kept alive through divine intervention and were even promoted (3:30), just as they and Daniel were previously promoted (2:48–49), their success in that way being an indication of the increase of the indestructible and enduring rule of God.

Just as his friends who were cast into the fiery furnace had emerged unimpaired, so Daniel was thrown into a lions' pit and he, too, emerged unimpaired. The lions, he asserted, did not impair him (לָא חַבְּלוּנִי, 6:23) and, indeed, when he was brought out of the lions' pit, no impairment (חֲבָל) was found on him (6:24), just as no impairment (חֲבָל) was found on his friends (3:25). This was so because he was found to have brought no impairment (חֲבוּלָה), and because he believed in God. Hence he was rescued, while his enemies were destroyed, the lions overpowering (שְׁלֵטוּ) them instead and crushing (הַדִּקוּ) their bones (6:25). Thus, "the servant of the living God" is not impaired, while the enemies are crushed, just as the stone hewn not by hands is supposed to crush all the other regimes. Once again, the prediction of Daniel 2 is already coming to pass: the foreigners are crushed, while the lowly Jewish exile is unimpaired. And this situation is the basis for praise of the living and eternal God, whose reign is said to be indestructible and enduring: "He is the living God who endures forever. His reign will not be impaired (לָא תִתְחַבַּל), and his dominion is till the end" (6:27). The survival of the faithful prompts the doxology about the durability of the rule of God. Indeed, the indestructible and enduring nature of the reign of God is evident in the survival of faith—when the people of God continue to bring no impairment upon others and believe in God.

Regimes Removed and Impaired

In Lenglet's analysis of the structure of Aramaic Daniel, the two innermost units—MT 3:31–4:34 and 5:1–29—parallel one another.[22] These inner units concern the freedom of the deity to grant or remove power, a theme already

---

22. Lenglet, "La structure littéraire," 169–90.

broached in 2:21. The opening and closing doxologies in the first passage
(3:31–33//4:31–32) suggest that at issue is the eternal rule of God over against
human rule, and it is remarkable that the terms for "kingship" and "dominion" are reiterated in the unit (3:33 [3×]; 4:14, 15, 19, 22, 23, 29, 31, 33), as
are the words "heaven" and "earth" (4:7, 8, 9, 10, 12, 17, 18, 19, 20, 22, 23,
28, 30, 31, 32, 33), and nowhere else in the book is the deity more frequently
called "the Most High God" (3:32; 4:14, 21, 22, 29, 31).

The metaphor of a verdant tree is applied to the king: at the beginning of
the scene, Nebuchadnezzar is said to be "luxuriating" (רַעְנַן), a term used elsewhere of the luxuriance of plants (e.g., Deut 12:3; 1 Kgs 14:23; Jer 11:16; Hos
14:9), once of a couch decorated with arboreal motifs (Song 1:16), and three
times of people thriving like plants (Pss 37:35; 52:10; 92:15). The metaphorical tree takes on cosmic proportions, for it is said to be at the center of the
earth (4:7), visible to the ends of the earth (4:8), providing sustenance and
shade for all living creatures (4:9), and its top reach the heavens (4:8; cf. Gen
11:4; Isa 14:13–14; Ezek 31:3). Nevertheless, it is an earthly tree and the
earthly nature of this tree is highlighted by the fact that a celestial being has to
descend from heaven (4:10, 20; cf. Gen 11:5) to bring about its destruction
(4:11, 20),[23] leaving behind nothing but the slightest trace of it, only the very
tip of the root, "the root of its root" (עִקַּר שָׁרְשׁוֹהִי, 4:12a, 20a). An imperative
from on high orders the impairment of the tree, חַבִּלוּהִי (4:20), the term ironically calling to mind the nonimpairment of those who mediate the eternal
reign of God (2:44; 3:25; 6:23, 24, 27; 7:11). And the very use of the term
calls attention to the contrasting fates of the powerful rulers on the one hand
and the lowly exiles on the other.

In a logic-defying sequence befitting a dream, the images morph into one
another. One moment Nebuchadnezzar is a tree (4:12a, 20a), the next moment he is a fettered animal (4:12b, 20b),[24] and then, just as suddenly, a human being with the mind of an animal (4:13). Yet, there is portentous
coherence in this bizarre dream. The tree that used to provide shade and food
for animals is now no longer able to provide. Instead, it has become a needy
animal, pitifully tethered and utterly dependent upon others for its survival.
Whereas animals had previously found shade under the tree, this animal is
now amazingly drenched in dew (טַל) from heaven. The similarity of the Ara-

---

23. The plural imperatives should probably be understood as charges to the divine
council (cf. Isa 40:1; 1 Kgs 22:19–22), another possible link with Deutero-Isaiah, suggests
Gammie ("Intention and Sources," 288).

24. Aramaic אֱסוּר and its Hebrew equivalent are always used for fetters and harnesses
(Judg 15:14; Eccl 7:26; Ezra 7:26) and never for a protective band, as many commentators
assume.

maic words for "dew" (טַל) in 4:12 and "shade" (טְלָל) in 4:9 ironically heightens the difference in the scenarios. The tree that had been at the center of the earth and that provided for all the animals of the earth is now itself an animal that is utterly reliant upon divine providence. The entire sequence makes the point that human rule is secondary to and dependent upon divine rule: "the Most High has power over the reign of mortals," and "he gives it to whomever he wills and he establishes it over even the lowliest of mortals" (4:14). The sovereign God is free to exalt the lowly or to humble the arrogant, to grant kingship or to remove it (4:33–34). The exaltation of the lowly in this case is evident in the success of Daniel through his imparting of insight. It is to him that the rule of God is given and through him that it is evident to the world.

The significance of the event is subsequently reiterated for Nebuchadnezzar's "son," Belshazzar: it is God who gave Nebuchadnezzar kingship so that the king could put to death whomever he wished and preserve whomever he wished, raise up high whomever he wished and bring down low whomever he wished (5:18–19). This characterization of royal power certainly describes the conduct of the king to this point in the narrative. Yet, as it is already stated in 2:21, it is the deity who "removes (מְהַעְדֵּה) kings and establishes kings." So, too, it is God who deposes the king and removes (הֶעְדִּיו) glory from kings (5:20) and "he gives it to whomever he wills and establishes it over whomever he wills" (5:21; cf. 4:14). The king's power is secondary and derived. In the context of Daniel 4–5, the lowly who is exalted over the arrogant is surely Daniel, whose lowly status is suggested by the king's reference to him as an exile (5:13). Comically, however, the king who, upon seeing the handwriting on the wall, "the knots of his loins were untied" (קִטְרֵי חַרְצֵהּ מִשְׁתָּרַיִן, 5:6), now faces a man who has a reputation of being able "to untie knots" (מְשָׁרֵא קִטְרִין, 5:12; קִטְרִין לְמִשְׁרֵא, 5:16),[25] implying not only that God humbles and exalts whomever God wills, but also that the rule of God may be manifest even in the ministrations of God's faithful but lowly servants: it is the lowly Judean exile who "unties knots."

The One Who Comes with the Clouds

The theme of the rule of God builds to a crescendo in Daniel 7, which a virtual scholarly consensus takes to be the book's "pivotal" chapter in more than one sense of the term. It is here, in what some perceive to be the

---

25. Whatever else the idiom might mean—solve a problem (cf. *b. Yebam.* 61a, 107b) or "unbind spells" (NEB)—the language clearly echoes the king's problem in 5:6—namely, he lost control of his bowels. See A. Wolters, "Untying the King's Knots: Physiology and Wordplay in Daniel 5," *JBL* 110 (1991) 91–97.

denouement of the entire book, that one finds the vision of one coming "with
the clouds of heaven as a human one" (7:12), a figure to whom is granted an
everlasting dominion that cannot be removed (לָא יֶעְדֵּה), a reign that cannot be
impaired (לָא תִתְחַבַּל, 7:13–14).[26]

This particular scene comes at the climax of a vision beginning with the
emergence of four terrible monsters from a turbulent "great sea" (7:2) that is
clearly a metaphor for the earth (7:17). This "great sea," even if its natural referent be the Mediterranean Sea (Ezek 47:10, 15, 19, 20), is an allusion to the
primordial ocean, known elsewhere in the Bible as "the great deep" (see Gen
7:11; Isa 51:10; Amos 7:4)—the chaotic waters that have been stilled by the
will of the divine warrior. As Hermann Gunkel argued long ago,[27] myth lies
in the background, for the monsters representing Babylon, Media, Persia, and
Greece all emerge from the sea, even though Greece alone is a maritime
power. The turbulence of "the great sea" suggests, therefore, a return to primeval chaos, the state of the cosmos before order was established. Indeed, the
Hebrew root for the disturbance (גיח) is used elsewhere of the turbulent sea
that God is said to have contained (Job 38:8), of the violent gush of a river (Job
40:23) and, most importantly, of a monster thrashing about in the waters (Ezek
32:2). Gunkel and others are right, therefore, to compare the "four winds of
heaven" (7:2) with the parallel passage in the Enuma Elish, where the storm
god Marduk subdues Tiamat by summoning "the four winds" against her
(Enuma Elish III 40–44). Yet, the role of the winds in cosmogony is found not
only in Mesopotamia; it is also evident in the west. According to an account
of Phoenician cosmogony attributed by Philo Byblius to Sanchuniathon, creation entailed the winds (Eusebius, *Praep. Ev.* 1.106, 7), and Damascius, too,
alludes to the role of the winds in Phoenician mythology (*de princ.* 125.C).

Such a world view is echoed in the Bible as well, where the wind is portrayed as an instrument used by God to bring order out of chaos (Gen 1:1–2)
and, significantly, this ordering by the wind is associated with the stilling of
the monsters from the sea (Job 26:12–13). In the vision of Daniel 7, however,
one finds a hint of the return of primeval chaos, because the very winds that
are supposed to bring order out of chaos now stir up the "great sea." Nothing

---

26. With other scholars, I take Daniel 7 to be a later reworking of the vision in chap. 2.
The latter vision, probably dated to the Persian period, concerns the four reigns in the first
half of the book, the last being the reign of Cyrus. Certainly there is nothing in this chapter
that *requires* a date later than the fourth or third centuries B.C.E. The former passage, however, is obviously dated to the second century B.C.E. and it recontextualizes the schema of
chap. 2 and now interprets the four reigns to refer to four world empires.

27. H. Gunkel, *Schöpfung und Chaos in Urzeit und Endzeit: Eine religionsgeschichtliche Untersuchung über Gen 1 und Ap Joh 12* (Göttingen: Vandenhoeck & Ruprecht, 1895) 327.

less than the rule of God is at stake in the vision, as creation appears to become undone.

Then, out of this chaos, there emerge, not one terrifying monster, as in the Enuma Elish, but four (7:3). In Ugaritic mythology, one finds a whole array of monsters associated with Sea and River, the enemies of Baal-Hadad who symbolize the threat to world order, including *tnn* (biblical *tannîn*), *ltn* (biblical Leviathan), and *šlyt d šbʿt rašm* "Potentate-with-Seven-Heads" (*CTU* 1.3.III. 38–47; 1.5.I.1–3, 27–31). Similarly in the Hebrew Bible, the sea monsters representing cosmic chaos are known as Tannin (Job 7:12; Ps 74:13; Isa 27:1; 51:9; Ezek 29:3; 32:2), Leviathan (Pss 74:14; 104:26; Job 40:25; Isa 27:1), and Rahab (Ps 89:11; Job 26:12; Isa 51:9). So one should perhaps not be too surprised to find a plurality of monsters arising from the chaotic sea. Furthermore, one suspects that the multiheaded monster of Ugaritic mythology but attested also in the Bible (Ps 74:13–14) may well be the mythic referent of the multihorned fourth beast in Daniel's vision, an imagery that is likely the background of the multiheaded dragon in Rev 12:3.

Nevertheless, the first three beasts in Daniel's vision are without parallel in mythology, as detractors of the history-of-religions approach are quick to point out. Rather, as E. Haag has observed, each of the creatures identified as analogy—the lion, the bear, and the leopard—has been employed as a figure in prophetic literature for the impending judgment of God and, indeed, all three animals are mentioned together in Hos 13:7–8 as evidence of divine judgment.[28] The mythological elements probably did not come directly from external sources but were mediated by way of Israelite traditions. In any case, the predators here are not simply a lion, a bear, a leopard. They are, rather, all hybrid and deformed; the hybrid character of these predators no doubt suggests uncleanness, while their deformity may portend ominous events on the horizon.[29] It seems as if the rule of God has been ceded to these grotesque and unclean predators that are now permitted to threaten the earth at will (cf. especially 7:6).

Yet, this is not all, for there appears a fourth beast that is not likened to any other. Some have identified this monster with the elephant,[30] although the

---

28. E. Haag, "Der Menschensohn und die Heiligen (des) Höchsten: Eine literar-, form- und Traditionsgeschichtliche Untersuchung zu Daniel 7," in *The Book of Daniel in the Light of New Findings* (ed. A. S. van der Woude; BETL 106; Leuven: Leuven University Press, 1993) 158–62.

29. So P. A. Porter (*Metaphors and Monsters: A Literary-Critical Study of Daniel 7 and 8* [ConBOT 20; Lund: CWK Gleerup, 1983] 16–29) has compared the deformities with those found in the Akk. *Šumma Izbu* omen texts.

30. U. Staub, "Das Tier met den Hörnern: Ein Beitrag zu Dan 7,7f.," *FZPhTh* 25 (1978) 356–97; O. Keel and U. Staub, *Hellenismus und Judentum: Vier Studien zu Daniel 7 und zur*

text itself, in contrast to the description of the other beasts, draws no analogy whatsoever with other creatures, indeed, stating that this beast is of a entirely different order (7:7). In fact, the destruction of this fourth beast is associated with the fourth regime in the dream of chap. 2, a regime that is said to be *"strong as iron*, inasmuch as iron *crushes* and smashes everything, so it shall *crush* and smash all these" (2:40). So the fourth monster is supposed to be *strong*, have teeth of *iron*, and to *crush*.

As in Ugaritic mythology, divine kingship and dominion are in question, as the forces of chaos are poised to take over.[31] These monsters arising from the sea represent the foreign nations hostile to the Israelites, indicating that the *Chaoskampf* has been historicized here and transformed into the *Völkerkampf*, as also elsewhere in the Bible: the unruly forces of the waters represent the hostile nations, constantly encroaching upon the domain of God, always threatening to return the earth to a state of chaos (see Isa 17:12–14; Pss 46:1–3; 93:3–4). Indeed, the rule of God appears to be at stake in history as in myth.

The scene of the monsters emerging from the chaotic "great sea" (7:2–8) is followed by a poetic depiction of a divine court (7:9–10), a scene similar to the portrayal in Ugaritic mythology of the divine assembly presided over by the high god, El. So in Daniel's vision, one finds the deity described as one whose head is "like lamb's wool," a description reminiscent of the Ugaritic characterization of El as a gray-bearded senior (*CTU* 1.3.V.23–25; 1.4.V.3–5; 1.18.I.11–12). The mythic background of the vision is further suggested by the plurality of thrones that are set up, even though Israelite theology would allow for only one to be enthroned (7:9). Similarly, a hymn from Ugarit celebrates the enthronement of El as judge (*CTU* 1.108), and there one finds a reference to "the years of El" (*šnt il, CTU* 108.27).

In the Ugaritic version of the story, the challenge is issued in the divine council by the emissaries of Sea, who demand the surrender of Baal. El and the majority of the other gods are ready to yield, but Baal rises to the challenge and goes forth to engage Sea in single combat, eventually defeating the chaos

---

Religionsnot unter Antiochus IV (OBO 178; Fribourg, Switzerland: Universitätsverlag / Göttingen: Vandenhoeck & Ruprecht, 2000).

31. The connections between Daniel 7 and Ugaritic literature, first argued by J. A. Emerton ("The Origin of the Son of Man Imagery," *JTS* 9 [1958] 225–42), rejected most notably by A. Ferch ("Daniel 7 and Ugarit: A Reconsideration," *JBL* 99 [1980] 75–86) and H. Kvanvig (*Roots of Apocalyptic* [WMANT 61; Neukirchen-Vluyn: Neukirchener Verlag, 1988] 389–44), has been ably defended recently by J. J. Collins, "Stirring Up the Great Sea: The Religio-Historical Background of Daniel 7," in *The Book of Daniel in the Light of New Findings* (ed. A. S. van der Woude; BETL 106; Leuven: Leuven University Press, 1993) 121–36; also in idem, *Daniel*, 283–94.

monster. By contrast, there is no evidence of divine indecisiveness in Daniel's vision, no hint of the possibility of surrender, no protracted battle between the forces of good and evil. Rather, there is only a brief allusion to divine judgment as some documents are laid open (7:10). The absolute rule of God is, thus, pointedly established. The fate of the cosmos depends not on the result of a protracted battle among the gods, as Canaanite mythology would have it, but on the unilateral judgment of the one enthroned as supreme ruler in the divine council.

The narrator then relates the destruction of the fourth monster (7:11–12). Other biblical texts speak of the slaying and piercing of the sea monsters by the sword (Isa 27:1; 51:9–10) or the crushing of their heads (Ps 74:12–13), but this monster will be burned, even as Mot, one of the chief enemies of Baal, is burned (*CTU* 1.6.30–37). Curiously, however, the other predators are not immediately annihilated; although their dominion is removed from them, their lives are prolonged for "a season and a time" (7:12). The absolute rule of God is in this way reiterated. Kingship and dominion are entirely God's to give or to take away whenever God wills. Indeed, the reference to "a season and a time" (וְעִדָּן זְמָן) echoes assertions elsewhere in the book that it is God who controls "the times and the seasons" (עִדָּנַיָּא וְזִמְנַיָּא, 2:21). Thus, while the most dangerous beast is immediately eliminated, threats to order in the world will persist for a duration to be determined by God alone. For the time being, the world will continue to be in need of divine intervention in some fashion or other.

In Ugaritic mythology, the ancient god El sits enthroned as a king, presiding over the divine council and issuing decrees. He does not rise to fight the chaos monsters personally. Instead, it is the youthful god, the storm deity Baal, known in the texts as *rkb ʿrpt* "the rider of clouds" (*CTU* 1.2.IV.8, 29; 1.3. II.40, III.38, IV.4, 6; 1.4.III.11, 18, V.60; 1.5.II.7; 1.10.I.7, III.36; 1.19.I.43; 1.92.37, 40) who rises to the challenge. The language of the deity coming on a cloud still finds echoes in the Bible, where Yhwh is often portrayed as coming upon a cloud to deliver people in distress (Deut 33:26; Isa 19:1; Ps 18:11// 2 Sam 22:11; Pss 68:4, 33; 104:3). This is surely the background of the imagery of the one who comes with the clouds of heaven (7:13). Indeed, the structure of the sentence suggests the importance of the allusion to the presence with the heavenly clouds, for the text fronts that particular metaphor: "Lo, with the clouds of the heavens, as a human, one comes." Significantly, too, just as the victorious rider of clouds in the Ugaritic myth is given "eternal kingship" and "everlasting dominion" (*CTU* 1.2.IV.7–10), so the one who comes with the clouds is said to be given dominion and glory that are eternal and cannot be impaired (7:13–14). As in Ugaritic mythology, where it is the prerogative

of the ancient god El to give and to remove kingship and dominion (see *CTU*
1.III.24–25), the vision implies by its juxtaposition of 7:13 with 7:14 that it is
the Ancient of Days, the El figure in the vision, who gives this champion the
trophies of eternal kingship and dominion.

Given that the imagery of the cloud-rider in Ugaritic mythology is always
used of Baal, the association of clouds with divine presence elsewhere, the
specific application of this imagery to Yhwh's theophany, and the mention of
heaven, it is astounding that the one who comes with the clouds is said to be
כְּבַר אֱנָשׁ (7:14). The interpreter's particular challenge here, however, is to sort
out the different levels and types of figuration.[32] Divine intervention is expressed in terms of the mythical metaphor of the theophanic cloud-rider, but
this divine presence is seen כְּבַר אֱנָשׁ. In the first place, the preposition sets the
cloud-rider in direct opposition to the predators that are likened to various
earthly creatures—*like* a lion (כְּאַרְיֵה, 7:4), *like* a human (כֶּאֱנָשׁ, 7:4), and *like* a
leopard (כִּנְמַר, 7:6). In these cases, the preposition indicates resemblance, as
suggested by the depiction of the second beast that *resembles* a bear (דָּמְיָה לְדֹב,
7:5). The pernicious monsters partly resemble various creatures that are elsewhere in the Bible used as agents of divine judgment, even as the agent of divine deliverance in 3:25 is said to resemble a divine being (דָּמֵה לְבַר־אֱלָהִין,
3:25). All this does not necessarily mean, however, that the divine champion
who comes with the clouds only resembles a בַּר אֱנָשׁ. The stakes have, after all,
been raised by the culminating danger of a fourth monster that has no analogy
whatsoever, except that its fourth position, its strength, its association with
iron, and its crushing action all together recall the fourth power in Nebuchadnezzar's dream of the four regimes. Indeed, given the association with that
earlier account, it seems reasonable to assume that the vision of the one coming with the clouds is a variant symbol of the stone hewn without hands, a vision of the reign of God manifested through the presence of lowly mortals. In
the seer's analogical imagination, divine presence is *seen as* mortal presence: "I
was *seeing* in the vision of the night, lo, with the clouds of heaven, *as* a mortal,
one coming" (7:13).

One notes that the expression בַּר אֱנָשׁ—like its equivalents in Hebrew,
בֶּן־אֱנוֹשׁ and בֶּן־אָדָם—is indeterminate (not "the Son of Man," as the KJV has
it), although a determinate plural form (בְּנֵי אֲנָשָׁא) is attested twice in Daniel,
both times referring to humanity in general (2:38; 5:21). The earliest attestation of the precise Aramaic expression is found on an eighth-century inscrip-

---

32. Cf. the discussion in K. Koch, *Das Daniel Buch* (EdF 144; Darmstadt: Wissenschaftliche Buchgesellschaft, 1980) 216–34; C. Colpe, "ὁ υἱὸς τοῦ ἀνθρώπου," *TDNT*
8.400–477 (= *TWANT* 8.403–81).

tion from Sefire (*KAI* 224:16), where it refers neutrally to "someone." The term corresponds to Ugaritic *bn adm*, a term referring generally to a human being (*CTU* 1.170.15), and to the same expression in Phoenician, where it is antithetical to *ʾlnm* 'gods' (*KAI* 48.4), and, of course, to Hebrew בֶּן־אָדָם, an expression that occurs 152 times in the Bible, often with the implication of human frailty, limitations, and mortality, as contrasted with the unlimited power and majesty of the transcendent God. Accordingly, the frequent address of Ezekiel as בֶּן־אָדָם (93 times), an address imitated also in Dan 8:17 (the terrified and vulnerable Daniel is called "human one"!), contrasts the terrified and vulnerable prophet with the transcendent God.[33] Elsewhere, too, the expression is used to convey the sense of a mere mortal, who only unexpectedly receives God's special attention and care (Ps 8:5; Job 25:6) and who certainly cannot be relied upon to save (Ps 146:3). And the related term בֶּן־אֱנוֹשׁ (Ps 144:3) carries the same connotations. Yet, the champion who comes with the clouds, whom the reader by dint of the cosmogonic allusion expects to be a divine figure, would appear כְּבַר אֱנָשׁ, as a mere mortal.[34] Against all the terrible predators comes one just like that. Indeed, just as Baal the cloud-rider in Canaanite mythology is finally given dominion and kingship (*CTU* 1.2.IV.8–10), so this champion in Daniel's vision, who comes with the clouds, will be given kingship and dominion so that "all peoples, nations, and languages should serve him" (7:14).

To some extent, what is to be given to this one is what God has hitherto given to human rulers such as Nebuchadnezzar (2:37; 5:18–19; cf. 7:6). This rule is, however, a temporal reality, a gift that can be removed (הֶעְדִּיו) at will, even if an extension is granted for a period (עַד־זְמַן וְעִדָּן, 7:12). By contrast, the kingship and dominion given to the one who comes with the clouds will be enduring, as the kingship and dominion of God are enduring (6:26).

Moreover, whereas human kingship may be removed (see the usage of עדה in 4:28; 5:20; 7:12, 26) and the edicts of human kings may be removed (see עדה in 6:9, 13), the rule that is given to the one who comes with the cloud will not be removed. The one who determines all this is, presumably, the God who is confessed as "the one who changes times and seasons, who removes kings and establishes kings" (2:21). It is this God who removes (עדה) the dominion

---

33. Cf. W. Zimmerli, *Ezekiel* (trans. R. E. Clements; Hermeneia; Philadelphia: Fortress, 1979) 1.131 (German original, *Ezechiel* [BKAT 13/1; Neukirchener-Vluyn: Neukirchener Verlag, 1969] 70).

34. Daniel 7 is by no means the earliest attempt to associate the divine figure with mortals. As P. G. Mosca ("Ugarit and Daniel 7: A Missing Link?" *Bib* 67 [1986] 496–517) has shown, there is already an earlier tradition that links the divine figure with his earthly counterpart, the human king.

of the beasts while allowing them an extension of life (7:12). This kingship will not be impaired (לָא תִתְחַבַּל, 7:14), just as the reign of God mediated through the lowly will not be impaired (חבל, 2:44; 3:25; 6:23, 24, 25, 27), while the reign of rulers such as Nebuchadnezzar may (see חַבְּלוּהִי in 4:20). Furthermore, as a result of the receipt of this kingship, "all nations and people and languages will serve him" (לֵהּ יִפְלְחוּן, 7:14, 27), the verb here being used in Daniel only in connection with divine veneration (Dan 3:12, 14, 17, 18, 28; 6:17, 21). This veneration is surely not different from the posture of Nebuchadnezzar before Daniel in 2:46–47. At issue, it seems clear, is not mere political hegemony but the sovereignty of God as manifested by the lowly—a mere mortal.

The Holy Ones of the Most High

Although the one who comes is referred to in the singular, the language of the gift of the indestructible and enduring reign of God in 7:14 inevitably links that figure to the recipients of this same gift in the first half of the book, namely, Daniel and his friends. This linkage is crucial for the interpretation of the one who comes with the cloud, who turns out to be one as well as many. Indeed, the seer appears to have imbued the divine rider of clouds with human form, as it were, and democratized that figure. The democratization is evident already in the interpretation in 7:18, where the promised reign is said to be given to a plurality of beings, called קַדִּישֵׁי עֶלְיוֹנִין probably meaning "the holy ones of the Most High."[35] The one who comes with the clouds appears, thus, to be at once one and many, and their reign that is "forever—forever and ever" (7:18) stands in stark contrast to the ephemeral regimes represented by the four terrible beasts (7:17).

The precise identity of these "holy ones" is vigorously debated, however. Following a lead by Otto Procksch,[36] Martin Noth has argued in an influential

---

35. The form עֶלְיוֹנִין (also in 7:22, 25, 27) is a plural of majesty and, as such, is used interchangeably with the singular form עֶלְיוֹן. Compare with the interchangeability of ʾlm and ʾl in various inscriptions (see the usage of ʾlm in KAI 26.C.iii.16, iv.19; 59.2; 120.1; 122.1, etc.) and, perhaps the references to the בְּנֵי אֵלִים in Pss 29:1; 89:7. Thus, קַדִּישֵׁי עֶלְיוֹנִין would be synonymous with Hebrew קְדוֹשֵׁי עֶלְיוֹן "the holy ones of Elyon" in CD 20.8. J. Goldingay ("Holy Ones on High in Dan 7:18," JBL 107 [1988] 495–97) has argued, however, that עֶלְיוֹנִין may be epexegetical or adjectival and that the phrase should be interpreted to mean "holy ones on high." Yet, one does not expect an adjectival -ôn ending in Aramaic, and neither עֶלְיוֹן nor עֶלְיוֹנִין is ever found in Aramaic as an adjective, except in the divine epithet אֵל עֶלְיוֹן (1QapGn 12:17; 20:12, 16; 21:2, 20; 22:15, 16, 21). It seems most likely, therefore, that עֶלְיוֹן and עֶלְיוֹנִין in Aramaic are taken over directly from Hebrew.

36. O. Procksch, "Der Menschensohn als Gottessohn," Christentum und Wissenschaft 3 (1927) 425–43, 473–81; idem, "Christus im Alten Testament," Neue kirchliche Zeitschrift 44 (1933) 57–83.

essay that the designation "holy ones" in the Old Testament is primarily used of God and other divine beings.[37] Indeed, the Hebrew term קְדֹשִׁים frequently refers to members of the divine council (Ps 89:6, 8; Zech 14:5; Job 5:1; 15:15; Sir 42:17), while in other cases it may be used as an alternative designation for the deity (// אֵל in Hos 12:1; דַּעַת קְדֹשִׁים // יִרְאַת יהוה in Prov 9:10; 30:3). In various Northwest Semitic inscriptions, too, the root *qdš* is also used in the same way: largely of divine beings, cultic representatives, sacred rituals, objects and places.[38]

To judge from the predominant usage of the Hebrew and Aramaic designation elsewhere, then, the expression "the holy ones" would point to celestial beings and, indeed, קָדוֹשׁ/קַדִּישׁ always do in Daniel (4:5, 6, 10, 14, 15, 20; 5:11; 8:13, 24; 7:18, 21, 22, 27). Nevertheless, the references to the devotees of Yhwh as "holy ones" may not be so easily set aside. To be sure, the terms קָדוֹשׁ and קְדֹשִׁים, when used of people, tend to occur in cultic contexts. Yet, Israel is called מַמְלֶכֶת כֹּהֲנִים וְגוֹי קָדוֹשׁ "a priestly kingdom and a holy nation" (Exod 19:6), and the people are charged to be קְדֹשִׁים because Yhwh is קָדוֹשׁ (Lev 11:44–45; 19:2; 20:7, 26). This does not mean that they are all cultic functionaries, as some pretenders to the office of priesthood once asserted (Num 16:3), cleverly manipulating the charge of holiness directed at all the people (Num 15:40), but that the ideal community of the elect would be dedicated to Yhwh, as priests are supposed to be. Indeed, Israel is supposed to be עַם קָדוֹשׁ "a holy people" (Deut 7:6; 14:2, 21; 26:19; 28:9), although only a faithful remnant may finally turn out to be so (see Isa 4:3). Accordingly, then, Yhwh's devotees are daringly addressed as "his holy ones" (קְדֹשָׁיו), a designation parallel to יְרֵאָיו "those who revere him" (Ps 34:10). And Ps 16:3 refers to קְדֹשִׁים אֲשֶׁר־בָּאָרֶץ "the holy ones that are on earth" (// אַדִּירֵי כָּל־חֶפְצִי־בָם "the magnificent ones in whom is my delight"), which sounds very much like a reference to human beings, although it is admittedly difficult to make sense of that interpretation in its present context. Perhaps the most important text for understanding the notion of "the holy ones" in Daniel is an old poem celebrating divine theophany in Deut 33:2–3a:

37. M. Noth, "Die Heiligen des Höchsten," in *Gesammelte Studien zum Alten Testament* (TB 6; Munich: Chr. Kaiser, 1957; orig. published in *NTT* 56 [1955] 146–61) = "The Holy Ones of the Most High," in *The Laws in the Pentateuch and Other Studies* (trans. D. R. Ap-Thomas; 2nd ed.; London: SCM, 1984) 215–28.

38. See *DNWSI* 2.994–97; P. Xella, "QDŠ: Semantica del 'Sacro' ad Ugarit," *Materiali Lessicali ed Epigrafici I* (Collezione di Studi Fenici 13; Rome: Consiglio Nazionale delle Richerche, 1982) 9–17.

Yhwh came from Sinai,
He shone from Seir for us,[39]
He beamed from Mount Paran.
With him were myriads of the holy ones,[40]
At his right hand, marched the divine ones;[41]
Yea, the purified of the peoples,[42]
All the holy ones are under your direction.[43]

The passage is particularly suggestive for the interpretation of the vision in Daniel 7, for it depicts a theophany of the divine warrior with his holy entourage. Indeed, S. R. Driver, who takes the MT at face value, imagines the deity coming "out of holy myriads" (MT: וְאָתָה מֵרִבְבֹת קֹדֶשׁ), that is, emerging from the divine council, as in Dan 7:10 and elsewhere.[44] The emphatic conjunctive particle אַף connects the earthly hosts with the heavenly one (cf. Pss 89:12; 96:10), suggesting that both the celestial and the terrestrial belong to the

---

39. Reading לָנוּ with LXX, Syr., Tg., and Vg.; the error in the MT (לָמוֹ) arose from a graphic confusion of *nun* and *mem* in the paleo-Hebrew script. While the tantalizing proposal to read לְעַמּוֹ "for his people" is certainly plausible (see I. L. Seeligmann, "A Psalm from Pre-Regal Times," *VT* 14 [1964] 76), it lacks textual support.

40. Reading אָתֹה־מ רִבְבֹת קֹדֶשׁ. The MT's מֵרִבְבֹת קֹדֶשׁ, presumes an otherwise unknown place-name. The common emendations to read מִמְּרִבַת קָדֵשׁ "from Meribat Qadesh," מְרִבַת "to Meribat Qadesh," and מֵעֲרָבַת קָדֵשׁ "from the steppes of Qadesh" are without textual support. The extant witnesses essentially support the MT's reading of "myriads": SamP (מרבבות), 4QpaleoDeutᶜ ([מרבבו[ת]), LXX (σύν μυριάσιν), Aq. (ἀπὸ μυριάδων ἁγιασμοῦ). Some witnesses, however, do not reflect the preposition מִן before "myriads" (LXX, Vg., Tg.), and some take אתה not as a verb but as a preposition (so SamP, LXX, Tg., Syr.). I read אָתֹה (assuming the 3rd masc. sing. suffix *-uhu > *-uh > -ōh) with the enclitic-*mem*. As for the form קֹדֶשׁ, it is a collective, as the Tg. correctly has it (see also the Vg.). This usage is found, too, in Exod 15:8, where בָּאֵלִים "among the gods" is parallel to בַּקֹּדֶשׁ, which the LXX correctly interprets as ἐν ἁγίοις. See H. S. Nyberg, "Deuteronomium 33:2–3," *ZDMG* 92 (1938) 335–36. See, too, Ps 68:18: בְּב(א) מִסִּנַי קֹדֶשׁ.

41. This reading follows the reconstruction proffered by F. M. Cross and D. N. Freedman (*Studies in Ancient Yahwistic Poetry* [SBLDS 21; Missoula, Mont.: Scholars Press, 1975] 106–7 = "The Blessing of Moses," *JBL* 67 [1948] 191–210): מימנ אשׁ(ר א)לם (assuming archaic orthography). Cf. LXX ἐκ δεξιῶν αὐτοῦ ἄγγελοι μετ' αὐτοῦ, where the last phrase is possibly a free rendering of Hebrew אשׁר אלים, where אשׁר is interpreted as a relative particle.

42. For this reading, see Cross, *Canaanite Myth and Hebrew Epic*, 101 n. 38. The root is cognate with Akk. *ebēbu* (adj., *ebbu*), which is used of cultic purity and holiness (see *CAD* E 1–8). So this term is a proper parallel to "holy ones."

43. The MT has קְדֹשָׁיו "his holy ones," but the LXX has οἱ ἡγιασμένοι (cf. Vg.), probably reading קֹדֶשׁ and taking it as a collective. For בְּיָד meaning "under the direction of," see Exod 38:21; Num 7:8.

44. S. R. Driver, *Deuteronomy* (ICC; 3rd ed.; Edinburgh: T. & T. Clark, 1901) 390, 392.

entourage of the immanent divine warrior. One may, indeed, point to the ABA′B′ structure of the quatrain that revolves around the juxtaposition of "the divine ones" with their earthly counterparts, "the purified of the peoples." While the term "the holy ones" at the end of the quatrain unmistakably refers to "the purified of the peoples," it also echoes divine "holy ones" at the beginning. The point is that "all the holy ones"—whether on earth or in heaven—will be at the disposal of the holy warrior who comes in theophany. As Miller has recognized with this and other theophanic texts (Judges 5, Psalms 68), there is a "fusion of the cosmic and the historical, the hosts of heaven and earth," a "synergism" of divine and human activities.[45] Such a convergence is evident, too, in a number of Qumran texts mentioning the קְדוֹשִׁים. While a majority of these clearly refer to angelic beings, some have been interpreted to refer to members of the human community, or at least to include them along with the celestial servants of God. Particularly in the *War Scroll* (1QM 3:4–5; 10:10; 12:7–9; 18:2), one finds evidence of the "fusion" or "synergism" of the divine and human, a fusion evident also in the *Similitudes of Enoch*, where the celestial "holy ones" are viewed as heavenly counterparts to the terrestrial "holy ones" (*1 En.* 47:2), and where the holy ones are also represented by one called "the human one" (*1 En.* 46:4; 62:1), as in Dan 7:12.

Certainly, in the case of Daniel 7, it becomes clear as the interpretation is laid out that the designation "holy ones of the Most High" refers not to angelic beings alone but also to God's faithful people on earth (7:21, 22, 25, 27). It is they, after all, who will be overwhelmed for a time (7:21–22) and be "worn down" (7:25).[46] Taking the text at face value, it seems obvious that "holy ones" are in some ways vulnerable to the threat of the ultimate chaos monster until the Ancient of Days comes and renders judgment. Here the images of 7:9–10 and 7:12–13 seem to coalesce, for the hitherto enthroned deity, the transcendent deity called the Ancient of Days (the El figure), now comes (אתה) just like the one who comes (אתה) with the clouds of heaven (the Baal figure). Images of divine transcendence and immanence have merged. Hence, in consequence of this intervention of the deity who is simultaneously

---

45. P. D. Miller, *The Divine Warrior in Early Israel* (HSM 5; Cambridge: Harvard University Press, 1975) 106, 156–57.

46. So Aram. בלי/בלא in all periods and dialects, but also Heb. בלה, Ug. *bly*, Arab. *baliya*, Eth. *balya*, etc., all with the basic meaning in the G-stem, "to be worn out." Noth ("The Holy Ones of the Most High," 224–25 = "Die Heiligen des Höchsten," 285–86) prefers to translate the verb "offend," citing Arab. *balā,* because he perceives the object of the verb to be the celestial holy ones. It is doubtful, however, whether this argument can be sustained in Classical Arabic. See E. W. Lane, *An Arabic-English Lexicon* (Edinburgh: Williams and Norgate, 1863) 1/1.255–57.

transcendent and immanent, evil power is removed (הֶעְדִּיו) and completely
destroyed (7:26), just as it is seen in the vision (7:11–12). By contrast, eternal
rule will be given to those he attacks, now called עַם קַדִּישֵׁי עֶלְיוֹנִין "the people
of the holy ones of the Most High," so that "all dominions shall serve him"
(לֵהּ יִפְלְחוּן) and obey (7:27; cf. 7:14). The antecedent of the 3rd masc. sing.
suffixes in מַלְכוּתֵהּ and לֵהּ is ambiguous, with most scholars taking it to point
to the people, the Most High, or to the one descending with the clouds. I
would submit, however, that all three are meant, for the one who comes with
the clouds, who mediates the eternal reign of God, is at once divine and human, at once one and many.

The expression עַם קַדִּישֵׁי עֶלְיוֹנִין is, of course, a problem for the view that
the holy ones refer only to celestial beings. Noth argues, therefore, that עַ
here means not "people" but "host" (Schar), a usage that is sufficiently well attested in the Bible,[47] including, one might add, two instances in Daniel (9:26;
11:15). Yet עַ used in this sense in the Bible always refers to earthly hosts—
humans and animals—and never to heavenly ones, which is hardly surprising,
since the word is used with the connotation of the host being mortal (e.g., Job
12:2) or even common (e.g., Jer 21:7; 22:4; Lev 4:27; Neh 5:1; 7:5; Sir 7:16;
16:17). In reference to the celestial host, the normal term is צָבָא, a term that,
unlike עַ, may be used of both the celestial and the terrestrial beings.

Importantly, צָבָא is used just so in Daniel, most notably in a cluster (five
times) in Dan 8:10–13, precisely in a passage about the aggression of the arrogant "little horn" presaged in the vision of Daniel 7. In Daniel 8, the pride-
ful aggression of the little horn—universally recognized as an allusion to
Antiochus Epiphanes—is expressed in mythopoeic terms. He is said to have
grown up to the host of heaven (צְבָא הַשָּׁמַיִם), causing some stars of that heavenly host to fall, and trampling upon them (8:10), an action reminiscent of the
aggression of the fourth beast in Daniel 7 (7:7, 19, 23). The host no doubt refers to the luminaries of the sky (Pss 33:6; 148:1–5; Isa 40:26; 45:12; Neh
9:6), although here as elsewhere (Ps 103:19–20), these luminaries are portrayed as members of the divine council—celestial beings who fight at the behest of Israel's God alongside their earthly counterparts (Judg 5:20; Josh
10:12–14). Accordingly, then, the rise of the arrogant little horn is depicted as
an insurrection against "the commander of the host" (8:11, שַׂר הַצָּבָא), a martial epithet that recalls the "commander of Yhwh's host" (שַׂר צְבָא יהוה), whom
Joshua had encountered as he led his people in holy war (Josh 5:13–15).
Clearly, in Israel's ideology of holy war, Yhwh's earthly host is thought to have

47. Noth, "The Holy Ones of the Most High," 223–24 = "Die Heiligen des Höchsten," 284–85.

had its divine counterpart, so that, while the earthly host fights, they are not alone, for a divine host fights alongside them (Deut 33:2–3; 2 Sam 5:22–25; 2 Kgs 6:15–18; Isa 13:4). Hence, even though the issue in Daniel 8 is the encroachment upon Mount Zion,[48] the text presents the event as a challenge to the hegemony of the deity in the divine council. The earthly rebel brings his צָבָא (Dan 8:12) against the deity's own צָבָא.

This account must be understood in light of its mythological background, namely, the various myths in the Levant concerning the fall of certain astral deities in the aftermath of a celestial coup d'état against the supreme ruler of the universe. The Ugaritic Baal cycle, for instance, relates an attempt by Athtar, the Morning Star (that is, Venus), to ascend the heights of Mount Ṣaphon to usurp the throne that rightfully belongs to Baal, although the rebel fails because of his inadequate stature (*CTU* 1.6.I.56–65). A possible reflex of that ancient myth is found in Isa 14:12–15, which depicts the fall of a certain "Day Star, son of Dawn." The arrogant challenger in this account ventured to ascend the heights of heaven, "above the stars of God" and up to "the mount of assembly" in the farthest reaches of Ṣaphon, the sacred mountain that in Canaanite lore was the home of the gods. This rebel, who dares to compare himself to the Most High, will, however, be cast down to Sheol. Myth is historicized in this Isaianic taunt song uttered against "the king of Babylon" (Isa 14:4), probably an allusion to the Assyrian invader, King Sargon II in the late eighth century B.C.E.[49] Now, in ways that echo the myth preserved in Isaiah 14, the apocalypticist envisages the "little horn" ascending to the host of heaven, and some of the heavenly host have been made to fall and are trampled (cf. Rev 12:3–4). The deity's sovereignty over the council is in question. The text cannot be taken to mean, however, that the rebel has literally cast the stars to the ground or that the members of the divine council have been removed from their heavenly stations. Rather, the attack is obviously on the earthly reflex of the heavenly host.

It can hardly be disputed that the allusion is to the aggression of Antiochus IV against the Jews that culminated in the desecration of the temple in

---

48. The target of the attack is called הַצְּבִי "the Beauty" (8:9), a designation reminiscent of the characterization in Zion theology of the city, "the beautiful holy mountain" (הַר צְבִי־קֹדֶשׁ, Dan 11:45), as beautiful (Pss 48:2–3; 50:2; Lam 2:15).

49. For the identification of the "king of Babylon" with Sargon II, see H. Winckler, *Die Keilinschriften und das Alte Testament* (3rd ed.; Berlin: Reuther & Reichard, 1902) 74–75; H. L. Ginsberg, "Reflexes of Sargon in Isaiah after 715 B.C.E.," *JAOS* 88/1 (1968) 493. Among the many arguments used in favor of this identification, arguably the most compelling is that Isa 14:19 refers to the abandonment of the king's corpse in an open field, a well-known fate suffered by Sargon II and remembered by his son and successor, Sennacherib.

167 B.C.E. Indeed, the portrayal of Antiochus in this fashion may have been prompted by his own increasingly pompous self-designations, evident in the coins minted during his reign, beginning simply with ΒΑΣΙΛΕΩΣ ΑΝΤΙΟ-ΧΟΥ, expanding to ΒΑΣΙΛΕΩΣ ΑΝΤΙΟΧΟΥ ΘΕΟΥ ΕΠΙΦΑΝΟΥΣ, and culminating with ΒΑΣΙΛΕΩΣ ΑΝΤΙΟΧΟΥ ΘΕΟΥ ΕΠΙΦΑΝΟΥΣ ΝΙΚΗΦΟ-ΡΟΥ.[50] Moreover, on coins with the latter two legends are portraits of the king, with stars adorning the loose ends of his royal diadem or a star above his portrait, adornments no doubt intended to suggest his divine and celestial character.[51] To the Jews, Antiochus had blasphemously claimed the sovereignty that properly belonged to God alone, imagining himself to have power like God over the waves of the sea (Ps 89:9) and the high mountains (see Isa 40:12), and thinking that he could "touch the stars" (2 Macc 9:9–10). Elsewhere in Daniel, too, this arrogance is depicted as an aggression against all gods and, indeed, against the "God of gods" (11:36–38). Mythological and literary allusions like these make plain that what is at issue theologically in this power struggle is the kingship and power and dominion of the Most High God.

If there remains any doubt regarding the identity of the host in 8:9–14, it is clarified in the interpretation (8:24–25). Whereas the vision depicts the aggression of the "little horn" in terms of an attack against the host of heaven, the interpretation speaks of the target of the aggression variously as "the people of the holy ones" (עַם קְדֹשִׁים), who are characterized as "numerous" (רַבִּים) and "mighty" (עֲצוּמִים), terms that echo the characterization of Israel as an elect people (Exod 1:6, 9; Deut 9:14; 26:5; Ps 35:18) but also are used of the celestial host (so Joel 2:11). Since the קְדֹשִׁים/קַדִּישִׁין may refer to both the celestial and terrestrial hosts of the deity, therefore, one should perhaps consider the construction עַם קְדֹשִׁים/קַדִּישִׁין to be neither a subjective genitive ("the people [belonging to/pertaining to] the holy ones")[52] nor an epexegetical genitive ("the people, the holy ones"),[53] but partitive ("the people of the holy ones," that is, the human elements among the holy ones). It is they, the human holy ones (cf. 12:7), who are attacked on earth.

Still, the aggression of the rebel is not against "the people of the holy ones" alone but also against heavenly authority—the "commander of the hosts" (שַׂר הַצָּבָא, 8:11) and, indeed, "the commander of commanders" (שַׂר שָׂרִים,

---

50. O. Mørkholm, *Studies in the Coinage of Antiochus IV in Syria* (Historisk-filosofiske Meddelelser utgivet af Det Kongelige Danske Videnskabernes Selskab 40/3; Copenhagen: Munksgaard, 1963) 68–74.

51. Ibid., 18.

52. Collins, *Daniel*, 315, 322.

53. Goldingay, *Daniel*, 146; O. Plöger, *Das Buch Daniel* (KAT 18; Gütersloh: Mohn, 1965) 105, 118.

8:15). The former title is probably a reference to Michael, Israel's own שַׂר (10:21; 12:1). The latter, if it is not an allusion to Michael as the archangel (cf. 10:13), must point to the deity as the quintessential divine warrior, "Yhwh of Hosts." In this sense, scholars who want to identify the one who comes with the clouds from heaven with a celestial being such as Gabriel or Michael are correct,[54] although one ought not to limit one's interpretation to any individual, whether celestial or terrestrial.

To the narrator, it is on the basis of such divine involvement that the threat of evil will be overcome. Despite the rebel's success through deceit "by his hand" (בְּיָדוֹ), he will be broken "not by hand" (בְּאֶפֶס יָד, 8:25), an expression that recalls the vision of the ultimate breaking of the empires through the agency of a stone hewn "not by hand" (Dan 2:34, 45). Indeed, countering the threats posed by the monstrous earthly rulers and even the mysterious and unseen powers that support them (10:13; cf. 10:20) stands the celestial "commander of the host," the archangel Michael, who is known as Israel's own "commander" (10:21; 12:1). It is this invisible, one might even say subliminal, presence in history—suggested by the mention of this "commander" at the beginning and the end of the historical recitation in 10:21–12:3—that assures one of the durability of divine rule despite the impression that history is dictated by political alliances, court intrigues, individual schemes, and military strategies. It is the sovereign God, the "one who changes times and seasons, who removes kings and establishes kings" (2:21), who determines the course of history. It is through this ruling presence that God's people will be vindicated in due time (12:1).

Resurrection

The affirmation of the indestructible and enduring nature of the rule of God through the elect does not mean, however, that the apocalypticist is oblivious to the actual consequences of oppression. Nor is the author overly sanguine about the faithfulness of all the covenant people. Indeed, it is acknowledged in the text that the enemy will be able to deceive some into betraying the covenant (11:32), no doubt a reference to the hellenizing Jews who collaborated with Antiochus (see 1 Macc 2:17–18). Still, there will be "those who know their God"—widely believed to be an allusion to active Jewish resistance of the Hasidim (1 Macc 2:19–22)—who will act with strength (Dan 11:32). And there are the מַשְׂכִּלִים, presumably the group with

---

54. So, for instance, N. Schmidt, "The 'Son of Man' in the Book of Daniel," *JBL* 19 (1900) 22–28; Collins, "Son of Man," 50–66; idem, *Daniel*, 310; Z. Zevit, "The Structure and Individual Elements of Daniel 7," *ZAW* 80 (1968) 385–96.

which Daniel and his friends are to be identified (see 1:4, 17; 9:13, 22, 25), who will bring understanding to many (לָרַבִּים, 11:33; cf. 12:10). They are described further as the ones "who bring many to righteousness" (מַצְדִּיקֵי הָרַבִּים, 12:3). Apart from their instructive role, however, these מַשְׂכִּלִים are viewed as utterly vulnerable: they stumble, are in captivity and plunder, receive scant help, and are "refined, purified, and cleansed" (11:33–35; cf. 12:10).[55] The portrayal is, as H. L. Ginsberg has shown, reminiscent of the depiction of the suffering servant in Deutero-Isaiah.[56] The מַשְׂכִּלִים bring understanding to "many" (רַבִּים) and they bring "many" (רַבִּים) to righteousness, just as Deutero-Isaiah's suffering servant bears the sins of "many" (רַבִּים) and brings "many" (רַבִּים) to righteousness (Isa 53:11–12).

Despite the suffering, humiliation, and even death, the servant in Deutero-Isaiah is supposed to have insight (יַשְׂכִּיל, Aq. ἐπιστημονισθήσεται; LXX συνήσει; Vg. *intelliget*)—one may even say, in the light of Daniel, be a מַשְׂכִּיל—and "rise, be lifted up, and be very high" (יָרוּם וְנִשָּׂא וְגָבַהּ מְאֹד, Isa 52:13), words that astoundingly echo the vision of God's exaltation as celestial king, רָם וְנִשָּׂא (Isa 6:1). For the apocalypticist, the decisive triumph of the rule of God comes in the resurrection of "many" (רַבִּים)—some to eternal life, others to eternal contempt. As for the מַשְׂכִּלִים, "they will radiate like the radiance of the firmament; yea, they who bring many to righteousness will be like the stars" (Dan 12:3; cf. Matt 13:43). This is a dramatic reversal of the situation described in 8:10, where the arrogant "little one" is depicted as one who ascends the heavens, casting down some of the hosts thereby. The seer envisions the vindication of the fallen מַשְׂכִּלִים in terms suggesting that the host of heaven are assuming once again their rightful stations in the heavens. Thus, we have here the motif of the exaltation of the lowly and the humiliation of the arrogant: the one who attempts to ascend to the stars (8:10; 11:36–37) is brought down, while whose who are fallen (8:10; 11:33–35) are exalted. Even the annihilation of "many" (11:44) will not preclude the prospect of this scenario, since "many" will be raised and "many" will be led to righteousness. The rule of God will be unimpaired and eternal after all; even death cannot impair it! According to the reading of Isa 53:11 evident in the Qumran witnesses (1QIsa[a], 1QIsa[b], 4QIsa[d]) concerning the servant of YHWH: "Out of his suffering one will see light" (cf. LXX, δεῖξαι αὐτῷ φῶς).

---

55. On the instructive function of the מַשְׂכִּלִים in the Qumran documents, see H. Kosmala, "Maśkîl," in *Studies, Essays and Reviews* (3 vols.; Leiden: Brill, 1978) 1.134–35.

56. H. L. Ginsberg, "The Oldest Interpretation of the Suffering Servant," *VT* 3 (1953) 400–404. See also W. H. Brownlee, "The Servant of the Lord in the Qumran Scroll," *BASOR* 132 (1953) 12–13.

The resurrection and exaltation of the מַשְׂכִּלִים will result, too, in the roaming about of many (יְשֹׁטְטוּ רַבִּים), "so that the knowledge may increase" (וְתִרְבֶּה הַדַּעַת, Dan 12:4).[57] Indeed, in the light of 12:4, one may discern another level of meaning in 12:3, for the root זהר is not only "to radiate" but also "to warn," which is what religious teachers do.[58] Many will radiate to bring insight to many more. So understood, the resurrection is not an end in itself, although it is a vindication of the מַשְׂכִּלִים. Rather, the resurrection is purposeful—that there may be an increase in "the knowledge." The vision thus corroborates the prophecy in Isa 53:11, inasmuch as the suffering servant will bring insight (יַשְׂכִּיל) and lead "many" to righteousness, and one "will find satisfaction through *his knowledge*" (יִשְׂבַּע בְּדַעְתּוֹ).

The apocalypticist's vision of the resurrection, thus, is an expression of confidence in the sovereignty of God, whose salvation extends, not only to those who are still alive when vindication comes (12:2), but also to those who have died (12:3). Death will not prove to be the ultimate triumph of evil, for in the possibility of resurrection, the promise of the eternal rule of God will nevertheless be worked out. There is, too, the promised growth of the mountain to become a great (רַב) mountain (2:35), for the מַשְׂכִּלִים, who are among the "many" (רַבִּים) to be raised, will lead "many" (רַבִּים) to righteousness, and "many" (רַבִּים) will roam about so that knowledge will increase (תִּרְבֶּה).

Conclusion

This essay has argued that there is substantial coherence in the characterization of the rule of God, unquestionably the most important theological theme in the book of Daniel. The two most significant passages, Daniel 2 and 7, present variant symbols of the same reality; the stone hewn not by hand from the mountain and the one coming with the clouds of heaven convey the divine origination of the earthly representation of the eternal divine rule. While it is affirmed that the power and authority of earthy rulers—even oppressive ones—are, indeed, given by God, the text is equally vehement in its insistence

---

57. Some commentators emend הדעת to read הרעה, citing the OG in part (although LXX-Theod., Syr., and Vg. all support the MT), while others proffer different etymologies for דעת. See D. W. Thomas, "Note on הדעת in Daniel xii 4," *JTS* 6 (1955) 226; J. Day, "*Daʿat* 'Humiliation,'" *VT* 30 (1980) 98–99. None of these moves is necessary, however. The scenario in Dan 12:4, in fact, reverses that in Amos 8:12, where there is a desperate but futile search for the Word of God. In the former case, there will not be an absence of divine knowledge, for many will bring understanding and "the knowledge."

58. So F. M. Cross *apud* Nickelsburg, *Resurrection*, 26 n. 85. As Nickelsburg points out, a similar pun on the verb is found in Sir 24:27, 32.

that these regimes are but ephemeral and subject to destruction and removal by the divine Sovereign. By contrast, the rule of God given to the stone hewn not by hand from the mountain, which is also portrayed as one who comes with the clouds of heaven, promises to be enduring, will not to be impaired, and is not a passing reality.

As for the identity of that imminent figure, it is to be sought in the first instance within the book itself. The promised coming of the stone hewn not by hands is fulfilled immediately, if only in a nascent manner, in the exaltation and increase of Daniel and his friends. They who are lowly and seemingly powerless are the ones given the "wisdom and power" that belong to the God, the Sovereign of history, who alone "removes kings and establishes kings" (2:20–23); they are the ones whom the apocalypticist blatantly associates with the heavenly host of God, the ultimate ruler of all (7:18–27). The enduring and indestructible character of the ruler of God is assured by the divine gift of insight (so chaps. 1–6) and through divine intervention in ways mysterious to mortals (so chaps. 7–12). It is through the quiet faith of those who impart insight and understanding, through the teaching of many by many, that the people who represent the rule of God on earth will grow to fill all the earth. Even death will not impair that rule of God, for death will be overcome by the possibility of resurrection.

Theological Anthropology at a Fulcrum: Isaiah 55:1–5, Psalm 89, and Second Stage Traditio in the Royal Psalms

SCOTT R. A. STARBUCK

Whitworth College, Gonzaga University

The Royal Psalms are commonly viewed either as windows to preexilic royal ideology or as seeds of postexilic biblical messianism. Indeed, they are both. Yet the tumult of the Babylonian exile reshaped what had existed formerly as royal hymns and prayers into *community psalms* giving witness to Yahweh's continuing election of Israel as well as to the elected people's relationship to a monarch-less royal office. The redactors of the Royal Psalms apparently believed the royal office or, in broad strokes, essential aspects thereof, had been bequeathed to the populace itself. At least this is the direction the textual evidence points when viewed within its ancient Near Eastern context. The redaction of the Royal Psalms, therefore, signals a radical shift in the theological appropriation of the royal covenant similar though not equivalent to a shift observable in Isa 55:3–5. An examination of the two provides a significant and variegated witness to Israel's developing theological anthropology and its indebtedness to royal theology.

Isaiah 55:1–5

More than 40 years ago Otto Eissfeldt enumerated significant verbal parallels between Psalm 89 and Isa 55:1–5.[1] Although Eissfeldt stated in conclusion that the relationship between the two texts was "only a formal and superficial one,"[2] the force of the linkages demonstrated for many the transfer of the royal covenant from the house of David to the whole people of Israel in Isa 55:1–5. Such a transfer held momentous implications for Israel's theological

---

Author's note: It is with a profound sense of gratitude that I return to a subject first researched and then written under the guidance of J. J. M. Roberts: *Doktorvater*, mentor, and cherished friend.

1. Otto Eissfeldt, "The Promises of Grace to David in Isaiah 55:1–5," in *Israel's Prophetic Heritage: Essays in Honor of James Muilenburg* (ed. B. W. Anderson and W. Harrelson; New York: Harper, 1962) 196–207.

2. Ibid., 206.

anthropology, in that the unique and privileged relationship between Yahweh and the Davidic house was now vulgarized, so to speak, among the populace. In scholarly literature, this transfer is often referred to as a *democratization* of the royal covenant, though the term itself is anachronistic, imprecise, and was not used by Eissfeldt himself.[3] Eissfeldt's position vis-à-vis the covenant was more the perspective recently iterated by Joseph Blenkinsopp, who finds the actual transfer of royal covenant doubtful, though the beneficence of "gratuitous acts of favor" likely.[4] Blenkinsopp asserts that, whereas royal metaphor and imagery are appropriated in terms of the deity's personal care, there is no "covenantal" or legal transfer indicated. The distinction between the two positions (that of actual covenantal *transfer* and that of the *gifting* of gratuitous acts of favor) is hardly subtle; each holds significantly different implications for Israel's theological anthropology.

Scholars remain divided about how to demarcate the whole of chap. 55, though there is general consensus that vv. 1–5 form an internal unit.[5] In v. 1 a new prophetic discourse is indicated by the emphatic particle הוֹי. As with many prophetic texts, legitimate questions can be raised about who is speaking in different sections of 55:1–5.[6] The introductory phrase in v. 3a, "Incline your ear (הַטּוּ אָזְנְכֶם), and come to me; hear (שִׁמְעוּ), that your soul (נַפְשְׁכֶם) may live," is most certainly the stylized voice of the prophet.[7] Since the imperative call to hear (שִׁמְעוּ שָׁמוֹעַ) in v. 2b anticipates the similar call in v. 3a, and since the purposed clause "that you might eat the good" (וְאִכְלוּ־טוֹב) in v. 2b mirrors the logic of v. 1b "and eat" (וְאָכֹלוּ), the whole of vv. 1–3a should be understood to be the voice of the prophet.

---

3. Regardless, scholars have largely adopted Eissfeldt's view, with or without using the language of "democratization"; e.g., Klaus Baltzer, *Deutero-Isaiah* (Hermeneia; Minneapolis: Augsburg Fortress, 2001) 470–71; Brevard S. Childs, *Isaiah* (OTL; Louisville: Westminster John Knox, 2001) 435–37; Walter Brueggemann, *Theology of the Old Testament: Testimony, Dispute, Advocacy* (Minneapolis: Augsburg Fortress, 1997) 619; Paul D. Hanson, *Isaiah 40–66* (Interpretation; Louisville: John Knox, 1995) 179; H. G. M. Williamson, *The Book Called Isaiah: Deutero-Isaiah's Role in Composition and Redaction* (Oxford: Clarendon, 1994) 112, 226; Claus Westermann, *Isaiah 40–66* (OTL; Philadelphia: Westminster, 1969) 283–86; Patricia Tull Willey, *Remember the Former Things: The Recollection of Previous Texts in Second Isaiah* (SBLDS 161; Atlanta: Scholars Press, 1997) 250–51.

4. Joseph Blenkinsopp, *Isaiah 40–55: A New Translation with Introduction and Commentary* (AB 19A; New York: Doubleday, 2002) 370.

5. See ibid., 367–71; Childs, *Isaiah*, 433; Baltzer, *Deutero-Isaiah*, 465–74; John N. Oswalt, *The Book of Isaiah* (NICOT; Grand Rapids: Eerdmans, 1998) 432–40; Westermann, *Isaiah 40–66*, 280–86. Cf. Hanson, *Isaiah 40–66*, 177–83.

6. See Baltzer, *Deutero-Isaiah*, 466.

7. See Isa 1:2, 10; 8:9; 28:23; 32:9; 42:23.

The prophetic discourse initiates an invitation in v. 1 with plural imperatives to *come*, *buy*, and *eat*, despite that fact that the community invited is defined as those without means to buy (אֵין־לוֹ כֶּסֶף לְכוּ). The likely cause for the
community's insolvency emerges in v. 2a through rhetorical confrontation:
"Why do you spend your money for that which is not bread, and your labor
for that which does not satisfy?" Though this is a stylized accusation, apparently those who are invited as thirsty and financially destitute had, in some
sense real or metaphorical, squandered their financial resources. They are not,
in other words, victims of circumstance. Their material poverty is also a poverty of wisdom. That clarified, the prophet enjoins the community to listen
intently (שִׁמְעוּ שָׁמוֹעַ) so that those in the community, properly informed,
might eat "the good" and their souls might luxuriate in abundance (בְּדֶשֶׁן).
Thus, vv. 1–2 exhibit a synthetic parallelism that serves to (1) gather the intended community, (2) confront the gathered community with accusation and
promise, and (3) prick the attention of the gathered community so that all
might intently hear/receive the divine oracle that follows in v. 3b.

The divine oracle conferred on the gathered community is formally a royal
grant:

> I will make with you an everlasting covenant (בְּרִית עוֹלָם),
> my steadfast sure love for David (חַסְדֵי דָוִד הַנֶּאֱמָנִים).
> See, I made him a witness (עֵד) to the peoples,
> a leader (נָגִיד) and commander of the peoples.

In terms of its language, this passage stands in a wider and ongoing theological movement associated with the Davidic covenant expressed in Psalm 89,
2 Samuel 7, and 2 Sam 23:1b–7. Each of these texts emerges from an ideological "background" framework signaled through word pairs and standard epithets.[8] Two notable language clusters surface in Isa 55:3: בְּרִית עוֹלָם (// 2 Sam
23:5) and חַסְדֵי דָוִד הַנֶּאֱמָנִים (// Ps 89:25, where עִמּוֹ occurs instead of דָּוִד).
These terms are standard verbal lexemes expressing the ideological motifs of
Royal Theology.

Although Blenkinsopp suggests translating חַסְדֵי דָוִד הַנֶּאֱמָנִים as "the tokens
of faithful love shown to David,"[9] thus indicating that God will show such
kindness and faithfulness to the populace *as was shown* to David, a more
straightforward reading of Isa 55:3b–4 simply views the oracular divine grant
once associated with David and his heirs reapplied to the gathered community,

---

8. On language "clusters," see J. C. Greenfield, "The 'Cluster' in Biblical Poetry,"
Sopher Mahir: Northwest Semitic Studies Presented to Stanislav Segert (ed. E. M. Cook; *Maarav*
5–6 [Santa Monica, Calif.: Western Academic Press, 1990]) 159–60.
9. Blenkinsopp, *Isaiah 40–55*, 367.

presumably exilic Israel.[10] The oracular grant, in its reference to the "everlasting covenant" (ברית עולם), shares identical phraseology with 2 Sam 23:5,
one of the texts in which the Davidic covenant is authenticated. In the same
way, the relationship between the imperatival invitation to come, buy, and
eat in vv. 1–2 and the oracular grant of vv. 3–4 is best understood in terms
of covenant-making and remaking.

Richard Clifford has noted that in *KTU* 1.23 6 the standard word pair *lḥm* //
šty ("eat" // "drink") occurs in context with the הוֹ cognate *ay*.[11] Though much
in this passage is disputed, a microcosm/macrocosm contrast is made in the
text around the theme of eating and drinking between the royal family of
Ugarit and the sons of El. In the introductory section of the tablet (*KTU* 1.23
7) the royal family of Ugarit is gathered, bid to eat bread and drink wine, and
then blessed with peace (*šlm*). Then, as the ritual-mythic text unfolds (presumably) in the hearing of the royal family, a contrast emerges between those
who were bid to eat as soon as they gathered (the royal family) and the offspring of El (Šahar and Šalim), who are granted permission to eat only after
years of wandering in the desert. Languishing at the gate leading to fertile land,
the gods plead: *hm* [1] *hm . w tn w nlhm . hm it*[   ]*tn . w nšt*, "if [there
is b]read, give to us that we may eat; if there is [wine], give to us that we may
drink" (*KTU* 1.23 72–73). The text, albeit broken, seems to indicate that the
gods are allowed to enter, eat, and drink.

In addition to sharing comparable language clustering with Isa 55:1–2,
KTU 1.23 also demonstrates a similar logic of royal investiture. The royal family of Ugarit is blessed and bid eat and drink, all the while a ritual drama unfolds in which the sons of El impair in the desert until they receive similar
access to divine bounty. In a sense then, Šahar and Šalim are not unlike the
gathered community of Isa 55:1–2 who, lacking the wherewithal to set their
own banquet, eat and drink only after receiving the divine grant. The royal
family of Ugarit, conversely, are bid eat and drink directly, thus affirming a
previous granting of divine favor. Significant to this observation is the recent
identification of Šahar and Šalim with the morning and evening manifestations
of the Venus star in Syria and Canaan; a star closely associated with kingship.[12]

10. The community addressed is presumably diaspora Israel, but not explicitly: "*all* who
thirst, come to the waters" (כל־צמא לכו למים).
11. Richard J. Clifford, "Isaiah 55: Invitation to a Feast," in *The Word of the Lord Shall
Go Forth: Essays in Honor of David Noel Freedman in Celebration of His Sixtieth Birthday* (ed.
C. L. Meyers and M. O'Connor; Winona Lake, Ind.: Eisenbrauns, 1983) 28.
12. R. Mark Shipp, *Of Dead Kings and Dirges: Myth and Meaning in Isaiah 14:4b–21* (Ac-
ademia Biblica 11; Atlanta: Society of Biblical Literature, 2002) 76–77.

The connection between eating and drinking and covenant-making and remaking is well known, as Kathryn Roberts aptly observes:

> ritual eating and drinking not only seals the covenant but also legitimates the enthronement of the human king and confers divine approval. Samuel anointed Saul as a ruler over Israel after a sacrifice and sacred meal on the sacral high place at Ramah (1 Samuel 9). When David brought the ark onto "Yahweh's mount of victory" in Jerusalem, he offered sacrifices and distributed shares to the worshiping community (2 Samuel 6–7). This feasting on Yahweh's mountain solidified David's role as sacral king, the king of Yahweh's choosing, and firmly established Jerusalem as his capital.[13]

One can hardly overemphasize the importance of the royal feast in terms of the ideology and legitimation of kingship as well as royal covenanting in the ancient Near East. A king's favor with the gods and populace was inextricably bound to his ability to sustain their cults as well as to lavish his court, if not the populace itself, with resplendent feasts.[14] Of course, and to the point, the human king provided (paid for) the food, as is illustrated in one set of texts in which Adad-nerari III of Assyria decrees a detailed list of expenditures for food-stuffs for rituals and feasts in the Temple of Ashur.[15] Customarily, the proof of the pudding, or better, the verification of the deity's oracular grant of favor, was inseparably linked to substantial wealth amassed by the king.

Returning to Isaiah 55 and the relationship between vv. 1–3a and the divine oracle of vv. 3b–4, it is now clear that the community that is invited to buy and then eat are invited *as if* they were kings on the cusp of receiving a divine grant, whereupon they would be expected to offer lavish sacrifice and throw a royal feast. Moreover, despite the absurdity of inviting them in their current state (being without means to provide for sacrifice and celebration), they are bid come nonetheless. Here, then, are two significant departures from the expected norm. First, the oracular "royal" grant is given to the entire populace. Second, the grant is given to people who, from every appearance, are incapable of fulfilling the royal charter. With *this* oracular grant, it is Yahweh himself who provisions the feast. Not only does the oracle of vv. 3b–4 reappropriate the royal covenant so that it now applies to the entire gathered

13. K. L. Roberts, "God, Prophet, and King: Eating and Drinking on the Mountain in First Kings 18:41," *CBQ* 62 (2000) 641.

14. In this regard one might think of the royal carvings depicting multitudes of attendants bearing upon their shoulders food for such feasts. See L. Kataja and R. Whiting, *Grants, Decrees, and Gifts of the Neo-Assyrian Period* (SAA 12; Helsinki: Helsinki University Press, 1995) 70.

15. Ibid., nos. 69, 71–77. Any number of similar examples could be adduced.

community, it is deity, not king (not even "king" as represented by the whole community), that sets table for the essential ratifying event of the covenant.

As the logic of the text advances, it is ambiguous as to whether v. 5 is a continuation of the divine oracle in vv. 3b–4 or commentary from the mouth of the prophet. The verse ends with the purposed statement, "for the sake of Yahweh your God, and for the sake of the Holy One of Israel. Indeed, he has beautified you!" which likely indicates a speaker other than Yahweh. Another possible indicator of a separate saying or section is the switch from plural to singular referents. However, as with v. 4, v. 5 begins with הֵן and explicates the purport of the transfer of the royal covenant from the Davidides to the gathered community: "See, you shall call nations that you know not, and nations that knew you not shall run to you." Just as to David, who was a leader and commander of the peoples (לְאֻמִּים), so the nations (גוֹי) will run to them.

The expectation that the nations would acknowledge Yahweh's suzerainty, and hence his earthly representative, is rooted in the royal theology of the Davidic-Solomonic empire and is explicit in Isa 2:2–4.[16] In Isa 55:1–5, the gathered community bequeathed the Davidic covenant becomes not only leader, commander, and witness to the nations, but hails peoples so that they come running, despite the fact that the community and the nations do not hold formal covenant relations; they are not *known* to one another. Importantly, here the nations are not viewed as vassals to the royal house as in earlier formulations of royal ideology,[17] but instead they are freely compelled and enlivened to be in proximity to Yahweh and his beautified people.

Given its covenantal "staging," Isa 55:1–5 posits an actual transfer of the Davidic covenant to the gathered community of Diaspora Israel; this is nothing less than the "transformation" of the Davidic covenantal tradition.[18] Yet, in this transformation the effect is not so much the depreciating or diluting of royal ideology and its multivalent conceptions of intimate relationship between deity and king; rather, the transfer of the royal covenant to the populace essentially transfers the eternal covenantal status of the Davidic house to everyman. Thus, in terms of Israel's theological anthropology, Isa 55:1–5 marks a fundamental shift in the valuation and conception of the ordinary human and his or her intrinsic and covenantal relationship with Yahweh.

Was the author of Isa 55:1–5 the first, however, to suggest such a radical and expansive shift in theological anthropology? Are there traces already within the royal traditions that paved the way for the transfer of the royal

---

16. See J. J. M. Roberts, "Zion in the Theology of the Davidic-Solomonic Empire," *The Bible and the Ancient Near East* (Winona Lake, Ind.: Eisenbrauns, 2002) 332.

17. See Psalm 47.

18. Childs, *Isaiah*, 436.

covenant to commoners? Although Eissfeldt did not perceive the full range of implications, his instinct to read Isa 55:1–5 in light of Psalm 89, a so-called Royal Psalm, was right on the mark. Not only does Isa 55:1–5 stem from the same ideological background as Psalm 89, its radical shift in theological anthropology was already potential, if not actual, in Stage 2 *traditio* of the Royal Psalms themselves.

Second Stage Traditio of the Royal Psalms

In the published revision of my doctoral dissertation written under J. J. M. Roberts, I argued that the so-called Royal Psalms attest a momentous stage in the ongoing refinement of Israel's theological anthropology.[19] At the conclusion of the study, significant verbal linkages between 2 Samuel 7, 2 Sam 23:1b–7, Psalm 89, and Isa 55:1–5 were cited as evidence of a shared *traditio* that betrays an ongoing and mutable theological assessment of the Davidic covenant. Here, I hope to advance the discussion a step further by elucidating a theological *fulcrum* within the *traditio* that hinges upon (a) the envisioned redistribution of that office to individual Israel in Stage 2 *traditio* similar to the redistribution in Isa 55:1–5 and (b) a singular theological focus on the "office" of human kingship in the biblical Royal Psalms in a Stage 3 *traditio*.

Royal Psalm Traditio Stages

The so-called Royal Psalms (Psalms 2, 18, 20, 21, 45, 72, 89, 101, 110, 132, and 144) are unique when compared with other royal hymns and prayers of the ancient Near East in their consistent omission of any reference to historical kings of Northern Israel or Judah as a protagonist within the body of the psalm. Rather than understanding the openness and generality of the Royal Psalms to indicate their popularity and reuse by historical royal courts as stock liturgy, the data suggests that the Royal Psalms attested in the Hebrew Psalter are at least one step removed from a royal court *traditum*.

When working with the Royal Psalms, the interpreter must distinguish between a psalm's *traditum* and its evolving *traditio*. On the one hand, a psalm's *traditum* is its (hypothetical) original composition, presumably authored for a court-sponsored event. On the other hand, a psalm's *traditio* includes the totality of processes and stages by which the individual psalm moved from its composition to its eventual placement and form in the Hebrew Psalter.[20] My

---

19. Scott R. A. Starbuck, *Court Oracles in the Psalms: The So-Called Royal Psalms in Their Ancient Near Eastern Context* (SBLDS 172; Atlanta: Scholars Press, 1999).

20. See Harry Nasuti, *Tradition History and the Psalms of Asaph* (SBLDS 88; Atlanta: Scholars Press, 1988) 1–24.

contention is that in each case the *traditum* of individual Royal Psalms would have referenced a specific king of Israel or Judah. It was in the *traditio*, then, that specific regnal names were excised, creating what we have come to call the genre "Royal Psalm." Since the avoidance of monarchical specificity necessarily refocused a Royal Psalm from the endowments and concerns of a particular king to, by the end of the *traditio* processes, the larger issue of "kingship" itself, the biblical Royal Psalms are properly defined as "psalms whose concern is the institution of Israelite kingship. Their protagonist is an unspecified king; hence he is a typological representative of the 'office' of the institution."[21]

Needless to say, such a refocusing from the *traditum* signals a strategic hermeneutical shift within the *traditio* of the Royal Psalms; that is from their (postulated) functions in specific historical royal courts of Israel to their theologically nuance-rich claims in the Hebrew Psalter. In brief, three major *traditio* stages can be outlined for the Royal Psalms:

- *Stage 1*: Usually referred to as the *traditum*, this stage accounts for the composition of the original text, presumably for a court-sponsored event. At this stage the Royal Psalm was historically and verbally anchored to a specific king.
- *Stage 2*: This stage occurred prior to the placement of Royal Psalms in the Psalter and is characterized by the editorial processes that excised specific references to monarchical protagonists within the Royal Psalms. In this stage monarchic imagery and metaphor within the Royal Psalms were preserved in order to be reappropriated by the general populace for worship and study.
- *Stage 3*: Often explored in terms of a psalm's canonical placement, this stage witnessed the inclusion of individual Royal Psalms in an evolving Hebrew Psalter. At the conclusion of this stage the Royal Psalms, now readable together thematically, necessarily focus on the "office" of kingship itself.

A differentiation between these *traditionsgeschichtliche* stages allows the interpreter a diachronic view of the ongoing interpretation of the Royal Psalms. Whereas Stage 1 and Stage 3 have actively been pursued among psalms scholars, Stage 2 has yet to be fully explored.

Traditio Stage 1

Stage 1 is necessarily dated to the preexilic period in which kingship, especially that of the Davidic house, was viable and active. Beginning with Wil-

---

21. Starbuck, *Court Oracles*, 206.

helm de Wette in 1811, scholars have rightly trusted the Royal Psalms to serve as windows into Israel's functional royal ideology.[22] The pioneering work of Hermann Gunkel demonstrated marked and inescapable continuities between the often mythic and propagandistic language of the Royal Psalms and the writings of the royal courts of Israel's neighbors.[23] Despite numerous refinements and expansions of Gunkel's groundbreaking work, the Royal Psalms remain, to this day, essential source material for the delineation of the Royal Theology and the Zion Tradition.[24] In no instance does one, however, observe an actual royal court *traditum* among the Royal Psalms. This is because in each case the Royal Psalms are themselves open and anonymous regarding protagonist, and there is no clear evidentiary warrant for concluding that the psalms would have been preserved lacking monarchical specificity in the pre-exilic period. That is, despite common assumptions to the contrary, there is no hard evidence that the anonymity of the Royal Psalms is due to a recurring use as stock liturgy. In fact, such an assumption is directly counter to the comparative evidence available.[25]

This means, then, that care must be taken when dating the Royal Psalms themselves. Specific content cues often point reasonably well to historical contexts within the monarchical period. While these cues most likely accurately reflect the *traditum*, the final shape of the Royal Psalm was fixed in the *traditio* at a later date after specific king names were excised.

Although no Royal Psalms have been preserved intact as *traditum*, a psalmic text found outside the Psalter has: 2 Sam 23:1b–7 (otherwise known as the "last words of David"). Whereas this hymnic text of seven verses did not find its way into the Hebrew Psalter, it was included in the Qumran *Psalms Scroll*, 11QPs[a] XXVII, due to its form as well as its Davidic attribution. The majority opinion holds that the oracle and its poetic framework should be dated to the early monarchical period based on its archaic elements:[26]

---

22. W. de Wette, *Commentar über die Psalmen* (Heidelberg: Mohr, 1811).

23. H. Gunkel, "Königspalmen," *Preußische Jährbucher* 158 (1914) 42–68.

24. See, for example, J. J. M. Roberts, "The Davidic Origin of the Zion Tradition" and "Zion in the Theology of the Davidic-Solomonic Empire," both in *The Bible and the Ancient Near East* (Winona Lake, Ind.: Eisenbrauns, 2002) 313–30 and 331–47, respectively.

25. Starbuck, *Court Oracles*, 67–102.

26. Ibid., 178–95. Frank M. Cross (*Canaanite Myth: Essays in the History of the Religion of Israel* [Cambridge: Harvard University Press, 1973] 234) attributes 2 Sam 23:1b–7 to the tenth century B.C.E. based on archaic elements. David Noel Freedman ("Divine Names and Titles in Early Hebrew Poetry," in *Pottery, Poetry, and Prophecy: Studies in Early Hebrew Poetry* [Winona Lake, Ind.: Eisenbrauns, 1980] 95) likewise assigns 2 Sam 23:1b–7 to the tenth century. P. K. McCarter (*II Samuel: A New Translation with Introduction and Commentary* [AB 9; Garden City, N.Y.: Doubleday, 1984] 483–86) favors an early date, though he considers

The oracle of David, son of Jesse,
    the oracle of the man whom ʾĒl raised up;[27]
the Anointed of the God of Jacob,
    the Favorite of the Strength of Israel:
The Spirit of Yahweh spoke through me,
    his word was upon my tongue;
the God of Jacob spoke,[28]
    to me the Rock of Israel said:
"He who rules over people as legitimate,
    is he who rules in the fear of God,
is like the light of morning as the sun rises,
    a morning without a cloud, out of the brightness,
    —grass from the earth after rain. . . ." [29]

In a more detailed treatment of 2 Sam 23:1–7, I argued that the *traditum* preserved in the MT dates to David's reign and was specifically used either in
connection to the covenanting ceremony with the elders of Israel at Hebron
(2 Sam 5:3) or in connection with the revolt of Sheba (2 Sam 20:1).[30] The
text's canonical placement suggests, however, that 2 Sam 23:1–7 was circulated independently and placed next to 2 Samuel 22 (// Psalm 18) as a constituent of a poetic interlude or appendix within the Deuteronomistic history. It
is notable that, whereas the text of 2 Samuel 22 (which is paralleled by Psalm
18) was adapted in a Stage 2 *traditio*, 2 Samuel 23 was not.

In comparative texts, it is often the case that the divine oracle to royalty
verbalizes monarchic specificity, the most basic and straightforward expression
being something along the lines of "Fear not, Ashurbanipal!"[31] In 2 Sam

---

v. 2 to be a gloss. Additionally, G. A. Rendsburg ("The Northern Origin of 'The Last
Words of David,'" *Bib* 69 [1988] 121) associates the poem with David during his stay at Ma-
hanaim. Two scholars, however, associate the poem with Solomon: A. Caquot, "La pro-
phétie de Nathan et ses échos lyriques," *Congress Volume: Bonn, 1962* (VTSup 9; Leiden:
Brill, 1963) 218; and T. Ishida, *The Royal Dynasties in Ancient Israel: A Study on the Formation
and Development of Royal-Dynastic Ideology* (BZAW 142; Berlin: de Gruyter, 1977) 107–8.

27. Reading הֻקַם אֵל with 4QSamᵃ.
28. Reading Ιακωβ with LXXᴸ and OL.
29. This stanza is very difficult and perhaps too corrupt in its preservation to translate
meaningfully, although the translation here mainly follows that of T. N. D. Mettinger,
"'The Last Words of David': A Study of Structure and Meaning in II Samuel 23:1–7," *SEÅ*
41–42 (1976–77) 154; and *HALAT* 2.565b. Apparently the poet mixed solar and fecundity
metaphors (see Ps 72:5–6 and Hos 6:3). A similar idea is expressed in an equally difficult
passage (Ps 110:3), in which the king is promised "dew" from the "womb of the dawn."
30. Starbuck, *Court Oracles*, 192–95.
31. Kataja and Whiting, *Grants, Decrees, and Gifts*, 38.

23:1–7, the less-common pattern is followed, by which *David, the son of Jesse*, is named in the poetic framework for the oracle, much in the same way that Zakur, king of Hamath, is named in the narrative introduction to Baal-shamayn's grant in an eighth-century B.C.E. dedicatory inscription:

1. The stele, which Zakir [*sic*], king of Hamath and Lu'ath, set up for Ilwer, [his lord].
2. I am Zakir [*sic*], king of Hamath and Lu'ath. A pious man was I, and Baal-shamayn [delivered]
3. me, and stood with me; and Baal-shamayn made me king in
4. Hadrach. Then Barhadad son of Hazael, king of Aram, organized against me an alliance of
5. [six]teen kings . . .
   . . . .
11. But I lifted up my hands to Baal-shamayn, and Baal-shamayn answered me, and Baal-shamayn [spoke]
12. to me through seers and messengers; and Baal-shamayn [said
13. to me], "Fear not, because it was I who made you king, [and I
14. shall stand] with you, and I shall deliver you from all [these kings who]
15. have forced a siege upon you. . . ."[32]

Despite the fact that the Zakur inscription is broken in places, it demonstrates that monarchic specificity in the *traditum* need not include specific reference to a royal name in the body of the oracle itself. Such a practice suggests that royal oracles were preserved as intact *traditum* within the Royal Psalms, whereas the surrounding framework could easily have been modified in Stage 2 of the *traditio*. For example, Ps 110:1, נאם יהוה לאדני "Oracle of Yahweh to my lord" may have been rather effortlessly adapted from a *traditum* such as נאם יהוה לאדני יְחִזְקִיָּהוּ "Oracle of Yahweh to my lord, Hezekiah," or even נאם יהוה לִיחִזְקִיָּהוּ "Oracle of Yahweh to Hezekiah."

Traditio Stage 2

The removal of regnal names within the *traditio* from the *traditum* (or even a secondary literary appropriation that skillfully circumscribed identifiers of monarchical specificity) indicates a shift from the use of Royal Psalms in the cult to their suitability for prayer and study. Prior to the exile, there is little reason to believe that the *institution* of kingship received such pointed focus in the cult. Even more, it is unclear how such a celebration of human kingship without overt connection to the ruling monarch would have been politically viable during Israel's monarchical period.[33]

---

32. *KAI* 202. Trans. *TSSI* 2.9–10. See also *ANET* 655–56.
33. Starbuck, *Court Oracles*, 67–102.

Unfortunately, there are no "fingerprints" to be found among the Royal Psalms that point definitively to Stage 2 redaction. As noted above, there are a number of places within the Royal Psalms that could easily have verbalized king names in an original *traditum*. Yet their poetic nature is malleable enough that the Royal Psalms redacted in the received *traditio* appear to have been composed "as is."

Fortuitously, outside the Psalter a Stage 2 redactional "fingerprint" (albeit somewhat "smudged") is recoverable in Isa 9:5, the centerpiece of a coronation titular oracle. It has long been recognized that this enumeration of throne names is dependent upon the Egyptian practice.[34] The sacral importance of the monarch's name is nowhere more patent than in the epigraphic remains of the Egyptians, which contain the Pharaoh's titulary and/or cartouche. The Egyptian titulary (*nkhbt*) comprised five great names (*rn wr*) that were given to the Pharaoh upon his accession to the throne.[35] The fourth name, the pronomen, is introduced by *n-sw-biat* "he who belongs to the sedge and the bee" and usually includes the theophoric component *R*ˀ. This name, the royal name assumed at the time of accession (i.e., the regnal name), is almost always written in a cartouche. The fifth and final title is similarly introduced by *sȝ R*ˀ "Son of Reˀ," followed by the family or personal name (or nomen) of the king. It, too, is usually written in a cartouche. The first four names of the titulary are throne names that give expression to the king's participation in the world of the gods.[36] The titulary is propagated throughout the kingdom after the king's accession. A similar pattern of "naming the royal name" is attested in Sumero-Akkadian and Hittite texts.[37]

---

34. J. J. M. Roberts, "Whose Child Is This? Reflections on the Speaking Voice in Isaiah 9:5," *The Bible and the Ancient Near East* (Winona Lake, Ind.: Eisenbrauns, 2002) 143–56; S. Morenz, "Ägyptische und davidische Königstitular," in *Religion und Geschichte des alten Ägypten* (Cologne: Böhlau, 1975) 401–3; M. Rehm, *Der königliche Messias im Licht der Immanuel-Weissagungen des Buches Jesaja* (Eichstätter Studien 1; Kevelaer: Butzon & Bercker, 1968) 130ff.; H. Wildberger, "Die Thronnamen des Messias, Jes. 9,5b," *TZ* 16 (1960) 314–32; and M. Crook, "A Suggested Occasion for Isaiah 9:2–7 and 11:1–9," *JBL* 68 (1949) 213–24.

35. See H. Frankfort, *Kingship and the Gods: A Study of Ancient Near Eastern Religion as the Integration of Society and Nature* (Oriental Institute Essay; Chicago: University of Chicago Press, 1978) 46–47; A. Gardiner, *Egyptian Grammar: Being an Introduction to the Study of Hieroglyphs* (3rd ed.; London: Oxford University Press, 1969) 71–76; and R. J. Leprohon, "Royal Ideology and State Administration in Pharaonic Egypt," *CANE* 1.276.

36. "[The titulary] sets the monarch apart from other men entirely. The mysterious powers in nature upon which man depends are somehow influenced by the king's actions. He shares their being; he vouchsafes their beneficial support of the community," Frankfort, *Kingship and the Gods*, 47.

37. See my *Court Oracles*, 76–83.

Sometimes objections are raised because Isa 9:5, as preserved in the MT, does not follow the Egyptian pattern *exactly*, since four throne names, not five, are voiced:[38]

> And one will call his name
> 1. He Who Proffers Wonders
> 2. Divine Warrior
> 3. Father of the Testament
> 4. Prince of Peace
> 5. _____

Roberts's tour de force article on this verse nevertheless demonstrates, without equivocation, the clear dependence of the text on the Egyptian pattern.[39] Where, then, is the expected *nomen*, or family name, which in the Egyptian pattern falls last in the fivefold sequence?

The MT of v. 6 attests an obvious anomaly (the unintelligible לםרבה), strongly suggesting an alteration has been made to the *traditum*. This anomaly, I suggest, is a redactional fingerprint betraying scribal redaction comparable to Stage 2 *traditio*. Hans Wildberger and others follow Albrecht Alt's suggestion that the verse, with a final *mem* occurring in medial position, betrays the fragmentation of a fifth name.[40] However, neither Alt's reconstruction (מרבה המשרה "one who increases dominion") nor Wildberger's (רב המשרה "great of dominion") has gained wide acceptance. This is primarily due to the fact that (1) neither adequately accounts for the introductory לם, which each scholar summarily drops completely or in part, and (2) neither proposed solution balances the obvious synonymous parallelism intended in v. 6. In my view, the most likely postulate to the oracle's *traditum* as well as the most likely explanation for the corrupted *traditio* attested in the MT is that an original reference to Hezekiah has been removed.

To begin with, if לם is bracketed from v. 6a and רבה is vocalized as a fem. sing. adjective modifying המשרה, then perfectly balanced and intelligible poetic bicola emerge (v. 6a–b):

> Great will be dominion,
>   and as for peace, there will be no end
> Upon the throne of David,
>   and upon his kingdom.

---

38. Most recently Blenkinsopp, *Isaiah 1–39*, 248; and Marvin A. Sweeney, *Isaiah 1–39: With an Introduction to Prophetic Literature* (FOTL 16; Grand Rapids: Eerdmans, 1996) 182.

39. Roberts, *Whose Child Is This?*

40. A. Alt, "Jesaja 8,23–9,6: Befreiungsnacht und Krönungstag," in *Kleine Schriften zur Geschichte des Volkes Israel* (Munich: Beck, 1953) 2.206–25; and H. Wildberger, *Isaiah 1–12: A Commentary* (Minneapolis: Fortress, 1991) 383–410.

This reading of the text is essentially reflected in the LXX (μεγάλη ἡ ἀρχὴ αὐτοῦ καὶ τῆς εἰρήνης αὐτοῦ οὐκ ἔστιν ὅριον ἐπὶ τὸν θρόνον Δαυιδ καὶ τὴν βασιλείαν αὐτοῦ). One might add to the Septuagintal confirmation that the terms רבה and אֵין־קֵץ occur as parallel word pairs in Job 22:5 ("Is not your wickedness great [רבה]? There is no end [אֵין־קֵץ] to your iniquities") just as they do in v. 6a as reconstructed above.

Still, there is the matter of the strange and obviously corrupted לְמ. If, as many students of Isaiah of Jerusalem think, Isa 8:23b–9:7 was intended for Hezekiah's coronation, then one could reasonably postulate that the fifth titular name might have been something like יְחִזְקִיָּהוּ יֵשֵׁב עֹלָם "Hezekiah reigns forever,"[41] or even יְחִזְקִיָּהוּ לְעֹלָם "Hezekiah forever!" This particular blessing following Hezekiah's name would be consistent with the Egyptian practice of adding a blessing after the *nomen*. For example, Harmhab's titulary is:

1. Horus: Mighty Bull, Ready in Plans
2. Favorite of the Two Goddesses; Great in Marvels in Karnak
3. Golden Horus: Satisfied with Truth, Creator of the Two Lands
4. King of Upper and Lower Egypt: Zeserkheprure, Setepnere
5. Son of Re: Mernamon, Harmhab, *given life* (emphasis mine).[42]

Since the bequest of a secure throne is a frequent blessing in the Egyptian titular,[43] it is easy to imagine that the promise of a long reign at the Judean king's coronation would have been not only appropriate but also earnestly desired. It is not evident why the redaction of an original oracle to Hezekiah was so clumsily rendered in the *traditio.* The tradition preserved in Ibn Ezra that the final *mem* was deliberately placed in medial position, on the one hand, to signal a terminus to the historical reign of Hezekiah and, on the other hand, to preserve the text's messianic vision, though unprovable and likely anachronistic, may not be far from the mark. Whatever the initial intent, the unique practice preserved a redactional fingerprint that is suggestive of processes in Stage 2 *traditio* of the Royal Psalms.

It is important to note at this point that the removal of monarchic specificity from individual Royal Psalms did not, in itself, necessarily redirect the focus of the psalm to the *institution* of kingship. Instead, for example, it is quite likely that Psalm 45 was preserved anonymously because it was sung routinely in nonroyal weddings.[44] Likewise, several of the Royal Psalms, though full of

---

41. See Ps 61:8.

42. *ARE*, 3.17.

43. See N.-C. Grimal, *Les termes de la propaganda royale égyptienne: De la XIXᵉ dynastie à la comquête d'Alexandre* (MPAIBL n.s. 6; Paris: Imprimerie Nationale, 1986) 189–94.

44. See J. J. M. Roberts, "The Enthronement of Yhwh and David: The Abiding Theological Significance of the Kingship Language of the Psalms," *CBQ* 64 (2002) 675–86, esp. 684.

strident metaphor, could easily have been appropriated by commoners in acts of devotion mirroring the leadership of a devout king (Psalms 20, 21, 101, and 144). Clearly Psalm 132 was appropriated and sung by pilgrims ascending to worship in the tradition.

Traditio Stage 3

Though it has been scholarly convention since the early nineteenth century to speak of a collection of Royal Psalms, it cannot be demonstrated the psalms identified by scholars as "royal" were in any way understood to be a related or a cohesive subgrouping prior to the Psalter's formation. Except for Psalms 2 and 89, there is little evidence for the purposeful and strategic placement of Royal Psalms in the editorial arrangements of the Psalter. Most of the Royal Psalms were included in the Psalter because of their prehistory as constituents of other subcollections.[45] Thus, it is likely that the Royal Psalms were preserved and circulated individually by a variety of means in a number of contexts and media. Any integrated relationship they might share is in little or no way due to the Stage 3 *traditio* processes by which they were included in the Psalter.

The striking exception to the "radical singularity" of the Royal Psalms is the canonical placements of Psalms 2 and 89. Three of the Royal Psalms occur at what have been called editorial "seams" of the Psalter: Psalms 2, 72, 89. Although Psalms 1 and 2 have received a plethora of scholarly attention, it is still not clear exactly when Psalm 1 was added as an introduction to the Psalter. Although most scholars assume that Psalm 2 was early on associated with the Davidic collections (Psalms 3–88), it remains speculative when Psalm 2 would have occupied the lead position to the Davidic collections. Wilson has suggested the possibility of a preexilic collection of Davidic psalms inclusive of Psalms 2–72.[46] However, since Psalm 3 begins with the superscription "A psalm of/for David: when he fled before Absalom, his son," and Psalm 72 ends with the postscript "Concluded are the prayers of David, the son of Jesse," and these editorial notations form the logical boundaries of the Psalms 3–72 subcollection, it seems unlikely that the non-superscripted Psalm 2 was subsequently added (alone) to the previously joined Books I and II.

The more likely case is that Psalm 2 was appended to a previously combined collection of "Davidic" psalms spanning Psalms 3–72, at the time when Book III of the Psalter was appended to Books I and II. This postulate is buttressed by the observation that over 85 percent of the psalms in Books I and II are attributed to David, while only five percent are attributed to the king in

---

45. See detailed analysis in my *Court Oracles*, 103–20.

46. G. Wilson, "The Use of Royal Psalms at the 'Seams' of the Hebrew Psalter," *JSOT* 35 (1986) 91.

Book III, neither Psalm 2 nor Psalm 89 holds Davidic attribution. This being the case, it makes sense to consider Psalms 2 and 89 to be constituents of a shared Stage 3 *traditio* focused on the endowments and fate of the "office" of kingship itself.

In fact, this is exactly what Wilson and others have successfully argued. The Davidic covenant, according to Wilson, is introduced at the head of Books I–III by Psalm 2 and then resounded throughout Psalms 3–88 by means of the overwhelming Davidic attributions. Psalm 89, then, voices issues of theodicy for a community that experienced the destruction of Jerusalem, the exile of the Hebrew nation, and the demise of the Davidic monarchy. Wilson explains: "for Psalm 89 the Davidic covenant is not only an event of the distant past, neither is it simply the source for later kingly authority, rather it is now a covenant *failed*. YHWH is depicted as rejecting his anointed king and renouncing the Davidic covenant."[47] Stage 3 of the *traditio*, then, used Psalms 2 and 89 to voice a lament over the excruciating lived-reality of the failure of the Davidic covenant.

Psalm 89

Clearly, the Stage 1 *traditio* of Psalm 89 was anchored to a particular time of crisis while a descendent of David sat upon the throne. Twice previous royal oracles are quoted within the psalm (vv. 4–5 and vv. 20–38) in order to lay the legal foundation for the psalmist's accusation commencing in v. 39: "But you have renounced and reviled, you have become enraged with your messiah!" Inclusive of the next 7 verses, 15 accusations are leveled by the psalmist against Yahweh. The psalmist is relentless in his indictment. The only reprieve is to be found in the lead verse of the next section of the psalm (v. 47), where the psalmist cries out: עד־מה יהוה "How long, O Yahweh?" Then, in vv. 47–52, the psalmist voices his desperate petition and pleads with God to revisit his commitment to his steadfast love that was promised by oath to David. The psalm's *traditum*, then, only makes sense in the context of a Judean king who is confronted with Yahweh's abandonment, at a time when the Davidic dynasty itself faced peril. The urgencies of the petitions and accusations of vv. 39–52 reflect a martial, hence also a judicial, context since in the ancient Near East warfare was interpreted as a judicial ordeal.[48] Walls have been breached (v. 41).

---

47. Ibid., 90.

48. See J. Van Seters's discussion of Merneptah's appointment to execute justice over the Libyans (*In Search of History: Historiography in the Ancient World and the Origins of Biblical History* [New Haven: Yale University Press, 1983; repr. Winona Lake, Ind.: Eisenbrauns, 1997] 156–57).

Fortifications lie in ruins (v. 41). The king has been defeated in battle (v. 44). His very ability to rule is at stake (v. 45). In short, these verses manifest Yahweh's abrogation of the royal covenant (v. 40).[49] Although impossible to confirm, Judah's vassalage after the death of Josiah at the hands of Pharaoh Neco and the subsequent deposing of Jehoahaz suggest a period likely for the psalm's original composition.[50] Presumably, the actual name of the beset king would have been vocalized, if not written within the psalm itself, in its *traditum*. Whereas Stage 3 *traditio* for Psalm 89, as stated above, refocused the force of the psalm from a petition for an individual king to the endowments and fate of the "office" of kingship itself within the structure of Books I–III of the Psalter, the psalm's Stage 2 *traditio* provided avenues for a monarchless community to continue to pray the psalm on their own behalf. This was accomplished, first and foremost, by the redaction of specific reference to a previously reigning king. By removing the *traditum*'s monarchic specificity, the redactors lifted the psalm's unrequited accusation from the historical record, offering it to the community itself for contemporary prayer. Psalm 89, thus reappropriated, is transformed from a preexilic lament for a unique king to a lament for the entire community in exile.

Additionally, there may be other remnants of Stage 2 *traditio* in Psalm 89. The MT v. 20 states that the divine oracle was given to Yahweh's loyal ones (לַחֲסִידֶיךָ) in a vision. Other Hebrew MSS attest the singular "loyal one," and though none of the versions supports this reading, a number of commentators have been inclined to emend the received text on the inference that the prophet Nathan is the intended referent.[51] Others have viewed David himself as the recipient.[52] It is likely that the MT's לַחֲסִידֶיךָ is secondary to the *traditum*

---

49. The king's confrontation of Yahweh (v. 50) is reminiscent of the complaint of Ramses II to Amun in the context of his attack on the Assyrians at Kadesh. The Kadesh battle inscriptions recount that Ramses II charged forward to meet the Hittite army but was abandoned by his troops. Just as in Ps 89:50 where the king implicates Yahweh's legal responsibility in the guise of a question (rather than a straightforward accusation), so too, Ramses II places his allegation as a query. Nevertheless, the language that Ramses II employs holds a legal force similar to the deposition of Yahweh's oath.

50. H.-J. Kraus, *Psalms 60–150: A Commentary* (Minneapolis: Augsburg, 1989) 784; and A. A. Anderson, *The Book of Psalms: Psalms 73–150* (NCB; Grand Rapids: Eerdmans, 1972) 631.

51. N.B. 2 Sam 7:17 and 1 Chr 17:15. See F. Nötscher, *Die Psalmen* (Würzburg: Echter-Verlag, 1952) 180; H. Gunkel, *Die Psalmen* (5th ed.; HKAT 2/2; Göttingen: Vandenhoeck & Ruprecht, 1933) 392; Cross, *Canaanite Myth*, 258; and Kraus, *Psalms 60–150*, 200 (but note his disclaimer and caution on p. 208).

52. G. W. Ahlström, *Psalm 89: Eine Liturgie aus dem Ritual des leidenden Königs* (Lund: C. W. K. Gleerup, 1959) 100. Dahood believed the reference to be to David himself, and

and that the text originally read a singular form of the noun. At the same time, rather than committing a copyist mistake, the MT and the Syr. attribute the oracle to the community itself consistent with Stage 2 *traditio*. In this regard, it is worth noting vv. 9 and 16 of Psalm 132, where חֲסִידִים is the complement of כֹּהֲנִים, and, together, the terms signify the temple community. Given this fact, coupled with the observation that חֲסִידִים is used elsewhere in the MT for the worshiping community of Israel, it is hard to escape the conclusion that the royal oracle was reappropriated in the Stage 2 *traditio* as if it were given to the community itself.[53] Likewise, in v. 51a the *traditum* likely read the singular,[54] rather than the MT's plural עֲבָדֶיךָ. Yet a similar reappropriation is evidenced in the MT, presumably emerging in the Stage 2 *traditio*, so that the petition to Adonai is refocused on the disposition of the exilic community itself, despite the uneasy shift to a 1st-person sing. subject in the second half of the bicolon.

Theological Anthropology at a Fulcrum

In his comparison of Isa 55:3b–4 with Psalm 89, Eissfeldt identified eight language clusters representing, essentially, two ideological motifs: the establishment of Yahweh's covenant (בְּרִית; Ps 89:4, 35) and Yahweh's loyalty // faithfulness pledged to the Davidic House (חֶסֶד // אָמַן / אֱמוּנָה; Ps 89:2, 3, 25, 29, 34, 50). Eissfeldt believed it entirely possible that Psalm 89 was known to Second Isaiah, since the two texts betrayed so many lexical parallels, though there was not enough evidence to say more than that they both stemmed from the same ideological background. Though emerging from the same royal theological traditions, the two texts, in Eissfeldt's mind, evidenced entirely different purposes. This is made clear at the conclusion of his study:

> In terms of content, the latter passage is entirely different from the former. In Ps. 89 the content of the promise is interpreted exclusively in the continued existence of the Davidic dynasty—the current threat that calls the validity of the

---

attempted to defend the consonantal text as a singular form with an archaic genitival ending or, alternatively, as a plural of majesty; see M. Dahood, *Psalms 50–100: A New Translation with Introduction and Commentary* (AB 17; Garden City, N.Y.: Doubleday, 1965) 316.

53. It should be noted, however, that certain textual traditions translate the plural referent in terms of the Davidic line. Some MSS of the LXX attest υἱοῖς "sons." This is somewhat strange since in most cases חֲסִידִים presented no problem for the translators of the LXX, who regularly used οἱ ὅσιοι. Likewise, 4Q236, although fragmentary, exhibits a much shorter line and offers בחרין "chosen ones." At Qumran חָסִיד was a self-referential epithet for the community.

54. Twenty-four Hebrew MSS and the Syr. attest the singular "your servant."

promise into question. Second Isaiah, however, places the promise before the fate of Israel and its royal house and declares its eternal validity.[55]

The comparison that Eissfeldt made, however, was a comparison between the *traditum* of Psalm 89 and Isa 55:1–5. The second stage *traditio* of Psalm 89, at least as outlined in this article, compares quite differently. In fact, both Second Isaiah and the second stage *traditio* of Psalm 89, as well as the other oracular Royal Psalms, view the collapse of the Davidic dynasty as the impetus to reframe the Davidic covenant in terms of the entire populace. Just as a beleaguered community is invited to a covenant feast and bequeathed the royal Davidic covenant in Isa 55:1–5, so too the same exilic community was able meaningfully to pray the so-called Royal Psalms on their own behalf in the psalms' second stage *traditio*. Similar to the ways by which Second Isaiah transforms the theology of the Davidic covenant of First Isaiah, the oracular Royal Psalms have been redacted and transformed to so that the one-time representative *for* all of Israel is now represented *through* all Israel. In terms of theological anthropology, this hermeneutical shift of royal traditions brings a similar perspective to an exilic counterpart, namely P, who maintained that *humanity*, not the king, is created in the image of God (בְּצֶלֶם אֱלֹהִים; Gen 1:27). Rather than existing as a gadfly mockery to the dispossessed in exile, Israel's royal traditions remained the theological-anthropological conduit through which the diaspora community reinterpreted its divinely given dignity, responsibility, and relationship with the Deity.

Though the Royal Davidic tradition would be interpreted in other ways, most notably culminating in eschatological expectations of a new "David," and though the Royal Psalms would be appropriated and used for such further developments, the theological advances made at the "fulcrum" with Isa 55:1–5 and the oracular Royal Psalms, namely the bequeathing of the royal office and its rights and responsibilities to the entire nation, remain one of the most significant advances in theological anthropology. It is an advance, inclusive of the identification with Jesus of Nazareth as the messianic Christ, that was affirmed in New Testament theology. In the words of 2 Tim 2:12: "if we endure, we will also reign with him."

---

55. Eissfeldt, "Promises of Grace," 206–7.

King Yahweh as the Good Shepherd: Taking Another Look at the Image of God in Psalm 23

BETH TANNER

New Brunswick Theological Seminary

It is with trepidation that any scholar attempts to provide a different look at Psalm 23. It is not only a beloved biblical text, but through its association with Jesus in art and media images, the image has become a religious icon.[1] The scene is both powerful and sentimentalized[2] and any interpretation of this psalm must take this image into account. But is this image of God as protector of the little lamb the complete picture of this psalm, or is there more to be considered when interpreting these words?

As a student of J. J. M. Roberts, I gained a wealth of knowledge, but more importantly I gained an invaluable perspective on the work of the biblical scholar. Professor Roberts teaches that in the most familiar texts, the ones appearing to provide nice comfortable images, are hidden great mysteries and complex pictures of God and humanity. He also stresses to his students and the academy that the culture and the church often domesticate the most jarring images of God and create their own meaning, while disregarding the texts' original ancient contexts.[3] Is this the case with Psalm 23? I argue that it is. The psalm does reflect God's protection and care, but it is the context in which this care and protection are guaranteed that is the focus of this investigation. I will point out how many of the images and, indeed, the opening title of the psalm

---

1. An internet search (www.google.com) for the image the Good Shepherd provided over 2,500 images from a variety of sources.

2. William L. Holladay, *The Psalms through Three Thousand Years* (Minneapolis: Fortress, 1993) 359–71.

3. For examples of this type of work, see J. J. M. Roberts, "Myth versus History: Relaying the Comparative Foundations," *CBQ* 38 (1976) 1–13; "Does God Lie? Divine Deceit as a Theological Problem in Israelite Prophetic Literature," *Congress Volume: Jerusalem* (VTSup 40; Leiden: Brill 1988) 211–20; and "The Motif of the Weeping God in Jeremiah and Its Background in the Lament Tradition of the Ancient Near East," *Old Testament Essays* 5 (1992) 361–74, all reprinted in *The Bible and the Ancient Near East: Collected Essays* (Winona Lake, Ind.: Eisenbrauns, 2002) 59–71, 123–31, and 132–42, respectively.

indicate that Yahweh should not be understood only as the peaceful shepherd but as the great and powerful shepherd king. The images of peace and tranquility so associated with this psalm are only one facet of Yahweh's kingship. When one looks closely at the images provided, a portrait of Yahweh as the king who controls both nature and humanity also emerges.

In pursuit of this focus, I will not address questions of form-critical analysis as my primary methodology. A great deal of competent work has already been published on that issue. Instead, this essay is concerned with the central question of what the psalm tells the reader about Yahweh when read in an ancient Near Eastern context. The words and images in the psalm will be compared with similar images both in the Hebrew Bible and in texts of surrounding cultures, and a case will be developed for a multifaceted picture of God's reign over the earth.

Preliminary Issues

Psalm 23 is certainly one of the most well-known of all psalms, but it is also vexing to scholars. It is a unique psalm, and its genre is difficult to identify. Gunkel characterizes it as a psalm of confidence, which he argues developed from the complaint psalms.[4] Kraus sees it as a prayer song, since Yahweh is addressed in the second person in vv. 4–5.[5] Most modern interpreters see it as a song of trust.[6] But others disagree. John Eaton has argued that it is a Royal Psalm in the sense that it was spoken by Israel's king to Yahweh.[7] Mark Smith proposes that the psalm should be understood as a pilgrimage song.[8] Much of this disagreement centers on just where one is to place the song's use in the cult. Gunkel and Kraus see it as directed in response to God for an answered complaint, and its placement after Psalm 22 certainly aids this interpretation. Likewise, Eaton sees it as a direct response to Psalm 22, but he argues that the opening reference of Psalm 23 to Yahweh as shepherd and the form of personal address show that the psalm is spoken by the king, most appropriately the Shepherd-King David.[9] Gerstenberger argues that the psalm is not from

---

4. Hermann Gunkel, *Introduction to the Psalms: The Genres of the Religious Lyric of Israel* (completed by J. Bergrich; trans. J. Nogalski; Macon, Ga.: Mercer University Press, 1998) 190.

5. Hans-Joachim Kraus, *Psalms 1–59* (trans. H. Oswald; Minneapolis: Augsburg, 1988) 305.

6. See, for example, Patrick D. Miller, *Interpreting the Psalms* (Philadelphia: Fortress, 1986) 112; or Peter C. Craigie, *Psalms 1–50* (WBC 19; Waco, Tex.: Word, 1983) 204.

7. John Eaton, *Kingship and the Psalms* (Sheffield: JSOT Press, 1986) 36–38. Dennis Pardee ("Structure and Meaning in Hebrew Poetry: The Example of Psalm 23," *MAARAV* 5–6 [Spring 1990] 239–80) also argues that the speaker is a king.

8. Mark S. Smith, "Setting and Rhetoric in Psalm 23," *JSOT* 41 (1988) 62.

9. Eaton, *Kingship*, 37.

cultic circles but from a very personal or familial situation. He argues that the close relationship shared by Yahweh and the psalmist must come from worship within a small family unit or clan.[10] Interestingly, Eaton uses a similar argument to associate the psalm with King David. What is clear is that the psalm is expressed in personal language, but the images used for Yahweh are not intimate. On the contrary, the images for Yahweh speak not of a personal God but of a mighty warrior king. This juxtaposition of personal address and powerful images of God is but one of the twists that will cause the reader to look at the contrasts in the psalm as part of its message.

Another question is the psalm's perspective on time. Is the poem speaking in the present tense or is it to be set in the future? Dahood maintains that this psalm is to be read as a future hope. He writes, "The psalmist is quite confident that Yahweh is his shepherd, who will guide him through the vicissitudes of life to the eternal bliss of Paradise."[11] Dahood sees the banquet as a future event. Likewise, Craigie's translation of the psalm is set in a future perspective.[12] Kraus and others who see the psalm as part of a cultic meal of thanksgiving place the psalm in the present; the meal is not one to be had in Paradise but one that is occurring in the present.[13] Freedman considers both ways of reading the psalm possible, "There are genuinely archaic features in the Psalm: e.g., . . . the tense system of the verbs, involving the alternation of imperfect and perfect verb forms, with no distinction of time or aspect."[14] The time frame of the psalm, then, is left to the interpreter and both translations are used in current contexts. The purpose of this essay, however, is to listen to the psalm in its ancient context and, in that context, literature was most often focused on the present. As Pardee notes, "The 'life' after death known very vaguely from Ugaritic texts is both spatially and qualitatively different from earthly life; I know of no Ugaritic or Biblical text which would permit the inference that the deceased 'dwell' in the temple of the deity."[15]

---

10. Erhard Gerstenberger, *Psalms: Part 1, with an Introduction to Cultic Poetry* (FOTL 14; Grand Rapids: Eerdmans, 1988) 114–15.

11. Mitchell Dahood, *Psalms I: 1–50* (AB 16; Garden City, N.Y.: Doubleday, 1965) 145.

12. Craigie, *Psalms 1–50*, 203–4. He uses the future tense, but there is no discussion about his reason for doing so.

13. Kraus, *Psalms 1–59*, 306. Similarly, Smith ("Setting and Rhetoric," 64) and Pardee ("Structure and Meaning," 240).

14. D. N. Freedman, "Twenty-Third Psalm," in *Pottery, Poetry, and Prophecy: Studies in Early Hebrew Poetry* (Winona Lake, Ind.: Eisenbrauns, 1980) 301; originally printed in *Michigan Oriental Studies in Honor of George G. Cameron* (ed. Louis L. Orlin et al.; Ann Arbor, Mich.: Department of Near Eastern Studies, University of Michigan, 1976).

15. Pardee, "Structure and Meaning," 279.

One additional point raised in academic discourse is germane to this discussion, the two images of Yahweh presented in the psalm. Verses 1–4 portray God as a shepherd, whereas vv. 5–6 provide a picture of God as host. Some scholars have attempted to make the shepherd image the encompassing one, arguing that it also includes an understanding as a host.[16] Others have been so convinced that the shepherd imagery is the single image that they emended the text to maintain the metaphor throughout the poem.[17] Freedman has argued that the two images are meant to be juxtaposed as a parallel to the question posed in Ps 78:19.[18] Miller holds the two images together with neither as the determinative portrait. He writes, "It [Psalm 23] has been properly recognized as a primal declaration of both (*a*) the basic trust of the one who knows he or she belongs to God, and (*b*) the nature of God's care for those who belong to the Lord."[19] The debate here points to another juxtaposition in this brief psalm. In this essay, I will argue that the structure of this psalm is even more complex than the representation of God as shepherd and host, but that every image can be understood under the rubric of Yahweh as king.[20]

Psalm 23: Its Images of Yahweh as King

Verse One: "The Lord Is My Shepherd"

The psalm opens with a title for God that is used often in the Hebrew Bible.[21] Craigie, who sees shepherd as a metaphor instead of a title, argues that shepherd expresses "the interrelated dimensions of *protection* and *care*."[22] Is

---

16. See for example, Bernhard W. Anderson, *Out of the Depths: The Psalms Speak for Us Today* (Philadelphia: Westminster, 1983) 208.

17. E. Power suggested that the word שלחן "table" in v. 5 be amended to שלח "weapon or spear" to preserve the shepherd image, reading "You hold a spear over against my adversaries" ("The Shepherd's Two Rods in Modern Palestine and in Some Passages in the Old Testament [Ps 23,4; Zach 22,7ss; 1 Sam 17,43]," *Bib* 9 [1928] 440).

18. Freedman, "Twenty-Third Psalm," 301–2; and Michael Barré and John Kselman, "New Exodus, Covenant, and Restoration in Psalm 23," in *The Word of the Lord Shall Go Forth: Essays in Honor of David Noel Freedman in Celebration of His Sixtieth Birthday* (ed. C. L. Meyers and M. O'Connor; Winona Lake, Ind.: Eisenbrauns, 1983) 97–98.

19. Miller, *Interpreting the Psalms*, 119.

20. Pardee makes a similar observation based on different criteria, "This combination of bucolic and royal imagery is only comprehensible in the context of royal ideology" ("Structure and Meaning," 272).

21. For example, God as a shepherd appears in a variety of texts in the Hebrew Bible either by the specific title רעה (Gen 49:24; Isa 40:11; Jer 31:10; Ezek 34:15; Ps 23:1, 28:9, 80:2) or by an image of the people as sheep (Isa 5:16–17, 49:9; Jer 50:19; Ezek 34:2–24; Zeph 3:13; Ps 79:13, 95:7, 100:3).

22. Craigie, *Psalms 1–50*, 205.

"shepherd" a metaphor or a title? Biblical and ancient Near Eastern textual evidence argues that the word be understood as a title and, even more specifically, as a royal title. God does provide protection and care, but as a function of God serving as king. For example, Isa 5:16–17 places the shepherd image beside the title יהוה צבאות "Yahweh of Hosts."[23]

> But the Lord of hosts is exalted by justice;
> and the Holy God shows himself holy by righteousness.
> Then lambs will graze as in their pasture, fatlings and kids will feed in the ruins.

Jer 31:10 uses the shepherd title in the context of God's power:

> Hear the word of the LORD, O nations, and declare it in the coastlands far away; say, "He who scattered Israel will gather him and will keep him as a shepherd a flock."[24]

The title *Shepherd* is also connected to the enthronement of Yahweh in Ps 95:6–7:

> O come, let us worship and bow down, let us kneel before the Lord, Our Maker! For he is our God, and we are the people of his pasture, the sheep of his hand.

and in Ps 80:1:

> Give ear, O Shepherd of Israel, you who lead Joseph like a flock!
> You who are enthroned upon the cherubim, shine forth.

Finally two additional texts, Ezek 34:1–24 and Zech 11:4–17, portray the kings of Israel as bad shepherds and God as the great shepherd: as shepherd, God will take back the sheep and will judge the leaders (Ezek 34:17, 20) and will repay the evil shepherds with violence (Zech 11:17). Both the title *Shepherd* and the image of God as Shepherd are associated with God's power, justice, and kingship. The psalm, then, opens, with a declaration that is equivalent to proclaiming "Yahweh is my king."

Further, the very structure of this first verse may also provide a poetic clue about how one is to hear this title. The psalm opens with a verbless clause, juxtaposing "Yahweh" and "shepherd." Only Psalms 93, 97, and 99 open with

---

23. The title "Yahweh of Hosts" is often used in the context of war and or Yahweh's rule over the nations. See Frank Cross, *Canaanite Myth and Hebrew Epic* (Cambridge: Harvard University Press, 1973), especially chaps. 5–7; and Patrick Miller, *The Divine Warrior in Early Israel* (Cambridge: Harvard University Press, 1973). Likewise, Psalm 80 opens with the title רעה ישראל "Shepherd of Israel" and also uses the title יהוה אלהים צבאות "Yahweh, God of hosts" twice and אלהים צבאות "God of hosts" twice.

24. Also Jer 50:19; similarly Isa 40:10–11; Zeph 3:13; Ps 95:7.

this same structure of "Yahweh" juxtaposed with a title, and the title is "king."[25] This structure further strengthens the evidence for "shepherd" as a title that is synonymous with "king."[26]

A multitude of ancient Near Eastern texts also use the title *shepherd* for the gods in the context of their function as king. The Sumerian god Enlil is referred to as "God Enlil, faithful Shepherd, Master of all countries, [faithful] Shepherd, . . . the lord who drew the outline of his land."[27] Marduk is also referred to as a shepherd of humans: "Most exalted be the Son, our avenger; let his sovereignty be surpassing, having no rival. May he shepherd the black-headed ones, his creatures";[28] and in his victory over Tiamat, "who the corpse of Tiamat carried off with *his* weapon; who directs the land—their faithful shepherd";[29] and in his rule over the other gods, "May he shepherd all the gods like sheep. . . . Because he created the spaces and fashioned the ground, Father Enlil called his name 'Lord of the Lands.' "[30] The image that opens the psalm, if read in the context of the biblical witness and the greater ancient Near Eastern literature, is of a powerful king god who will make the world just by a powerful hand, a god who controls humans and other gods.

"I Do Not Lack"

Many scholars have noted that Psalm 23 uses uncommon vocabulary.[31] I am arguing that it is this very vocabulary that provides important clues to reading the psalm as one proclaiming Yahweh's kingship.[32] The word חסר is one such word. It is used in several contexts where the powerful God is providing for the needs of the human; see Gen 8:3, 5 where the waters *diminish*;

---

25. Granted Psalm 23 uses the personal term "my shepherd," whereas the Enthronement Psalms use the 3rd-person "king," but despite this difference, which was discussed above, the parallel is striking.

26. Pardee argues that the psalm "is only comprehensible in the context of royal ideology" ("Structure and Meaning," 272).

27. *ANET* 337.

28. Ibid., 69.

29. Ibid., 71.

30. Ibid., 72.

31. For example, Freedman writes, "the vocabulary while unusual is quite comprehensible" ("Twenty-Third Psalm," 275).

32. Freedman (ibid., 276–77) used a similar process of investigating the vocabulary of Psalm 23. He focuses his research, however, on the psalm's connection to the exodus and wilderness narratives, arguing that "the poet has adapted the main elements in the Exodus tradition to encourage and enhance personal piety." His evaluation is helpful, and the connections he makes also point to an event that has as its center an understanding of Yahweh as king (Exod 15:18).

Deut 2:7 where Moses tells the people God provided for them in the wilderness so that *they lacked nothing*; Deut 8:9 where God promised to bring the people into a land where they *will lack nothing*; 1 Kgs 17:14, 16 where the widow's jar of oil *will not lack*; Isa 51:14 where God will make sure that the oppressed *do not lack* bread. The use of the word is often associated with God's providing food but is also seen in God's control over the waters of chaos and care for the poor and weak. Interestingly, God's provision is causative but is not the subject of the sentence. The person does not lack, because Yahweh, the Shepherd-King, provides for humanity.

Verse Two: "In Green Pastures, He Makes Me Lie Down;
To Still Waters He Leads Me" [33]

The image of the shepherd here is a dual one. At one level this verse places the poem firmly within an agricultural setting. The green field and the brook are the background for much of the art and media images based on this text. The image is one of care, but this image also fits well with the image of God as King. The first verb of the verse (רבץ) is in the *Hiphil*, implying that the "shepherd" has power over the person, "he causes me to lie down." The person saying these words acknowledges that Yahweh is the one in the relationship with the most power. Second, the imagery here is consistent with the ways that kings (both divine and human) are to provide for the people of their flock. Typical in this regard is the characterization of Yahweh in Ezek 34:13–15:

> I will bring them out from the peoples and gather them from the countries . . . and I will feed them on the mountains of Israel, by the watercourses . . . I will feed them with good pasture . . . there they shall lie down in good grazing land . . . I will myself be the shepherd of my sheep, and I will make them lie down.

Likewise, Zeph 3:13b offers, "Then they will pasture and lie down, and no one will make them afraid."

The image of providing green pasture is also seen in several ancient Near Eastern descriptions of the king. Tomback uses several texts to show that this image of lying down in green pasture is to be equated with a righteous king's reign. [34] He notes, for example, Hammurabi's claim in the epilogue to the Code of Hammurabi, "I made the people lie down in safe pastures, I did not

---

33. In this article, I am translating the psalm as close to the Hebrew as possible, using the gender grammatically encoded in the words. This perspective is for academic purposes only and is not a comment on the use of inclusive language in modern contexts.

34. Richard Tomback, "Psalm 23:2 Reconsidered," *JNSL* 10 (1982) 93–94.

allow anyone to frighten them."[35] This imagery also applies to the god Marduk, "who provides grazing and drinking places."[36]

So in an ancient Near Eastern context, the imagery of the psalm is agricultural, but it is also an image of the shepherd-king who is charged with the welfare of the people. In addition, the imagery of the sheep grazing at peace is closely associated with the removal of enemies that threaten the flock. The security comes only after the shepherd-king has vanquished all the enemies and their threats.[37]

Verse Three: "My Life He Renews; He Leads Me in Paths of Righteousness for His Name's Sake"

It is here in v. 3 that the image of an actual shepherd and sheep begins to erode. While one can easily picture sheep eating and drinking and possibly having their נפש renewed (or returned, depending on how the verb is translated), sheep being led down paths of righteousness are a strain on the metaphor.

The first image is of God renewing or returning my נפש. The verb, שוב, is quite common and often indicates a return from sin or error. What is unusual in this verse is not the word but the form of the word. The *Poel* form is used. Is the verb form a clue to a different meaning? God is the subject of the *Poel* form in all but two occurrences, and when God is the subject, God is acting either for the good of the people (Isa 49:5, 58:12; Jer 50:19; Ezek 39:27; Ps 60:3) or in judgment (Ezek 38:4; 39:2). Interestingly, this word is used twice in Jeremiah, and both times it is in reference to the shepherd image. In Jer 50:6, "the shepherds have turned the people away (שובבום),"[38] while in 50:19, "I (God) will return (שבבתי) Israel to its pasture and it shall feed on Carmel . . . its hunger shall be satisfied."[39] These other occurrences illustrate that God acts as a king, providing both "good" and "judgment" over the people and the leaders. The form of the verb indicates a more holistic understanding of "life renewed," meaning both physical life and the good and justice a righteous king gives to the community.

---

35. Ibid., 94.

36. *ANET* 69.

37. Bernard Batto has pointed to similar descriptions that refer to God's eschatological reign of peace (Lev 26:5–6; Ezek 34:25–31; and Zech 8:10–12). He argues that these descriptions derive from ancient Near Eastern language depicting the divine sovereign's control over the world that is manifested via agricultural bounty, "The Covenant of Peace: A Neglected Ancient Near Eastern Motif," *CBQ* 49 (1987) 197–211.

38. Reading with the Q, against the K (שובבים).

39. Contra Timothy Willis, who argues that the *Poel* form should be read as "he herds me in," thus maintaining the shepherd image from v. 2 ("A Fresh Look at Psalm XXIII 3A," *VT* 37 [1987] 104–6).

The next colon, "in paths of righteousness, he leads me for his name's sake," moves the reader further away from an exclusively agricultural setting and strengthens the image of kingship. The word used for "lead" (נחה) is never used of animals. It is most often used of God in the context of God's leading the individual, Israel, or other nations.[40] Several passages also indicate that God is leading to a place of safety or rest (Ps 77:21[20]; 78:53; 107:30).

The term "paths of צדק"[41] is also not one associated with domestic animals. The word for path (מעגל) appears to come from a root associated with a "calf" or "heifer," but it is always used to indicate a life course, instead of an actual trodden path.[42] This is not the way of animals. Indeed this indicates another type of "leading," a leading that is less physical and more associated with a leading such as in the way of the Torah, a path that Israel's leader is to exemplify (Psalm 72).[43]

The final phrase moves to God's motivation for leading the people—for his name's sake. This is royal language. The people are irrelevant here, except as they show forth God's leadership. Ezekiel prophesies that Yahweh will bring the people out of exile for his name's sake (Ezek 20:19–20). In similar fashion, Moses appeals to God in Exod 32:11–12 to "change his mind" for the sake of God's reputation, not because of anything the people can do for God. In both cases God saves the people to show forth God's greatness and rule.

Verse Four: "Even if I Walk in the Valleys of Deep Darkness, I Do Not Fear Evil for You Are with Me; Your Rod and Your Staff, They Comfort Me"

The form dramatically changes in v. 4. Directly on the heels of God's leading of the human for God's purpose, the focus shifts without warning from God as the subject of the verb to the psalmist as subject. The form also changes

---

40. The word appears 39 times, and 33 times the subject is God. Also, of 6 other times it is used, 4 of them refer to kings (Num 23:7; 1 Sam 22:4; 1 Kgs 10:26; 2 Kgs 18:11).

41. I have used the term "paths of righteousness" to preserve the construct form of the poem, but the meaning of צדק is difficult to capture in English. A better understanding may be "right paths," as argued by Miller (*Interpreting the Psalms*, 114).

42. BDB, 722. The path here is one set by God for good (Isa 26:7, 59:8; Ps 17:5, 65:12[11]; Prov 4:11, 26; 5:21) or a bad or wicked path of humans (Ps 140:6[5]; Prov 2:15, 18; 5:6). Interestingly, the other use of this word is for a type of military entrenchment used of both Saul's and David's armies (2 Sam 17:20; 24:5).

43. Miller (*Interpreting the Psalms*, 115) has made a similar observation, noting, "but the activity of God here may be understood as either leading the psalmist to walk in the way of justice and righteousness (cf. Prov 2:9, 4:11)—a meaning that would be especially appropriate if the one who speaks were originally the king—or leading the trusting one to walk in safe and correct paths where no harm will befall (Pss 5:9, 16:11)."

from the real to the hypothetical.[44] Most scholars continue the theme of the person being led here, but this interpretation denies the abrupt change of perspective.[45] God's role here has become passive, and the psalmist takes control. Previously God is directly involved in the path of the person, but here what is presented is presence, not leadership.[46] Does this indicate a change in the relationship between the psalmist and God because of the psalmist's act, or does the psalm continue to indicate God's care and protection of the psalmist?

The verse is further complicated by difficulties of translation. One of the issues in translating this psalm has been exactly how to understand the word צלמות. Is it a compound word that combines the word for "shadow" (צל) with the word for "death" (מות), as the well-known translation "the shadow of death" indicates? Or does it originate from the Semitic root *ṣlm* meaning to be dark, as in a dark or black valley? Either way, the reference is to some place that is fearful and threatening. Likewise, the phrase "I do not fear evil" sheds no light on the meaning of the verse and, indeed, may further complicate it. The Hebrew word רע has a wide semantic range, meaning everything from distress to an external threat of malice.[47] Instead of "evil" as it is understood in a modern sense, the phrase may be better translated "I do not fear any bad event or harm."[48] Either way, the outcome is never a good or peaceful one for the one experiencing "evil," no matter what form that "evil" may take. In summary, while certainty in meaning eludes the translator, there is no doubt here that the path the psalmist is taking is one of danger and possibly even death.

What is left to the interpreter is to decide how one is to understand the changing roles of the human/sheep and the God/Shepherd. If the psalm is read

---

44. The two lines of the verse begin with prepositions that must be read as conditional clauses. B. Waltke and M. O'Connor (*Introduction to Biblical Hebrew Syntax* [Winona Lake, Ind.: Eisenbrauns, 1990] 638) explain that the phrase גם כי introduces the protasis of an "irreal conditional" sentence: "Even if I walk . . . I do not fear . . . because (then) God is with me."

45. For example, see Kraus, *Psalms 1–59*, 307; or Craigie, *Psalms 1–50*, 207.

46. Pardee ("Structure and Meaning," 272) recognizes this change, noting, "In the second section, the sheep-herding terminology continues but the 'speaker' acts and YHWH by means of his surrogates reacts."

47. BDB gives the definition of רע as bad, evil, distress, injury, or calamity (948). The word is used of humans: "against you alone I have sinned, and I have done *evil* in your eyes" (Ps 51:6[4]), and "an assembly of *evildoers* surround me" (Ps 22:17[16]); of God: "and God changed his mind concerning the *evil* that he planned to bring on his people" (Exod 32:14); as a way of life: "turn aside from *evil* and do good" (Ps 34:14); or even of a wild animal: "then we will say that an *evil* animal devoured him" (Gen 37:20).

48. Kraus translates the phrase "I fear no harm" (*Psalms 1–59*, 304), and Dahood translates "I shall fear no danger" (*Psalms I*, 145).

as celebrating Yahweh's kingship, this passage could be seen in the same light as the surprising warning in Ps 95:7b–11, which is also stated as a conditional situation.[49] Despite confidence in Yahweh's kingship, there is still human autonomy. If the metaphor in v. 3 symbolizes a way of life (path of righteousness), then does this juxtaposition remind the reader of the other path?[50] Could this image be a connection to the kings of Israel and Judah, who chose their own ways instead of following Yahweh? Or could it relate to the covenantal promise to David in 2 Samuel 7, which stated that God will be with the Davidic line forever, even when they stray? This reading, then, would be reminiscent of the curses associated with a covenant between a suzerain and vassal, reminding the reader that following one's own way is fraught with danger.

One thing is certain, the change in perspective in this verse is significant, and this verse may not be as much of a comfort as it is a confession of the potential for human sin. The poetry here does not allow for a reading of God's gently leading the person into "that great good night." On the contrary, it is clear here that the psalmist is suggesting that he might walk into danger by his own power, but even in dangers created by one's own doing, God is present.[51]

Verse Four: "Your Rod and Your Staff, They Comfort Me"

The conditional phrasing continues, as does God's passive role. "Even if I walk in the valleys of deep darkness, I will not fear evil for you are with me; your rod and your staff, they comfort me." How does God's presence relate to the comfort provided by the "rod" and "staff"? Had God transferred power or protection to these objects, or do they represent a role or even a title for Yahweh?

From a greater ancient Near Eastern perspective, the image of these implements is strongly associated with royalty. Richard Corney states that "evidence for their [mace and staff] use as royal regalia in antiquity is much more plentiful than the evidence for their pastoral use."[52] In both art and in documents,

---

49. "O that today you would listen to his voice! Do not harden your hearts as at Meribah, as on the day at Massah in the wilderness, when your ancestors tested me, and put me to the proof, though they had seen my work" (Ps 95:7b–9).

50. This would be especially appropriate in the context of the book of Proverbs, where מעגל is used for a good or right path (Prov 2:9; 4:11) and for a wrong or wicked path (Prov 2:15, 18).

51. This verse may have the same sense as Psalm 139, where the psalmist flees from God, yet always finds God wherever he may flee.

52. Richard Corney, "'Rod and Staff' (Psalm 23:4): A Double Image?" in *On the Way to Nineveh: Studies in Honor of George M. Landes* (ed. Stephen L. Cook and S. C. Winter; ASOR Books 4; Atlanta: Scholars Press, 1999) 32.

one or both of these implements mark human kingship. Hammurabi is described in the prologue to his laws as "the lord, adorned with scepter and crown." Earlier in the same document, he is described as "caus[ing] justice to prevail in the land, to destroy the wicked and the evil that the strong might not oppress the weak."[53] Likewise in Neo-Babylonian sources, Nabonidus is recorded as praying that he may have "scepter and just staff forever."[54] In the greater ancient Near Eastern context, then, these implements are not only associated with kingship but more precisely with just and righteous kingship. The comfort they provide appears to be in their representation of kingship, not in any innate properties that the implements possess.

The specific Hebrew words used for "rod" and "staff" also are more applicable to the role of king than to the role of common shepherd. Indeed, the writer had a whole host of words to select for "your rod" and "your staff," and the ones selected are both uncommon choices.[55] The first word, שֵׁבֶט, most often means "tribe," but when it is understood as a staff or rod, it is most often a rod of judgment or justice.[56] It also has direct royal imagery, being used to represent earthly kings three times (Ezek 19:11; Amos 1:5; Zech 10:11), and as God's reign in Psalm 45, where it is tied directly with justice,

> Your throne, O God, endures forever and ever,
> Your royal scepter is a scepter of equity;
> you love righteousness and hate wickedness.

This scepter or rod never carries the sense of providing security or comfort, nor is it used as a word for an actual shepherd's staff. The image is jarring. This is the insignia for the king-god who will judge the earth, and the other passages where it is used in the Hebrew Bible are far from comforting. Furthermore, this specific rod is directly connected to the control of the Davidic line in another conditional statement in 2 Sam 7:14–15a:

> I (Yahweh) will be a father to him, and he shall be a son to me. When he commits iniquity, I will punish him with a rod (שֵׁבֶט) such as mortals use, with blows inflicted by humans. But I will not remove my steadfast love from him.

---

53. *ANET* 164, 165.

54. S. Langdon, *Die neubabylonischen Königsinschriften* (Vorderasiatische Bibliothek 4; Leipzig: Hinrichs, 1912) 226.

55. Yet as noted by Corney, commentators have looked to only one way of defining these instruments, that of the tools of a shepherd in the field ("Rod and Staff," 31).

56. Note, for example, 2 Sam 7:14, 18:4; Isa 9:3; 10:5, 24; 11:4; 14:29; Mic 4:14; Ezek 20:37; Ps 2:9; 89:33[32]; Prov 13:4; 22:8, 15; 23:13, 14; 26:3; 29:15). Pardee has made a similar assertion, stating that this word could be understood "as the judge's rod or king's scepter" ("Structure and Meaning," 275).

The second implement, מִשְׁעֶנֶת, appears only eleven times in the Hebrew Bible. The word is also never used as a shepherd's staff, but does appear to have the sense of a walking stick (2 Kgs 4:29, 31; Zech 8:4). When applied to nations, it indicates a broken (destroyed) nation (2 Kgs 18:21; Isa 36:6; Ezek 29:6). A staff that is used for the support of individuals (the old in Zech 8:4) is also used to portray the nations as the broken staff that God has destroyed.

The two words used here have an ambiguous meaning. They are certainly not the staffs of simple shepherds but carry a meaning of power and judgment when used by the king. At the same time, these are the implements of a just and righteous king, who rules with equity. The conditional phrases here may function as noted in Psalm 95 and 2 Samuel 7, as a warning of what happens when one chooses to take the path into his/her own hands; the rod here is not one of gentle prodding but of decisive judgment. The "comfort," then, is not only of God's presence but also of God's righteous reign that will maintain order, even if correction of the psalmist is part of that righteous reign. The image of this verse serves to "confess" another function of Yahweh's reign: that of order over chaos and human action. The comfort does not come from the implements themselves, but from their representation of Yahweh's kingship.

Verse Five: "You Spread before Me a Table in Front of My Enemies;
You Cover My Head with Oil; My Cup Is Overfilled"

Most commentators note that the image of God changes in this verse from one of shepherd to one of host.[57] Several commentators have argued that in a traditional agricultural meaning, this change in imagery is not that jarring. After all, Abraham was both a shepherd and a great host. Larry Herr notes that, even in current times, the hospitality of the Bedouin is legendary.[58] But the text indicates that this is much more than the hospitality that a shepherd or herdsman would offer to a passing stranger; this is a table spread *in front of* (נֶגֶד) "my enemies." As in the verses that precede it, the conflicting images cause the reader to pause and contemplate the meaning. As if to complicate the scene even more, the subject changes back to God and the conditional phrasing of v. 4 returns to the action of God in the present. The appearance of the enemies is as surprising as is the change of subject in v. 4. The enemies are clearly adversaries of the psalmist ("*my* enemies") but appear, not in the context of acts of the psalmist, but at table in God's house. It is difficult to make

---

57. Craigie writes, "Although the focus of the psalmist now shifts, v 5 forms a transition from the imagery of the shepherd to that of present and future banquets of thanksgiving" (*Psalms 1–50*, 207).

58. Larry Herr, "An Off-Duty Archaeologist Looks at Psalm 23," *BR* 8 (April 1992) 48.

the case that they are associated with the path of the psalmist in "the dark valleys," since v. 4 was in the form of a conditional statement. These enemies appear in the most unexpected place, and the reader has no context in which to understand the nature of the enemies or their purpose. The psalm itself also offers no aid, moving quickly from a mention of the enemies to the banqueting festivities.

Does an image of Yahweh as king aid in understanding what the psalmist is telling us about God in v. 5? As in the previous verses, the meaning of the words and images in their greater ancient context does offer additional information. The שֻׁלְחָן "table" of this verse is used most often for two types of tables: the table of the king[59] or the table of Yahweh.[60] These tables are places of peace and protection.

The word is used in 2 Samuel, where Mephibosheth, Jonathan's son, is told by David, "I will restore to you all the land of your grandfather Saul, and you yourself shall eat at my table always" (2 Sam 9:7). The king's table is offered as a sign of protection, but this table should also be understood as a victory table, since David's table is offered to the only living male of his enemy, Saul. Mephibosheth's presence as a protected guest shows to all that it is David's kingdom, not Saul's.[61]

There are general references to Yahweh's table and specific references to the table in the temple that holds the bread of presence (Exod 25:23–30) that is "before me always." This is a table set up directly before the throne of Yahweh and is to be tended with ceremony and great care. This table of Yahweh offers peace and a source of security within the temple. Other texts, however, offer a different picture of the banquet table of Yahweh. Ezek 39:17–20 is a passage that speaks clearly of Yahweh's victory table.

> Assemble and come, gather from all around to the sacrificial feast that I am preparing for you. . . . You shall eat the flesh of the mighty and drink the blood of the princes of the earth. . . . You shall eat fat until you are filled and drink blood until you are drunk at the sacrificial feast I am preparing for you. And you shall

---

59. See Judg 1:7; 1 Sam 20:34; 2 Sam 9:7, 10, 11, 13; 19:29; 1 Kgs 2:7; 4:27; 10:5; 13:20; 18:19; Dan 11:27.

60. See many references to the table for the bread of presence in the temple: Exod 25:23 and 17 more times; Lev 24:6; Num 3:31; 4:7; 1 Kgs 7:48; Ezek 40:39 and 7 more times; 1 Chr 28:16 and 7 more times. Also there are several references to "the table of Yahweh": Ezek 39:20; 41:22; 44:16; Mal 1:12; Ps 78:19; Job 36:16.

61. A similar situation is indicated in 2 Kgs 25:27–30. Here the king of Babylon brings the exiled King Jehoiachin to his table, an act of graciousness, but also an act of demonstrating power in the region.

be filled at my table with horses and chariots, with warriors and all kinds of soldiers, says the LORD God.

The context of the rest of the chapter speaks of God's executing justice and restoring the fortunes of Jacob. Philip Stern has noted that there is a parallel in a text about Anat.

> She [Anat] arranges seats for the warriors,
> Arranges tables for the soldiers,
> Footstools for the heroes. . . .
> (skip 5 lines; Anat is filled with joy and triumph)
> She plunges her knees indeed in the blood of soldiers,
> Her hips in the gore of warriors,
> Until she has had her fill of fighting in the house.[62]

In both of these texts, the enemies are not invited to eat at the banquet but, indeed, are the banquet! This table is spread by the divine and victorious king-god. Likewise, the table of the bread of presence, while offering peace and security, can also remind the ancient reader that God's gracious table sat in Jerusalem only after the land and Jerusalem were taken from "my enemies." So to an interpretation of a peaceful scene here should be added the image of God's victory table in Ezekiel, where the enemies are not enemies who are now friends but enemies who are "broken staffs," present at the table to show forth the power of the great king-warrior. This is not just a table of hospitality offered by a Bedouin shepherd, but the table of the great Shepherd, where enemies sit to show God's majesty and control of all.

The meaning of the word used for "enemies" continues this complex image of the power of God. The noun, צוֹרֵר, or צַר, is often used of enemies of a warring or national nature.[63] But the use of this vocable in the psalms is mixed, referring to general enemies where their identity is unclear, as well as personal enemies and national enemies. So, depending on the interpreter's perspective, the enemy here could be warring foes, and the banquet scene could be portrayed as in Ezekiel or in the Anat narrative; it could also be enemies closer to the psalmist.[64] Either view of the enemy fits well with the kingship image of Yahweh: whether national enemies, as is often the case in

---

62. Philip D. Stern, "The 'Bloodbath of Anat' and Psalm xxiii," *VT* 44 (1994) 120–25, esp. 121, citing *KTU* 1.3.II.20–23, 27–29.

63. See, for example, צֹרֵר in Exod 23:22; Num 10:9; 25:17, 18; 33:55; Esth 8:1; 9:10, 24; and צַר in Deut 32:41; 33:7; Josh 5:13; 2 Sam 24:13; Isa 1:24; 9:10; 26:11; 59:18; 63:81; 64:1; Jer 30:16; 46:10; 50:7; Ezek 30:16; 39:23; Amos 3:11; Mic 5:8.

64. Pardee argues that the "enemies" must be part of the royal imagery ("Structure and Meaning," 276).

narratives texts, or the nondescript enemy used within the Psalter, only a
powerful suzerain god can provide a table with the enemies in full sight.
The second half of the verse continues the description of the banquet
scene, but the words used are unusual and difficult to translate. Interestingly,
English translations introduce a royal image by using the word *anoint* (e.g.,
"You anoint my head with oil," NRSV) that does not convey the meaning of
the Hebrew text. The psalm uses a phrase that appears nowhere else in the
Hebrew Bible, דשנת בשמן ראשי. The verb has a meaning of "to be fat" and
indicates not a royal anointing of the king but a good and prosperous situation.[65] Does this lack of royal anointing destroy the royal imagery? It is certainly problematic if one is arguing that the speaker is the king of Israel.
However, I have argued that the focus is on Yahweh as king, a king who is not
anointed, so the absence of the word משח does not affect Yahweh's kingship.[66]
The dual image of king and warrior that has been noted above is also present
in this phrase. In Ps 20:3 the wish is made that "God will grow fat with your
sacrifices," indicating a desire for blessing. But in Isa 34:6–7 "growing fat" has
a violent meaning:

> The LORD has a sword: it is sated with blood;
> It is made fat with fat (מחלב). . . .
> Their land shall be soaked with blood,
> and their soil made fat with fat (מחלב).

The second phrase, "my cup is overfilled," continues the image of bounty
but is also difficult to translate. The difficulty is understanding the exact meaning of the verbless clause כוסי רויה. Based on the verbal structure, it appears
that the filled cup is a direct result of placing oil on the head, rather than of
pouring in wine. However, this phrase could have a dual meaning, indicating

---

65. The verb דשן occurs 11 times. Twice the meaning refers to bowls in the temple and
the meaning is unclear (Exod 27:3; Num 4:13). In Proverbs, the word occurs 4 times indicating that goodness or trust in the Lord will cause a person "to grow fat" (Prov 11:25;
13:4; 15:30; 28:25).

66. Others have argued that the words of Ps 23:5 can be seen as "evoking" the anointing
of a king (Freedman, "Twenty-Third Psalm," 297). Barré and Kselman argue that this
anointing connects to Psalm 89, where the king is anointed (v. 21); see further connections
as Yahweh will destroy the king's enemies and that God's covenant will be with the king
forever ("New Exodus," 106). But it is just as possible that the psalmist purposely did not
use משח to remind the king of his human nature since there are as many parallels in
Nathan's warning to David in 2 Sam 7:8–9 as there are in Psalm 89: "Thus says the LORD
of Hosts, I took you from the pasture, from *following the sheep* to be prince over my people
Israel, and *I have been with you* wherever you went, and I have cut off *all your enemies* from
before you."

both the abundance of oil (as in Psalm 133) and the abundance of wine at a victory banquet in the house of the king-god.

Verse Six: "Surely Goodness and Steadfast Love Will Pursue Me All the Days of My Life, and I Will Dwell in the House of Yahweh for the Length of Days"

Just as God's rod and staff provide comfort, here goodness and steadfast love will pursue the psalmist. The choice of word here should also remind the reader of the enemies. Often translated as "follow," the verb רדף has more a sense of "pursue" or "chase."[67] What was once "evil" pursuit is now pursuit by God's blessings. The psalm ends with the same sense of protection that was offered by green pastures and the king's table, a protection that will last until the end of the psalmist's days.

Conclusion

When read against an ancient background, a more nuanced picture of Psalm 23 emerges. The vocabulary used and the images evoked provide a picture of Yahweh as the great Shepherd-King and the psalmist as a vassal to that king. The psalm, as Pardee notes, is indeed royal, even if the royal imagery is more muted than in the classic Psalms of Enthronement.

The picture of the human is also interesting.[68] Referred to in "I" language, the psalmist is not portrayed as powerful; on the contrary, the only act the psalmist takes by his own volition is one that leads to danger and possibly even death. If the speaker is the king, as Eaton and Pardee have argued, the message here is not to praise the king but to put him squarely in his place (as in 2 Samuel 7). The human is the vassal, and only by following the suzerain will the psalmist arrive at the place offered in v. 6.

One further point: the multiple juxtapositions noted throughout the psalm are disorienting. The reader is forced to confront questions of the relationship of the "I" to the great shepherd-king; the question of the time frame portrayed

---

67. Modern translators appear to be trying to connect this phrase to the imagery of the sheep by using the term "follow," but the verb has the sense of being chased or pursued by enemies. For example, see Exod 14:4, 8, 9; Josh 2:5, 7; 8:6, 7; 10:19; 2 Sam 20:6, 7, 10, 13; 2 Kgs 9:27.

68. I have avoided commenting on the traditional questions of form criticism. Pardee and Eaton may indeed be correct; the original speaker may be the king of Israel. But the answer remains speculative. It is just as possible that this psalm is intended as a warning to the king. In the same manner, the date of the psalm is impossible to determine. The only context that the postbiblical reader is given is the series of poems themselves that make up the Psalter.

in the poem; surprising vocabulary; multiple imagery; twists in the subject of the lines; and the appearance of "my enemies" in the very place where one would expect rest. This disorientation serves the king-vassal relationship well. There is comfort and peace only when Yahweh's reign is seen fully (vv. 1–3 and 6), but at the same time, the path to God's kingdom of peace is not without tension (vv. 4–5). "Evil" is present in the psalmist and in others, and only God can rectify the situation. Yahweh will judge the world, and righteous kingship does not come without judgment on both the enemies and the psalmist.

The modern interpretation of Psalm 23 argues for God as providing the psalmist with protection and comfort. What is not as clear is God's power in the equation. God is indeed a shepherd, but this shepherd has power over both the psalmist and the enemies. God does not guide for the sake of the psalmist but to show forth God's righteous reign. The psalmist, instead of being totally passive, is indeed a human with full capacity to turn to his own way. The psalm may portray a future hope, but it is also a strong reflection of the tensions of the present life. The psalm is a confession of God's royal reign, and only from that perspective does it offer the comfort sought by the psalmist.

Part 3

Historical and Lexical Studies

The Crux of Psalm 22:17c: Solved at Long Last?

MICHAEL L. BARRÉ

St. Mary's Seminary and University

This festschrift dedicated to J. J. M. Roberts, one of my professors during my doctoral studies at The Johns Hopkins University, has as its theme "David and Zion." Old Testament scholars will agree that Roberts has made significant contributions to our understanding of the Zion traditions. But they also recognize the many other contributions that he has made to our understanding of OT texts. In this paper I shall highlight a significant discovery he published some years ago on a long-standing *crux interpretum* in a psalm from the first collection of Davidic psalms in the Psalter—Psalm 22. In addition, I shall offer my own contribution to this discovery. It is a privilege to present this study in honor of my esteemed teacher.

Roberts's Proposal

Over the years many have attempted to solve the *crux* of Ps 22:17, specifically the colon: כָּאֲרִי יָדַי וְרַגְלָי. Thirty years ago, Roberts published an article proposing a solution to this problematic text.[1] Agreeing with the widespread view that the problematic term כארי represents one of many examples in the MT of the confusion of the letters *waw* and *yod* and that the form in question should be parsed as a 3rd masc. pl. verb, Roberts was the first to propose that the verb derived from a verbal root כרי hitherto unattested in Biblical Hebrew but attested in Akkadian (*karû*) and Syriac (*kry*), a root whose literal meaning is "to be(come) short."[2] In this paper I shall present evidence to corroborate his thesis that the Hebrew term in question does derive from this verb, although I shall propose a somewhat different translation. I shall further argue, however, that the "problem" with this passage involves not only v. 17c (כארי) but also the verb in the next colon, v. 18a (אספר).

---

1. J. J. M. Roberts, "A New Root for an Old Crux: Ps. XXII 17c," *VT* 23 (1973) 247–52.
2. At least four different verb stems from the root כרי have so far been identified (*HALAT*, 472–73). The third of these is a tris legomenon and the fourth is a hapax legomenon, a conjectural reading of the passage under discussion.

287

Roberts notes in his article that all of the ancient versions except the Targum read a 3rd masc. pl. verb for כארי,[3] the most important being the LXX with ὤρυξαν "they dug."[4] In addition to this we now have the evidence of XHev/Se 4, which has כארו. Gregory Vall has criticized Roberts's reading of the word as כָּרוּ, claiming that he "dismisses the 'intrusive' א too facilely" and that, "without admitting it, he is in fact emending the text." Both claims are totally unfounded. To judge from these critical remarks it would appear that Vall is unaware of the fact that in the MT medial ʾalep is occasionally used to represent ā (as is ʾalif commonly in Arabic). For example, Neh 13:16 has the word דָּאג "fish," for the usual דָּג. From the context as well as the witness of the ancient versions[5] there is no doubt whatsoever that this is simply an unconventional spelling of the word for "fish" with a medial ʾalep as a mater lectionis for ā. Hence Roberts's explanation of the ʾalep in Ps 22:17 is hardly "facile." In his article he cites Friedrich Delitzsch, who documented a number of examples of the use of ʾalep as a mater in the MT, including ʾalep for ā.[6] The year after Roberts's publication Eduard Y. Kutscher came out with his study on the language of the Great Isaiah Scroll from Qumran Cave I, in which he documented many further examples of the use of ʾalep in the pre-Christian period as a mater for ā (as well as for a, and ē).[7] Hence, it is not only possible but most likely that כארו (XHev/Se 4) reflects this late orthographic convention and that the verb in question is indeed from the root כרי as Roberts argued.

As for Vall's criticism that Roberts has "emended the text" (which Vall himself proceeds to do in his article, with the far more drastic emendation of כארי to אסרו!),[8] it is important to point out that the ʾalep here is not a "scribal error" that needs to be "corrected," a fact of which Roberts was not unaware. Rather, it is a late, now well-attested orthography, no more an error than is final he representing ā or e. In point of fact, there is no need to remove the medial ʾalep in order to arrive at the "correct" reading of the term, but since it represents a late orthography most scholars would prefer to normalize the spelling of the verb in the direction of Standard Biblical Hebrew and delete it.

---

3. For the reading of the various ancient versions, see Gregory Vall, "Psalm 22:17b: 'The Old Guess,'" JBL 116 (1997) 45–56.

4. This almost certainly reflects a Vorlage with כרו, from I כרי (see HALAT, 472).

5. LXX, ἰχθὺν; Vg. pisces; Syr. nwnʾ.

6. Roberts, "A New Root for an Old Crux," 248 n. 3, cites Delitzsch, Die Lese- und Schreibfehler im Alten Testament (Berlin: de Gruyter, 1920) §31, who provides a number of examples of ʾalep = ā.

7. Eduard Y. Kutscher, The Language and the Linguistic Background of the Isaiah Scroll (1QIsᵃ) (Leiden: Brill, 1974) 160–62.

8. Vall, "Psalm 22:17b," 52–56.

Thus the only correction that needs to be made in v. 17c is the emendation of *yod* to *waw* in כארי.

Regarding the translation of this verb, the most important evidence Roberts presents in support of his proposed solution is an Akkadian diagnostic text:

šumma ina muršišu pāšu ṣabitma qātāšu u šēpāšu ik-ta-ra-a ul mišitti murussu ittiq[9]

Roberts's translation of this text is very close to that of the *Chicago Assyrian Dictionary*:

> If in his sickness his mouth is paralyzed and his hands and his feet are shrunken, it is not a stroke, his sickness will pass.[10]

When he applies the information from this passage to the interpretation of Ps 22:17c, he renders the cognate verb from the root כרי slightly differently: "My hands and my feet are shriveled up."[11]

A connection of the psalm passage with Akkadian diagnostic tradition is certainly a possibility, and other connections of such texts with OT passages have been competently argued.[12] The Babylonians were not only regarded in the ancient Near East as the leading experts in astronomy, they were also renowned for their knowledge of medicine.

One may question, however, whether "shrink" or "shrivel" accurately describes the precise pathology reflected in this text. If the verb in fact describes a shrinking of these members, how can such a condition simply go away, as the apodosis suggests?[13] A clue to the verb's meaning here may be provided

---

9. René Labat, *Traité akkadien de diagnostics et pronostics médicaux* (2 vols.; Leiden: Brill, 1951) 1.160, line 30. The line is cited in *CAD* K 229. Oddly, Labat reads the verb here (written DIB-*iq*) as a perfect form, *ētetiq*. But almost certainly a present-future form should be read in the apodosis, namely, *ittiq*. The present-future is used in virtually all of the apodoses in this work—for example, *iballuṭ* "he will recover"; *imât* "he will die"; *itebbi* "he will get up (out of his sick-bed)"; *murussu ezzibšu* "his illness will leave him," etc. Note *murussu ittiqšu* "his illness will pass from him" in a similar passage cited by Nils P. Heeßel, *Babylonisch-assyrische Diagnostik* (AOAT 43; Münster: Ugarit-Verlag, 2000) 64.

10. Roberts, "A New Root for an Old Crux," 251. The translation of *CAD* K, which appeared in 1971, is: "If in his sickness his mouth is paralyzed [and] hands and his feet are shrunken, this is not a stroke, his sickness will disappear" (p. 229).

11. Roberts, "A New Root for an Old Crux," 252.

12. See Shalom M. Paul, "An Unrecognized Medical Idiom in Canticles 6,12 and Job 9,21," *Bib* 59 (1978) 545–47; Michael L. Barré, "New Light on the Interpretation of Hosea VI 2," *VT* 28 (1978) 465–67; idem, "Bulluṭsa-rabi's Hymn to Gula and Hosea 6:1–2," *Or* 50 (1981) 241–45.

13. I am grateful to Prof. Robert D. Biggs of the Oriental Institute of the University of Chicago for his private communication to me on this point: "I would say that *karû* is definitely not 'shrunken, shriveled'."

by *pāšu ṣabitma* in the protasis, which indicates some kind of "paralysis" of the mouth. This medical context may suggest that *karû* refers not to a change in the size or appearance of the hands and feet but rather to something like paralysis, i.e., a temporary loss of the use of these members. Most likely the term refers to a pathology in which the muscles of the extremities *contract* involuntarily. At least three Assyriologists translate the term "contract" in these diagnostic texts.[14]

Another problem is the form of the verb. Roberts describes *ik-ta-ra-a* as a Gt form (*iktarâ*), but this is difficult, because this form of the verb would suggest some mutual action of the two extremities upon each other.[15] Wolfram von Soden takes it as a Gtn preterite (*iktarrâ*).[16] There are several unmistakable examples of the Gtn of this verb in other diagnostic texts in which the subject is again the patient's feet (e.g., [*i*]*k-te-ner-ra-a*).[17] The Gtn form indicates a repeated or recurrent action. Now it does not seem likely that hands and feet would keep shrinking or shriveling over and over, a fact that renders such translations of the term doubtful. On the other hand, it is possible for their muscles to behave spasmodically, alternating between relaxing and contracting. In the contracted state the affected members might cause the digits to draw inward so that the hand or foot appears to be "shorter" than normal. Extremities so affected cannot function and thus become temporarily "lame."[18]

14. Labat, *Traité*, 161; von Soden, *AHw*, 452; and Heeßel, *Babylonisch-assyrische Diagnostik*, 44, 411. So also Jeremy Black et al., *The Concise Dictionary of Akkadian* (SANTAG 5; Wiesbaden: Harrassowitz, 2000) 150. Heeßel is somewhat inconsistent in his rendering of *karû*. At times he translates it literally as *kurz werden* (*Babylonisch-assyrische Diagnostik*, 108, 411) and once as *schrumpfen*, which can mean either "to shrink" or "shrivel" (ibid., 208). At other times, however, he renders it *zusammenziehen*, by which he evidently means "to contract" (ibid., 411). Most significantly, he translates it this way when he includes it in a series of other terms that he lists under the heading "Unnormale und auffällige Bewegungen" (ibid., 44). "Contract" seems to fit as a kind of *movement* of these body parts, whereas "shrink" and "shrivel" do not.

15. I am grateful to Prof. Jerrold Cooper of The Johns Hopkins University for his comment on this issue: "The form could well be a Gtn. . . . The only other thing it could be is a perfect, or a Gt, but you'd have to be able to show there was a reason to assume so" (private communication).

16. Von Soden translates this form of the verb in passages where feet are the subject by *sich i*[*mmer*] *w*[*ieder*] *zusammenziehen* = "to keep contracting" (*AHw*, 452). Cf. *The Concise Dictionary of Akkadian*, 150: "contract repeatedly."

17. Labat, *Traité*, 142:8′.

18. The question naturally arises whether a text describing hands and feet as being "short" has any connection with a usage of verbs with this meaning together with "hand" in several Semitic languages. In Arabic, Syriac, and Biblical Hebrew such verbs (Arab. and

I would emphasize, however, that the hypothesis I am proposing here does not absolutely require the adoption of one of these three proposed translations to the exclusion of the others. As we shall see in the following sections of this paper, the most important point is that this medical language describes hands and feet that—because of whatever pathological condition—have (at least temporarily) *ceased to function.*

Since virtually all commentators assume that the "problem" with this section of Psalm 22 consists solely in the term כארי, commentators have given little if any attention to the immediately following colon, v. 18a. As I noted above, however, I believe that part of the problem lies in v. 18a as well. The MT of this colon reads: אֲסַפֵּר כל עצמותי. The standard translation runs something like "I can count all my bones" (RSV). I maintain that such a line does not fit either with the structure or with the context of this psalm, which is concerned with assault by enemies, and hence the term in question must be emended.[19] I propose that the text originally read ספד כל עצמותי. The word ספד is to be parsed either as a 3rd masc. pl. verb with the final -*ū* unexpressed in the orthography (סָפְדוּ) or an infinitive absolute serving as a finite verb (סָפֹד).[20]

A few of the ancient textual witnesses provide some basis for this reading. First, although the critical edition of the LXX agrees with the MT on the

---

Heb. קצר, Syr. *kry*) are associated with "hand." Edward W. Lane translates the Arabic idiom "to have little/no power," as in *qaṣura yaduhu*, "He had little or no power" (*Arabic-English Lexicon* [2 vols.; London: Williams and Norgate, 1863–93] 2533). In Modern Arabic *qāṣir/qaṣīr al-yad* means to be unable or powerless to do something (Hans Wehr, *Dictionary of Modern Written Arabic* [Ithaca, N.Y.: Spoken Language Services, 1976] 768–69). In Syriac the verb is found with "hand" in the *Aphel*: *ʾkry ʾÿdyhwn mn*) "He made their hands too 'short' to . . ." = "He made them unable to . . . , prevented them from . . ." (cf. J. Payne Smith, *A Compendious Syriac Dictionary* [Oxford: Clarendon, 1903; repr. Winona Lake, Ind.: Eisenbrauns, 1998] 224). In Biblical Hebrew קצר occurs with יד in five OT texts and the meaning is again "to be powerless" (Num 11:23; 2 Kgs 19:26; Isa 37:27; 50:2; 59:1). But although it is tempting to postulate a connection with the Akkadian passage, there is less of a relationship than meets the eye. (1) In Arabic, Syriac, and Hebrew the singular "hand" is used in the idiom, never the dual. This is because only the *singular* form is used as a metaphor for power. But the diagnostic text has "hands." (2) In the three languages the idiom never occurs with "foot" or "feet," since this member is never used as a metaphor for power, whereas the Akkadian text has "hands" *and* "feet." (3) The protases of Akkadian diagnostic texts have as their purpose to describe the medical condition of the patient, and so the use of metaphor is out of the question in such passages.

19. I will discuss this position in the subsequent sections of this essay in which I deal with structure and context.

20. See Bruce K. Waltke and Michael O'Connor, *An Introduction to Biblical Hebrew Syntax* (Winona Lake, Ind.: Eisenbrauns, 1990) §35.5.

reading of this word (ἐξηρίθμησα "I numbered"),[21] some manuscripts read a plural here (ἐξηρίθμησαν "they numbered").[22] In his translation of the Psalms *iuxta Septuaginta* Jerome was evidently working from a manuscript that had the plural form, because his translation is *dinumeraverunt* "they (have) numbered." Admittedly, since the difference between these two readings comes down to the presence or absence of a final *nu*, the variation could theoretically be explained on the grounds of inner-Greek corruption.

There is another ancient textual witness, however, that has a 3rd-pl. verb here. It is based neither on the LXX nor the Vg. but rather on the Hebrew text. I refer to the reading of the Syr.: *wᵓyllw kwlhwn gᵼrmy*[23] "and all my bones wailed."[24] This reading of the verb as *ᵓyllw* "they wailed" can only be explained by assuming that it reflects (ו)ספד in its Hebrew *Vorlage*. Because of the confusion of *dalet* and *reš* through all periods of Hebrew paleography, it is easy to see how ספד could be confused with the far more common root ספר and read as such. A scribe, coming across this term, could easily have interpreted it as an infinitive absolute form and then "modernized" it to a finite verb, in this case the 1st sing. form with the *ᵓalep* prefix. As for the plausibility of this scribal procedure, note the recent comment of Bruce K. Waltke on how post-biblical scribes dealt with this obsolescent grammatical form:

> Scribes sometimes modernized archaic features of a verse. In Num 15:35 the S[amaritan] P[entateuch] replaces the old infinitive absolute construction of the MT (*rāgōm*) . . . [with] the imperative, *rigmû*, stone.[25]

Waltke also notes that "Qumran biblical manuscripts often shift the infinitive absolute forms to finite forms."[26] Therefore the change of ספר (< ספד) to אספר was not an error in the sense of a miscopying. It was a deliberate change made to the text, a type of scribal intervention that at this point is well documented.[27]

---

21. Alfred Rahlfs, *Psalmi cum Odis* (Septuaginta Vetus Testamentum Graecum 10; 2nd ed.; Göttingen: Vandenhoeck & Ruprecht, 1967) 110.

22. Frederick Field (*Origenis Hexaplorum Quae Supersunt* [2 vols.; Oxford: Clarendon, 1875] 2.119]) lists the plural form as what Origen read in the LXX column of his Hexapla.

23. See *The Book of Psalms* (The Old Testament in Syriac according to the Peshiṭta Version 2/3; Leiden: Brill, 1980) 22.

24. For another example in the MT of all one's bones metaphorically uttering sound, see Ps 35:10: כל עצמותי תאמרנה "All my bones shall say. . . ."

25. Bruce K. Waltke, "How We Got the Hebrew Bible: The Text and Canon of the Old Testament," in *The Bible at Qumran: Text, Shape, and Interpretation* (ed. Peter W. Flint; Studies in the Dead Sea Scrolls and Related Literature; Grand Rapids: Eerdmans, 2001) 45.

26. Waltke and O'Connor, *An Introduction to Biblical Hebrew Syntax*, 595 n. 57.

27. See Robert Polzin, *Late Biblical Hebrew: Toward an Historical Typology of Biblical Hebrew Prose* (HSM 12; Missoula, Mont.: Scholars Press, 1976) 43–44; Erling Hammershaimb,

The meaning of the original verb may be more precisely defined. The word סָפַד was a technical term in Biblical Hebrew and Akkadian for lamenting the dead and originally referred to the specific mourning *gestus* of striking the breast.[28] From this it came to denote funeral lamentation in a more general sense, including making mournful sounds.[29] In the majority of its occurrences in the MT it refers specifically to mourning for the dead and is at times in parallelism with קָבַר "to bury."[30] The bones of the psalmist are pictured here as not simply lamenting but intoning his own funeral dirge in anticipation of his enemies' vanquishing him and finishing him off. Thus I would translate something like, "All my bones have intoned my funeral dirge." The appropriateness of this translation in the context will be demonstrated below.

Further evidence for reading the verb סָפַד in v. 18a comes from another Akkadian diagnostic text only recently published that contains the Akkadian cognates of both כרי and סָפַד:

> *šumma ūmīšu irrikūma qātāšu u sēpāšu ikrâ murussu inakkiršumma elišu isappidūma iballuṭ*[31]

If his days are long[32] and (the muscles of?) his hands and feet contract: his illness will take a turn (for the worse)[33] and they will make the funeral lamentation over him—but (then) he will recover.

"On the So-Called *Infinitivus Absolutus* in Hebrew," in *Hebrew and Semitic Studies Presented to Godfrey Rolles Driver* (ed. David Winton Thomas and W. D. McHardy; Oxford: Clarendon, 1963) 91.

28. See Mayer I. Gruber, *Aspects of Non-Verbal Communication in the Ancient Near East* (2 vols.; Studia Pohl 12; Rome: Pontifical Biblical Institute Press, 1980) 436–56.

29. Ibid., 438–46.

30. 1 Sam 25:1; 28:3; 1 Kgs 13:29, 30; 14:13, 18; Jer 16:4, 6; 25:33. See Yitzhak Avishur, *Stylistic Studies of Word-Pairs in Biblical and Ancient Semitic Literatures* (AOAT 210; Kevelaer: Butzon & Bercker / Neukirchen-Vluyn: Neukirchener Verlag, 1984) 294.

31. Heeßel, *Babylonisch-assyrische Diagnostik*, 180, line 95'. The untranscribed text reads: DIŠ KI.MIN ŠU.II-*šú* u GÌR.II-*šú* ik-ra-a GIG-*su* KÚR-*šum-ma* UGU-*šú* KI.MIN TIN. The signs represented by the first KI.MIN ("ditto") can be seen from line 90' (U₄.MEŠ-*šú* GÍDDA.MEŠ-*ma*), and those by the second from line 93' (*i-sap-pi-du-ma*). Heeßel's translation is, "Wenn *dito* (und) seine Hände und seine Füße kurz werden: Seine Krankheit wird sich für ihn ändern und (während) sie (schon) über ihn trauern wird er gesunden" (ibid., 185).

32. This probably means, "If he is of advanced age."

33. The Akk. verb *nakāru* can mean to change for the better or for the worse (see *CAD* N/1 164). In this text, since the reference to the change is followed immediately by the notice that people are performing funeral lamentations over the patient, it must denote a change for the worse.

What is striking here is not only the use of the same verbs in both texts, verbs that rarely if ever again appear together in either language,[34] but even more the fact that in both texts ספד/*sapādu* serves to express the rare topos of *proleptic funeral lamentation*—that is, lamentation for someone who is *not yet dead*, a topos attested in several Akkadian literary texts.[35] Below I shall demonstrate the proleptic character of this verb in Ps 22:18a.

Structure

No proposed solution to the difficulties of Ps 22:17–18 can be persuasive on philological grounds alone. In order to be convincing, such a proposal must fit well into the structure of the psalm as well as the context in which these verses are situated. Numerous previous attempts at a solution have run aground because they failed to take these factors sufficiently into consideration. In this section, I shall discuss the structure of Part II of Psalm 22—that is, the section within which the controverted verses occur. I shall demonstrate that the translation of vv. 17c–18a proposed in the foregoing section fits the structure and context of this psalm very well.

---

34. In light of this evidence, I would propose that in Ps 22:17c the hapax legomenon כרי is not to be classified as yet another Hebrew root to be added to the four already recognized in the lexicons (cf. *HALAT*, 472–73) but rather as a loanword from Akkadian.

35. I present here the three texts in translation only (all but the first are my own translation). The first is from *Ludlul bēl nēmeqi* II 114–15 (for the text, see Wilfred G. Lambert, *Babylonian Wisdom Literature* [Oxford: Clarendon, 1960; repr. Winona Lake, Ind.: Eisenbrauns, 1996] 46; see also Benjamin R. Foster, *Before the Muses: An Anthology of Akkadian Literature* [2 vols.; Bethesda, Md.: CDL, 1993] 1.317):

> My grave stood open, my funeral goods were ready;
> *Before I was even dead*, lamentation for me was over.

The second is from an Akkadian poem discovered at Ugarit (for the text, see Jean Nougayrol et al. [eds.], *Ugaritica V* [Mission de Ras Shamra 16; Paris: Imprimérie Nationale, 1968] 267, lines 9′–10′; see also Foster, *Before the Muses*, 1.326):

> My family gathered to bow (in grief over me) *before my time*,
> My kinfolk were present and stood to make lamentation (over me).

The third text comes from a Babylonian prayer to Ishtar. It is clear from the remainder of the poem that the protagonist is still living (for the text, see W. G. Lambert, "Three Literary Prayers of the Babylonians," *AfO* 19 [1959–60] 52; see also Marie-Joseph Seux, *Hymnes et prières aux dieux de Babylonie et d'Assyrie* [LAPO 8; Paris: Cerf, 1976] 196–97):

> His professional mourners asse[mbled] his family,
> [His] kinfolk gathered for bitter lamentation over him.

While the structure of many poetic compositions in the MT, including psalms, continues to be a matter of debate, we are fortunate in that this is not—or should not be—the case for Psalm 22. Evidence for a tripartite division is so overwhelming that any denial of this must be considered unreasonable. I shall not enter here into a thorough discussion of the psalm's structure but will first point out a few salient structural features of the poem as a whole and then go into a more detailed examination of the structural unit in which the verses under discussion are situated.

As to the overall division of the poem, its three major divisions are vv. 2–12, 13–22, and 23–32.[36] Some of the rhetorical devices marking off the Part I are (1) the presence of אלי "my God" at the beginning (v. 2 [twice]) and end (v. 11) of this section; (2) the inclusion formed by derivatives of the root רחק "to be far away" in vv. 2b and 12. That a new section (Part III) begins with v. 23 and extends to the end of the poem is undeniable, since the entire mood of the poem changes abruptly from lament to praise precisely at this juncture. Moreover, vv. 23–32 are bracketed by an inclusion formed by two occurrences of the root ספר in the "intensive" form (*Piel/Pual*) in vv. 23 and 31.

The identification of Parts I and III of the poem leaves a central section, Part II (vv. 13–22), by process of elimination. Moreover, these verses contain several structural features that confirm that they form a single poetic unit. One of these is the inclusion formed by the word "mouth" (פה) in vv. 14 and 22; this word occurs only in these two places in the psalm. But the most striking feature is the chiastic arrangement of three terms for certain animals in this stanza: bovines, canines, and leonine(s) in vv. 13–17 and in vv. 21–22.[37] The canine and leonine terms are the same at the beginning and the end of the unit: כלבים in v. 17 and כלב in v. 21, and אריה in vv. 14b and 22a. The bovine terms, however, are different: פרים "young bulls" in v. 13 and רמים "wild oxen" in v. 22b. This animal chiasmus marks off vv. 13–22 as a self-contained section of Psalm 22.[38]

---

36. See the excellent study by John S. Kselman, "'Why Have You Abandoned Me?': A Rhetorical Study of Psalm 22," in *Art and Meaning: Rhetoric in Biblical Literature* (ed. David Clines et al.; JSOTSup 19; Sheffield: JSOT Press, 1982) 172–98. Kselman divides the poem into the three major divisions I have indicated (pp. 183–88).

37. Ibid., 187–88. See also Nicolaas H. Ridderbos, "The Psalms: Style-Figures and Structure," *OTS* 13 (*Studies on Psalms*; 1963) 56.

38. One immediately evident corollary of this structural feature has to do with the MT's כארי in v. 17a. Even though ארי is a variant of the longer term for lion, אריה, which occurs in vv. 14b and 22a, it is highly unlikely that the poet would have spoiled this carefully constructed, structurally significant chiasmus by introducing "lion" a third time in Part II of the psalm.

Aside from the animal chiasmus, another noticeable structural feature of Part II is the repetition of the verb סבבוני "they have surrounded me" in vv. 13 and 17. Each has as its subject one of the plural animal terms ("young bulls" in v. 13a and "dogs" in v. 17a) and each is paralleled in the subsequent colon by another term meaning "to surround" with the 1st sing. suffix (כתרוני in v. 13b and הקיפוני in v. 17b). The repetition of סבבוני // synonym marks the two major subdivisions of Part II, namely, vv. 13–16 and 17–22, which I shall designate Stanza A and Stanza B, respectively. Note that each of the stanzas also contains another phrase, namely, כל עצמותי "all my bones" (vv. 15b and 18a).

Part II, Stanza A

13 Many YOUNG BULLS *have surrounded me,*   A
     the strong ones of Bashan have encompassed me.
14 They have opened their MOUTHs against me
     (like) a rending and roaring LION.   B
15 I have been poured out like water,
     all my bones have become disjointed.
   My heart has become like wax,
     it has melted in the midst of my bowels.
16 My palate has dried up like a potsherd,
     my tongue has stuck to[39] the roof of my mouth[40]—
     in the dust of death you have set me down![41]

---

39. Since דבק "cling to, stick to" requires a preposition (ל, אל, ב, etc.), most likely the מ of מלקוחי should be read as the preposition ב. The מ in the MT would then be one of many examples of the scribal confusion between ב and מ. If this emendation is correct, this hapax legomenon should not be read as מלקוח but לקוח*. See the following note.

40. BDB had translated מלקוחי "jaws," deriving it from the root לקח "to take," a translation followed by many. But it is hardly doubtful that the term in question is cognate with Arab. ḥalq, ḥulqūm; Eth. ḥelq; Akk. lī/āqu, etc., meaning "palate" or possibly "gullet" (cf. LXX λάρυγγι; Vg. *faucibus*; Syr. ḥky). Since the usual Biblical Hebrew term for "palate," חך, appears as the "A-word" in the previous colon, the author uses this rare synonym as the "B-word."

41. The MT reads: ולעפר־מות תשפתני "and in the dust of death you set me down," deriving the verb from שפת "to place something (down) on something" (e.g., a pot on the fire [2 Kgs 4:38; Ezek 24:3]). But here again the versions suggest rather a *qtl* verb, in which case the initial *taw* represents a dittography from the preceding מות (LXX κατήγαγές με, Vg. *deduxisti me* [*iuxta LXX*], Syr. *šdytny* "you have brought me down" [Vg. *iuxta Hebraeum* has *detraxisti me*]). These readings probably reflect a Vorlage with שְׁפַתָּנִי. Note that 4QPs^f reads [שופט] here, which indicates that, despite the obvious errors, this manuscript read a *qtl* rather than a *yqtl* form, as did the versions mentioned above.

Part II, Stanza B

17 Indeed, DOGS *have surrounded me,*   C
    a pack of those who would harm (me) has encircled me.
    My hands and my feet have gone lame,
18   *all my bones* have intoned my funeral lament.
    They [my enemies] are staring at/gloating over me;
19   they are dividing my garments among themselves,
    they are casting the lot for my clothing.
20 But you, O Lord, do not be far away;
    O my strength, hasten to my aid!
21 Deliver my soul from the sword,
    my precious life(?) from the hand of the DOG.   C′
22 Save me from the MOUTH of the LION,   B′
    from the horns of the WILD OXEN answer me![42]   A′

Let us look at the first subdivision, Stanza A (vv. 13–16). Contentwise, this unit may be divided into the following components:

13   Enemies surround the psalmist
14   Further hostile actions of enemies against the psalmist
15–16b   The psalmist's reaction to his enemies' actions
16c   Address to Yahweh (change to 2nd-person verb)

At least three of these four elements are also present in the second subdivision:

17ab   Enemies surround the psalmist
17c–18a
18b–19   Further hostile actions of enemies against the psalmist
20–22   Address to Yahweh (change to 2nd-person verb)

Theoretically, vv. 17c–18b, which contain the controversial verbs, could be fit into the structure in several ways. They could be taken as a continuation of the actions of the psalmist's foes against him, extending to v. 19. In this case his hands, feet, and bones would be *objects* of the verbs in question. This is how most interpreters and translations have understood these lines. Alternatively, these lines could be taken as a parallel subunit to vv. 15–16b, in which case they would continue the theme of the psalmist's reaction to his enemies' hostilities against him from Stanza A. In this case, the poet's hands, feet, and

---

42. I take עניתני here as a perfect precative form, thus virtually an imperative in sense. In this I follow Mitchell Dahood in his commentary (*Psalms I: 1–50* [AB 16; Garden City, N.Y.: Doubleday, 1966] 142), although I do not follow his translation ("make me triumph"). Kselman ("Why Have You Abandoned Me?" 174) earlier translated the verb "you have answered me!" but now concurs that it is a precative perfect (private communication).

bones would be *subjects* of the verbs in these lines. Which of these choices is
correct? Does the poem provide any clues to guide the interpreter here?

I believe it does. The first and most obvious clue is the phrase כל עצמותי in
v. 15b, which is the subject of its verb. It is repeated in v. 18a, forming an
inclusion that links these two sections. But the connection goes further. In
vv. 15b–16 it is followed by references to other parts of the psalmist's body
that continue the theme of terrified reaction.[43] After noting that the psalmist
has virtually turned to water out of fear of his enemies (v. 15a), vv. 15b–16b
list four of his body parts that likewise *react* to the daunting threat of his foes.[44]

Verse	Body Part(s)	Predicate
15b	all my bones	have become disjointed
15c	my heart	has become like wax
15d		has melted in the midst of my bowels
16a	my palate	has become as dry as a potsherd
16b	my tongue	has stuck to the roof of my mouth

These verses have a connection with Stanza B in that vv. 17c–18 also mention
parts of the psalmist's body. In fact, they mention three such parts, concluding
with "all my bones":

17c	my hands	
17c	my feet	have gone lame
18a	all my bones	have intoned my funeral dirge

These two sections of the middle stanza thus contain altogether a series of
seven parts of the body (actually, six parts with one repeated). The repetition
of "all my bones" (which occurs only in these two places in the psalm) forms
a clear inclusion. The schema also shows that these are accompanied by *seven*
verbs.[45] The fact that the three parts in vv, 17c–18a complete the series of
seven and conclude with an inclusion constitutes structural evidence that they
perform the same function within the poem as the first four in vv. 15b–16b.
As I have argued above, these three body parts are to be taken as subjects of
their respective verbs, as are each of the other four in vv. 15b–16b.

With this information in mind, we can now schematize the two subunits
as follows:

---

43. Body parts of the psalmist are not mentioned in this psalm outside of vv. 13–22.

44. Two other body parts are mentioned in these verses: מעי "my innards" (v. 15b) and
מלקוחי "my palate" (v. 16b). But these are not subjects of verbs that denote the psalmist's
reactions.

45. The poet did not simply assign one verb to each of the seven body parts as one might
expect. Rather, "my heart" in v. 15cd is the subject of two verbs, whereas "my hands" and
"my feet" in v. 17a share a single verb.

Part II, Stanza A

A	13	Enemies surround the psalmist
B	14	Further hostile actions of enemies against the psalmist
C	15–16b	The psalmist's reaction to his enemies
D	16c	Address to Yahweh (change to 2nd-person verb)

Part II, Stanza B

A′	17ab	Enemies surround the psalmist
C′	17c–18a	The psalmist's reaction to his enemies
B′	18b–19	Further hostile actions of enemies against the psalmist
D′	20–22	Address to Yahweh (change to 2nd-person verb)

The two subunits of the middle stanza contain the same four basic parts, except that (1) the middle two are inverted in Stanza B, and (2) the length of certain of the components differs: C is longer than C′ (6 cola vs. 2 cola), whereas D′ is longer than D (1 colon vs. 6 cola).

I now summarize with regard to the structure of the poem. The emendation of the two verbs in vv. 17c–18a proposed above results in a text that fits very well with the *structure* of the poem. The two verbs in question are, like those connected with the other four body parts in Stanza B, all *qtl* forms.[46] *All* the body parts function as the *subject* of their respective verbs.[47]

Context

We must now see whether the proposed emendations yield a text that fits well into the *context* of Psalm 22. As I have already suggested, the two verbs under consideration parallel those in vv. 15–16b insofar as the verbs in both sections describe the *terror* of the psalmist *in reaction to* the menacing actions of

---

46. The possible exceptions to this pattern occur in vv. 15 and 16. The last colon of v. 15 reads: נָמֵס בְּתוֹךְ מֵעָי, referring to the heart. Now the form נָמֵס can be parsed either as the 3rd masc. sing. *qtl* Qal form or the Qal participle. The LXX takes it as the latter (τηκό-μενος), as does the Vg. (*liquescens* [*iuxta LXX*] and *liquefacta* [*iuxta Hebraeum*]). The Syr., on the other hand, takes it as a pl. *qtl* form: *w'tmsyw* "and they have melted" (perhaps taking "all my bones" together with "my heart" as subjects). In v. 16 the first word, יָבֵשׁ, is clearly a *qtl* form and was so understood by the ancient versions (LXX ἐξηράνθη; Vg. *aruit*; Syr. *ybš*). The problem comes in the next colon: לְשׁוֹנִי מֻדְבָּק מַל קֹוחִי. The text should probably read: לְשׁוֹנִי דְבַק בְּלְקוֹחִי־ם (see Horace D. Hummel, "Enclitic *Mem* in Northwest Semitic, Especially Hebrew," *JBL* 76 [1957] 99). Note that the versions evidently read the *qtl* 3rd masc. sing. דָּבַק, not the participle מֻדְבָּק (LXX κεκόλληται; Vg. *adhesit*; Syr. *ybq*).

47. Cf. 1QH 8:32–35 (+ 4Q428), which, like Ps 22:13–22, contains *seven* parts of the poet's body reacting to the menacing of his foes. Some of the language is based on Psalm 22. All of the verbs connected with these parts of the body are either *qtl* or *wyqtl* forms. (On this text, see below.)

his enemies. This is certainly clear in vv. 15–16b. All of the images in v. 15 describe in various ways the disintegration of the psalmist in the face of such fear. They portray him "going to pieces" from sheer terror, to use a modern idiom. This could be understood as a reaction to both of the enemies' actions described in vv. 13–14, surrounding and roaring at him, or only to the first. He virtually turns to water, which elsewhere in the OT is used as a reaction stemming from great fear.[48] Then his bones become disjointed. The topos of one's bones being affected by terror appears elsewhere in Hebrew literature.[49] Finally, his heart melts, an expression that likewise appears elsewhere in the OT to describe a terrified reaction.[50]

The next two images in vv. 15–16b refer to things that happen to the psalmist's speech, specifically his palate and his tongue (v. 16ab). These describe his loss of the ability to speak in the face of such terror. On closer inspection, one notes that these images not only describe reactions to the enemies' actions in general but appear to correspond specifically to v. 14, which I have labeled in the schema as "further hostile actions of the enemies against the psalmist." Both v. 14 and v. 16ab explicitly mention the *mouth* or parts thereof. In v. 14 the enemies open their mouth against the psalmist like a roaring (שׁאג) lion. In reaction to this the psalmist, who had earlier roared out (שׁאגתי [v. 2b]) his lament to God, becomes mute with terror,[51] unable to utter a single sound to defend himself or cry for help. One could argue, then, that the psalmist's reactions involving his palate and tongue (v. 16ab) are a direct reaction to this "oral behavior" of his enemies rather than to their action of surrounding him.

In the context, vv. 17c–18a would be expected to continue the theme of the psalmist's terrorized reaction to the menacing actions of his enemies. On this reading v. 17c would refer to his hands and feet having (temporarily) ceased to function, just as his tongue has ceased to function in the immediately preceding image (v. 16ab).[52] Surrounded by his enemies, the psalmist be-

---

48. Job 3:24; 20:16.

49. Job 4:14; Dan 5:6; 1QH 7:4.

50. Deut 1:25; Josh 2:11; 5:1.

51. See Job 29:8–10, where Job relates that in former times he presented such a formidable appearance that people were overawed at the sight of him. As part of this picture he mentions (v. 10) that "the voice of nobles was hushed, and their tongue cleaved to the roof of their mouth [ולשׁונם לחכם דבקה]" (RSV). See also 1QH 5:31.

52. It may be worth noting here that the same sequence—nonfunctioning mouth followed immediately by nonfunctioning extremities—also appears in the diagnostic text pointed out by Roberts, where *pāšu ṣabit* "his mouth is paralyzed" precedes *qātāšu u šēpāšu iktarrâ* "his hands and his feet keep contracting."

comes immobilized with terror. His hands no longer function, meaning that he cannot fend off his attackers or defend himself against them. His feet no longer function, meaning in this context that he cannot run away even if escape were possible. This colon thus describes a natural reaction to being completely surrounded by fearsome enemies. The inability to use his feet to run away is particularly appropriate here. Once again it expresses the opposite of the enemies' action. His enemies surround him, a verb implying walking on foot, whereas he has become unable to walk altogether.

The context strongly supports such an interpretation—namely, that the focus of the hands/feet image here is one of immobility rather than physical suffering. Further evidence that this understanding of v. 17c is on track may be found in several of the *hodayoth* from Qumran. Several of these contain phrases that are clearly based on language from Psalm 22.[53]

1QH 7:1–5

ותטבע]ב{בבץ רגלי	[ ] אני נאלמתי] [ ]
אזני משמוע דמים	] זרו]ע נשברת מקניה
כי בליעל עם הופע יצר הוותם	שעו עיני מראות רע
ועצמי יתפרדו	השם לבבי ממחשבת רוע
ותכמי עלו כאניה בזעף חרישית	וירועו כול אושי מבניתי
מהוות פשעם	ויהם לבי לכלה
	ורוח עועיים תבלעני

[. . .] I became mute [. . .]
[(My) ar]m was fractured at the elbow,[54]
   and my *foot* was sunk in the mire;[55]
My eyes were shut because of seeing (their) evil,
   my ears (were deaf) because of hearing of (their) bloodshed;
My heart was horrified because of (their) perverse scheming,
   for Belial (is present) when their baneful impulse appears.

---

53. Roberts ("A New Root for an Old Crux," 249–50) argued that the cola of vv. 17c–18a are related in that both express physical afflictions. But if one reads v. 18c as I have suggested, it does not refer to a real physical affliction but to the *figurative* image of bones lamenting. Similarly the basic intent of v. 17c is not to emphasize the psalmist's physical suffering but rather, using contemporary medical terminology, that his hands and feet cannot function. In the present context this means that he cannot fend off his enemies or run away from them. Both images are therefore metaphorical.

54. Based on Job 31:22.

55. Based on Jer 38:22.

And all *the foundations of my frame* were shattered,
   and *my bones* became disjointed;
And *my entrails* heaved like a ship in a raging storm,
   and *my heart* palpitated as if it would perish;
A sensation of staggering engulfed me[56]
   because of the baneful power of their iniquity.

1QH 8:32–35 (+ 4QH . . .)

ויגר כמים לבי   וימס כדונג בשרי

ותשבר זרועי מקניה   ומעוז מותני היה לבהלה

[רג]לי נלכדה בכבל   [ואי]ן להניף יד

ואין לשלוח פעם   וילכו כמים ברכי

            ולא מצפד לקול רגלי

      [   ] זרועי רותקו בזקי משכיל

My heart has been poured out like water,
   and *my flesh* has become like wax;
the strength of my loins[57] has turned into horror.
My arm is fractured at the elbow
   so that I cannot move my hand.
My foot has been caught in fetters,
   my knees flow like water;
I cannot take a (single) pace
   or a step to run away swiftly.[58]
[   ] *my arms* are bound with chains that cause stumbling. . . .

The 1QH 7 passage contains the phrase עצמי יתפרדו "my bones have become disjointed," a clear allusion to Ps 22:15b, since there is no other passage in the MT in which these two words are associated. Note that the poet's afflictions

---

56. Based on Isa 19:14. The word רוח here is not to be taken as a continuation of the storm imagery. From the Isaiah passage it is clear that רוח עועיים means "a spirit of stumbling," which in modern parlance would equate to something like "a sensation, feeling of stumbling"—that is, dizziness or disorientation.

57. In this context of body parts, מעוז מותני (lit., "the strength of my loins") is possibly a euphemism for the *membrum virile*. To my knowledge the expression is otherwise unattested in ancient Hebrew.

58. This line is rather difficult. It would literally translate something like: "It was not (possible) to stretch forth the sole (of my foot) or (take a) step to the fleetness of my feet." The word קול here is certainly not "voice" but *scriptio plena* for Biblical Hebrew קל, from the root קלל "to be light/swift," attested only in Jer 3:9 (there with the nuance of "lightness"). Here with רגל it must mean "swiftness," as in the idiom קל רגלים (2 Sam 2:18).

are poetic ways of describing his *reaction to* the baneful actions (הוות) of the sons of darkness. Some of these reactions are similar to those in Ps 22:13–22: the poet becomes mute (cf. Ps 22:16ab), his bones become disjointed (cf. Ps 22:15a), his heart reacts strongly (cf. Ps 22:15cd), and finally there is a reference to his arm and foot. This is not exactly "hands" and "feet" but the image is very close. Both poems cited here, from columns 7 and 8, contain an allusion to Job 31:22b, which might be translated "Let my arm be fractured at the elbow" or the like.

How does such an image function as part of one's reaction to enemies? The complaint here is not the physical pain of such a trauma but the fact that it renders the poet incapable of using his hand, presumably to defend himself. This is clear from the line that follows in 1QH 8: ואי[ן] להניף יד "so that I cannot move my hand." The reference to the foot has the same function in both poems. In 1QH 7 it is an allusion to Jer 38:22. In this passage the women of the palace mock King Zedekiah by telling him that when the time comes to *escape* from the Babylonians he will find his foot "stuck in the mire." In other words, the image suggests the inability to escape in the time of danger.[59] In 1QH 8 the reference to the foot is followed by lines that indicate the inability to *take a step* or *run away*. In summary, these later poems corroborate the view that the "hands and feet" image in Ps 22:17c has to do not with physical suffering but with *immobility* and the consequent inability to escape the clutches of one's foes.

Turning to v. 18a, we can say that this verse too can be understood as a reaction to the enemies surrounding the psalmist in v. 17ab. His bones intoning his funeral lament can be taken as the despairing cry of one so surrounded and hopelessly outnumbered. However, another interpretation is possible, which supplements rather than excludes this interpretation. Just as the psalmist's reaction of becoming mute in v. 16b is connected with the "further hostile actions of the enemies against the psalmist" in v. 14 (opening their mouths against him like a roaring lion), so his reaction in v. 18a is most likely connected with the "further hostile actions of the enemies against the psalmist," namely, their dividing his clothes among them (vv. 18b–19)—a *hysteron proteron*.[60] As noted above, the verb ספר implies that the psalmist is virtually intoning his own

---

59. That the image in question relates to escape is clear from the next verse in Jeremiah: "And you yourself shall not escape [לא־תמלט] their hand, but shall be seized by the king of Babylon" (RSV).

60. See Walter Bühlmann and Karl Scherer, *Stilfiguren der Bibel: Ein kleines Nachschlagewerk* (2nd ed.; Giessen: Brunnen, 1994) 50–51. See also Z. Rodriguez, "El *hysteron-proteron* en la poesía bíblica hebrea," *EstBib* 58 (2000) 399–415. I am grateful to John S. Kselman for bringing these publications to my attention.

funeral lament, so little is his hope of coming out of this situation alive. He considers himself as good as dead. This action is related to the subsequent verses, vv. 18b–19.

The final member of the septad of body parts, "all my bones," which climaxes the series, is followed immediately by a tricolon composed of vv. 18b–19 that begins with a "resumptive" הַמָּה, which is necessary in order to inform the reader that the subject of the plural verbs is no longer the psalmist's bones but rather the enemies from v. 17a. This second series of enemy actions against the psalmist in Stanza B can be properly understood only if they are seen in the Sitz im Leben of conquest in battle. First, the idiom רָאָה בְ- in v. 18b signals the decisive defeat of an enemy and the victor's triumphant gloating over his vanquished foe. This idiom appears a number of times in the OT and also in the Mesha Stele in a context that refers to the death of the foe.[61] Second, the reference to dividing the psalmist's clothing has its origin also in the language of warfare and is simply a variation on the theme of the victors dividing up the spoils of war. Both of these idioms, but in particular the second, present the image of the psalmist's being treated as already killed (or mortally wounded) in battle. His enemies are already claiming his garments as spoils of war and removing them, as one would from the slain on a battlefield.

This "further action of the enemies against the psalmist" thus corresponds closely to his action in v. 18a, which I would take as an anticipated reaction to his enemies' actions. It is no coincidence that v. 18a is the last element in the series of seven parts of the psalmist's body that react to his enemies' threats. The image of all one's bones making lament is also metaphorical, so that in this case it may refer to the totality of the psalmist's being expressing despair for his life. At this point he has no option but to turn to Yahweh in a desperate, final plea for help (vv. 20–22). The fact that Yahweh answers this prayer and delivers him from death interestingly corresponds to the last word of the diagnostic text cited above—*iballuṭ* "he shall live/recover."[62]

---

61. Ezek 28:17–19; Mic 7:10; *KAI* 181.7 (the Mesha Stele). Note especially the last, which reads: וארא בה ובבתה וישראל אבד עבד עלם "And I gazed in triumph over him and over his house, and Israel *has perished forever.*"

62. I tentatively suggest that this may be reflected in the conclusion of the poem, that is, in vv. 30c–31a:

{וְ}נַפְשִׁי לֹא חִיָּה   ⟨וְ⟩זַרְעִ⟨י⟩ יַעַבְדֶנּוּ

He has indeed restored my soul to life,
and my progeny shall serve him.

Regarding the emendations to the text, note the following. The Syr. lacks the copula at the beginning of the first colon, and the LXX reads a copula at the beginning of the second. Both also read a 1st sing. pronominal suffix on נפש rather than the 3rd masc. sing. (as in the

Verse	Action of Enemies	Verse	Psalmist's Reaction	Body Part(s)	Reaction Manifested by
Part II, Stanza A					
13	surround psalmist	15	disintegration		being poured out like water
				1	*bones* become disjointed
				2	*heart* becomes like wax, melts
14	roar at psalmist	16ab	aphasia	3	*palate* dries up
				4	*tongue* sticks to roof of mouth
		16c	address to God (complaint)		
Part II, Stanza B					
17ab	surround psalmist	17c	immobility	5, 6	*hands/feet* go lame
18b	gloat over psalmist	18a	despair	7	*bones* intone funeral lament
19	divide the spoil				
		20–22	address to God (plea)		

Conclusion

It is a commonplace today in studies in Biblical Hebrew poetry to note how Israelite poets make frequent use of formulaic expressions in creating their poems. But poets are not confined to these poetic building-blocks. Every now and then a creative author will make use of an unusual image. I believe that this is what has happened in the case of Ps 22:17c–18a. The psalmist could have expressed the idea of immobility in his hands and feet by using formulas readily available to him, but he chose to use a metaphor drawn from the medical terminology of his day, ultimately going back to Akkadian diagnostic vocabulary. This image, together with the subsequent rare motif of proleptic funeral lament, creates a striking climax to the series of seven body parts and

---

MT). Restoring a 1st sing. suffix to זרע is not necessary (although I have done so here), since the suffix on נפש could serve "double-duty." Finally, I read לא as the emphatic particle לְאִ/לוּ. The phrase נֶפֶשׁ חִיָּה is identical in meaning to the frequent expression in Akk. literature, *bulluṭu napišta* "to cause (one's) vital force to live (again)" (see *CAD* B 58–61).

seven verbs in Part II of Psalm 22 that express the poet's terrorized reaction to the actions of his foes. This climax, in turn, throws into greater relief the divine deliverance implicit in Part III of the psalm.

Doves in the Windows: Isaiah 60:8 in Light of Ancient Mesopotamian Lament Traditions

WALTER C. BOUZARD, JR.
Wartburg College

The message of Isaiah 60, rooted in a reworking of themes long familiar from the Royal Zion tradition,[1] represents Trito-Isaiah's attempt to resuscitate the flagging hopes of the returned exiles in the face of oppressive historical circumstances.[2] The prophet holds before his auditors a vision of Jerusalem as a light in the world's darkness by which the earth shall be illumined and toward which both the people of God and the nations of the world shall converge. The universal character of the prophet's vision is seen particularly in vv. 4–7, 9, 10–14, and 16: exiled children of Daughter Zion and even foreign nations will travel to the city of God, bringing their wealth, glory, and offerings to the temple. Those who will stream toward Jerusalem include peoples whose lands are found south of Palestine (Midian/Ephah, Sheba, Kedar, and Nebaioth, vv. 6–7), as well as representatives from the coastland regions and far away Tarshish (v. 9).[3]

Author's note: I am pleased to offer this essay in honor of Professor J. J. M. Roberts, a man whose scholarship, teaching, and personal discipleship have shaped me in greater measure than he could know.

1. On the Royal Zion tradition, see J. J. M. Roberts, "Zion in the Theology of the Davidic-Solomonic Empire," in *Studies in the Period of David and Solomon and Other Essays* (ed. T. Ishida; Winona Lake, Ind.: Eisenbrauns, 1982) 93–108; R. E. Clements, *God and Temple* (Philadelphia: Fortress, 1965) 40–78; and the monograph by Ben C. Ollenburger, *Zion the City of the Great King: A Theological Symbol of the Jerusalem Cult* (JSOTSup 41; Sheffield: JSOT Press, 1987).

2. On the critical questions involved in the historical location of Trito-Isaiah, see Christopher R. Seitz, "Isaiah, Book of (Third Isaiah)," *ABD* 3.501–7 and the bibliography cited there.

3. On the several suggestions for the location of Tarshish, see David W. Baker, "Tarshish (Place)," *ABD* 6.331–33, and the bibliography cited there. Elsewhere, Sidney B. Hoenig ("Tarshish," *JQR* 69 [1979] 181–82) argues, primarily on the basis of the similarity between the Hebrew noun and the Greek θαλάσσης, that throughout the entire Bible "tarshish" is consistently understood as a general expression for "sea" and is thus not to be identified with a particular geographic location. Hoenig's thesis seems not to have found widespread acceptance.

Between the mention of these various peoples, however, appears the bicola question of v. 8, translated in the NRSV as follows: "Who are these that fly
like a cloud, and like doves to their windows?" While this verse presents no
obvious textual or translational difficulties, the conceptual link between the
ones who are "like doves" and the sacrificial animals mentioned in v. 7a, the
reference to the temple in v. 7b, or the exiles returning on the ships of Tarshish in v. 9 remains elusive, as does the meaning of the verse as a whole. Perhaps for this reason commentators generally refrain from treating this verse.
When Isa 60:8 finds mention at all in the secondary literature, the two similes
are understood as poetic depictions of the ships of Tarshish mentioned in the
following verse.[4] This solution, however, is neither particularly convincing
nor satisfying for the following reasons.

First, assuming for the moment that עב is here properly understood as
"cloud," one notes that nowhere else in the Hebrew Scriptures are clouds or
doves associated with sailing vessels. One must conjecture that the prophet
had in mind a vast armada of white-sailed ships approaching from the west and
that this, in turn, put him in mind of a cloud and doves. But, if this is a correct
assessment of the cloud/dove imagery, the first colon of v. 9 and its reference
to the coastlands seems awkwardly inserted, whether one assumes the MT's
"for the coastlands shall wait for me" or one corrects the text, as in the translation of John L. McKenzie, "for the ships are assembled for me."[5] That is, the
standard interpretations strain to identify the imagery of v. 8 with that of v. 9.
As will be shown, however, this association may be far less likely than linking
v. 8 with the reference to altar and temple in v. 7. Indeed, references to doves

4. The verse is frequently omitted in the discussion of commentators. For example,
Claus Westermann (*Isaiah 40–66* [trans. David M. G. Stalker; OTL; Philadelphia: Westminster, 1969] 359) and Paul D. Hanson (*Isaiah 40–66* [Interpretation; Louisville: Westminster
John Knox, 1995] 221) refrain from treating the verse at all. When the passage does find its
way into the commentaries, most follow some version of the view of G. von Rad (*Old Testament Theology* [2 vols.; New York: Harper & Row, 1962–65] 2.295), who understands the
verse as a poetic description of the sea vessels mentioned in v. 9. See, for example, the works
of John N. Oswalt, *The Book of Isaiah Chapters 40–66* (NICOT; Grand Rapids: Eerdmans,
1998) 543; R. N. Whybray, *Isaiah 40–66* (NCBC; Grand Rapids: Eerdmans, 1975) 233;
and A. S. Herbert, *The Book of the Prophet Isaiah, Chapters 40–66* (CBC; Cambridge: Cambridge University Press, 1975) 158. So, too, the paraphrastic reading provided by the TEV:
"What are these ships that skim along like clouds, Like doves returning home?"

5. John L. McKenzie, *Second Isaiah: Introduction, Translation, and Notes* (AB 20; Garden
City, N.Y.: Doubleday, 1968) 174. Similarly, Whybray (*Isaiah 40–66*, 233–34) emends אִיִּים
to צִיִּים ("ships") and repoints יְקַוּוּ as יְקֻוּ ("will be assembled"): "for me (the) ships will be
assembled." Alternatively, he proposes that v. 9 could be amended to read כְּלֵי אִיִּים יְקֻוּ "the
vessels of the coastlands will be assembled."

typically appear in contexts having explicitly to do with mourning and catastrophe, not excluding a catastrophe that falls upon the city and the temple.

Second, the terms used for cloud (עב) and window (ארבה) often find explicit association with God's divine presence. Having said that, one must admit immediately that epiphanic connotations for these two nouns are not universal in the Hebrew scriptures. The noun עב sometimes simply signifies rain clouds[6] and, occasionally, finds employment in a simile that emphasizes ephemerality.[7] Frequently, however, the noun does appear in epiphanic contexts: God is often depicted as appearing in clouds,[8] as riding upon clouds,[9] or as being present, though obscured, by clouds.[10] Even when the term simply signals rain clouds, however, mastery of the clouds is always understood to be within God's purview, and human attempts to usurp that realm are regarded as hubris.[11] Similarly, the noun ארבה twice signifies no more than ordinary holes in earthly structures.[12] Nevertheless, while it is inarguable that this noun's basic denotative meaning is rooted in the concrete realities of domestic architecture and daily life, it remains the case that, when the noun is employed elsewhere, it refers to the windows of the heavens (ארבת השמים) that are fixed in the firmament and controlled by God and through which the rain falls.[13] Thus, the presence of these two nouns, appearing as they do in proximity with references to altar and temple in v. 7, at least raises a question relative to the propriety of the conclusion that the ones "like the doves" are simply to be understood as poetic depictions of ships hastening from the west in v. 9. Therefore, one may well ask anew, with the prophet, who are these ones like a dove? Further, what does this verse signify?

The following comments intend to support the thesis that, in the imagery employed in this verse and through the chapter, Trito-Isaiah at once evokes and reverses a trope quite familiar to his listeners by means of their familiarity with the Mesopotamian communal lament compositions: whereas in that literature, a dove's abandonment of the temple signified divine abandonment of temple, city, and people, the prophet uses the image of doves returning to the city and temple as a simile for the hope of restoration of both God's house and Jerusalem's population.

---

6. 1 Kgs 18:44–45; Job 26:8; 36:29; 37:11, 16; 38:34; Ps 147:8; Eccl 11:3–4; 12:3.
7. Job 30:15; Isa 18:4, 44:22.
8. Exod 19:9, Judg 5:4, Ps 77:17–19.
9. Ps 104:3, Isa 19:1.
10. Job 22:14, Ps 18:12–13 [= 2 Sam 22:12–13].
11. Job 20:4–7, Isa 14:13–14.
12. Hos 13:3, a chimney; Eccl 12:3, windows, perhaps used metaphorically for eye sockets.
13. Gen 7:11; 8:2; Isa 24:18; 2 Kgs 7:2, 19; Mal 3:10.

The image of the returning dove (יונה) alighting on a window provides an important interpretive clue. Of the occurrences of this noun in the Hebrew Bible, the majority appear in ritual texts in which two pigeons (יונים) or two turtledoves (תורים) serve as sacrificial substitutes for an offering of a sheep.[14] No significant distinction seems to be made between the two species of birds in these texts. The latter observation applies as well to the appearance of יונה and תור in the Song of Songs, where both terms appear as zoomorphic similes intended to depict the beauty or tender cooing of the beloved.[15] The word יונה also appears several times in Gen 8:8–12 as the creature whose behavior signaled the abatement of the chaos waters in the flood story.[16] Beyond these references, however, the characteristics of the dove that emerge in the poetic texts are the moan-like noises issued by the birds and their shared penchant for inhabiting remote or desolated places. Evidently, the vulnerable pigeon or turtledove, whose cooing suggested human moaning to a number of biblical poets[17] and whose normal habitat included remote or destroyed areas,[18] provided an

---

14. Lev 1:14; 5:7, 11; 12:8; 14:22, 30; 15:14, 29; Num 6:10. For further details, see G. Johannes Botterweck, "יונה yônâ," *TDOT* 6.39.

15. Song 2:12 [תור]; 1:15; 2:14; 4:1; 5:2, 12; 6:9 [יונה].

16. The noun תור also appears in Gen 15:9 in connection with Abram's covenant ritual. Interestingly, Christopher T. Begg ("The Birds in Genesis 15,9–10," *BN* 36 [1987] 7–11) discovers yet another solid association between this תור, as well as the bird mentioned in Ps 74:19–20 ("The Covenantal Dove in Psalm 74:19–20," *VT* 37 [1987] 78–81), and Mesopotamian texts. In particular, Begg sees the references to these birds as a reflection of Sumerian treaty rituals, as in the case of the famous Sumerian "Vulture Stela," wherein doves are sent to the temple of a deity with news of the treaty-making. A translation of the "Vulture Stela" is provided by J. S. Cooper, *Reconstructing History from Ancient Inscriptions: The Lagash-Umma Border Conflict* (SANE 2/1; Malibu: Undena, 1993) 45–47.

17. Nah 2:5–7; Isa 59:11, 38:14; compare with Ps 74:19.

18. Ps 55:6–8, Jer 48:28, Ezek 7:16, Hos 11:10–11 [compare with Hos 7:11], Ps 68:12–14. That a discernible relationship exists between Ps 68:13 and 14 is, admittedly, far from assured. It may be that the women are understood, collectively, as the dove. If so the latter's adorning silver and gold include the spoil gotten in the wake of kings routed by Yahweh's command. Here then, as elsewhere in the poetic texts, the dove would stand as a metaphor for the people, as it appears to be in Ps 74:19. W. F. Albright ("A Catalogue of Early Hebrew Lyric Poems," *HUCA* 23 [1950] 1–38) believes that vv. 13–14a and 14b represent separate incipits. Nevertheless, Albright's thesis is often vigorously challenged, as are the particulars of his assessment of this psalm. See A. Weiser (*The Psalms* [OTL; Philadelphia: Westminster, 1962] 481–82], M. Dahood (*Psalms II: 51–100* [AB 17; Garden City, N.Y.: Doubleday, 1968] 133), A. A. Anderson (*The Book of Psalms* [NCB; London: Oliphants, 1972] 1.481–82), H.-J. Kraus (*Psalms 60–150* [Minneapolis: Augsburg Fortress, 1989] 48), J. Gray ("A Cantata of the Autumn Festival: Psalm LXVIII," *JSS* 22 [1977] 2–26), and Christopher T. Begg ("The Messenger Dove in Ps 68,12–14," *ETL* 63 [1987] 117–18) for alternative proposals.

apt image for the effect alien invasion and that event's inevitable destruction has on human beings. With the lone exception of Isa 60:8, the image otherwise finds employment in contexts that, strikingly, have to do with a catastrophe. The disaster is, moreover, normally one of national consequences, such as the invasion and the destruction of the city and its temple.[19] For example, Ezek 7:16 notes that, should any survivors of the city escape destruction, "they shall be found on the mountains, like doves of the valleys, all of them moaning over their iniquity." The preexilic prophecy of Nah 2:7 concerning the destruction of Nineveh likewise illustrates the point: "It is decreed that the city be exiled, its slave women led away, moaning like doves and beating their breasts."

The origin and significance of the dove image are illuminated by the Mesopotamian communal laments known as *balags*. These ritual lamentations, developed from the Sumerian city laments and used continuously in the rituals of successive Mesopotamian empires until the close of the first millennium,[20] by virtue of temporal, geographic and cultural proximity, seem likely to have been familiar to the returning exiles who had been exposed to Babylonian worship and, quite probably, to preexilic Judeans as well.[21] The specific reference to a returning dove finds clarification in the *balag* known by its incipit *a-še-er gi₆-ta*.[22] Following a description of the devastating storm of Enlil

---

19. See the texts cited above and, especially, Nah 2:5–7, Jer 48:28, Ezek 7:16.

20. On the origin and history of *balags*, see Mark E. Cohen, *Balag-Compositions: Sumerian Lamentation Liturgies of the Second and First Millennium* B.C. (Sources from the Ancient Near East 1/2; Malibu: Undena, 1974) 9–15; *The Canonical Lamentations of Ancient Mesopotamia* (Potomac: Capital Decisions, 1988) 1.11–44.

21. A full recitation of the complex scholarly debate relative to the question of literary influence by the cuneiform tradition on specific Hebrew texts surpasses the scope of the present article. For a thorough discussion of the matter pursuant to an argument for such influence, see my *We Have Heard with Our Ears, O God: Sources of the Communal Laments in the Psalms* (SBLDS 159; Atlanta: Scholars Press, 1997) 15–51, where important older contributions by Folker Willesen ("The Cultic Situation of Psalm LXXIV," *VT* 11 [1952] 289–306), Thomas F. McDaniel ("The Alleged Sumerian Influence upon Lamentations," *VT* 18 [1968] 198–209), and W. C. Gwaltney ("The Biblical Book of Lamentations in the Context of Near Eastern Lament Literature," in *Scripture in Context II* [ed. W.W. Hallo, J. C. Moyer, and L. G. Perdue; Winona Lake, Ind.: Eisenbrauns, 1983] 191–211), as well as more recent publications by scholars such as Paul Wayne Ferris, Jr. (*The Genre of Communal Lament in the Bible and the Ancient Near East* [SBLDS 127; Atlanta: Scholars Press, 1992]), Jeffrey Tigay ("On Evaluating Claims of Literary Borrowing," in *The Tablet and the Scroll: Near Eastern Studies in Honor of William W. Hallo* [ed. Mark E. Cohen, Daniel C. Snell, and David B. Weisberg; Bethesda, Md.: CDL, 1993] 250–55), and F. W. Dobbs-Allsopp (*Weep, O Daughter of Zion: A Study of the City-Lament Genre in the Hebrew Bible* [Rome: Pontifical Biblical Institute, 1993]) are considered in detail.

22. *Balag* 50 according to the NA catalog *4R² 53*. The translations for this *balag* and those that follow are by Cohen, in *Canonical Lamentations*.

(b+139–154)[23] and the defilement of both the sanctuary and the goddesses'
image in the sanctuary by the enemy (b+155–162),[24] the goddess describes
herself as a frightened dove who must abandon both her temple and city:

> Like a frightened dove, I spend the day (huddled) against the rafters.
> Like a flying bat, I disappear among the crevices.
> It causes me to fly about in my house like a bird.
> It causes me to fly about my city like a bird.
> In my house it screeches right behind me.
> As for me, the lady, in my city it screeches right behind me.
> How I pour out in my house, "You are no longer my house!"
> How I pour out in my city, "You are no longer my city!"
> How I pour out in my cella, "You are no longer my cella!"
> "I can no longer enter it!" I utter. Its wealth has been consumed.
> "I can no longer . . . !" I utter, Its laughter has dried up. (b+166–176)[25]

Later in this same composition, however, the simile is abandoned; now the
goddess seemingly describes the fate of a real creature that inhabits the temple's
window:

> The window where I focus attention has been destroyed. Its dove flies away.
> The dove of the window has abandoned her nest. Where can she fly to?
> The bird has abandoned its built nest. Where can she fly to?
> Its men have abandoned the cella which was founded there. Where can they
>   go to? (b+258–261)[26]

That Israel was familiar with the concept of nesting birds finding safe haven
in the temple is illustrated by Ps 84:4, albeit the passage uses different words
to describe the winged creatures:

> Even the sparrow (צִפּוֹר) finds a home,
>   and the swallow (דְּרוֹר) a nest for herself,
>   where she may lay her young,
> at your altars, O Lord of hosts,
>   my King and my God.

---

23. Ibid., 2.721.

24. Ibid., 2.721–22.

25. Ibid., 2.722. Compare with similar expressions in the *balag urú-ḫul-a-ke₄*, lines
a+28–29, a+68–74, *Canonical Lamentations*, 1.261–62.

26. Ibid., 2.724. That the goddess was also regularly associated with the dove in ancient
Near Eastern iconography has been demonstrated by Othmar Keel ("Perspektiven der Forschung," in *Altorientalische Miniaturkunst: Die ältesten visuellen Massenkommunikationsmittel.
Ein Blick in die Sammlungen des Biblischen Instituts der Universität Freiburg Schweiz* [ed. O. Keel
and C. Uehlinger; Mainz am Rhein: von Zabern, 1990] 126–27).

Ps 55:7–9, moreover, well demonstrates the fact that Israel was familiar with the lament motif of the fleeing dove:

> And I say, "O that I had wings like a dove!
> I would fly away and be at rest;
> truly, I would flee far away;
> I would lodge in the wilderness;
> I would hurry to find a shelter for myself
> from the raging wind and tempest."

Nor is the mention of the fleeing dove in this text the only point of correspondence between Israel's lament tradition and that of Mesopotamia: this passage, like the *balag a-še-er gi₆-ta* quoted above, also joins the motif of the devastating storm and its effects upon the dove.

In the Mesopotamian lament traditions the destruction of the temple spells the end of the normal resting place for the dove: the creature is forced to abandon its nesting place in the window of the temple. This fact doubtless accounts for several references in the *balags* expressing the idea that the dove "hovers about" as a consequence of the temple's destruction. That is, the dove, like the goddess, is homeless and wandering: "Its crenellated wall has been destroyed. Its dove hovers about."[27]

The link between the dove imagery in Isa 60:8 and the motifs of the Mesopotamian *balag* is also consistent with the 2nd-person fem. sing. address present throughout the biblical poem. God speaks directly to the city, here as elsewhere (for example, Lamentations 1; 2:14–19) personified as woman. Although the feminine personification of cities has been considered to be a West Semitic phenomenon since the publication of two seminal articles by Aloysius Fitzgerald,[28] a recent reevaluation of Fitzgerald's evidence by Peggy L. Day has dealt that hypothesis a serious blow.[29] Instead, it appears that this poetic feature represents an Israelite adaptation of the Mesopotamian "weeping goddess" motif, a motif that manifests itself as early as the Sumerian city laments

---

27. ᵈ*UTU-gin₇ è-ta aḫù*, line 143 (*Canonical Lamentations*, 1.111). Compare with *é tùr-gin₇ nigin-na-àm*, line 19 (*Canonical Lamentations*, 1.84) and *mu-tin nu-nuz dím-ma*, line a+12 (*Canonical Lamentations*, 1.243) for identical statements.

28. A. Fitzgerald, "The Mythological Background for the Presentation of Jerusalem as a Queen and False Worship as Adultery in the Old Testament," *CBQ* 34 (1972) 403–16; "BTWLT and BT as Titles for Capital Cities," *CBQ* 37 (1975) 170–80.

29. Peggy L. Day, "The Personification of Cities as Female in the Hebrew Bible: The Thesis of Aloysius Fitzgerald, F.S.C.," *Reading From This Place: Social Location and Biblical Interpretation*, vol. 2: *Social Location and Biblical Interpretation in Global Perspective* (ed. Fernando F. Segovia and Mary Ann Tolbert; Minneapolis: Fortress, 1995) 283–302.

and that is both ubiquitous in and characteristic of the *balag* compositions.[30] In those texts the goddess laments, often in laborious detail, the destruction of both her temple and the city in which it is located. Throughout the present chapter, the feminine city is addressed and reassured of her coming restoration and glory. If, as I contend, the present chapter represents another example of Israel's adaptation of this motif, then the persona uttering the words of v. 8 must be the personified city herself.[31] This is far from a unique example; a similar shift in speakers within prophetic and poetic texts, including the appearance of the feminine voice of the personified city, has been uncovered in Lamentations[32] and Jer 10:19–25.[33] Verse 8 and the evident shift in speakers that the verse manifests can be understood as the city's response and wonderment to the promise of restoration given in vv. 1–7 and, especially, in the description of the exiles who would be returned from afar.

At just this juncture, however, a potentially serious objection can be raised. In the *balag*s, as well as in Psalm 55, the coming of a storm signals the divinely wrought destruction and precipitates the departure of the dove. One might object that a true reversal of this imagery would require that the return of the doves be balanced by the departure of the storm clouds. In v. 8, however, the movement of the two is parallel, not set in opposition; both doves and cloud arrive together. In response to this objection, however, one may note the following.

First, the larger context of this poem itself suggests a reversal of fortune in which the destitute and forsaken city is promised a restoration of its prominence and prosperity. Images of darkness banished by the presence of Yahweh's glory (vv. 1–2) or Yahweh himself (vv. 19–20) bracket an extended report of the return of Jerusalem's native children (vv. 4–10) and the arrival of Gentile worshipers (vv. 11–16). Renewed material wealth will be carried into the city by all peoples; the Lord himself will bring gifts of peace, righteousness, salvation, and praise (vv. 17–18). Verse 13 summarizes the general tone and

---

30. Dobbs-Allsopp, *Weep, O Daughter of Zion*, 75–90; compare with Tikva Frymer-Kensky, *In the Wake of the Goddesses: Women, Culture, and the Biblical Transformation of Pagan Myth* (New York: Free Press, 1992) 170.

31. For a discussion of this phenomenon, see Barbara Bakke Kaiser, "Poet as 'Female Impersonator': The Imagery of Daughter Zion as Speaker in Biblical Poems of Suffering," *JR* 67 (1987) 164–82.

32. Dobbs-Allsopp, *Weep, O Daughter of Zion*, 75–90, especially p. 85.

33. J. J. M. Roberts, "The Motif of the Weeping God in Jeremiah and Its Background in the Lament Tradition of the Ancient Near East," *Old Testament Essays* 5 (1992) 361–74; repr. in *The Bible and the Ancient Near East: Collected Essays* (Winona Lake, Ind.: Eisenbrauns, 2002) 132–42; Bouzard, *We Have Heard with Our Ears, O God*, 181–82.

theme of the chapter: "Whereas you have been forsaken and hated, with no one passing through, I will make you majestic forever, a joy from age to age." That is, as Yahweh and Yahweh's glory return to Jerusalem, the city and the temple are made once more habitable. The larger context is absolutely consistent with the notion that imagery of the divine abandonment of cella and city, such as one finds in the Mesopotamian lament materials, is being reversed in this poem in order to bring about a restoration hope.

Second, the reference to the cloud in v. 8 does not seem to be a reference to an impending storm. Clouds are little mentioned either in the *balag* material or the Bible in connection with the deity's destructive storm. Instead, one finds reference to a "raging wind" (מרוח סעה) and a "tempest" (סער)[34] as the metaphor for divine destruction. As noted above, within the Hebrew tradition, clouds tend to signal the presence of God rather than signaling an agent of God's destruction per se. If "cloud" is the word meant here, therefore, the image would seem to be saying something about objects—or persons—who are borne toward the city in connection with God's power and presence. This too is consistent with the larger context of the poem.

It seems likely, however, that עב in v. 8 does not signify a cloud after all. The text reads כעב תעופינה and is translated in the NRSV "they fly like a cloud." The translation assumes the trilateral root עוב or עיב "cloud" and ignores the presence of the definite article with the prefixed *kap*. However, one can perhaps explain the presence of the definite article if the noun in question comes not from the middle weak root just mentioned but instead from the geminate עבב. If so, עב, here prefixed with a definite article, may well refer to a specific architectural feature found on the temple. The noun is, admittedly, rare in the Hebrew Bible. It occurs only in three other places: 1 Kgs 7:6, where it refers to some architectural feature of the palace associated with a pillared porch; and twice in Ezek 41:25–26, where it seems to refer to a wooden structure, attached to a porch (אולם) located just outside the nave of the temple. For want of a better term, the NRSV renders עב as "canopy" in these three instances. If, in fact, the prophet had this architectural feature of the temple in mind (as the presence of the definite article with the preposition suggests), v. 8 could be translated as follows: "Who are these? They fly in the canopy like doves to their (the canopy's) windows."

This suggested translation requires further brief comment. First, the translation assumes that the conjunction *waw* of וכיונים, if it is to be translated at all,

---

34. See Ps 55:9 and Jer 25:32, respectively. Compare with Ps 83:15–17. On the use of these terms in the Hebrew Scriptures, see my *We Have Heard with Our Ears, O God*, 131–33.

should be understood as an explicative.[35] Alternatively—and more likely, given the presence of the comparative *kap* (כעב)—the *waw* may simply be pleonastic.[36] In either instance, the translation is not affected. Second, this translation does not assume graphic confusion of the prepositions *bet* and *kap*. Although the strong possibility of graphic confusion between these two radicals is amply demonstrated elsewhere,[37] there are several examples where the preposition *kap* absorbs other prepositions, including *bet*, and is best translated, as here, with a spatial or locative meaning.[38] The likelihood of this suggested translation is furthered by the nearby—if enigmatic—association of windows (here חלונים) with the עב in Ezek 41:26; it appears that the עב had windows on or near it. The suggested translation also helps to explain the otherwise odd association of a fem. pl. noun (יונים) with a noun suffixed with a masc. pl. ending (ארבתיהם); the עב (plural עבים) is that which has windows.

Finally, the proposed translation is attractive, in my view, because it satisfactorily links the verse with the references to the temple and altar in the preceding verse and that, be it noted, without altering the received text. Just as flocks and rams will be brought and accepted at the altar of the temple, doves will return to the temple precincts both as symbols of the gathering peoples and as a sign of Jerusalem and the temple's restoration. Just as in the Mesopotamian lament traditions the destruction of the temple spells the end of the normal resting place for the dove and the deity, so here the return of doves points the prophet's auditors to the return of divine glory and peace. On the other hand, the proposed translation also accords well with the unaltered MT of v. 9. There one reads that "the coastlands shall wait for me." This verse is, of course, reminiscent of Isa 51:5 (and, to a lesser degree, of 42:4) where God promises swiftly to bring near the divine deliverance and salvation. The promise of this coming deliverance, explicitly named in 51:5, is again conveyed in 60:8, albeit there in the image of the returning dove.

---

35. On *waw* as an explicative, see Ronald J. Williams, *Hebrew Syntax: An Outline* (2nd ed.; Toronto: University of Toronto Press, 1976) 71; Choon Leong Seow, *A Grammar for Biblical Hebrew* (2nd ed.; Nashville: Abingdon, 1995) 284. Compare with 1 Sam 17:40, Gen 4:4.

36. As in Isa 44:1; 2 Sam 13:20, and 15:34. See Williams, *Hebrew Syntax*, 71; Seow, *A Grammar*, 286.

37. See Ernst Würthwein, *The Text of the Old Testament* (trans. Erroll F. Rhodes; Grand Rapids: Eerdmans, 1979) 107; and P. Kyle McCarter, Jr., *Textual Criticism: Recovering the Text of the Hebrew Bible* (Philadelphia: Fortress, 1986) 44 and the examples cited there.

38. For example, Isa 5:17, "as in their pastures"; 23:15, "in the song of the harlot"; 28:21 and 29:7, "as in a dream." Compare with M. O'Connor, *Hebrew Verse Structure* (Winona Lake, Ind.: Eisenbrauns, 1980) 122; Bruce K. Waltke and M. O'Connor, *An Introduction to Biblical Hebrew Syntax* (Winona Lake, Ind.: Eisenbrauns, 1990) 204; E. Kautzsch (ed.), *Gesenius' Hebrew Grammar* (2nd ed.; trans. A. E. Cowley; Oxford: Clarendon, 1910) 376.

The Mesopotamian laments, as laments, never undertake a description of the restoration of the temple or its precincts. Indeed, because the original cultic raison d'être of these compositions was to avert any wrath of the deity that may have been accidentally incurred on the occasions when temples were renovated,[39] one would expect a description neither of the goddess's city nor of its temple's restoration. However, the hope of restoration for both Jerusalem, personified as a female, and especially its temple is precisely what the prophet means to instill in his auditors. As a part of this proclamation, Trito-Isaiah reverses an image quite familiar to his listeners by means of their familiarity with the *balag* compositions: even as the dove once abandoned the temple, the dove will be seen flying to the windows of God's "glorious house" (v. 7) on the soon-to-come day of Jerusalem's exaltation. This verse strongly suggests Israel's familiarity with this aspect of the Mesopotamian lament tradition, here transformed by the prophet into a message of restoration hope.

---

39. Cohen, *Balag-Compositions*, 11; compare with *Canonical Lamentations*, 39.

The Pride of Jacob

JOEL S. BURNETT

Baylor University

Various interpretations of Psalm 47 have tended to place its original setting in Jerusalem.[1] Alternatively, some have suggested that this psalm is "Northern" in origin.[2] One reason cited for this suggestion is the psalm's use of the phrase *gĕ'ôn ya'ăqōb* "the Pride of Jacob" (v. 5).[3] On the whole, this expression has received relatively little attention in the way of scholarly comment. The phrase occurs in three other instances in the Hebrew Bible—Amos 6:8, 8:7; and Nah 2:3. Typically, it is regarded in each instance as a poetic embellishment by which some aspect of the people's "pride" is mentioned. In Ps 47:5, where it is described as the "inheritance" that Yahweh has chosen for his people, the expression has usually been understood as a reference to the land of Canaan.[4]

Author's note: This essay is offered in honor of J. J. M. Roberts and in appreciation for his decisive guidance in and influence on my own study of the Bible and the ancient Near East.

1. See, e.g., A. F. Kirkpatrick, *The Book of Psalms* (CBC; Cambridge: Cambridge University Press, 1902); Hermann Gunkel, *Introduction to Psalms: The Genres of the Religious Lyric of Israel* (completed by J. Begrich; trans. J. D. Nogalski; Mercer Library of Biblical Studies; Macon, Ga.: Mercer University Press, 1998) 66–69; Sigmund Mowinckel, *The Psalms in Israel's Worship* (trans. D. R. Ap-Thomas; 2 vols.; Nashville: Abingdon, 1962) 1.188; Hans-Joachim Kraus, *Psalms 1–59: A Commentary* (trans. H. C. Oswald; Minneapolis: Augsburg, 1988) 86–89, 465–70; André Caquot, "Le psaume 47 et la royauté de Yahwé," *RHPR* 39 (1959) 311–37; E. Lipiński, *La royauté de Yahwé dans la poésie et le culte de l'ancien Israël* (Brussels: Paleis der Academiën, 1965) 432–51; Leo G. Perdue, "'Yahweh Is King over All the Earth': An Exegesis of Psalm 47," *ResQ* 17 (1974) 85–98; and J. J. M. Roberts, "The Religiopolitical Setting of Psalm 47," *BASOR* 221 (1976) 129–32.

2. H. Louis Ginsberg, *The Israelian Heritage of Judaism* (Texts and Studies of the Jewish Theological Seminary of America 24; New York: Jewish Theological Seminary of America, 1982) 33–34. Arguing for the Northern origins of the Korahite Psalms as a whole (to which Psalm 47 belongs) are John P. Peters, *The Psalms as Liturgies* (New York: Macmillan, 1922) 273–95; Michael D. Goulder, *The Psalms of the Sons of Korah* (JSOTSup 20; Sheffield: JSOT Press, 1982), on Psalm 47, specifically, pp. 151–59; and Gary A. Rendsburg, *Linguistic Evidence for the Northern Origin of Selected Psalms* (SBLMS 43; Atlanta: Scholars Press, 1990) 57, 59. See also, following Rendsburg and Goulder, William L. Holladay, *The Psalms through Three Thousand Years: Prayerbook of a Cloud of Witnesses* (Minneapolis: Fortress, 1993) 28–32.

3. Ginsberg, *Israelian Heritage*, 33–34.

4. See James Muilenburg, "Psalm 47," *JBL* 63 (1944) 240; Kraus, *Psalms 1–59*, 468.

In Nah 2:3 it has been understood as a designation either for the Southern Kingdom of Judah or, alternatively, for the Northern Kingdom of Israel.[5] The use of the expression in Amos 6:8—"I abhor the Pride of Jacob"—is usually understood in reference to the hubristic arrogance of Northern Israelite society.[6] These instances, being poetic in nature and allegedly not having the same referent, are usually discussed somewhat in isolation from one another.[7] A cohesive explanation that accounts for all of these instances is lacking.

Set apart even further is the interpretation of the fourth instance, Amos 8:7. Here the phrase is found in the context of an oath by Yahweh, who swears by "the Pride of Jacob." Interpreters have rightly recognized that Yahweh "swears by" himself only and that in this case *gĕʾôn yaʿăqōb* must in some sense be a designation for the deity.[8] The lack of a satisfactory explanation for the phrase

---

5. Walter A. Maier, *The Book of Nahum: A Commentary* (St. Louis: Concordia, 1959) 227–28; cf. J. J. M. Roberts, *Nahum, Habakkuk, and Zephaniah: A Commentary* (OTL; Louisville: Westminster John Knox, 1991) 64–65.

6. James Luther Mays, *Amos: A Commentary* (OTL; Philadelphia: Westminster, 1969) 118; Hans Walter Wolff, *Joel and Amos: A Commentary of the Books of the Prophets Joel and Amos* (Hermeneia: Philadelphia: Fortress, 1977) 282; Wilhelm Rudolph, *Joel-Amos-Obadja-Jona* (KAT 13/2; Gütersloh: Mohn, 1971) 223.

7. See, e.g., Muilenburg, "Psalm 47," 240; Peter Craigie, *Psalms 1–50* (WBC 19; Waco, Tex.: Word, 1983) 349; Shalom Paul, *Amos: A Commentary on the Book of Amos* (Hermeneia; Minneapolis: Fortress, 1991) 214; Mays, *Amos*, 118, 145; Maier, *The Book of Nahum*, 227–28; Ginsberg (*Israelian Heritage*, 33–34) who in connection with Psalm 47 mentions the occurrences in Amos but not the one in Nahum; cf. Roberts, *Nahum, Habakkuk, and Zephaniah*, 64, who mentions all of the instances, noting that the expression is used alternatively with "positive" and "negative" connotations.

8. Friedrich Horst, "Der Eid im Alten Testament," *Gottes Recht: Gesammelte Studien zum Recht im Alten Testament* (Munich: Chr. Kaiser, 1961) 306; repr. from *EvT* 17 (1957); Rudolph, *Joel-Amos-Obadja-Jona*, 264; with less certainty, Mays, *Amos*, 145. The effort, based on an observed sense of irony, to explain "the Pride of Jacob" in Amos 8:7 as not being in reference to the deity is seen to be absurd in its articulation. As Paul explains, "The Lord swears by the very attribute of the people that he has formerly condemned (6:8), that is, by the same pride and arrogance that are exhibited in their very words cited in the previous verses" (*Amos*, 260). A similar explanation alleging a sarcastic divine oath is offered early on by Julius Wellhausen (*Die kleinen Propheten übersetzt und erklärt* [Skizzen und Vorarbeiten 5; repr., Berlin: Reimer, 1963] 93). The lack of cogency in this explanation is made clear by the remarks of Mays, who states mildly, "an oath sworn by the very sin condemned is strange" (*Amos*, 145), and of Saul Olyan, who (speaking in connection with Amos 8:14) observes, "No one swears by a transgression" ("The Oaths of Amos 8.14," in *Priesthood and Cult in Ancient Israel* [ed. G. A. Anderson and S. M. Olyan; JSOTSup 125; Sheffield: JSOT Press, 1991] 149). This objection still obtains where the oath is attributed to the creative activity of a school of Amos (as in the interpretation of Wolff, *Joel and Amos*, 328). Alternatively, Rudolph, noting a similar sense of intended irony in the passage, suggests that "the

that reconciles its occurrence as an ostensible divine designation with its use elsewhere is a further problem of interpretation. The apparent use of the expression as a divine epithet in at least one instance suggests that in the other passages, too, the phrase may be more than a mere poetic flourish. In any case, a reexamination of these passages is warranted both for their own sake and in the hopes of shedding some light on the meaning and significance of *gě'ôn ya'ăqōb* as a designation of the divine. Related to this discussion is the question of whether the expression had an original "Northern" orientation or whether it may have belonged to religious and political traditions associated with Jerusalem. In any case, a coherent explanation that accounts for all occurrences of the expression is needed.

The Noun *ga'ôn* in Biblical Hebrew

One might begin by considering the first element of the expression, the noun *gā'ôn*. This term, which is derived from the third-weak root *g'w/y* "to rise, to be high or exalted"[9] can often have the negative sense of inappropriate pride (Job 35:12; Ps 59:13; Prov 8:13; 16:18; Isa 13:11; 16:6; Jer 48:29; Zeph 2:10). Alternatively, it can refer to pomp or majesty without a necessarily pejorative connotation (Isa 14:11; Ezek 7:20; Job 38:11). This latter sense is best illustrated in instances in which *gā'ôn* refers to the majestic power of Israel's god (Job 37:4; 40:10), which insures security for his people (Isa 24:14; Mic 5:3) and evokes terror from his enemies (Exod 15:7; Isa 2:10, 19, 21).

In some instances the term is used figuratively for an object or feature of prominence. Thus *gě'ôn hayyardēn* "the pride of the Jordan" refers to the thick, lush vegetation along the banks of the river (Jer 12:5; 49:19; 50:44; Zech 11:3). Similarly, in Lev 26:19–20 the construct expression *gě'ôn 'uzzěkem*, "the pride of your might," is used in connection with the agricultural productivity of Israel's land.

Gā'ôn occurs most frequently in association with cities. Jer 13:9 speaks of "the pride of Judah and the great pride of Jerusalem" (*'et-gě'ôn yěhûdâ wě'et-gě'ôn yěrûšālaim hārāb*). In an oracle against Jerusalem, Ezekiel reminds the personified city of her bygone time of affluence and security with the expression *yôm gě'ônāyik* "the day of your pride" (16:56). Likewise, in v. 49 the *gā'ôn* of

Pride of Jacob" refers both to might and affluence as a source of inappropriate pride and to Yahweh as the rightful source of the people's pride. While this explanation accounts for the expression's use with both a divine and a non-divine referent in Amos, it fails to account for the instances in Ps 47:5 and Nah 2:3.

9. As are the nouns *gē'â*, *ga'ăwâ*, *gē'ût*, and *gēwâ*, which overlap *gā'ôn* in its various nuances in meaning.

Jerusalem's "sister" Sodom is linked with "abundance of food and prosperous ease," all of which the city is condemned for possessing without helping the poor and the orphan.

The book of Ezekiel uses the construct expression *gĕʾôn ʿōz* "pride of might" in reference to cities and to prominent features of cities.[10] Ezek 30:6–7 predicts

> *wĕnāpĕlû sōmĕkê miṣrayim wĕyārad gĕʾôn ʿuzzāh*
> *mimmigdōl sĕwēnâ[11] baḥereb yippĕlû-bāh nĕʾum ʾădōnāy yhwh*
> *wĕnāšammû bĕtôk ʾărāṣôt nĕšammôt wĕʿārāyw bĕtôk-ʿarîm naḥărābôt tihyeynâ*

"The ones supporting Egypt will fall, and the pride of its might will go down; from Migdol to Syene, those within it shall fall by the sword," says the Lord Yahweh.

"They shall be devastated among devastated lands; its cities shall be among desolate cities."

Here *gĕʾôn ʿuzzāh* "the pride of [Egypt's] might" parallels "the ones supporting Egypt," that is, its fortified cities "from Migdol to Syene"—a merism standing not only for these two fortress towns at the northern and southern extent of the country, respectively, but also for all the fortified towns throughout Egypt. The passage goes on to describe the anticipated destruction of cities and strongholds throughout the land of Egypt (vv. 13–17). In v. 18, the expression *gĕʾôn ʿuzzāh* is used again in describing the defeat of the Egyptian border fortress city Tahpanhes. The verse elaborates on the city's defeat: "a cloud will cover it, and its daughter towns will go into exile."

This expression is used in Ezek 7:24 to describe the anticipated attack by foreign armies on the Jerusalem temple. In this passage Yahweh is quoted to say concerning his people:

> *wĕhišbattî gĕʾôn ʿuzzām[12] wĕniḥălû miqdĕšêhem*

I will bring to an end the pride of their might; their sanctuary[13] will be taken as a possession.

---

10. See Lev 26:19, mentioned above, in which *gĕʾôn ʿuzzĕkem* refers to the productivity of the land.

11. The syntax of this phrase both here and in 29:10 suggests that the final *he* is directive, as reflected in the LXX (*heōs suēnēs*).

12. Here and with *miqdĕšêhem*, following the reading reflected in the LXX.

13. See other passages in which the Jerusalem temple is denoted by *miqdāš* in the plural: *ben-ʾādām śîm pānêkā ʾel-yĕrûšālaim wĕhaṭṭēp ʾel-miqdāšîm* "Mortal, set your face toward Jerusalem, and let your speech flow toward the sanctuary" (Ezek 21:7); *miqdĕšê bêt yhwh* "the sanctuary of the house of Yahweh" (Jer 51:51). The plural form may indicate the composite nature of the temple complex.

In this instance, the prominent urban feature referenced by *gĕʾôn ʿōz* is the Jerusalem temple. Immediately following the account of Ezekiel's receiving both word of Jerusalem's fall and the restoration of his ability to speak (33:21–22), an oracle is presented describing utter devastation throughout the land upon Jerusalem's destruction (vv. 23–29). Along with the statements that Yahweh "will make the land a desolation and a waste" and that "the hills of Israel will be desolate, without anyone passing through them," this oracle includes the assertion *wĕnišbat gĕʾôn ʿuzzāh* "the pride of its might will be brought to an end" (v. 28). Our same construct expression is found in the related, earlier passage, in which, following the death of the prophet's wife, his speech is taken away and Jerusalem's fall is predicted (24:15–27); there we find the following statement attributed to Yahweh:

> *hinnî mĕhallēl ʾet-miqdāšî gĕʾôn ʿuzzĕkem mahmad ʿênêkem ûmahmal napšĕkem*
>
> I myself will defile my sanctuary, the pride of your might, the object of your eyes' desire and your life's compassion. (v. 21)

In this passage, it is clear that for Judah "the pride of your might" (*gĕʾôn ʿuzzĕkem*) is the Jerusalem temple itself, the anticipated violation of which will be central to the devastation and dismay of Yahweh's people upon the fall of their capital. Verse 25 quotes Yahweh further in describing the fall of his people's capital city as

> *yôm qahtî mēhem ʾet-māʿuzzām mĕśôś tipʾartām ʾet-mahmad ʿênêhem wĕʾet-maśśāʾ napšām*
>
> the day on which I take from them their stronghold, the exultation of their glory, the desire of their eyes, the uplifting of their life.

The same kind of language of desire and yearning that was used specifically in reference to the temple in v. 21 is found here more broadly in connection with the whole of Jerusalem, with emphasis on its strength and security as a fortified city. Within this passage (24:15–27), the construct expression *gĕʾôn ʿōz* is used in connection with Jerusalem's temple and fortifications, prominent features of the city.

Gāʾôn is used in prophetic descriptions of a new Jerusalem. In Isaiah 4, which predicts a restored Jerusalem that has been purged of iniquity by Yahweh's cleansing judgment, the "pride and splendor" (*lĕgāʾôn ûlĕtipʾeret*) of the city's surviving inhabitants will not be any feature of the city itself but the "fruit of the land" (*pĕrî hāʾāres*, v. 2). In this renewed Jerusalem, the typically urban features of the once disobedient city are replaced by more pastoral ones as points of pride, a motif consistent with the reference to agricultural bounty as *gĕʾôn ʿōz in Lev 26:19–20 (mentioned above). The portrayal of a gloriously restored Jerusalem in Isaiah 60 includes the promise that the city will become gĕʾôn ʿôlām "a pride everlasting" (v. 15). Here as in other instances, the noun gāʾôn designates prominent cities and the features of these cities that make them prominent.

The noun's association with cities is even more impressive in a number of construct expressions following the pattern gĕʾôn X "the Pride of X," which are used in designating prominent foreign capitals. In Zech 10:11, the fall of Nineveh is recalled in archetypal fashion with the statement that "the Pride of Assyria shall be brought down" (wĕhûrad gĕʾôn ʾaššûr).[14] Isa 13:19 calls Babylon tipʾeret gĕʾôn kaśdîm "the Splendor of the Pride of the Chaldeans." In Zech 9:5–6, gĕʾôn pĕlištîm "the Pride of the Philistines" is used in parallel with Ashdod, Ashkelon, Gaza, and Ekron, members of the Philistine pentapolis. In Isa 23:9, Tyre is called gĕʾôn kol ṣĕbî "the Pride of all Beauty." In Ezekiel 32, a "lament over Pharaoh the king of Egypt" (v. 2) predicts that invading Babylonian troops will "despoil the Pride of Egypt; all of its crowd will be annihilated" (wĕšādĕdû ʾet-gĕʾôn miṣrayim wĕnišmad kol-hămônāh, v. 12).[15]

As these passages demonstrate, the noun gāʾôn is frequently used in reference to prominent cities and features of cities—especially defenses, and, in the case of Jerusalem, the temple. Whether the focus is the "pride" of the city or the city itself as the "pride" of the nation and its people, a persistent association of the noun gāʾôn with cities is to be observed. In this connection, it is useful to bear in mind the full semantic range of gāʾôn, which is conveniently translated "pride" here but, rooted as it is in the sense of being "high" or "lofty," can also in the appropriate context be rendered "exaltation" or "majesty." This sense is most fitting in connection with ancient cities in general, which were ideally—for purposes of defensibility, among other things—situated in elevated, hilltop locations. More specifically, the royal connotations thus conveyed would be compatible with the designation of capitals by expressions following the pattern gĕʾôn X, which could thus be rendered "the *Majesty* of X." The recognition of gāʾôn's persistent association with cities and these related considerations provide an obvious framework of associations within which to understand the expression gĕʾôn yaʿăqōb. That is to say, one might consider whether our expression functions as a city designation in one or any of its occurrences. To that end, a closer look at the relevant passages is warranted.

14. Here "the Pride of Assyria" is paralleled by "the Scepter of Egypt" (šēbeṭ miṣrayim); see the reference to Jerusalem as the "Scepter of Judah" (šēbeṭ yĕhûdâ) in Ps 78:68.

15. The verbs in this passage are often used to describe the destruction of cities—šdd: Ar (Isa 15:1), Kir (15:1), Tyre (23:10), Nebo (Jer 48:1), Heshbon (49:3), Nineveh (Nah 3:7); šmd: the cities of Israel (Mic 5:13), the strongholds of Canaan (Isa 23:11).

A Closer Examination of *gě'ôn ya'ăqōb*

Amos 6:8

Amos 6 presents a condemnation of "the House of Israel" (vv. 1, 14)—that is, of the Northern Israelite Kingdom, and of its leadership in the capital, "those who feel secure on Mount Samaria" (*habbōṭěḥîm běhar šōmrōn*, v. 1).[16] After an unfavorable comparison with other kingdoms and their capitals in v. 2—Calneh, Hamath, and "Gath of the Philistines"—the passage offers a vivid description of the unconcerned affluence and self-absorption that characterize the lifestyle of the royal city's elite, "those who lie on beds of ivory . . . who drink from bowls of wine and anoint themselves with the finest of oils but are not sickened by the breaking of Joseph" (vv. 4–6). This disdainful description culminates in Yahweh's pronouncement of judgment by the following oath (v. 8):

> *mětā'ēb 'ānōkî 'et-gě'ôn ya'ăqōb*
> *wě'arměnōtāyw śānē'tî*
> *wěhisgartî 'îr ûmělō'āh*

I abhor[17] the pride of Jacob;
I hate its strongholds;
I will deliver up the city and that which fills it.

Quite clearly, "the city" mentioned here is none other than the capital itself. Accordingly, the term *gā'ôn* (the basic meaning of which, as mentioned above, has to do with being "high" or "exalted") in the sense both of physical loftiness and of royal prominence is most fitting as part of an epithet for "Mount Samaria." With its hilltop setting, fortifications, impressive buildings, and overall opulence as described in Amos 6, Samaria was quite worthy of the designation.

---

16. It is debatable whether or not the mention of Zion in v. 1 is original to the passage (1:2a notwithstanding); either way, the references to "Mount Samaria" (v. 1), "House of Israel" (vv. 1, 14), and "Joseph" (v. 6) make clear that the focus of the passage—as is the case for the book as a whole (see 2:6–16)—is the Northern Israelite Kingdom and its capital.

17. That MT *mětā'ēb* stands in place of original *mt'b* "abhor, loath," which is reflected in the versions (e.g., LXX *bdelussomai*), is borne out by the parallelism between *t'b* and *śn'* elsewhere in the text (5:10). Any one of a number of explanations would account for the MT reading: *mt'b* as a biform of *mt'b* (cf. *g'l* for *g'l* "to be defiled, polluted" in Isa 59:3; Zeph 3:1; Mal 1:7; Lam 4:14; see Rudolph, *Joel-Amos-Obadja-Jona*, 222; Paul, *Amos*, 213 n. 4); aural scribal error due to the weakening of gutturals (see Paul, ibid.; note, again, the *g'l* = *g'l* interchange in the passages cited); or deliberate scribal "correction" (Theodor Nöldeke, *Neue Beiträge zur semitischen Sprachwissenschaft* [Strassburg: Trübner, 1910] 69; Wolff, *Joel and Amos*, 281–82).

Of course, Samaria's majesty in terms of its physical impressiveness was interrelated with its importance as a political and religious center. Samaria served as the Northern Israelite royal capital from the time of its founding by Omri and became an important religious center as well. The books of 1 and 2 Kings mention a "temple of Baal" (*bêt habbaʿal*) built there by Ahab and later destroyed in Jehu's purge (1 Kgs 16:32; 2 Kgs 10:18–27). The existence of a prominent sanctuary in Samaria in the eighth century is implied by the series of oaths cited in Amos 8:14, which mentions Samaria in parallel with the sanctuary sites Dan and Beer-sheba.[18] Central to Micah's description of the coming fall of the city of Samaria is the smashing of its divine images (1:6–7), an act that figures prominently in Assyrian descriptions of the pillaging of foreign cities and their temples.[19] That Samaria was a principal location where, in characteristically Northern Israelite fashion, Yahweh was worshiped in connection with tauromorphic imagery is implied by reference to the "bull of Samaria" in Hos 8:5, 6.[20] The inscriptional mention of "Yahweh of Samaria" at Kuntillet ʿAjrud[21] would seem to suggest that the Northern capital was a major worship center for the deity.[22] In its grandeur as the foremost city of the Northern Israelite Kingdom, Samaria was known as "the big sister" of Jerusalem (Ezek 16:46) and "the head of Ephraim" (Isa 7:9). Thus its designation as "the Pride of Jacob" was most appropriate.

---

18. The existence of a cult sanctuary at Beer-sheba is indicated not only by the dismantled horned altar excavated there but also by the reference in Amos 5:5 to Beer-sheba (along with Bethel and Gilgal) as a worship site and by the mention in 2 Kgs 23:8 of a "high place" there that was destroyed by Josiah; see Amiḥai Mazar, *Archaeology of the Land of the Bible: 10,000–586 B.C.E.* (New York: Doubleday, 1992) 495–96; see also Olyan, "The Oaths of Amos 8.14," 136–38.

19. For references to the Assyrians' pillaging and destroying divine statues of defeated enemies, see Morton Cogan, *Imperialism and Religion: Assyria, Judah and Israel in the Eighth and Seventh Centuries B.C.E.* (SBLMS 19; Missoula, Mont.: Scholars Press, 1974) 22–41.

20. See also Hos 10:5, which refers to the bull of Beth-aven (literally, "House of wickedness," a slur for Bethel; see 4:15). The Deuteronomist's description of Jeroboam's installment of bull statues for worship at Bethel and Dan appears to be paradigmatic for the whole of the Northern Kingdom throughout its history (1 Kgs 12:27–33; 2 Kgs 10:29; 17:16). The relative dearth of information regarding worship in Samaria (or any other aspect of Samaria, for that matter) in Dtr, while in one respect surprising, is understandable in light of this source's preoccupation with the altar of Bethel, whose dismantlement in Josiah's reform was roughly contemporary with the composition of Dtr[1] (1 Kgs 16:24; cf. 1 Kgs 12:32–13:32; 2 Kgs 23:15–20).

21. Z. Meshel, "Kuntillet ʿAjrud," *ABD* 4.107.

22. As Olyan explains, this datum is decisive evidence for the existence of a Yahwistic sanctuary in Samaria; Saul M. Olyan, *Asherah and the Cult of Yahweh in Israel* (SBLMS 34; Atlanta: Scholars Press, 1988) 34–35.

We may now consider whether the use of *gěʾôn yaʿăqōb* as a designation for a city, specifically Samaria, in Amos 6:8 sheds light on the expression's meaning in other passages. I will return to the other occurrence of *gěʾôn yaʿăqōb* in the book of Amos (8:7) after considering the other relevant passages.

Nahum 2:3

The book of Nahum opens with its introduction as "an oracle concerning Nineveh" (1:1). Into the elaborate description of the fall of the city in chap. 2, a comment has been inserted, contrasting the scene of Nineveh's devastation with the restoration of *gěʾôn yaʿăqōb* (v. 3).[23] In the fullest sense of poetic justice, the point of this contrast seems to be that the destruction of Assyria and its capital Nineveh brings about the restoration of "the Pride of Jacob." If the expression here is an epithet for Samaria, as it clearly is in Amos 6:8, then the specific contrast implied would be that between the anticipated restoration of the desolate city of Samaria and the devastation of the capital of its conqueror, so vividly portrayed in Nahum 2. The immediate context of this passage and that of the book as a whole, centering as they do on the Assyrian capital, provide the appropriate framework within which to understand the intended meaning of the parenthetical remark in 2:3. This meaning would seem to be that the violent end befalling Nineveh is to be mirrored in an equally dramatic but positive reversal of fortunes for Samaria, namely, the recovery of the city's prominent existence. Thus in Nah 2:3, as in Amos 6:8, "the Pride of Jacob" serves as a designation for the Northern Israelite capital, Samaria.

In this passage, *gěʾôn yaʿăqōb* is accompanied by the expression *gěʾôn yiśrāʾēl*. The latter occurs elsewhere only in Hos 5:5 and 7:10, where it is mentioned in parallel with Ephraim (5:5) and in the context of "the wickedness of Samaria" (7:1). While more will be said below regarding the precise nuance of "the pride of Israel" in these Hosea passages, one might safely conclude at this point in the discussion that it is a variant of "the Pride of Jacob."[24]

---

23. See Roberts's (*Nahum, Habakkuk, and Zephaniah*, 64–65) dismissal of the interpolation as a later parroting of "older prophetic motifs and expressions."

24. See the comments of Roberts, *Nahum, Habakkuk, and Zephaniah*, 65; compare the claim by Maier (*The Book of Nahum*, 227–28) that in Nah 2:3 "Jacob" denotes Judah, and "Israel" refers to the Northern Kingdom. While on occasion "the house of Jacob" may have the Southern Kingdom of Judah as its referent (e.g., Jer 5:20), whenever "Jacob" and "Israel" occur together, they tend to be synonymous variants and not opposites within the frame of reference of the divided monarchy; see the passages cited by Maier.

Psalm 47:5

The next occurrence of *gĕʾôn yaʿăqōb* to be discussed is Ps 47:5, which reads

> *yibḥar-lānû ʾet-naḥălātô*
> *ʾet gĕʾôn yaʿăqōb ʾăšer-ʾāhēb*
>
> He (Yahweh) has chosen for us his inheritance,
> the Pride of Jacob, which he loves. [25]

That "the Pride of Jacob" in this psalm refers to Jerusalem may be inferred from Ps 78:68, a passage that is strikingly similar to 47:5 in its formulation:

> *wayyibḥar ʾet šēbeṭ yĕhûdâ*
> *ʾet-har ṣiyyôn ʾăšer ʾāhēb*
>
> And he has chosen the tribe of Judah,
> Mount Zion, which he loves.

The parallels in form and phraseology in these passages, especially the use of prefixed forms of *bḥr* and the phrase *ʾăšer ʾāhēb* in the same place in both texts, would make "the Pride of Jacob" in Ps 47:5 the equivalent of "Mount Zion" in Ps 78:68. As in the identification of "Mount Samaria" by this expression in Amos 6:8, the designation of Jerusalem as "the Pride of Jacob" would be in keeping with the use of the noun *gāʾôn* in the identification of cities, especially in construct expressions of the pattern *gĕʾôn* X. While the possibility suggested by this parallel (i.e., that "the Pride of Jacob" in this passage refers to Jerusalem) is quite plausible, uncertainty regarding the literary and historical relationship between these two passages calls for restraint in making conclusions based on the parallel alone.

---

25. The only textual issue for the verse is a relatively simple one, namely, the choice of the reading *naḥălātô*—which is reflected in the LXX and the Syriac and which, as Roberts points out ("The Religio-political Setting of Psalm 47," 130), is commended by the thematic and verbal correspondence with Deut 32:8–9 and Psalm 82 (see also other references to Yahweh's "inheritance," e.g., Jer 2:7; 16:18, and other examples to be discussed below)—in preference to *naḥălātēnû* in the MT, which is easily explained as a scribal error triggered by the 1st-person common pl. pronominal suffix in the preceding word. The rest of the verse, as represented by the MT and the other textual witnesses, is textually and grammatically without problems. Regarding Roberts's contention of a stylistic difficulty in the verse (ibid., 130 and n. 9), it may be observed that wherever *bāḥar* is used (as in this verse) with a direct object and an indirect object prefixed by the preposition *l-*, it is usually the *indirect* object that precedes the direct object (and not vice versa); the only exceptions involve syntactic or grammatical constructions not analogous to the one in Ps 47:5: Job 34:4, in which the verb is a passive *Niphal*; 1 Sam 2:28, in which the verb is an infinitive absolute; 8:18, in a relative clause in which the direct object is represented by the heading particle *ʾăšer*; and Ps 135:4, in which the direct object is placed before the verb for emphasis.

However, the preliminary conclusion that *gěʾôn yaʿăqōb* in Ps 47:5 is a designation for Jerusalem may be tested by considering the term with which it is in apposition in 47:5, namely, (Yahweh's) *naḥălâ* "inheritance." The appositional relationship between the two makes *gěʾôn yaʿăqōb* an identification for Yahweh's *naḥălâ*.[26] Elsewhere in the Hebrew Bible, Yahweh's *naḥălâ* refers to the land of Israel or to the Israelites in that land as Yahweh's inalienable possession.[27] According to Deut 32:8–9, when Elyon "apportioned the nations as an inheritance," "divided humankind," and "established the boundaries of the peoples according to the number of the gods,"[28] Jacob was assigned to Yahweh as *ḥebel naḥălātô* "the measured portion of his inheritance." The heavy use of territorial terminology (*gěbūlōt, ḥēleq, ḥebel*) in this passage indicates that, along with the population, the land is also in view.[29] Precluding any understanding of *naḥălâ* in Ps 47:5 as being in reference to the people is the simple fact that the term is in reference not to "Jacob" but to "*the Pride of Jacob*."[30] This meaning is in keeping with a primarily territorial sense of the *naḥălâ* of Yahweh in a number of other passages, especially those employing the construct expression *naḥălat yhwh/ʾĕlōhîm*, which always refers to Israelite territory as Yahweh's

26. For the relevant points in the discussion of apposition, see Bruce K. Waltke and M. O'Connor, *An Introduction to Biblical Hebrew Syntax* (Winona Lake, Ind.: Eisenbrauns, 1990) 12.1–5, esp. 12.3e; GKC §131f–h; Paul Joüon and T. Muraoka, *A Grammar of Biblical Hebrew* (Subsidia biblica 14/1; Rome: Pontifical Biblical Institute, 1993) §131h, i, k.

27. See the discussions by Gerhard von Rad, "Verheissenes Land und Jahwes Land im Hexateuch," *ZDPV* 66 (1943) 191–204; Friedrich Horst, "Zwei Begriffe für Eigentum (Besitz): נַחֲלָה und אֲחֻזָּה," in *Verbannung und Heimkehr: Beiträge zur Geschichte und Theologie Israels im 6. und 5. Jahrhundert v. Chr.* (ed. A. Kuschke; Tübingen: Mohr, 1961) 135–56; Herbert Chanan Brichto, "Kin, Cult, Land and Afterlife: A Biblical Complex," *HUCA* 44 (1973) 1–50; Samuel E. Loewenstamm, "*nḥlt yhwh*," in *Studies in Bible, 1986* (ed. S. Japhet; Scripta Hierosolymitana 31; Jerusalem: Magnes, 1986) 155–92; E. Lipiński, "נָחַל *nāḥal*, נַחֲלָה *naḥălâ*," *TDOT* 9.330–33. The biblical and extrabiblical evidence (especially evidence from Mari) related to *naḥălâ* indicates that at its basis the term refers to an inalienable estate of land conferred either through inheritance along lines of kinship or as royal land grant (see Horst, "Zwei Begriffe für Eigentum," 152; Abraham Malamat, "Pre-Monarchical Social Institutions in Israel in the Light of Mari," *History of Biblical Israel: Major Problems and Minor Issues* [Leiden: Brill, 2001] 36–40; cf. Harold D. Forshey, "The Construct Chain *naḥălat yhwh/ʾĕlōhîm*," *BASOR* 220 [1975] 51–53; see also Bernard F. Batto, "Land Tenure and Women at Mari," *JESHO* 23 [1983] 209–39, esp. 227–29).

28. Following the reading *bny ʾlwhym* attested in 4QDeutʲ and implied by *aggelōn theou* in the LXX.

29. See, for example, Ps 105:11 (= 1 Chr 16:18): *lěkā ʾettēn ʾet-ʾereṣ-kěnāʿan ḥebel naḥălatkem* "To you I have given the land of Canaan as the measured portion of your inheritance." Cf. Loewenstamm, "*nḥlt yhwh*," 186; Horst, "Zwei Begriffe für Eigentum," 142.

30. Cf. Roberts, "The Religio-political Setting of Psalm 47," 129–30.

inalienable possession (1 Sam 26:19; 2 Sam 14:16; 20:19; 21:3).[31] In 2 Sam
20:19, the expression is applied to the city of Abel Beth-Maacah—which apparently had long stood as a large and significant city ("a mother in Israel")
near Israel's northern border—not as an epithet unique to the city but as an
identification of it as part of the greater *naḥălat yhwh*.[32] What stands out about
this passage is that the expression *naḥălat yhwh*, which usually denotes the
whole of Yahweh's special land, is used in designating a specific and special
part of that land.

The broader religious context for our understanding of Yahweh's "inheritance" can be found in West Semitic mythic tradition, in which the term has a
special significance in designating the landed holdings of a deity or a special
part of that territory. All of the occurrences of the noun *nḥlt* in Ugaritic are in
reference to the territorial possessions of various gods: *arṣ nḥlth* "the land of his
inheritance," designating the domains of Mot (*KTU* 1.4 VIII 13–14; 1.5 II 16)
and of Kothar (*KTU* 1.3 VI 16) and *ǵr nḥlty* "the mountain of my inheritance"
in reference to Baal's abode on Zaphon (*KTU* 1.3 III 30; 1.3 IV 20).[33] In the
same way, Yahweh's *naḥălâ* is to be understood as his special place of possession, within which he dwells. The use of the term "inheritance" in connection

---

31. While in 2 Sam 14:16 and 21:3 the people may be implied along with the land, in
each case the primary referent is the land; cf. Forshey, "The Construct Chain *naḥălat
yhwh/ʾĕlōhîm*," 51–53; Horst, "Zwei Begriffe für Eigentum," 142. Compare further Loewenstamm ("*nḥlt yhwh*," 159–61), who objects to distinguishing either land or people as
primary in at least one of these passages (2 Sam 14:16). Compare further the different understanding of the last passage offered by Theodore J. Lewis ("The Ancestral Estate [נַחֲלַת
אֱלֹהִים) in 2 Samuel 14:16," *JBL* 110 [1991] 597–612), who proposes understanding *ʾĕlōhîm*
in this instance according to its occasionally-attested meaning "the dead" (see, e.g., 1 Sam
28:13). Working against this interpretation, for which Lewis makes an otherwise thorough
and compelling case, is the occurrence of *ʾĕlōhîm* with the meaning of God five other times
in this passage, all in the speech of the woman from Tekoa. Among these instances is a reference to Israel under David as the "people of God" (*ʿam ʾĕlōhîm*, v. 13; see also vv. 11, 14,
17 [2x]), an expression which, in view of the connections between *ʿam* and *naḥălâ*—as discussed in the bibliography cited here—favors a compatible meaning for *naḥălat ʾĕlōhîm*.
Nonetheless, the passage, along with the argument-by-analogy it presents, are at best vague
in places (especially v. 14), and it may involve a deliberate play on different meanings of *ʾĕlōhîm*, which would potentially be consistent with the cogent explanation Lewis offers. In any
case, the meaning of *naḥălâ* as irrevocable landed possession and the implications of that
meaning for the expression *naḥălat yhwh* are borne out in Lewis's thorough discussion of the
term and in previous scholarship treating it; see especially pp. 597–600, 605–9.

32. On this instance of *naḥălat yhwh* being "confined to a specific domain," see Malamat, "Pre-Monarchical Social Institutions," 38–39.

33. This observation is made by Richard J. Clifford, *The Cosmic Mountain in Canaan and
the Old Testament* (HSM 4; Cambridge: Harvard University Press, 1972) 69–71.

both with the broader realm of the deity and with a more delimited location within that realm is found in Ugaritic myth, where Kothar's "land of inheritance" (*arṣ nḥlth*) is in poetic parallel with "the throne on which he sits" (*ksu ṯbth*, *KTU* 1.3 VI 16). Furthermore, Mot's "land of inheritance" (*arṣ nḥlth*) is paralleled not only with "the throne on which he sits" (*ksu ṯbth*) but also with "his city" (*qrth*, *KTU* 1.4 VIII 11–13; 1.5 II 15–16). According to the mythic conceptualization expressed in these passages, the deity's "inheritance" is, properly speaking, the place of his enthronement and, by extension, the surrounding territory.[34] In striking similarity to the descriptions of the abodes of Ugaritic Mot and Kothar, Psalm 47's reference to Yahweh's "inheritance" is intimately linked to his dwelling "on his sacred throne" (*yāšab ʿal-kissēʾ qodšô*, v. 9). What one might infer from Ps 47:5, 9 in isolation is reinforced by the Ugaritic parallels: namely, that as Yahweh's place of enthronement, his "inheritance" in v. 5 refers to a specified location in relation to which a more extended domain might be defined.

Even further light is shed on Yahweh's *naḥălâ* in Psalm 47 by the discussion of a passage that is crucial to any discussion of Yahweh's "inheritance," the Song of the Sea (Exod 15:1–18). The designation of Baal's dwelling on Zaphon as *ǵr nḥlty* "the mountain of my inheritance" (*KTU* 1.3 III 30; 1.3 IV 20, mentioned above) has an exact parallel in this ancient Hebrew poem, which refers to Yahweh's possession and place of dwelling as *har naḥălātĕkā* "the mountain of your inheritance" (v. 17). The parallel belongs to a larger mythic pattern attested in Ugaritic and early Hebrew poetry, the basic elements of which are described by Cross as follows: "(1) the combat of the Divine Warrior and his victory at the Sea, (2) the building of a sanctuary on the 'mount

---

34. The broader mythic concept is rightly articulated by Horst in connection with these Ugaritic passages and is brought to bear on Exod 15:1–18 (to be discussed below); Horst, "Zwei Begriffe für Eigentum," 141. The part of Horst's explanation to which Loewenstamm ("*nḥlt yhwh*," 168) objects is dependent on their shared identification of Yahweh's "mount of inheritance" in Exod 15:17 as Zion, an identification that is to be rejected; see below. Slightly different are the possible implications of Clements's explanation that in West Semitic ("Canaanite") religion the god's ownership of the larger territory is expressed in the metaphor of enthronement, which is associated with a specified location within that land (*God and Temple* [Philadelphia: Fortress, 1965] 11, 52–53). Within Clements's larger discussion, this specifically West Semitic notion of enthronement is not necessarily dependent on or implied by the mythic and cultic conceptualization of the cosmic mountain, which Clements identifies as an important feature of the religion of the broader ancient Near East. On the idea of the cosmic mountain in West Semitic religion, see Clifford (*The Cosmic Mountain*) and, following him, Jon D. Levenson, *Sinai and Zion: An Entry into the Jewish Bible* (Minneapolis: Winston, 1985) 130–36.

of possession' won in battle, and (3) the god's manifestation of 'eternal' king-ship."[35] The Divine Warrior's "mountain of inheritance" won in battle is de-scribed by Cross as "the special seat of the deity, either his cosmic shrine or its earthly counterpart."[36] That Yahweh's "mountain of inheritance" refers to a specific shrine is clear from its description as his "abode of holiness" (*nĕwê qod-šekā*, v. 13);[37] the *mqdš* "holy place/sanctuary" "established" by Yahweh's own "hands," and as "the established place for your dwelling, that you, Yahweh, have made" (*mākôn lĕšibtĕkā pāʿaltā yhwh*);[38] from which "Yahweh will reign forever and ever" (*yhwh yimlōk lĕʿōlām wāʿed*, v. 18).[39] In this regard, the ex-pression's use in Exodus 15 corresponds to its Ugaritic counterpart, in which Baal's "mountain of inheritance" is associated with his "holy (place)/sanctu-ary" (*qdš*, KTU 1.3 III 30; 1.3 IV 20). Within the Divine Warrior tradition, the earthly form of the deity's place of dwelling and enthronement won in battle, that is, of his "mountain of inheritance," is the hill of his sanctuary. Thus Yahweh's *har naḥălâ* in Exod 15:17 is to be understood as a specific sanc-tuary site.

A dimension of the Song of the Sea that goes beyond the Divine Warrior tradition is that the deity shares his triumph and rewards with his special people. Through his victory at the sea, Yahweh "redeems" his people (v. 13). In establishing his "mountain of inheritance" as his dwelling, he not only takes up residence there himself but also "plants" his people in that place (v. 17). All of this is carried out at the expense of the other nations, beginning with Egypt and then with the enemies surrounding Israel, who are summarily cowed by Yahweh's might so that his people may "pass by" unharmed (v. 16). The priv-ileging of the Divine Warrior's special people is thus described within the

35. Frank Moore Cross, Jr., *Canaanite Myth and Hebrew Epic: Essays in the History of the Religion of Israel* (Cambridge: Harvard University Press, 1973) 142.

36. Idem, "The Song of the Sea and Canaanite Myth," *JTC* 5 (1968) 23.

37. Early on Frank Moore Cross, Jr., and David Noel Freedman ("The Song of Mi-riam," *JNES* 14 [1955] 240, 248) understood this expression as a reference to Yahweh's desert sanctuary, an interpretation developed by Freedman ("Early Israelite History in the Light of Early Israelite Poetry," in *Unity and Diversity: Essays in the History, Literature, and Religion of the Ancient Near East* [ed. H. Goedicke and J. J. M. Roberts; Baltimore: Johns Hopkins University Press, 1975] 6–8); see also Cross, *Canaanite Myth and Hebrew Epic*, 142. See the reference in Ps 93:5 to Yahweh's Temple (*bêtĕkā*) as *nwh qdš* (4QPsb).

38. In the description of Solomon's dedication of the temple in Jerusalem, similar lan-guage (*mĕkôn šibtekā*) is used to describe both Yahweh's heavenly dwelling place (1 Kgs 8:39, 43, 49 = 2 Chr 6:30, 33, 39) and the sanctuary built as its earthly counterpart (1 Kgs 8:13 = 2 Chr 6:2): *haššāmayim mĕkôn šibtekā* (1 Kgs 8:39, 43, 49 = 2 Chr 6:30, 33, 39).

39. Cross, "The Song of the Sea and Canaanite Myth," 24; idem, *Canaanite Myth and Hebrew Epic*, 142.

framework of the old mythic pattern. "Settlement" is implied here only to the degree that Yahweh himself settles on the mountain of his sanctuary, this in accordance with the Divine Warrior tradition.[40] Thus the oft-suggested understanding of *har naḥălātĕkā* as having a dual meaning, according to which it is said to denote not only the sanctuary site but also the land of Canaan west of the Jordan (hence, "the *hill country* of your inheritance"), while possible, is not necessary.[41] What is beyond doubt, as observed above, is that Yahweh's "mountain of inheritance" designates a specific shrine location.

A number of possibilities have been suggested for the identification of the site in question. The frequently encountered view that Yahweh's mount and sanctuary referenced in the Song of the Sea is Zion is inconsistent with the early date of the poem.[42] Freedman understands a reference to a desert sanctuary at

---

40. The conquest and settlement traditions include neither Edom (v. 15) nor Philistia (v. 14), the latter being explicitly excluded in Josh 11:22 and 13:2–3; cf. 15:45–47, which reflects subsequent Judean territorial claims (v. 63).

41. For the suggestion that both ideas are present, see, e.g., Malamat, "Pre-Monarchical Social Institutions," 39; Lipiński, *TDOT* 9.330; Cross, *Canaanite Myth and Hebrew Epic*, 142. The presence of both ideas is reconciled alternatively in an explanation offered by Wellhausen and later Noth that this passage refers to the whole of Canaan as Yahweh's dwelling or sanctuary; however, as Clements (*God and Temple*, 52 n. 2) points out, this idea is not stated as such elsewhere in the Hebrew Bible. Similarly, Levenson (*Sinai and Zion*, 136), based on the semantic ambiguity of *har* "hill/hill country" suggests that in the passage the entire land is understood as the deity's mountain abode, from which Israel's god rules the cosmos. While the sacred mountain is often depicted as being central for his people and for the other nations, the equation of the broader land and the sacred mountain, in any sense, does not seem to find support elsewhere in the Hebrew Bible or in the Ugaritic texts. Compare the understanding of the expression as referring solely to the land as a whole and not to a specific site (as expressed in J. J. M. Roberts, "The Davidic Origin of the Zion Tradition," *JBL* 92 [1973] 343).

42. Those who claim a reference to Zion in Exodus 15 include Clements, *God and Temple*, 52–55; Horst, "Zwei Begriffe für Eigentum," 141; Jörg Jeremias ("Lade und Zion: Zur Entstehung der Ziontradition," in *Probleme biblischer Theologie* [ed. H. W. Wolff; Munich: Chr. Kaiser, 1971] 196–97; Loewenstamm, "*nḥlt yhwh*," 166–70; Malamat, "Pre-Monarchical Social Institutions," 39. The arguments dating the poem's composition to premonarchic times (see William Foxwell Albright, *Yahweh and the Gods of Canaan: A Historical Analysis of Two Contrasting Faiths* [London: School of Oriental and African Studies, University of London: 1968; repr. Winona Lake, Ind.: Eisenbrauns, 1994] 1–52; Cross and Freedman, "The Song of Miriam"; Cross, "The Song of the Sea and Canaanite Myth"; idem, *Canaanite Myth and Hebrew Epic*, 121–44; David A. Robertson, *Linguistic Evidence in Dating Early Hebrew Poetry* [SBLDS 3; Missoula, Mont.: SBL, 1972]), which were recognized as sound from early on (see Brevard S. Childs, *The Book of Exodus: A Critical, Theological Commentary* [OTL; Philadelphia: Westminster, 1974] 245–46), have continued to be upheld (Susan Niditch, *Ancient Israelite Religion* [New York: Oxford University Press, 1997] 30). With regard to the dating

Mount Sinai.[43] Cross has suggested Gilgal, pointing out that the "mountain-ous" characterization of the sanctuary has to do primarily with the conventional mythical language and concepts employed and need not require being dramatically evident in the topography of the site.[44] Regardless of the identification of the specific shrine, the term *naḥălâ* is clearly used in this context in reference to a particular sanctuary site designated as Yahweh's dwelling from which he rules and which, as the most sacred part of his realm, can be under-

---

of Exodus 15, very little has changed since Roberts made the following observation two decades ago: "If one rejects [Albright, Cross, Freedman, and Robertson's] dating, one must at least answer their arguments, which, as far as I am aware, no one has bothered to do" ("Zion in the Theology of the Davidic-Solomonic Empire," in *Studies in the Period of David and Solomon and Other Essays* [ed. T. Ishida; Winona Lake, Ind.: Eisenbrauns, 1982] 95). The most noteworthy attempt at a recent challenge has come from Martin L. Brenner (*The Song of the Sea: Ex 15:1–21* [Berlin: de Gruyter: 1991] 9–11), who, though citing in the negative Albright, Cross, and Freedman (*Song of the Sea*, 9–11), does not even mention David Robertson's study or include it in his bibliography. Brenner's contention that those arguing for an early date of this poem "have not given any way of distinguishing the Song from a later composition seeking to be archaic sounding" (p. 10) is simply incorrect and does not acknowledge the overarching point made in all of these studies that the clustering of archaic linguistic features to the exclusion of corresponding later features, as does indeed occur in the Song of the Sea, is proof of an early date as opposed to later archaizing imitation, which is characterized by a mixture of older and later features. Brenner's treatment of specific linguistic features relevant to dating fails to engage arguments made decades earlier and relies on flawed reasoning. For example, with respect to the pronominal suffix -*mô/û*, a linguistic feature on which Brenner places the utmost emphasis for dating the poem, he makes much over the fact that it occurs in the Song of the Sea with verbs and not with nouns; however, he fails to acknowledge that there is *no* noun with a 3rd-person-pl. pronominal suffix in the poem (pp. 33–36), a fact pointed out in the earlier literature (Cross and Freedman, "Song of Miriam," 245). He then seeks to reinforce this incomplete observation with suspect reasoning when he argues that the form "as a verbal suffix appears twenty-three times in all the Scripture, and the Song contains nine of them. The highest elsewhere is two. It is obvious that it is intentional and artificial, both because of the high number of appearances and because it cannot be just coincidence that it always appears here after verb forms" (p. 33). Brenner's operative assumption that the frequency and consistency of a form indicates "intentional and artificial" archaizing (as opposed to a genuinely archaic composition) is baffling. (For the same reasoning, see GKC §91.*l*.3.) Brenner's apparently insufficient understanding of principles basic to the typological dating of Hebrew poetry and of Exodus 15 in particular and his failure to engage both the literature and the specific arguments for the early dating of the poem place his own very precise attribution of the Song of the Sea to Persian-period "Asaphites" on a precarious footing, to say the least (pp. 174–88).

43. Freedman, "Early Israelite History," 6–8.

44. Cross, "The Song of the Sea and Canaanite Myth," 21–24; idem, *Canaanite Myth and Hebrew Epic*, 142–43. This point is reiterated by Clifford, *Cosmic Mountain*, 139 and n. 57.

stood as Yahweh's *naḥălâ* in a superlative sense. This meaning of *naḥălâ* in Exod 15:17 reinforces the initial impression that its use in Psalm 47 has a specific location in view, as implied both by the mention of Yahweh's dwelling "on his sacred throne" (*yāšab ʿal-kissēʾ qodšô*, v. 9) and by the comparison with Ps 78:68 (see above).

Like the Song of the Sea, Psalm 47 celebrates in connection with Yahweh's *naḥălâ* his distinct preference for his people at the expense of the other nations. In this respect vv. 4 and 5 belong together:

> He subdued peoples beneath us
> and nations under our feet.
> He chose for us his inheritance,
> the Pride of Jacob, which he loves.

Similar to Exodus 15, in Psalm 47 Yahweh subdues the other nations and shares his "inheritance" with his own people by assigning them to his own special abode. Again, the earthly counterpart of the deity's heavenly abode is his sanctuary (see above). Reference to a sanctuary site is implied by the mention of various aspects of public worship activity throughout the psalm: a gathering of people (*ʾsp*, v. 10), clapping of hands (v. 2), shouts of joy, the blowing of the shofar (v. 6), and singing (vv. 7–8). These details provide further confirmation of the conclusion that Yahweh's *naḥălâ*, and hence "the Pride of Jacob," denotes a specific worship site.

While the location of Yahweh's shrine referenced in Exodus 15 may be debatable (see discussion above), there can be no doubt regarding the sanctuary in question in Psalm 47. As a psalm extolling Yahweh as "great king over all the earth" (v. 3), this poem belongs together with other psalms celebrating Yahweh's enthronement (Psalms 93; 95–99), in which the earthly seat of Yahweh's rule over the other nations (96:7, 10; 99:1) and their gods (95:3; 96:4–5; 97:7, 9) is Jerusalem (97:8; 99:2).[45] Also to be noted are the close thematic and verbal

---

45. Form-critical analysis of the Psalter, beginning with Gunkel, grouped these psalms together as Psalms of Yahweh's Enthronement (see Gunkel, *Introduction to the Psalms*, 66–81). Irrespective of the merits or deficiencies of a thesis of a regular cultic festival associated with these and other psalms—whether in the form argued by Mowinckel (*The Psalms in Israel's Worship*) or alternatively by Aubrey R. Johnson (*Sacral Kingship in Ancient Israel* [2nd ed.; Cardiff: University of Wales Press, 1967]), by Artur Weiser (*The Psalms: A Commentary* [trans. H. Hartwell; OTL; Philadelphia: Westminster, 1962]), by Hans-Joachim Kraus (*Worship in Israel: A Cult History of the Old Testament* [trans. G. Buswell: Richmond: John Knox, 1966]), or by Gunkel himself (*Introduction to the Psalms*, 69–81)—the recognition of the correspondences among these psalms in terms of content and phraseology is sound. In addition to the basic thematic unity of these psalms as described, one might note that, with the exceptions of Psalms 95 and 98, which refer to Yahweh as *melek gādôl* (95:3) and *hammelek*

correspondences of Psalm 47 with Psalms 46 and 48, which extol Zion as "the city of God" (46:5; 48:2, 9) and refer to Yahweh not only as "the God of Jacob" (ʾĕlōhê yaʿăqōb, 46:8, 12; cf. gĕʾôn yaʿăqōb in 47:5) but also as Elyon, a title of divine supremacy (46:5; 47:3; also 97:9),[46] and as "Great King" (melek rāb, 48:3; melek gādôl, 47:3), exercising dominion over the other nations (46:7; 47:2–4, 8–10; 48:5–8).[47] The theology thus espoused is the Zion tradition, the basic and essential elements of which, as explicated by Roberts, are Yahweh's rule as king and his choice of Jerusalem as his place of dwelling.[48]

The theme associated with Yahweh's naḥălâ both in Exodus 15 and in Psalm 47, namely, Yahweh's privileging of his people before the other nations, is compatible with and no doubt foundational for the Zion tradition's emphases on Yahweh's protection of Zion from foreign enemies and on the blessings of the divine presence for God's people in Zion.[49] As our passage explains, the

---

(98:6), all of these psalms contain the assertion mlk yhwh "Yahweh is/has become king" (as in 47:9, accounting for the preference for ʾĕlōhîm over yhwh as the favored divine designation in Psalms 42–83, the "Elohistic Psalter").

46. For the understanding of Elyon and its importance within the Zion tradition (on which, see below), see Roberts, "Davidic Origin of the Zion Tradition," 331–42; idem, "The Religio-political Setting of Psalm 47," 129–32; and "Zion in the Theology of the Davidic-Solomonic Empire," 94 and n. 3.

47. Such connections among these psalms (along with Psalm 45) are recognized by Jerome F. D. Creach as being at the basis of the shaping of this portion of the Psalter (Yahweh as Refuge and the Editing of the Hebrew Psalter [JSOTSup 217; Sheffield: Sheffield Academic Press, 1996] 87). Psalms 46, 47, and 76 were associated with one another in Gunkel's form critical categories as Zion Psalms; see Gunkel, Introduction to the Psalms, 258.

48. J. J. M. Roberts, "Zion in the Theology of the Davidic-Solomonic Empire," 93–108; see also idem, "The Davidic Origin of the Zion Tradition"; "The Religio-political Setting of Psalm 47"; "Zion Tradition," IDBSup, 985–87; "In Defense of the Monarchy: The Contribution of Israelite Kingship to Biblical Theology," in Ancient Israelite Religion: Essays in Honor of Frank Moore Cross (ed. P. D. Miller Jr., P. D. Hanson, and S. D. McBride; Philadelphia: Fortress, 1987) 377–396, esp. 378, 386–87; "The Enthronement of Yhwh and David: The Abiding Theological Significance of the Kingship Language of the Psalms," CBQ 64 (2002) 675–86. For a review of scholarship on the Zion tradition, see Ben C. Ollenburger (Zion the City of the Great King: A Theological Symbol of the Jerusalem Cult [JSOTSup 41; Sheffield: JSOT Press, 1987] 15–19), who describes the tradition as "a coherent 'theological conception' which underlies most of the Psalms and is articulated above all in [the] Songs of Zion as well as in the creation Psalms, the Psalms of Yahweh's kingship and the royal Psalms" (p. 16.) As Ollenburger recognizes, the Zion tradition finds expression in other portions of the Hebrew Bible as well, mainly among the prophets. On Psalm 47 specifically as an expression of the Zion tradition, see Roberts, "Zion Theology in the Davidic-Solomonic Empire," 94 n. 3; idem, "The Religio-political Setting of Psalm 47."

49. On these and other themes belonging to the Zion tradition, see Roberts, "Zion in the Theology of the Davidic-Solomonic Empire," 94.

people's enjoyment of the divine presence involves Yahweh's choice of his "inheritance" not only as his own dwelling place but also as that of his people (v. 5). From the recognition of this psalm's place squarely within the Zion tradition, it follows that, as the seat of Yahweh's enthronement and the location of the deity's beneficent presence before his power, Yahweh's "inheritance" in v. 5 must be none other than Jerusalem itself.[50]

This conclusion is confirmed by the use of the term *naḥălâ* in the description of Jerusalem's fall in Ps 79:1:

> *ʾĕlōhîm bāʾû gôyîm bĕnaḥălātekā*
> *ṭimmĕʾû ʾet-hêkal qodšekā*
> *śāmû ʾet-yĕrûšālaim lĕʿiyyîm*

> O God, nations have entered your inheritance;
> they have defiled your holy temple;
> they have placed Jerusalem in ruins.

In the poetic parallelism of Jerusalem, the temple, and Yahweh's "inheritance," the latter is intimately associated with—if not equated with—the city and its sanctuary.[51]

Thus, as the appositional equivalent of the *naḥălâ* of Yahweh, *gĕʾôn yaʿăqōb* in Ps 47:5 can only be understood as a designation for Jerusalem. As discussed above, the noun *gāʾôn*, on the basis both of its associations with prominent cities and city features and of its basic meaning "height, exaltedness, prominence," is most appropriate as a designation for a hilltop capital, as suggested

---

50. By comparison, the reasons adduced by Ginsberg (*Israelian Heritage*, 33–34) for suggesting Northern origins for Psalm 47 are unconvincing, to say the least: the claim that the *Hiphil* participle *maśkîl* "one who acts prudently" in Amos 5:13 is a second occurrence of the noun of the same form (which occurs outside of psalm superscriptions only in Ps 47:8); the simple fact that "the Pride of Jacob" also occurs in Amos; and speculation that Amos 6:8 ("I abhor the Pride of Jacob") is a response to "the Pride of Jacob, which he loves" in Ps 47:5 (cf. Ps 78:68, cited above). Against the hypothesis of Northern origins for the Korahite Psalms as a group (as in Peters, *Psalms as Liturgies*, 273–95; and Goulder, *The Psalms of the Sons of Korah*), see the assignment of their origins to Jerusalem by Martin J. Buss, "The Psalms of Asaph and Korah," *JBL* 82 (1963) 387. Among the linguistic indications that Rendsburg (*Linguistic Evidence*) cites for Northern origins of the whole collection of Korah Psalms is the "double plural" *nĕdîbê ʿammîm* in Ps 47:10 (the only occurrence of a "double plural" identified in all the Korah Psalms!), though he concedes that "double plurals occur elsewhere in the Bible where northern provenance is not indicated" (pp. 36, 57). None of the other features that Rendsburg identifies as reflecting a "Northern" character for the Korah Psalms occurs in Psalm 47.

51. Noting the "cultic significance of the term 'inheritance,'" Clements compares Pss 79:1 and 47:5 with similar results, though with more emphasis on the temple itself; *God and Temple*, 55 n. 1.

by use of *gě'ôn ya'ăqōb* in reference to "Mount Samaria" in Amos 6. This hint of the topographical prominence of Jerusalem is in keeping both with the city's relative elevation and more importantly with the Zion tradition's mythic representation of Zion as being a high mountain, a theme that finds its most notable expression in the description of the hill of Zion as *yarkětê ṣāpôn* "the Heights of Zaphon" (Ps 48:3).[52] Of course, long before the founding of Samaria, it was Jerusalem that had served as the political and religious center of the nation. In light of these considerations, one can see that *gě'ôn ya'ăqōb* was a most fitting epithet for Jerusalem.

The expression's occurrence in Amos 8:7 remains to be examined more closely (see below). The preceding discussion of the other three instances shows *gě'ôn ya'ăqōb* to have been used as an epithet for capital cities, a usage in keeping both with the use of the noun *gā'ôn* in connection with prominent cities and with the identification of various foreign capitals by phrases following the construct pattern *gě'ôn* X (see above). In one case (Ps 47:5) the title is taken up in the context of the Zion tradition as a designation for the Davidic capital Jerusalem; in the other two (Amos 6:8; Nah 2:3), it refers to the subsequently established capital of the Northern Kingdom, Samaria. In the interest of better understanding the expression and its origin, one might consider further its role as a title for cities.

Gě'ôn ya'ăqōb as City Epithet

In Psalm 47, "the Pride of Jacob" occurs in the context of the Zion tradition, which was certainly in place no later than the eighth century and was most likely established, as Roberts has persuasively demonstrated, during the early monarchy in Jerusalem under David and Solomon.[53] According to Roberts, the original setting for Psalm 47 was "a cultic celebration of Yahweh's imperial accession, based on the relatively recent victories of David's age."[54] In view of these considerations alone, it seems likely that "the Pride of Jacob" was used as a title for Jerusalem before it was used for Samaria. Yet there is more to consider.

---

52. See Roberts, "Zion in the Theology of the Davidic-Solomonic Empire," 94, 99–100.

53. As Roberts points out, the Zion tradition "permeates" the message of Isaiah ("Zion in the Theology of the Davidic-Solomonic Empire," 107–8). For Roberts's arguments on the dating of the Zion tradition, see ibid., 105–8; "The Davidic Origin of the Zion Tradition," 338–39; and "Zion Tradition," 986.

54. As Roberts goes on to conclude, "Such a religio-political *Sitz im Leben* must assume an early date for Psalm 47, but there is nothing in the psalm which argues against its antiquity, and the content as well as the archaic use of emphatic *l* and *'im* meaning 'to,' argue for it" ("The Religio-political Setting of Psalm 47," 132).

In light of the noun *gā'ôn*'s frequent association with cities, including the designation of various capitals as *gĕ'ôn* X "the Pride of X," one may safely assume that *gĕ'ôn ya'ăqōb* originated as a city epithet and not as a slogan or title of some other sort that was secondarily applied to a city. Both Jerusalem and Samaria, the two cities designated by this title in the Hebrew Bible, were founded as royal capitals having no tribal associations or established place within Israelite tradition.[55] For each city, this circumstance was by design, in an effort to ensure a politically neutral capital that the king could more easily control and around which the kingdom's constituencies might be united. Ironically, this political strength was at the same time a weakness; that is, the lack of existing tribal associations severely limited the ability to achieve unified loyalty to the city as a legitimate political center. The latter problem, however, was not insurmountable. Whereas established divisions and rivalries would have constituted potentially formidable barriers to elevating an existing Israelite city as capital, a new (or newly Israelite) city could be brought in line with commonly shared tradition. To be sure, these factors were operative in the selection of Jerusalem and Samaria alike. That is to say, both cities from their beginnings as royal capitals required legitimization in terms of common Israelite tradition. The coining of a city epithet like "the Pride of Jacob" would represent a larger effort to portray the new royal capital as being in continuity with traditional (i.e., premonarchic), common Israelite identity, a legitimization that would have transcended sectional or tribal divisions and that would have softened objections to the capital as a royal institution.

Israel's premonarchic heritage is not infrequently invoked in support of the royal ideology centering on David and Zion. This occurs in various allusions to Israel's ancestral and tribal past in connection with David and with his capital, Jerusalem. 2 Sam 23:1 calls David "the anointed of the God of Jacob, the darling of the Stronghold of Israel" (*mĕšîaḥ 'ĕlōhê ya'ăqōb ûnĕ'îm zimrat yiśrā'ēl*).[56]

---

55. The well-known traditions of the founding of these two cities as Israelite capitals highlight the status of each as a royal possession. Jerusalem, upon its capture by the king and "his men" (2 Sam 5:6), is known as "the City of David" (vv. 7, 9). Prior to being built into a city, the hill of Samaria is purchased by Omri (1 Kgs 16:24). The reference to Samaria as "the head of Ephraim" (Isa 7:9, mentioned above) involves the use of Ephraim as a designation for the Northern Israelite Kingdom (as in Isa 9:9, 21; 11:13; Jer 31:9–20; Ezek 37:16–19; Hos 5:3, 5, 12, 13), a usage that is itself based on the territorial (and not the tribal) sense of Ephraim.

56. On the text and translation of this verse, see P. Kyle McCarter, Jr., *II Samuel: A New Translation with Introduction, Notes, and Commentary* (AB 9; New York: Doubleday, 1984) 476–77, 480. Yahweh is called *'uzzî wĕzimrat(î)* "my strength and my stronghold" in Exod 15:2; Isa 12:2; Ps 118:14.

Psalm 132, which explicitly declares Yahweh's choice of Zion as his dwelling and the Davidic king as his earthly regent, begins

> Remember, O Yahweh, for David's sake
>   all his affliction
> how he swore to Yahweh
>   and vowed to the Mighty One of Jacob (*ʾăbîr yaʿăqōb*):
> "I will not enter the tent of my house
>   . . . .
> until I find a place for Yahweh,
>   a dwelling for the Mighty One of Jacob (*ʾăbîr yaʿăqōb*)." (vv. 1–5)

This psalm goes on to celebrate what is, of course, the premier example of David's appropriation of Israel's premonarchic religious legacy in support of his royal capital, namely, his bringing the ark of Yahweh, the central divine symbol of the Israelite tribal league, into Jerusalem.[57] Psalm 46, which extols Jerusalem as "the city of God, the holiness of the habitation of the Most High," refers to Yahweh also as "the God of Jacob" (vv. 8, 12). Psalm 99, which lauds Yahweh as king in Jerusalem (vv. 1–4), celebrates his establishment of justice, equity, and righteousness "in Jacob" (v. 4) and invokes the authority of Moses, Aaron, and Samuel (v. 6). Even as the summoning of Israel's premonarchic heritage places in continuity with that heritage the king and his capital, there is no mistaking the priority given to the latter. As Ps 122:4 states regarding Jerusalem, "to there, the tribes, the tribes of Yah, go up." More poignantly, Ps 87:2 asserts, "Yahweh loves the gates of Zion more than all the dwellings of Jacob." It is in this vein that Psalm 47 mentions Abraham (v. 10) and refers to Jerusalem as *gěʾôn yaʿăqōb*.[58] Like the relocation of the ark to Jerusalem, the appropriation of the ancestral name Jacob in a title for the city would have served not only to bring the new capital into the flow of Israel's established, unifying traditions but also to reinforce the city's prominence and centrality. As "the Pride of Jacob," Jerusalem is not simply identified as the center of

---

57. On the significance of David's transfer of the ark to Jerusalem, see Jeremias, "Lade und Zion," 183–98.

58. Note the coupling of "Jacob" and "Abraham" as parallels in the harkening back to ancestral and tribal ideals at the conclusion of Micah (7:20):

> *tittēn ʾĕmet lěyaʿăqōb ḥesed lěʾabrāhām*
> *ʾăšer-nišbaʿtā laʾăbōtênû mîmê qedem*

> You will grant faithfulness to Jacob, loyalty to Abraham,
> as you have sworn to our fathers from days of old.

royal authority but is celebrated as the culmination of Israel's ancestral and tribal heritage.[59]

Within common Israelite tradition as reflected in the Hebrew Bible, "Jacob," like "Israel," was used in the naming both of the people and of its eponymous ancestor.[60] Accordingly, the name Jacob was claimed as a national designation for the united kingdom and, during the divided monarchy, for both Northern and Southern Kingdoms.[61] It is quite reasonable to suppose that, with the establishment of the monarchy under David and Solomon, not only the institutionalization of a central capital but also the designation of Israel's capital as "the Pride of Jacob" might have come to be in place. In fact, it would be during the inception of kingship that the need for the legitimization of the new capital in terms of premonarchic Israelite identity, as described above, would be most acute, whereas an already well-established kingship would itself lend authority to a new capital without the same need for buttressing by nonroyal tradition. With the transfer of kingship to the North upon its secession from the united monarchy, not only would the title Israel be regarded by the Northern tribes as proper to its own rightful heritage, but also "the Pride of Jacob" would be "retained" as the title of the royal capital now that the institution of monarchy had become normative for "Israel."[62] Thus it is not difficult to comprehend how *gěʾôn yaʿăqōb*, having originated as

---

59. These various examples of the appropriation of Israel's tribal heritage go along with the early monarchy's reshaping of league values and institutions, as described by Cross, *From Epic to Canon: History and Literature in Ancient Israel* (Baltimore: Johns Hopkins University Press, 1998) 20–21.

60. The designation of the people as a whole as Jacob at a relatively early time is attested in the Song of Moses (Deut 32:9, 15), which is among the earliest examples of Hebrew poetry; for its eleventh-century dating, see Otto Eissfeldt, *Das Lied Moses: Deuteronomium 32,1–43 und das Lehrgedicht Asaphs Psalm 78 samt einer Analyse der Umgebung des Mose-Liedes* (Berlin: Akademie, 1958) 41–43; William Foxwell Albright, "Some Remarks on the Song of Moses in Deuteronomy XXXII," *VT* 9 (1959) 339–46; David Noel Freedman, *Pottery, Poetry, and Prophecy: Studies in Early Hebrew Poetry* (Winona Lake, Ind.: Eisenbrauns, 1980) 77.

61. For the united monarchy: 2 Sam 23:1; for the Northern Kingdom: Amos 7:2, 5; Hos 12:3; for the Southern Kingdom: Mic 3:1, 8; Obad 10. For other examples, see the dictionaries.

62. Notwithstanding the possible (though not necessary) topographical implication of *gāʾôn* in its association with cities, it is reasonable to suppose that the epithet might have been applied initially in the Northern Kingdom to Shechem (1 Kgs 12:25), which had served as a political and religious center prior to the monarchy, or more likely to Tirzah (14:17; 15:21, 33; 16:6, 8, 9, etc.), the name of which means "pleasantness" or "beauty" and which, during its time as the Northern capital, perhaps rivaled Jerusalem in its physical impressiveness (Song 6:4).

a title for Jerusalem, would have eventually been used also in reference to Samaria. At the same time, it is unlikely that a title created as a designation for Samaria would come to be used for the older capital, Jerusalem.

In summary, the royal city—either Jerusalem (Ps 47:5) or Samaria (Amos 6:8; Nah 2:3)—being "elevated," both in the sense of its hilltop location and in the sense of its status as political and religious capital, was appropriately designated by the term *gā'ôn* and, more specifically, by the title *gĕ'ôn ya'ăqōb*, which follows a pattern used in the epithets of other capitals. The use of the ancestral name in the title represents an effort to establish an association between the royal capital and traditional common Israelite identity, a much needed legitimization for Jerusalem and Samaria, both of which were founded as royal capitals having no tribal associations. The expression's use as a city epithet probably had its origin as a designation for Jerusalem and then was transferred later on to the Northern Kingdom with Omri's establishment of Samaria.

Gĕ'ôn ya'ăqōb as Divine Designation

We now return to the fourth and final occurrence of the expression under discussion, Amos 8:7. Here the expression appears in the introduction of an oath: *nišba' yhwh big'ôn ya'ăqōb* "Yahweh has sworn by the Pride of Jacob." As noted above, Yahweh "swears by" himself only. Therefore, *gĕ'ôn ya'ăqōb* in this case must be understood in some sense as a designation for the divine.

It has been observed that *gĕ'ôn ya'ăqōb* corresponds to the pattern of divine epithets discussed by Alt as designating the "gods of the Fathers," epithets such as *'ĕlōhê 'abrāhām, 'ĕlōhê yiṣḥāq, 'ĕlōhê ya'ăqōb*.[63] This pattern would seem to resonate with other patriarchal associations sounded in Psalm 47 by the mention of Abraham (v. 10). A particularly striking correspondence is noted between *gĕ'ôn ya'ăqōb* and *'ăbîr ya'ăqōb* "the Mighty One of Jacob." These observations suggest the very alluring possibility that *gĕ'ôn ya'ăqōb* originated as an epithet of the ancestral deity.

However, expressions such as *'ăbîr ya'ăqōb* are always and unambiguously used in reference to the deity, while, as we have seen, *gĕ'ôn ya'ăqōb* is not. The same distinction would apply in the comparison between *gĕ'ôn ya'ăqōb* and another construct expression suggested as being analogous to our expression,

---

63. Karl Heinz Ratschow, "Epikrise zum Psalm 47," *ZAW* 53 (1935) 173. For this deity type identified by Albrecht Alt, see idem, "The God of the Fathers," in *Essays on Old Testament History and Religion* (trans. R. A. Wilson; Oxford: Blackwell, 1966) 1–77; trans. and repr. from Alt, *Der Gott der Väter: Ein Beitrag zur Vorgeschichte der israelitischen Religion* (BZAW 3; Stuttgart: Kohlhammer, 1929).

namely, *nēṣaḥ yiśrā'ēl* "the Eminence of Israel."[64] Furthermore, the latter epithet occurs only once (1 Sam 15:29) and seems to be an interpolation from a time much later than the preexilic context of *gě'ôn ya'ăqōb*.[65] Thus our expression is not strictly analogous to the divine epithet types that would seem to provide a framework for understanding its meaning and usage as a divine designation.

Such a framework does emerge, though, as one gives attention to other oaths in the book of Amos. In his discussion of Amos 8:14, Saul Olyan has noted the important connection between oaths and worship sanctuaries and the significance of that connection for that passage.[66] This correlation is observed in Hos 4:15, which reads

> *wě'al-tābō'û haggilgāl*
> *wě'al-ta'ălû bêt 'āwen*
> *wě'al-tiššābě'û ḥay yhwh*
>
> And do not come to Gilgal,
> And do not go up to Beth-Aven,
> And do not swear, "By the life of Yahweh."

The association of oaths with shrines is explained by the fact that, as described by Horst, the cultic oath invoked contact with the *Lebenssphäre* of the deity.[67] That is, the oath invoked the presence of the deity as known in the deity's cult place, the latter either being implied or mentioned explicitly. The oaths of Amos 8:14 invoke the divine presence as known specifically at the sanctuary sites of Dan and Beer-sheba. As discussed above, the paralleling of these two cult sites with Samaria in this passage implies that the latter also was the location of a sanctuary.[68] In any case, this correlation between oaths and worship sites suggests that the citing of an oath in Amos may involve reference to the deity's presence as associated with a specific sanctuary location.

The book of Amos features not one but three oaths attributed to Israel's god. Besides the one introduced in 8:7, two other such oaths occur with the following introductions:

> *nišba' yhwh běqodšô*
> Yahweh has sworn by his holiness. . . . (4:2)

---

64. See Mays, *Amos*, 145.
65. P. Kyle McCarter, Jr., *I Samuel: A New Translation with Introduction and Commentary* (AB 8; New York: Doubleday, 1980) 268.
66. More specifically, Olyan discusses Israelite shrines in connection with religious pilgrimage; "The Oaths of Amos 8.14," 127, 145–48.
67. Horst, "Der Eid im Alten Testament," 298.
68. On the difficulties posed by *'ašmat šōměrôn* (MT), see Olyan, "The Oaths of Amos 8.14," 148–49.

nišbaʿ yhwh běnapšô
Yahweh has sworn by his life. . . . (6:8)[69]

These oath introductions are identical in formula to our passage in 8:7:

nišbaʿ yhwh bigʾôn yaʿăqōb
Yahweh has sworn by the pride of Jacob. . . .

Again, the same formula is followed in each case. What is also clear is that in each instance Yahweh swears by himself in some sense. In both 4:2 and 6:8, this divine self-reference is accomplished by the mention of one of the deity's own attributes, his "holiness" and his "name," respectively. One might proceed by giving further consideration to these divine attributes as mentioned in other parts of the Hebrew Bible, especially those in which a sanctuary location is in view.

First, Yahweh's "holiness" (*qōdeš*), mentioned in 4:2, occurs in various construct phrases denoting Yahweh's presence both in the heavenly abode[70] and on earth[71] and often stands alone in designating places set apart by God's sacred presence, such as the tabernacle and its courts[72] and the temple and its precincts.[73] Thus the most sacred space within the temple is designated by the superlative expression *qōdeš haqqŏdāšîm* "the most holy place," literally, "the greatest holiness" (1 Kgs 6:16; 7:50; 8:6; etc.), that is, the space in which the divine presence is most potently manifest. Jerusalem itself, the more extended locus of the divine presence, is called *měqôm qodšô* "the place of his holiness" (Ezra 9:8; Ps 24:3), *ʿîr haqqōdeš* "the city of holiness" (Isa 48:2; etc.), *har qodšî* "the mountain of my holiness" (Isa 11:9; etc.), *har haqqōdeš* "the mountain of holiness" (Isa 27:13; Jer 31:23), and simply (Yahweh's) *qōdeš* (Ps 20:3). Regarding his faithfulness to the royal line of David, a matter of utmost relevance to the destiny of Jerusalem, Yahweh swears in Ps 89:36 by his holiness, that is, by his presence made available in the cult in the holy city. The holy city in

---

69. The expansion of *yhwh* to *ʾădōnāy yhwh* in 4:2 and 6:8, as attested in the MT and at Murubaʿat, apparently had not occurred in the Vorlage to the LXX; see Wolff, *Joel and Amos*, 130, 190, 203, 279.

70. *Měʿôn qodšěkā* "the place of your holiness" (Deut 26:15, etc.); *hêkal qodšô* "the palace/temple of his holiness" (Mic 1:2, etc.); *kissēʾ qodšô* "the throne of his holiness" (Ps 47:9); *měrôm qodšô* "the height of his holiness" (Ps 102:20); *zěbûl qodšěkā* "the lofty abode of your holiness" (Isa 63:15).

71. *ʾAdmat qōdeš* "holy ground" (Exod 3:5; Josh 5:15); *har qōdeš ʾělōhîm* "the mountain of the holiness of God/(the) god(s)" (Ezek 28:14).

72. E.g., Exod 38:24; 40:9; Lev 10:4, 17, 18; Num 3:28; for more examples, see the dictionaries.

73. 1 Kgs 8:10; Ezek 42:14; 44:27; Pss 63:3; 68:25.

connection with which Yahweh swears by his *qōdeš* in Amos 4 is, of course, not Jerusalem but "Mount Samaria" (v. 1). As with Jerusalem, the perception of Yahweh's sacred presence in Samaria would be rooted in his sanctuary and cult in the capital.[74] This implied reference to Yahweh's cultic presence in this context is reinforced by the mention of cultic activity at the older Northern sanctuaries of Bethel and Gilgal (vv. 4–5). Like the sacrifices, tithes, and offerings mentioned in connection with those shrines, the swearing of an oath in connection with "Mount Samaria," as attributed to Yahweh in 4:2, is a practice associated with the worship sanctuary in that location. As discussed elsewhere in the Hebrew Bible, Yahweh's *qōdeš* regularly refers to his cultically available presence in the religious capital. In light of the observed connection between oaths and sanctuaries, this understanding of Yahweh's *qōdeš* in Amos 4:2 seems quite clear.

Mention of Yahweh's *nepeš* "breath/life" as found in 6:8, is relatively rare in the Hebrew Bible and, when it occurs, is usually in reference to God's "self."[75] Its use in this context does not seem out of place, as oaths are often sworn by "the life" (*ḥay/ḥê*) of Israel's god,[76] and, as implied in Ps 24:4, human oaths can be taken by Yahweh's *nepeš*. Like Amos 6:8, Jer 51:14 presents a divine oath in which Yahweh swears by his own *nepeš*. The term *nepeš* is used to describe Yahweh's favor in Isa 42:1, where Yahweh's servant is called the one "in whom my *nepeš* delights," and in Yahweh's description of an anticipated faithful priest, "who shall do according to my *lēb* and my *nepeš*," in 1 Sam 2:35.[77] In Isa 1:14, Yahweh's conditional rejection of acts of worship in Jerusalem is stated as follows: "Your new moons and appointed festivals my *nepeš* hates." In Jer 6:8, Yahweh threatens Jerusalem with destruction, which will result when "my *nepeš* turns away from you." In 15:1, the notion of the refusal of Yahweh's *nepeš* to turn "toward" his people is paralleled with their rejection from his "presence" (*pānîm*). Thus in Jeremiah, Yahweh's "life" refers to his favorable presence and his protection of his people. This concept is further illustrated in Jeremiah's temple sermon (7:1–15), which is predicated on the notion that the nation's welfare and security result from Yahweh's beneficent presence dwelling in the central sanctuary (v. 4)—earlier at Shiloh

---

74. For the evidence and arguments pertaining to the existence of a major sanctuary in Samaria, see the discussion above.

75. H. Seebass, "נֶפֶשׁ *nepeš*," *TDOT* 9.516.

76. In addition to Amos 8:14 (cited above), see the numerous examples listed in the dictionaries; also note the circumlocution *ḥê(-)napšĕkā*, by which human figures of authority are referenced in oaths. For the translation of *ḥay/ḥê* in oaths, see Moshe Greenberg, "The Hebrew Oath Particle *Ḥay/Ḥê*," *JBL* 76 (1957) 34–39.

77. Ibid.

(v. 12) and then in Jerusalem (vv. 4, 7). As we have seen, the context of the divine oath in Amos 6, like that of the oath in chap. 4, is "Mount Samaria" (6:1). The favorable presence of Yahweh, centered in the god's dwelling in the sanctuary, is understood by the city's inhabitants as being manifest in the might and opulence of the capital, as elaborately described in this passage. It is in this context that Yahweh takes up the oath by his *nepeš*, asserting his contempt for the capital and its strongholds and his intention to deliver up the city to destruction (v. 8). Again, oaths regularly relate to cult places. By reference to his *nepeš*, the deity summons as oath witness his cultic presence in the capital, which is usually manifest in the grandeur of the city but whose presumed removal will result in the city's (and hence the nation's) destruction. In the invocation of Yahweh's "life" in Amos 6:8, as with the invocation of his "holiness" in 4:2, the divine attribute invoked as witness to the oath represents the deity's cultic presence in the capital, insuring the validity and the consequences of the oath for the nation as a whole.

Again, in each of these two oaths, the attribute of Yahweh named is one that stands for his presence in the royal and religious capital. Other biblical examples of Yahweh's attributes' representing the divine presence are well known, such as his "face/presence" mentioned in Jer 15:1 and in Exod 33:14–15 and his "name" in Jer 7:14 and extensively in Deuteronomy.[78] Both are examples of divine hypostasis, whereby one of the deity's attributes is perceived to be hypostatized or reified and standing for the deity.[79] As texts from the fifth-century Jewish colony at Elephantine attest, Yahweh ("Yahu," as he is called in these texts) was worshiped in the form of his hypostatized attributes (e.g., Anath-Yahu, "the Sign [of the active presence] of Yahu").[80] It is in this sense, as hypostatic forms of the divine presence, that Yahweh's "holiness" and his "life" are invoked as witnesses to his oaths in Amos 4:2 and 6:8. These hypostases, so closely associated with Samaria itself, serve as surrogates for Yahweh in the context of his own swearing of oaths, specifically, oaths promising the overthrow of the nation of which Samaria is the capital.

The invocation of divine attributes representing Yahweh's presence in Samaria in Amos 4:2 and 6:8 suggests a similar meaning and function for "the

---

78. Of relevance to our oaths in Amos is the fact that one can likewise swear by the "name" of Yahweh (Isa 48:1).

79. P. Kyle McCarter, Jr., "Aspects of the Religion of the Israelite Monarchy: Biblical and Epigraphic Data," in *Ancient Israelite Religion: Essays in Honor of Frank Moore Cross* (ed. P. D. Miller Jr., P. D. Hanson, and S. D. McBride; Philadelphia: Fortress, 1987) 147–48.

80. Ibid.; William Foxwell Albright, *From the Stone Age to Christianity: Monotheism and the Historical Process* (2nd ed.; Garden City, N.Y.: Doubleday, 1957) 373.

Pride of Jacob" invoked in the third instance of the oath introduction formula in 8:7. Again, Yahweh can take an oath by himself only. That is to say that, like Yahweh's *qōdeš* and *nepeš*, *gĕʾôn yaʿăqōb* (which, as we have seen, is used elsewhere as an epithet for the political and religious capital) must in some sense represent the divine presence, specifically, the divine presence in Samaria.

As noted, the close association of Yahweh's "holiness" and "life" as hypostatic forms of the divine presence with the royal and religious capital is due to the location in the capital of the deity's sanctuary, in which the presence of the deity is made accessible through the cult. In addition to the deity's hypostatized attributes, another way in which the divine presence associated with the cult can be represented is in the personification of the divine sanctuary, a phenomenon well attested in texts from throughout the ancient Near East.[81] The premier example of this phenomenon is the Aramaic deity Bethel.[82] Israelite worship of divine Bethel is quite clearly indicated in Jer 48:13. In the Elephantine documents, one finds the personification and adoration of Bethel and of Herem-Bethel (i.e., the extended temple precinct)[83] as surrogates for Yahweh. Both the representation of the deity by the sanctuary and the extension of the recognized divine presence from the temple to the city as a whole are observed in a blessing found in Babylonian letters:

> Uruk^KI *u Eanna ana šar mātāti bēlīya likrubū*
> May Uruk and Eanna be gracious to the king of countries, my lord.[84]

In this benediction, the goddess Ishtar is represented in the personified forms of her temple precinct, Eanna, and, by extension, her city, Uruk. Though not necessarily involving either personification or deification, the tendency to extend the recognition of the divine presence from the sanctuary proper to the broader sacred area, even to the city as a whole, is observable in the Hebrew Bible in the case of Jerusalem. As the more extended locus of the divine presence centered in the temple, Zion is called *mĕqôm qodšô* "the place of his holiness" (Ezra 9:8), *ʿîr haqqōdeš* "the city of holiness" (Isa 48:2; etc.), *har qōdeš* "mountain of holiness" (Ps 48:2; etc.), *ʿîr ʾĕlōhîm qōdeš miškĕnê ʿelyôn* "the city

---

81. McCarter, "Aspects of the Religion of the Israelite Monarchy," 147–48; J. Philip Hyatt, "The Deity Bethel and the Old Testament," *JAOS* 59 (1939) 81–98.

82. William Foxwell Albright, *Archaeology and the Religion of Israel* (Garden City, N.Y.: Doubleday, 1969) 164–65; Wolfgang Röllig, "Bethel בית(י)אל," *DDD* 173–75.

83. McCarter, "Aspects of the Religion of the Israelite Monarchy," 147; cf. Albright, *Archaeology and the Religion of Israel*, 167–68.

84. Cited by Hyatt, "The Deity Bethel," 92.

of God, the holiness of the habitation of Elyon" (Ps 46:5),[85] and simply (Yahweh's) *qōdeš* (Pss 20:3; 24:3). These designations reflect a recognition of the sacred presence as emanating from the most sacred place (*qōdeš haqqōdāšîm*) within the temple proper to the more extended area of Zion, the hill of the sanctuary.

This extension of the recognized divine presence to the sanctuary hill as a whole is compatible with the mythic conceptualization of the deity's abode as a sacred mountain in West Semitic tradition.[86] With reference again to Jerusalem—for which we of course have more information than we do for Samaria—the recognition of the city as a manifestation of the divine presence finds a place within the Zion tradition, according to which, as mentioned above, Jerusalem is "the city of God, the holiness of the habitation of Elyon" (Ps 46:5). This idea receives especially strong expression in Psalm 48, which calls Zion "the city of our God, the mountain of his holiness" (v. 2) and equates Zion with "the heights of Zaphon" (*yarkĕtê ṣāpôn*, v. 3), Baal's mountain abode in Ugaritic myth. According to Psalm 48, the power and presence of Israel's god are revealed in the city's fortifications, as stated in v. 4:

> *ʾĕlōhîm bĕʾarmĕnôtêhā nôdaʿ lĕmiśgāb*
> Within [Zion's] citadels, God has made himself known as a strong tower.

For attacking armies and adoring worshipers alike—though with very different consequences—Yahweh's might is overwhelmingly evident at the very sight of the city (vv. 5–9). The psalmist's invitation to walk around the city and marvel at its fortifications (vv. 13–14) culminates in the exclamation: "This is God, our God forever and ever" (*zeh ʾĕlōhîm ʾĕlōhênû ʿôlām wāʿed*, v. 15). Here the fortified might of Jerusalem is commended as a concrete manifestation of the divine presence.[87] The terms in which this affirmation is expressed suggest the deification of the city, a notion that is by no means unthinkable, in light of the description at Ugarit of Zaphon—the mountain abode of Baal in Ugaritic myth, with which Zion is equated in this psalm (v. 3)—as *il ṣpn* "divine Zaphon" (*KTU* 1.3.III.29, IV.19; 1.47.1).[88] In Psalm

---

85. The reading *qōdeš*, as indicated by the second column of the Hexapla, is preferable to the MT's *qĕdōš* in that the adjectival form regularly refers to places in attributive usage and not as a substantive.

86. See the discussion above.

87. Levenson's explanation that the sight of the city serves as a visual "medium of revelation" for the verbal declaration that "this is Israel's God for all eternity" (*Sinai and Zion*, 147–51) begs the question of the referent of "this," as it stands both in v. 4 and in the interpretation offered.

88. Marvin H. Pope and Jeffrey H. Tigay, "A Description of Baal," *UF* 3 (1971) 121–22.

48 we see that, just as the divinized sanctuary in a Yahwistic context can be construed to represent the divine presence (as in Jer 48:13 and Elephantine Bethel), so the sanctuary mount and the city as a whole can be understood as a concrete manifestation of the more extended presence of Israel's god.

It is in this sense that Amos 8:7, in the divine oath threatening the overthrow of the Northern Israelite Kingdom, invokes the divine presence as understood to be manifest in its capital Samaria by using an epithet elsewhere applied to the city, namely, "the Pride of Jacob." Like the references to Yahweh's "holiness" and "life" in 4:2 and 6:8, respectively, "the Pride of Jacob" in 8:7 refers to the deity's presence in the capital. While the first two oaths do so by reference to hypostatized attributes of Yahweh associated with the religious capital, 8:7 does by reference to the city itself, which is perceived as the extended locus of the deity's cultically available presence. Once again, the connection between oaths and sanctuaries is relevant. Both the hypostatized attributes of the deity and the city mount, that is, the divine dwelling extended, represent manifestations of the cultically available presence of Israel's god. In this case, the divine presence stands ready to guarantee the devastation of the land and its capital promised in the oaths.

It bears noting that this reference to the divine presence manifest in Mount Samaria does not *require* the title "the Pride of Jacob"; rather, it assumes it. That is to say, the expression is primarily a designation for the city, and it is by use of that city epithet that the presence of the deity known in the city so named is invoked in Yahweh's threat against the nation and the city itself. It is in this way that Israel's god can be said both to swear by (8:7) and to despise (6:8) "the Pride of Jacob." In similar fashion, the variant of the expression found in Hosea, "the Pride of Israel" (5:5; 7:10), testifies against the nation.[89] The mention of the people's "reeling" in response suggests a depiction of divine judgment, "the Pride of Israel" being in reference to the divine presence in the capital, standing in judgment over the nation.[90]

Summary

The expression "the Pride of Jacob" (*gĕʾôn yaʿăqōb*) was most likely first used in reference to Jerusalem in an effort to establish a legitimizing association between the new royal capital and traditional (i.e., premonarchic) common Israelite identity. With the secession of the Northern tribes and the transfer of monarchic institutions, such as a royal capital, to the North, the epithet would

---

89. Hos 5:5; 7:10; "the Pride of Israel" also occurs as a variant for "the Pride of Jacob" in Nah 2:3, which is discussed above.

90. See the identification of this phrase as a divine epithet in BDB, 145.

have been claimed by the North as the rightful title of the capital of "Israel." Eventually the epithet was used in reference to Samaria, which, like Jerusalem before it, was founded as a royal capital having no tribal affiliations and in need of legitimization by common Israelite tradition. In one instance (Amos 8:7), the epithet is used where the capital Samaria is referenced as a concrete manifestation of the presence of Israel's god, Yahweh. It is only in this secondary sense that "the Pride of Jacob" appears as a divine designation.

Bashan, Symbology, Haplography, and Theology in Psalm 68

Princeton Theological Seminary

It is always precarious to venture into a heated area of debate. No area of biblical research is more vexing than the text of the Psalter and its poetry, and within this collection no psalm remains so obtuse to the exegete and theologian as Psalm 68.

In 1911, H. Gunkel offered this sane assessment: "Unter allen Büchern des Alten Testamentes ist vielleicht dasjenige, das dem geschichtlichen Verständnis die größten Schwierigkeiten entgegenstellt, das Buch der Psalmen."[1] In 1942, R. Tournay lamented the many emendations for bringing coherence in the psalms that had been appearing in critical publications and opined that Psalm 68 "est sans contredit l'un des joyaux de l'Ancien Testament."[2] Indeed, Psalm 68 deserves its title as the "Psaume Titan." In 1950, W. F. Albright offered the learned opinion that "Psalm 68 has always been considered with justice as the most difficult of all the Psalms."[3] J. A. Emerton refers to Psalm 68 as "notoriously problematical" in terms of text and interpretation.[4] P. D. Miller wisely cautions that Psalm 68 is an "ancient and vexing psalm" and that the problems it presents are "vast." He also advises that "recent discoveries and studies have

---

Author's note: I am pleased to dedicate this research and these reflections to a friend and colleague for twenty years, J. J. M. Roberts, whose work on Psalm 68 is a major contribution to biblical research.

1. H. Gunkel's "Die Psalmen" was originally published in *Deutschen Rundschau* 38 (1911) and republished in *Zur Neueren Psalmenforschung* (Wege der Forschung 192; Darmstadt: Wissenschaftliche Buchgesellschaft, 1976) 19–54.

2. R. Tournay, "Le Psaume LXVIII," *RB* 51 (1942) 227–45 [= *Vivre et Penser* 2]; the quotations are from p. 227.

3. W. F. Albright, "A Catalogue of Early Hebrew Lyric Poems (Psalm LXVIII)," *HUCA* 23 (1950–51) 1–39; the quotation is from p. 7.

4. J. A. Emerton, "The 'Mountain of God' in Psalm 68:16," in *History and Interpretations of Early Israel: Studies Presented to Eduard Nielsen* (ed. A. Lemaire and B. Otzen; Leiden: Brill, 1993) 24–37; see p. 24.

produced new insights into the psalm."[5] H.-J. Kraus held the same opinion, which is a consensus: "There is hardly another psalm in the Psalter which in its corrupt text and its lack of coherence precipitates such serious problems for the interpreter as Psalm 68."[6]

The purpose of the present essay is to publish discoveries that appeared as I was completing a six-year project that seeks to comprehend serpent iconography and symbology in antiquity. This search led me to the appearance of Bashan in Ps 68:23[22]. Eventually I became persuaded that clearly some consonants have been lost in the first colon, and these must constitute one beat and be in synonymous parallelism to the parallel beat in the second colon of the bicolon. My work thus addresses the widely held perspective that the text is corrupt and Psalm 68 lacks coherence. The following study progresses with nine successive questions:

1. What is the meaning of "Bashan" in Ps 68:23[22]?
2. Does "Bashan" not mean simply an area of land that is east of the Sea of Galilee?
3. Should "Bashan" be translated "dragon-snake"?
4. Is one word missing from Ps 68:23[22]?
5. What is the date of Psalm 68, especially v. 23[22], and is Canaanite culture evident in it?
6. Is Psalm 68 a "catalogue"?
7. Are the words in 68:23[22] shaped by an echo from earlier in Psalm 68?
8. Should one seek for an understanding of Ps 68:23[22] by appealing to context?
9. What has been learned?

1. What Is the Meaning of "Bashan" in Psalm 68:23[22]?

What does בשן denote or connote in the Hebrew Bible? This focused question evoked the present research. A noun בשן may appear in the Hebrew Bible only twice: Deut 33:22 and Ps 68:23[22]. The classical biblical lexicons

---

5. P. D. Miller, *The Divine Warrior in Early Israel* (Cambridge: Harvard University Press, 1973) 102.

6. H.-J. Kraus, *Psalms 60–150* (trans. H. C. Oswald; Minneapolis: Augsburg, 1989) 47. J. P. Fokkelman argues that "this great psalm" yields to a "varying play of ideas" and reveals an "incredible richness of meanings" (p. 83); see Fokkelman, "The Structure of Psalm LXVIII," in *In Quest of the Past* (ed. A. S. van der Woude; OtSt 26; Leiden: Brill, 1990) 72–83.

do not distinguish a noun separate from the more common, homographic place-name, however, and provide only one meaning for בָּשָׁן: the land of Og that is east of Lake Kennereth. What does this noun mean? Is there perhaps another meaning for Bashan in Biblical Hebrew?

2. Does "Bashan" Not Mean Simply an Area of Land That Is East of the Sea of Galilee?

In time-honored lexicons of Biblical Hebrew, בָּשָׁן appears with only one clear meaning. For example, in Gesenius' *Handwörterbuch über das Alte Testament* (1962 [17th ed.]), BDB, and Koehler-Baumgartner (1985) "Bashan" denotes only a place. Only one meaning is provided. Not only the lexicons but also the commentaries of the Psalter show that the meaning of the Hebrew noun בָּשָׁן was once clear to scholars, the transliterated proper name Bashan,[7] which was identified as the kingdom of Og, the territory east of the Jordan, extending from the Jabbok River to Mount Hermon.[8] In this area is Mount Bashan, which is due east of the Yarmuk River and rises 5,905 feet above the plain.[9]

Hence, many—perhaps most—translators presented a rendering of Ps 68:22[23] that assumes the poet is referring to the well-known land east of the Kennereth (the Sea of Galilee) and south of Mount Hermon. Here are examples of the usual translation:

> The Lord said, "I will bring back from Bashan,
> I will bring *them* back from the depths of the sea." [NKJV]

> (He is) the Lord who says,
> "I will bring back from Bashan,
> I will bring back from the depths of the sea,
> so that you may shake the blood off your feet,
> (and) the tongues of your dogs may have a portion
> from the enemy!" [M. E. Tate][10]

> The Lord has spoken:
> "From Bashan I will bring [you] back,
> bring [you] back from the depths of the sea,

---

7. In the Hellenistic and Roman periods the region was called "Batanea." See J. C. Slayton, "Bashan," *ABD* 1.623–24. With different vocalization the consonants can denote Beth Shan (Scythopolis); see N. Jechielis's *Aruch Completum sive Lexicon Vocabula et Res, quae in Libris Targumicis, Talmudicis et Midraschicis*, 1.207.

8. See, for example, BDB, 143.

9. For a map, see Y. Aharoni et al. (eds.), *The Carta Bible Atlas* (4th ed.; Jerusalem: CARTA, 2002) pl. 8.

10. M. E. Tate, *Psalms 51–100* (WBC 20; Dallas: Word, 1990) 161.

so that your foot 'may bathe'
in blood,
and the tongues of your dogs
may have their portion of the enemies." [H.-J. Kraus][11]

Adonai said, I'll bring back from Bashan;
I'll bring back from the abysses of the sea,
To let you bathe your feet in the blood of your foes,
And even your dogs' tongues will share in it! [S. Terrien][12]

In favor of this rendering is the observation that in the first colon there is a place (Bashan) that is parallel in the second colon to another place (the sea). What is the poet thinking when he links "Bashan" and "the sea"? What is the poetic and theological understanding behind "Bashan" and "the sea"? It is far from clear what relation exists between Bashan and sea. Are they synonymous or antithetical? Should the mythology behind the bicolon be enunciated so that Bashan (symbolizing the land) is parallel to Yam (symbolizing the sea)? Such questions put in doubt the widely held assumption that "Basan est le type de la haute montagne."[13]

The customary translation, presented above, is far from lucid and transparent. What or whom is "the Lord" bringing back? Why is the Lord bringing "you," "them," "it" (or some similar concepts) back? Does the poem reflect Canaanite or Israelite cultures and myths? Why is there nothing in colon one to parallel "from the depths of" in colon two? If God is calling Israel's enemies to judgment, then Bashan is most likely not a place, since it would be within greater Israel or the Holy Land.[14] These questions reveal that research needs to be focused on Psalm 68; each of these questions will be answered in the following presentation of years of studying the serpent and serpent iconography in the Levant.

3. Should "Bashan" Be Translated "Dragon-Snake"?

Does this noun בשׁן have a meaning in addition to the place? The translator of the Septuagint in Ps 68[67]:23[22] seems to have been somewhat confused; after about the seventh century C.E., in later minuscules, the text is presented with a capitalized "from" and a transliterated "Bashan" (Ἐκ Βασαν). The text

---

11. H.-J. Kraus, Psalms 60–150, 45.
12. S. Terrien, The Psalms (Eerdmans Critical Commentary; Grand Rapids: Eerdmans, 2003) 487.
13. Tournay, "Le Psaume LXVIII," 239.
14. I am grateful to H. Lichtenberger for this suggestion.

is ancient, since it has influenced the Vulgate.[15] The translator of the passage in the Peshiṭta has rendered מבשן with the interesting ܪܝܫܐ ܕܒܝܬ ܫܢܐ "from the house of teeth," or better idiomatically, "from the edge of a steep rock."[16] There is no variant to v. 23[22] in Hebrew, and there is no reason to postulate a variant.[17] The Peshiṭta text probably resulted from a Syriac scribe's guess concerning the meaning of the Hebrew. That translation presents a meaning-ful rendering of Psalm 68[67 in the LXX, but 68 in the Peshiṭta]. A lucid, even meaningful, rendering, however, should not be confused with an accurate translation of the original Hebrew.

We receive no help in understanding this Hebrew noun, בשן, from the hundreds of manuscripts found in the Qumran caves.[18] The word does not appear; a similar-looking form is found, however; but the form is the noun "tooth" with a preformative *beth*. In the *Copper Scroll* we find "in a rock peak (or cliff)" (בשן הסלע, which is literally "in the tooth of a rock"). The form in the *Temple Scroll*, בשן, is again simply "tooth" plus the preposition (11QT 61:12 [an echo of the *lex talionis* following Deut 19:21]). Both passages in these scrolls parallel what we observed regarding the Peshiṭta of Psalm 68. Thus, while we have more data for ascertaining the meaning of the noun and form in antiquity, there is still no convincing evidence in extant Hebrew manuscripts that בשן denoted a snake.

The most help in comprehending בשן as having a second meaning, "dragon-snake," comes from cognate languages.[19] The Ugar. *bṯn*[20] and the

---

15. Compare the Vulgate: *Dixit Dominus: "Ex Basan convertam,* ‖ *convertam in profundum maris."*

16. The Syriac is an idiomatic expression; John Mard, apud *Bibliotheca Orientalis Clementino-Vaticana* 2.227, uses the same phrase but with the Syriac word for lion, which qualifies and explains the whole phrase: "from the house of the teeth of a lion" (i.e., "from within a lion's mouth surrounded by teeth" or simply, idiomatically, "from a lion's teeth"). See R. Payne Smith, *Thesaurus Syriacus* (2 vols.; Oxford: Clarendon, 1879–1901) 2.4231.

17. No variant is cited in *BHS* for this construct. This lack of variants suggests that scribes found a meaning in Psalm 68. This psalm is not preserved in the Qumran *Psalms Scroll* (11QPsᵃ); while Ps 68:1–4 and 13–17 appear in 11QPsᵈ, v. 23[22] has not been found at Qumran.

18. The word is not cited in M. Sokoloff, *A Dictionary of Jewish Palestinian Aramaic* (2nd ed.; Ramat Gan: Bar Ilan University Press / Baltimore: Johns Hopkins University Press, 2002). It is not discussed in E. Qimron, *The Hebrew of the Dead Sea Scrolls* (HSS 29; Atlanta: Scholars Press, 1986).

19. I checked the rumor that in Modern Hebrew, *bašan* denotes the large black snake in the Golan—the region of ancient Bashan gives its name to a snake. The rumor is false.

20. Ugaritic *bṯn* becomes *bšn* in Hebrew and is equal to *bšm* in Akkadian, with the *n* to *m* shift. I am grateful to Prof. J. J. M. Roberts for discussing this issue with me.

Akk. *bašmu* are cognate to the Heb. *bšn* and the Aram. *ptn*. These terms are
equal to the Arab. *bathan*.[21] All these nouns denote some type of "dragon" or
"snake." The new and expanded Koehler-Baumgartner indicates that the Heb.
בשן denotes a type of serpent similar to פתן "cobra."[22] As already intimated,
the key to the Hebrew may now be found in Ugar. *btn*, which signifies a
mythological dragon-snake akin to תנין "dragon."[23]

M. Dahood, who wisely employs Ugaritic to shine light upon dark passages
in the Psalter, perceives that Bashan in Ps 68:23[22] refers to a dragon-snake
or serpent:

> The Lord said:
> "I stifled the Serpent,
> muzzled the Deep Sea."[24]

In his notes Dahood points out that "*bāšān* is another name for Leviathan, as
appears from UT 67:I:12."[25] The translators of the NEB also opted to bring out
a reference to a snake in Ps 68:23[22]: "from the Dragon." It is clear that in
antiquity Bashan meant not only a mountain but also a mythological dragon-
snake.

4. Is One Word Missing from Psalm 68:23[22]?

Is not some restoration needed in Ps 68:23[22]? Surely, a phrase in the first
colon needs to parallel "the depths of" in the second colon.[26] Long ago, W. F.
Albright insightfully contended that Ps 68:23[22] is a passage with at least one
word missing.[27] He restored the second colon as follows:

מ(מחץ) בשן אשב

The bicolon thus restored means:

21. Spirantized *t* in Hebrew sometimes becomes unspirantized in Aramaic, and *b* shifts
to *p*. See פתן "snake," in Sokoloff, *A Dictionary of Jewish Palestinian Aramaic*, 456.

22. *HALOT*, 1.165.

23. See F. C. Fensham, "Ps 68:23 in the Light of Recently Discovered Ugaritic Tablets,"
JNES 19 (1960) 292–93. I was encouraged to discover that Fensham restores and translates
Ps 68:3 as follows: "From the hole of the snake (or Bashan) I will bring back" (p. 293).

24. M. Dahood, *Psalms II: 51–100* (AB 17; Garden City, N.Y.: Doubleday, 1968) 131.

25. Ibid.,145.

26. It is conceivable, *prima facie*, that the verb repeated in both lines is due to dittography, but this possibility disappears upon further reflection. The poetic form is probably step
parallelism, in which the last word in the first stichos reappears at the beginning of the second stichos. This is precisely the case with Ps 68:23[22].

27. Albright, "Catalogue of Early Hebrew Lyric Poems."

> Yhwh said,
> From (smiting) the Serpent I return,
> I return from destroying the Sea!

This meaning depends on the presupposition or perception:

- that Psalm 68 is a catalogue of the beginnings of poems,
- that v. 23[22] is the *incipit* of a poem,
- that one cannot appeal to a general context for this verse,
- that a word has been lost,
- that this word is מחץ,
- that the Psalm is to be interpreted in light of south Canaanite, especially Ugaritic poems,[28]
- and that the verb אשב is a *Qal*, "I will return," and not a *Hiphil*, "I will bring back" [this seems to demand an emendation of the text from אשיב to אשב].[29]

Most drastic, as Albright admitted, is the emendation of ממצלות to מצמת. The change of the *lamedh* to a *mem* is extreme. It is an emendation "for which no similarity of form or mechanical error of a copyist can be adduced."[30] This admission reveals that perhaps there may be a less-drastic solution to understanding this verse.[31] Moreover, Albright claimed that one should not appeal to context in rendering this verse, since Psalm 68 is basically a catalogue containing *incipits* from early Canaanite or Hebrew poems.

What seems persuasive now, so many years after Albright's ingenious conclusion? It seems obvious that the Ugaritic language and Canaanite myths are essential in understanding the Psalms,[32] that the rhythm and meter demands restoring a word in colon one, and that this restoration must be in line with the synonymous *parallelismus membrorum* of the bicolon so that the restoration is harmonious with *"from the depths of* the sea" or some similar understanding, as in Albright's restoration and rendering.

---

28. Note Albright's words: "The bicolon is undoubtedly of Canaanite origin; the name *YHWH* has displaced original *Ba'al*" (ibid., 27).

29. A. Weiser suggested a minor emendation to *'āšûb*. See his *Psalms* (trans. H. Hartwell; OTL; Philadelphia: Westminster, 1962) 480.

30. Albright, "Catalogue of Early Hebrew Lyric Poems," 28.

31. M. E. Tate rightly states that Albright's rendering demands "obviously too much emendation" but that Bashan as "serpent" has been accepted by many experts. See Tate, *Psalms 51–100*, 167.

32. Surprisingly, Psalm 68 is not mentioned in Y. Avishur's *Studies in Hebrew and Ugaritic Psalms* (Jerusalem: Magnes, 1994).

Albright argued that we "must almost certainly insert מחץ here in order to complete both sense and metric form. These three consonants were presumably lost "by a combination of vertical haplography and *homoioarkton*."[33] Most importantly, Albright rightly perceived that בשׁן denoted a serpent in v. 23[22]. He was the first scholar to argue that this noun must mean a serpent; and he derived this meaning from an intimate understanding of Akkadian, Syrian Arabic, and especially Ugaritic.[34]

Returning now to the perception that "Bashan" meant "serpent" in early western Semitic,[35] this meaning is now certain, especially because of a reading in a Ugaritic text. This mythological text, *KTU* 1.82 (= *PRU* 2.1 [RS 15.134]),[36] also provides some data to guide us in restoring the first colon of Ps 68:23[22], which clearly has one beat missing, and the missing consonants contained an idea parallel to "from the depths of" the sea in the second colon.

The Ugaritic text is a discussion between Baal and Anat after their victory over the dragon Tannin. In line 6 we find *ḥr.bṭnm*,[37] which means "the hole (or den) of snakes."[38] C. Virolleaud took *ḥr.bṭnm* to mean "trou de vipéres" and drew attention to the famous חר פתן in Isa 11:8, which denotes "the den of a cobra." On the basis of the poetic meter and syntax and in light of the Ugaritic phrase, which was perhaps a cliché, the meaning of Ps 68:23[22] may be restored. Thus, I suggest restoring מחר before בשׁן "[from the den of] the dragon-snake." The context suggests that "them" in colon one and two is understood to be implied (as is typical in Semitics).[39]

What then is the meaning of the passage? The implied "them" refers to "God's enemies" mentioned in the previous verse (68:22[21]). The "God of our salvation" will bring back "his enemies" from far distant regions: "the [den of] the snake" and "the depths of the sea." It seems that the God of salvation, the one to whom belongs "escape from death," is bringing his enemies into judgment. God will bring all the enemies to salvation or judgment. Not

---

33. Albright, "Catalogue of Early Hebrew Lyric Poems," 27.

34. See Albright, "New Light on Early Canaanite Language and Literature," *BASOR* 46 (1932) 19; and idem, "Catalogue of Early Hebrew Lyric Poems," 27.

35. See D. J. A. Clines, *The Dictionary of Classical Hebrew* (Sheffield: Sheffield Academic Press, 1995) 2.281, in which a second meaning is given to בשׁן: "snake."

36. There is no *CTA* number. I am grateful to Prof. J. M. de Tarragon for helping me comprehend the nomenclature of Ugaritic research (a nightmare of sigla, as is Qumranology).

37. Reading *ḥr* instead of *ḥw*, with C. Virolleaud, *PRU*, 4–5 and pl. 4.

38. Also, see line 35 of the reverse of this same text (*KTU* 1.82): rev. ᶜl *bṭnt.trtḥ*. Virolleaud, *PRU*, 6.

39. Semitics abounds with indefinite or assumed pronouns. The Semitic mind, ancient and modern, feels it redundant to supply what is obviously implied.

only those still alive (68:22[21]) but also those who are in the den of the dragon-snake (those buried in the earth) or in the depths of the sea (those who died at sea). God will bring forth for judgment all who have died, either on land or on sea. Thus, it is not necessary to emend the text, which is always a precarious act, to obtain, as Gunkel did, a translation that is appealing: "From the furnace of fire I will bring them back."[40] The restoration and emendation reveals that Gunkel correctly understood the intended meaning: God will bring back [a completed act] all enemies for judgment.

The meaning of Psalm 68, especially vv. 19–24[18–23] is similar to other strains in biblical theology. God brings into judgment all—including all in heaven and on the earth (or in its waters). Recall how similar Psalm 68 now is to Amos 9:2–3,

> Though they dig into Sheol,
> From there my hand shall take them;
> Though they ascend (into) heaven,
> From there I will bring them down;
> And though they hide themselves on top of Carmel,
> From there I shall search and take them;
> Though they hide from my sight at the bottom of the sea,
> From there I shall command the serpent,
> And he shall bite them.

According to Amos 9, the "top of Carmel" represents the land, and it is parallel to "the bottom of the sea," which signifies the waters. This is virtually identical to Psalm 68, in which "[the den of] the dragon-snake" represents the land and is parallel to "the depths of the sea," which represents the waters. In both passages the author is proclaiming that God will bring all to judgment—those who died on land or sea.

This interpretation of Ps 68:23 was originally imagined to be weak and perhaps speculative. Now, it seems that my exegesis is sound and established. A stunning confirmation of the meaning I see in this verse is found, quite to my surprise in the *Midrash on the Psalms*. The rabbis saw that Ps 68:23 referred to the places in which the dead are located: in the earth or in the sea. This verse received the following exposition in the *Midrash on the Psalms*:

> *The Lord said: "I will bring again from Bashan"* (Ps. 68:23)—that is, bring those whom wild beasts devoured; *"I will bring My people again from the depths of the sea" (ibid.)*—that is, bring those who drowned in the depths for the hallowing of the Name. [Or, reading the end of the verse, *I will bring them again from the depths*

---

40. H. Gunkel, *Die Psalmen* (Göttingen: Vandenhoeck & Ruprecht, 1929 [4th ed.], 1968 [5th ed.]) ad loc.

of the sea, and taking the word *them* to refer to the enemies of Israel, the verse
means that] even as the Holy One, blessed be He, requited Og, the king of
Bashan, and requited Pharaoh and the Egyptians at the Red Sea, so will the
Holy One, blessed be He, requite the mighty men of wicked Edom.[41]

Obviously, I prefer to interpret Ps 68:23 to mean that God is the eternal judge
who will bring all the dead back for judgment, those who are buried in the
land or in the sea. We should not expect the rabbis to imagine that the sacred
text needed emendation or restoration. Thus, we learn how to improve our
exegesis and exposition from the rabbis, who recited the ancient traditions in
a "living language."

It now becomes clearer that in Biblical Hebrew "Bashan" can denote a
mythical snake: a dragon-snake. With this lexical insight and a restored text,
meter, and *parallelismus membrorum*, we can appreciate the synonymous *parallelismus membrorum* between "[from the den of] the dragon-snake" (מחר בשן)
and "from the depths of the sea" (ממצלות ים).[42] It is possible, perhaps probable, that this section of Psalm 68 (now vv. 23–24[22–23]) once read:

> The Lord spoke:
> "[From the den of] the dragon-snake I will bring (them) back,
> I will bring (them) back from the depths of the sea,
> So that your foot might crush (them) in blood,
> And the tongues of your dogs (may have) their portion from (your) enemies."

This rendering restores an original מחר בשן.[43] The original 3 + 3 meter is also
restored; thus, the bicolon has a harmonious rhythm of 3 + 3 followed by 3 +
3.[44] Experts apparently overlooked the missing beat in the first colon: they

---

41. W. G. Braude, *The Midrash on Psalms* (Yale Judaica Series 13; New Haven: Yale University Press, 1959) 546.

42. The noun מצלות is the fem. pl. of צולה "abyss," "deep," or "depths." See Isa 44:27.

43. The word חר can denote a "hole" for people (1 Sam 14:11, Job 30:6) or a "den" for
animals (Nah 2:13[12]). How can we explain the loss of a noun in Ps 68:23? On the one
hand, copyists often miss a word in transcribing, and one does not have to appeal to ho-
moeoteleuton. The Qumran Scrolls, including the carefully copied biblical sacred texts,
abound with supralinear corrections; that is, a word was missed by a copyist and he or a later
scribe placed it above the line. These words added above others supply words or even
clauses that were missed in transcribing. On the other hand, if the text had been read out
loud and the laryngeal not carefully enunciated, then "ḥur" may have been lost in poor elo-
cution or hearing (obviously, some elderly scribes may have benefited by a hearing aide).
Thus, we should assume that some of our texts are missing words and realize that they may
not have been so extremely cryptic originally.

44. In its present form v. 23[22] is 2 (The Lord said) + 2 (I will bring back from the
dragon-snake) + 3 (I will bring back from the depths of the sea). For a seminal study of

may not have observed that אמר אדני, which begins what we call v. 23[22], is outside the meter of the first colon and was intended to introduce the bicolon.

5. What Is the Date of Psalm 68, Especially Verse 22[23], and Is Canaanite Culture Evident in It?

Most experts of the Psalter correctly date Psalm 68 early; that is, they place the origin of the Psalm long before the exilic period.[45] A very early date for the traditions in Psalm 68 seems demanded, since God is associated with Mount Bashan.[46] Note S. Terrien's translation of 68:16,

> The mount of Bashan would be the mount of God,
> Mount of a thousand hills, the mount of Bashan.[47]

The text continues to stress that this "mount of Bashan" is where God desires to dwell, and that he will "dwell (in it) forever" (לנצח; Ps 68:16–17[15–16]).[48] Such an affirmation is impossible not only in Judea but also in Israel after the monarchy or at least after the sixth century B.C.E. It is quite misleading to interpret Ps 68:16[15] as a verse, like others, in which there is a "repeated mention of the sanctuary of Jerusalem."[49] The elevation of Jerusalem over all other sanctuaries is a belief that arose with the arrival of the ark in Jerusalem, with David,[50] and was emphasized by at least the sixth century B.C.E., with the editor known as "the Deuteronomist" (Dtr), advocated by M. Noth,[51] or with the slightly earlier Deuteronomistic School, espoused by E. W. Nicholson and M. Weinfeld.[52] The traditions of this school, among other tendencies,

---

Canaanite rhythm, see F. M. Cross, "Notes on a Canaanite Psalm in the Old Testament," *BASOR* 117 (1950) 19–21.

45. A. Caquot ("Le Psaume LXVIII," *RHR* 167 [1970] 147–82) concludes that Psalm 68 is a hymn of victory composed during the time of Hezekiah.

46. Psalm 68 seems to presuppose a worship of some god, perhaps originally Baal (now edited to Yhwh) on Mount Bashan. Mowinckel rightly perceived that Psalm 68, in its present form, reflects the Jerusalem cult, but opined that it reflected "an old originally North Israelite psalm." See S. Mowinckel, *The Psalms in Israel's Worship* (2 vols.; trans. D. R. Ap-Thomas; Oxford: Blackwell, 1962) 2.152–43.

47. Terrien, *Psalms*, p. 486.

48. Perhaps the editor of Psalm 68 omitted an earlier "in it" or "on Bashan" in the last colon of v. 17.

49. The words of Weiser, *Psalms*, 488.

50. See esp. C. L. Seow, *Myth, Drama, and the Politics of David's Dance* (Atlanta: Scholars Press, 1989).

51. M. Noth, *Überlieferungsgeschichtliche Studien* (Schriften der Königsberger Gelehrten Gesellschaft 18/2; Halle [Saale]: Niemeyer, 1943).

52. E. W. Nicholson, *Deuteronomy and Tradition* (Philadelphia: Fortress, 1967); M. Weinfeld, *Deuteronomy and the Deuteronomic School* (Oxford: Clarendon, 1972; repr. Winona

emphasized that Jerusalem, and only Jerusalem, was the abode of Yhwh. Thus, the celebration of Bashan as God's abode considerably antedated this tendency that became the authoritative definition of Judaism.

This point needs emphasizing today in light of the publications of the so-called minimalists. The claim that Jerusalem alone is Yhwh's home clearly antedates the sixth century B.C.E. As recorded in 1 Kgs 11:36, 15:4; and 2 Kgs 8:19, God gave David and his descendants a lamp in Jerusalem.[53] The Zion tradition definitively shapes Ps 78:68 and 132:13, and as J. J. M. Roberts states, "its crystallization point must still be sought in the Davidic-Solomonic era."[54] Perhaps Psalm 68 is as early as Albright suggested—in the Solomonic period. Following S. Mowinckel's claim that Psalm 68 reflects a Jerusalem festival (as we shall see), Anderson offers a viable suggestion that the Sitz im Leben is the Autumnal Festival, when Yhwh's kingship was celebrated and his mighty deeds acclaimed.[55] Surely, the traditions we have isolated in Psalm 68, especially v. 16, must antedate the Zion tradition that in the tenth century B.C.E. began to be dogma. Note Roberts's words:

> The fundamental point necessary for the formation of the Zion tradition was the belief that Yahweh had chosen Jerusalem as his permanent abode. That dogma could not date much later than David's decision to move the ark to Jerusalem, and certainly not later than the decision to build the temple there.[56]

There is a major tension in Psalm 68. Verse 16[15], "the mountain of Elohim (is) the mountain of Bashan," clashes with v. 30[29], "your temple at Jerusalem." Verse 30[29] clearly refers to Solomon's temple.[57] How should one resolve this tension? It seems prima facie evident that vv. 16[15] and 23[22] preserve traditions that both antedate the monarchy and reflect the popular Canaanite myth about Baal residing on Mount Bashan and how he defeated Bashan (the dragon-snake). Most likely, v. 30[29] reflects the hand of the Elo-

---

Lake, Ind.: Eisenbrauns, 1992); see especially "The Centralization of Worship: The Chosen Place and the 'Name' Theology," pp. 324–26.

53. See esp. F. M. Cross, *Canaanite Myth and Hebrew Epic* (Cambridge: Harvard University Press, 1973) 274–89. Cross dates "the fundamental composition of the Deuteronomistic history in the era of Josiah"; that is, to "the late Kingdom." He makes room for "only minor modification by a member of the Deuteronomistic school in the Exile" (p. 289).

54. Roberts, *The Bible and the Ancient Near East: Collected Essays* (Winona Lake, Ind.: Eisenbrauns, 2002) 343.

55. Anderson, *Psalms*, 1.482.

56. Roberts, *The Bible and the Ancient Near East*, 345.

57. Roberts (ibid., 344) argues that v. 30 must date "after Solomon's construction of that edifice" (i.e., the temple).

hisitic editor who brought early Canaanite lore into line with Jerusalem's Yahwistic theology.

6. Is Psalm 68 a "Catalogue"?

The psalm is not easy to comprehend. The verses do not seem to flow smoothly and logically. Is Psalm 68 fundamentally a catalogue of early Hebrew poems, as Albright argued long ago? Albright's solution is rather drastic and assumes that a catalogue of incipits would be included into the Psalter.

Is there no coherency in Psalm 68? Was Hans Schmidt correct to suggest that Psalm 68 is a collection of independent songs?[58] Is the psalm a chaotic miscellany? If so, then why have Israelites in Solomon's temple and Jews in the Second Temple and for millennia, and through changing times, found meaning in the psalm?

Most scholars have not been persuaded by Albright's attempt to solve the seeming disjunctions that define this psalm. Many experts have followed Mowinckel, mutates mutandes, in seeing Psalm 68 in its final edited form with some unity and as a processional psalm for the Jerusalem cult. K. Schaefer calls Psalm 68 "A Triumphal Parade" and sees it as "a hymn to God's power and majesty."[59] Thus, it is helpful to quote Mowinckel's conclusion. He grouped Psalms 24, 68, 118, and 132 as festal procession psalms. Of them he wrote:

> They can only be understood in connexion with a vision of the procession itself and its different acts and scenes. The interpreter has to use both the descriptions of such cultic processions and the allusions to them in other Old Testament texts, and his own imagination, to recall a picture of the definite situation from which such a psalm cannot be separated. Only thus it is possible to find the inner connexion between the apparently incoherent stanzas of, e.g., Ps. 68.[60]

This interpretation gives pride of place to v. 25 in Psalm 68; which obviously follows the verse in focus now, v. 23[22]. Note Mowinckel's translation of this verse:

> We are seeing thy processions, O God,
> The procession of my God and my King in the sanctuary,
> Singers in front, musicians behind,
> Between them girls with tambourines (Ps. 68.25 [actually 25–26]).[61]

---

58. H. Schmidt, *Die Psalmen* (HAT 1/15; Tübingen: Mohr [Siebeck], 1934) 125–31.
59. K. Schaefer, *Psalms* (Berit Olam; Collegeville, Minn.: Liturgical Press, 2001) 163.
60. Mowinckel, *The Psalms in Israel's Worship*, 1.5.
61. Ibid., 1.11.

Mowinckel tended to read Psalm 68 in its present (corrupt) form and with an eye on vv. 25–26. There is far more discontinuity than he allows,[62] even when we try to imagine the procession toward the enthronement of Yhwh. One should admit, moreover, that there is nothing in vv. 25–26 that suggests, let alone demands, that one think about Jerusalem and its temple. These verse may reflect an original, very early procession at Bethel, Shiloh, Dan, or even a Canaanite sanctuary, as at Meggido, Beth Shan (which may have been confused with Bashan),[63] or on Mount Bashan. Yet in its present setting, vv. 25–26 are followed by v. 30[29], which refers to "your temple in Jerusalem."

Mowinckel's general insight regarding some unity in Psalm 68, among or behind the *disjecta membra*, allows for the following reflections concerning echoes and connections within Psalm 68. As we proceed, we must keep in mind the pioneering influence of Albright and the obvious echoes in Psalm 68 from Canaanite cults and myths.

Surely Psalm 68 belongs with Psalms 27, 36, 40, 41, 89, 94, 108, and 144; these are classed as *psalms of mixed types*.[64] Psalm 68 is thus not merely a catalogue of early Hebrew poems, as Albright concluded.[65] Even if one is convinced that Psalm 68 is essentially a catalogue of incipits, one should admit that in some passages there is a remnant of an original, extremely early poem or extended selections from an early poem.[66] At least a later compiler—the Elohistic editor—placed similar thoughts sometimes contiguously. Most likely, Psalm 68 obtains more unity when one understands that it reflects a yearly procession within the temple cult. Thus, one should seek to understand

---

62. See esp. H.-J. Kraus, *Psalms 60–150*, 48.

63. The Hebrew בשׁן can also denote Beth Shan; see N. Jechielis, *Aruch Completum*, 1.207.

64. See T. Craven, *The Book of Psalms* (Collegeville, Minn.: Liturgical Press, 1992) 23.

65. S. Mowinckel claimed that Psalm 68 is essentially a unity. See Mowinckel's disagreement with Albright in *Der achtundsechzigste Psalm* (Oslo: Dybwad, 1953); especially see pp. 1–78. In the early 1960s, F. M. Cross ("The Divine Warrior in Israel's Early Cult," in *Biblical Motifs* [ed. A. Altmann; Cambridge: Harvard University Press, 1966] 11–30) followed his teacher, Albright: "Apparently each couplet is the *incipit* of a longer liturgical piece" (p. 25). Anderson finds Albright's atomistic approach "rather unlikely." Anderson contends that Psalm 68 does not fit the major psalm-types, although it is close to the *Gattung* of hymns. Under the influence of Mowinckel, he labels Psalm 68 "a song of procession." Anderson, *Psalms* (NCB; London: Oliphants, 1972) 1.481.

66. See P. D. Miller: "The possibility of an older unified poem underlying this one cannot be completely denied, but the present state of the text points much more clearly to a piecing together of isolated bits of poetry or *incipits*." Miller leans toward Albright ("various parts of this psalm were not originally connected") but judges that Albright has atomized this psalm too severely (*The Divine Warrior in Early Israel*, 103).

68:23[22] within its immediate context and in light of earlier verses. Generations of Israelites and Jews, subsequent to its editing, would have read Psalm 68 with an ear open to the contextual meaning of words and images.

Terrien indicates that Psalm 68 "reveals a rather spectacular structure of eleven strophes." One of them is our focal point: vv. 23–26. Terrien insightfully concludes that these verses reflect an editor's fascination with temple music.[67] Tournay rightly pointed out that our key verse, Ps 68:23, is not to be read in isolation: "Cette strophe fait corps avec la précédente."[68] As Roberts perceived, while parts of Psalm 68 lack clarity, "there are large blocks where there are more logical connections than one would expect in a random collection of incipits."[69] Roberts sees vv. 22–24 as "connected"; they "may lead into the description of the processional in vv. 25–28."[70] Roberts, and many other Semitic experts, are intermittently influenced by Mowinckel's claim that the Sitz im Leben is a procession in the Jerusalem temple.

Mowinckel saw Psalm 68 as devoid of meaning until we comprehend it within its edited context: a cultic processional psalm for the enthronement of Yhwh in Jerusalem, perhaps during the New Year Festival and the Festival of Lights at Tabernacles.[71]

Mowinckel was probably correct that Psalm 68 is related to some festival in Jerusalem, but he may have been incorrect that it is Sukkot (the Feast of Tabernacles). Equally possible, and probably more likely, is the possibility that Psalm 68 was associated with Shavuot (Pentecost, Feast of Weeks, or Day of Firstfruits) and not only in the Herodian temple but also in Solomon's temple before the exile.

Early, perhaps in pre-Solomonic and certainly preexilic times, Shavuot was the time to celebrate the wheat harvest (Deut 16:9–11). By at least 100 B.C.E., Shavuot was the festival par excellence for celebrating the giving of Torah and the Sinai Covenant. Perhaps not originally, but certainly finally, Psalm 68 was associated with Shavuot. Note how Ps 68:18[17] provides traditions for the celebration of Sinai at Shavuot:

> God's chariots (רכב אלהים) (are) twenty thousand,
> (Indeed) thousands of thousands;

---

67. Terrien, *Psalms*, 489. For the form and structure of Psalm 68, according to Terrien, see the diagram on p. 490.

68. Tournay, "Le Psaume LXVIII," 238.

69. Roberts, *The Bible and the Ancient Near East*, 345. Roberts found Albright's thesis of incipits "unconvincing."

70. Ibid.

71. Mowinckel, *The Psalms in Israel's Worship*, 1.5, 11, 125, 170; 2.152–53.

The Lord is among them (as in) Sinai (סיני),
in the Holy (Place) (בקדש).

How do we now know that Psalm 68 was associated with Shavuot? Two reasons: a scroll from Qumran is shaped by this psalm, and the scroll is liturgically linked with Shavuot.

The *Angelic Liturgy* (or *Songs of the Sabbath Sacrifice*) clearly antedates 100 B.C.E. and certainly embodies ancient traditions. In this scroll Psalm 68 echoes, and the context of the specific song is, the liturgical celebrations immediately after Shavuot.[72] Psalm 68 has shaped the *Angelic Liturgy*. This document was popular at Qumran,[73] but it also represents non-Qumran traditions. Four observations prove the point that Psalm 68 was associated with Shavuot (the Festival of Weeks).

First, Ps 68:17–20 with the focus on "God's chariots" has, with Ezekiel's merkavah vision, provided the poet with numerous expressions and concepts, including the following: "his glorious chariots" (מרכבות כבודו), mentioned twice; "wondrous chariots" (כבוד מרכבות); and the "chariot throne" (כסא מרכבה). All of these appear in *Sabbath Song* 12. Perhaps Ps 68:34[33] has also shaped the 12th *Sabbath Song*; note that this verse exhorts the singing of praise to the Lord, who "chariots" in the heaven:

To the One who rides (לרכב) on the heaven of heavens of old;
Indeed, He sends out His voice, a mighty voice.

Second, the author or compiler of Ps 68:35[34] adds that God's "strength (is) in the clouds" (ועזו בשחקים). Clearly this thought was appealing to the author of *Sabbath Song* 12, who supplies a vision of heavenly worship in God's chariot-throne tabernacle, in which the angels exalt over "the powerful acts of the Go[d of eternity]" (גבורות אלו[ה]י עולמים).

Third, the verb for God "to dwell," לשכן, in Ps 68:19[18] probably supplied the similar concept "and when they settle (or dwell)," ובשוכן, in line 12 of *Sabbath Song* 12 (4Q405 frgs. 20–22 col. ii). The fragment of this portion of the scroll is dated to about 50 B.C.E. Perhaps "in the tabernacle" (במשכ[ן]) of *Sabbath Song* 12 is also an echo of Ps 68:19[18]. The same seems to apply to the idea, but expressed with a different word, that beneath the "luminous firmament" is God's "glorious seat (or dwelling)" (מושב כבודו).

Fourth, the praise to God who "will dwell forever" (ישכן לנצח) on his holy mountain, found in Ps 68:17[16], most likely provided resonating themes in

---

72. J. R. Davila also points out that Psalm 68 influenced the perception of Shavuot in rabbinic traditions; see his *Liturgical Works* (Grand Rapids: Eerdmans, 2000) 149.

73. Traditions about the storm-god shape Psalm 68 and 4QBerakhot, but the latter does not quote Psalm 68.

the *Angelic Liturgy.* Perhaps this concept from Psalm 68 has helped shape the concept of "the God of [eter]nity" (עולﬦ[עולﬦ] אלוהי) in *Sabbath Song* 12.

Surely, in many ways Psalm 68 has influenced the mind of the author of *Sabbath Song* 12. It is not one element but the way that the elements are related and their liturgical setting that ground *Sabbath Song* 12 with Psalm 68. In evaluating these echoes, it is imperative to perceive that the authors of the *Angelic Liturgy* knew the Hebrew Bible—especially the Psalter—by heart; but they never directly quoted from it in their creative compositions.

Without any doubt *Sabbath Song* 12 is associated with Shavuot. The setting is for "the twelf⟨th⟩ [Sa]bbath [on the twenty-first of] the third [month.]" This Sabbath follows Shavuot; thus, there is a connection between Psalm 68 and Shavuot (the Festival of Weeks), according to the traditions in the *Angelic Liturgy.* As J. R. Davila states, the use of Psalm 68 in the *Angelic Liturgy* is "further evidence of its early exegetical use in association with the Festival of Weeks."[74] He was dependent on C. A. Newsom, who argued convincingly that Ps 68:17–20, along with 1 Kgs 19:12 and Ezekiel 1, 3, and 10, were "drawn upon" by the poet as he explained how the chariot throne praises God in *Sabbath Song* 12.[75] And, as already noted, this song immediately followed Shavuot (the Festival of Weeks);[76] hence, Psalm 68 was at least by the second century B.C.E. associated not only with a festival but specifically with Shavuot.

We should not judge the ideas in Psalm 68 in terms of the logical progression of post-Enlightenment logic. There is hardly a logical progression in Ugaritic and Mesopotamian hymns (and certainly little or no progression in some sections of the *Hodayot* or *Odes of Solomon*).[77] Even today those who live in the West tend to appreciate logic, while those in the East often find it annoying and misrepresentative of life.

7. Are the Words in 68:23[22] Shaped by an Echo from Earlier in Psalm 68?

Recognizing that Psalm 68 reflects some unity, we may look for possible echoes of our restored text. The restored noun חר "den" seems to echo הר "mountain" in a preceding verse. These echoes would be heard when the

74. Davila, *Liturgical Works,* 148.

75. C. A. Newsom and J. H. Charlesworth, *Angelic Liturgy: Song of the Sabbath Sacrifice* (Princeton Theological Seminary Dead Sea Scrolls Project 4B; Tübingen: Mohr Siebeck / Louisville: Westminster John Knox, 1999) 8. For the text and translation of the *Angelic Liturgy,* see this edition.

76. See Newsom, Charlesworth, Strawn, and Rietz in *Angelic Liturgy,* 4.

77. R. H. Charles misled scholars by emending, without any manuscript support, the conclusion of *The Parables of Enoch,* as I have frequently pointed out; see *OTP* 1, ad loc.

psalm was read out loud (as were all ancient literary texts). The two Hebrew nouns for "den" and "mountain" sound similar. They are virtually indistinguishable when the speaker does not bring out the force of the laryngeal; and from Qumran we know the plosive quality of the laryngeals waned during the Second Temple period [e.g. the ע and א are sometimes confused].

By choosing his words carefully, a poet, or the compiler, may echo in 68:23[22] a passage in Ps 68:16[15].[78] Note v. 16[15]:

> A mountain of God (is) the mountain of Bashan;
> A mountain [of many] peaks (is) the mountain of Bashan.[79]

In this verse הר־בשן appears in colon one and in colon two. The poet then proceeds to develop his thought, so that a similar phrase evolves into the meaning "the den of the dragon-snake." Note how similar the two passages appear:

> har-ʾĕlōhîm har-bāšān
> har gabnunnîm har-bāšān (Ps 68:16[15])

This text seems to be echoed in the restored text:

> miḥur bāšān ʾāšîb
> ʾāšîb mimmĕṣulōt yām

Just as an echo of a sound bouncing off mountains does not identically reproduce the original sound, so the repetitive har-bāšān (bis) is echoed in memory when one hears ḥur bāšān. Even if Psalm 68 is fundamentally a compilation of incipits, some postexilic readers would likely have heard the echo. It is also conceivable that the two passages, now vv. 16[15] and 23[22], were originally much closer than in the miscellany of disjoined thoughts. Both verses reflect early Canaanite myths: "Bashan" as the abode of God and "Bashan" as the enemy of Baal [the likely Urtext]. The similar lexemes are not only harmonious but most likely were created by the same poet.

Such a reader—and perhaps the Elohistic editor—may have perceived an evolution of thought from Mount Bashan as the place where God dwells for-

---

78. See the reflections of Emerton, which are focused on Ps 68:16, in "The 'Mountain of God' in Psalm 68:16," 24–37. He rightly suggests that v. 16 may be a question, indicating that Yhwh does not dwell on Bashan, which some Israelites may have confused with Hermon.

79. S. A. Geller (Parallelism in Early Biblical Poetry [HSM 20; Missoula, Mont.: Scholars Press, 1979] 213) takes hr ʾlhm to mean "O mighty mountains." Also, see D. Winton Thomas, "A Consideration of Some Unusual Ways of Expressing the Superlative in Hebrew," VT 3 (1953) 209–24.

ever (68:16–17[15–16]) to the extremities in which God's enemies now hide (68:20–24[19–23]). We have amassed additional data to demonstrate that בשׁן once also denoted a "dragon-snake." Surely, it is not wise now to follow the advice of H.-J. Kraus, who argues that in Ps 68:23[22] Bashan is "certainly a designation for the 'highest height.'"[80]

8. Should One Seek for an Understanding of Psalm 68:23[22] by Appealing to Context?

The context suggests that the thought of v. 23 flows from v. 20 through v. 22. In 68:23[22] the poet (through the paronomasia of double entendre) is drawing attention to the power of "the God of salvation" (68:21[20]). God will bring everything and everyone to judgment; that is, bring them back from a place poetically representing Sheol (the den of the dragon-snake and the depths of the sea).[81] The Warrior-God, Yhwh, is bringing all his enemies to judgment.

My interpretation is not far from that of P. D. Miller. Note how he renders vv. 22–24:

> How "Yahweh" has smitten
> The head of his enemies
> The head of the "wicked (?)"
> Roaming in his guilt.
> The Lord said:
> *I muzzled the Serpent,*
> *I muzzled the Deep Sea.*
> That you may wash
> Your feet in blood,
> The tongues of your dogs
> From the enemies their portion. (?)[82]

Miller was focused on the image of the "Divine Warrior in Early Israel." I am focusing on "Bashan" as denoting a dragon-snake. Miller rightly found

---

80. Kraus, *Psalms 60–150*, 55.

81. Although Anderson (*Psalms*, 1.494) prefers the rendering "I will bring them back from Bashan," he understands that God's enemies are to be brought to punishment from any place to which they may have fled. One should note that Anderson was constrained to provide commentary on an established text, the RSV. In *Psalms 51–100*, Tate draws attention to a dissertation that contains the argument that God brings his enemies back from anywhere they may be; see J. P. LePeau, *Psalm 68: An Exegetical and Theological Study* (Ph.D. Dissertation, University of Iowa, 1981).

82. After completing my study of Psalm 68, I found Miller's insightful research; see Miller, *The Divine Warrior in Early Israel*, 110 (italics mine).

Albright's emendations "too extreme and actually unnecessary" (p. 111). Miller's translation, and especially his exegesis, also is deeply influenced by Ugaritic. He focuses on ʿnt III 37–38 (= *KTU* 1.3 III 37–38),[83] which he renders as follows:

> I muzzled Tannin, I muzzled him.
> I smote the twisting Serpent.[84]

In contrast to Miller, I prefer to see Ps 68:23[22] in light of *KTU* 1.82 instead of *KTU* 1.3 III 37–38. I take the verb אשיב in Ps 68:23[22], in which it appears in colons one and two, as a *Hiphil* from the familiar שוב (with most scholars) and not as Miller, who follows Dahood,[85] from שבם "muzzled," which is a verb known from Ugaritic and Arabic but is not obviously extant in Biblical Hebrew.[86]

9. What Has Been Learned?

Lexicographically, we have learned that there is now abundant evidence that בשן signifies a mythological snake in early Biblical Hebrew;[87] it denoted a mythical snake-like monster. In light of 18 nouns that denote "serpent" or "snake" in Biblical Hebrew, and for some consistency between Hebrew text and English translation, I suggest that Bashan be represented by "dragon snake."[88]

Haplography abounds in the Qumran Scrolls, including the biblical texts.[89] The rhythm and meter of the bicolon and the poetic form, synonymous *paral-*

---

83. For the text, see A. Herdner, ed., *Corpus des tablettes en cunéiformes alphabétiques* (Mission de Ras Shamra 10; Paris: Imprimerie Nationale, 1963) 1.17.

84. See Miller, "Two Critical Notes on Psalm 68 and Deuteronomy 33," *HTR* 57 (1964) 240; and Miller, *The Divine Warrior in Early Israel*, 111. Contrast Roberts's (*The Bible and the Ancient Near East*, 344) rendering; he attaches the *mem* in colon 1 to the end of אדני, as an enclitic, and takes the verb to be a *Hiphil*:

> The Lord said, "I will repulse the Serpent,
> I will muzzle the depths of the Sea."

85. Dahood, "Mišmār 'Muzzle' in Job 7:12," *JBL* 80 (1961) 270–71.

86. The probability that *šmr* meant "muzzle"—esp. in Job 8:12—should not lead to the far more speculative suggestion that שבם meant "muzzle" also, let alone in Biblical Hebrew. In Job 8 "set a guard over me" is not far from the concept of "place a muzzle on me." The verb שבר appears in a negative sense in Job 10:14.

87. For a discussion of Bashan in Deut 33:22, see my "Biblical Hebrew Terms for Various Types of Snakes" (in press).

88. See the preceding note.

89. I have seen a fragment of Leviticus in which a word was left out by the copyist and then restored by him (most likely) or another hand. I hope to announce the recovery of this text, which has an interesting variant, in the near future.

lelismus membrorum, demand some restoration, as Albright indicated. My restoration recognizes the "severely corrupted text"[90] and does not appeal to any emendation, which many experts have concluded that Psalm 68 must receive. It is not an unfounded speculation. It restores the meter and the *parallelismus membrorum*. That is, *"the den of* the dragon-snake" is parallel and synonymous to *"the depths of* the sea." The passage fits the early Canaanite mythic origins of this psalm that reflects how Baal defeated the gods named Yamm and Bashan. This dating of the *traditions* behind Psalm 68 is in line with many experts who follow Albright in tracing these *traditions* to pre-Solomonic Canaanite culture.[91] As Miller contends, "when verse 23 is translated correctly, we see that Yahweh's enemies are also the monsters of the cosmos." Miller then salutes Albright for being "one of the first to call attention to this theme in the verse and particularly to the mention of the serpent Bašan."[92] Albright's insight was developed in a creative and brilliant manner by F. M. Cross and D. N. Freedman, who argued that *bāšān* denoted a "serpent," or "viper." Cross and Freedman appealed to proto-Sinaitic and Ugar. *bṯn* "serpent" and Arab. *bathan* "viper."[93]

The echoes we have discerned in Psalm 68 were most likely heard by many who read the psalm out loud, in Hebrew, for centuries before the burning of the temple by Titus in 70 C.E. There is an ideological progression from the Mount of Bashan to the den of the dragon-snake called Bashan. The final edited form of Psalm 68 indicates that the psalm was most likely used in the Jerusalem cult as a processional song chanted by the Levites and perhaps others during a festival in the temple, most likely Shavuot.

The Psalter is a deposit of the praises of God and the way that his power and grace shaped creation and define history. The Israelites and Jews celebrated Yhwh; in the past and future he conquers the enemies. This theme shapes Psalm 68, appearing in vv. 1, 21, and 23.[94]

The theological and poetic thought of 68:23[22] seems now to be clear. Yhwh is the All-Powerful Judge who will find all the enemies and punish them, because Yhwh is the God of salvation. Indeed, the present research

---

90. The words of Weiser in his *Psalms*, 481.

91. See, e.g., Miller, *The Divine Warrior in Early Israel*, 102–13; and Roberts, *The Bible and the Ancient Near East*, 344 (in which Roberts argues convincingly for archaic linguistic features and mythological elements that point to many contacts with the Baal myth).

92. Miller, *The Divine Warrior in Early Israel*, 111.

93. F. M. Cross and D. N. Freedman, "The Blessing of Moses," *JBL* 67 (1948) 191–210; the quotation is from p. 195.

94. See the reflections by H.-J. Kraus in *Theology of the Psalms* (trans. K. Crim; Minneapolis: Fortress, 1992), esp. p. 128.

helps us hear the chanting of priests and others in the Second Temple, and perhaps also in the Solomonic temple: הָאֵל לָנוּ אֵל לְמוֹשָׁעוֹת.[95]

95. Ps 68:21.

The "Dying and Rising God": A Survey of Research from Frazer to the Present Day

TRYGGVE N. D. METTINGER

Lund University

It is natural for people who have spent three decades or more in academe to look back and reflect. When I consider my own scholarly life in retrospect, one intense semester stands out in special light: the spring semester of 1984, which I spent in Princeton. It was Jimmy Roberts who brought me there to teach Hebrew Bible. That semester had a decisive effect on the direction of my own future work. Jimmy Roberts, with his double professional competence in Assyriology and Hebrew Bible, made me realize, more than ever before, the immense amount of perspective and depth that a scholar gains by studying ancient Israel in the light of the rest of the ancient Near East.

Jim and I first met in Tokyo at the 1979 International Symposium for Biblical Studies. There Jim contributed a masterly study of the structural features of the Zion-Sabaoth theology, which has since been compulsory reading in my part of the world.[1]

In the Zion-Sabaoth theology, Israel's God is sometimes denoted as a God who "lives" (2 Sam 22:47 = Ps 18:47) or as "the living God" (Ps 84:3).[2] We may of course ask in which way the ancient Near Eastern phenomenon of gods who die and return might shed light on such biblical formulations. A first step in the direction of such a study is to acquaint oneself with the intense scholarly debate on this aspect of Semitic religions. My contribution to the festschrift for a scholar who has demonstrated mastery of the field of "the Bible and the ancient Near East" is therefore a capsule survey of research on "dying

---

1. J. J. M. Roberts, "Zion in the Theology of the Davidic-Solomonic Empire," in *Studies in the Period of David and Solomon and Other Essays: Papers Read at the International Symposium for Biblical Studies, Tokyo, 5–7 December, 1979* (ed. Tomoo Ishida; Winona Lake, Ind.: Eisenbrauns, 1982) 93–108.

2. On this designation of God, see provisionally T. N. D. Mettinger, *In Search of God: The Meaning and Message of the Everlasting Names* (Philadelphia: Fortress, 1982) 82–91 with literature.

and rising gods." The following definition by Jonathan Z. Smith of "dying and rising gods" is the basis for my own usage of the label in this essay:

a generic appellation for a group of male deities found in agrarian Mediterranean societies who serve as the focus of myths and rituals that allegedly narrate and annually represent their death and resurrection.[3]

Jonathan Z. Smith and the Dying and Rising Gods

Even though the concept of the dying and rising god had a long prior history, there is no doubt that it owes its life to a large extent to James G. Frazer ([1906] 1914).[4] Having lived healthily for some decades, the dying and rising god lost much of his vigor due to the severe attack by Roland de Vaux in 1933. He then led a somewhat endangered life in the scholarship of the last half of the twentieth century, until he apparently died the death of a thousand wounds at the hands of Jonathan Z. Smith.

According to Smith, "all the deities that have been identified as belonging to the class of dying and rising deities can be subsumed under the two larger classes of disappearing deities or dying deities. In the first case, the deities return but have not died; in the second case, the gods die but do not return."[5] Death and resurrection are not combined in the "biography" of one single deity. In the case of Adonis, "only late texts, largely influenced by or written by Christians, claim that there is a subsequent day of celebration for Adonis having been raised from the dead."[6] Smith seems to have issued the death certificate for the idea of dying and rising gods; he takes the final step when he celebrates the secondary burial in his *Drudgery Divine*.[7]

Nevertheless, even after J. Z. Smith's contributions, the issue continued to be discussed by Mark S. Smith and H.-P. Müller.[8] Both scholars were equally skeptical about the existence of dying and rising deities in the ancient Near East. It is clear, then, that a number of major scholars in Bible and comparative

---

3. Jonathan Z. Smith, "Dying and Rising Gods," *ER* 4.521–27, esp. 521.
4. James G. Frazer, *Adonis, Attis, Osiris* (part 4.1 of *The Golden Bough*; 3rd ed. [published as a separate work, 1906]; London: Macmillan, 1914).
5. J. Z. Smith, "Dying and Rising Gods," 522.
6. Ibid.
7. Jonathan Z. Smith, *Drudgery Divine: On the Comparison of Early Christianities and the Religions of Late Antiquity* (Jordan Lectures in Comparative Religion 14; Chicago: University of Chicago Press, 1990) 85–115.
8. Mark S. Smith, *The Ugaritic Baal Cycle* (VTSup 55; Leiden: Brill, 1994) 69–75; H.-P. Müller, "Sterbende und auferstehende Vegetationsgötter? Eine Skizze," *TZ* 53 (1997) 74–82.

religion now find the idea of dying and rising deities untenable. In the following survey of research I shall sketch the main developments that have led to the present consensus, beginning with Frazer's contribution and what could be called the birth of the dying and rising gods. Then each of the following deities will be considered separately: Dumuzi/Tammuz, Adonis, and Baal. At the end of my contribution I shall try to identify some major features of the discussion surveyed.

Frazer and Baudissin

In the third edition of *The Golden Bough* (part 4.1), James G. Frazer presented the fascinating trinity of "Adonis, Attis, Osiris."[9] This part of his work was obviously a follow-up to his third volume, entitled *The Dying God*, in which he discussed the killing of the divine king and the death and resurrection of the corn spirit. Although Adonis was presented as the paramount example of the dying god, Frazer also listed a whole array of gods who belong together as representatives of one particular type of deity: "Under the names of Osiris, Tammuz, Adonis, and Attis, the peoples of Egypt and Western Asia represented the yearly decay and revival of life, especially of vegetable life, which they personified as a god who annually died and rose again from the dead."[10] Frazer explicitly identified Tammuz and Adonis and suggested that the true name of the deity was Tammuz, while the appellation Adonis was merely a Semitic title of honor, meaning "lord," that had been wrongly understood by the Greeks to be a proper name.[11]

What Frazer submitted was thus a naturist explanation of the dying and rising deity: this type of god is a personification of the seasonal cycle of vegetation. This naturist explanation, however, is combined with a euhemerist[12] one: behind the dying god looms a sacred, or even divine king, who will be slain when his fertility wanes.[13]

From the mythological material Frazer turned to the more fragmentary evidence for the Adonis ritual. Specifically, he discussed the festivals for Adonis in Alexandria and Byblos as known from the works of Theocritus (*Idyll* 15)

9. On the various editions of *The Golden Bough*, see Robert Ackerman, *J. G. Frazer: His Life and Work* (Cambridge: Cambridge University Press, 1987) 95–110, 164–79, 236–57; and J. Z. Smith, *Drudgery Divine*, 91–92 nn. 13–14.

10. *Golden Bough*, 4.1, 6.

11. Ibid., 6–7.

12. Thus named after Euhemerus, who held that the gods had been historical persons of ancient times.

13. *Golden Bough*, 4.1, 13–30.

and Lucian (*De dea syria* §§6–7). In both of these contexts, he found references to the resurrection of Adonis.[14]

An important chapter is devoted to the gardens of Adonis.[15] Frazer said,
without qualification, "Perhaps the best proof that Adonis was a deity of vegetation, and especially of the corn, is furnished by the gardens of Adonis, as
they were called. These were baskets or pots filled with earth, in which wheat,
barley, lettuces, fennel, and various kinds of flowers were sown and tended for
eight days, chiefly or exclusively by women."[16]

W. Baudissin was another scholar at the beginning of the twentieth century
who devoted a monograph to various issues related to the dying and rising
deity. It is obvious that Baudissin and Frazer agreed on one essential point: that
there are gods who are thought to die and return to life. To Baudissin, Adonis
was an *Auferstehungsgott*, a "dying and rising deity." The Phoenician triads comprised the city god, the young god, and his spouse. Of these, it is especially the
young god who is identified as the god who returns to life and who later appears, in one of his manifestations, as a healing god, insofar as the recuperation
from illness can be thought of as awaking from death.[17]

Baudissin devoted a brief, but important, section to a discussion of the cultic celebration of Adonis's resurrection. One might argue that the celebration
of the resurrection was borrowed from the Osiris complex by the Adonis cult.
Baudissin, however, found this assumption unnecessary, because the idea of
the resurrection of a god of nature (*Naturgott*) was not foreign to the North
Semites. He hypothesized that the annual celebration of mourning for the god
necessarily presupposed his *Wiederaufleben*, his "returning to life": if the god
was the focus of annual mourning rites, then it must have been thought that
he came back to life every year. Baudissin thus attempted to show that the idea
of Adonis's resurrection was no late newcomer, possibly dating back as early
as the times of the Old Testament prophets. Any relation to the Osiris tradition would be of a very early date.[18]

Another part of Baudissin' s argument that is of interest to us concerned the
relations between Adonis, Eshmun, and Tammuz.[19] Taking exception to Frazer, he considered Adonis and Tammuz to be two different deities.[20]

---

14. Ibid., 225.
15. Ibid., 236–59.
16. Ibid., 236.
17. Wolf Wilhelm Baudissin, *Adonis und Esmun: Eine Untersuchung zur Geschichte des Glaubens an Auferstehungsgötter und an Heilgötter* (Leipzig: Hinrichs, 1911) 52.
18. Ibid., 133–37.
19. Ibid., 345–84.
20. Ibid., 368.

There are, then, clear differences between Frazer and Baudissin. While Frazer, due to his anthropological orientation, devoted much energy to defending a specific theory of the prehistorical roots of the myth of Adonis, Baudissin was thoroughly oriented toward the historical tangibles, leaving euhemerist speculations aside. In particular, he took exception to Frazer's ideas about the cultic expressions of the Adonis myth.[21] Nevertheless, both scholars understood Adonis as being a dying and rising deity. Baudissin's position was made clear already in the subtitle of his book: Adonis belongs among the *Auferstehungsgötter.*

In the following I shall deal with the discussion as it continued after Frazer and Baudissin. My presentation will not follow a strict chronological order but a systematic one. I shall deal first with Tammuz, then with Adonis, and finally with Baal. The main purpose of this discussion is to determine how scholars have dealt with the question of the very existence of the alleged type. Are there any deities who die and then rise from the dead? Adopting a Popperian perspective, I will give particular importance to the works of scholars who have voiced a critique of this assumption.

Tammuz and Marduk

In the field of Assyriology, the twentieth century has witnessed a protracted discussion of Dumuzi/Tammuz and related figures.[22] In works from the first decades of the century by Zimmern and then notably by Langdon (1914), Tammuz was discussed in more or less Frazerian terms.[23] Langdon spoke of "a cult of sorrow, death and resurrection."[24]

Very early, Marduk became interesting to scholars inspired by Frazer. In a work on the Babylonian New Year festival, Zimmern argued, on the basis of the text *KAR* 143, that the ideas of Tammuz had been transferred to Marduk.[25] This suggestion played an important role in subsequent studies. In 1955, however, von Soden demonstrated that the crucial text was a work of

---

21. Ibid., vi–vii.

22. Note O. R. Gurney ("Tammuz Reconsidered: Some Recent Developments," *JSS* 7 [1962] 147–60) for a survey of research on Tammuz.

23. Heinrich Zimmern, *Der babylonische Gott Tamūz* (Abhandlungen der königl. Sächsischen Gesellsch. der Wiss., Phil.-hist. Klasse 27; Leipzig: Teubner, 1909) 699–738; and Stephen Langdon, *Tammuz and Ishtar: A Monograph upon Babylonian Religion and Theology, Containing Extensive Extracts from the Tammuz Liturgies and All of the Arbela Oracles* (Oxford: Clarendon, 1914).

24. Ibid., 1.

25. Heinrich Zimmern, *Zum babylonischen Neujahrsfest: Zweiter Beitrag* (Berichte über die Verhandl. der königl.Sächsischen Gesellsch. der Wiss., Phil.-hist. Klasse 70/5. Leipzig: Teubner, 1918) 2–3.

propaganda, composed in Assyria, which had nothing to do with either the death and resurrection of Marduk or the New Year festival.[26]

The discussion about Dumuzi/Tammuz peaked with the publication of Moortgat's work in 1949 on the Tammuz figure in ancient Near Eastern art.[27] Moortgat claimed to find representations of this deity in a number of Sumerian and Babylonian sculptures and advanced the theory that the symbolism employed in these works were expressions of a secret mystery-cult that advocated a belief in the immortality of the soul.

The reaction to his claims was, however, strongly critical. F. R. Kraus, in his review of the book, rejected both its method and its results.[28] By then, Kramer had already published an important cuneiform tablet from the Yale collection with the hitherto missing conclusion to the Sumerian myth of Inanna's descent to the netherworld.[29] This text clearly demonstrated that Inanna came back from the netherworld only to hand Dumuzi over to her demoniac retinue, the *gallu*, to be put to death as a substitute for herself.[30] Since it has generally been believed that Inanna went down to the netherworld in order to liberate her lover, the recovery of the ending of this Sumerian myth is an extremely important datum in the files on dying and rising deities. Then, in 1966, Kramer announced that he had now adopted a new reading of a crucial line in the text to the effect that Dumuzi had to spend only one-half of the year in the netherworld, and his sister, the other half.[31]

In a 1962 essay Kramer made two observations about the putative resurrection of the dying god:

1. Regarding the Sumerian mythology of Dumuzi, we now have access to texts from which the myth of Dumuzi can be reconstructed in detail. There is no trace in this Sumerian mythology of a poem about Dumuzi's resurrection.

2. In the Assyrian "Descent of Ishtar" the goddess's emergence from the netherworld is followed by an epilogue that creates great interpretive difficulties. Gurney found here "a clear allusion to the rising of Tammuz from the

---

26. W. von Soden, "Gibt es ein Zeugnis dafür dass die Babylonier an die Wiederaufstehung Marduks geglaubt haben?" *ZA* n.s. 17 (1955) 130–66. I cannot here enter into a discussion of other contributions to the debate about the so-called Marduk ordeal texts.

27. Anton Moortgat, *Tammuz: Der Unsterblichkeitsglaube in der altorientalischen Bildkunst* (Berlin: de Gruyter, 1949).

28. F. R. Kraus, "Zu Moortgat, 'Tammuz,'" *WZKM* 52 (1953) 36–80.

29. S. N. Kramer, "'Inanna's Descent to the Nether World': Continued and Revised," *JCS* 5 (1951) 1–17.

30. See also, for instance, *ANET*[3] 52 n. 6.

31. S. N. Kramer, "Dumuzi's Annual Resurrection: An Important Correction to 'Inanna's Descent,'" *BASOR* 183 (1966) 31.

underworld" but discounted its value by saying that "the whole passage is obviously a late addition—perhaps specifically Assyrian—which has displaced the original end of the poem."[32]

Yamauchi made some further observations about the epilogue. In agreement with Gurney, he found it closely associated with the mourning rituals for Tammuz but was able to specify: "In the last three days of the month of Tammuz in the summer, the figure of the god was laid out for burial in a rite known as *taklimtu*."[33] Yamauchi suggested that the reference to the rising of Tammuz should be understood in light of this ritual and accounts for both the rising of Tammuz and of the dead as "the ascent of the spirits to partake of the offerings made for the dead."[34]

It must be concluded then that the optimism during the first decades of the twentieth century for finding support for the resurrection of Dumuzi/Tammuz was dampened subsequently by such hard-core evidence as the recovery of the previously missing ending of Inanna's Descent.

Adonis

Few deities of antiquity have been as divergently assessed as Adonis. The explanation for this lies partly in the nature of the sources, which are derived mainly from Greek antiquity. However, a number of characteristics seem to indicate that the Greek Adonis had a long Oriental pedigree. Besides, the apparent analogy between Adonis and Christ certainly makes Adonis a rather controversial figure.

Three scholars were particularly prominent among those who have scrutinized the idea of the dying and rising deity: Roland de Vaux, Paul Lambrechts, and Günther Wagner. In 1933, de Vaux published a paper that criticized the two most essential points in Frazer's construct.[35] The first concerned the symbolism of the Adonis gardens. Although these gardens were considered reminiscent of the gardens of Osiris that symbolized the renascence of the god, in fact they symbolize the short life of vegetation and the ephemeral existence of

---

32. Gurney, "Tammuz Reconsidered," 152–54.

33. Edwin M. Yamauchi, "Additional Notes on Tammuz," *JSS* 11 (1966) 10–15, esp. 11. The noun in question is a derivation from the verb *kullumu(m)* and means "display"; see *AHw*, 1307, "Zeigen," "Schaustellung"; it probably refers to the display of the corpse or the grave goods of Tammuz.

34. Yamauchi, "Additional Notes on Tammuz," 13. Gurney ("Tammuz Reconsidered," 157) had made reference to the *taklimtu* but did not connect this with the rising of the god.

35. R. de Vaux, "Sur quelques rapports entre Adonis et Osiris," *RB* 42 (1933) 31–56; reprinted in *Bible et Orient* (Paris: Cerf, 1967) 379–405.

the hero. For this reason, de Vaux found it impossible to subscribe to Frazer's interpretation of these "gardens." A second criticism pertained to the dating of the belief in Adonis's resurrection. De Vaux was able to make this criticism on source-critical grounds. Taken in isolation, Lucian does not prove that there was an actual historical celebration of Adonis's resurrection. Neither does the witness of the later writers prove its existence, since these writers are clearly dependent on Origen and Cyril of Alexandria. De Vaux concluded that there is no reliable attestation for a resurrection feast for Adonis outside Alexandria and that even in Alexandria the feast was not celebrated before the second or third centuries C.E., it being a late borrowing from the Osiris cult.[36] These two main points, concerning the nature of the Adonis gardens and the date of a resurrection feast, predominate in much of what has been published since on the topic.

The next major contribution was made by Lambrechts, who devoted special attention to the resurrection motif and wrote in the vein of de Vaux. In the case of Tammuz, the texts contain a long series of lamentations. The resurrection motif, however, is completely absent.[37] Similarly, in connection with Adonis, the symbolism of the Adonis gardens focuses on the rapid wilting of the sprouts.[38] In the textual material there is a difference between a group of older texts and a group of more recent ones. The older texts contain a sequence describing first the celebration of the return of the god and his holy marriage and then the mourning commemorating his death, thus yielding a sequence of return followed by death.[39] This sequence is found in, for instance, Theocritus. It is only in a group of more recent texts (Lucian, Origen, Cyril) that clear evidence can be found of a celebration of Adonis's resurrection. This development occurred no earlier than the second century C.E. Furthermore, Lambrechts agreed with de Vaux that the notion of a resurrection originated in the Osiris cult.[40]

Wagner, in his magisterial 1962 monograph *Das religionsgeschichtliche Problem von Römer 6,1–11*, devoted some 200 pages to the issue of the dying and rising god and arrived at the conclusion that there is no clear evidence for the resurrection of Tammuz.[41] Adonis was not a god of vegetation in general but of spring vegetation that would wither during the summer drought. The re-

---

36. Ibid., 404.

37. Paul Lambrechts, "La 'résurrection' d'Adonis," *Annuaire de l'institut de philologie et d'histoire orientales et slaves* (Brussels) 13 (1955) 208–40, esp. 216.

38. Ibid., 221–23.

39. Ibid., 225–31.

40. Ibid., 231–35.

41. Günter Wagner, *Das religionsgeschichtliche Problem von Römer 6,1–11* (ATANT 39; Zurich: Zwingli, 1962) 151, 155.

sultant sequence was, then, from life to death.[42] In addition, the Adonis feast took place in the middle of the summer, which is not the appropriate time for a celebration of resurrection.[43] Already in Theocritus, Adonis was a sort of *Unterweltsgott*[44] who appeared on earth once a year to receive the rites of mourning. Such a return cannot be termed a resurrection.[45] This idea of Adonis's resurrection can be considered to have arisen quite late due to an innovative development in which three factors were of importance: (a) influences from syncretistic cults, (b) competition with Christianity, and (c) the influence of the Osiris cult.[46]

Will (1975) made an original contribution to this discussion. He denied that there was ever a profound transformation in the rites of Adonis. He explained what we find in the Church Fathers as a later reading of the Adonis rites through glasses colored by the Christian beliefs of these writers. In this way Will claimed to have reconstituted a "uniform pagan tradition": Greco-Roman paganism did not know a resurrection of Adonis; the alleged evidence for a resurrection of Adonis is due to a Christian misreading.[47]

Colpe (1969) to a great extent followed the same reasoning as de Vaux, Lambrechts, and Wagner. After discussing Adonis, Attis, and Osiris, Colpe concluded that these gods cannot be considered dying and rising deities of vegetation.[48] Their myths have no basic pattern in common. The treatment of these gods in prior scholarly discussion has often been determined by one specific interest: "Dieses Interesse ist das der Religionswissenschaft des 18. und 19. Jahrhunderts überhaupt, die als Wissenschaft Religionskritik, und d.h. de facto: Christentumskritik sein wollte."[49]

Detienne conceptualized Adonis differently from the agrarian figure presented earlier by Frazer. Instead, Detienne sketched a complex of myths with a basic contrast between Adonis (spices and seduction) and Demeter (cereals and abstinence), summarized in a graphic survey of the main features of the Adonia

---

42. Ibid., 187–88.
43. Ibid., 194–99.
44. Ibid., 189.
45. Ibid., 207.
46. Ibid., 210. Note, however, that it was clear to Wagner that there was no resurrection proper of Osiris; see p. 130.
47. E. Will, "Le rituel des adonies," *Syria* 52 (1975) 93–105, esp. 101–3.
48. C. Colpe, "Zur mythologischen Struktur der Adonis-, Attis- und Osiris-Überlieferungen," in *lišān mitḫurti: Festschrift Wolfram Freiherr von Soden zum 19.4.1968 gewidmet von Schülern und Mitarbeitern* (ed. K. Bergerhof et al.; AOAT 1; Kevelaer: Butzon & Bercker / Neukirchen-Vluyn: Neukirchener Verlag, 1969) 23–44, esp. 42–44.
49. Ibid., 42.

(celebrating Adonis) and the Thesmophoria (celebrating Demeter).[50] He then devoted ample space to the Adonis gardens.[51] The entire ancient tradition, from Plato onward, indicates that these gardens bore no fruit and were in fact fundamentally sterile. The Greek Adonis was thus hardly an agrarian deity.

Most recently, new and important insights have been brought to the discussion by Ribichini who, like Baudissin, works with both classical and Semitic sources. Ribichini, however, is unique in the sharp distinction he makes between Adonis the Greek *hero*[52] and the Adonis of the Oriental sources. This is apparent in the title of his 1981 book, *Adonis: Aspetti "orientali" di un mito greco*. The first part of the book deals with the Greek *hero*. One of the main conclusions of this work is that the Greek Adonis does not reflect a single Oriental deity. Instead, he is a mixture of various Oriental traditions that have been elaborated on in a Greek context.[53] Ribichini also notes the difference between the pictures we get from mythology and from the cult as reflected in the classical sources. In the mythology, there is no mention of a victorious return of the hero from death. The order is instead first life, then death. In a papyrus text, Adonis inhabits the netherworld and is counted among the chthonic gods. In the cult, however, there is a return, but this is only a temporary and periodical one. There is no true and permanent resurrection.[54]

With regard to the Adonis of the Orient, Ribichini finds a deity proper and not a hero of the Greek type. Although Ribichini draws a negative conclusion about a resurrection of Adonis in the Greek material, he is somewhat more open to the possibility of a resurrection of the Oriental Adonis as known from Lucian.[55]

In addition, Ribichini devotes some attention to the relation between Adonis and Tammuz. His conclusion is that there is no clearly evident historical line representing a development from Dumuzi/Tammuz to Adonis.[56]

In order to account for the genesis of the Adonis beliefs, Ribichini argues that there was a mythic and ritual pattern associated with the cult of defunct

---

50. Marcel Detienne, *The Gardens of Adonis: Spices in Greek Mythology* (trans. Janet Lloyd; Princeton: Princeton University Press, 1994) 82 [orig. French, 1972].

51. Ibid., 99–122.

52. In Greek antiquity, a hero was a man of superhuman qualities, favored by the gods; a demigod.

53. S. Ribichini, *Adonis: Aspetti "orientali" di un mito greco* (Rome: Consiglio nazionale delle ricerche, 1981) 42, 45, 142–43, 192.

54. Ibid., 133–40.

55. Ibid., 156–59.

56. Ibid., 181–92.

royal figures in Syria and Palestine during the Bronze Age.[57] This point is developed further in a later monograph.[58] The cult of divinized defunct kings in Ebla, Mari, and Ugarit is of special interest as an important part of the background. Notably the Ugaritic *rpum* and *mlkm* are important in this context.

In 1995, Ribichini was able to conclude: "It is probable that the cult of Adonis in Byblos continued the worship of a Phoenician . . . 'Baal' conceived [of] as a dying and rising god."[59]

In the case of Adonis, there is thus a respectable research tradition that finds insurmountable difficulties for the conclusion that Adonis was a dying and rising deity. That he was such a god is clearly a minority position, and moreover, one that has not been argued in dialogue and confrontation with opponents.

Baal

As this discussion reveals, the figures of Adonis and Tammuz stood at the center of the debate inaugurated by Frazer. Although Ugaritic material has played a role in the contributions of Colpe and Ribichini, surprisingly little attention has usually been paid to Ugarit regarding the dying and rising god as a specific type in the history of religions.

In 1963 W. H. Schmidt could speak of "Baals Tod und Auferstehung."[60] Within a decade, however, de Moor assumed a different position. He called attention to the "twin-brother" (*mt̠*) that Baal begets with the heifer (*KTU* 1.5.V:17–26): "Disguised as Baʿlu this offspring will die in his stead, as if he were a kind of *šar pūḫi*, the famous substitute-king of Babylonia. . . . Baʿlu himself will experience apparent death only."[61]

The idea that only a substitute of Baal descends to the netherworld was taken up by Gibson. He also draws certain additional conclusions from this: "The cheating of death by Baal, with its implication that it was not Baal himself but a substitute victim that was killed by Mot, is an intriguing notion; it ought, if true, to dampen not a little the enthusiasm of those who theorize

---

57. Ibid., 194–97.

58. S. Ribichini, *Poenus advena: Gli dei fenici e l'interpetazione classica* (Rome: Consiglio nazionale delle ricerche, 1985) 41–73, esp. 63–73.

59. S. Ribichini, "Adonis," *DDD*, cols. 12–17, esp. 14. It should be noted that Edouard Lipiński (*Dieux et déesses de l'univers phénicien et punique* [Orientalia lovaniensia analecta 64; Leuven: Peeters, 1995] 90–105, 97) reached similar conclusions.

60. W. Schmidt, "Baals Tod und Auferstehung," *ZRGG* 15 (1963) 1–13.

61. J. C. de Moor, *The Seasonal Pattern of the Ugaritic Myth of Baʿlu* (AOAT 16; Kevelaer: Butzon & Bercker / Neukirchen-Vluyn: Neukirchener Verlag, 1971) 188.

about a dying and rising god in Canaanite religion and the possible effects of such a concept on Israelite religion."[62]

In 1989, these problems were taken up anew by Waterston, however, who expressly took exception to the idea of a substitute: "I cannot agree with Gibson that the body buried by ʿAnat is that of a surrogate conceived by Baʿal and a heifer. There is no indication in the text that this is so. . . . Gibson's view is based on the supposition that Baʿal does not die, but surely this would make nonsense of the subsequent events."[63]

Mark S. Smith prefers to understand Baal as a disappearing deity: "Using the language for Baal's disappearance, perhaps like that of Telepine, does not make Baal a 'dying and rising god' like Adonis and Tammuz, but only a weather-god, whose powers and presence wax and wane in language reminiscent of the seasons."[64] Smith then returns to the issue in a challenging article in which he purports to issue the death certificate for the category of dying and rising gods. Smith here gives an overall treatment of the relevant questions and deals with all the relevant gods and especially with Baal. The death of Baal of Ugarit is a subcategory of the disappearance that we know from Anatolian gods. The death and return of Baal in the Baal Cycle is to be seen in the light of *KTU* 1.161.[65] "Baal's death reflects the demise of Ugaritic kings, but his return to life heralds the role of the living king to provide peace for the world. Death is the form which the disappearance of Baal takes."[66]

Regarding the Ugaritic Baal, there is obviously no consensus. Some scholars hold that he only disappears, like Telepine. Others agree that there are references to death but that it is only a substitute that dies, having been killed by Mot. Others seem to regard Baal as a dying and rising deity.

Where Do We Stand?
An Attempt at an Evaluation

We have surveyed almost a century of research. Some general observations can now be made. To begin with, it seems fairly obvious that the fundamental role of Christ's death and resurrection in the Christian religion has been important below the surface of the debate. Part of the hidden agenda seems

---

62. J. C. L. Gibson, "The Last Enemy," *SJT* 32 (1979) 151–69, esp. 159–60.

63. A. Waterston, "Death and Resurrection in the A.B. Cycle," *UF* 21 (1989) 425–34, esp. 431.

64. M. S. Smith, *The Ugaritic Baal Cycle*, 72–73.

65. Idem, "The Death of 'Dying and Rising Gods' in the Biblical World: An Update, with Special Reference to Baal in the Baal Cycle," *SJOT* 12 (1998) 257–313, esp. 289–313.

66. Ibid., 307–8.

sometimes to have been either to deprive the Christian religion of the claim to uniqueness, or alternatively, to present conclusions that would demonstrate that Christianity could not possibly have been influenced by ideas of a dying and rising god, since the idea of this resurrection was later than the first Christian century.

In surveying the discussion, it is easy to see that the evidence from Ugarit has not yet made any profound impact. As evident from the survey, the two main foci of the debate have been Tammuz and Adonis. The discussion about the situation in "Mesopotamian religion" can be described as a process of progressive reduction. There has been a gradual dampening of the enthusiasm for describing various gods in terms of a dying and rising deity. The order of elimination was first Marduk, then Dumuzi, and finally, Tammuz. Part of this major turn in the debate had already taken place by the 1950s. It was also in the 1950s that Lambrechts published his heavy critique of the assumption that Adonis was a dying and rising deity, though Lambrechts' 1955 essay had been anticipated in important respects by de Vaux in 1933. The lines of the discussion thus seemed to converge, and the *Lebensraum* for the dying and rising god was gradually reduced.

Thus, during the last half of the century, it was fairly clear that there was no connection to be made between the ideas of resurrection and Dumuzi/Tammuz. It is also a given that the ideas about a resurrection in connection with Adonis were very late. Those who criticized the idea of Adonis as a dying and rising deity often argued that these references to resurrection were very late, mainly from the Christian Era, and adduced various explanations for the presence of resurrection ideas in connection with Adonis. Thus, de Vaux argued that these ideas were a late borrowing from the cult of Osiris and that the resurrection of Adonis was first attested in third-century C.E. Alexandria. Lambrechts was in agreement concerning the Egyptian origin of the idea. Although Wagner, too, reckoned with the possible influence of Osiris ideas, he adduced another explanation as well: an alleged competition with Christianity. Will, for his part, denied the presence of any notions at all of Adonis as a rising deity. The supposed presence of such notions was merely due to a misreading of the evidence: Origen, Cyril, and others saw the Adonis rites from their Christian perspective.

It may well be that the very terminology "dying and rising deities" has been too charged with Christological associations. Some scholars have preferred to speak of "disappearing deities," an important category in Hittite mythology.[67]

---

67. See G. Beckman, "Mythologie, A. II: Bei den Hethitern," *RLA* 8.564–72, esp. 566–67.

Bianchi prefers a still wider category and speaks of deities who undergo various "vicissitudes," including death, disappearance, and marginalization of various kinds.[68]

Whatever the future fate of the dying and rising god, the history of this category in twentieth-century scholarship has been one of initial triumph and subsequent demise.

---

68. U. Bianchi, "Initiation, mystères, gnose," in *Initiation* (ed. C. J. Bleeker; Studies in the History of Religions 10; Leiden: Brill, 1965) 154–71.

Isaiah at Princeton One Hundred Fifty Years Ago and Now: Joseph Addison Alexander (1809–1860) and J. J. M. Roberts (1939–)

THOMAS H. OLBRICHT
Pepperdine University (Emeritus)

Princeton Theological Seminary, founded in 1812, has a rich heritage in Old Testament studies.[1] For its first 120 years, Princeton was famous for a traditional Reformed (Calvinistic) approach. A change of directions in 1929 may not have been as radical as the conservatives insisted; nevertheless, after that date new appointees identified more readily with the consensus of critical scholarship found in the foremost European and North American seminaries and universities. One manner of appraising old and new interests and directions in Old Testament studies at Princeton is to compare the approaches to Isaiah by Joseph Addison Alexander and J. J. M. Roberts. J. A. Alexander, Professor of Oriental and Biblical Literature at Princeton Theological Seminary, 1840–51, published the major commentary on Isaiah by a Princeton Theological Seminary professor prior to 1930.[2] J. J. M. Roberts, William Henry Green Professor of Old Testament Literature at Princeton Theological Seminary since 1979, is slated to publish a major commentary on Isaiah 1–39 in the Hermeneia Commentary Series. While it is premature to offer a definitive analysis of Roberts's perspectives, he has published several essays that make clear his interests and directions (conveniently reprinted in *The Bible and the Ancient Near East: Collected Essays*).[3]

---

1. Mary Ann Taylor, *The Old Testament in Old Princeton School (1812–1932)* (San Francisco: Mellen Research University Press, 1992).

2. Joseph Addison Alexander, *The Earlier Prophecies of Isaiah* (New York: Wiley and Putnam, 1846), and *The Later Prophecies of Isaiah* (New York: Wiley and Putnam, 1847). Subsequently these two volumes were edited by John Eadie and republished as one volume under the title *Commentary on the Prophecies of Isaiah* (New York: Scribner, 1867); this later work in turn has been reissued, with a new introduction by Merril C. Unger, by Kregel (Grand Rapids, 1992).

3. J. J. M. Roberts, *The Bible and the Ancient Near East: Collected Essays* (Winona Lake, Ind.: Eisenbrauns, 2002).

Joseph Addison Alexander

Charles Hodge was the first well-trained biblical scholar at Princeton Theological Seminary.[4] But his interests soon turned to theology. His groomed successor, Joseph Addison Alexander, was a son of the first professor at Princeton, Archibald Alexander.[5] J. A. Alexander came in contact with the cutting-edge German Old Testament critics, their methods and views during a visit to Germany in 1833–34.[6] He shared the German love of languages and philology. He was already a person of thoroughness and rigor, but what he witnessed in Germany reinforced his prior habits. In the 1840s and 1850s, as a biblical commentator, Alexander emulated German scholarship better than any other American. Theologically, however, he remained loyal to basic perspectives established by his father and perpetuated by Charles Hodge.

When Alexander arrived in Europe, he quickly made his way to Halle, no doubt on the counsel of Charles Hodge, who had only recently returned from there. Alexander spent his time reading widely, especially in biblical scholarship, studying biblical languages, and attending lectures by German scholars and visiting with them. Some of the professors he heard lecture were Tholuck on ethics, Galatians, and Psalms; Rödiger on Hebrew syntax; Fuch on Genesis; Pott on Sanskrit; and Wegschneider on 1 Corinthians and James. He read commentaries by de Wette, Rosenmüller, Klaus, and Ewald.[7] In January 1834

---

4. Thomas H. Olbricht, "Charles Hodge as an American New Testament Interpreter," *Journal of Presbyterian History* 57 (1979) 117–33.

5. Joseph Addison Alexander (1809–60) was born in Philadelphia. He received most of his early education from his father. He was especially adroit at languages. He studied Latin as early as he did English, and at ten could read the Old Testament in Hebrew. He entered Princeton in 1824 and graduated in 1826 summa cum laude. The next two years he spent in private study, mainly of Near and Middle Eastern languages. In 1830 he was appointed Adjunct Professor of Ancient Languages and Literature at Princeton. After a year of study and travel in Europe, he was appointed Instructor in 1834 at Princeton Theological Seminary. In 1840 he was appointed Professor of Oriental and Biblical Literature. From 1851 to 1859 he held the Chair of Biblical and Ecclesiastical History, and from 1859 to 1860, Professor of Hellenistic and New Testament Literature. Henry Covington Alexander, *The Life of Joseph Addison Alexander* (2 vols.; New York: Scribners, 1870). See also J. H. Moorhead, "Joseph Addison Alexander: Common Sense, Romanticism, and Biblical Criticism at Princeton," *Journal of Presbyterian History* 53 (1975) 51–66; Thomas H. Olbricht, "Joseph Addison Alexander," *Dictionary of Biblical Interpretation* (ed. John H. Hayes; Nashville: Abingdon, 1999) 24–25.

6. These include Charles Hodge, Edward Robinson, and Ira Chase. See Thomas H. Olbricht, "Alexander Campbell in the Context of American Biblical Studies, 1810–1874," *ResQ* 33 (1991) 20–24.

7. Henry Covington Alexander, *The Life of Joseph Addison Alexander*, 434.

Alexander traveled to Berlin and there came in contact with Biesenthal, Schleiermacher, Ritter, and Hengstenberg. Next he went to Tübingen, where he heard Ewald lecture.[8]

During the following decades Alexander wrote a three-volume commentary on Psalms (1850), two-volume commentaries on Isaiah (1846, 1847) and Acts (1857), and single-volume commentaries on Mark (1858) and Matthew (posthumous, 1861). Of these various works, according to John Eadie, "his crowning labour, his imperishable monument, is his Commentary on Isaiah."[9] The Isaiah commentary was his most scholarly by intention. It was by far the most erudite American commentary up to the time of its publication, as well as the most scholarly commentary on Isaiah by an English-speaking author. Alexander explained that a series of expository sermons on the text might better please the clergy, the typical audience for commentaries of the time, but he averred that preachers, better than scholars, are capable of relating the importance of the text to their parishioners.

> Let the professional interpreter content himself with furnishing the raw material in a sound and merchantable state, without attempt to prescribe the texture, colour, shape, or quantity of the indefinitely varied fabrics into which it is the business of the preacher to transform it.[10]

Alexander's comments on Isa 2:1–4 disclose his typical approach in the commentary. He first sums up the pericope, opining that

> the Prophet sees the church, at some distant period, exalted and conspicuous, and the nations resorting to it for instruction in the true religion, as a consequence of which he sees war cease and universal peace prevail, vers. 2–4.[11]

He then tackled the problem that these verses may also be found in Mic 4:1–3. He grouped the proposed solutions of the scholars into five categories: (1) Isa 2:2–4 had been accidentally transferred from a motto (Justi, Eichhorn, Bertholdt, Credner); (2) both prophets quote from Joel (Vogel, Hitzig, Ewald); (3) both prophets quote from an older writer now unknown (Koppe, Rosenmüller, Maurer, de Wette, Knobel); (4) Micah quotes from Isaiah (Vitringa, Lowth, Beckhaus, Umbreit); and (5) Isaiah quotes from Micah (J. D. Michaelis, Gesenius, Hendewerk, Henderson). He concluded that, because the statement

---

8. Taylor, *The Old Testament in Old Princeton School*, 95–97.

9. John Eadie, editor's preface to *The Prophecies of Isaiah Translated and Explained*, by Joseph Addison Alexander (New York: Scribner, 1870) v–vi.

10. Alexander, *The Earlier Prophecies of Isaiah*, xiv. All the citations in this essay refer to pagination in the 1870 edition, reprinted by Kregel (Grand Rapids, 1992).

11. Ibid., 96.

more clearly fits the context in Micah, it seems likely that Isaiah took this statement from Micah. But he was also open to the possibility that both "adopted a traditional prediction current among the people in their day, or that both received the words directly from the Holy Spirit."[12] He was more concerned with the inspiration of the pericope than its source. "So long as we have reason to regard both places as authentic and inspired, it matters little what is the literary history of either."[13] Alexander noted that the rabbins considered the passage to pertain to "the days of the Messiah"[14] and that the one who is to teach is the Messiah. He alleged, without defending his claim, that the text gives prominence to the (Christian) church so that it can attract the surrounding nations. He did not address the issue of the historical source of this elevated status of Zion. He did, however, make several observations on grammar and vocabulary.

Alexander more than adequately demonstrated his familiarity with many of the commentators on Isaiah, past and present, significant and insignificant. His greatest contribution had to do with philology, where he exhibited an almost exhaustless search through scholarship of all stripes, including the various translations and versions. One cannot but be impressed with his industry in this regard. In the preface Alexander set forth his rationale for depending heavily upon German scholarship.

> The prominence given to modern German writers has arisen not from choice but from necessity, because their labours have been so abundant, because their influence is so extensive, and because one prominent design of the whole Work is to combine valuable processes and products of the new philology with sounder principles of exegesis. Hence too the constant effort to expound the book with scrupulous adherence to the principles and usages of Hebrew syntax as established by the latest and best writers.[15]

Alexander was, however, critical of what he considered radical German scholarship. In the midst of comments on the unity of Isaiah, Alexander wrote,

> After the middle of the eighteenth century, a memorable change took place in Germany, as to the method of interpreting Isaiah. . . . As the skeptical criticism of the classics was the model upon which that of the Hebrew text was formed, so a like imitation of the classical methods of interpretation became generally current. The favourite idea now was, that the Hebrew books were to be treated simply and solely as remains of ancient Jewish literature, and placed, if not upon

12. Ibid.
13. Ibid.
14. Ibid., 97.
15. Ibid., xvi.

a level with the Greek and Roman books, below them, as the products of a ruder period and a less gifted race. . . . Instead of prophecies, and psalms, and history, the talk was now of poems, odes, orations, and mythology. The ecclesiastical and popular estimate of the books as sacred went for nothing, or was laughed at, as a relic of an antiquated system. This change, although apparently confined to technicalities, could never have been wrought without a deep defection from the ancient faith, as to the inspiration of the Scriptures.[16]

Extreme examples of this German approach, he argued, were characteristic of Eichhorn, Hitzig, Knobel, and Hendewerk. At the same time, he saw indications that more recently the best German scholars had backed off from the radical perspectives.

From this extreme position . . . De Wette and Gesenius receded, as they did from the critical extravagance of multiplying authors and reducing the ancient prophecies to fragments. They admitted, not only that many portions of Isaiah had reference to events still future when he wrote, but also that he was inspired, reserving to themselves the right of putting a convenient sense on that equivocal expression.[17]

Alexander likewise noted that the recent German critics were generally more open to accepting the Masoretic Text as essentially correct and without need of constant revision.

In an introduction of almost 80 pages, Alexander discussed first the role of the prophet. Although he believed that etymologies of words would not supply a complete answer, he nonetheless considered philological investigation necessary to discover prophetic roles through examining the various persons who were identified as prophets. Alexander concluded that a prophet is one "who speaks (or the act of speaking) for God, not only in his name and by his authority, but under his influence, in other words by divine inspiration."[18] His speech was not limited to the future, but also had to do with the past and present.[19] The key to the prophetic role was inspiration. The inspiration was plenary, that is, adequate to the attainment of its end.[20]

---

16. Ibid. 23.
17. Ibid., 24.
18. Ibid., 2.
19. Ibid., 3.
20. Ibid., 5. Roberts has published scattered reflections on prophecy and prophets. Two apropos essays in the collected volume are "Of Signs, Prophets, and Time Limits: A Note on Psalm 74:9" and "A Christian Perspective on Prophetic Prediction," in *The Bible and the Ancient Near East*, 274–81 and 406–18, respectively.

In regard to inspiration Alexander was more concerned with a conviction of its presence than with the specific manner in which it came about. He believed that God inspired through various means and opposed Hengstenberg, who argued for the prophet's being mostly inspired while in a state of ecstasy.[21] In Alexander's view,

> the prophets were clearly represented as infallible, *i.e.* incapable of erring or deceiving, with respect to the matter of their revelation. How far this object was secured by direct suggestion, by negative control, or by an elevating influence upon the native powers, is a question of no practical importance to those who hold the essential doctrine that the inspiration was in all cases such as to render those who were inspired infallible. Between this supposition and the opposite extreme, which denies inspiration altogether, or resolves it into mere excitement of the imagination, and the sensibilities, like the afflatus of a poet or an orator, there seems to be no definite and safe position.[22]

Alexander argued that the most usual mode of inspiration was an immediate vision.

Throughout the commentary, Alexander was interested in structures in Isaiah, both macro and micro. His observations were the conventional literary ones of the times, neither the Ramian rational structures of a previous century nor the *Formsgeschichte* of a century later. He argued at length that the eighth-century prophet Isaiah of Jerusalem was the author of the whole of Isaiah and that, therefore, there was a unity to the entire work.

> This book not only forms a part of the Old Testament Canon as far as we can trace it back, but has held its place there without any change of form, size, or contents, of which the least external evidence can be adduced. The allusions to this Prophet, and the imitations of him, in the later books of the Old Testament, are not confined to any one part of the book or any single class of passages. The apocryphal writers who make mention of it, use no expression which imply that it was not already long complete in its form and size. The same thing seems to be implied in the numerous citations of this book in the New Testament. . . . We find accordingly a long unbroken series of interpreters, Jewish and Christian, through a course of ages, not only acquiescing in this general statement, but regarding all the passages and parts of which the book consists, as clearly and unquestionably genuine.[23]

In the introduction to the first volume, Alexander declared what he believed were the false presuppositions of the German exegetes: they treated

---

21. Alexander, *The Earlier Prophecies of Isaiah*, 6.
22. Ibid., 5.
23. Ibid., 13–14.

scripture as any other document and declared the inauthenticity of certain parts on the same grounds aside from any sense of inspiration. He charged that the main reason the last 27 chapters of Isaiah were attributed to a later author is that all the details presuppose events after the Babylonian exile.

> The first and main objection to the doctrine that Isaiah wrote these chapters, although variously stated by the writers who have urged it, is in substance this: that the prophet everywhere alludes to the circumstances and events of the Babylonish exile as those by which he was himself surrounded, and with which he was familiar, from which his conceptions and his images are borrowed, out of which he looks both at the future and the past, and in the midst of which he must as a necessary consequence have lived and written.[24]

He argued that an inspired prophet could write words of consolation for sorrows that would not be experienced for ages. Other arguments against the Isaiah authorship had to do with diction, phraseology, and style. Such arguments, he maintained, were inconclusive even in the writings of the best scholars.[25]

With respect to Isa 7:14, a highly controversial topic among the critical scholars at that time, Alexander argued that the vocable *ʿalmâ* should be translated "virgin." "It is enough for us to know that that a virgin or unmarried woman is designated here as distinctly as she could be by a single word."[26] As to who this child is, he presented three possibilities: (1) that the birth was only a natural birth in days of Isaiah; (2) that the passage refers to two distinct children, the second being the Messiah; and (3) that these statements refer exclusively to the Messiah.[27] In conjunction with the first option, he examined the views of Jerome, Kimchi, Abarbanel, Isenbiehl, Bauer, Cube, Steudel, Hitzig, Michaelis, Eichhorn, Paulus, Hensler, Ammon, Aben Ezra, Jarchi, Faber, Plüschke, Gesenius, Maurer, Hendewerk, and Knobel. In regard to the second, he mentioned Junius, Usher, Calvin, Grotius, Clericus, Barnes, Lowth, and Dathe. On the third, he cited Michaelis, Henderson, Cocceius, Vitringa, Rosenmüller, Ewald, and Hengstenberg. He rejected aspects of the views of most of these commentators, without finding a single one with whom he could fully agree. He concluded "that the choice lies between the supposition of a double sense and that of a reference to Christ exclusively, but in connection with the promise of immediate deliverance to Ahaz."[28] He opined, however,

---

24. Ibid., 61.
25. Ibid., 17–19.
26. Ibid., 168.
27. Ibid., 166–73.
28. Ibid., 172.

that "the two particular interpretations which appear to be most plausible and least beset with difficulties, are those of Lowth and Vitringa, with which last Hengstenberg's is essentially identical."[29] At times he seemed to prefer the reference as only specifying the Messiah, not welcoming wholeheartedly a double fulfillment, but he often argued for latitude within established parameters. His final conclusion was that

> there is no ground, grammatical, historical, or logical, for doubt as to the main point, that the Church in all ages has been right in regarding this passage as a signal and explicit prediction of the miraculous conception and nativity of Jesus Christ.[30]

It is clear that Alexander was committed to a rigorous lexicographical and syntactical scrutiny of the text. He was less focused on historical settings, in part because data and documents for historical insights from the Mesopotamian world were miniscule as compared with those available at the end of the twentieth century. He was certainly not intent upon discovering the sources for various developments within Israel, whether endemic or exterior. He was chiefly concerned that the text be honored as sacrosanct from the standpoint of inspiration and that Messianic statements, which he believed referred to Jesus Christ, be recognized and highlighted. In keeping with Scottish Princetonian epistemology he held that proper interpretation was to be adjudicated by a commonsensical marshaling of evidences and reasons.[31]

J. J. M. Roberts

Roberts, born in Winters, Texas, is a graduate of Abilene Christian University, and holds an S.T.B. and Ph.D. from Harvard Divinity School and Harvard University, respectively. He has taught at Dartmouth, The University of Toronto, The Johns Hopkins University, and Princeton Theological Seminary.[32]

---

29. Ibid.

30. Ibid.

31. On Alexander's hermeneutics, see Taylor, *The Old Testament in Old Princeton School*, 165–66.

32. William Henry Green Professor of Old Testament Literature. S.T.B., Harvard University Divinity School; Ph.D., Harvard University. His teaching and research interests are comparative studies between Mesopotamian and Israelite religion, Old Testament prophecy, Semitic languages, and Hebrew lexicography. Roberts is currently working on a commentary on Isaiah 1–39 for the Hermeneia series. He has served on the editorial boards of *JBL*, *CBQ*, *BASOR*, and *Restoration Quarterly*, and was OT editor for the SBLDS and a member of the NRSV translation committee. Presently, he is the coeditor of the Princeton Classical Hebrew Lexicon Project.

Roberts, in prior publications, has disclosed central interests that will emerge as he produces a commentary on Isaiah 1–39. He has set out unique insights through locating specifics and larger views in the context of especially Mesopotamian religion.[33] He continually offers perspectives on the text that are both similar and contrastive with surrounding views of the times. Roberts continues to work within the trajectories of his mentors G. Ernest Wright, Frank Moore Cross Jr., and William L. Moran, who were all students of William F. Albright, and therefore himself remains broadly within the Albright school.[34] Nevertheless, Roberts has questioned many details in regard to the manner in which biblical theology allegedly stands radically over against perspectives that come out of its environment.[35] He has relentlessly pursued his own contention that

> there is a need for a far more rigorous attempt to understand both the OT material and the nonbiblical material in their own settings, and before making comparative judgments one should also be clear that the material being compared or contrasted is really comparable.[36]

He is also interested in the nature of prophecy, to what extent it was predictive, and the distinguishing marks of true prophecy in contrast with false.[37]

---

33. His Harvard Ph.D. dissertation completed in 1969 was: "The Early Akkadian Pantheon: A Study of the Semitic Deities Attested in Mesopotamia before UR III." The dissertation was published as: J. J. M. (Jimmy Jack McBee) Roberts, *The Earliest Semitic Pantheon: A Study of the Semitic Deities Attested in Mesopotamia before Ur III* (Baltimore: Johns Hopkins University Press, 1972).

34. Notice that Roberts employs essays of William F. Albright as the framework for his own essay "The Ancient Near Eastern Environment" (*The Bible and the Ancient Near East*, 3–43). See also *The Scholarship of William Foxwell Albright: An Appraisal* (ed. Gus W. Van Beek; Atlanta: Scholars Press, 1989); and Thomas H. Olbricht, "The American Albright School," *ResQ* 9 (1966) 241–48.

35. As, for example: G. Ernest Wright, *The Old Testament against Its Environment* (Naperville, Ill.: Allenson, 1957). Note the observations of Brevard S. Childs, *Biblical Theology in Crisis* (Philadelphia: Westminster, 1970) 39–50. For Roberts's own rigorous critique, see his essays "Divine Freedom and Cultic Manipulation in Israel and Mesopotamia" (in *Unity and Diversity: Essays in the History, Literature, and Religion of the Ancient Near East* [ed. H. Goedicke and J. J. M. Roberts; Baltimore: Johns Hopkins University Press, 1975] 181–90; reprinted in *The Bible and the Ancient Near East*, 72–82) and "The Ancient Near Eastern Environment" (in *The Hebrew Bible and Its Modern Interpreters* [ed. Douglas A. Knight and Gene M. Tucker; Philadelphia: Fortress / Chico, Calif.: Scholars Press, 1985] 75–121; reprinted in *The Bible and the Ancient Near East*, 3–43).

36. Roberts, *The Bible and the Ancient Near East*, 23.

37. Roberts's translation of the Mari prophetic texts indicates his interest and expertise in comparing Hebrew and Mari prophecy. "The Prophetic Texts in Transliteration and English Translation," *The Bible and the Ancient Near East*, 157–253.

Especially apropos to Isaiah is his interest in Zion as the place of God's dwelling and influence as well as the center for Davidic hegemony. Roberts argues that in Isaiah this royal theology finds its strongest prophetic voice.[38]

Obviously Roberts departs from Alexander's commitment to the unity of Isaiah. He even denies the value of trying to interpret it as a unified whole while accepting its multiauthorship.

> One could, however, take Lindbeck's claim for canonical and narrational unity as a claim that the reading of a particular passage in a prophetic book should be controlled by the literary arrangement of oracles in the book. Brevard Childs clearly makes such a claim when he argues that the placement of Isaiah 40–66 in the same scroll with the oracles of Isaiah of Jerusalem has dehistoricized the oracles of Second Isaiah so that they should be read canonically as though they were from the eighth century B.C.E. In my opinion, this is sheer nonsense, and it certainly cannot claim the support of the history of interpretation. It is true that Isaiah 40–66 was attributed to Isaiah of Jerusalem because these chapters were included in the same book as the oracles of the eighth-century prophet, but in terms of the actual interpretation of individual passages the ancient Christian interpreters paid very little attention to the literary shape of the book. Classical interpretation of a prophetic book actually interpreted discrete passages, not the prophetic book as a whole. Prophetic books were read, not as coherent, unified wholes, but as collections of discrete prophecies, each of which could stand on its own as a word of God.[39]

I will take up Roberts's "Yahweh's Foundation in Zion (Isaiah 28:16)" as a point of departure for comparing and contrasting his approach with that of Alexander, who wrote 140 years earlier.[40] I will also refer to other pertinent essays of Roberts. As he opens the essay, Roberts explains the significance of Isa 28:16 for the larger work.

> Isa 28:16 is also the central verse in the larger pericope of which it is a part, so that the satisfactory resolution of its internal difficulties is essential to an adequate interpretation of this larger context. What is more, this larger context seems to involve some of the most central issues in Isaiah's theology, so in the case of Isa 28:16 the struggle to resolve the technical difficulties is at the same time a struggle to understand one of Isaiah's central theological affirmations.[41]

---

38. Patrick Miller, preface to *The Bible and the Ancient Near East*, vii–xii.

39. Roberts, "Historical-Critical Method, Theology, and Contemporary Exegesis," *The Bible and the Ancient Near East*, 399.

40. Idem, "Yahweh's Foundation in Zion (Isaiah 28:16)," in ibid., 292–310. My citations are to this publication (originally published in *JBL* 106 [1987] 27–45).

41. Ibid., 292.

Roberts commenced with comments on textual, lexicographical, stichometric, and syntactical difficulties. In this he reflects the empirical approach of the Albright school in which the data must be sorted through before conclusions are drawn. Though Alexander lived in a period in which Baconianism was a catchword, he was more inclined to state a case first and then marshal the evidence.[42] In his commentary on Nahum, Habakkuk, and Zephaniah, Roberts's approach is much the same as in the essay under consideration.[43] His tendency is always to offer conclusions after a careful examination of the pertinent detail.

In his discussion of the textual and lexical problems, Roberts assembles a massive array of cognate examples from other Old Testament texts and versions, including the Masoretic Text, the Septuagint, the Peshitta, the Targum, Saadya, the Vulgate, as well as extrabiblical examples from Qumran and cognates from Ugaritic and Egyptian sources; to these he adds the opinions of medieval and later Jewish commentators and the grammatical analyses of GKC.[44] Roberts maintains that the "foundation" of Isa 28:16 is the power of God's presence in the temple as the result God's people being faithful to him.

Alexander in his exposition of this same text was much more interested in establishing that the foundation was the New Testament Messiah, a matter on which Roberts does not comment, as I shall discuss below. Alexander wrote,

> This foundation is neither the temple (Ewald), nor the law (Umbreit), nor Zion itself (Hitzig), nor Hezekiah (Gesenius), but the Messiah, to whom it is repeatedly and explicitly applied in the New Testament (Rom. ix. 33, x. 11; 1 Peter ii. 6). The same application of the text is made by Jarchi, and according to Raymund Martini (in his Pugio Fidei) by the Targum of Jonathan, although the word *Messiah* is now wanting in the Chaldee text.[45]

---

42. Theodore Dwight Bozeman, *Protestants in an Age of Science: The Baconian Ideal and Ante-bellum American Religious Thought* (Chapel Hill: University of North Carolina Press, 1977).

43. J. J. M. Roberts, *Nahum, Habakkuk, and Zephaniah: A Commentary* (Louisville: Westminster John Knox, 1991).

44. Roberts, "Yahweh's Foundation in Zion," 292–303.

45. Alexander, *The Earlier Prophecies of Isaiah*, 454. Roberts is not sealed off to such statements as this one, or the possibility of New Testament fulfillment, but he does not discuss this particular text in that light. In "A Christian Perspective on Prophetic Prediction" (*The Bible and the Ancient Near East*, 406–18) he argues that prophecy always involves a mystery and the complexity that accompanies it. But he obviously endeavors to locate the first meaning of a prophecy in its original setting, in contrast with Alexander, who sometimes ignores original settings so as to adumbrate Christological implications. This is clear in Roberts's discussion of passages that acquired a later messianic interpretation (see "The Old Testament Contribution to Messianic Expectation," *The Bible and the Ancient Near East*, 376–89). He wrote, "It would seem that both prophets expected a new embodiment of the Davidic ideal,

Alexander, in contrast to Roberts, more frequently cited the work of other scholars than that of ancient texts. He did refer occasionally, however, to targumic and Septuagint readings, to the medieval commentator Kimchi, and to Arabic cognates. He also mentioned Edward Robinson's observations on the immense stones still remaining at the foundation of the Jerusalem walls.[46] His independent work in the ancient languages, however, is not as thoroughgoing and detailed as that of Roberts. Roberts, like Alexander, offers a commonsensical approach by ruling out the use of vocables that are not altogether parallel, on the one side, and adopting those that make sense in terms of what can be known, on the other side.

It is interesting how nearly alike the translations of Roberts and Alexander are. Roberts has proceeded step by step through observations of parallel usage and commonsense conclusions regarding what Isaiah may mean in order to arrive at his translation. It is precise and polished.

> Therefore, thus says the Lord Yahweh:
> Look, I am about to lay in Zion a stone,
> A massive stone, a cornerstone valuable for a foundation,
> A foundation which will not shake for the one who trusts.[47]

The translation of Alexander is more succinct, but somewhat abrupt.

> Therefore thus saith the Lord Jehovah,
> Behold I lay in Zion a stone,
> A stone of proof, a corner stone of value,
> Of a firm foundation; the believer will not be in haste.[48]

Without extensive probing, Alexander arrived at a translation that is similar to Roberts's, with two exceptions. The first difference is that Roberts translates *bōḥan* in the third line "a massive stone," while Alexander translates it "a stone of proof." Roberts argues that "*bōḥan* should be connected with *baḥan* another

---

but both expected a refining judgment on the nation beforehand. That is certainly the case with Isaiah, who envisioned a humbling of the royal house and of the royal city before both would experience a new embodiment of the ancient ideal (Isa 1:21–26; 11:1–9; 32:1–8). Nonetheless, it also seems certain that Isaiah expected this new David in the near future. His use of very similar language in his coronation oracle for Hezekiah probably suggests that, for a time at least, he expected Hezekiah to fulfill these expectations" (pp. 382–83). See also Roberts, "The Divine King and the Human Community in Isaiah's Vision of the Future," ibid., 348–57.

46. Alexander, *The Earlier Prophecies of Isaiah*, 454–55. His reference is to E. Robinson, *Biblical Researches in Palestine and Adjacent Regions* (3 vols.; London: John Murray, 1841) vol. 1.

47. Roberts, "Yahweh's Foundation in Zion," 302.

48. Alexander, *The Earlier Prophecies of Isaiah,*" 454.

loanword from Egypt which means 'fortress, tower, watch tower.'"[49] After presenting occurrences elsewhere in Isaiah, and in Qumran materials, Roberts argues that a massive fortress stone is what is envisioned. Alexander argued that the Hebrew term literally means "stone of proof." He rejected Calvin's sense of this meaning, that it was a stone by which other stones were to be tested. Roberts also rejected this denotation. Alexander believed that *bōḥan* was the stone that had been tried and was sufficient, which comes closer to Roberts's conclusion, but he had no Qumran documents from which to note parallel connotations.

A second difference lies in the last phrase, which Roberts translates "a foundation which will not shake for the one who trusts." Alexander's explanation of the meaning "shake" is essentially the same as that of Roberts: "will not shake the one who trusts." Roberts, however, argues that "will not shake" has Qumran parallels and that the verb clause modifies the foundation and not the believer,[50] whereas for Alexander it is the believer who cannot be shaken. Alexander translated the last phrase as "the believer will not be in haste." He understood the meaning as having to do with firmness: "*Will not be in haste*, i.e. will not be impatient, but will trust the promise, even though the execution be delayed."[51] Accordingly, Alexander translated the firmness as being in the believer and not in the foundation.

At this point in the essay Roberts turns to the larger issues, and here we discover key differences of interest. Roberts argues that 28:1–4 was originally addressed to the Northern Kingdom at the time of the Syro-Ephraimite War.[52] Alexander did not bother with a specific time frame but simply observed that "It was obviously written before the downfall of Samaria, but how long before is neither ascertainable nor of importance to the exposition of the prophecy."[53] Roberts gave some attention to the form of the pericope arguing that these materials from 28:1 belong together with 28:16, which is the central verse of the section 28:14–22, against Brevard Childs, who contended that 28:16–17a constitutes an independent oracle.[54] Concerning the sense of the section, Roberts asserts,

---

49. Roberts, "Yahweh's Foundation in Zion," 296.
50. Ibid., 301.
51. Alexander, *The Earlier Prophecies of Isaiah,*" 455.
52. Roberts, "Yahweh's Foundation in Zion," 302.
53. Alexander, *The Earlier Prophecies of Isaiah,* 444.
54. Roberts, "Yahweh's Foundation in Zion," 303.

On the one hand, Yahweh is building a very solid structure with an unshakable foundation. On the other hand, the rival refuge constructed by the human rulers of Jerusalem will be swept away by the first rainstorm.[55]

The first of the larger issues is the temple within the Zion tradition. The Zion theology in the histories, in Psalms, and in the Prophets has been a major focus of Roberts since at least 1973, when he published a study on "The Davidic Origin of the Zion Tradition."[56] He brought insights from his 1969 dissertation "The Early Akkadian Pantheon: A Study of the Semitic Deities Attested in Mesopotamia before Ur III" to bear on the matter. He argues that the imagery of "Yahweh as the founder of Jerusalem and its temple"[57] goes back to the golden age of the Davidic-Solomonic period.[58] He refers to several passages that identify Yahweh as the founder of Jerusalem or the builder of Zion, including Isa 8:18 and 14:32.[59] It is at this point that we note a major divergence from Alexander, who has little interest in the historical background of the claims for Zion because he is inclined to interpret all statements of this sort as pertaining to the future establishment of the church. Regarding 14:32 he wrote, "What answer was given to the messengers of the nation (i.e. the messengers sent to them) when Jehovah founded Zion (or the Christian Church) and the afflicted of his people sought refuge in it?"[60]

The stability of the foundation, Roberts argues, is further affirmed in 28:17 by the declaration that the foundation will be tested by line and plummet. Roberts throws a whole new light on such testing by presenting materials that attest to the special efforts of Neo-Babylonian kings to find the original foundation of temples whenever they undertook any reconstruction. The kings believed that strict attention to such details was necessary in order to please the deities.[61] The materials from which one might obtain these sorts of insights were, for the most part, unavailable to Alexander in the nineteenth century.

Roberts's second larger issue pertains to a contrast between the sure foundation that Yahweh was laying and the worthless structure being erected by the Judean kings. Their handiwork is destined to collapse "under a violent rainstorm" (Isa 28:17). Roberts found the same imagery in Isa 30:12–14. He proposes that the kings attempted to reinforce the fortifications so as to with-

---

55. Ibid., 304.
56. Idem, "The Davidic Origin of the Zion Tradition," *JBL* 92 (1973) 329–44.
57. Idem, "Yahweh's Foundation in Zion," 304.
58. Idem, "The Davidic Origin of the Zion Tradition," in *The Bible and the Ancient Near East*, 330.
59. Idem, "Yahweh's Foundation in Zion," 304–5.
60. Alexander, *The Earlier Prophecies of Isaiah*, 312.
61. Roberts, "Yahweh's Foundation in Zion," 305–6.

stand the inevitable Assyrian retaliation. He further notes that there is now considerable archaeological evidence for Hezekiah's reconstruction in the fortification of Jerusalem.[62] But such construction also served as a metaphor identifying the political treaties into which the kings were entering in order to acquire chariots and cavalry especially from Egypt. These reconstructions, however, will be swept away by a torrent, and only the foundations that God has established in Zion will stand.[63] Alexander noticed these claims but did little to heighten the contrast between the solid work of Yahweh and that of the kings. He did note the bulging wall, however, and declared that a downfall "springing from internal causes" is the most appropriate in this connection, rather than that of mere external violence, however overwhelming.[64]

Finally, Roberts argues that this passage cuts to the heart of Isaiah's message regarding the defense of Jerusalem. "Metaphorically drawing on the ancient temple ideology of the Zion tradition, Isaiah contrasted the solid foundation Yahweh was laying to the government's flimsy fortifications, hastily built on inadequate foundations."[65] It was God's presence in the city that provided security. If God's people are to be truly secure, they must follow his blueprints in regard to justice and righteousness. The effort of the leaders to gain security through political alliances and military preparation was doomed to failure. In order to reinforce the walls, they became guilty of injustice and oppression by instituting forced labor and destroying houses of the less affluent. "The prophetic word suggests that Israel's true security would come by giving relief to the citizens who were paying for the royal fortifications with their houses, labor, taxes, and time."[66] The ones who trusted God could find ways of promoting righteousness and justice even in their endeavors to improve fortification and diplomacy.

Alexander clearly understood the references to justice and righteousness in a different way. For him, they had to do, not with fair treatment of the oppressed, but with a strict adherence to the laws of God. He translated 28:17, "And I will place judgment for a line and justice for a plummet, and hail shall sweep away the refuge of falsehood, and the hiding-place waters shall overflow."[67] It becomes clear how he envisioned this judgment in his comments on 28:12:

---

62. Ibid., 308.
63. Ibid., 307–8.
64. Alexander, *The Earlier Prophecies of Isaiah*, 477.
65. Roberts, "Yahweh's Foundation in Zion," 308–9.
66. Ibid., 309.
67. Alexander, *The Earlier Prophecies of Isaiah*, 455.

The sense is not, that the true way to rest is to give rest to the weary; the latter expression is a kind of parenthesis, as if he had said, This is the true rest, let the weary enjoy it. By *this* we are therefore to understand, not compassion and kindness to the suffering, but obedience to the will of God in general. This is the true rest which I alone can give, and the way to which I have clearly marked out. . . . To *give rest to the weary* does not mean to cease from warlike preparations, or to relieve the people from excessive burdens, whether of a civil or religious kind, but simply to reduce to practice the lesson which God had taught them.[68]

Alexander did not focus, to any extent, on Isaiah's concern for the oppressed and the needy. In his introductory remarks on Isaiah 1 he stresses the sins of the people that led to idolatry and does not mention 1:17 regarding justice for the oppressed, the orphan, and the widow.[69] In his comments on 1:17 he does not elaborate on the welfare of the oppressed but essentially paraphrases the text.[70]

Conclusions

Joseph Addison Alexander at the middle of the nineteenth century produced the first major scholarly commentary on Isaiah in America, as well as the first by an English author. It was a landmark effort, not in the mode of typical English commentaries that focused primarily on homiletical application. Before the century was over, not only continental biblical scholars, but also the foremost American scholars, following in the wake of Alexander, had moved on to new interests regarding authorship and backgrounds. But Alexander, in addition to his lexicographical and historical interests, was especially interested in the Christological ramifications of Isaiah. Because of these combined factors his commentary was never given its just due by the scholarly guild nor was it ever popular with ministers, even though conservative publishers have kept it in print to the present.

What then is new at Princeton on Isaiah in the work of J. J. M. Roberts? Alexander drew upon an impressive range of lexicographical materials and the research of prior commentators so as to throw light upon Isaiah. Roberts, however, brings to bear an even more extensive sweep of data from the ancient setting in order to explain the vocabulary, allusions, and historical backgrounds of Isaiah. He can do this in part because of an impressive array of new finds since the middle of the nineteenth century. Adequate materials were

---

68. Ibid., 452–53.
69. Ibid., 79–80.
70. Ibid., 89.

available to Alexander, however, so that he could have accomplished some of the same ends; but his interests lay elsewhere. Roberts is committed to a rigorous pursuit of backgrounds materials in order to throw an accurate light on both the extrabiblical conceptions and the conceptions of the biblical text.

Second, Roberts has a deep commitment to ascertaining the primary meaning of the text through a scrutiny of the historical setting of Isaiah. He does not deny certain "double" meanings or write that it is improper to bring Isaian texts to bear upon later events, even those that are Christological. We cannot, anticipate, however, that much Christological comment will occur in his Hermeneia commentary. Alexander, in contrast, focused almost immediately upon the inspiration of the text and its value for Christological insight into the New Testament.

One of the chief interests of Roberts is to situate Isaiah in a trajectory regarding the origins, the fleshing out, and the nuances of the Zion traditions and their ramifications for theology. We can anticipate, therefore, that the significance of Zion within the Yahwistic tradition will provide several occasions for theological reflection as Roberts works his way through Isaiah 1–39.

Finally, Roberts in his determination to understand texts in their original setting has taken the position that texts throughout First Isaiah are sometimes out of place chronologically and that materials of later authors have been added to the prophecies of Isaiah of Jerusalem, notably the portions known as Second Isaiah and Third Isaiah. He is much more sensitive to historical settings and to literary forms than was Alexander, even though Alexander gave some attention to both.

Why Perez?
Reflections on David's Genealogy in Biblical Tradition

KATHARINE DOOB SAKENFELD
Princeton Theological Seminary

In a time when the very existence of the historical David has been challenged in some quarters and the dating of the composition of many Old Testament materials continues to engender heated debate, a look at the genealogy
of this hero of Judahite tradition may seem misplaced. The goal of this essay
is not to contribute directly to either of those debates, although I continue to
view David as a historical character (though probably without a mighty empire) and to regard much biblical material as preexilic. Rather, the goal is to
suggest how context may enhance our understanding of these genealogical
traditions as part of the canonical portrait of King David.

We begin with a review of the basic structure and individual names in the
genealogies in Ruth 4 and 1 Chronicles 2. The list in Ruth 4:18–22 begins
with Perez and proceeds by a perfectly repetitious and symmetrical linear[1]
method to name the direct line of descendants: Hezron, Ram, Amminadab,
Nahshon, Salmon, Boaz, Obed, Jesse, and finally David. No "asides" giving
comments about any of the names are incorporated. Two among these names
show textual variants in the tradition. Ram is known in some LXX manuscripts as Arran, and in others as Aram (the version of the name that appears
in the New Testament genealogy of Matt 1:3, 4). Hebrew *slmn* appears with
an alternate spelling, *slmh*, even within the Leningrad codex (compare Ruth
4:20, 21), and these variants persist in the Hebrew manuscript traditions as
well as in some LXX manuscripts and some versions. While no exact pattern

---

Author's note: This essay is offered in grateful appreciation to J. J. M Roberts for his scholarly
work, especially in the area of Davidic theology, and for his friendship over more than three
decades, beginning with our student years.

1. As widely described in genealogical studies, genealogies are of two basic types. "Linear" genealogies proceed in a direct line of descent (typically father to a son to that son's
son, etc.) over generations. "Segmented" genealogies list the several children of one father,
then in turn list the various children of each of those children.

appears, the fact of the variations may be of significance, as will be suggested below.

In 1 Chronicles the Davidic genealogy is of course set in a far larger context going back to creation (Adam). For the purposes of this essay our primary focus is upon the tribe of Judah, whose descendants follow immediately after the list of the twelve sons of Israel in 1 Chr 2:1. The genealogy of Judah begins with a segmented, albeit incompletely filled out, structure through Perez and Hezron down to Ram. At this point (2:10) the list switches to linear reporting from Ram to Amminadab, Nahshon, Salma, Boaz, Obed, Jesse, interrupted only by the note that Nahshon was "prince of the sons of Judah." After naming Jesse, the genealogy branches out again to list all the children of Jesse, with the male offspring numbered so that it is clear that David is the seventh son, followed by the names of their two sisters and the sons of each of those sisters. In subsequent paragraphs the genealogical report returns to the segmented style account of other sons of Hezron (Jerahmeel and Caleb, who had been listed in v. 9) and to Hezron himself by another marriage. The list of names of the direct line leading to David is identical to the one found in Ruth, and indeed only the same two names, Ram and Salma (in 1 Chronicles MT *slm'* with *'aleph*, not with *he* or *nun* as in Ruth), again appear in variant spellings in the LXX and versions.

Much ink has been spilled in trying to determine the relative ages of these lists, whether one was borrowed or both used a third source, and whether the genealogy at the end of the story of Ruth was integral to the composition or was subsequently appended. I follow Bush's linguistic arguments[2] for dating the Hebrew of Ruth to approximately the time of the exile, and I join most commentators in placing Chronicles sometime during the Persian era. The arguments for the dating of Ruth are not such that they can be necessarily extended to the genealogy given in Ruth 4:18–22, and the original or secondary character of that genealogy cannot in my view be finally determined. Thus the question of possible direction of dependence cannot be decided by dating the two main texts, and this essay will not attempt to resolve the question. Our focus, rather, will be upon features of the genealogies that lead the reader's attention to the key characters, and particularly to King David.

The Chronicler's picture of Hezron's other descendants, the Jerahmeelites and particularly the Calebites, is complex and even unclear, perhaps because of melding of sources.[3] The line through Ram, by contrast, has no branches or further elaboration, neither here nor elsewhere in biblical tradition. This

2. Frederic W. Bush, *Ruth, Esther* (WBC 9; Dallas: Word 1996) 18–30.

3. See discussion in Roddy Braun, *Chronicles* (WBC 14; Waco, Tex.: Word, 1986) 25–35. For a review of major theories of sources and composition of 1 Chronicles 1–9 from

contrast is the first feature to be noted that functions to highlight David. Various commentators have suggested that the overall organization of the Chronicler's presentation of the Judahite tribe gives David a central place; the sharp contrast between linear and segmented presentation should be added to these organizational features as a further strategy.

Of the names in the line leading to David, Judah, Perez, Nahshon, Boaz, Obed, and Jesse are known from narrative contexts, whereas Hezron, Ram, Amminadab, and Salmon are not. We look first at the latter group. Hezron is known elsewhere only as one of those who went down to Egypt.[4] Amminadab is mentioned elsewhere only as the "father of Nahshon" (thus identifying Nahshon) when Nahshon appears in narrative, and as the father of Aaron's wife Elisheba, brother of Nahshon (in a segmented genealogical list, Exod 6:23). Neither Ram, son of Hezron, nor Salmon, son of Nahshon, of David's genealogy receives any mention elsewhere in biblical material beyond the Chronicles and Ruth verses.

It is noteworthy, however, that the names Ram and Salmon both do appear attached to other individuals in the Chronicler's genealogy. The other Ram is listed as a son of Jerahmeel (1 Chr 2:25, 27), thus as a grandson of Hezron and a nephew of the Ram of the Davidic ancestral line. As with the Ram of the Davidic line, no other details or references are available for his Jerahmeelite nephew. In the case of Salma/Salmon, we find in 1 Chr 2:51 and 54 a listing of Salma,[5] son of Hur, who was son of Caleb, who was a son of Hezron. Related details in the text draw our attention to this second Salma. First, the name of this second Salma's grandmother (Caleb's wife) is given as Ephrathah (1 Chr 2:50; cf. 2:19);[6] furthermore, this second Salma is named as the father

---

Wellhausen forward, see Manfred Oeming, *Das wahre Israel: Die "genealogische Vorhalle" 1 Chronik 1–9* (BWANT 7/8; Stuttgart: Kolhammer, 1990) 108–15. Most recently, Gary N. Knoppers (" 'Great among His Brothers,' but Who Is He? Heterogeneity in the Composition of Judah," *Journal of Hebrew Scriptures* 3 [2000–2001], article 4; online: http://www.arts.ualberta.ca/JHS [accessed July 22, 2002]) has provided a helpful methodological categorization of the major approaches to this issue in recent literature.

4. In making the narrative/nonnarrative categorization, I treat Obed here as a narrative character, even though only his birth and naming are recorded (Ruth 4). Hezron does receive mention in Genesis 46 in the larger context of the report of Jacob's travel to Egypt with his family; but the name is merely part of a list making up the seventy persons. Hence, he has no individual narrative function.

5. Spelling variations appear in some LXX manuscripts for v. 51, where he is Salomon or Sama.

6. 1 Chr 2:24a probably includes another reference to this Ephrathah, if one follows the LXX. H. G. M. Williamson's suggestion for the solution to this difficult verse is attractive. He accepts the LXX for v. 24a (". . . Caleb went in to Ephrathah") and then treats the

of Bethlehem (vv. 51, 54).[7] Significantly, both Bethlehem and Ephrathah appear in the Ruth narrative and in association with David in other traditions. Bethlehem is of course the home village of Naomi's family and of Boaz, and it is the place within Judah where Ruth's marriage to Boaz and the birth of Obed take place. David's connection to Bethlehem is furthered in biblical narrative tradition through the identification of his father as "Jesse the Bethlehemite" in the narrative of David's anointing (1 Sam 16:1, 4). The possible connection of the woman's name Ephrathah from 1 Chronicles 2 to the book of Ruth and to David is more complex. In biblical material Ephrathites are sometimes associated with an area of Ephraim, well north of Bethlehem (cf. Judg 12:15; 1 Sam 1:1; 1 Kgs 11:26). In the book of Ruth, however, the term "Ephrathite" appears in the phrase "Ephrathites from Bethlehem in Judah" (1:2), thus identifying Naomi's husband as from a family line in this southern location. Ephrathah and Bethlehem appear in parallelism as place names in the blessing recorded in Ruth 4:11. This specific association of Ephrathah with Bethlehem appears in two other biblical texts. In 1 Sam 17:12 David is described as "a son of an Ephrathite of Bethlehem in Judah, named Jesse"; and Mic 5:1[2] looks forward to a new and upright ruler from the clan of "Bethlehem of Ephrathah."

Although the genealogical material in Chronicles associates Bethlehem with a Calebite branch of the descendants of Hezron, rather than the line through Ram, the reappearance of the name Salma as "father of Bethlehem," together with the grandmother's name, Ephrathah, suggests that we are dealing with variant old traditions of the association of these terms. The appearance of the second Ram in the Jerahmeelite branch of Hezron's line may be simply coincidence. Yet no other Ram or Salma/Salmon is known from elsewhere, and no other information is given beyond what is given in these genealogical lists. Indeed, as we have seen, even the exact names of these two

---

phrase "and the wife of Hezron [was] Abijah" within v. 24b as a misplaced gloss on v. 21. See Williamson, "Sources and Redaction in the Chronicler's Genealogy of Judah," *JBL* 98 (1979) 354–55. Other scholars have followed Wellhausen's suggested reading that interprets Ephrathah as a wife of Hezron whom Caleb married after his father's death; see, e.g., E. M. Luker, "Ephrathah," *ABD* 2.557. Wellhausen's proposal, which seems to me less likely than Williamson's, might place Ephrathah as a direct named matriarchal ancestor of David, along with Tamar and Ruth (so Luker), but the reconstruction, even if accepted, does not specify which of Hezron's sons might have been born of that relationship.

7. In 1 Chr 4:4, Salma's father, Hur, "the firstborn of Ephrathah" (cf. 2:50), is apparently listed as the "father of Bethlehem," although the word order is awkward.

individuals do not seem clearly set in the tradition.[8] The uniqueness of these names, together with the refrences to Ephrathah and Bethlehem that point toward associating the second Salma with the Davidic context, may suggest that memories of the heritage of Judah's great leader were evoked by fluid older traditions around the name Ram as well.

Whatever other functions the Calebite and Jerahmeelite genealogies may serve in the Chronicler's design, the aim of highlighting David is furthered by the introduction of these reverberations of the names and places so specifically associated with the story of David's ancestry and origins in narrative and prophetic memory (Ruth, Samuel, Micah). Why do we know nothing at all of Ram and Salmon of the linear genealogy of David? Given the other occurrences of the two names in the 1 Chronicles genealogy, one might imagine that their appearance in the linear genealogy functioned in part to set David apart from related (through Hezron) Jerahmeelite and Calebite groups, while at the same time allowing David some form of connectedness to both. Unfortunately this must remain speculative, since there is not sufficient information about these groups to propose a specific sociohistorical setting.[9]

We turn now to those in the genealogy about whom the tradition offers us some narrative information. The name about whom the least can be said is Obed. The narrative of Ruth 4 simply reports that he was born and that the women of Bethlehem recognized in him one who would care for Naomi in her old age. Their exclamation, "a son is born to Naomi," which was of course not biologically true, expresses a reversal of the loss of offspring and inability to bear more sons that was the heart of Naomi's words to her daughters-in-law in chap. 1. The naming of the boy is strange, with no suitable pattern or wordplay such as is typical of many naming scenes in biblical material. Although the narrative suggests that this child should carry on the line of Naomi's deceased son Mahlon (4:5, 10), the genealogy connects Obed only to his biological

---

8. To be sure, other names show variants within the MT between the Chronicler and other traditions (e.g., Achan/Achar) and within Chronicles itself (e.g., Chelubai/Caleb, although some have questioned whether the same person is in fact remembered). As these examples show, the phenomenon of name variants is not restricted to unknown individuals. It is striking, nonetheless, that in this set genealogy of David such variants are restricted to the two otherwise unknown names who also appear in other related genealogical lists.

9. Fluidity of genealogies involving rearranging of relationships, addition of names, and telescoping of names has been well documented both for contemporary oral societies and for written texts of various ancient Near Eastern cultures by Robert R. Wilson in his *Genealogy and History in the Biblical World* (New Haven: Yale University Press, 1977).

father, Boaz.[10] Beyond the narrative of Ruth 4 and the two genealogies, we find no further reference to Obed. This absence of reference is striking in a way that the absence of further mention of the more distant ancestors Ram or Salmon is not. The story of Samuel's visit to Jesse (1 Samuel 16) would seem to have been an obvious place in which the tradition might have added "son of Obed," and yet it did not happen. Whether the Davidic genealogy was established relatively early or much later, it did not have an impact on a key related text.

The Chronicler provides the appropriate clue to the significance of our next lesser-known figure, Nahshon; he was "prince (or leader, *nsy'*) of the sons of Judah," a title ascribed to him in Num 2:3. This Nahshon ben Amminadab is remembered in the book of Numbers as the representative of Judah in the wilderness era. He, along with representatives of each of the other tribes, assisted Moses with the tasks of taking a census (Num 1:7), leading Judah to its camp position (2:3), presenting the tribe's dedicatory offering (7:12, 17), and leading Judah when the people departed from the wilderness of Sinai (10:14). In each case except the opening census, Judah was given the position of preeminence, holding the first honored position to the east of the tabernacle in the camp, presenting its offering first, leading the entire tribal procession in the march forward when camp was broken. Thus King David came from the line of the figure remembered as the key Judahite of the wilderness era. Although most scholars today would reject the possibility of an organized twelve-tribe federation in this early pre-land period, the memory of a named ancestral figure associated with a Judahite group is certainly plausible.

In Exod 6:23 we find one additional reference to Nahshon. In a genealogical context we learn that Aaron's wife, Elisheba, was the sister of Nahshon. This brief notice is incorporated into a text devoted mainly to describing the segmented genealogy of the Levites. It seems likely that through this device the tradition sought to use David's Judahite ancestor to associate David more closely with the Aaronid line. While the remembrance of the name Nahshon may be old, it is possible that this connection to the Aaronids may have developed separately, perhaps in the context of disputes about competing official priesthoods.

Before turning to a discussion of Perez and Boaz, whom the narrative of Ruth calls us to consider together, I must make some comments about the overall structure of the genealogy. In Ruth 4:18–22, we find a total of ten

---

10. Although many commentators find this ignoring of Mahlon surprising, it is exactly the same pattern that we find with Perez, who is remembered genealogically only in relation to Judah. See below.

names, extending from Perez through David. Within this list, the name found in seventh position is Boaz, who of course is the central male character of the story that was preserved to tell its readers something of the ancestry of David. Sasson has proposed that a ten-person lineage for important figures may have been a convention known to the genealogists. He argues further that attention could be drawn to a particular name in any genealogy by a convention of placing that person in the seventh slot.[11] Methodologically, Sasson's proposal is difficult to demonstrate, since if these features exist, they are only two of many possible conventions and neither appears regularly enough or obviously enough even in the Bible, much less in the ancient Near Eastern sources, to be described as a norm. In fact, Sasson admits that in many examples in the biblical materials he cannot make an argument for the significance of the seventh name. Thus it may or may not be by design that the Ruth genealogy culminates with David in the tenth position and features Boaz in the seventh. The pattern does not appear in the same way Chronicles, where the linear genealogy begins with Ram, although David does appear there as the seventh son of the seventh ancestor (Jesse).

Supposing that the numerical design in the Ruth genealogy might have been deliberate (the individuals in positions seven and ten are obviously central in this instance), then one must ask what "editing" may have been done by the compiler to produce this end result. First of all, the list is surely idealized in some way in relation to biblical chronology overall, for ten generations is not sufficient to cover the traditional time period from the descent to Egypt till the accession of David. The time span of the genealogy, seven generations from Perez to Boaz and three more from Boaz to David, does not correlate easily with the length of time supposedly passed either according to the biblical tradition or according to modern historians.[12] That a genealogy may have

---

11. Jack M. Sasson, *Ruth* (2nd ed.; Biblical Seminar 10; Sheffield: JSOT Press, 1989) 183–84. Regarding the ten-generation convention, he follows Abraham Malamat, "King Lists of the Old Babylonian Period and Biblical Genealogies," *JAOS* 88 (1968) 163–73. Sasson develops his proposal concerning the seventh position in detail in "A Genealogical 'Convention' in Biblical Chronography?" *ZAW* 90 (1978) 171–85. Wilson (*Genealogy and History*, 64), in a study broader than Malamat's, finds that most Mesopotamian royal genealogies are shorter, typically just three generations deep, but sometimes ranging up to six or eight generations.

12. The biblical text itself is not completely clear about the length of time of the sojourn in Egypt, since Gen 15:13 mentions 400 years of slavery but Gen 15:16 refers to the return of the "fourth generation." The genealogies of Moses (Exod 6:16–20 and Num 26:57–59) do indeed present him as the great-great-grandson of Jacob [Jacob/Israel > Levi > Kohath > Amram > Moses]. By this reckoning, the fourth generation contemporary of

been truncated in some way is not problematic; indeed, the ancient Near Eastern examples analyzed by Wilson demonstrate that such abbreviation was practiced. Omission of names from various points in Mesopotamian lists can be seen in cases of historical kings known from independent sources. Such "telescoping" is most evident in lengthier lists, but it is even attested in three-generation genealogies.[13]

Sasson proposes that the list of ten and the seventh place of Boaz in Ruth 4 is achieved by beginning with Perez rather than with his father, Judah. He considers Judah a more likely starting point, and of course Judah is mentioned in the text (4:12).[14] Nielsen, while apparently accepting the importance of the seventh and tenth slots, correctly observes that Sasson's explanation is far from self-evident. If the author of the genealogical verses was free to edit a received list, then it seems reasonable that he might have eliminated another name such as Ram or Salmon, about whom nothing is otherwise known, or any of the other names who are not featured in the Ruth narrative, in order to keep the better known and more important Judah as head of the list. She concludes that the author did not do this "because he was not free to do so."[15]

While we cannot finally know why the genealogist in Ruth chose to begin with Perez, we may suggest a confluence of several factors. Although his goal may not have been to display the seven/ten pattern, it seems unlikely that he would not have noticed this result and even considered it desirable. Did he have a choice about the intervening names? And why did he not begin with Judah?

As indicated earlier in this essay, it cannot in my view finally be determined whether the Chronicler and Ruth drew independently upon an older source

---

Moses in the wilderness era from the Ruth genealogy should be Ram [Jacob/Israel > Judah > Perez > Hezron > Ram], not Nahshon, son of Amminadab (two generations later). Of course individuals in different lines may have been imagined to have lived briefer or longer periods, and Nahshon is mentioned in Exod 6:20 as a brother-in-law of Aaron. Following this genealogical and narrative correlation of Nahshon with Moses, Aaron, and the wilderness era allows for four intervening generations (Salma, Boaz, Obed, Jesse) to the time of David. The number is insufficient when counting a traditional 40 years per generation and using the biblical tradition of 480 years from the Exodus to the founding of the Jerusalem temple (1 Kgs 6:1); one would look for about ten generations. The number is likewise insufficient when counting a more typical scholarly estimate of 25 years per generation and calculating from an archaeologically suggested Iron I emergence of Israel in the land to the traditional date for the reign of David at ca. 1000 B.C.E.; although the count may be closer, one would expect about six generations, if indeed such a calculation is possible at all.

13. Wilson, *Genealogy and History*, 64–69.

14. Sasson, *Ruth*, 184.

15. Kirsten Nielsen, *Ruth: A Commentary* (trans. Edward Broadbridge; OTL; Louisville: Westminster John Knox, 1997) 97.

or whether the Chronicler copied from Ruth or vice versa. Whichever of the three options is preferred, it remains the fact that the two versions of the genealogy are identical. Given the fluidity in detail that is characteristic of so many biblical genealogies, whether the other material in Chronicles or the variety of traditions in Genesis,[16] the exact reproduction of David's genealogy in two places, including the otherwise unknown persons, is remarkable. The other major example of a longer royal linear genealogy in the biblical tradition (other than the Chronicler's summation of the king list descended from Solomon, 1 Chr 3:10–24) is that of Saul; as Malamat has pointed out, the pertinent texts (1 Sam 9:1; 14:50–51) are shorter, less clear, and less consistent than those for David.[17] This evidence from other genealogies corroborates Nielsen's suggestion. David's genealogy is likely to have been established sufficiently in corporate memory that changes even with regard to unknown individuals were not possible. The list of names was fixed.

Yet the question remains why the genealogy in Ruth begins with Perez. Is it only or even primarily to establish the seventh and tenth positions, or may other factors be at work as well? One clue, if it can be deciphered, certainly lies in the reference to Perez in the villagers' blessing upon Boaz prior to his marriage (Ruth 4:12). Thus we come to a consideration of Perez in narrative tradition and the relationship of this tradition to the circumstances of Boaz in the Ruth narrative. The Ruth blessing joins with the genealogy of 1 Chr 2:4 in making specific reference to Tamar as the mother of Perez, as is recounted in full narrative detail in Genesis 38. The other references to Perez are in the genealogical lists of Genesis 46 and Numbers 26. The Numbers clan lists are strictly of males, organized by tribes; the only females who appear are the five daughters of Zelophehad, who had no sons. The Genesis list is also of males belonging to the sons of Jacob (tribal names); Jacob's wives and concubines are mentioned in order to organize the main subgroups, but no details are given concerning the mothers of the next generation. Yet in both Gen 46:12 and Num 26:19 the tradition is careful to indicate that Er and Onan, Judah's two eldest sons, died and did not go down to Egypt. The Chronicler certainly appears cognizant of the Genesis 38 narrative, because he specifies, "Now Er, Judah's firstborn, was wicked in the sight of the Lord, and he put him to death" (1 Chr 2:3; remarkably, this text makes no mention of the death of

---

16. See Wilson, *Genealogy and History*, 197: while the basic structure of the major tribal units is fixed, individual names "are added to or omitted from otherwise parallel versions of the genealogies, and in some cases the genealogical relations of the names themselves are changed."

17. Malamat, "King Lists," 171–72.

Judah's second son, Onan, although he is listed in the immediately preceding verse). From this evidence it appears that omission of a reference to Tamar in connection with Perez occurs only where the structure of a genealogy militates against the inclusion of any such "extraneous" allusions.

What then may be the functions of the reference to Tamar, Judah, and the house of Perez together in Ruth 4? The comparison of Boaz's future house with the house of Perez evokes a whole range of themes. Some have suggested that a large number of descendants is in view, since children are mentioned;[18] but this surely does not exhaust the possibilities. Indeed children are a feature of all three phases of the blessing of vv. 11–12.

The reference to Tamar as mother of Perez, however, sets in motion a whole train of allusive connections between her story and that of Ruth. To begin quite apart from the two women, both stories are set in motion by the death of male offspring. Er dies at God's displeasure for an unspecified reason; Onan dies for disobedience to a specific law. Ruth 1 does not explain the deaths of Elimelech, Mahlon, and Chilion, although rabbinic tradition suggests their disobedience in moving from Bethlehem to Moab. In both cases, it is the death of the males through whom descent is expected that initiates the action. Then in both narratives it is the initiative of the female protagonist that sets a course toward resolution and the birth of the next generation: Perez is analogous to Obed. While the actions of Tamar and Ruth are certainly not identical, the similarities can scarcely be overlooked. Possibly both women are non-Israelites.[19] Each of their stories seems to relate at least tangentially to the concept of levirate marriage, although no consistent pattern of law and practice can be discerned in the biblical material.[20] Each prepares deliberately to make herself attractive to the male protagonist; each deliberately engineers the encounter; each encounter is set in a context of community agricultural festivities; each woman is in need of economic security (although this point is not developed explicitly in the Tamar narrative); each takes a great personal risk (although this point is not developed explicitly in the Ruth narrative); each is declared in the right/worthy by the man.

---

18. See, for example, C. F. Mariottini, "Perez," *ABD* 5.226.

19. Tamar's ethnicity is never made explicit in the biblical tradition. Later Jewish tradition regarded her as of Gentile descent. See Marshall D. Johnson, *The Purpose of the Biblical Genealogies with Special Reference to the Setting of the Genealogies of Jesus* (2nd ed.; Cambridge: Cambridge University Press, 1988) 154.

20. For an extensive discussion of this issue, see Bush, *Ruth, Esther*, 221–27. I concur with Bush that the family responsibility portrayed in the Ruth story is understood better as a moral obligation than as the prescriptive legal obligation outlined in the legislation of Deut 25:50.

Through these parallels between the two women, Judah and Boaz are seen to be parallel as well; but the dominant theme is one of contrast rather than similarity. Each man does become progenitor of an important child through an unexpected relationship and a process initiated by a woman. But in Judah's case the action is required because of his own fault in sending Tamar away and withholding Shelah from her. In Boaz's case, by contrast, the existence of the nearer kinsman suggests that Boaz has not failed in any duty. Ruth's initiative in fact spurs him to go beyond his normal responsibility in order to resolve the situation. Despite much vocabulary with potential sexual overtones in the threshing floor scene, the overall direction of the narrative suggests that sexual intercourse does not take place until after the marriage. Judah seeks a tryst, whereas Boaz resists the opportunity available to him. The parallels of the two women, combined with these contrasts between the two men, suggest that the narrator is right to couch the villagers' blessing in terms of comparison with Perez rather than with Judah.

Finally, we may ask about the place of the "house of Perez" in Judahite tradition. Here we must return to the witness of the Chronicler. As is generally recognized, 1 Chronicles 1–9 gives primary attention to the tribes of Judah and Levi in order to establish the theological importance of the Davidic line and the priestly house for the historical narrative to follow. Among the offspring of Judah, the descendants of Zerah and of Shelah (the two surviving sons besides Perez who are known from the Genesis tradition) receive only six verses total (2:6–8; 4:21–23). By contrast, the line of Perez through his son Hezron is provided in extensive detail.[21] Thus it is indeed the line of Perez that becomes a great house in the memory of the past represented by the Chronicler. The comparison drawn in Ruth 4:12 is highly appropriate. The narrator would not have been likely to base a blessing comparsion on Hezron, about whom tradition reported nothing beyond his name, when his father, Perez, was available with all the potential for narrative allusion outlined above.

We have found that the beginning of the Ruth genealogy with Perez and the blessing of 4:12 are indeed well coordinated. We have proposed that the list of names following Perez was most likely fixed well enough in tradition that modification would not have been realistic, even though some of the names were known only from that list. It appears also that the narrative contrast between Boaz and Judah reflected negatively upon Judah, thus discouraging any possibility of beginning the Ruth genealogy with his name. Because

---

21. Perez's second son, Hamul, is mentioned in 1 Chr 2:5, as he is in Gen 46:12 and Num 26:21. But no descendants are referenced. Thus, the line of principal interest is that of the branches of the Hezronites.

Hezron was unknown, beginning with him was also not a likely option, despite his centrality as the immediate ancestor of all major Judahite groups in the Chronicler's overall presentation. The name of Perez, however, is able to evoke a surplus of meaning through the circumstances of his conception. In these respects, the Ruth tradition shows greater affinity to Genesis than to Chronicles, despite the exact parallelism of the two Davidic genealogies. The ascribing of the seventh and tenth positions to Boaz and David in the Ruth genealogy may have been intentional, but the impact of this numerical feature seems more likely to be a "bonus," because other more substantive features of text and tradition press toward the recording of the Ruth genealogy in this form.

Indexes

Index of Authors

Index of Scripture

Old Testament / Hebrew Bible

Note: When there are two sets of numbers, the first number refers to the Hebrew versification; the number in brackets is the English verse number.

Genesis
1   148, 168–169, 171, 174, 183
1–3   174
1–9   169
1:1   168
1:1–2   168, 230
1:1–2:3   143
1:1–2:4   168
1:2   169–171
1:6   170
1:6–10   169
1:9   170
1:26   143, 173–174, 179, 182–183
1:27   143, 265
1:28   179
2   158
2–3   174
2:1–3   172–173
2:2   143
2:10–14   158
2:24   173
3:5   173
4:4   316
5   185
5:1–3   185
6:2   173
6:4   173
7:11   169–170, 230, 309
8   171
8:2   169–171, 309
8:3   171, 272
8:5   272

Genesis (cont.)
8:8–12   310
9   171
9:2   182
9:6   182
9:10–17   170
9:13–17   169, 171, 175
9:14   37, 171, 175
11   111
11–12   119
11:4   228
11:5   228
11:7   173
11:26   119
11:26–27   118
11:26–32   118, 121
11:27   119
11:28   118–119
11:28–30   118–119
11:31   119–120
12–22   114–115
12:1   117, 121
12:1–4   111–115, 117, 121–123
12:3   91
12:4   113, 116–120
12:5   120–121
12:10   112–113
12:10–12   114
12:10–20   116, 123
13:1   118
13:7   115
13:10   30, 45, 122
14:19   167
15   115–116

Genesis (cont.)
15:1   115
15:2–3   115
15:4–5   115
15:9   310
15:13   411
15:13–16   115
15:16   411
15:17   33
15:17–21   115
17:17   116
17:18–20   116
18:28   30
19   36
19:13   30, 45
19:14   45
19:29   30, 45
20   116
20:1–8   114
21:28   43
22   111–112, 114–116, 123
22:12   123
24:3   165
24:7   165
30:2   58
30:3–8   121
31:13   54
31:42   55
33:20   43
36:6   120
37:20   276
38   413
38:29   41
39:21   221

Judges (cont.)
5:4   36, 309
5:4–5   171
5:14   205, 208
5:20   240
5:26   44
5:31   206
6–8   200
6–9   199
6:1   206, 214
6:1–6   205
6:1–10:5   206
6:7–10   203, 205, 210
6:10   204
6:11   207, 209
6:15   207, 209
6:24–27   210
6:27   209
7:1–8   209
7:2   209–210
7:18–20   209
7:24–25   208
8:1–3   205, 208
8:4   209
8:13–17   210–211
8:18   209
8:18–21   211
8:21   209
8:22   209
8:23   200, 202, 208–212
8:24–26   210
8:24–27   204
8:24–28   211
8:27   206, 210
8:28   205–206
8:29–30   210
8:30   211
8:31   211
8:33–35   204
8:35   211
9   200, 211
9:5   205
9:49   33
9:53–54   200
9:56   211

Judges (cont.)
10:1   207
10:1–5   206
10:6   204, 214
10:6–16   205
10:6–16:31   206
10:8   206
10:10–14   205
11:1   207
11:24   163
12:1   33
12:1–6   205
12:7   206
12:8   207
12:8–15   206
12:12   207
12:13   207
12:15   408
13:1   205–206, 214
13:2   207, 216
13:5   205
14:3   214
14:7   214
15:9–17   208
15:14   228
16:23–31   216
16:31   206
17–18   211
17–21   201, 203, 213–214, 217
17:6   200, 203, 212–213
17:7   215
18:1   201, 212
19–21   37, 208, 211, 215
19:1   201, 212, 215
19:10–12   136
19:25   57
19:29–30   201
20:1   215
20:8   215
20:17–25   215
20:18   215
20:18–25   215
20:33–36   215

Judges (cont.)
21:25   200, 203, 212–213

1 Samuel
1:1   408
2:5   30
2:10   44
2:19   15
2:28   328
2:35   345
3:3   138
4:1–5:5   131
4:4   131, 139
4:10–5:2   137
5:6–7:2   131
6:6   57
6:18   29
6:21   136
7–12   201
7:1–2   129–130
8:5   201
8:7   201
8:18   328
9   251
9:1   413
9:15–16   136
9:16   136
10–31   201
10:1   4, 136
10:26   212
11:7   201
12:12   163
13   13
13:1–14:46   133
13:7–14   134
13:13–14   5
13:14   104, 201
14:11   360
14:19   133
14:36–37   134
14:38–45   134
14:50–51   413
15   13, 15
15:1–34   5
15:1–16:13   3

Jonah
1:9 167
1:19 165
4:5 32

Micah
1–2 79
1–3 79, 83–84, 87, 92
1–5 94
1:2 79, 85, 344
1:2–7 84–85, 92–93,
95–96
1:4 84
1:6–7 326
1:7 84, 89
1:8–9 93
1:9 80, 84
1:10–16 91
1:11 84
1:21–26 92
2:1–5 84, 89, 93
2:3 45
2:4 84
2:9 80
2:12–13 86–89, 93–
94
3 83
3–5 79, 95
3:1 79–80, 341
3:1–4 83
3:1–7 93
3:3 80
3:5 80
3:5–8 83, 93
3:9 80, 85
3:9–12 83–85, 93
3:11 84
3:12 85, 90, 93
4 85
4–5 79, 92–93
4:1 225
4:1–2 85
4:1–3 389
4:1–4 44, 83, 85–86,
93
4:1–5 86, 93

Micah (cont.)
4:2 86
4:3 85
4:3–4 94
4:5 86, 163
4:6–7 93–94
4:6–8 86, 88–90
4:7 87
4:8 88, 90
4:9–10 86, 89
4:11–12 85
4:11–13 86, 88–89,
93
4:14 278
5 89, 94
5:1 408
5:1–5 89, 93
5:2 89–90
5:2–6 86
5:3 321
5:4–5 85, 89
5:6–8 90, 93–94
5:7–9 86
5:8 85, 281
5:9–14 85
5:10 29
5:13 324
6–7 79
6:1 79
6:1–8 95
6:6–8 91
7:10 304
7:20 340

Nahum
1:1 327
1:6 33
2 327
2:3 319–321, 327,
338, 342, 349
2:5–7 310–311
2:7 311
2:8 40, 51
2:13[12] 360
3:7 324
3:13 31

Habakkuk
3:3–5 171
3:9 33

Zephaniah
1:7–8 59
1:11 28
1:14 28
1:15 28, 36
1:16 28
1:17 28
1:18 28
2:10 321
2:13–15 84
2:15 40, 51
3:1 325
3:4 32
3:13 270–271, 273
3:15 163

Haggai
2:17 150

Zechariah
1:16 46
2:4 44
3:10 85
8:4 279
8:10–12 274
9–14 47
9:5–6 324
9:13 33
10:11 278, 324
11:3 321
11:4–17 271
11:17 271
13:7 42
14:5 237
14:9 164
14:16–19 44

Malachi
1:7 325
1:12 280
1:14 165
3:10 309

New Testament

Deuterocanonical Literature